Selected as one of the Amazon Best Books of 2015 in the Cookbooks and Food Writing category
AMAZON ON THE COMPLETE VEGETARIAN COOKBOOK

"The sum total of exhaustive experimentation . . . anyone interested in gluten-free cookery simply shouldn't be without it."
NIGELLA LAWSON ON *THE HOW CAN IT BE GLUTEN-FREE COOKBOOK*

"The editors at America's Test Kitchen, known for their meticulous recipe testing and development, are back at it again. This time, they've trained their laser-eyed focus on reduced-sugar baking. . . . Cooks with a powerful sweet tooth should scoop up this well-researched recipe book for healthier takes on classic sweet treats."
BOOKLIST ON *NATURALLY SWEET*

"An exceptional resource for novice canners, though preserving veterans will find plenty here to love as well."
LIBRARY JOURNAL (STARRED REVIEW) ON *FOOLPROOF PRESERVING*

"The 21st-century *Fannie Farmer Cookbook* or *The Joy of Cooking.* If you had to have one cookbook and that's all you could have, this one would do it."
CBS SAN FRANCISCO ON *THE NEW FAMILY COOKBOOK*

"This book upgrades slow cooking for discriminating, 21st-century palates—that is indeed revolutionary."
THE DALLAS MORNING NEWS ON *SLOW COOKER REVOLUTION*

"The go-to gift book for newlyweds, small families or empty nesters."
ORLANDO SENTINEL ON *THE COMPLETE COOKING FOR TWO COOKBOOK*

"Some 2,500 photos walk readers through 600 painstakingly tested recipes, leaving little room for error."
ASSOCIATED PRESS ON *THE AMERICA'S TEST KITCHEN COOKING SCHOOL COOKBOOK*

"A one-volume kitchen seminar, addressing in one smart chapter after another the sometimes surprising whys behind a cook's best practices. . . . You get the myth, the theory, the science and the proof, all rigorously interrogated as only America's Test Kitchen can do."
NPR ON *THE SCIENCE OF GOOD COOKING*

"A terrifically accessible and useful guide to grilling in all its forms that sets a new bar for its competitors on the bookshelf. . . . The book is packed with practical advice, simple tips, and approachable recipes."
PUBLISHERS WEEKLY (STARRED REVIEW) ON *MASTER OF THE GRILL*

"This book is a comprehensive, no-nonsense guide . . . a well-thought-out, clearly explained primer for every aspect of home baking."
THE WALL STREET JOURNAL ON *THE COOK'S ILLUSTRATED BAKING BOOK*

"A beautifully illustrated, 318-page culinary compendium showcasing an impressive variety and diversity of authentic Mexican cuisine."
MIDWEST BOOK REVIEW ON *THE BEST MEXICAN RECIPES*

"Buy this gem for the foodie in your family, and spend the extra money to get yourself a copy too."
THE MISSOURIAN ON *THE BEST OF AMERICA'S TEST KITCHEN 2015*

"This comprehensive collection of 800-plus family and global favorites helps put healthy eating in an everyday context, from meatloaf to Indian curry with chicken."
COOKING LIGHT ON *THE AMERICA'S TEST KITCHEN HEALTHY FAMILY COOKBOOK*

"There are pasta books . . . and then there's this pasta book. Flip your carbohydrate dreams upside down and strain them through this sieve of revolutionary, creative, and also traditional recipes."
SAN FRANCISCO BOOK REVIEW ON *PASTA REVOLUTION*

"The perfect kitchen home companion . . . The practical side of things is very much on display . . . cook-friendly and kitchen-oriented, illuminating the process of preparing food instead of mystifying it."
THE WALL STREET JOURNAL ON *THE COOK'S ILLUSTRATED COOKBOOK*

"RELY ON THIS DOORSTOPPER FOR EXPLICIT AND COMPREHENSIVE TAKES ON RECIPES FROM BASIC TO SOPHISTICATED."
TOLEDO BLADE ON *THE COMPLETE AMERICA'S TEST KITCHEN TV SHOW COOKBOOK*

"The entire book is stuffed with recipes that will blow your dinner-table audience away like leaves from a sidewalk in November."
SAN FRANCISCO BOOK REVIEW ON *THE COMPLETE COOK'S COUNTRY TV SHOW COOKBOOK*

"Further proof that practice makes perfect, if not transcendent. . . . If an intermediate cook follows the directions exactly, the results will be better than takeout or Mom's."
THE NEW YORK TIMES ON *THE NEW BEST RECIPE*

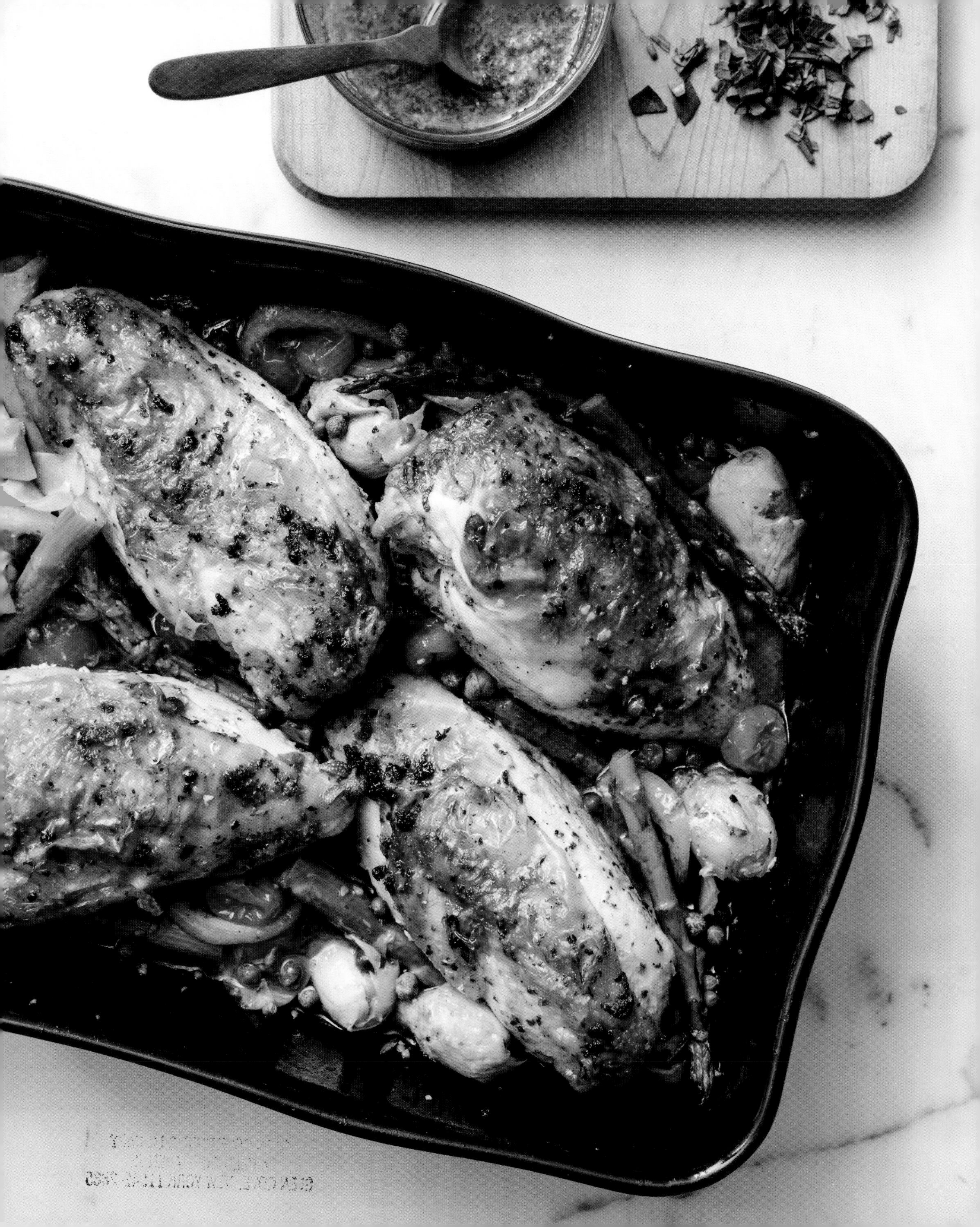

THE COMPLETE
MAKE-AHEAD
COOKBOOK

From Appetizers to Desserts
500 Recipes You Can Make in Advance

THE EDITORS AT

AMERICA'S TEST KITCHEN

Library of Congress Cataloging-in-Publication Data
Names: America's Test Kitchen (Firm)
Title: The complete make-ahead cookbook : from appetizers to desserts 500
    recipes you can make in advance / the editors at America's Test Kitchen.
Description: Brookline, MA : America's Test Kitchen, [2017] | Includes index.
Identifiers: LCCN 2017005153 | ISBN 9781940352886
Subjects: LCSH: Make-ahead cooking. | LCGFT: Cookbooks.
Classification: LCC TX714 .C6423 2017 | DDC 641.5/55--dc23
LC record available at https://lccn.loc.gov/2017005153

**AMERICA'S — ®
TEST KITCHEN**

AMERICA'S TEST KITCHEN
17 Station Street, Brookline, MA 02445

Manufactured in the United States of America
10 9 8 7 6 5 4 3 2 1

Distributed by Penguin Random House Publisher Services
Tel: 800–733–3000

Pictured on front cover: Best Chicken Parmesan (page 158)
Pictured on back cover: Individual Chicken Pot Pies for the Freezer (page 173),
Indoor Barbecue Ribs (page 218), Kale Salad with Roasted Sweet Potatoes
and Pomegranate Vinaigrette (page 86), Ultimate Seven-Layer Dip (page 24),
Sausage and Broccoli Rabe Lasagna (page 129)

CHIEF CREATIVE OFFICER Jack Bishop
EDITORIAL DIRECTOR, BOOKS Elizabeth Carduff
EXECUTIVE EDITOR Julia Collin Davison
EXECUTIVE FOOD EDITOR Suzannah McFerran
SENIOR EDITORS Debra Hudak, Stephanie Pixley, and Anne Wolf
ASSOCIATE EDITORS Leah Colins, Melissa Drumm, Lawman Johnson,
    Nicole Konstantinakos, and Russell Selander
TEST COOKS Kathryn Callahan, Afton Cyrus, Joseph Gitter,
    Katherine Perry, and Esther Reynolds
EDITORIAL ASSISTANT Alyssa Langer
DESIGN DIRECTOR, BOOKS Carole Goodman
PRODUCTION DESIGNER Reinaldo Cruz
GRAPHIC DESIGNER Katie Barranger
PHOTOGRAPHY DIRECTOR Julie Bozzo Cote
SENIOR STAFF PHOTOGRAPHER Daniel J. van Ackere
STAFF PHOTOGRAPHER Steve Klise
PHOTOGRAPHY PRODUCER Mary Ball
ADDITIONAL PHOTOGRAPHY Keller + Keller, Anthony Tieuli,
    and Carl Tremblay
FOOD STYLING Isabelle English, Catrine Kelty, Kendra McKnight,
    Marie Piraino, Elle Simone Scott, and Sally Staub
PHOTOSHOOT KITCHEN TEAM
    SENIOR EDITOR Chris O'Connor
    TEST COOKS Daniel Cellucci and Matthew Fairman
    ASSISTANT TEST COOKS Mady Nichas and Jessica Rudolph
PRODUCTION DIRECTOR Guy Rochford
SENIOR PRODUCTION MANAGER Jessica Lindheimer Quirk
PRODUCTION MANAGER Christine Walsh
IMAGING MANAGER Lauren Robbins
PRODUCTION AND IMAGING SPECIALISTS Heather Dube,
    Sean MacDonald, Dennis Noble, and Jessica Voas
COPY EDITOR Cheryl Redmond
PROOFREADER Elizabeth Wray Emery
INDEXER Elizabeth Parson

Contents

Welcome to America's Test Kitchen

This book has been tested, written, and edited by the folks at America's Test Kitchen, a very real 2,500-square-foot kitchen located just outside of Boston. It is the home of *Cook's Illustrated* magazine and *Cook's Country* magazine and is the Monday-through-Friday destination for more than 60 test cooks, editors, and cookware specialists. Our mission is to test recipes over and over again until we understand how and why they work and until we arrive at the "best" version.

We start the process of testing a recipe with a complete lack of preconceptions, which means that we accept no claim, no technique, and no recipe at face value. We simply assemble as many variations as possible, test a half-dozen of the most promising, and taste the results blind. We then construct our own recipe and continue to test it, varying ingredients, techniques, and cooking times until we reach a consensus. As we like to say in the test kitchen, "We make the mistakes so you don't have to." The result, we hope, is the best version of a particular recipe, but we realize that only you can be the final judge of our success (or failure). We use the same rigorous approach when we test equipment and taste ingredients.

All of this would not be possible without a belief that good cooking, much like good music, is based on a foundation of objective technique. Some people like spicy foods and others don't, but there is a right way to sauté, there is a best way to cook a pot roast, and there are measurable scientific principles involved in producing perfectly beaten, stable egg whites. Our ultimate goal is to investigate the fundamental principles of cooking to give you the techniques, tools, and ingredients you need to become a better cook. It is as simple as that.

To see what goes on behind the scenes at America's Test Kitchen, check out our social media channels for kitchen snapshots, exclusive content, video tips, and much more. You can watch us work (in our actual test kitchen) by tuning in to *America's Test Kitchen* or *Cook's Country from America's Test Kitchen* on public television or on our websites. Listen to test kitchen experts on public radio (SplendidTable.org) to hear insights that illuminate the truth about real home cooking. Want to hone your cooking skills or finally learn how to bake—with an America's Test Kitchen test cook? Enroll in one of our online cooking classes. If the big questions about the hows and whys of food science are your passion, join our Cook's Science experts for a deep dive. However you choose to visit us, we welcome you into our kitchen, where you can stand by our side as we test our way to the best recipes in America.

f facebook.com/AmericasTestKitchen
twitter.com/TestKitchen
youtube.com/AmericasTestKitchen
instagram.com/TestKitchen
pinterest.com/TestKitchen
google.com/+AmericasTestKitchen

AmericasTestKitchen.com
CooksIllustrated.com
CooksCountry.com
CooksScience.com
OnlineCookingSchool.com

The Make-Ahead Kitchen

INTRODUCTION

Getting dinner on the table every night of the week is a challenge for most home cooks. Countless books have tried to address the problem with fast recipes, but they're not always the best solution, and certainly not the only lane to a good dinner. While fast recipes have their place, you may still find yourself prepping ingredients and monitoring a skillet for 45 minutes on a night when you just don't have the time. Enter *The Complete Make-Ahead Cookbook*. It presents the canon of American home cooking from the make-ahead perspective: more than 500 versatile, fresh recipes from appetizers to desserts plus an entire chapter devoted to the holidays, the Super Bowl of stressful cooking. The promise of this book is clear and very simple: Every recipe has information in a carefully crafted box that provides every possible make-ahead option (see next page for more information). Even experienced cooks have questions when it comes to making recipes in advance, and our test cooks provide all the answers.

So how will this book help you get dinner on the table more easily? First, we spell out the time required to make each recipe so you know how much hands-on active time is needed to make a recipe and also how much total time is ultimately involved. (Recipes with 30 minutes or less of active time are tagged as Easy.) A Freeze It icon indicates which recipes are ideal for that purpose. The rest is really up to you and what sort of cook you are. Are you willing to make a big batch of stew on Sunday so some can go in the freezer, meaning dinner is solved for multiple nights now and in the future? Or would you rather spend just a few minutes the night before to ensure an easy dinner the following night by applying a spice-rub to flank steak to give it flavor (it requires only a quick sear to finish) and making a fresh corn and bean salad ahead in just 15 minutes to go with it? There are many options across the book for easy prep-ahead meals such as this that give you a serious jump start on dinner the next night, as well as recipes you can fully assemble, like Chicken Baked in Foil (page 150) and Stuffed Eggplant (page 272), and then simply store—ready to be baked when you walk in the door. Comforting casseroles are here too, along with one-dish meals, fresh main-course salads, and numerous sides and desserts that can all be made in advance.

When it comes to entertaining, one of the hardest things is plotting out, with confidence, what you can make in advance so on the day of the party everything isn't left to the last minute. There are many company-worthy recipes throughout the book along with holiday recipes; once you plan your menu, you can use the make-ahead boxes accompanying each recipe to organize your game plan. You'll no longer worry that your stuffed mushrooms will be soggy or your fruit cobbler lackluster come serving time. Plus, inventive recipes like make-ahead Turkey Gravy (page 324) or Tiramisù (page 361) that you can freeze will be your aces in the hole.

This book is your ticket to a lifetime of easier meal planning, make-ahead cooking, and entertaining. It's not a prescription for cooking for the freezer or cooking ahead on weekends. It helps you do the type of make-ahead cooking you want to do and are willing to do. There is no need to buy dozens of Tupperware containers and embark on a cooking marathon. Simply browse through the hundreds of options across the book and start planning and cooking. Follow the tips and strategies laid out in this book to become a more organized and efficient make-ahead cook.

THE MANY LANES TO DINNER (WITH ALL THE DETAILS)

If making a batch of homemade chicken soup for another day, do you store it before or after adding the rice or noodles? Is it safe to roll and stuff chicken in advance? How about a raw meatloaf or meatballs? Should pie be stored on the counter or in the fridge? How many hours ahead can you make whipped cream? For each recipe in this book, you will find a box detailing the best kitchen-tested make-ahead options. For some recipes, this is as simple as storing a partly finished dish for a day or two, and then continuing with the next step in the recipe exactly as it is written. For others, stopping and starting a recipe may require some different instructions, such as increasing baking time or reserving some salad dressing. But don't worry—we spell everything out, every time. The box will tell you how long you can store something before the quality starts to deteriorate, and if it needs to be refrigerated. If we give you the option to freeze something like lasagna (see below), we'll also tell you whether or not you need to defrost it before cooking and whether to increase the baking time. By carefully following the instructions in the boxes, you're guaranteed great results every time.

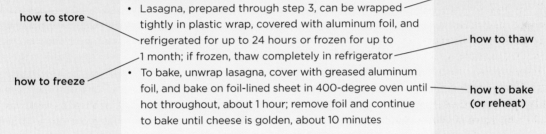

how to store

how to freeze

TO MAKE AHEAD

- Lasagna, prepared through step 3, can be wrapped tightly in plastic wrap, covered with aluminum foil, and refrigerated for up to 24 hours or frozen for up to 1 month; if frozen, thaw completely in refrigerator
- To bake, unwrap lasagna, cover with greased aluminum foil, and bake on foil-lined sheet in 400-degree oven until hot throughout, about 1 hour; remove foil and continue to bake until cheese is golden, about 10 minutes

how to wrap

how to thaw

how to bake (or reheat)

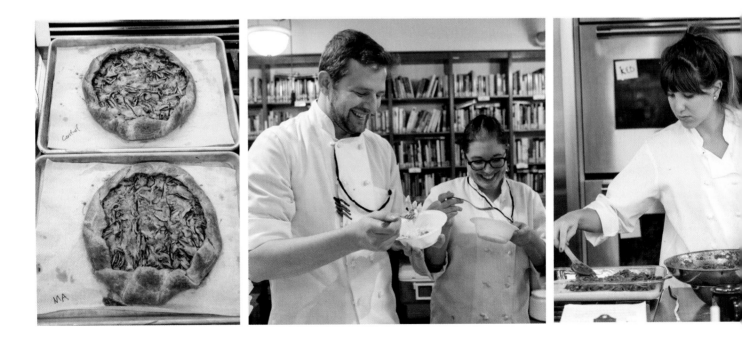

We wanted all the food we made ahead to taste as good as (or better than) its freshly prepared counterpart. While all of the recipes in this book are designed to be made straight through and served, we actively tested and tasted storing dishes along the way. We always tasted the food that had been stored in the fridge or freezer alongside a just-made version as our control. Through our thorough testing, we learned a few tricks to guarantee the best possible results. Whether you are stashing food in the freezer, holding it for a couple days in the fridge, or prepping entrées ahead so they are ready to cook the next day, here are some tips to ensure the very best results.

1. Build Flavor Overnight with Rubs and Marinades

Bold spice rubs and marinades infuse meat, poultry, and fattier fish (such as salmon and swordfish) with flavor, especially if you build in time for them to work their magic overnight. We've found that the most important ingredient in any spice rub or marinade is salt; not only does salt enhance flavor, it also helps proteins retain their natural juices when cooked and so prevents the meat from drying out. In a marinade or rub, salt draws the other flavors into the meat, seasoning the meat throughout as in the case of Thick-Cut Pork Chops (page 209). Most marinades and spice rubs are a snap to prepare and rely on pantry ingredients, and sometimes there's an added benefit beyond flavor: Applying a rub and air-drying a chicken in the fridge overnight (see page 179) will result in ultracrisp, crackly skin as well as incredibly moist, flavorful meat.

2. Loosen and Refresh

In some cases, when we tried to reheat things like soups and braises after they had been stored in the fridge, they ended up dry or too thick. To compensate, we added some extra liquid as needed during reheating. A splash or two of hot water easily refreshed pasta salads and helped us get the perfect consistency. We learned to store grains and their dressings separately to keep them vibrant.

3. The Benefits of Chilling

Of course you can use your fridge to store things like casseroles and salads for the next day, but in some cases, chilling a dish can actually improve it. When it comes to dips like Classic Hummus (page 20) and Herbed Spinach Dip (page 16), a stay in the fridge helps their flavors to meld, making them a natural choice for make-ahead appetizers. Our tasters generally thought that reheated soups and stews tasted better the next day; after a stint in the fridge their flavors were more integrated and fuller tasting. Many burgers and cakes, such as Black Bean Burgers (page 258) and Maryland Corn and Crab Cakes (page 253), also benefit from chilling; they firm up and hold together better when you cook them. And desserts like Icebox Cheesecake (page 356), Chocolate Pots de Crème (page 362), and Summer Berry Pie (page 379) require some time in the fridge to set up properly—a fact you can use to your advantage when entertaining.

4. Making Pasta Ahead

In general, pasta salads do well when made ahead. We found that cooking the pasta beyond al dente ensures that it stays tender once cooled. That's because as the pasta cools, its starches firm up, giving the pasta a chewy, slightly hard texture. We also rinse the cooked pasta to remove excess starches that would make the pasta stick together and clump when stored overnight. Some pasta casseroles freeze well, but unfortunately soups with a pasta component in them are not the best choice for making ahead and don't freeze well because the noodles absorb too much liquid and become bloated and mushy. You can, however, freeze the soup without the pasta and then stir the uncooked pasta into the soup when simmering to reheat it.

5. To Thaw or Not to Thaw

We did a lot of testing to determine the best way to freeze and reheat casseroles, pies, and more. For the best results, we found that frozen raw casseroles need to thaw completely in the refrigerator before being baked; this helps to preserve moisture and flavor since freezing dries out food. Frozen casseroles are basically big blocks of ice; they can take up to 48 hours to thaw so plan accordingly. To test if a casserole is fully thawed, stick a knife in the middle. We found that unbaked double-crust fruit pies freeze well because they are relatively small and less dense than casseroles; they can go straight into the oven without defrosting first. Remember that not every baking dish can go from freezer to oven; see page 8 for more information.

6. Add Certain Ingredients at the Last Minute

When making a dish ahead, we found it was best to wait to add certain ingredients until just before serving. The reasons for this vary: In some recipes, it was to preserve the texture of ingredients like cherry tomatoes, delicate greens, or toasted nuts; in other recipes, it was to ensure the best, brightest flavor of ingredients such as lemon zest and herbs. In still other recipes, such as some that called for oil-cured olives, we left them out until the end of cooking to make sure their potent flavor didn't overwhelm the dish on serving day. We add frozen peas last so they will retain their color, since they need only to be heated through.

7. Boost Flavor Before Serving

Tossing a dish with a marinade, sauce, or dressing before storing is a great way to build deep flavor, but we found that the flavors often needed refreshing before serving. To avoid making extra work on the day we wanted to serve the dish, we simply reserved some marinade to make a quick sauce or saved some dressing to toss in just before serving. Brightening the sauce or dressing with extra vinegar or citrus juice helped to reawaken the flavors. In some recipes, such as our Pasta Salad with Pesto (page 134), we discovered that stirring in some reserved pesto just before serving not only freshened up the flavor of the stored dish, but also brightened the color and made it more appealing.

When thinking about storing food in a container, there are a lot of questions. Does it fit in the fridge or freezer? Will it leak if it tips over? Can you microwave in it? Should you worry about possible health risks with plastics containing bisphenol-A (BPA)? In search of a storage container that would put these questions to rest, we ran eight 8-cup rectangular and square containers made from purportedly safer BPA-free plastic through a battery of tests. In a separate series of tests, we tried out three containers made from glass, a worry-free yet heavy and breakable alternative to plastic.

Close Encounter

There are two main categories of food storage containers: those with seals that close by pressing all around the rim, and those that close with snap down flaps that project like wings from the lid. Five of the eight plastic containers we tested relied on snap seal flaps, though we found that the tightness of the seal was more important than the style of lid.

In addition to their sealing power, we also found that containers differed in how easy they were to close. Some took force to snap—threatening pinched fingers—and a lot of wiggling to align the lid. One particularly fussy unit wouldn't close unless its lid was fitted in a particular (yet poorly indicated) direction.

Testing Usability

Besides a snug lid, there are a few other practical concerns. First was odor absorption. While we found that most of the glass and polypropylene containers were resistant to odors, one of the "disposable" supermarket containers didn't fare so well—even after a run through the dishwasher, we could detect odors of previously stored food.

Second, a truly convenient storage container should cope with the freezer or microwave without warping, melting, or staining. We froze chili and then microwaved it in the containers until hot. We detected no plastic scents or flavor, but one "disposable" container softened and then rehardened as it cooled; another's snap flaps warped and then wouldn't lock. Chili stained them all, but a few dishwasher cycles removed most traces.

Third, a storage container is serviceable only if it fits in the prescribed storage space. After weeks of cramming containers into freezers and refrigerators, we preferred low, flat rectangles that slide onto any shelf, leaving room for other items, and simple, stackable, flat—not bulbous—lids. But there's also a food-quality reason to opt for flat: more efficient chilling and heating. After 24 hours in the freezer, water in tall containers was still liquid at the center but frozen solid in lower, flatter models. In the microwave, the chili in deep containers overheated at the edges before heating through in the middle.

THE BOTTOM LINE

One plastic container worked nicely out of the box, survived all our tests, and met all our long-term goals. Our winner sealed tightly and easily; resisted warping, stains, and smells; and fit easily among the contents of our refrigerator. It performed perfectly even after taking more than 50 trips through the dishwasher. This might be the last container we'll have to buy for quite a while.

PLASTIC STORAGE CONTAINERS

We highly recommend our plastic container winner, **Snapware Airtight**. Its simple snap-down lid sealed easily throughout testing. Though it allowed a few drops of water through in an initial submersion test, after dishwashing the seal was perfect. Its flat, rectangular shape encourages quick cooking or heating and stacks easily, with the lid attaching to the bottom.

GLASS STORAGE CONTAINERS

Many consumers have decided to avoid plastic storage containers after learning about the possible ill effects of microwaving in plastic, leading to the resurgence of glass food storage. Only one aced all our tests and was equal to the top-ranked plastic container—if it weren't considerably heavier and more prone to breakage, we'd consider choosing glass as our favorite storage container.

The **Kinetic Go Green GlassLock** had a neat, tight, reliable seal, good capacity, and solid performance in every test. If you are concerned about microwaving food in plastic storage containers, this is the one to choose. Downside: The glass container has a deep, tall shape, which is less preferable than the shallower, flatter shape of our favorite plastic container for quick cooling, freezing, and heating.

Keeping an organized and well-stocked kitchen is key to successful make-ahead cooking, so it's important to have the right wraps and zipper-lock bags on hand in addition to containers. These items will help you store food easily and safely and prevent contamination and off-flavors.

Plastic Wrap

When you want to stash a dish in the fridge or freezer without transferring it to a storage container, covering it with plastic wrap is the simplest way to keep the dish airtight. Plastic wrap can be made from two distinctly different substances. Some manufacturers use a food-safe version of PVC; others use low-density polyethylene (LDPE). The main difference? PVC clings but is not impermeable; LDPE is impermeable but has far less cling. Clingy PVC wraps are preferable if you are transporting food or are worried about spills and leaks, but to keep foods fresh longer, select plastic wraps made from LDPE. If the plastic wrap doesn't adhere easily to the dish, dampen the edge of the dish with a wet paper towel to help the plastic stick. Our all-around winner is **Glad Cling Wrap Clear Plastic**.

Aluminum Foil

We reach for aluminum foil constantly in the test kitchen. We use it to line baking sheets for easy cleanup, to cover dishes when baking to prevent them from drying out, to wrap food in a pouch so it will steam gently in the oven, and to protect dishes from off-flavors in the freezer. We find heavy-duty foil easier to work with and recommend you stock extra-long rolls as well as standard 12-inch rolls. While parchment is typically used to cook food *en papillote*, or in a pouch, we find aluminum foil easier to work with. To make a tidy foil packet that can be refrigerated for up to 24 hours, see page 151.

Zipper-Lock Bags

Plastic zipper-lock bags are a must in the make-ahead kitchen. They are great for holding meat and marinade in the fridge overnight and handy for freezing sauces so you can store them flat—a bonus if you are short on freezer space. You can also use them to freeze individual items like breaded chicken cutlets or veggie burgers, making it easy to take out and defrost just what you need. We recommend buying freezer-safe zipper-lock bags because they are made of thicker plastic than standard bags, making them sturdier and better at protecting food from off-flavors in the fridge or freezer. Readily available, the best supermarket option is **Ziploc Brand Freezer Bags**

Ziploc Brand Freezer Bags with Easy Open Tabs

with Easy Open Tabs but we highly recommend **Elkay Plastics Ziplock Heavy Weight Freezer Bags** as the best all-around option (order at webrestaurantstore.com). When storing food in a zipper-lock bag, be sure to press out as much air as possible before sealing the bag. When transferring raw meat to a zipper-lock bag, it can be difficult to keep the opening from coming in contact with the meat. To guarantee a clean seal, fold back the last 2 to 3 inches of the bag into a cuff. To make filling the bag with soup or sauce easier, place it in a measuring cup and fold the cuff over the sides of the cup.

Elkay Plastics Ziplock Heavy Weight Freezer Bags

LABEL IT

It's easy to lose track of what's in your freezer and when you put it there so it's essential to label everything. Some storage bags have a place for just this task so keep a permanent marker to use on these; masking tape is handy to have around for all sorts of other labeling. We also like to place a sticky note on top of the wrapped food that lists the finishing ingredients and instructions; even better, we photocopy the recipe and place it on top of the wrapped dish. Wrap the whole thing in an extra layer of plastic wrap. In the rush before dinner you'll have all the information you need to finish the dish without having to dig up the recipe again.

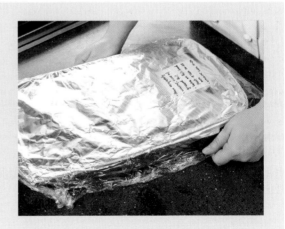

ESSENTIAL EQUIPMENT

You don't need a lot of specialty equipment to make food ahead, but there are definitely things that will make your job easier and more efficient. An array of casserole dishes, baking sheets, and wire racks is essential. And if you plan to make big-batch stews, chilis, pasta sauces, and braises, a good Dutch oven is a must-have. A slow cooker is an added bonus, to use as a hands-off way to get ahead on future meals or when entertaining. Here's a rundown of what you need to stock your make-ahead kitchen.

Casserole Dishes and Pie Plates

When it comes to making casseroles, classic 13 by 9-inch casserole dishes are essential. While the straight sides and sharp corners of a metal baking pan are ideal for making bar cookies and sheet cakes, we prefer glass dishes for casseroles; our favorite is the **Pyrex Easy Grab 3-Quart Oblong Baking Dish**. We also prefer glass dishes for pies; we like the **Pyrex Bakeware 9 Inch Pie Plate**. The tempered glass of our low-priced favorite Pyrex dishes won't react with acidic foods, it's safe for use with metal utensils, and its transparency easily lets you track browning. Plus, Pyrex can safely go directly from freezer to oven, while ceramic dishes can't—the sudden temperature change will cause them to crack. So if you're planning to freeze your casserole or pie, use Pyrex. However, keep in mind that Pyrex is not broiler-safe. While this shouldn't matter for pies, we do sometimes broil casseroles to crisp the topping. In these cases, we like the **HIC Porcelain Lasagna Baking Dish**. This dish has large, convenient handles and straight sides for easy serving.

Disposable Pans

When making and storing pies and casseroles, our winning glass Pyrex dishes are our preferred option. But in some cases, we realize that disposable pans have value, such as when bringing a casserole to a friend or to share at a party, and perhaps even for storing food in your own freezer so that your glass baking dishes are free to use when you need them. For those occasions, we like **Glad Ovenware**, which are made from oven-safe plastic (safe to 400 degrees), not aluminum. We know that disposable pans can be flimsy, making it difficult to transfer them in and out of the oven, especially when they're hot. Plus, food cooked in disposable pans tends not to brown as well as it would in metal or glass baking dishes. We solve both problems by putting the disposable pan on a metal baking sheet in the oven.

Dutch Oven

A good Dutch oven comes in handy whether you are making soup or doing some big-batch cooking. We put our Dutch ovens to work making hearty stews, braises, and pasta sauces. Because it's heavier and thicker than a skillet, a Dutch oven retains and conducts heat more evenly and effectively, so it's perfect for dishes that have long simmering times. We like a Dutch oven that holds at least 6 quarts, with a wide bottom for more efficient browning. Our favorite Dutch oven is the **Le Creuset 7¼ Quart Round Dutch Oven** while our Best Buy is the **Cuisinart 7 Quart Round Covered Casserole**; it's a little smaller but offers excellent performance at a more affordable price.

Pyrex Easy Grab 3-Quart Oblong Baking Dish

Pyrex Bakeware 9 Inch Pie Plate

HIC Porcelain Lasagna Baking Dish

Le Creuset 7¼ Quart Round Dutch Oven

Cuisinart 7 Quart Round Covered Casserole

Rimmed Baking Sheets

One of our favorite kitchen workhorses is the rimmed baking sheet. We frequently pull this piece of equipment into service for our make-ahead dishes; it's perfect for roasting a large cut of meat or for baking chicken pieces on top of hearty vegetables (see page 166). Baking sheets make it easy to spread out chicken fingers, veggie burgers, or cookie dough balls to quick-freeze them for an hour before storing them. We highly recommend the **Nordic Ware Baker's Half Sheet**. This sturdy pan browns evenly and won't bend or warp. We recommend that you have at least two on hand. We also like to put them to work in other ways: Make-ahead dinners like casseroles can take up a lot of space in the fridge. You

can use a baking sheet as an extra "shelf" by placing it on top of a casserole dish and then placing smaller items on the baking sheet.

Wire Racks

In the test kitchen, wire racks and rimmed baking sheets go hand in hand. Baking food on a wire rack set in a rimmed baking sheet allows air to circulate all around the food, helping it to brown evenly. We use this technique to achieve even cooking and the best texture, as for our Crispy Breaded Cod Fillets (page 235) and Breaded Pork Chops (page 208). And we use a wire rack set in a baking sheet to air-dry our roast chicken (see page 179) and Cornish game hens (see page 183) for ultracrispy skin. Wire racks are also handy for keeping cooked foods such as Batter Fried Chicken (page 160), Falafel (page 257), and Yeasted Waffles (page 343) warm in a low oven while maintaining their crisp or crunchy exterior. It's essential to get a wire rack that will fit inside your baking sheet; we like the **Libertyware Half Size Sheet Pan Cooling Rack** for its sturdy central support bar and extra feet.

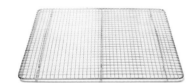

Slow Cooker

In this book, we focused on how a slow cooker can be your make-ahead ally as a hands-off helper in making big-batch pasta sauces, large roasts, and holiday side dishes that can save precious space in your oven and on your stovetop on those marathon cooking days. Even if you choose not to make a side dish in the slow cooker from start to finish (see pages 330–331 for our holiday slow-cooker sides), you can still use the appliance to your advantage when cooking for a holiday or large group. Mashed potatoes, squash, and stuffing can all be held in the slow cooker on the low

setting for a couple of hours before serving, freeing up valuable stovetop space. Our favorite slow cooker is the **KitchenAid 6-Quart Slow Cooker with Solid Glass Lid**.

REFRIGERATOR/FREEZER THERMOMETER

A thermometer is a proven aid in limiting the spread of food-borne illness. Maintaining the proper refrigerator and freezer temperature is essential to keep food as safe as possible. A good refrigerator thermometer will tell you if your fridge and freezer are cooling properly. Check regularly to ensure that your refrigerator is between 35 and 40 degrees; your freezer should be 0 degrees or below. We tested both analog and digital thermometers and our favorite is a digital model that takes two temperatures at once, simultaneously monitoring the temperature in both the freezer and the refrigerator. The **Maverick Cold-Chek Digital Refrigerator/Freezer Thermometer** sticks to the wall of the freezer and has a long wire probe that runs to the refrigerator. It has a clear digital display and a built-in sensor that sounds an alarm when the temperature needs adjusting.

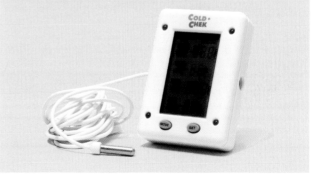

KNOW YOUR REFRIGERATOR

Knowing the best place to store different items in the refrigerator is the best way to ensure that food will stay fresh longer. Here's what you need to know about storing food in the fridge.

Where to Store Produce

KEEP IN THE FRONT OF THE FRIDGE

These items are sensitive to chilling injury and should be placed in the moderate zone in the front of the fridge.

Berries	Corn on the cob	Peas
Citrus	Melons	

BEST IN THE CRISPER

These items do best in the humid environment of the crisper.

Artichokes	Chiles	Mushrooms
Asparagus	Cucumbers	Peppers
Beets	Eggplant	Radishes
Broccoli	Fresh herbs	Scallions
Cabbage	Green beans	Summer squash
Carrots	Leafy greens	Turnips
Cauliflower	Leeks	Zucchini
Celery	Lettuce	

CHILL ANYWHERE

These items are not prone to chilling injury and can be stored anywhere in the fridge (including its coldest zones), provided the temperature doesn't freeze them.

Apples	Cherries	Grapes

ON THE COUNTER

Some produce is sensitive to chilling injury and subject to dehydration, internal browning, and/or pitting if stored in the refrigerator.

Apricots	Mangos	Pears
Avocados*	Nectarines	Pineapples
Bananas*	Papayas	Plums
Kiwis*	Peaches	Tomatoes

*Once they've reached their peak ripeness, these fruits can be stored in the refrigerator to prevent overripening, but some discoloration may occur.

Track the Temperature

A thermometer will tell you if your fridge is cooling properly. Check regularly to ensure that your refrigerator is between 35 and 40 degrees. Different foods are safest at different temperatures; see the chart below for our recommendations. For more information about our favorite thermometer, see page 9.

FOOD	IDEAL TEMP
Fish and Shellfish	30 to 34 degrees
Meat and Poultry	32 to 36 degrees
Dairy Products	36 to 40 degrees
Eggs	38 to 40 degrees
Produce	40 to 45 degrees

Refrigerator Microclimates

We often think of our refrigerator as having a single temperature, but every refrigerator has its own microclimates, with warmer, cooler, and more humid zones. You can make this temperature variation work to your advantage by learning about the different temperature zones.

COLD ZONE **BACK, TOP TO MIDDLE** The top and middle shelves at the back of the fridge are normally the coldest, with temperatures as low as 34 degrees. Meat, dairy, and produce that are not prone to chilling injury should be stored here.

MODERATE ZONE **FRONT, MIDDLE TO BOTTOM** The areas at the front of the refrigerator, from the middle to the bottom shelves, are the most moderate, with temperatures above 37 degrees. Put eggs, butter, and fruits and vegetables that are sensitive to chilling injury here.

HUMID ZONE **CRISPER DRAWER** Crispers provide a humid environment that helps keep produce with a high water content from shriveling and rotting. However, if the humidity is too high, water can accumulate and hasten spoilage. You can regulate humidity by adjusting the vents; the more cold air that is let in, the less humid the environment.

KNOW YOUR FREEZER

Keeping your freezer stocked is a great way to lighten your cooking load on nights you most need the extra time, whether you opt to stash fully prepared dinners or elements of a meal there. To ensure that food is safe to eat, make sure your freezer stays below 0 degrees. Although properly wrapped food kept at this temperature will be safe to eat for a while, we recommend using frozen food within a month for peak quality. Be sure to carefully label everything so that you know what you're defrosting and when it was made.

Temperature

Many freezers can be too warm. Track the temperature of your freezer with an inexpensive refrigerator/freezer thermometer (page 9). According to food safety experts, your freezer should register 0 degrees Fahrenheit or colder at all times.

Air Flow

Keep foods away from the vents in the back wall and don't overpack the freezer; this allows the air to circulate more efficiently, freezing foods faster.

The Warmest Spot

The door shelves are the warmest spots in most freezers. They are good places to store frequently used items and foods less prone to spoiling, such as coffee beans, bread, butter, and nuts.

The Coldest Spot

The rear center is the coldest spot in a freezer, making it the best place to quick-freeze individual items or to store casseroles and containers of sauces while they freeze, because the foods will freeze rapidly, preventing moisture loss.

Shelf Space

Many top-mounted freezers are short on shelf space. Use portable wire cabinet shelving (available at most home goods stores) to organize your food and to maximize the air flow, ensuring a quick and thorough freeze. Clear some shelf space to quick-freeze individual items—the quicker they are frozen, the less moisture loss they will suffer when defrosted.

FROZEN ASSETS: 10 THINGS TO ALWAYS KEEP IN YOUR FREEZER

Sure, keeping a fully composed dish in your freezer is one way to make dinner easier on busy nights, but keeping recipe components in your freezer can help streamline meals on nights that you have a little bit of time to cook.

1 VEGETABLES Peas, pearl onions, and chopped onions are great frozen options. In many applications, frozen peas are preferable to fresh. To save time, and that unused half onion, you can chop a bunch of onions at once and freeze them in portions in zipper-lock bags; they last for about one month.

2 SLICED MEAT Keeping 1 or 2 pounds of sliced flank steak, boneless, skinless chicken breasts, or pork tenderloin in the freezer can be a weeknight lifesaver; having meat at the ready means you'll have a jump start on a simple stir fry (pages 151 and 193), with the bulk of the prep work done.

3 COOKED SHREDDED MEAT Flavorful spiced shredded chicken, pork, or beef can be portioned out and frozen. With your freezer stocked, making quick homemade burritos, tostadas, or enchiladas requires only a few pantry staples and a minimum of additional prep work.

4 SHRIMP We recommend purchasing bags of still-frozen shrimp and defrosting them as needed at home. You can quickly thaw them under running water in just a few minutes.

5 PASTA SAUCE Make your own sauce (pages 112–119), store some in the freezer, and dinner is only minutes away.

6 PESTO Stirred into pasta, pesto makes a great quick vegetarian meal (see pages 136–137). It can also be used to flavor simple steamed veggies, to top chicken or fish, to dollop on pizza, or as a spread for sandwiches.

7 HOMEMADE BROTH Broth tastes worlds better when you make it yourself (see pages 46–47) to use in recipes. It keeps in the freezer for up to one month.

8 DINNER ROLLS, BISCUITS, AND TORTILLAS On a busy weeknight, a bread accompaniment warm out of the oven can help to turn a salad, soup, or bowl of chili into a meal.

9 PIE DOUGH When planning your pie making, remember that rounds of pie dough (pages 370–371) freeze beautifully. Let the dough thaw overnight before assembling and baking a fresh pie.

10 COOKIE DOUGH Keeping frozen cookie dough on hand means that you can bake as many, or as few, cookies as you like whenever you want (note that this technique only applies to drop cookies; see pages 386–389).

EIGHT RULES FOR SAFER (AND MORE EFFICIENT) FOOD STORAGE

While developing our make-ahead recipes, we wrapped dozens of casseroles; stashed countless stews and braises in the fridge overnight; and prepped, marinated, and stored all sorts of recipe components. Here's what you need to know about wrapping food and storing it safely so that it will retain its freshness.

1. Refrigerate Cooked Food in Airtight Containers

To keep cooked food fresh, store it in an airtight storage container or zipper-lock bag, or cover it tightly with plastic wrap. To maximize your refrigerator space, seal a bowl with plastic wrap, then cover it with an appropriate-size plate and stack another dish on top. If you can't fit a large dish (such as a baking sheet or a Dutch oven) in your fridge, transfer the food to smaller containers. As an added bonus, this can help the food to cool faster by increasing its surface area. Never store cooked food near or below raw meat in the fridge.

2. Store Raw Meat and Seafood Properly

Raw meat should be refrigerated promptly after purchase in the back of the fridge where it's coldest; make sure that it is well wrapped and never stored on shelves that are above other food, especially when thawing. Fish and seafood should be stored on a bed of ice.

3. Know How to Store Your Produce

In general, it's a good idea to store produce in the packaging in which it was sold. The ready-made packaging is specially designed to let out the ripening gases that cause spoilage while protecting the produce from the drying effects of the air. If you buy loose lettuce, greens, fresh herbs, berries, or mushrooms, store them in a partially open plastic bag lined with paper towels. If you wash produce before storing, be sure to dry it thoroughly; moisture promotes the growth of mold.

4. Keep Frozen Foods Cold (and Organized)

For safety reasons, frozen foods should stay at 0 degrees or colder. It's best to cool food before freezing because the quicker foods freeze, the smaller the ice crystals that form. And remember to label everything you freeze with the contents and date so you don't end up with mystery soups or casseroles past their prime. Containers should be mostly full with about ½ inch of headroom to allow for expansion; if there's more than ½ inch of headroom in the container, place a piece of plastic wrap directly on the surface of the food to prevent freezer burn. And keep in mind that not everything will freeze well—refer to the Freeze It icons throughout the book for our tested recommendations.

5. Freeze Some Items Individually

Quick-freezing individual items like chicken nuggets, veggie burgers, and balls of cookie dough before storing makes it easy to grab just what you need without having to thaw the entire package. Simply freeze the items on a tray for about 1 hour, then transfer to a zipper-lock bag. Or place portions in a zipper-lock bag, press out the air, being sure the portions do not touch, fold the bag over in the center, and freeze.

6. Avoid Refreezing Food

While the U.S. Department of Agriculture says that it is technically safe to refreeze food once it has been defrosted (as long as it is refrozen within four days), we don't recommend it. The texture of refrozen food will suffer considerably due to the amount of moisture lost in thawing. Try dividing items like stews or sauces into smaller containers and portioning out raw meat and other ingredients before you freeze them so that it's easy to defrost only what you will use.

7. Wrap It Well

To wrap a pie, casserole dish, large platter, or baking sheet, lay a piece of plastic wrap about twice as long as the dish on the counter, set the dish on top parallel to the plastic, then bring the edges together over the top. Lay a second piece of plastic about twice as wide as the dish on the counter, set the dish on top perpendicular to the plastic, then bring the edges together and press to seal tightly. Casseroles and pies stored in the freezer require an added layer of protection; after wrapping the dish with plastic, wrap it again with a layer of aluminum foil; this will prevent odors in the freezer from affecting the dish.

8. Use Zipper-Lock Bags as Space Savers

When storing food in a zipper-lock bag, be sure to press out as much air as possible before sealing the bag. Zipper-lock bags are also a space-saving way to store soups and sauces for the freezer: Fill the bag, seal it tightly, and freeze it flat on a baking sheet. Once frozen, the bags can be stacked or stored upright wherever there's room.

AVOID THE DANGER ZONE

Keep in mind that within the "danger zone" of 40 to 140 degrees, bacteria double about every 20 minutes. As a general rule, food shouldn't stay in this zone for more than 2 hours (1 hour if the room temperature is over 90 degrees).

COOL ON THE COUNTER, NOT IN THE FRIDGE It might seem like a convenient shortcut to put a hot dish into the fridge to cool, but this will cause the temperature in the refrigerator to rise, potentially making it hospitable to the spread of bacteria. Always cool foods to room temperature (about 75 degrees) before transferring them to the fridge. The FDA recommends cooling foods to 70 degrees within 2 hours after cooking, and to 40 degrees within another 4 hours.

DEFROST IN THE FRIDGE Defrosting should always be done in the refrigerator, not on the counter, where bacteria can multiply rapidly. Always place food on a plate or in a bowl while defrosting to prevent any liquid it releases from coming in contact with other foods. Most food will take 24 hours to thaw fully with larger casseroles taking up to 48 hours.

REHEAT CAREFULLY When food is reheated, it should be brought through the danger zone quickly—don't let it come slowly to a simmer. Make sure that leftover sauces, soups, and casseroles reach at least 165 degrees, using an instant-read thermometer to determine when they're at the proper temperature.

Appetizers

◼ EASY (30 minutes or less active time)   ◼ FREEZE IT
Photo: Stuffed Mushrooms

Our creamy spinach dip is made using frozen spinach and gets its big flavor from fresh herbs and a hit of hot sauce.

Herbed Spinach Dip

MAKES ABOUT 1½ CUPS   **EASY**

ACTIVE TIME 15 MINUTES

TOTAL TIME 15 MINUTES (PLUS 1 HOUR CHILLING TIME)

WHY THIS RECIPE WORKS Spinach dip doesn't have to be bland or boring. For a spinach dip to really taste good, we found that both the ingredients and the method were key. We packed tons of flavor into our spinach dip with herbs, red bell pepper, scallions, garlic, and even a little kick of hot sauce. For the mixing method, we used the food processor to help distribute the spinach evenly throughout the dip. This method also made it easy to add other flavors to the dip for our creative variations. The garlic must be minced or pressed before going into the food processor or the dip will contain large chunks of garlic. Serve with crudités.

10 ounces frozen chopped spinach, thawed and squeezed dry
½ red bell pepper, chopped fine
½ cup sour cream
½ cup mayonnaise
½ cup fresh parsley leaves
3 scallions, sliced thin

1 tablespoon fresh dill or 1 teaspoon dried
1 garlic clove, minced
¼ teaspoon hot sauce
Salt and pepper

Process all ingredients with ½ teaspoon salt and ¼ teaspoon pepper in food processor until well combined, about 1 minute. Transfer to serving bowl, cover, and refrigerate until flavors have blended, at least 1 hour. Season with salt and pepper to taste before serving.

VARIATIONS

Spinach Dip with Blue Cheese and Bacon   EASY
Omit bell pepper, dill, hot sauce, and salt. Add ⅓ cup crumbled blue cheese to food processor with spinach. Sprinkle with 2 slices cooked, crumbled bacon before serving.

Cilantro-Lime Spinach Dip   EASY
Omit bell pepper, dill, and hot sauce. Add ¼ cup fresh cilantro leaves, 1 tablespoon chopped canned chipotle chile in adobo sauce, ½ teaspoon grated lime zest, 1 tablespoon lime juice, ½ teaspoon light brown sugar, and ⅛ teaspoon ground cumin to food processor with spinach.

TO MAKE AHEAD
• Dip can be refrigerated for up to 24 hours
• To serve, bring to room temperature and season with salt and pepper to taste

Creamy Blue Cheese Dip

MAKES ABOUT 2½ CUPS   **EASY**

ACTIVE TIME 10 MINUTES

TOTAL TIME 10 MINUTES (PLUS 30 MINUTES CHILLING TIME)

WHY THIS RECIPE WORKS The key to full-flavored blue cheese dip is to use a combination of dairy ingredients—namely, sour cream and mayonnaise. Whenever we tried to eliminate either one of these, tasters complained of seriously compromised flavor. Serve with crudités, potato chips, or Buffalo Wings (page 40).

6 ounces blue cheese, crumbled (1½ cups)
½ cup buttermilk, plus extra as needed
1 garlic clove, minced
6 tablespoons mayonnaise
⅓ cup sour cream
2 tablespoons white wine vinegar
½ teaspoon sugar
Salt and pepper

Using fork, mash blue cheese, buttermilk, and garlic together in serving bowl until mixture resembles cottage cheese. Stir in mayonnaise, sour cream, vinegar, sugar, ½ teaspoon salt, and ½ teaspoon pepper. Add extra buttermilk as needed to adjust dip consistency. Cover and refrigerate until flavors have blended, at least 30 minutes. Season with salt and pepper to taste before serving.

> **TO MAKE AHEAD**
> - Dip can be refrigerated for up to 2 days
> - To serve, bring to room temperature and season with salt and pepper to taste

Roasted Red Pepper and Walnut Dip

MAKES ABOUT 2 CUPS   EASY
ACTIVE TIME 15 MINUTES
TOTAL TIME 30 MINUTES

WHY THIS RECIPE WORKS Our quick version of this Middle Eastern dip starts with jarred roasted red peppers. We flavored them with cumin and cayenne and added honey and molasses for sweetness and a velvety texture. Toasted walnuts and wheat crackers lent complexity and richness, amplifying the sweet, smoky, and savory flavors that are unique to this dip. We've had good luck using Carr's Whole Wheat Crackers in this recipe. Serve with pita chips.

1½ cups jarred roasted red peppers, rinsed and patted dry
 1 cup walnuts, toasted
 ¼ cup plain wheat crackers, crumbled
 3 tablespoons lemon juice
 2 tablespoons extra-virgin olive oil
 1 tablespoon molasses
 1 teaspoon honey
 ¾ teaspoon salt
 ½ teaspoon ground cumin
 ⅛ teaspoon cayenne pepper
 1 tablespoon minced fresh parsley (optional)

Pulse all ingredients except parsley in food processor until smooth, about 10 pulses. Transfer to serving bowl, cover, and refrigerate for 15 minutes. Sprinkle with parsley, if using, before serving.

> **TO MAKE AHEAD**
> - Dip can be refrigerated for up to 2 days
> - To serve, bring to room temperature, season with lemon juice, salt, and cayenne to taste, and sprinkle with parsley, if using

OLIVE OIL–SEA SALT PITA CHIPS

SERVES 8   EASY
ACTIVE TIME 10 MINUTES
TOTAL TIME 30 MINUTES (PLUS COOLING TIME)

Both white and whole-wheat pita breads will work well here. We prefer the larger crystal size of sea salt or kosher salt; if using table salt, reduce the amount of salt by half.

 4 (8-inch) pita breads
 ½ cup extra-virgin olive oil
 1 teaspoon sea salt or kosher salt

1. Adjust oven racks to upper-middle and lower-middle positions and heat oven to 350 degrees. Using kitchen shears, cut around perimeter of each pita and separate into 2 thin rounds.

2. Working with 1 round at a time, brush rough side generously with oil and sprinkle with salt. Stack rounds on top of one another, rough side up, as you go. Using chef's knife, cut pita stack into 8 wedges. Spread wedges, rough side up and in single layer, on 2 rimmed baking sheets.

3. Bake until wedges are golden brown and crisp, about 15 minutes, switching and rotating sheets halfway through baking. Let cool before serving.

VARIATION
ROSEMARY-PARMESAN PITA CHIPS   EASY
Reduce amount of salt to ½ teaspoon. Toss salt with ½ cup grated Parmesan and 2 tablespoons minced fresh rosemary before sprinkling over pitas.

> **TO MAKE AHEAD**
> Pita chips can be stored at room temperature for up to 3 days

PREPARING PITA FOR CHIPS

1. Using kitchen shears or scissors, cut around perimeter of each pita to yield 2 thin rounds.

2. Brush rough sides of each round with oil, season with salt, and stack them. Using chef's knife, cut stack into 8 wedges.

EASY, CREAMY DIPS WITH CRUDITÉS

For creamy dips that draw a crowd, you need a rich but well-balanced base matched with fresh and assertive flavorings. These dips are almost as easy as store-bought options, but with a lot more flavor. For our base, we tested mayonnaise, sour cream, yogurt, buttermilk, heavy cream, cottage cheese, and cream cheese in all possible combinations. Mayonnaise and sour cream made the strongest pairing. The mayonnaise contributed the body, richness, and velvety texture we wanted in a creamy dip, while sour cream heightened the flavor. Adding a few flavor-charged ingredients let us take the dips in different directions without making the process too complicated.

TO MAKE Combine all ingredients in medium bowl until smooth and creamy. Transfer dip to serving bowl, cover with plastic wrap, and refrigerate until flavors are blended, at least 1 hour.

CAESAR DIP WITH PARMESAN AND ANCHOVIES
SERVES 4 TO 6 `EASY`
ACTIVE TIME 10 MINUTES
TOTAL TIME 10 MINUTES (PLUS 1 HOUR CHILLING TIME)

- 1 cup mayonnaise
- ½ cup sour cream
- ¼ cup grated Parmesan cheese
- 1 tablespoon lemon juice
- 1 tablespoon minced fresh parsley
- 2 garlic cloves, minced
- 2 anchovy fillets, rinsed and minced
- ⅛ teaspoon pepper

GREEN GODDESS DIP
SERVES 4 TO 6 `EASY`
ACTIVE TIME 10 MINUTES
TOTAL TIME 10 MINUTES (PLUS 1 HOUR CHILLING TIME)

- ¾ cup mayonnaise
- ¾ cup sour cream
- ¼ cup minced fresh parsley
- ¼ cup minced fresh chives
- 2 tablespoons minced fresh tarragon
- 1 tablespoon lemon juice
- 2 garlic cloves, minced
- ⅛ teaspoon salt
- ⅛ teaspoon pepper

CHIPOTLE-LIME DIP WITH SCALLIONS
SERVES 4 TO 6 `EASY`
ACTIVE TIME 10 MINUTES
TOTAL TIME 10 MINUTES (PLUS 1 HOUR CHILLING TIME)

- 1 cup mayonnaise
- ½ cup sour cream
- 3 scallions, sliced thin
- 2 garlic cloves, minced
- 1 tablespoon minced canned chipotle chile in adobo sauce plus ½ teaspoon adobo sauce
- 1 teaspoon grated lime zest plus 1 tablespoon juice

CREAMY HORSERADISH DIP
SERVES 4 TO 6 `EASY`
ACTIVE TIME 10 MINUTES
TOTAL TIME 10 MINUTES (PLUS 1 HOUR CHILLING TIME)

- ¾ cup mayonnaise
- ¾ cup sour cream
- 2 scallions, sliced thin
- ¼ cup prepared horseradish, squeezed of excess liquid
- 1 tablespoon minced fresh parsley
- ⅛ teaspoon pepper

TO MAKE AHEAD ▷

- Dips can be refrigerated for up to 2 days
- To serve, bring to room temperature and season with salt and pepper to taste

How To Make Crudités

A platter of crudités and dips provides an easy and healthy make-ahead appetizer. Preparing your own is less expensive and the vegetables will taste fresher.

TO BLANCH Some vegetables need to be blanched (see below) and shocked in ice water to help preserve their color and crisp texture. Bring 6 quarts water and 2 tablespoons salt to a boil in a large pot over high heat. Cook the vegetables, one type at a time, until slightly softened but still crunchy at the core, following the times listed. Transfer the blanched vegetables immediately to a bowl of ice water until completely cool and then drain and pat dry.

BELL PEPPERS

Slice off top and bottom of pepper and remove seeds and stem. Slice down through side of pepper, unroll it so that it lies flat, then slice into ½-inch-wide strips.

BROCCOLI AND CAULIFLOWER

Place head of broccoli or cauliflower upside down on cutting board and use chef's knife to trim off florets close to heads. Cut larger florets into bite-size pieces by slicing down through stem. Blanch broccoli and cauliflower (separately) for 1 to 1½ minutes.

CARROTS AND CELERY

Slice both celery and peeled carrots lengthwise into long, elegant lengths rather than short, stumpy pieces.

GREEN BEANS

Line beans up in row on cutting board and trim off inedible stem ends with 1 slice. Blanch beans for 1 minute.

RADISHES

Choose radishes with green tops still attached so each half has leafy handle for grasping and dipping. Trim each radish and slice in half through stem.

SNOW AND SNAP PEAS

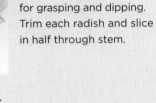

Use paring knife to snip off tip of pod and pull along flat side to remove tough, fibrous string that runs along straight side of snow and snap peas. Blanch snow and snap peas separately for 15 seconds.

TO MAKE AHEAD ▸

- Crudités can be refrigerated for up to 2 days; store raw vegetables wrapped in damp paper towels in a zipper-lock bag and blanched vegetables in an airtight container
- Celery and carrot sticks can also be refrigerated by standing them in a glass with a few ice cubes in the bottom for extra freshness

To give our hummus the perfect silky texture, we process canned chickpeas with olive oil and tahini.

Classic Hummus

MAKES ABOUT 2 CUPS   **EASY**

ACTIVE TIME 20 MINUTES

TOTAL TIME 20 MINUTES (PLUS 30 MINUTES SITTING TIME)

WHY THIS RECIPE WORKS For a flavorful, silky-smooth hummus that puts supermarket versions to shame, we started with canned chickpeas. We used the food processor to simplify the preparation; instead of laboring over the fussy job of removing the chickpeas' tough skins, we simply pureed the unskinned chickpeas into a velvety emulsion with olive oil and tahini for the perfect texture.

¼ cup water

3 tablespoons lemon juice

6 tablespoons tahini

2 tablespoons extra-virgin olive oil, plus extra for drizzling

1 (15-ounce) can chickpeas, rinsed

1 small garlic clove, minced

½ teaspoon salt

¼ teaspoon ground cumin
   Pinch cayenne pepper

1 tablespoon minced fresh cilantro or parsley

1. Combine water and lemon juice in small bowl. In separate bowl, whisk tahini and oil together. Set aside 2 tablespoons of chickpeas for garnish.

2. Process remaining chickpeas, garlic, salt, cumin, and cayenne in food processor until almost fully ground, about 15 seconds. Scrape down bowl with rubber spatula. With processor running, add lemon juice mixture in steady stream. Scrape down bowl and continue to process for 1 minute. With processor running, add tahini mixture in steady stream and process until hummus is smooth and creamy, about 15 seconds, scraping down bowl as needed.

3. Transfer hummus to serving bowl, cover with plastic wrap, and let sit at room temperature until flavors meld, about 30 minutes.

4. Sprinkle with reserved chickpeas and cilantro, drizzle with extra oil to taste, and serve.

VARIATIONS

Artichoke-Lemon Hummus   **EASY**

Omit cumin and cilantro and increase lemon juice to ¼ cup (2 lemons). Rinse 1 cup jarred baby artichoke hearts packed in water and pat dry; chop ¼ cup artichokes and set aside for garnish. Process entire can of chickpeas (do not reserve 2 tablespoons) along with remaining ¾ cup artichokes and ¼ teaspoon grated lemon zest. Garnish hummus with reserved artichokes, 2 teaspoons minced fresh parsley or mint, and extra oil to taste.

Roasted Red Pepper Hummus   **EASY**

Omit water, cumin, and cilantro. Process entire can of chickpeas (do not reserve 2 tablespoons) with ¼ cup jarred roasted red peppers that have been rinsed and patted dry. Garnish hummus with 2 tablespoons toasted sliced almonds, 2 teaspoons minced fresh parsley, and extra oil to taste.

> **TO MAKE AHEAD**
>
> • Reserved chickpeas and hummus, prepared through step 3, can be refrigerated separately for up to 4 days
> • To serve, bring to room temperature and continue with step 4

Guacamole

SERVES 4 TO 6   **EASY**

ACTIVE TIME 15 MINUTES

TOTAL TIME 15 MINUTES

WHY THIS RECIPE WORKS As party dips go, it's hard to beat good guacamole, but many versions are as smooth and bland as baby food. Our guacamole is all about bold flavor and great texture. For the base, we mashed one avocado and then gently folded in two diced avocados for just the right chunky texture. We flavored our guacamole with onion, fresh herbs, spices, and a few other add-ins to keep this party favorite interesting. Very ripe avocados are key to this recipe. Serve with tortilla chips.

3 ripe avocados
¼ cup chopped fresh cilantro
1 jalapeño chile, stemmed, seeded, and minced
2 tablespoons finely chopped onion
2 tablespoons lime juice
2 garlic cloves, minced
Salt
½ teaspoon ground cumin

1. Halve 1 avocado, remove pit, and scoop flesh into medium bowl. Add cilantro, jalapeño, onion, lime juice, garlic, ¾ teaspoon salt, and cumin and mash with potato masher (or fork) until mostly smooth.

2. Halve and pit remaining 2 avocados. Carefully make ½-inch crosshatch incisions in flesh with butter knife, cutting down to but not through skin. Insert spoon between skin and flesh, gently scoop out avocado cubes, and add to mashed mixture. Gently mash until mixture is well combined but still coarse. Season with salt to taste. Serve.

> **TO MAKE AHEAD**
> • Guacamole can be refrigerated for up to 24 hours with plastic wrap pressed directly against its surface
> • To serve, bring to room temperature and season with lime juice and salt to taste

Tomatillo Salsa

MAKES ABOUT 2 CUPS   **EASY**
ACTIVE TIME 30 MINUTES
TOTAL TIME 35 MINUTES (PLUS 30 MINUTES SITTING TIME)

WHY THIS RECIPE WORKS *Salsa verde* (literally meaning "green sauce") is perhaps more common on the authentic Mexican table than tomato-based *salsa fresca*. We wanted a tangy, well-balanced tomatillo salsa recipe that highlighted the green, citrusy notes of the fruit. While some salsa verde recipes use raw tomatillos, most cook them either by boiling or roasting. Cooking softens the fruit, which can be quite firm, and mellows its acidity. We found that charring half under the broiler and leaving the other half raw produced a salsa with a clean, fresh flavor and subtle, smoky nuances. We combined the tomatillos with the traditional salsa verde seasonings—jalapeño, onion, garlic, cilantro, lime juice, and salt—in the bowl of a food processor, and pulsed the salsa to a chunky consistency. Serve with tortilla chips or as an accompaniment to grilled steaks, chicken, or fish.

1 pound tomatillos, husks and stems removed, rinsed well and dried
1 teaspoon vegetable oil
1 small white onion, chopped
1 jalapeño chile, stemmed, halved, and seeded
½ cup fresh cilantro leaves
2 tablespoons lime juice
1 garlic clove, minced
Salt
2 teaspoons extra-virgin olive oil
Sugar

1. Adjust oven rack 6 inches from broiler element and heat broiler. Line rimmed baking sheet with aluminum foil. Toss half of tomatillos with vegetable oil and transfer to prepared sheet. Broil until tomatillos are spotty brown and skins begin to burst, 7 to 10 minutes. Transfer tomatillos to food processor and let cool completely.

2. Halve remaining tomatillos and add to food processor with broiled tomatillos. Add onion, jalapeño, cilantro, lime juice, garlic, and ¼ teaspoon salt. Pulse until slightly chunky, 16 to 18 pulses. Transfer salsa to serving bowl, cover, and let sit at room temperature for at least 30 minutes. Stir in olive oil and season with salt and sugar to taste before serving.

> **TO MAKE AHEAD**
> • Salsa can be refrigerated for up to 2 days
> • To serve, bring to room temperature and season with salt and sugar to taste

PREPARING TOMATILLOS FOR SALSA

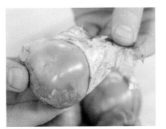

1. Pull papery husks and stems off of tomatillos; discard.

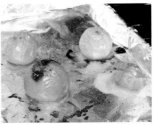

2. Broil half of tomatillos until skins are spotty brown, leaving other half raw to add to salsa later.

CROSTINI AND TOPPINGS

Crostini—Italian for "little toasts"—are simply small slices of toasted or grilled bread, usually made with baguette or ciabatta, that make a perfect base for cheeses, vegetables, dips, spreads, or pâtés. We found that thin slices of baguette were the best choice for our crostini recipe. Baking the toasts for 10 minutes in a 400-degree oven turned them crisp enough to hold even hefty toppings, and rubbing the hot toasts with a raw garlic clove added just the right subtle garlicky flavor. Finally, brushing them with olive oil added richness and moisture.

CROSTINI

MAKES 25 TO 30 TOASTS EASY
ACTIVE TIME 15 MINUTES
TOTAL TIME 35 MINUTES
You can also serve these little toasts next to a dip or alongside a soup, stew, or salad. Crostini taste best straight from the oven.

- 1 large (12- to 15-inch) baguette, sliced ¼ inch thick on bias
- 1 garlic clove, peeled and sliced in half
- 2 tablespoons extra-virgin olive oil
  Salt and pepper

Adjust oven rack to middle position and heat oven to 400 degrees. Arrange bread in single layer on baking sheet. Bake bread until dry and crisp, about 10 minutes, flipping slices over halfway through baking. Rub garlic clove over 1 side of each piece of toasted bread, then brush with oil. Season with salt and pepper to taste, and serve.

▸ TO MAKE AHEAD

Crostini can be stored at room temperature for up to 8 hours before serving

ARUGULA PESTO AND GOAT CHEESE TOPPING

SERVES 8 TO 10 EASY
ACTIVE TIME 20 MINUTES
TOTAL TIME 20 MINUTES

- 5 ounces (5 cups) baby arugula
- ¼ cup extra-virgin olive oil, plus extra for serving
- ¼ cup pine nuts, toasted
- 1 tablespoon minced shallot
- 1 teaspoon grated lemon zest plus 1 teaspoon juice
  Salt and pepper
- 1 recipe Crostini
- 2 ounces goat cheese, crumbled (½ cup)

Pulse arugula, oil, pine nuts, shallot, lemon zest and juice, ½ teaspoon salt, and ¼ teaspoon pepper in food processor until mostly smooth, about 8 pulses, scraping down sides of bowl as needed. Spread arugula mixture evenly on toasts, top with goat cheese, and drizzle with extra oil to taste. Serve.

▸ TO MAKE AHEAD

- Pesto can be covered with 1 tablespoon oil and refrigerated for up to 2 days; bring to room temperature before serving
- Assemble and garnish crostini just before serving

ARTICHOKE HEART AND PARMESAN TOPPING

SERVES 8 TO 10 EASY
ACTIVE TIME 20 MINUTES
TOTAL TIME 20 MINUTES
While we prefer the flavor and texture of jarred whole baby artichoke hearts, you can substitute 6 ounces frozen artichoke hearts, thawed and patted dry, for the jarred.

- 1 cup jarred whole baby artichoke hearts packed in water, rinsed and patted dry
- 2 tablespoons extra-virgin olive oil, plus extra for serving
- 2 tablespoons chopped fresh basil
- 2 teaspoons lemon juice
- 1 garlic clove, minced
  Salt and pepper
- 2 ounces Parmesan cheese, 1 ounce grated fine, 1 ounce shaved
- 1 recipe Crostini

Pulse artichokes, oil, basil, lemon juice, garlic, ¼ teaspoon salt, and ¼ teaspoon pepper in food processor until coarsely pureed, about 6 pulses, scraping down sides of bowl as needed. Add grated Parmesan and pulse to combine, about 2 pulses. Spread artichoke mixture evenly on toasts and top with shaved Parmesan. Season with pepper and drizzle with extra oil to taste. Serve.

▸ TO MAKE AHEAD

- Artichoke mixture can be refrigerated for up to 4 days; bring to room temperature before serving
- Assemble and garnish crostini just before serving

RICOTTA, TOMATO, AND BASIL TOPPING

SERVES 8 TO 10   EASY
ACTIVE TIME 20 MINUTES
TOTAL TIME 30 MINUTES

We prefer the rich flavor of whole-milk ricotta; however, part-skim ricotta can be substituted. Do not use fat-free ricotta.

- 1 pound cherry tomatoes, quartered
  Salt and pepper
- 5 tablespoons shredded fresh basil
- 1 tablespoon extra-virgin olive oil, plus extra for serving
- 10 ounces (1¼ cups) whole-milk ricotta cheese
- 1 recipe Crostini

Toss tomatoes with 1 teaspoon salt in colander and let drain for 15 minutes. Transfer drained tomatoes to bowl, toss with ¼ cup basil and oil, and season with salt and pepper to taste. In separate bowl, combine ricotta with remaining 1 tablespoon basil and season with salt and pepper to taste. Spread ricotta mixture evenly on toasts, top with tomato mixture, and drizzle lightly with extra oil to taste. Serve.

> **TO MAKE AHEAD**
> - Tomato mixture and ricotta mixture can be refrigerated separately for up to 24 hours; bring to room temperature before serving
> - Assemble and garnish crostini just before serving

BLACK OLIVE TAPENADE AND RICOTTA TOPPING

SERVES 8 TO 10   EASY
ACTIVE TIME 20 MINUTES
TOTAL TIME 20 MINUTES

We prefer the rich flavor of whole-milk ricotta; however, part-skim ricotta can be substituted. Do not use fat-free ricotta.

- ¾ cup pitted kalamata olives
- 1 small shallot, minced
- 2 tablespoons extra-virgin olive oil, plus extra for serving
- 1½ teaspoons lemon juice
- 1 garlic clove, minced
- 10 ounces (1¼ cups) whole-milk ricotta cheese
  Salt and pepper
- 1 recipe Crostini
- 2 tablespoons shredded fresh basil

Pulse olives, shallot, oil, lemon juice, and garlic in food processor until coarsely chopped, about 10 pulses, scraping down sides of bowl as needed. Season ricotta with salt and pepper to taste. Spread ricotta mixture evenly on toasts, top with olive mixture, and drizzle with extra oil to taste. Sprinkle with basil before serving.

> **TO MAKE AHEAD**
> - Olive tapenade and ricotta mixture can be refrigerated separately for up to 2 days; bring to room temperature before serving
> - Assemble and garnish crostini just before serving

Fresh ingredients and bold Tex-Mex flavors form the contrasting textures and layers of this classic party dip.

Ultimate Seven-Layer Dip

SERVES 8 TO 10
ACTIVE TIME 40 MINUTES
TOTAL TIME 1 HOUR

WHY THIS RECIPE WORKS We reduced every layer of this iconic dip down to its essential flavors and designed our recipe to emphasize them. We used canned black beans that we processed with garlic, chili powder, and lime juice. To keep the sour cream layer from watering down our dip, we combined it with cheese to give it more structure. We made the salsa and guacamole layers simple to ensure that they would come together easily and stay fresh and vibrant. This recipe is usually served in a clear dish. For a crowd, double the recipe and serve in a 13 by 9-inch glass baking dish. If you don't have time to make fresh guacamole as called for, simply mash three avocados with 3 tablespoons lime juice and ½ teaspoon salt. Serve with tortilla chips.

4 large tomatoes, cored, seeded, and chopped fine
2 jalapeño chiles, stemmed, seeded, and minced
3 tablespoons minced fresh cilantro
6 scallions (2 minced; 4 green parts only, sliced thin)
2 tablespoons plus 2 teaspoons lime juice (2 limes)
 Salt
1 (15-ounce) can black beans, drained but not rinsed
2 garlic cloves, minced
¾ teaspoon chili powder
1½ cups sour cream
1 pound pepper Jack cheese, shredded (4 cups)
1 recipe (3 cups) Guacamole (page 20)

1. Toss tomatoes, jalapeños, cilantro, minced scallions, 2 tablespoons lime juice, and ⅛ teaspoon salt in bowl. Let stand until tomatoes begin to soften, about 30 minutes. Strain through fine-mesh strainer, discard liquid, and return to bowl.

2. Meanwhile, pulse black beans, garlic, chili powder, ⅛ teaspoon salt, and remaining 2 teaspoons lime juice in food processor until mixture resembles chunky paste, about 15 pulses. Spread bean mixture evenly over bottom of 8-inch square baking dish or 1-quart glass bowl.

3. Wipe out food processor, add sour cream and 2½ cups pepper Jack, and pulse until smooth, about 15 pulses. Spread sour cream mixture evenly over bean layer. Top evenly with remaining 1½ cups pepper Jack, followed by guacamole and, finally, drained tomato mixture. Sprinkle with sliced scallion greens before serving.

VARIATION
Ultimate Smoky Seven-Layer Dip
Add 1 to 3 teaspoons minced canned chipotle chile in adobo sauce to food processor with black beans. Sprinkle with 4 slices cooked, crumbled bacon before serving.

> **TO MAKE AHEAD**
> - Dip can be refrigerated for up to 24 hours
> - To serve, bring to room temperature and sprinkle with scallion greens

Roasted Artichoke Dip

SERVES 8 TO 10
ACTIVE TIME 35 MINUTES
TOTAL TIME 1 HOUR 10 MINUTES

WHY THIS RECIPE WORKS For our version of this classic hot dip, we focused on packing in great artichoke flavor under a golden, crispy crust. We replaced tinny canned artichokes with the cleaner taste of jarred artichokes. For the perfect creamy texture, we used mayonnaise and cream cheese as the base for the dip. Finally, we added some Parmesan to the bread-crumb topping to kick it up a notch. While we prefer the flavor and texture of jarred whole baby artichoke hearts, you can substitute 18 ounces of frozen artichoke hearts; do not thaw the frozen artichoke hearts. This dip is best served warm. Serve with crackers or a thinly sliced baguette.

TOPPING

2 slices hearty white sandwich bread, torn into quarters
2 tablespoons grated Parmesan cheese
1 tablespoon unsalted butter, melted

DIP

3 cups jarred whole baby artichoke hearts packed in water, rinsed and patted dry
2 tablespoons olive oil
Salt and pepper
1 onion, chopped fine
2 garlic cloves, minced
1 cup mayonnaise
4 ounces cream cheese, softened
1 ounce Parmesan cheese, grated (½ cup)
2 tablespoons lemon juice
1 tablespoon minced fresh thyme
Pinch cayenne pepper

1. FOR THE TOPPING Pulse bread in food processor until coarsely ground, about 12 pulses. Toss bread crumbs with Parmesan and melted butter.

2. FOR THE DIP Adjust oven rack to middle position and heat oven to 450 degrees. Line rimmed baking sheet with aluminum foil. Toss artichokes with 1 tablespoon oil, ½ teaspoon salt, and ¼ teaspoon pepper on prepared sheet. Roast artichokes, stirring occasionally, until browned at edges, about 25 minutes. When cool enough to handle, chop artichokes coarse. Reduce oven temperature to 400 degrees.

3. Meanwhile, heat remaining 1 tablespoon oil in 10-inch skillet over medium-high heat until shimmering. Add onion and cook until softened, 5 to 7 minutes. Stir in garlic and cook until fragrant, about 30 seconds. Transfer onion mixture to large bowl.

4. Stir mayonnaise, cream cheese, Parmesan, lemon juice, thyme, and cayenne into onion mixture until uniform, smearing any lumps of cream cheese against side of bowl with rubber spatula. Gently fold in artichokes and season with salt and pepper to taste. Transfer mixture to 1-quart baking dish and smooth top. Sprinkle topping evenly over dip.

5. Bake dip until hot throughout and topping is golden brown, 20 to 25 minutes. Let dip cool for 5 minutes before serving.

▸ TO MAKE AHEAD

Dip, prepared through step 4, can be refrigerated for up to 3 days

Buying Processed Artichokes

Artichokes are served boiled, baked, stuffed, braised, and more. They are used in everything from soups and stews to risotto, paella, and pasta. But while fresh artichokes have their place, they're limited by seasonality, so many recipes turn to prepared artichokes as a flavorful alternative. When buying processed artichokes, avoid marinated versions; we prefer to control the seasonings ourselves. We also don't recommend canned hearts, which tend to taste waterlogged and have large, tough leaves. We think that smaller whole jarred artichoke hearts labeled "baby" or "cocktail" are best. (If the label doesn't say this, look for specimens no larger than 1½ inches in length.) Our favorite brand is Pastene Baby Artichokes, which are nicely tender with a sweet, earthy flavor. If you can't find jarred baby artichokes, frozen artichoke hearts will work in certain recipes.

Baked Brie en Croûte

SERVES 6 TO 8 **EASY**
ACTIVE TIME 15 MINUTES
TOTAL TIME 50 MINUTES (PLUS 30 MINUTES COOLING TIME)

WHY THIS RECIPE WORKS Freezing the Brie for 20 minutes is a trick we discovered to keep the cheese from melting too much during baking (note that you can freeze the Brie for a lot longer). Also, while this recipe calls for apricot preserves or hot pepper jelly, other fruit preserves or chutney can be used. Use a firm, fairly unripe Brie for this recipe. To thaw frozen puff pastry, let it sit either in the refrigerator for 24 hours or on the counter for 30 minutes to 1 hour. Serve with crackers or bread.

1 (9½ by 9-inch) sheet puff pastry, thawed
1 large egg, lightly beaten
1 (8-ounce) wheel firm Brie cheese
¼ cup apricot preserves or hot pepper jelly

1. Line rimmed baking sheet with parchment paper. Roll puff pastry into 12-inch square on lightly floured counter. Using pie plate or other round guide, trim pastry to 9-inch circle with paring knife. Brush edges lightly with beaten egg.

2. Place Brie in center of pastry and wrap pastry around cheese, leaving small circle of Brie exposed on top.

3. Freeze Brie for 20 minutes. Adjust oven rack to middle position and heat oven to 425 degrees. Brush pastry with egg and transfer to prepared baking sheet. Bake wrapped cheese until pastry is deep golden brown, 20 to 25 minutes.

4. Transfer to wire rack. Spoon preserves into exposed center of Brie and let cool for about 30 minutes. Serve.

> **TO MAKE AHEAD** ▶
>
> Wrapped Brie, prepared through step 2, can be refrigerated for up to 24 hours or frozen for up to 1 month

WRAPPING BRIE IN PUFF PASTRY

1. Lift pastry up over cheese, pleating it at even intervals and leaving opening in center where Brie is exposed.

2. Press pleated edge of pastry up into rim, which will later be filled with preserves or jelly.

Pimento Cheese

MAKES ABOUT 3 CUPS   EASY

ACTIVE TIME 20 MINUTES

TOTAL TIME 20 MINUTES

WHY THIS RECIPE WORKS Equally at home with a sleeve of saltines or melted on a burger or a sandwich, pimento cheese is a flavorful Southern spread. We used sharp cheddar for its moderately intense flavor and creamy consistency (extra-sharp cheddar tended to be more crumbly), and shredded it with both the large and small holes of a box grater to give the cheese a cohesive yet chunky consistency. A couple of tablespoons of cream cheese kept the mixture spreadable, even right out of the fridge, and a ratio of ⅔ cup mayo to 1 pound cheese gave it a creamy texture. Worcestershire and lemon juice added brightness and depth without overpowering the cheese. You will need one 4-ounce jar of pimentos for this recipe. Yellow cheddar cheese is traditional, but you can substitute white cheddar cheese. Serve pimento cheese with crackers or crudités or use as a sandwich spread.

⅔ cup mayonnaise

2 tablespoons cream cheese, softened

1 teaspoon lemon juice

1 teaspoon Worcestershire sauce

¼ teaspoon cayenne pepper

1 pound yellow sharp cheddar cheese

⅓ cup pimentos, patted dry and minced

1. Whisk mayonnaise, cream cheese, lemon juice, Worcestershire, and cayenne together in large bowl.

2. Shred 8 ounces cheddar on large holes of box grater. Shred remaining 8 ounces cheddar on small holes of box grater. Stir pimentos and all cheddar into mayonnaise mixture until thoroughly combined. Serve.

> **TO MAKE AHEAD** ▶
>
> • Pimento cheese can be refrigerated for up to 1 week
> • To serve, bring to room temperature

Marinated Artichokes

SERVES 8   EASY

ACTIVE TIME 15 MINUTES

TOTAL TIME 15 MINUTES (PLUS 3 HOURS CHILLING TIME)

WHY THIS RECIPE WORKS The key to this quick and easy appetizer is prep-free jarred artichokes. Baby artichoke hearts have a bright acidity and nice bite, and when marinated with herbs and aromatics they develop a wonderfully complex flavor. We tossed the artichokes in a lively mixture of olive oil, fresh herbs, and lemon zest and juice; the artichokes absorbed the bold flavors of the dressing during chilling. While we prefer the flavor and texture of jarred whole baby artichoke hearts, you can substitute 18 ounces of frozen artichoke hearts, thawed, patted dry, and quartered if whole, for the jarred. Make sure to dry the artichokes thoroughly before tossing them with the marinade or they will be watery. Serve with thin breadsticks.

¼ cup minced fresh parsley or basil

1 shallot, minced

¾ teaspoon grated lemon zest plus 2 tablespoons juice

1 garlic clove, minced

  Salt and pepper

¾ cup extra-virgin olive oil

3 cups jarred whole baby artichoke hearts packed in water, rinsed and patted dry

1. Whisk parsley, shallot, lemon zest and juice, garlic, ¼ teaspoon salt, and ⅛ teaspoon pepper together in bowl. Whisking constantly, drizzle in oil. Gently fold artichoke hearts into dressing, cover, and refrigerate until flavors meld, at least 3 hours.

2. To serve, transfer artichoke hearts to serving bowl and season with salt and pepper to taste.

TO MAKE AHEAD ►

- Marinated artichokes can be refrigerated for up to 24 hours
- To serve, bring to room temperature and season with salt and pepper to taste

Marinated Olives

SERVES 8   EASY

ACTIVE TIME 15 MINUTES

TOTAL TIME 15 MINUTES (PLUS 4 HOURS 30 MINUTES CHILLING AND SITTING TIME)

WHY THIS RECIPE WORKS You can buy a wide variety of prepared olive products, but with just a little effort you can put together marinated olives with a lot more flavor and freshness. The most important step is to start with good olives and good olive oil. We used green and black olives with pits (pitted olives tend to have less flavor), packed in brine, not oil. On top of the usual aromatics—garlic, thyme, and red pepper flakes—we added shallot, fresh oregano, and grated lemon zest. Make sure to bring the mixture to room temperature before serving or the oil will look cloudy and congealed. Serve with toothpicks and a thinly sliced baguette or crackers.

1 cup brine-cured green olives with pits
1 cup brine-cured black olives with pits
¾ cup extra-virgin olive oil
1 shallot, minced
2 teaspoons grated lemon zest
2 teaspoons minced fresh thyme
2 teaspoons minced fresh oregano
1 garlic clove, minced
½ teaspoon red pepper flakes
½ teaspoon salt

Rinse olives thoroughly, then drain and pat dry with paper towels. Toss olives with oil, shallot, lemon zest, thyme, oregano, garlic, pepper flakes, and salt in bowl, cover, and refrigerate for at least 4 hours. Let sit at room temperature for at least 30 minutes before serving.

TO MAKE AHEAD ►

- Olive mixture can be refrigerated for up to 4 days
- To serve, bring to room temperature

Shallow frying canned chickpeas in olive oil deepens their nutty flavor and makes them supercrisp.

Crispy Spiced Chickpeas

SERVES 6   EASY

ACTIVE TIME 25 MINUTES

TOTAL TIME 25 MINUTES

WHY THIS RECIPE WORKS Chickpeas aren't just for salads and curries anymore. Tossed in oil and roasted, these beans become ultracrisp and deeply nutty in flavor—the perfect cocktail snack. Most recipes call for roasting chickpeas in the oven, but we found they never became crisp enough. Switching to the stovetop and frying the chickpeas in olive oil gave us the big crunch factor we were seeking. A quick toss in a sweet and savory mixture of sugar and smoked paprika made our chickpeas incredibly addictive. Make sure to dry the chickpeas thoroughly with paper towels before placing them in the oil. In order to get crisp chickpeas, it is important to keep the heat high enough to ensure the oil is simmering the entire time. After about 12 minutes, test for doneness by removing a few chickpeas and placing them on a paper towel to cool slightly before tasting. If they are not quite crisp yet, continue to cook 2 to 3 minutes longer, checking occasionally for doneness.

1 teaspoon smoked paprika
1 teaspoon sugar
½ teaspoon salt
¼ teaspoon pepper
1 cup extra-virgin olive oil
2 (15-ounce) cans chickpeas, rinsed and patted dry

Combine paprika, sugar, salt, and pepper in large bowl. Line rimmed baking sheet with paper towels. Heat oil in Dutch oven over high heat until just smoking. Add chickpeas to oil and cook, stirring occasionally, until deep golden brown and crisp, 12 to 15 minutes. Using slotted spoon, transfer chickpeas to prepared baking sheet to drain briefly, then toss with spices. Serve.

TO MAKE AHEAD

Chickpeas can be stored at room temperature for up to 24 hours

Spiced Nuts

SERVES 8 TO 10 **EASY**
ACTIVE TIME 15 MINUTES
TOTAL TIME 50 MINUTES (PLUS 30 MINUTES COOLING TIME)

WHY THIS RECIPE WORKS Salty spiced nuts are a deceptively easy and unassuming appetizer. Done correctly, however, they pack a double punch of flavor and protein that makes a perfect addition to your party snacks. Most recipes are made with a heavily sugared syrup that causes the nuts to clump awkwardly and leaves your hands a sticky mess. We wanted to develop a recipe that was both tasty and neat. Tossing the nuts in a mixture of egg white, water, and salt gave them a nice crunch when baked and helped the spices adhere. Using this basic technique, you can vary the spices for a mix that fits your menu. If you can't find superfine sugar, process granulated sugar in a food processor for 1 minute. If desired, you can use a mixture of the recommended nuts equaling 1 pound instead of 1 pound of a single type of nut.

⅔ cup superfine sugar
2 teaspoons cumin
1 teaspoon cayenne pepper
1 teaspoon paprika
1 large egg white
1 tablespoon water
1 teaspoon salt
1 pound pecans, cashews, walnuts, or whole unblanched almonds

1. Adjust oven racks to upper-middle and lower-middle positions and heat oven to 275 degrees. Line 2 rimmed baking sheets with parchment paper. Mix sugar, cumin, cayenne, and paprika together in bowl.

2. In medium bowl, whisk egg white, water, and salt together. Add nuts and toss to coat. Sprinkle spices over nuts, toss to coat, then spread evenly over prepared sheets. Bake until nuts are dry and crisp, about 50 minutes, stirring occasionally.

3. Let nuts cool completely on sheets, about 30 minutes. Break nuts apart and serve.

VARIATION

Cinnamon-Spiced Nuts **EASY**

Substitute 2 teaspoons ground cinnamon, 1 teaspoon ground ginger, and 1 teaspoon ground coriander for cumin, cayenne, and paprika.

TO MAKE AHEAD

Nuts can be stored at room temperature for up to 1 week

Classic Deviled Eggs

MAKES 12 EGG HALVES **EASY**
ACTIVE TIME 30 MINUTES
TOTAL TIME 1 HOUR

WHY THIS RECIPE WORKS The best deviled eggs start with the best hard-cooked eggs. Conventional wisdom insists that older eggs peel more easily than fresh eggs but we wanted to be able to start with eggs of any age and still end up with flawlessly smooth peeled results. Instead of a cold-water start, we used our recipe for Easy-Peel Hard-Cooked Eggs, which calls for placing cold eggs directly into hot steam. This denatures the outermost egg white proteins, causing them to shrink away from the shell membrane and making it easy to slip off the eggshells after cooking. Fresh herbs, cider vinegar, Dijon, Worcestershire sauce, and cayenne elevated the flavor of the filling, and we also created two variations: one with aromatic curry powder and another with crisp bacon and fresh chives. This recipe can be doubled. If you prefer, use a pastry bag fitted with a large plain or star tip to fill the egg halves.

1 recipe Easy-Peel Hard-Cooked Eggs (page 88)
3 tablespoons mayonnaise
1 tablespoon minced fresh parsley, plus 12 small whole parsley leaves for garnishing
1 teaspoon cider vinegar
1 teaspoon Dijon mustard
¼ teaspoon Worcestershire sauce
Pinch cayenne pepper

Our deviled eggs start with flawless easy-peel hard-cooked eggs that are made in a steamer basket.

1. Peel eggs and halve lengthwise with paring knife. Transfer yolks to bowl; arrange whites on serving platter. Mash yolks with fork until no large lumps remain. Add mayonnaise and use rubber spatula to smear mixture against side of bowl until thick, smooth paste forms, 1 to 2 minutes. Add minced parsley, vinegar, mustard, Worcestershire, and cayenne and mix until fully incorporated.

2. Transfer yolk mixture to small heavy-duty plastic bag. Press mixture into 1 corner and twist top of bag. Using scissors, snip ½ inch off filled corner. Squeezing bag, pipe yolk mixture into egg white halves. Garnish with parsley leaves before serving.

VARIATIONS

Curry Deviled Eggs

MAKES 12 EGG HALVES EASY

    1 recipe Easy-Peel Hard-Cooked Eggs (page 88)
    3 tablespoons mayonnaise
    1 tablespoon minced fresh parsley, plus 12 small whole parsley leaves for garnishing
 1½ teaspoons lemon juice
    1 teaspoon curry powder
    1 teaspoon Dijon mustard
      Pinch cayenne pepper

1. Peel eggs and halve lengthwise with paring knife. Transfer yolks to bowl; arrange whites on serving platter. Mash yolks with fork until no large lumps remain. Add mayonnaise and use rubber spatula to smear mixture against side of bowl until thick, smooth paste forms, 1 to 2 minutes. Add minced parsley, lemon juice, curry powder, mustard, and cayenne and mix until fully incorporated.

2. Transfer yolk mixture to small heavy-duty plastic bag. Press mixture into 1 corner and twist top of bag. Using scissors, snip ½ inch off filled corner. Squeezing bag, pipe yolk mixture into egg white halves. Garnish with parsley leaves before serving.

Bacon and Chive Deviled Eggs

MAKES 12 EGG HALVES EASY

    2 slices bacon, chopped fine
    1 recipe Easy-Peel Hard-Cooked Eggs (page 88)
    2 tablespoons mayonnaise
    1 teaspoon Dijon mustard
    1 tablespoon minced fresh chives
    2 teaspoons distilled white vinegar
  ⅛ teaspoon salt
      Pinch cayenne pepper

1. Cook bacon in 10-inch skillet over medium heat until crispy, 5 to 7 minutes. Using slotted spoon, transfer bacon to paper towel–lined plate. Reserve 1 tablespoon fat.

2. Peel eggs and halve lengthwise with paring knife. Transfer yolks to bowl; arrange whites on serving platter. Mash yolks with fork until no large lumps remain. Add mayonnaise and mustard and use rubber spatula to smear mixture against side of bowl until thick, smooth paste forms, 1 to 2 minutes. Add reserved bacon fat, chives, vinegar, salt, and cayenne and mix until fully incorporated. Stir in three-quarters of bacon.

3. Transfer yolk mixture to small heavy-duty plastic bag. Press mixture into 1 corner and twist top of bag. Using scissors, snip ½ inch off filled corner. Squeezing bag, pipe yolk mixture into egg white halves. Sprinkle with remaining bacon before serving.

TO MAKE AHEAD ▶

Filled deviled eggs can be refrigerated for up to 24 hours; garnish just before serving

We top sweet figs with bold blue cheese and honey before wrapping them with buttery prosciutto.

Prosciutto-Wrapped Figs with Gorgonzola

SERVES 8 TO 10 **EASY**

ACTIVE TIME 25 MINUTES

TOTAL TIME 25 MINUTES

WHY THIS RECIPE WORKS Few food pairings are more perfect than savory, salty prosciutto and sweet, fresh figs. To add another layer of sweet-salty complexity and textural interest to this appetizer, we also incorporated bold, pungent blue cheese and golden honey into the mix. We started by halving the figs to make them easier to eat. For the cheese, tasters preferred creamy, assertive Gorgonzola. Small mounds of the cheese, placed in the center of each fig before adding the honey, offered a rich, bold counterpoint to the figs' tender flesh and sweet flavor. Briefly microwaving the honey ensured that it was easy to drizzle over the cheese-stuffed figs. Finally, we wrapped each fig in a thin slice of prosciutto. To guarantee the ham stayed put, we stuck a toothpick through the center of each fig. Be sure to choose ripe figs for this recipe. They not only taste best but also yield easily when mounding the blue cheese gently into the centers.

2 ounces Gorgonzola cheese
16 fresh figs, stemmed and halved lengthwise
1 tablespoon honey
16 thin slices prosciutto (8 ounces), cut in half lengthwise

Mound 1 teaspoon Gorgonzola into center of each fig half. Microwave honey in bowl to loosen, about 10 seconds, then drizzle over cheese. Wrap prosciutto securely around figs, leaving fig ends uncovered. Secure prosciutto with toothpick and serve.

> **TO MAKE AHEAD**
> • Wrapped figs can be refrigerated for up to 8 hours
> • To serve, bring to room temperature

Cheddar Cheese Coins

SERVES 10 TO 12 **EASY** **FREEZE IT**

ACTIVE TIME 30 MINUTES

TOTAL TIME 1 HOUR 50 MINUTES (PLUS COOLING TIME)

WHY THIS RECIPE WORKS We wanted to come up with a simple, foolproof homemade cracker that would be cheesy, buttery, and just a little spicy—and that we could stash in the freezer. We started with a full 8 ounces of cheese and a touch of salt, cayenne, and paprika. We used the food processor to combine the dry ingredients and the shredded cheese, which helped to keep our cheese coins tender by limiting the handling of the dough. Adding a little cornstarch with the flour further ensured that the coins baked up flaky and buttery. We processed the dry ingredients with chilled butter until the mixture resembled wet sand, added water, and processed until the dough came together. Next, we rolled the dough into logs, refrigerated them until firm, and then sliced them into thin coins before baking until lightly golden and perfectly crisp.

8 ounces extra-sharp cheddar cheese, shredded (2 cups)
1½ cups (7½ ounces) all-purpose flour
1 tablespoon cornstarch
½ teaspoon salt
¼ teaspoon cayenne pepper
¼ teaspoon paprika
8 tablespoons unsalted butter, cut into 8 pieces and chilled
3 tablespoons water

The dough for these easy cheesy homemade crackers can be kept in the freezer for up to a month.

1. Process cheddar, flour, cornstarch, salt, cayenne, and paprika in food processor until combined, about 30 seconds. Scatter butter pieces over top and process until mixture resembles wet sand, about 20 seconds. Add water and process until dough forms ball, about 10 seconds. Transfer dough to counter and divide in half. Roll each half into 10-inch log, wrap in plastic wrap, and refrigerate until firm, at least 1 hour.

2. Adjust oven racks to upper-middle and lower-middle positions and heat oven to 350 degrees. Line 2 rimmed baking sheets with parchment paper. Unwrap logs and slice into ¼-inch-thick coins, giving dough quarter turn after each slice to keep log round. Place coins on prepared sheets, spaced ½ inch apart.

3. Bake until light golden around edges, 22 to 28 minutes, switching and rotating sheets halfway through baking. Let coins cool completely on sheets before serving.

VARIATIONS
Parmesan and Rosemary Cheese Coins
`EASY` `FREEZE IT`

Substitute 8 ounces finely grated Parmesan for cheddar, black pepper for cayenne, and 1 teaspoon minced fresh rosemary for paprika.

Gruyère, Mustard, and Caraway Cheese Coins
`EASY` `FREEZE IT`

Substitute Gruyère for cheddar. Add 1 teaspoon caraway seeds to food processor with spices. Substitute ¼ cup whole-grain mustard for water.

▶ TO MAKE AHEAD

- Dough, prepared through step 1, can be refrigerated for up to 3 days or frozen for up to 1 month; if frozen, thaw completely before continuing with step 2
- Alternatively, baked coins can be stored at room temperature for up to 3 days

Fresh Vegetable Spring Rolls

MAKES 8 SPRING ROLLS
ACTIVE TIME 1 HOUR
TOTAL TIME 1 HOUR

WHY THIS RECIPE WORKS Fresh spring rolls should offer a pleasing contrast in texture (soft wrapper, chewy noodles, and crunchy vegetables) and in flavor (fresh mint, basil, and cilantro; peanuts, spicy chiles, and salty sauce). But too often, spring rolls disappoint, with gummy noodles and bland vegetables. We set out to develop a recipe for foolproof spring rolls with fresh, bright flavors. We started by boiling the rice noodles and then tossed them with carrot, peanuts, and jalapeño in a combination of lime juice, fish sauce, and sugar. Before rolling the filling in the rice paper wrappers, we soaked the wrappers in water just long enough to make them pliable. Finally, we made a spicy hoisin-peanut sauce for dipping. If you can't find Thai basil, do not substitute regular basil; its flavor is too gentle to stand up to the assertive flavors in the filling. Mint makes a better substitute. Be sure to make only one spring roll at a time to keep the wrappers moist and pliable.

HOISIN-PEANUT DIPPING SAUCE
¼ cup creamy peanut butter
¼ cup hoisin sauce
¼ cup water
2 tablespoons tomato paste
1 teaspoon Asian chili-garlic sauce (optional)
2 teaspoons vegetable oil
2 garlic cloves, minced
1 teaspoon red pepper flakes

We toss the rice noodles and vegetables for our fresh spring rolls with a bright mix of lime juice, fish sauce, and sugar.

SPRING ROLLS

2½ tablespoons lime juice (2 limes)
1½ tablespoons fish sauce
1 teaspoon sugar
3 ounces rice vermicelli
1 teaspoon salt
1 large carrot, peeled and shredded
⅓ cup chopped dry-roasted peanuts
1 jalapeño chile or 2 Thai chiles, stemmed, seeded, and minced
1 large cucumber, peeled, halved lengthwise, seeded, and cut into matchsticks
4 leaves red leaf lettuce or Boston lettuce, halved lengthwise
8 (8-inch) round rice paper wrappers
½ cup fresh Thai basil or mint, small leaves left whole, medium and large leaves torn into ½-inch pieces
½ cup fresh cilantro leaves

1. FOR THE DIPPING SAUCE Whisk peanut butter, hoisin, water, tomato paste, and chili-garlic sauce, if using, together in bowl. Heat oil, garlic, and pepper flakes in small saucepan over medium heat until fragrant, 1 to 2 minutes. Stir in peanut butter mixture and bring to simmer. Reduce heat to medium-low and cook, stirring occasionally, until flavors meld, about 3 minutes. (Sauce should have ketchup-like consistency; if too thick, add water, 1 teaspoon at a time, until proper consistency is reached.) Transfer sauce to bowl and let cool to room temperature.

2. FOR THE SPRING ROLLS Combine lime juice, fish sauce, and sugar in bowl.

3. Bring 4 quarts water to boil in large pot. Remove from heat, stir in rice vermicelli and salt, and let sit, stirring occasionally, until noodles are tender but not mushy, about 10 minutes. Drain noodles, transfer to medium bowl, and toss with 2 tablespoons fish sauce mixture.

4. Toss carrot, peanuts, and jalapeño with 1 tablespoon fish sauce mixture in small bowl. Toss cucumber with remaining 1 tablespoon fish sauce mixture in separate bowl.

5. Arrange lettuce on platter. Spread clean, damp dish towel on counter. Fill 9-inch pie plate with 1 inch room-temperature water. Submerge each wrapper in water until just pliable, about 2 minutes; lay softened wrapper on towel. Scatter about 6 basil leaves and 6 cilantro leaves over wrapper. Arrange 5 cucumber sticks horizontally on wrapper, leaving 2-inch border at bottom. Top with 1 tablespoon carrot mixture, then arrange about 2½ tablespoons noodles on top of carrot mixture. Fold bottom of wrapper up over filling. Fold sides of wrapper over filling, then roll wrapper up into tight spring roll. Set spring roll on 1 lettuce piece on platter. Cover with second damp dish towel.

6. Repeat with remaining wrappers and filling. Serve with dipping sauce, wrapping lettuce around exterior of each roll.

> **TO MAKE AHEAD**
> - Sauce can be refrigerated for up to 3 days; to serve, bring to room temperature and adjust consistency with hot water as needed
> - Spring rolls can be covered with clean, damp dish towel and refrigerated for up to 4 hours before serving

Classic Shrimp Cocktail with Horseradish Cocktail Sauce

SERVES 6 **EASY**
ACTIVE TIME 25 MINUTES
TOTAL TIME 35 MINUTES (PLUS 1 HOUR CHILLING TIME)

WHY THIS RECIPE WORKS Our take on this party staple boasts tender, sweet shrimp and a lively, well-seasoned cocktail sauce. Rather than simply boiling the shrimp, we cooked them in a simple mixture of water and seasonings to infuse the shrimp with as much flavor as possible. Old Bay seasoning contributed a perceptible depth of flavor to the shrimp. To avoid overcooking, we brought the water and aromatics to a boil, took the pot off the heat, and then added the shrimp, leaving them to poach for 7 minutes. This method delivered perfectly tender, not rubbery, shrimp every time. Buy refrigerated, prepared horseradish, not the shelf-stable kind, which contains preservatives and additives.

SHRIMP

- 2 teaspoons lemon juice
- 2 bay leaves
- 1 teaspoon salt
- 1 teaspoon black peppercorns
- 1 teaspoon Old Bay seasoning
- 1 pound extra-large shrimp (21 to 25 per pound), peeled and deveined

HORSERADISH COCKTAIL SAUCE

- 1 cup ketchup
- 2 tablespoons lemon juice
- 2 tablespoons prepared horseradish, plus extra for seasoning
- 2 teaspoons hot sauce, plus extra for seasoning
- ⅛ teaspoon salt
- ⅛ teaspoon pepper

1. FOR THE SHRIMP Bring lemon juice, bay leaves, salt, peppercorns, Old Bay, and 4 cups water to boil in medium saucepan for 2 minutes. Remove pan from heat and add shrimp. Cover and steep off heat until shrimp are firm and pink, about 7 minutes.

2. Meanwhile, fill large bowl with ice water. Drain shrimp, plunge immediately into ice water to stop cooking, and let sit until cool, about 2 minutes. Drain shrimp and transfer to bowl. Cover and refrigerate until thoroughly chilled, at least 1 hour.

3. FOR THE COCKTAIL SAUCE Stir all ingredients together in small bowl and season with additional horseradish and hot sauce as desired. Arrange shrimp and sauce on serving platter and serve.

> **TO MAKE AHEAD**
>
> Cooked shrimp and cocktail sauce can be refrigerated separately for up to 24 hours

Broiled Coriander-Lemon Shrimp

SERVES 8 TO 10 **EASY**
ACTIVE TIME 30 MINUTES
TOTAL TIME 40 MINUTES

WHY THIS RECIPE WORKS For the easiest-ever version of shrimp cocktail that serves a crowd, we bypassed the traditional method of poaching and instead used the high heat of the broiler and a spice

Cooking 2 pounds of flavorful shrimp for a party takes just minutes using a spice rub and the broiler.

rub to give the shrimp great flavor. The little bit of sugar in our simple rub caramelized quickly under the broiler, adding good color to the outside of the shrimp and helping to bring out the fresh, sweet shrimp flavor. Instead of a traditional horseradish cocktail sauce, we paired the broiled shrimp with a creamy and lemony tarragon sauce. Other fresh herbs, such as dill, basil, cilantro, or mint, can be substituted for the tarragon. It's important to dry the shrimp thoroughly before tossing with the oil. We prefer to use jumbo shrimp here, but extra-large shrimp (21 to 25 per pound) can be substituted; if using smaller shrimp, reduce the broiling time by 1 to 2 minutes.

CREAMY TARRAGON SAUCE

- ¾ cup mayonnaise
- 3 tablespoons lemon juice
- 2 scallions, minced
- 2 tablespoons minced fresh tarragon
- ¼ teaspoon salt
- ⅛ teaspoon pepper

SHRIMP

¾ teaspoon salt

¾ teaspoon ground coriander

¼ teaspoon pepper

¼ teaspoon sugar

   Pinch cayenne pepper

2 pounds jumbo shrimp (16 to 20 per pound), peeled and deveined

2 tablespoons extra-virgin olive oil

1. FOR THE CREAMY TARRAGON SAUCE Stir all ingredients together in serving bowl. Cover and refrigerate until flavors have blended, at least 30 minutes.

2. FOR THE SHRIMP Adjust oven rack 3 inches from broiler element and heat broiler. Combine salt, coriander, pepper, sugar, and cayenne in small bowl. Pat shrimp dry with paper towels, then toss with oil and spice mixture in large bowl.

3. Spread shrimp in single layer on rimmed baking sheet. Broil shrimp until opaque and light golden in spots, 4 to 6 minutes. Transfer shrimp to serving platter and serve with sauce.

TO MAKE AHEAD ▶

- Sauce and shrimp, prepared through step 2, can be refrigerated separately for up to 24 hours
- To cook, season sauce with salt, pepper, and lemon juice to taste and continue with step 3

A boiling-water dough produces thin and flaky pancakes that brown and crisp evenly when cooked in a cast-iron skillet.

Scallion Pancakes with Dipping Sauce

SERVES 4 TO 6   **FREEZE IT**

ACTIVE TIME 1 HOUR

TOTAL TIME 1 HOUR 30 MINUTES

WHY THIS RECIPE WORKS Scallion pancakes are full of rich flavor and flaky golden-brown layers. The secret to these hidden depths is all in the method. We used boiling water, which helped keep the pancake dough firmer and less sticky. This made it easier to complete the rolling, coiling, and rerolling process required to shape the pancakes. Then we cooked the pancakes one at a time in a hot skillet, first covered to cook the pancake through and then uncovered to crisp up the exterior. A simple slit cut in the center of each pancake allowed steam to escape, which resulted in more even browning and better crisping. The finishing touch was a quick sweet-salty dipping sauce. We strongly recommend weighing the flour for the pancakes. For this recipe we prefer the steady, consistent heat of a cast-iron skillet. For an accurate measurement of boiling water, bring a full kettle of water to a boil and then measure out the desired amount.

DIPPING SAUCE

1 scallion, sliced thin

2 tablespoons soy sauce

1 tablespoon water

2 teaspoons rice vinegar

1 teaspoon honey

1 teaspoon toasted sesame oil

   Pinch red pepper flakes

PANCAKES

1½ cups (7½ ounces) plus 1 tablespoon all-purpose flour

¾ cup boiling water

7 tablespoons vegetable oil

1 tablespoon toasted sesame oil

1 teaspoon kosher salt

4 scallions, sliced thin

1. FOR THE DIPPING SAUCE Whisk all ingredients together in small bowl.

2. FOR THE PANCAKES Using wooden spoon, mix 1½ cups flour and boiling water in bowl to form rough dough. When cool enough to handle, transfer dough to lightly floured counter and knead until it forms ball that is tacky but no longer sticky, about 4 minutes (dough will not be perfectly smooth). Cover loosely with plastic wrap and let rest for 30 minutes.

3. While dough is resting, stir together 1 tablespoon vegetable oil, sesame oil, and remaining 1 tablespoon flour.

4. Divide dough in half. Cover 1 half of dough with plastic wrap and set aside. Roll remaining dough into 12-inch round. Drizzle 1 tablespoon oil-flour mixture over surface and then use pastry brush to spread evenly over entire surface. Sprinkle with ½ teaspoon salt and half of scallions. Roll dough into cylinder. Coil cylinder into spiral, tuck end underneath, and flatten spiral with your palm. Cover with plastic wrap and repeat with remaining dough, oil-flour mixture, salt, and scallions.

5. Place 12-inch cast-iron skillet over low heat for 10 minutes. Place 2 tablespoons oil in skillet and increase heat to medium-low. Roll first pancake into 9-inch round. Cut ½-inch slit in center of pancake. Place pancake in pan (oil should sizzle). Cover and cook until pancake is slightly puffy and deep golden brown on underside, 1 to 1½ minutes. (If underside is not browned after 1 minute, turn heat up slightly. If it is browning too quickly, turn heat down slightly.)

6. Drizzle 1 tablespoon oil over pancake. Use pastry brush to distribute oil over entire surface. Carefully flip pancake. Cover and cook until second side is deep golden brown, 1 to 1½ minutes. Uncover skillet and flip pancake. Cook uncovered until very deep golden brown and crispy on underside, 30 to 60 seconds. Flip and cook second side until very deep golden brown and crispy, 30 to 60 seconds. Transfer to wire rack. Repeat with remaining oil and pancake. Cut each pancake into 8 wedges and serve with dipping sauce.

TO MAKE AHEAD

Uncooked pancakes, prepared through step 4, can be layered between parchment paper, wrapped tightly in plastic wrap, and refrigerated for up to 24 hours or frozen for up to 1 month; if frozen, separate and let thaw for 15 minutes before continuing with step 5

Mayonnaise, a beaten egg, and a stint in the fridge make our mini crab cakes firm enough to pan-fry without crumbling.

Cocktail Mini Crab Cakes

SERVES 6 TO 8
ACTIVE TIME 45 MINUTES
TOTAL TIME 1 HOUR 15 MINUTES

WHY THIS RECIPE WORKS We really like to taste the crab in our crab cakes, especially the ones in miniature hors d'oeuvre form. But they usually have way more binder than meat, making them

ROLLING OUT SCALLION PANCAKES

1. Roll out dough into 12-inch round. Brush with oil and flour; sprinkle with salt and scallions.

2. Roll up dough round into cylinder.

3. Coil cylinder, tucking end underneath, then flatten.

4. Roll out flattened spiral into 9-inch round; cut slit.

closer to dough balls than seafood specialties. Our version is different: We kept both binder and seasonings to a minimum to let the sweet crab flavor really sing. For the binder we used fine dry bread crumbs that didn't overwhelm the crab. We also included mayonnaise and an egg to keep the crabmeat moist and help hold everything together. To further ensure they held their shape, we chilled the cakes briefly before pan-frying them. Great crab cakes begin with top-quality crabmeat. Look for fresh jumbo lump, which indicates the largest pieces and highest grade. The amount of bread crumbs you add will depend on the juiciness of the crabmeat. If the cakes won't hold together once you have added the egg, add more bread crumbs, 1 tablespoon at a time.

CRAB CAKES

1	pound jumbo lump crabmeat, picked over for shells
4	scallions, green parts only, minced
¼	cup mayonnaise
2–4	tablespoons fine dry bread crumbs
1	tablespoon chopped fresh parsley
1½	teaspoons Old Bay seasoning
	Salt and ground white pepper
1	large egg, lightly beaten
½	cup all-purpose flour
6	tablespoons vegetable oil

CHIPOTLE MAYONNAISE

¼	cup mayonnaise
¼	cup sour cream
2	teaspoons minced canned chipotle chile in adobo sauce
1	small garlic clove, minced
2	teaspoons minced fresh cilantro
1	teaspoon lime juice

1. FOR THE CRAB CAKES Gently mix crabmeat, scallions, mayonnaise, 2 tablespoons bread crumbs, parsley, and Old Bay in bowl, being careful not to break up crab lumps. Season with salt and white pepper to taste. Carefully fold in egg with rubber spatula until mixture just clings together. Add more crumbs if necessary.

2. Line rimmed baking sheet with parchment paper. Using generous tablespoon, form mixture into 24 cakes, each 1½ inches in diameter and ½ inch thick; place cakes on prepared sheet. Cover with plastic wrap and chill for 30 minutes.

3. FOR THE CHIPOTLE MAYONNAISE Combine all ingredients in bowl, cover, and refrigerate for 30 minutes.

4. Adjust oven rack to middle position and heat oven to 200 degrees. Line baking sheet with double layer of paper towels. Spread flour in shallow dish. Lightly dredge crab cakes in flour.

5. Heat 3 tablespoons oil in 12-inch nonstick skillet over medium-high heat until shimmering. Add half of crab cakes to skillet and cook until crisp and brown on both sides, 2 to 4 minutes, flipping halfway through cooking. Transfer cakes to prepared sheet and place in oven to keep warm.

6. Pour off fat from skillet and wipe clean with paper towels. Return skillet to medium-high heat, add remaining 3 tablespoons oil, and heat until shimmering. Repeat cooking with remaining crab cakes. Serve crab cakes with chipotle mayonnaise.

> **TO MAKE AHEAD**
>
> - Uncooked crab cakes, prepared through step 2, can be refrigerated for up to 24 hours
> - Chipotle mayonnaise can be refrigerated for up to 2 days; to serve, bring to room temperature and season with lime juice and salt to taste

Stuffed Mushrooms with Parmesan and Thyme

SERVES 6 TO 8
ACTIVE TIME 40 MINUTES
TOTAL TIME 1 HOUR 15 MINUTES

WHY THIS RECIPE WORKS Forget about leathery, dried-out stuffed mushrooms with bland, watery filling; these are meaty bites full of great savory flavor. To get rid of excess moisture before stuffing, we roasted the mushrooms gill side up until their juice was released and they were browned; we then flipped them gill side down to let the liquid evaporate. To create the filling, we chopped the mushroom stems in the food processor and sautéed them with garlic and wine. Cheese bound the filling together, and a final hit of acid brightened the earthy, savory flavor. Once you know how easy it is to make great stuffed mushrooms, you'll want to try all our savory flavor variations.

24	large white mushrooms (1¾ to 2 inches in diameter), stems removed and reserved
¼	cup olive oil
	Salt and pepper
1	small shallot, minced
2	garlic cloves, minced
¼	cup dry white wine
1	ounce Parmesan cheese, grated (½ cup)
1	teaspoon minced fresh thyme
1	teaspoon lemon juice

1. Adjust oven rack to middle position and heat oven to 425 degrees. Line rimmed baking sheet with aluminum foil. Toss mushroom caps with 2 tablespoons oil, ¼ teaspoon salt, and ⅛ teaspoon pepper in large bowl. Arrange caps gill side up on prepared sheet and roast until juice is released, about 20 minutes. Flip caps and roast until well browned, about 10 minutes.

2. Meanwhile, pulse reserved stems, shallot, garlic, and ⅛ teaspoon pepper in food processor until finely chopped, 10 to 14 pulses. Heat remaining 2 tablespoons oil in 8-inch nonstick skillet over medium heat until shimmering. Add processed mixture and cook until golden brown and moisture has evaporated, about 5 minutes. Stir in wine and cook until nearly evaporated and mixture thickens slightly, about 1 minute. Transfer to bowl, let cool slightly, then stir in Parmesan, thyme, and lemon juice. Season with salt and pepper to taste. Flip caps gill side up. Divide stuffing evenly among caps.

3. Return caps to oven and bake until stuffing is heated through, 5 to 7 minutes. Serve.

VARIATIONS

Stuffed Mushrooms with Cheddar, Fennel, and Sage
Substitute ¼ cup shredded sharp cheddar cheese for Parmesan, ½ teaspoon fennel seeds and ½ teaspoon dried sage for thyme, and malt vinegar for lemon juice. Add ¼ teaspoon red pepper flakes to cooked stuffing.

Stuffed Mushrooms with Olives and Goat Cheese
Substitute ¼ cup crumbled goat cheese for Parmesan, 1 teaspoon minced fresh oregano for thyme, and red wine vinegar for lemon juice. Add 3 tablespoons chopped pitted kalamata olives to cooked stuffing.

Stuffed Mushrooms with Chorizo and Manchego
In step 2, before adding processed mixture to pan, cook 1½ ounces Spanish-style chorizo sausage, cut into ¼-inch pieces, until lightly browned, about 2 minutes; stir in processed mixture and cook as directed. Substitute ¼ cup shredded Manchego cheese for Parmesan, 2 tablespoons minced fresh parsley for thyme, and sherry vinegar for lemon juice. Add ½ teaspoon paprika to cooked stuffing.

Stuffed Mushrooms with Bacon and Blue Cheese
In step 2, before adding processed mixture to pan, cook 2 slices finely chopped bacon until crispy, about 5 minutes; stir in processed mixture and cook as directed. Substitute ¼ cup crumbled blue cheese for Parmesan, 2 tablespoons minced fresh chives for thyme, and cider vinegar for lemon juice.

▸ TO MAKE AHEAD ▸
- Stuffed mushrooms, prepared through step 2, can be refrigerated for up to 24 hours
- To bake, continue with step 3, increasing baking time to 10 to 15 minutes

We parcook jalapeño halves in the oven before stuffing them to ensure tender chiles.

Stuffed Jalapeños
SERVES 6 TO 8
ACTIVE TIME 40 MINUTES
TOTAL TIME 50 MINUTES

WHY THIS RECIPE WORKS A cousin of traditional Mexican *chiles rellenos* (stuffed green chiles), these Tex-Mex appetizers are a party favorite. The heat of the jalapeños is perfectly tempered by the cream cheese filling, and a fried coating gives them appealing crunch. But the process of making them at home is labor-intensive, and many recipes turn out unremarkable results. We wanted a recipe for stuffed jalapeños that would eliminate the fuss and play up the flavor. We decided to skip the breading and deep-frying, since these techniques were time-consuming and messy. To adjust our recipe to work in the oven, we cut the chiles in half and parcooked them at a high heat. This slightly softened their flesh and drove off extra moisture. For our filling, we combined cream cheese with mild cheddar, Monterey Jack, bread crumbs, and an egg yolk for a creamy yet stable texture. Bacon, cilantro, scallions, lime juice, and cumin rounded out the flavor of the filling. Once stuffed, the jalapeños needed only about 10 more minutes in the oven to become perfectly browned and tender.

6 slices bacon

12 jalapeño chiles, halved lengthwise with stems left intact, seeds and ribs removed

Salt

4 ounces mild cheddar cheese, shredded (1 cup)

4 ounces Monterey Jack cheese, shredded (1 cup)

4 ounces cream cheese, softened

2 scallions, sliced thin

3 tablespoons minced fresh cilantro

2 tablespoons panko bread crumbs

1 large egg yolk

2 teaspoons lime juice

1 teaspoon ground cumin

1. Adjust oven rack to upper-middle position and heat oven to 500 degrees. Set wire rack in rimmed baking sheet. Cook bacon in 12-inch nonstick skillet over medium heat until crisp, 7 to 9 minutes. Using slotted spoon, transfer bacon to paper towel–lined plate. When bacon is cool enough to handle, chop fine and set aside.

2. Season jalapeños with salt and place cut side down on prepared rack. Bake until just beginning to soften, about 5 minutes. Remove jalapeños from oven and reduce oven temperature to 450 degrees. When cool enough to handle, flip jalapeños cut side up.

3. Mix cheddar, Monterey Jack, cream cheese, scallions, cilantro, panko, egg yolk, lime juice, cumin, and bacon in bowl until thoroughly combined. Divide cheese mixture among jalapeños, pressing into cavities.

4. Bake jalapeños until tender and filling is lightly browned, 9 to 14 minutes. Let cool for 5 minutes. Serve.

▶ TO MAKE AHEAD ▶

Stuffed jalapeños, prepared through step 3, can be refrigerated for up to 24 hours

Mini Chicken Empanadas

SERVES 6 TO 8   **FREEZE IT**

ACTIVE TIME 1 HOUR

TOTAL TIME 1 HOUR 30 MINUTES

WHY THIS RECIPE WORKS Making empanadas is a labor of love. Our bite-size version streamlines the process by using store-bought pie dough and a filling that requires no cooking other than the chicken. The remaining ingredients—sharp cheddar cheese, lime juice, cilantro, chipotle, and green olives—don't require a lot of coaxing, either. For a finishing touch, we used the food processor to create a vibrant salsa that came together in minutes. To make this dish spicier, reserve the jalapeño seeds and add them

Store-bought pie dough and a spicy mostly no-cook filling make short work of assembling mini empanadas.

with the jalapeño. Our favorite store-bought pie dough is Wholly Wholesome 9" Certified Organic Traditional Bake at Home Rolled Pie Dough.

EMPANADAS

1 (6- to 8-ounce) boneless, skinless chicken breast, trimmed

Salt and pepper

1 tablespoon vegetable oil

4 ounces sharp cheddar cheese, shredded (1 cup)

½ cup pitted green olives, chopped fine

¼ cup minced fresh cilantro

2 teaspoons lime juice

1 teaspoon minced canned chipotle chile in adobo sauce

2 packages store-bought pie dough

SALSA

1 small onion, quartered

1 green bell pepper, stemmed, seeded, and quartered

1 jalapeño chile, stemmed, seeded, and minced

2 tablespoons fresh cilantro leaves

½ teaspoon salt

2 tomatoes, cored and chopped coarse

⅓ cup white wine vinegar

3 tablespoons extra-virgin olive oil

1. **FOR THE EMPANADAS** Adjust oven rack to middle position and heat oven to 425 degrees. Pat chicken dry with paper towels and season with salt and pepper. Heat oil in 12-inch nonstick skillet over medium-high heat until just smoking. Add chicken and cook until browned on 1 side, about 3 minutes. Flip chicken over, add ½ cup water, and cover. Reduce heat to medium and continue to cook until thickest part of breast registers 160 degrees, 5 to 7 minutes longer. Transfer chicken to cutting board. When cool enough to handle, shred chicken into bite-size pieces.

2. Combine shredded chicken, cheddar, olives, cilantro, lime juice, and chipotle in bowl. Season with salt and pepper to taste. Cover bowl with plastic wrap and refrigerate until needed.

3. Line rimmed baking sheet with parchment paper. Using 3½-inch round cutter, cut circles out of dough rounds (6 circles per round); discard scraps.

4. Working with half of dough circles at a time, place 2 teaspoons empanada filling in center of each. Moisten edges of dough circles with water, then fold dough over filling into half-moon shape. Pinch edges to seal, then crimp with fork to secure. Arrange empanadas on prepared sheet.

5. **FOR THE SALSA** Pulse onion, bell pepper, jalapeño, cilantro, and salt in food processor until minced, about 10 pulses, scraping down sides of bowl as needed. Add tomatoes and pulse until chopped, about 2 pulses. Transfer to serving bowl and stir in vinegar and oil. Let salsa sit at room temperature until flavors meld, about 30 minutes.

6. Bake empanadas until golden, 20 to 25 minutes, rotating sheet halfway through baking. Let cool for 5 minutes, then serve with salsa.

> **TO MAKE AHEAD**
>
> - Empanadas, prepared through step 4, can be refrigerated for up to 3 days or frozen for up to 1 month (do not thaw before baking)
> - Salsa can be refrigerated for up 24 hours; to serve, bring to room temperature and season with salt to taste

Chicken Satay with Spicy Peanut Dipping Sauce

SERVES 10 TO 15

ACTIVE TIME 45 MINUTES

TOTAL TIME 1 HOUR 15 MINUTES

WHY THIS RECIPE WORKS Any dish that comes with its own handle is bound to be an appetizer favorite, and this Southeast Asian dish of marinated, grilled meat has deep flavor to match its

Party-ready spicy chicken skewers easily pick up great grilled flavor indoors from the broiler.

convenient form. We set out to bring this dish indoors for a simple but satisfying appetizer. A marinade of brown sugar, soy sauce, ketchup, and hot sauce guaranteed moist, full-flavored meat. The intense, direct heat of the broiler approximated a grill. Our peanut dipping sauce has sweet, tart, and spicy elements that echo the marinade for a fresh, bright finish. Covering the exposed ends of the skewers with aluminum foil protects them from burning. Freezing the chicken for 30 minutes will make it easier to slice into strips. You will need thirty 6-inch wooden skewers for this recipe.

SKEWERS

¼ cup soy sauce

¼ cup vegetable oil

¼ cup packed dark brown sugar

¼ cup minced fresh cilantro

4 scallions, sliced thin

3 tablespoons ketchup

2 garlic cloves, minced

1 teaspoon hot sauce

2 pounds boneless, skinless chicken breasts, trimmed and sliced diagonally into ¼-inch-thick strips

SPICY PEANUT DIPPING SAUCE

½ cup peanut butter, creamy or chunky
¼ cup hot water
3 tablespoons lime juice (2 limes)
2 scallions, sliced thin
2 tablespoons ketchup
1 tablespoon soy sauce
1 tablespoon packed dark brown sugar
1 tablespoon minced fresh cilantro
1½ teaspoons hot sauce
1 garlic clove, minced

1. FOR THE SKEWERS Combine soy sauce, oil, sugar, cilantro, scallions, ketchup, garlic, and hot sauce in medium bowl, add chicken, and toss to combine. Cover and refrigerate for at least 30 minutes. Weave chicken onto skewers.

2. FOR THE SPICY PEANUT DIPPING SAUCE Whisk peanut butter and hot water together in medium bowl. Stir in lime juice, scallions, ketchup, soy sauce, sugar, cilantro, hot sauce, and garlic. Transfer to serving bowl.

3. Adjust oven rack 6 inches from broiler element and heat broiler. Set wire rack in aluminum foil–lined rimmed baking sheet. Lay skewers on prepared rack and cover skewer ends with foil. Broil until fully cooked, about 8 minutes, flipping skewers halfway through broiling. Serve with peanut sauce.

VARIATION

Beef Satay with Spicy Peanut Dipping Sauce

To make the beef easier to slice, freeze it for 15 minutes.

Substitute 2 pounds flank steak for chicken. Cut flank steak in half lengthwise, freeze for 30 minutes, then slice each piece across grain into ¼-inch-thick strips.

TO MAKE AHEAD

- Skewers, prepared through step 1, can be refrigerated for up to 24 hours
- Sauce can be refrigerated for up to 2 days; to serve, bring to room temperature, season with lime juice to taste, and adjust consistency with water as needed

Buffalo Wings

SERVES 8 TO 10
ACTIVE TIME 45 MINUTES
TOTAL TIME 1 HOUR

WHY THIS RECIPE WORKS Great Buffalo wings boast juicy meat and a crisp coating, as well as a spicy, slightly sweet, and vinegary sauce. But dry, flabby wings are often the norm and the sauce can be scorchingly hot. We wanted perfectly cooked wings coated in a well-seasoned sauce. We coated the wings with cornstarch for a super-crisp exterior and deep-fried (rather than roasting, sautéing, or pan-frying) the wings for the best texture. Then we deepened the flavor of the traditional sauce by adding brown sugar and cider vinegar. And for heat, we chose Frank's RedHot Original Sauce, which is traditional; however, it's not very spicy, so we added a little Tabasco for even more kick. Serve with our Creamy Blue Cheese Dip (page 16) and sliced carrots and celery.

SAUCE

4 tablespoons unsalted butter
½ cup hot sauce, preferably Frank's RedHot Original Cayenne Pepper Sauce
2 tablespoons Tabasco sauce or other hot sauce, plus more to taste
1 tablespoon packed dark brown sugar
2 teaspoons cider vinegar

WINGS

2 quarts vegetable oil
3 tablespoons cornstarch
1 teaspoon salt
1 teaspoon pepper
1 teaspoon cayenne pepper
3 pounds chicken wings, cut at joints, wingtips discarded

1. FOR THE SAUCE Melt butter in small saucepan over low heat. Whisk in hot sauces, sugar, and vinegar until combined. Remove from heat.

2. FOR THE WINGS Adjust oven rack to middle position and heat oven to 200 degrees. Line baking sheet with several layers of paper towels. Heat oil in large Dutch oven over medium-high heat to 350 degrees.

3. While oil heats, mix cornstarch, salt, pepper, and cayenne together in bowl. Dry chicken with paper towels and place pieces in large bowl. Sprinkle spice mixture over wings and toss until evenly coated.

4. Fry half of chicken wings until golden and crisp, 10 to 15 minutes. Using slotted spoon, transfer wings to prepared sheet and keep warm in oven. Return oil to 350 degrees and repeat with remaining wings.

5. Combine sauce and fried chicken wings in large bowl and toss well to coat. Serve immediately.

TO MAKE AHEAD ▶

- Fried wings and sauce, prepared through step 4, can be refrigerated separately for up to 24 hours; to reheat, place wings on wire rack set in baking sheet, let sit at room temperature for 30 minutes, then reheat in 400-degree oven until hot, 8 to 10 minutes; microwave sauce until hot, about 1 minute, before tossing with reheated wings
- Alternatively, fried wings, prepared through step 4, can be held in 200-degree oven for up to 2 hours

PREPARING CHICKEN WINGS

Using kitchen shears or sharp chef's knife, cut through wing at joints and discard wingtip.

Cornstarch helps to create a crust on our Korean wings that stays supercrispy long after being tossed with the sauce.

Korean Fried Chicken Wings

SERVES 8 TO 10
ACTIVE TIME 45 MINUTES
TOTAL TIME 1 HOUR

WHY THIS RECIPE WORKS One bite of this exceptionally crunchy, sweet-spicy style of fried chicken and you'll be hooked. To get the ideal exterior that would stay crispy even under a layer of sauce, we followed tradition and double-fried the wings. We tried different types of coatings for our chicken—a simple dusting of cornstarch, a light batter of flour, cornstarch, and water, and a heavy batter of eggs, cornstarch, and water. We preferred the flour, cornstarch, and water batter, which yielded a light, crisp crust. A rasp-style grater makes quick work of turning the garlic into a paste. *Gochujang*, Korean hot red chili paste, can be found in Asian markets and some supermarkets; use the larger amount for spicier wings. If you can't find gochujang, substitute an equal amount of Sriracha sauce and add only 2 tablespoons of water to the sauce.

SAUCE

- 1 tablespoon toasted sesame oil
- 1 teaspoon garlic, minced to paste
- 1 teaspoon grated fresh ginger
- ¼ cup water
- 3 tablespoons sugar
- 2–3 tablespoons gochujang
- 1 tablespoon soy sauce

WINGS

- 2 quarts vegetable oil
- 1½ cups water
- 1 cup all-purpose flour
- 3 tablespoons cornstarch
- 3 pounds chicken wings, cut at joints, wingtips discarded

1. FOR THE SAUCE Combine sesame oil, garlic, and ginger in large bowl and microwave until mixture is bubbly and fragrant but not browned, 40 to 60 seconds. Whisk in water, sugar, gochujang, and soy sauce until smooth; set aside.

2. FOR THE WINGS Heat oil in large Dutch oven over medium-high heat to 350 degrees. While oil heats, whisk water, flour, and cornstarch in second large bowl until smooth. Set wire rack in rimmed baking sheet and set aside.

3. Place half of wings in batter and stir to coat. Using tongs, remove wings from batter one at a time, allowing any excess batter to drip back into bowl, and add to hot oil. Increase heat to high and cook, stirring occasionally to prevent wings from sticking, until coating is light golden and beginning to crisp, about 7 minutes. (Oil temperature will drop sharply after adding chicken.) Transfer wings to prepared rack. Return oil to 350 degrees and repeat with remaining wings. Reduce heat to medium and let second batch of chicken rest for 5 minutes.

4. Heat oil to 375 degrees. Carefully return all chicken to oil and cook, stirring occasionally, until exterior is deep golden brown and very crispy, about 7 minutes. Transfer to rack and let stand for 2 minutes.

5. Add chicken to sauce and toss well to coat. Return chicken to rack and let stand for 2 minutes to allow surface to set. Serve immediately.

TO MAKE AHEAD

- Fried wings and sauce, prepared through step 4, can be refrigerated separately for up to 24 hours; to reheat, place wings on wire rack set in baking sheet, let sit at room temperature for 30 minutes, then reheat in 400-degree oven until hot, 8 to 10 minutes; microwave sauce until hot, about 1 minute, before tossing with reheated wings
- Alternatively, fried wings, prepared through step 4, can be held in 200-degree oven for up to 2 hours

To prevent our tart from being soggy, we salt and drain the tomatoes and line the crust bottom with grated Parmesan.

Tomato and Mozzarella Tart

SERVES 4 TO 6 **EASY**

ACTIVE TIME 25 MINUTES

TOTAL TIME 1 HOUR

WHY THIS RECIPE WORKS Falling somewhere between pizza and quiche, a tomato and mozzarella tart shares the flavors of both but with a unique problem: Some sort of pastry crust is required, but the moisture in the tomatoes can make it soggy. We set out to make a tart that would have a solid bottom crust and great vine-ripened flavor. For a perfectly flaky but rigid crust, we used a two-step baking method—we parbaked the unfilled crust until golden and then baked it again once the topping had been added. Waterproofing the crust with egg wash and using two kinds of cheese in layers prevented sogginess. We also salted the sliced tomatoes for 30 minutes and then gently pressed them with paper towels to remove excess juice. For the best flavor, use authentic Parmesan cheese and very ripe, flavorful tomatoes.

1 (9½ by 9-inch) sheet puff pastry, thawed
1 large egg, lightly beaten
1 ounce Parmesan cheese, grated (½ cup)

2 plum tomatoes, cored and sliced ¼ inch thick
½ teaspoon salt
4 ounces mozzarella cheese, shredded (1 cup)
2 tablespoons extra-virgin olive oil
1 garlic clove, minced
2 tablespoons chopped fresh basil

1. Adjust oven rack to lowest position and heat oven to 425 degrees. Line rimmed baking sheet with parchment paper. Lay puff pastry in center of parchment and fold over edges of pastry to form ½-inch-wide crust. Using paring knife, cut through folded edge and corners. Brush edges with egg. Sprinkle Parmesan evenly over crust bottom, then poke uniformly with fork. Bake until crust is golden brown and crisp, 15 to 20 minutes. Let cool on wire rack.

2. Meanwhile, spread tomatoes over several layers of paper towels. Sprinkle with salt and let drain for 30 minutes.

3. Sprinkle mozzarella evenly over cooled crust bottom. Press excess moisture from tomatoes using additional paper towels. Shingle tomatoes evenly over mozzarella. Whisk olive oil and garlic together, then drizzle over tomatoes. Bake until cheese has melted and shell is deep golden, 10 to 15 minutes.

4. Let cool on wire rack for 5 minutes. Gently slide tart onto cutting board, sprinkle with basil, slice, and serve.

TO MAKE AHEAD ▶

Tart shell, prepared through step 1, can stored at room temperature for up to 2 days

FORMING PASTRY SHELL

Fold short edges of pastry over by ½ inch. Repeat with long edges. Using paring knife, cut through folded edges and corners of tart shell.

Rustic Caramelized Onion Tart with Goat Cheese

SERVES 8
ACTIVE TIME 40 MINUTES
TOTAL TIME 50 MINUTES

WHY THIS RECIPE WORKS Topped with caramelized onions, fresh herbs, and goat cheese, this rustic tart is a winning appetizer that is easy to make, especially if you rely on store-bought pizza dough. Make sure your oven is really hot (500 degrees), as this is crucial for a crisp crust. Also, we found it best to use just a small amount of very flavorful toppings to prevent the thin dough from being weighed down. If your pizza dough is refrigerated, let it come room temperature for 30 minutes before using.

¼ cup extra-virgin olive oil
1 pound onions, halved and sliced ¼ inch thick
1¼ teaspoons minced fresh thyme
½ teaspoon brown sugar
Salt and pepper
8 ounces pizza dough
4 ounces goat cheese, crumbled (1 cup)
2 tablespoons minced fresh parsley, scallion, basil, dill, or tarragon

1. Heat 1 tablespoon oil in 12-inch nonstick skillet over medium-low heat until shimmering. Stir in onions, 1 teaspoon thyme, sugar, and ¼ teaspoon salt. Cover, and cook, stirring occasionally, until onions have softened and released their liquid, about 10 minutes.

This easy, savory tart uses pizza dough as the crust and is baked quickly in a superhot oven so it's really crisp.

Uncover, increase heat to medium-high, and continue to cook, stirring often, until onions are deeply browned, 10 to 15 minutes.

2. Adjust oven rack to lowest position and heat oven to 500 degrees. Brush rimmed baking sheet with 1 tablespoon oil. Place dough on lightly floured counter. Press and roll dough into 14 by 8-inch oval. Transfer dough to prepared baking sheet, reshape as needed, and gently dimple with your fingertips.

3. Brush dough with remaining 2 tablespoons oil and season with pepper. Scatter caramelized onions, goat cheese, and remaining ¼ teaspoon thyme evenly over dough, leaving ½-inch border around edge.

4. Bake until tart is deep golden brown, 8 to 12 minutes, rotating sheet halfway through baking. Sprinkle with parsley, cut into 16 equal pieces, and serve warm.

TO MAKE AHEAD ▶

• Caramelized onions, prepared through step 1, can be refrigerated for up to 3 days
• Assembled tart, prepared through step 3, can be held at room temperature for up to 4 hours before baking

Soups, Stews, and Chilis

■ EASY (30 minutes or less active time)   ■ FREEZE IT
Photo: Carrot-Ginger Soup with Classic Croutons

Our chicken stock recipe delivers maximum flavor from just six ingredients and is great to make and store in the freezer.

Chicken Stock

MAKES 8 CUPS EASY FREEZE IT

ACTIVE TIME 15 MINUTES

TOTAL TIME 1 HOUR 40 MINUTES

WHY THIS RECIPE WORKS Rather than simmering a whole chicken, we found that cutting parts into small pieces released flavor in less time since more surface area of the meat was exposed. More bone marrow, key for both flavor and a thicker consistency, was also exposed. Sweating the chicken pieces further sped along the release of flavor. Use a meat cleaver or the heel of a chef's knife to cut the chicken. Discard any meat left over after straining the stock; it will be flavorless. Thighs can be substituted for the legs, backs, and wings. Make sure to use a 7-quart or larger Dutch oven.

  1 tablespoon vegetable oil
  3 pounds whole chicken legs, backs, and/or wings, hacked into 2-inch pieces
  1 onion, chopped
  8 cups water
  2 teaspoons salt
  2 bay leaves

1. Heat oil in Dutch oven or stockpot over medium-high heat until just smoking. Brown half of chicken lightly on all sides, about 5 minutes; transfer to large bowl. Repeat with remaining chicken using fat left in pot, and transfer to bowl.

2. Add onion to fat left in pot and cook until softened, about 3 minutes. Return browned chicken and any accumulated juices to pot, cover, and reduce heat to low. Cook, stirring occasionally, until chicken has released its juices, about 20 minutes.

3. Add water, salt, and bay leaves and bring to boil. Cover, reduce heat to gentle simmer, and cook, skimming as needed, until stock tastes rich and flavorful, about 20 minutes longer.

4. Remove large bones from pot, then strain stock through fine-mesh strainer. Let stock settle for 5 to 10 minutes, then defat using wide, shallow spoon or fat separator before using.

TO MAKE AHEAD

Stock can be refrigerated for up to 4 days or frozen for up to 1 month

Beef Stock

MAKES 8 CUPS FREEZE IT

ACTIVE TIME 35 MINUTES

TOTAL TIME 2 HOURS 30 MINUTES

WHY THIS RECIPE WORKS We wanted a flavorful, full-bodied beef stock without having to buy and roast pounds of big and expensive beef bones. We found that just a pound of ground beef, which releases its flavor quickly and is relatively inexpensive, a few vegetables, water, and wine—plus a few other enhancements—produced a rich, velvety stock in just 1½ hours of simmering. We sautéed mushrooms with the onions to create an even more flavorful fond, resulting in stock with a meaty, roasted flavor. Tomato paste and soy sauce enhanced the meaty flavor even more. We prefer 85 percent lean ground beef for this recipe; 93 percent lean ground beef will work, but the stock will be less flavorful. Make sure to use a 7-quart or larger Dutch oven for this recipe.

  1 teaspoon vegetable oil
  1 pound white mushrooms, trimmed and quartered
  1 large onion, chopped
  1 pound 85 percent lean ground beef
  2 tablespoons tomato paste
  ½ cup dry red wine
  8 cups water
  1 large carrot, peeled and chopped
  1 large celery rib, chopped

2 tablespoons soy sauce
2 teaspoons salt
2 bay leaves

1. Heat oil in Dutch oven or stockpot over medium-high heat until just smoking. Add mushrooms and onion and cook, stirring often, until onion is browned and golden brown fond has formed on bottom of pot, 8 to 12 minutes.

2. Stir in ground beef and cook, breaking up meat with wooden spoon, until no longer pink, about 3 minutes. Stir in tomato paste and cook until fragrant, about 30 seconds. Stir in wine, scraping up any browned bits, and cook until nearly evaporated, 1 to 2 minutes.

3. Stir in water, carrot, celery, soy sauce, salt, and bay leaves and bring to boil. Cover, reduce heat to gentle simmer, and cook, skimming as needed, until stock tastes rich and flavorful, about 1½ hours.

4. Strain stock through fine-mesh strainer. Let stock settle for 5 to 10 minutes, then defat using wide, shallow spoon or fat separator before using.

TO MAKE AHEAD

Stock can be refrigerated for up to 4 days or frozen for up to 1 month

Vegetable Broth Base

MAKES ABOUT 1¾ CUPS BASE OR ABOUT 1¾ GALLONS BROTH **EASY** **FREEZE IT**

ACTIVE TIME 25 MINUTES
TOTAL TIME 25 MINUTES

WHY THIS RECIPE WORKS To make a vegetable concentrate with bold and balanced flavor, we swapped in celery root and leeks for the usual celery and onion. To give the broth more savory flavor and complexity, we added dried onion, tomato paste, and soy sauce. A hefty dose of salt ensured that the broth was well seasoned and kept the base from freezing solid, so we could store it in the freezer for months and easily remove a tablespoon at a time. For the best balance of flavors, measure the prepped vegetables by weight. Kosher salt aids in grinding the vegetables.

2 leeks (5 ounces), white and light green parts only, chopped, and washed thoroughly (2½ cups)
2 carrots (3 ounces), peeled and cut into ½-inch pieces (⅔ cup)
½ small celery root (3 ounces), peeled and cut into ½-inch pieces (¾ cup)
½ cup (½ ounce) fresh parsley leaves and thin stems
3 tablespoons dried minced onion

2 tablespoons kosher salt
1½ tablespoons tomato paste
3 tablespoons soy sauce

1. Process leeks, carrots, celery root, parsley, dried minced onion, and salt in food processor, pausing to scrape down sides of bowl frequently, until paste is as fine as possible, 3 to 4 minutes. Add tomato paste and process for 1 minute, scraping down sides of bowl every 20 seconds. Add soy sauce and continue to process for 1 minute. Transfer mixture to airtight container and tap firmly on counter to remove air bubbles. Press small piece of parchment paper flush against surface of mixture, cover tightly. and freeze.

2. TO MAKE 1 CUP BROTH Stir 1 tablespoon fresh or frozen broth base into 1 cup boiling water. If particle-free broth is desired, let broth steep for 5 minutes, then strain through fine-mesh strainer before using.

TO MAKE AHEAD

Broth base can be frozen for up to 6 months

NOTES FROM THE TEST KITCHEN

Freezing Broth
Whether we're using homemade or store-bought broth, we frequently have some extra left after cooking. To save the leftover amount, we either store it in an airtight container in the refrigerator for up to four days or freeze it for up to one month using one of these methods.

FOR SMALL AMOUNTS Pour the broth into ice cube trays. After the cubes have frozen, remove them and store them in a zipper-lock bag. Use cubes for pan sauces, stir-fry sauces, and vegetable braises.

FOR MEDIUM AMOUNTS Ladle the broth into nonstick muffin tins (each muffin cup will hold about one cup). After the broth has frozen, store the "cups" in a large zipper-lock bag. "Cups" are good for casseroles and braising/steaming/poaching liquid.

FOR LARGE AMOUNTS Line a 4-cup measuring cup with a zipper-lock bag (it holds the bag open so you can use both hands to pour) and pour in the cooled broth. Seal the bag (double up if you wish) and lay it flat to freeze. This is a good option for soup, stew, rice, or gravy.

For rich-tasting broth, we use bone-in chicken thighs and then poach boneless breasts to use as meat for the soup.

Classic Chicken Noodle Soup

SERVES 8 TO 10   **FREEZE IT**

ACTIVE TIME 1 HOUR

TOTAL TIME 2 HOURS 20 MINUTES

WHY THIS RECIPE WORKS Our classic chicken soup starts the old-fashioned way, with a from-scratch broth. But instead of using a whole chicken we turned to chicken thighs, which kept things easier; they also added intense, meaty flavor to the broth. To cut down on greasiness, we removed the skin after browning. Since most people prefer white meat in their chicken soup, we poached boneless, skinless chicken breasts in the broth, removing them to add to the soup at the end. With the broth and the meat taken care of, we turned our attention to the soup with an eye toward keeping things simple and traditional. Onion, carrot, celery, and some fresh thyme fit the bill. As for the noodles, cooking them right in the broth intensified their flavor. Note that the thighs are used only to flavor the broth, but once the broth is strained, the meat can be shredded and used for chicken salad or a pot pie. If you prefer dark meat in your soup, you can omit the chicken breasts and add the shredded thigh meat instead.

BROTH

- 4 pounds bone-in chicken thighs, trimmed
  Salt and pepper
- 1 tablespoon vegetable oil
- 1 onion, chopped
- 12 cups water
- 2 bay leaves
- 1 pound boneless, skinless chicken breasts, trimmed

SOUP

- 1 tablespoon vegetable oil
- 1 onion, chopped fine
- 1 carrot, peeled and sliced thin
- 1 celery rib, halved lengthwise and sliced thin
- 2 teaspoons minced fresh thyme or ½ teaspoon dried
- 6 ounces (4 cups) wide egg noodles
- ¼ cup minced fresh parsley
  Salt and pepper

1. FOR THE BROTH Pat chicken thighs dry with paper towels and season with salt and pepper. Heat oil in Dutch oven over medium-high heat until just smoking. Add half of chicken and cook until deep golden on first side, about 6 minutes. Flip and continue to cook until lightly browned on second side, about 2 more minutes; transfer to plate and remove skin. Repeat with remaining thighs.

2. Pour off fat left in pot, then add onion and cook over medium heat until just softened, about 3 minutes. Add thighs, water, bay leaves, and 1 tablespoon salt, cover, and simmer for 30 minutes. Add chicken breasts and continue to simmer until broth is rich and flavorful, about 15 minutes.

3. Strain broth into large container, let stand for at least 10 minutes, then skim fat from surface with large spoon. Meanwhile, transfer chicken breasts to cutting board, let cool slightly, and shred into bite-size pieces using 2 forks.

4. FOR THE SOUP Heat oil in now-empty Dutch oven over medium-high heat until shimmering. Add onion, carrot, and celery and cook until onion has softened, 3 to 4 minutes. Stir in thyme and broth and simmer until vegetables are tender, about 15 minutes.

5. Add noodles and shredded breast meat and simmer until noodles are just tender, about 5 minutes. Off heat, stir in parsley and season with salt and pepper to taste. Serve.

> **TO MAKE AHEAD**
> - Soup and shredded chicken, prepared through step 4, can be refrigerated separately for up to 2 days or frozen for up to 1 month; if frozen, thaw completely in refrigerator
> - To reheat, bring soup, covered, to gentle simmer, stirring often, and continue with step 5

Italian Chicken Soup with Parmesan Dumplings

SERVES 4 TO 6
ACTIVE TIME 1 HOUR
TOTAL TIME 2 HOURS

WHY THIS RECIPE WORKS This rustic Northern Italian specialty features tender, plump dumplings deeply flavored with Parmesan and served in a light chicken broth. We modernized the classic recipe, making it more hearty and a bit easier by adding flavor to store-bought broth using browned chicken thighs. We used a little of the rendered chicken fat along with extra cheese to boost the savory flavor of the dumplings while egg whites kept them light. Fennel, carrots, and escarole complemented the shredded chicken and the flavorful dumplings. To ensure that the dumplings remain intact during cooking, hand-roll them until their surfaces are smooth and no cracks remain.

1½ pounds bone-in chicken thighs, trimmed
    Salt and pepper
1 teaspoon vegetable oil
1 fennel bulb, 1 tablespoon fronds minced, stalks discarded, bulb halved, cored, and cut into ½-inch pieces
1 onion, chopped fine
2 carrots, peeled and cut into ¾-inch pieces
½ cup dry white wine
8 cups chicken broth
1 Parmesan cheese rind, plus 3 ounces Parmesan, shredded (1 cup)
2 slices hearty white sandwich bread, torn into 1-inch pieces
2 large egg whites
¼ teaspoon grated lemon zest
    Pinch ground nutmeg
½ small head escarole (6 ounces), trimmed and cut into ½-inch pieces

1. Pat chicken dry with paper towels and season with salt and pepper. Heat oil in Dutch oven over medium-high heat until just smoking. Add chicken, skin side down, and cook until well browned, 6 to 8 minutes. Transfer chicken to plate and remove skin.

2. Pour off all but 1 teaspoon fat from pot and reserve 1 tablespoon fat for dumplings. Add fennel bulb, onion, carrots, and ½ teaspoon salt and cook over medium heat, stirring occasionally, until vegetables soften and begin to brown, 5 to 7 minutes. Stir in wine and cook, scraping up any browned bits, until nearly dry,

about 2 minutes. Return chicken to pot; add broth and Parmesan rind and bring to boil. Reduce heat to low, cover, and simmer until chicken is tender and registers 175 degrees, about 30 minutes. Transfer chicken to clean plate. Discard Parmesan rind. Cover broth and remove from heat. When cool enough to handle, use 2 forks to shred chicken into bite-size pieces; discard bones.

3. While broth is simmering, adjust oven rack to middle position and heat oven to 350 degrees. Pulse bread in food processor until finely ground, 10 to 15 pulses. Measure out 1 cup bread crumbs and transfer to parchment paper–lined rimmed baking sheet (set aside remainder for another use). Bake until lightly browned, about 5 minutes. Transfer to large bowl and set aside to cool completely.

4. Pulse shredded Parmesan in now-empty food processor until finely ground, 10 to 15 pulses. Transfer Parmesan to bowl with cooled bread crumbs and add reserved 1 tablespoon fat, egg whites, lemon zest, ⅛ teaspoon pepper, and nutmeg. Mix until thoroughly combined, then refrigerate for 15 minutes.

5. Working with 1 teaspoon dough at a time, roll into balls and place on parchment-lined sheet (you should have about 28 dumplings).

6. Return broth to simmer over medium-high heat. Add escarole and chicken and return to simmer. Add dumplings and cook, adjusting heat to maintain gentle simmer, until dumplings float to surface and are cooked through, 3 to 5 minutes. Stir in fennel fronds, season with salt and pepper to taste, and serve.

TO MAKE AHEAD

- Soup, shredded chicken, and dumplings, prepared through step 5, can be refrigerated separately for up to 24 hours
- To reheat, bring soup, covered, to gentle simmer, stirring often, and continue with step 6

SHREDDING CHICKEN

To shred chicken into bite-size pieces, hold fork in each hand with tines facing down. Insert tines into cooked meat and gently pull forks away from each other, breaking meat apart and into thin, bite-size strands.

Our French onion soup gets its rich flavor from caramelized onions and two kinds of broth.

Ultimate French Onion Soup

SERVES 6

ACTIVE TIME 1 HOUR 30 MINUTES

TOTAL TIME 4 TO 5 HOURS

WHY THIS RECIPE WORKS There is no denying the appeal of a great bowl of French onion soup, with its rich broth, caramelized onions, and nutty Gruyère-topped bread. For a rich soup, we caramelized the onions a full 2½ hours in the oven and then deglazed the pot several times with water, before adding a combination of chicken broth, beef broth, and more water. For the classic crouton topping, we warded off sogginess by toasting the bread before floating it in the soup, and we sprinkled the toasts with a modest amount of nutty Gruyère so that its flavor wouldn't overwhelm the soup. Sweet onions, such as Vidalia or Walla Walla, will make the soup overly sweet. Use broiler-safe crocks and keep the rim of the bowls 4 to 5 inches from the broiler element to obtain a proper gratinée of melted, bubbly cheese. If using ordinary soup bowls, sprinkle the toasted bread slices with Gruyère and return them to the broiler on the baking sheet until the cheese melts, then float them on top of the soup.

SOUP

4 pounds onions, halved and sliced ¼-inch-thick through root end

3 tablespoons unsalted butter, cut into 3 pieces

Salt and pepper

2¾ cups water, plus extra as needed

½ cup dry sherry

4 cups chicken broth

2 cups beef broth

6 sprigs fresh thyme, tied together with kitchen twine

1 bay leaf

CHEESE CROUTONS

1 (12-inch) baguette, sliced ½ inch thick

8 ounces Gruyère cheese, shredded (2 cups)

1 tablespoon chopped fresh parsley

1. FOR THE SOUP Adjust oven rack to lower-middle position and heat oven to 400 degrees. Generously spray inside of Dutch oven with vegetable oil spray. Add onions, butter, and 1 teaspoon salt, cover, and bake until onions wilt slightly and look moist, about 1 hour.

2. Stir onions thoroughly, scraping bottom and sides of pot. Partially cover pot and continue to cook in oven until onions are very soft and golden brown, 1½ to 1¾ hours longer, stirring onions thoroughly after 1 hour.

3. Carefully remove pot from oven (pot will be hot) and place over medium-high heat. Being careful of hot pot, continue to cook onions, stirring and scraping pot often, until liquid evaporates, onions brown, and bottom of pot is coated with dark crust, 20 to 25 minutes. (If onions begin to brown too quickly, reduce heat to medium. Also, be sure to scrape any browned bits that collect on spoon back into onions.)

4. Stir in ¼ cup water, thoroughly scraping up browned crust. Continue to cook until water evaporates and pot bottom has formed another dark crust, 6 to 8 minutes. Repeat deglazing 2 or 3 more times, until onions are very dark brown.

5. Stir in sherry and cook until evaporated, about 5 minutes. Stir in chicken broth, beef broth, 2 cups more water, thyme bundle, bay leaf, and ½ teaspoon salt, scraping up any remaining browned bits. Bring to simmer, cover, and cook for 30 minutes. Discard thyme bundle and bay leaf.

6. FOR THE CHEESE CROUTONS Adjust oven rack to middle position and heat oven to 400 degrees. Lay baguette slices on rimmed baking sheet and bake until dry, crisp, and lightly golden, about 10 minutes, flipping slices over halfway through baking.

7. Position oven rack 8 inches from broiler element and heat broiler. Set individual broiler-safe crocks on baking sheet. Season soup with salt and pepper to taste and fill each crock with about

1½ cups soup. Top each bowl with 1 or 2 baguette slices (do not overlap slices) and sprinkle evenly with Gruyère. Broil until cheese is melted and bubbly around edges, 3 to 5 minutes. Let cool for 5 minutes, sprinkle with parsley, and serve.

TO MAKE AHEAD

- Soup, prepared through step 5, can be refrigerated for up to 3 days
- To reheat, bring soup, covered, to gentle simmer, stirring often, and continue with step 6

Turkish Tomato, Bulgur, and Red Pepper Soup

SERVES 6 TO 8 **EASY** **FREEZE IT**

ACTIVE TIME 30 MINUTES

TOTAL TIME 1 HOUR

WHY THIS RECIPE WORKS This rustic soup has onion and red bell peppers and a solid flavor backbone thanks to garlic, tomato paste, white wine, dried mint, smoked paprika, and red pepper flakes. For additional smokiness, canned fire-roasted tomatoes did the trick. For the grain, we turned to bulgur. When stirred into the soup, it absorbed the surrounding flavors and released starch that created a silky texture. (When we made the soup ahead, we refrigerated or froze it without the bulgur and simply added it in when we reheated it.) Don't confuse bulgur with cracked wheat, which has a much longer cooking time and will not work in this recipe.

- 2 tablespoons extra-virgin olive oil
- 1 onion, chopped
- 2 red bell peppers, stemmed, seeded, and chopped
  Salt and pepper
- 3 garlic cloves, minced
- 1 teaspoon dried mint, crumbled
- ½ teaspoon smoked paprika
- ⅛ teaspoon red pepper flakes
- 1 tablespoon tomato paste
- ½ cup dry white wine
- 1 (28-ounce) can diced fire-roasted tomatoes
- 4 cups chicken or vegetable broth
- 2 cups water
- ¾ cup medium-grind bulgur, rinsed
- ⅓ cup chopped fresh mint

1. Heat oil in Dutch oven over medium heat until shimmering. Add onion, bell peppers, ¾ teaspoon salt, and ¼ teaspoon pepper and cook until softened and lightly browned, 6 to 8 minutes.

Both dried mint and fresh mint add flavor to this bulgur-enriched smoky tomato and red bell pepper soup.

Stir in garlic, dried mint, smoked paprika, and pepper flakes and cook until fragrant, about 30 seconds. Stir in tomato paste and cook for 1 minute.

2. Stir in wine, scraping up any browned bits, and simmer until reduced by half, about 1 minute. Add tomatoes and their juice and cook, stirring occasionally, until tomatoes soften and begin to break apart, about 10 minutes. Stir in broth and water and bring to simmer.

3. Stir in bulgur, reduce heat to low, cover, and simmer gently until bulgur is tender, about 20 minutes. Season with salt and pepper to taste. Serve, sprinkling individual portions with fresh mint.

TO MAKE AHEAD

- Soup, prepared through step 2, can be refrigerated for up to 3 days or frozen for up to 1 month; if frozen, thaw completely in refrigerator
- To reheat, bring soup, covered, to gentle simmer, stirring often, and continue with step 3

We use dried chickpeas in this soup and flavor the broth with a Parmesan rind, bay leaves, and orange zest.

Sicilian Chickpea and Escarole Soup

SERVES 6 TO 8 **EASY**

ACTIVE TIME 30 MINUTES

TOTAL TIME 2 HOURS (PLUS 8 HOURS TO SOAK CHICKPEAS)

WHY THIS RECIPE WORKS In Sicily, chickpeas are the favored legume to use in soup. In this version the mild bean shares the stage with escarole. We knew that dried chickpeas were the way to go for our traditional soup because we could infuse them with lots of flavor as they cooked. For aromatics, we started with the classic flavors of the region: onion, garlic, oregano, and red pepper flakes. We also added fennel; its mild anise bite complemented the nutty chickpeas. A strip of orange zest added a subtle citrus note, while a Parmesan rind bolstered the chickpeas' flavor with richness and complexity. When stirred in for the last 5 minutes of cooking, the escarole leaves wilted until velvety, while the stems retained a slight crunch. To speed up the process if you're tight on time, you can use our quick-salt-soak method for the beans: In step 1, combine the salt, water, and chickpeas in a Dutch oven and bring to a boil over high heat. Remove the pot from the heat, cover, and let stand for 1 hour. Drain and rinse the beans well and proceed with the recipe. The Parmesan rind can be replaced with a 2-inch chunk of the cheese. We do not recommend freezing this soup as the chickpeas become unappealingly mushy.

Salt and pepper
1 pound (2¾ cups) dried chickpeas, picked over and rinsed
2 tablespoons extra-virgin olive oil, plus extra for serving
2 fennel bulbs, stalks discarded, bulbs halved, cored, and chopped fine
1 small onion, chopped
5 garlic cloves, minced
2 teaspoons minced fresh oregano or ½ teaspoon dried
¼ teaspoon red pepper flakes
5 cups vegetable broth
1 Parmesan cheese rind, plus grated Parmesan for serving
2 bay leaves
1 (3-inch) strip orange zest
1 head escarole (1 pound), trimmed and cut into 1-inch pieces
1 large tomato, cored and chopped

1. Dissolve 3 tablespoons salt in 4 quarts cold water in large container. Add chickpeas and soak at room temperature for at least 8 hours or up to 24 hours. Drain and rinse well.

2. Heat oil in Dutch oven over medium heat until shimmering. Add fennel, onion, and 1 teaspoon salt and cook until vegetables are softened, 7 to 10 minutes. Stir in garlic, oregano, and pepper flakes and cook until fragrant, about 30 seconds.

3. Stir in 7 cups water, broth, Parmesan rind, bay leaves, orange zest, and chickpeas and bring to boil. Reduce to gentle simmer and cook until chickpeas are tender, 1¼ to 1¾ hours. Off heat, discard bay leaves and Parmesan rind (scraping off any cheese that has melted and adding it back to pot).

4. Stir in escarole and tomato and cook until escarole is wilted, 5 to 10 minutes. Season with salt and pepper to taste. Sprinkle individual portions with grated Parmesan, drizzle with extra oil, and serve.

TO MAKE AHEAD

- Soup, prepared through step 3, can be refrigerated for up to 3 days
- To reheat, bring soup, covered, to gentle simmer, stirring often, and continue with step 4

Tuscan White Bean Soup

SERVES 6 TO 8
ACTIVE TIME 40 MINUTES
TOTAL TIME 2 HOURS 40 MINUTES

WHY THIS RECIPE WORKS This soup is comprised of only two components: tender, creamy beans and a broth perfumed with garlic and rosemary. We tossed out the rules about how to prepare dried beans for this recipe. First, we skipped the presoak (soaked beans exploded once cooked), instead simmering them right in what would become the broth for our soup. We cooked them until just barely done and let residual heat gently cook them through to ensure even cooking. We also added salt to the pot, something typically thought to cause the beans' exteriors to toughen. We felt the salt actually helped keep the beans from bursting, and it also seasoned them nicely. Adding onion, garlic, bay leaf, and pancetta to our cooking broth gave the beans a welcome depth of flavor. We liked the large size of cannellini beans. For a more authentic soup, place a small slice of lightly toasted Italian bread in the bottom of each bowl and ladle the soup over the bread. To make this soup vegetarian, omit the pancetta and add a piece of vegetarian Parmesan cheese rind to the pot along with the halved onion and unpeeled garlic in step 1. We do not recommend freezing this soup as the beans become unappealingly mushy.

- 6 ounces pancetta, cut into 1-inch cubes
- 12 cups water, plus extra as needed
- 1 pound (2½ cups) dried cannellini beans, picked over and rinsed
- 1 large onion, unpeeled and halved, plus 1 small onion, chopped
- 7 garlic cloves (4 unpeeled, 3 minced)
- 1 bay leaf
  Salt and pepper
- ¼ cup extra-virgin olive oil, plus extra for serving
- 1 sprig fresh rosemary
  Balsamic vinegar

1. Cook pancetta in Dutch oven over medium heat until just golden, 8 to 10 minutes. Add water, beans, halved onion, unpeeled garlic cloves, bay leaf, and 1 teaspoon salt and bring to boil over medium-high heat. Cover partially, reduce heat to low, and simmer, stirring occasionally, until beans are almost tender, 1 to 1¼ hours. Remove pot from heat, cover, and let stand until beans are tender, about 30 minutes.

2. Drain beans in colander set over medium bowl, reserving cooking liquid (you should have about 5 cups; if not, add enough water to reach 5 cups). Discard pancetta, onion, unpeeled garlic

To achieve the best texture, we skip presoaking dried cannellini beans and cook them right in the broth.

cloves, and bay leaf. Spread beans in even layer on rimmed baking sheet and let cool.

3. While beans are cooling, heat oil in now-empty pot over medium heat until shimmering. Add chopped onion and cook, stirring occasionally, until softened, 5 to 6 minutes. Stir in minced garlic and cook until fragrant, about 30 seconds. Add cooled beans and reserved cooking liquid. Increase heat to medium-high and bring to simmer.

4. Submerge rosemary in liquid, cover, and let stand off heat for 15 to 20 minutes. Discard rosemary sprig and season with salt and pepper to taste. Ladle soup into bowls, drizzle with extra oil, and serve, passing vinegar separately.

> **TO MAKE AHEAD**
> - Soup, prepared through step 3, can be refrigerated for up to 3 days
> - To reheat, bring soup, covered, to gentle simmer, stirring often; adjust consistency with hot water as needed and continue with step 4

To ensure creamy, well-seasoned lentils with intact skins, we soak them in a warm brine before cooking them.

Hearty Spanish-Style Lentil and Chorizo Soup with Kale

SERVES 6 TO 8 **FREEZE IT**

ACTIVE TIME 40 MINUTES

TOTAL TIME 2 HOURS

WHY THIS RECIPE WORKS This sustaining soup pairs dried lentils with flavor-packed sausage. Neither entirely brothy nor creamy, the soup features whole lentils suspended in a thick broth. *Lentilles du Puy,* also called French green lentils, are our first choice for this recipe due to their resilience to softening in the fridge or freezer. Brown, black, or regular green lentils will also work (note that cooking times will vary depending on the type used); do not use red or yellow lentils. If Spanish-style chorizo is not available, kielbasa sausage can be substituted. Red wine vinegar can be substituted for the sherry vinegar. We prefer sweet smoked paprika for this recipe.

1 pound (2¼ cups) lentils, picked over and rinsed
  Salt and pepper
1 large onion

5 tablespoons extra-virgin olive oil
1½ pounds Spanish-style chorizo sausage, pricked with fork several times
3 carrots, peeled and cut into ¼-inch pieces
3 tablespoons minced fresh parsley
3 tablespoons sherry vinegar, plus extra for seasoning
2 bay leaves
⅛ teaspoon ground cloves
12 ounces kale, stemmed and cut into ½-inch pieces
2 tablespoons sweet smoked paprika
3 garlic cloves, minced
1 tablespoon all-purpose flour

1. Place lentils and 2 teaspoons salt in heatproof container. Cover with 4 cups boiling water and let soak for 30 minutes. Drain well.

2. Meanwhile, finely chop three-quarters of onion (you should have about 1 cup) and grate remaining quarter (you should have about 3 tablespoons). Heat 2 tablespoons oil in Dutch oven over medium heat until shimmering. Add chorizo and cook until browned on all sides, 6 to 8 minutes. Transfer chorizo to large plate. Reduce heat to low and add chopped onion, carrots, 1 tablespoon parsley, and 1 teaspoon salt. Cover and cook, stirring occasionally, until vegetables are very soft but not brown, 25 to 30 minutes. If vegetables begin to brown, add 1 tablespoon water to pot.

3. Add lentils and vinegar to vegetables; increase heat to medium-high; and cook, stirring frequently, until vinegar starts to evaporate, 3 to 4 minutes. Add 7 cups water, chorizo, bay leaves, and cloves; bring to simmer. Reduce heat to low, cover, and cook for 15 minutes. Stir in kale and cook until lentils and kale are tender, about 15 minutes. Off heat, remove chorizo from lentils and discard bay leaves. When chorizo is cool enough to handle, cut in half lengthwise, then cut each half into ¼-inch-thick slices.

4. Heat remaining 3 tablespoons oil in small saucepan over medium heat until shimmering. Add paprika, grated onion, garlic, and ½ teaspoon pepper; cook, stirring constantly, until fragrant, 2 minutes. Add flour and cook, stirring constantly, 1 minute longer. Stir paprika mixture into lentils and continue to cook until flavors have blended and soup has thickened, 10 to 15 minutes. Return chorizo to soup.

5. Stir in remaining 2 tablespoons parsley and heat through, about 1 minute. Season with salt, pepper, and up to 2 teaspoons vinegar to taste, and serve.

TO MAKE AHEAD

- Soup, prepared through step 4, can be refrigerated for up to 3 days or frozen for up to 1 month; if frozen, thaw completely in refrigerator
- To reheat, bring soup, covered, to gentle simmer, stirring often; adjust consistency with hot water as needed and continue with step 5

Curried Vegetarian Lentil Soup

SERVES 4 TO 6 **FREEZE IT**
ACTIVE TIME 45 MINUTES
TOTAL TIME 1 HOUR 30 MINUTES

WHY THIS RECIPE WORKS This simple and appealing soup takes complete advantage of the delicate, firm-tender bite and deep, earthy flavor of properly prepared lentils. We started by sautéing plenty of aromatics; we then added the lentils and cooked them until the vegetables were softened and the lentils had darkened, which helped them hold their shape and boosted their flavor. We deglazed the pan with white wine before adding the broth and water and simmering the lentils until tender. Pureeing part of the soup ensured that the broth had a luscious consistency. *Lentilles du Puy*, also called French green lentils, are our first choice for this recipe because they don't soften in the fridge or freezer. Brown, black, or regular green lentils will also work (note that cooking times will vary depending on the type used).

- 2 tablespoons extra-virgin olive oil
- 1 large onion, chopped fine
- 2 carrots, peeled and chopped
- 3 garlic cloves, minced
- 1 teaspoon curry powder
- 1 (14.5-ounce) can diced tomatoes, drained
- 1 bay leaf
- 1 teaspoon minced fresh thyme
- 1 cup lentils, picked over and rinsed
  Salt and pepper
- ½ cup dry white wine
- 4½ cups vegetable broth
- 1½ cups water
- 3 tablespoons minced fresh parsley

1. Heat oil in Dutch oven over medium-high heat until shimmering. Stir in onion and carrots and cook until vegetables begin to soften, about 2 minutes. Stir in garlic and curry powder and cook until fragrant, about 30 seconds. Stir in tomatoes, bay leaf, and thyme and cook until fragrant, about 30 seconds. Stir in lentils and ¼ teaspoon salt. Cover, reduce heat to medium-low, and cook, stirring occasionally, until vegetables are softened and lentils have darkened, 8 to 10 minutes.

2. Uncover, increase heat to high, add wine, scraping up any browned bits, and bring to simmer. Stir in broth and water and bring to boil. Partially cover pot, reduce heat to low, and simmer, stirring occasionally, until lentils are tender but still hold their shape, 30 to 35 minutes.

3. Discard bay leaf. Puree 3 cups soup in blender until smooth, then return to pot.

4. Warm soup over medium-low heat until hot, about 5 minutes. Stir in parsley, season with salt and pepper to taste, and serve.

TO MAKE AHEAD

- Soup, prepared through step 3, can be refrigerated for up to 3 days or frozen for up to 1 month; if frozen, thaw completely in refrigerator
- To reheat, bring soup, covered, to gentle simmer, stirring often; adjust consistency with hot water as needed and continue with step 4

NOTES FROM THE TEST KITCHEN

Storing and Reheating Soup

Soups, stews, and chilis make a generous number of servings, and they're easy enough to freeze in small batches so you can reheat them whenever you like. First you'll need to cool the soup. As tempting as it might seem, avoid transferring hot soup straight to the refrigerator; you may speed up the cooling process, but you'll also increase the fridge's internal temperature to unsafe levels, which is dangerous for all the other food stored in the fridge. We find that letting the soup cool on the countertop for an hour helps the temperature drop to about 85 degrees, at which point the soup can be transferred safely to the fridge. If you don't have an hour to cool your soup or stew at room temperature, you can divide it into a number of storage containers to allow the heat to dissipate more quickly, or you can cool the soup rapidly by using a frozen bottle of water to stir the contents of the pot.

To reheat soups and stews, we prefer to simmer them gently on the stovetop in a sturdy, heavy-bottomed pot, but a spin in the microwave works too. Just be sure to cover the dish with a plate to prevent a mess (we don't recommend using plastic wrap). And note that while most soups freeze just fine, those that contain dairy or pasta do not. In soups that contain dairy or pasta, the dairy curdles as it freezes and the pasta turns bloated and mushy. Instead, make and freeze the soup without including the dairy or pasta component. After you have thawed the soup and it has been heated through, you can stir in the uncooked pasta and simmer until just tender, or stir in the dairy and continue to heat gently until hot (do not boil).

½ small sweet onion or 2 large shallots, minced

⅓ cup sherry vinegar

2 garlic cloves, minced

  Salt and pepper

5 cups tomato juice

8 ice cubes

1 teaspoon hot sauce (optional)

  Extra-virgin olive oil

1. Combine tomatoes, bell peppers, cucumbers, onion, vinegar, garlic, and 2 teaspoons salt in large (at least 4-quart) bowl and season with pepper to taste. Let sit until vegetables just begin to release their juices, about 5 minutes. Stir in tomato juice, ice cubes, and hot sauce, if using. Cover and refrigerate to blend flavors, at least 4 hours.

2. Discard any unmelted ice cubes and season soup with salt and pepper to taste. Serve cold, drizzling individual portions with oil.

TO MAKE AHEAD ▶

Soup, prepared through step 1, can be refrigerated for up to 2 days

We let the chopped vegetables in our gazpacho stand briefly in a sherry vinegar marinade so they absorb flavor.

Classic Gazpacho

SERVES 8 TO 10   EASY

ACTIVE TIME 20 MINUTES

TOTAL TIME 25 MINUTES (PLUS 4 HOURS CHILLING TIME)

WHY THIS RECIPE WORKS To showcase the brightness of fresh vegetables in our gazpacho, we chopped the vegetables by hand to retain their color and firm texture. A sherry vinegar marinade guaranteed well-seasoned vegetables, while tomato juice and ice cubes provided the liquid. Chilling our soup for at least 4 hours was critical to allow the flavors to develop and meld. This recipe makes a large quantity because the leftovers are so good, but it can be halved. Traditionally, more of the same diced vegetables that are in the soup are used as a garnish, so cut some extra. Serve in chilled bowls with Garlic Croutons (page 58), chopped pitted black olives, chopped hard-cooked eggs, and finely diced avocados.

1½ pounds tomatoes, cored and cut into ¼-inch pieces

2 red bell peppers, stemmed, seeded, and cut into ¼-inch pieces

2 small cucumbers (1 cucumber peeled, both sliced lengthwise, seeded, and cut into ¼-inch pieces)

Creamless Creamy Tomato Soup

SERVES 6 TO 8   EASY   FREEZE IT

ACTIVE TIME 30 MINUTES

TOTAL TIME 45 MINUTES

WHY THIS RECIPE WORKS A warm bowl of tomato soup brings out the kid in all of us. Our homemade version satisfies a grown-up palate with its creamy texture and fresh taste. We wanted a tomato soup that would have velvety smoothness and a bright tomato taste, without using any flavor-dulling cream. We started with canned tomatoes for their convenience and year-round availability. Sautéing an onion in olive oil ramped up the sweet notes of the tomatoes and a little brown sugar balanced the tomatoes' acidity. A surprise ingredient—slices of crustless white bread torn into pieces and blended into the soup—helped give our tomato soup luxurious body without adding cream. Make sure to purchase canned whole tomatoes in juice, not in puree. If half of the soup fills your blender by more than two-thirds, process the soup in three batches. For an even smoother soup, pass the pureed mixture through a fine-mesh strainer after blending it. Serve with Classic Croutons (page 58).

¼ cup extra-virgin olive oil, plus extra for serving

1 onion, chopped fine

3 garlic cloves, minced

1 bay leaf

Pinch red pepper flakes (optional)

2 (28-ounce) cans whole peeled tomatoes

3 slices hearty white sandwich bread, crusts removed, torn into 1-inch pieces

1 tablespoon packed brown sugar

2 cups chicken or vegetable broth

2 tablespoons brandy (optional)

Salt and pepper

Chopped fresh chives

1. Heat 2 tablespoons oil in Dutch oven over medium-high heat until shimmering. Add onion, garlic, bay leaf, and pepper flakes, if using. Cook, stirring often, until onion is translucent, 3 to 5 minutes. Stir in tomatoes and their juice. Using potato masher, mash until no pieces bigger than 2 inches remain. Stir in bread and sugar and bring soup to boil. Reduce heat to medium and cook, stirring occasionally, until bread is completely saturated and starts to break down, about 5 minutes. Discard bay leaf.

2. Transfer half of soup to blender. Add 1 tablespoon oil and process until soup is smooth and creamy, 2 to 3 minutes. Transfer to large bowl and repeat with remaining soup and remaining 1 tablespoon oil. Return soup to clean, dry pot and stir in broth and brandy, if using.

3. Return soup to brief simmer over medium heat. Season with salt and pepper to taste. Serve, sprinkling individual bowls with chives and drizzling with extra oil.

> **TO MAKE AHEAD**
>
> • Soup, prepared through step 2, can be refrigerated for up to 3 days or frozen for up to 1 month; if frozen, thaw completely in refrigerator
> • To reheat, bring soup, covered, to gentle simmer, whisking often; adjust consistency with hot water as needed and continue with step 3

Carrot-Ginger Soup

SERVES 6 **EASY** **FREEZE IT**

ACTIVE TIME 30 MINUTES
TOTAL TIME 1 HOUR 10 MINUTES

WHY THIS RECIPE WORKS With its combination of cooked carrots and carrot juice, this soup delivers well-rounded, fresh carrot flavor. Using a mixture of grated fresh ginger and crystallized ginger gave us bright, refreshing ginger flavor with a moderate kick of heat. For a silky-smooth texture, we added a touch of baking soda to help break down the carrots and ginger. Serve the soup with Classic Croutons (page 58).

2 tablespoons unsalted butter

2 onions, chopped fine

¼ cup minced crystallized ginger

1 tablespoon grated fresh ginger

2 garlic cloves, peeled and smashed

Salt and pepper

1 teaspoon sugar

2 pounds carrots, peeled and sliced ¼ inch thick

4 cups water

1½ cups carrot juice

2 sprigs fresh thyme

½ teaspoon baking soda

1 tablespoon cider vinegar

Chopped fresh chives

Sour cream

1. Melt butter in large saucepan over medium heat. Stir in onions, crystallized ginger, fresh ginger, garlic, 2 teaspoons salt, and sugar. Cook, stirring often, until onions are softened but not browned, 5 to 7 minutes.

2. Stir in carrots, water, ¾ cup carrot juice, thyme sprigs, and baking soda. Increase heat to high and bring to simmer. Reduce heat to medium-low, cover, and simmer gently until carrots are very tender, 20 to 25 minutes.

3. Discard thyme sprigs. Working in batches, process soup in blender until smooth, 1 to 2 minutes. Return soup to clean, dry pot and stir in vinegar and remaining ¾ cup carrot juice.

4. Return soup to brief simmer over medium heat. Season with salt and pepper to taste. Serve, sprinkling individual bowls with chives and topping with sour cream.

> **TO MAKE AHEAD**
>
> • Soup, prepared through step 3, can be refrigerated for up to 3 days or frozen for up to 1 month; if frozen, thaw completely in refrigerator
> • To reheat, bring soup, covered, to gentle simmer, whisking often; adjust consistency with hot water as needed and continue with step 4

PUREEING SOUP SAFELY

To prevent getting sprayed or burned when pureeing hot soup, work in small batches and fill blender only two-thirds full. Hold lid in place with dish towel and pulse several times before blending continuously.

Butternut Squash Soup

SERVES 4 TO 6   FREEZE IT

ACTIVE TIME 50 MINUTES

TOTAL TIME 1 HOUR 20 MINUTES

WHY THIS RECIPE WORKS For this soup, we started by microwaving large chunks of squash to speed up the cooking process. We then slowly caramelized the parcooked squash in a Dutch oven until a thick brown fond developed. Deglazing the pot gave the soup the deep flavor of roasted squash in a fraction of the time. To further enhance the soup's vegetable flavor, we chose vegetable broth over chicken and used an aromatic base of leeks, fresh thyme, and bay leaf. Do not use prepeeled squash in this recipe. Chicken broth can be substituted for the vegetable broth. Serve with Cinnamon-Sugar Croutons (recipe follows).

2½ pounds butternut squash, peeled, seeded, and cut into 2-inch chunks (about 7 cups)

2 tablespoons unsalted butter

1 leek, white and light green parts only, quartered lengthwise, sliced thin, and washed thoroughly (about 1½ cups)

Salt and pepper

4 cups vegetable broth

1–2 cups water

2 sprigs fresh thyme

1 bay leaf

Pinch cayenne pepper

Sour cream

¼ cup roasted pepitas

1. Place squash in bowl, cover, and microwave until paring knife glides easily through flesh, 14 to 18 minutes, stirring halfway through microwaving. Carefully transfer squash to colander set in bowl (squash will be very hot) and drain for 5 minutes; reserve liquid.

2. Melt butter in Dutch oven over medium-high heat. Add squash, leek, and 1 teaspoon salt; cook, stirring occasionally, until squash pieces begin to break down and brown fond forms in bottom of pot, 10 to 13 minutes.

3. Stir in 2 cups broth, scraping up any browned bits. Add remaining 2 cups broth, reserved squash liquid, 1 cup water, thyme sprigs, bay leaf, and cayenne. Increase heat to high and bring to simmer. Reduce heat to medium and simmer until leeks are fully tender, 6 to 7 minutes.

4. Discard bay leaf and thyme sprigs. Working in batches, process soup in blender until smooth, 1 to 2 minutes.

5. Return pureed soup to clean, dry pot and return to brief simmer over medium heat, thinning with up to 1 cup water to desired consistency. Season with salt and pepper to taste. Serve, topping individual bowls with sour cream and sprinkling with pepitas.

VARIATION

Curried Butternut Squash and Apple Soup   FREEZE IT

Use a sweet apple such as Golden Delicious, Jonagold, or Braeburn.

Add 1 large apple, peeled, cored, and quartered, to bowl with squash in microwave in step 1. After squash pieces begin to break down in step 2, stir in 1½ teaspoons curry powder and cook until fragrant, about 30 seconds. Omit thyme and bay leaf in step 3.

TO MAKE AHEAD ▶

- Soup, prepared through step 4, can be refrigerated for up to 3 days or frozen for up to 1 month; if frozen, thaw soup completely in refrigerator
- To reheat, bring soup, covered, to gentle simmer, whisking often, and continue with step 5

CLASSIC CROUTONS

MAKES 3 CUPS   EASY

ACTIVE TIME 5 MINUTES

TOTAL TIME 40 MINUTES

Either fresh or stale bread can be used, although stale bread is easier to cut and crisps more quickly in the oven.

6 slices hearty white sandwich bread, crusts removed, cut into ½-inch cubes (3 cups)

3 tablespoons unsalted butter, melted, or extra-virgin olive oil

Salt and pepper

Adjust oven rack to middle position and heat oven to 350 degrees. Toss bread with melted butter, season with salt and pepper, and spread onto rimmed baking sheet. Bake until golden brown and crisp, 20 to 25 minutes, stirring halfway through baking. Let cool and serve.

VARIATIONS

GARLIC CROUTONS   EASY

Whisk 1 minced garlic clove into melted butter before tossing with bread.

CINNAMON-SUGAR CROUTONS   EASY

Toss buttered bread with 6 teaspoons sugar and 1½ teaspoons ground cinnamon before baking.

TO MAKE AHEAD ▶

Croutons can be stored at room temperature for up to 3 days

Steaming open the clams and using their steaming liquid for the broth gives our chowder maximum clam flavor.

New England Clam Chowder

SERVES 6
ACTIVE TIME 50 MINUTES
TOTAL TIME 1 HOUR 25 MINUTES

WHY THIS RECIPE WORKS This recipe is chock-full of clams and classic briny, creamy chowder flavor. Starting with the clams, we settled on medium-size littlenecks or cherrystones since they offered good value and taste. We steamed the clams open instead of shucking them, which was easier and yielded clam broth. We also found that a ratio of 2 cups of our homemade broth to 3 cups of bottled clam juice gave enough clam taste without being too salty. We chose Yukon Gold potatoes, as their moderate levels of starch and moisture blended seamlessly with this creamy chowder. Thickening the chowder with flour helped to stabilize it, as it can otherwise easily separate and curdle. Cream turned out to be essential, but our chowder needed only a minimal amount; just 1 cup provided richness without overpowering the flavor of the clams. Finally, we chose bacon rather than salt pork, a traditional component of chowder, to enrich the flavor with a subtle smokiness. Serve with oyster crackers.

3 cups water
6 pounds medium hard-shell clams, such as cherrystones, scrubbed
2 slices bacon, chopped fine
2 onions, chopped fine
2 celery ribs, chopped fine
1 teaspoon minced fresh thyme or ¼ teaspoon dried
⅓ cup all-purpose flour
3 (8-ounce) bottles clam juice
1½ pounds Yukon Gold potatoes, peeled and cut into ½-inch pieces
1 bay leaf
1 cup heavy cream
2 tablespoons minced fresh parsley
Salt and pepper

1. Bring water to boil in Dutch oven over medium-high heat. Add clams, cover, and cook for 5 minutes. Stir clams thoroughly and continue to cook, covered, until they begin to open, 2 to 7 minutes. Transfer clams to large bowl as they open; let cool slightly. Discard any clams that refuse to open.

2. Measure out and reserve 2 cups clam steaming liquid, avoiding any gritty sediment that settles on bottom of pot. Remove clam meat from shells and chop coarse.

3. Add bacon to clean, dry pot and cook over medium heat until crisp, 5 to 7 minutes. Stir in onions and celery and cook until vegetables are softened, 5 to 7 minutes. Stir in thyme and cook until fragrant, about 30 seconds. Stir in flour and cook for 1 minute.

4. Gradually whisk in bottled clam juice and reserved clam steaming liquid, scraping up any browned bits and smoothing out any lumps. Stir in potatoes and bay leaf and bring to boil. Reduce heat to gentle simmer and cook until potatoes are tender, 20 to 25 minutes. Stir in cream and return to brief simmer. Off heat, discard bay leaf.

5. Stir in parsley and season with salt and pepper to taste. Stir in chopped clams, cover, and let warm through, about 1 minute. Serve.

TO MAKE AHEAD

- Chopped clams and chowder, prepared through step 4, can be refrigerated separately for up to 24 hours
- To reheat, bring chowder, covered, to gentle simmer, stirring often; adjust consistency with hot water as needed and continue with step 5

To ensure perfectly cooked fish in our soup, we gently poach slices of cod off the heat in a rich, flavorful broth.

Provençal Fish Soup

SERVES 6 TO 8 **EASY** **FREEZE IT**

ACTIVE TIME 25 MINUTES

TOTAL TIME 1 HOUR 10 MINUTES

WHY THIS RECIPE WORKS Every country with a coastline boasts its own version of fish soup; our Provence-inspired version is not only easy to make, it also boasts a richly flavored broth fragranced with fennel, paprika, saffron, and orange zest. We chose thick cod fillets, wanting a firm fish that would not break apart too easily. The problem then came in building the soup base. Initial tests with premade fish stock produced soups that overpowered the fish's own mild flavor. To cook the fish perfectly, we left it in big slices so that they wouldn't break apart too much. We tried simmering the fish over low heat, but when we employed direct heat, the fish was overcooked by the time it was served. We decided on a more unconventional method: We placed the fish in the pot, shut off the heat, and let it poach gently. This technique was undeniably successful and the fish was perfectly cooked. Finally, we had a hearty, fragrant fish soup with perfect broth and perfect fish. This method lends itself well to making ahead, as all the work is in building a flavorful broth, which can be done ahead of time. Halibut can be substituted for the cod.

> 1 tablespoon extra-virgin olive oil, plus extra for serving
> 6 ounces pancetta, chopped fine
> 1 fennel bulb, 2 tablespoons fronds minced, stalks discarded, bulb halved, cored, and cut into ½-inch pieces
> 1 onion, chopped fine
> 2 celery ribs, chopped fine
> Salt and pepper
> 4 garlic cloves, minced
> 1 teaspoon paprika
> ⅛ teaspoon red pepper flakes
> Pinch saffron threads, crumbled
> 1 cup dry white wine or dry vermouth
> 4 cups water
> 2 (8-ounce) bottles clam juice
> 2 bay leaves
> 2 pounds skinless cod fillets, 1 inch thick, sliced crosswise into 6 equal pieces
> 2 tablespoons minced fresh parsley
> 1 tablespoon grated orange zest

1. Heat oil in Dutch oven over medium heat until shimmering. Add pancetta and cook, stirring occasionally, until beginning to brown, 3 to 5 minutes. Stir in fennel pieces, onion, celery, and 1½ teaspoons salt and cook until vegetables are softened and lightly browned, 12 to 14 minutes. Stir in garlic, paprika, pepper flakes, and saffron and cook until fragrant, about 30 seconds.

2. Stir in wine, scraping up any browned bits. Stir in water, clam juice, and bay leaves. Bring to simmer and cook until flavors meld, 15 to 20 minutes. Off heat, discard bay leaves.

3. Nestle cod into cooking liquid, cover, and let sit until fish flakes apart when gently prodded with paring knife and registers 140 degrees, 8 to 10 minutes. Gently stir in parsley, orange zest, and fennel fronds and break fish into large pieces. Season with salt and pepper to taste. Serve, drizzling individual portions with extra oil.

TO MAKE AHEAD ▶

- Soup, prepared through step 2, can be refrigerated for up to 24 hours or frozen for up to 1 month; if frozen, thaw completely in refrigerator
- To reheat, bring soup, covered, to gentle simmer, stirring often; remove pot from heat and continue with step 3

Classic Beef Stew

SERVES 6 TO 8 **FREEZE IT**

ACTIVE TIME 1 HOUR

TOTAL TIME 3 HOURS 45 MINUTES TO 4 HOURS 15 MINUTES

WHY THIS RECIPE WORKS We wanted to create a foolproof beef stew that would be rich and satisfying, with fall-apart meat and tender vegetables draped in a rich brown gravy. To begin, we chose chuck-eye roast for its great flavor and cut it into pieces. We bypassed the step of searing the meat by cooking the stew uncovered in the oven. This not only helped brown the exposed meat but also let some of the moisture evaporate, concentrating the sauce's flavor. Along with traditional stew components like onions, garlic, red wine, and chicken broth, we also added tomato paste, which is rich in glutamates—compounds that give meat its savory taste and contribute considerable flavor. Potatoes, carrots, and peas rounded out our updated take on beef stew. Use a good-quality medium-bodied wine, such as a Côtes du Rhône or Pinot Noir, for this stew. Try to find beef that is well marbled with white veins of fat. Meat that is too lean will come out slightly dry.

4 pounds boneless beef chuck-eye roast, pulled apart at seams, trimmed, and cut into 1- to 1½-inch pieces
  Salt and pepper
3 tablespoons vegetable oil
2 tablespoons unsalted butter
2 onions, chopped
3 garlic cloves, minced
¼ cup all-purpose flour
1 tablespoon tomato paste
1 cup dry red wine
2½ cups chicken broth, plus extra as needed
1 pound carrots, peeled and sliced 1 inch thick
2 bay leaves
1 tablespoon minced fresh thyme or 1 teaspoon dried
1½ pounds red potatoes, unpeeled, cut into 1-inch pieces
1 cup frozen peas
3 tablespoons minced fresh parsley

1. Adjust oven rack to lower-middle position and heat oven to 325 degrees. Pat beef dry with paper towels and season with salt and pepper. Heat 2 tablespoons oil in Dutch oven over medium-high heat until just smoking. Add half of meat and cook, stirring occasionally, until well browned, 7 to 10 minutes, reducing heat if pot begins to scorch; transfer to bowl. Repeat with remaining 1 tablespoon oil and remaining beef.

2. Melt butter in now-empty pot over medium-low heat. Add onions and 1 teaspoon salt and cook, stirring often, until softened, 5 to 7 minutes. Stir in garlic and cook until fragrant, about

30 seconds. Stir in flour and tomato paste and cook, stirring constantly, until golden, about 1 minute. Slowly whisk in wine, scraping up any browned bits. Gradually whisk in broth until smooth and bring to simmer.

3. Stir in browned meat, carrots, bay leaves, and thyme and bring to simmer. Cover, place pot in oven, and cook for 1 hour. Stir in potatoes and continue to cook in oven, covered, until meat is just tender, 1½ to 2 hours longer. Remove pot from oven and discard bay leaves.

4. Stir peas into stew, cover, and let stand for 10 minutes. Season with salt and pepper to taste. Serve, sprinkling parsley over individual portions.

TO MAKE AHEAD

- Stew, prepared through step 3, can be refrigerated for up to 3 days or frozen for up to 1 month; if frozen, thaw completely in refrigerator
- To reheat, bring stew, covered, to gentle simmer, stirring often; adjust consistency with hot water as needed and continue with step 4

CUTTING STEW MEAT

1. Pull apart roast at its major seams (delineated by lines of fat and silverskin). Use knife as necessary.

2. With knife, trim off excess fat and silverskin.

3. Cut meat into 1 to 2-inch pieces, according to recipe.

Modern Beef Burgundy

SERVES 6 TO 8 **FREEZE IT**

ACTIVE TIME 1 HOUR 10 MINUTES

TOTAL TIME 5 HOURS TO 5 HOURS 30 MINUTES

WHY THIS RECIPE WORKS Classic *boeuf bourguignon* is the ultimate example of how rich, savory, and satisfying a beef stew can be: By gently simmering large chunks of well-marbled meat in beef stock and a good amount of red wine, you end up with fork-tender beef and a braising liquid that's transformed into a silky, full-bodied sauce. But most recipes require many hours of work, so we set out to streamline the technique while maintaining the stew's bold, appealing flavor. Well-marbled chuck-eye roast gave our stew meaty flavor. To eliminate the time-consuming step of searing the beef, we cooked the stew uncovered in a roasting pan in the oven so that the exposed meat browned as it braised. This method worked so well that we also used the oven, rather than the stovetop, to render the salt pork and to caramelize the traditional mushroom and pearl onion garnish. Salting the beef before cooking and adding some anchovy paste and porcini mushrooms enhanced the meaty savoriness of the dish without making our recipe too fussy. If the pearl onions have a papery outer coating, remove it by rinsing them in warm water and gently squeezing individual onions between your fingertips. Two minced anchovy fillets can be used in place of the anchovy paste. To save time, salt the meat and let it stand while you prep the remaining ingredients. Serve with mashed potatoes or buttered noodles.

- 4 pounds boneless beef chuck-eye roast, pulled apart at seams, trimmed, and cut into 1- to 1½-inch pieces, scraps reserved
  Salt and pepper
- 6 ounces salt pork, cut into ¼-inch pieces
- 3 tablespoons unsalted butter
- 1 pound cremini mushrooms, trimmed, halved if small or quartered if large
- 1½ cups frozen pearl onions, thawed
- 1 tablespoon sugar
- ⅓ cup all-purpose flour
- 4 cups beef broth
- 1 (750-ml) bottle red Burgundy or Pinot Noir
- 5 teaspoons unflavored gelatin
- 1 tablespoon tomato paste
- 1 teaspoon anchovy paste
- 2 onions, chopped coarse
- 2 carrots, peeled and cut into 2-inch lengths
- 1 garlic head, cloves separated, unpeeled, and crushed
- 2 bay leaves
- ½ teaspoon black peppercorns
- ½ ounce dried porcini mushrooms, rinsed
- 10 sprigs fresh parsley, plus 3 tablespoons minced
- 6 sprigs fresh thyme

1. Toss beef and 1½ teaspoons salt together in bowl and let stand at room temperature for 30 minutes. Adjust oven racks to lower-middle and lowest positions and heat oven to 500 degrees.

2. Combine salt pork, beef scraps, and 2 tablespoons butter in large roasting pan and roast on upper rack until well browned and fat has rendered, 15 to 20 minutes. Meanwhile, toss cremini mushrooms, pearl onions, remaining 1 tablespoon butter, and sugar together on rimmed baking sheet. Roast on lower rack, stirring occasionally, until moisture released by mushrooms evaporates and vegetables are lightly glazed, 15 to 20 minutes. Transfer vegetables to large bowl, cover, and refrigerate.

3. Remove roasting pan from oven and reduce oven temperature to 325 degrees. Whisk flour into rendered fat until no dry flour remains. Whisk in broth, 2 cups wine, gelatin, tomato paste, and anchovy paste until combined. Add onions, carrots, garlic, bay leaves, peppercorns, porcini mushrooms, parsley sprigs, and thyme sprigs to pan, then arrange beef in single layer over top. Add water as needed to come three-quarters up side of beef (beef should not be submerged). Return roasting pan to oven and cook until meat is tender, 3 to 3½ hours, stirring after 1½ hours and adding water to keep meat at least half-submerged.

4. Using slotted spoon, transfer beef to bowl with cremini mushrooms and pearl onions; cover and set aside. Strain braising liquid through fine-mesh strainer set over large bowl, pressing on solids to extract as much liquid as possible; discard solids. Stir in remaining wine and let cooking liquid settle, 10 minutes. Using large spoon, skim excess fat from surface of stew.

5. Transfer liquid to Dutch oven and bring mixture to boil over medium-high heat. Simmer briskly, stirring occasionally, until sauce is thickened to consistency of heavy cream, 15 to 20 minutes. Reduce heat to medium-low, stir in beef and mushroom-onion garnish, cover, and cook until just heated through, 5 to 8 minutes.

6. Season with salt and pepper to taste, stir in minced parsley, and serve.

TO MAKE AHEAD

- Stew, prepared through step 5, can be refrigerated for up to 3 days or frozen for up to 1 month; if frozen, thaw completely in refrigerator
- To reheat, bring stew, covered, to gentle simmer, stirring often; adjust consistency with hot water as needed and continue with step 6

Daube Provençal

SERVES 4 TO 6 **FREEZE IT**

ACTIVE TIME 1 HOUR

TOTAL TIME 3 HOURS 45 MINUTES TO 4 HOURS 15 MINUTES

WHY THIS RECIPE WORKS *Daube Provençal*, also known as *daube niçoise*, has all the elements of the best French fare: tender beef, a luxurious sauce, and complex flavors. We wanted to translate the flavors of Provence—olive oil, olives, garlic, wine, herbs, oranges, tomatoes, mushrooms, and anchovies—into a beef stew. We chose briny niçoise olives, bright tomatoes, floral orange zest, and the regional flavors of thyme and bay. Anchovies added complexity without a fishy taste, and salt pork contributed rich body. A whole bottle of wine added bold flavor. Serve this stew with egg noodles or boiled potatoes. If niçoise olives are not available, kalamatas can be substituted. Cabernet Sauvignon is our favorite wine for this recipe, but Côtes du Rhône and Zinfandel also work. We prefer to use chuck-eye roast, but any boneless roast from the chuck will work. Because they are added just before serving, use canned whole tomatoes and dice them yourself—uncooked, they are more tender than canned diced tomatoes.

2 cups water

¾ ounce dried porcini mushrooms, rinsed

3½ pounds boneless beef chuck-eye roast, pulled apart at seams, trimmed, and cut into 2-inch pieces

1½ teaspoons salt

1 teaspoon pepper

¼ cup extra-virgin olive oil

5 ounces salt pork, rind removed

1 pound carrots, peeled and sliced 1 inch thick

2 onions, halved and sliced ⅛ inch thick through root end

2 tablespoons tomato paste

4 garlic cloves, sliced thin

⅓ cup all-purpose flour

1 (750-ml) bottle dry red wine

1 cup chicken broth

4 (3-inch) strips orange zest, sliced thin lengthwise

3 anchovy fillets, rinsed and minced

5 sprigs fresh thyme, tied together with kitchen twine

2 bay leaves

1 (14.5-ounce) can whole peeled tomatoes, drained and chopped

1 cup pitted niçoise olives

2 tablespoons minced fresh parsley

1. Microwave 1 cup water and mushrooms in covered bowl until steaming, about 1 minute. Drain mushrooms in fine-mesh strainer lined with coffee filter, reserving ¼ cup liquid, and chop mushrooms. Set mushrooms and reserved liquid aside.

Our favorite beef for stews is flavorful boneless chuck-eye roast that we trim and cut into pieces.

2. Adjust oven rack to lower-middle position and heat oven to 325 degrees. Pat beef dry with paper towels and season with salt and pepper. Heat 2 tablespoons oil in Dutch oven over medium-high heat until shimmering. Add half of beef and cook without moving until well browned, about 2 minutes per side; transfer to bowl. Repeat with remaining oil and remaining beef.

3. Reduce heat to medium and add salt pork, carrots, onions, tomato paste, and garlic to now-empty pot; cook, stirring occasionally, until light brown, about 2 minutes. Stir in flour and cook, stirring constantly, about 1 minute. Slowly add wine, scraping up any browned bits. Add broth, remaining 1 cup water, and beef with any accumulated juices. Increase heat to medium-high and bring to simmer.

4. Stir in mushrooms and their liquid, orange zest, anchovies, thyme bundle, and bay leaves, arranging beef so it is completely covered by liquid; partially cover pot and place in oven. Cook until fork slips easily in and out of beef (meat should not be falling apart), 2½ to 3 hours. Discard salt pork, thyme, and bay leaves. Using large spoon, skim excess fat from surface of stew.

5. Add tomatoes and olives and cook over medium-high heat until heated through, about 1 minute. Cover pot and let stew sit, about 5 minutes; stir in parsley and serve.

> **TO MAKE AHEAD**
>
> - Stew, prepared through step 4, can be refrigerated for up to 3 days or frozen for up to 1 month; if frozen, thaw completely in refrigerator
> - To reheat, bring stew, covered, to gentle simmer, stirring often; adjust consistency with hot water as needed and continue with step 5

Pork Vindaloo

SERVES 4 TO 6 **EASY** **FREEZE IT**

ACTIVE TIME 30 MINUTES

TOTAL TIME 3 HOURS

WHY THIS RECIPE WORKS Vindaloo is a complex, spicy dish that has both Indian and Portuguese influences. The hallmark of vindaloo is its interplay of sweet and sour flavors. It features tender meat in a thick reddish-orange sauce with a delicately balanced flavor. The heat of the spices is tamed by the sweetness of the sugar and the acidity of the tomatoes and vinegar. Onions and garlic add pungency, and mustard seeds lend their unique flavor and punch. We used pork butt for the meat, as it turned meltingly tender and remained moist. Pork butt roast is often labeled Boston butt in the supermarket. Serve with basmati rice.

3 pounds boneless pork butt roast, trimmed and cut into 1-inch pieces

3 onions, chopped

1 tablespoon vegetable oil

Salt and pepper

3 tablespoons paprika

8 garlic cloves, minced

4 teaspoons garam masala

⅛ teaspoon cayenne pepper

2 tablespoons all-purpose flour

3 cups chicken broth

1 tablespoon mustard seeds

2 teaspoons sugar

1 (14.5-ounce) can diced tomatoes

2 tablespoons red wine vinegar

¼ cup minced fresh cilantro

1. Adjust oven rack to lower-middle position and heat oven to 325 degrees. Combine pork, onions, oil, ¼ teaspoon salt, and ⅛ teaspoon pepper in Dutch oven over medium heat. Cook,

We brown the pork in this spicy stew on the stovetop then move the pot to the oven to gently finish cooking.

stirring often, until released pork juices nearly evaporate and meat begins to brown, 20 to 25 minutes, reducing heat if necessary to prevent scorching.

2. Stir in paprika, garlic, garam masala, and cayenne and cook until fragrant, about 1 minute. Stir in flour and cook for 1 minute. Slowly stir in broth, mustard seeds, and sugar, scraping up any browned bits and smoothing out any lumps. Stir in tomatoes with their juice and vinegar, cover, transfer to oven, and cook until pork is tender, about 2 hours. Remove pot from oven. Using large spoon, skim excess fat from surface of stew.

3. Stir in cilantro and season with salt and pepper to taste. Serve.

> **TO MAKE AHEAD**
>
> - Stew, prepared through step 2, can be refrigerated for up to 3 days or frozen for up to 1 month; if frozen, thaw completely in refrigerator
> - To reheat, bring stew, covered, to gentle simmer, stirring often; adjust consistency with hot water as needed and continue with step 3, seasoning with vinegar to taste

Pork Posole

SERVES 8 TO 10

ACTIVE TIME 1 HOUR 20 MINUTES

TOTAL TIME 3 HOURS 30 MINUTES

WHY THIS RECIPE WORKS *Posole rojo*, or red posole, is a rich stew with a deep and earthy flavor profile. Authentic versions are made with bones from the head, neck, shank, and feet of a pig, supplemented with meat from the shoulder or loin. The bones provide rich, porky flavor and give the stew body, but we discovered that we could simplify by using a bone-in pork butt roast. Splitting the roast into small chunks allowed for easier cooking; the chunks cooked faster and were easier to shred. We skipped browning and instead parcooked the meat gently with onions and garlic to develop flavor in the broth. Chicken broth provided savory depth, while canned tomatoes added lively acidity and color. We liked the rich, slightly sweet flavor of ancho chiles, which we soaked and pureed into a thick paste. We mixed most of the puree into the stew, saving the rest to add later for those who wanted extra heat. We added the hominy only after the meat was cooked and removed from the pot; this gave the hominy enough time to absorb flavor from the broth but not become mushy. For an accurate measurement of boiling water, bring a full kettle of water to a boil and then measure out the desired amount. Serve with lime wedges, diced avocado, and/or sliced radishes.

1 (5-pound) bone-in pork butt roast
  Salt and pepper
2 tablespoons vegetable oil
2 large onions, chopped coarse
5 garlic cloves, minced
6 cups chicken broth
1 (14.5-ounce) can diced tomatoes
1 tablespoon minced fresh oregano or 1 teaspoon dried
3 dried ancho chiles, stemmed and seeded
1½ cups boiling water
3 (15-ounce) cans white or yellow hominy, rinsed

1. Adjust oven rack to lower-middle position and heat oven to 300 degrees. Trim thick skin and excess fat from meat and cut along muscles to divide roast into large pieces of various sizes; reserve bones. Season pork with salt and pepper.

2. Heat oil in Dutch oven over medium heat until shimmering. Add onions and ¼ teaspoon salt and cook until softened, 8 to 10 minutes. Stir in garlic and cook until fragrant, about 30 seconds. Add pork and bones and cook, stirring often, until meat is no longer pink on outside, about 8 minutes. Stir in broth, tomatoes and their juice, oregano, and ½ teaspoon salt and bring to simmer, skimming foam from surface as needed. Cover, place pot in oven, and cook until pork is tender, about 2 hours.

3. Meanwhile, soak anchos in bowl with boiling water until softened, about 20 minutes. Process anchos and soaking liquid in blender until smooth, about 30 seconds. Strain through fine-mesh strainer into bowl, using rubber spatula to help pass chili mixture through strainer. Measure out and reserve ¼ cup ancho mixture for serving.

4. Remove pot from oven. Transfer pork to cutting board, let cool slightly, then shred into bite-size pieces using 2 forks; discard bones. Stir hominy and remaining ancho mixture into pot and bring to simmer over medium heat. Reduce heat to low, cover, and simmer gently until flavors meld, about 30 minutes. Stir shredded pork into stew.

5. Cook stew until heated through, about 2 minute, then season with reserved ancho mixture, salt, and pepper to taste. Serve.

TO MAKE AHEAD

- Stew and reserved ¼ cup ancho mixture, prepared through step 4, can be refrigerated separately for up to 3 days
- To reheat, bring stew, covered, to gentle simmer, stirring often; adjust consistency with hot water as needed and continue with step 5

NOTES FROM THE TEST KITCHEN

Using Dried Chiles

Different types of dried chiles have wildly varying flavors. While store-bought chili powder is great for many dishes, it is often worth toasting and grinding dried chiles at home. Here are a few we use in our stews and chilis.

CHIPOTLE We use these more than any other dried chile. Smoky, sweet, and moderately spicy, they are jalapeños that are smoked and dried. They are sold as is or canned in adobo, a tangy tomato-and-herb sauce. We like canned chipotles; they can be added straight to dishes, and leftovers last up to two weeks in the refrigerator or for months when frozen.

ANCHO These chiles are dried poblanos and are a dark mahogany red. They have a relatively mild flavor with a slightly fruity sweetness.

ÁRBOL These Mexican chiles are bright red and quite hot, and have a bright, slightly smoky flavor.

A rich lamb shank adds meaty flavor to dried white beans as they slowly braise together in the oven.

Moroccan Lamb and White Bean Stew

SERVES 6 TO 8

ACTIVE TIME 1 HOUR

TOTAL TIME 2 HOURS 30 MINUTES (PLUS 8 HOURS TO SOAK BEANS)

WHY THIS RECIPE WORKS These Moroccan-style white beans are cooked in a warm-spiced tomatoey base. We decided to use a lamb shank to season our stew, searing and then slowly braising the lamb in the oven with the beans. Moroccan-inspired spices gave the dish a deeply flavorful backbone, and chicken broth lent savory depth. We chose dried beans over canned so that the beans would cook at the same rate as the lamb, leaving us with creamy, rich beans that could withstand both long braising and a reheat. You can substitute 1 pound of lamb shoulder chops (blade or round bone), 1 to 1½ inches thick, trimmed and halved, for the lamb shank; reduce the browning time in step 2 to 8 minutes. If you are pressed for time you can "quick-soak" your beans. Simply combine the salt, water, and beans in a large Dutch oven and bring to a boil over high heat. Remove the pot from the heat, cover and, let stand for 1 hour. Drain and rinse the beans well before using. For more information on soaking beans, see page 314.

Salt and pepper
1 pound (2½ cups) dried great Northern beans, picked over and rinsed
1 (12- to 16-ounce) lamb shank
1 tablespoon extra-virgin olive oil, plus extra for serving
1 onion, chopped
1 red bell pepper, stemmed, seeded, and chopped fine
2 tablespoons tomato paste
3 garlic cloves, minced
2 teaspoons paprika
2 teaspoons ground cumin
1½ teaspoons ground ginger
¼ teaspoon cayenne pepper
½ cup dry white wine
4 cups chicken broth
2 tablespoons minced fresh parsley

1. Dissolve 3 tablespoons salt in 4 quarts cold water in large container. Add beans and soak at room temperature for at least 8 hours or up to 24 hours. Drain and rinse well.

2. Adjust oven rack to lower-middle position and heat oven to 350 degrees. Pat lamb dry with paper towels and season with salt and pepper. Heat oil in Dutch oven over medium-high heat until just smoking. Brown lamb on all sides, 10 to 15 minutes; transfer to plate. Pour off all but 2 tablespoons fat from pot.

3. Add onion and bell pepper to fat left in pot and cook over medium heat until softened and lightly browned, 5 to 7 minutes. Stir in tomato paste, garlic, paprika, cumin, ginger, cayenne, and ⅛ teaspoon pepper and cook until fragrant, about 30 seconds. Stir in wine, scraping up any browned bits. Stir in broth, 1 cup water, and beans and bring to boil.

4. Nestle lamb into beans along with any accumulated juices. Cover, transfer pot to oven, and cook until fork slips easily in and out of lamb and beans are tender, 1½ to 1¾ hours, stirring every 30 minutes.

5. Remove pot from oven. Transfer lamb to cutting board, let cool slightly, then shred into bite-size pieces using 2 forks. Stir shredded lamb back into beans; discard excess fat and bone.

6. Stir in parsley and season with salt and pepper to taste. Adjust consistency with extra hot water as needed. Serve, drizzling individual portions with extra oil.

> **TO MAKE AHEAD**
> - Stew, prepared through step 5, can be refrigerated for up to 3 days
> - To reheat, bring stew, covered, to gentle simmer, stirring often; adjust consistency with hot water as needed and continue with step 6

Best Chicken Stew

SERVES 6 TO 8

ACTIVE TIME 1 HOUR

TOTAL TIME 2 HOURS 30 MINUTES

WHY THIS RECIPE WORKS We wanted a chicken stew with succulent bites of chicken, tender vegetables, and a truly robust gravy. To build a flavorful base, we browned chicken wings; their collagen converted to gelatin during cooking and enriched the gravy. A few strips of bacon, crisped in the pot before we browned the wings in the rendered fat, lent porky depth and just a hint of smoke, while soy sauce and anchovy paste further enhanced the savory flavor of the stew. Adding the chicken thighs to the pot later allowed the meat to stay tender and moist. Mashed anchovy fillets (rinsed and dried before mashing) can be used instead of anchovy paste. Use small red potatoes measuring 1½ inches in diameter.

  2 pounds boneless, skinless chicken thighs, halved crosswise and trimmed
     Kosher salt and pepper
  3 slices bacon, chopped
  1 pound chicken wings, cut at joints
  1 onion, chopped fine
  1 celery rib, minced
  2 garlic cloves, minced
  2 teaspoons anchovy paste
  1 teaspoon minced fresh thyme or ¼ teaspoon dried
  5 cups chicken broth
  1 cup dry white wine, plus extra for seasoning
  1 tablespoon soy sauce
  3 tablespoons unsalted butter, cut into 3 pieces
  ⅓ cup all-purpose flour
  1 pound small red potatoes, unpeeled, quartered
  4 carrots, peeled and cut into 1-inch pieces
  2 tablespoons chopped fresh parsley

1. Adjust oven rack to lower-middle position and heat oven to 325 degrees. Arrange chicken thighs on baking sheet and lightly season with salt and pepper; cover with plastic wrap and set aside.

2. Cook bacon in Dutch oven over medium-low heat, stirring occasionally, until fat renders and bacon browns, 6 to 8 minutes. Using slotted spoon, transfer bacon to medium bowl. Add chicken wings to pot, increase heat to medium, and cook until well browned on both sides, 10 to 12 minutes; transfer wings to bowl with bacon.

3. Add onion, celery, garlic, anchovy paste, and thyme to fat in pot; cook, stirring occasionally, until dark fond forms in bottom of pot, 2 to 4 minutes. Increase heat to high; stir in 1 cup broth, wine, and soy sauce, scraping up any browned bits; and bring to boil. Cook, stirring occasionally, until liquid evaporates and

The rich, robust gravy of this stew starts with browning chicken wings in rendered bacon fat.

vegetables begin to sizzle again, 12 to 15 minutes. Add butter and stir to melt; sprinkle flour over vegetables and stir to combine. Gradually whisk in remaining 4 cups broth until smooth. Stir in wings and bacon, potatoes, and carrots; bring to simmer. Transfer to oven and cook, uncovered, for 30 minutes, stirring once halfway through cooking.

4. Remove pot from oven. Use wooden spoon to draw gravy up sides of pot and scrape browned fond into stew. Place over high heat, add thighs, and bring to simmer. Return pot to oven, uncovered, and continue to cook, stirring occasionally, until thighs offer no resistance when poked with fork and vegetables are tender, about 45 minutes longer. Discard wings.

5. Season stew with up to 2 tablespoons extra wine and salt and pepper to taste. Sprinkle with parsley and serve.

▸ TO MAKE AHEAD

- Stew, prepared through step 4, can be refrigerated for up to 3 days
- To reheat, bring stew, covered, to gentle simmer, stirring often; adjust consistency with hot water as needed and continue with step 5

Chickpea Stew with Spinach, Chorizo, and Smoked Paprika

SERVES 4 TO 6

ACTIVE TIME 50 MINUTES

TOTAL TIME 1 HOUR 15 MINUTES

WHY THIS RECIPE WORKS We adapted a traditional chickpea and spinach tapas dish into a robust stew. For the flavor backbone, we stuck with the Spanish flavors of saffron, garlic, smoked paprika, and cumin. Tasters also liked chorizo, which added meaty richness. Curly-leaf spinach was the best choice for its sturdy texture in this brothy dish. We wilted it and then set it aside before building the base with canned chickpeas and aromatics. Including the chickpeas' starchy canning liquid gave the dish more body. Finally, we added a picada, a bread crumb–based mixture often used as a thickener. It gave the dish a velvety texture and flavor boost. The stew can be served over rice or with crusty bread. If you can't find curly-leaf spinach, substitute flat-leaf; do not substitute baby spinach. Chopped or whole unsalted almonds can be substituted for the slivered almonds; they may require longer processing times.

PICADA

- ¼ cup slivered almonds
- 2 slices hearty white sandwich bread, torn into quarters
- 2 tablespoons extra-virgin olive oil
- ⅛ teaspoon salt
  Pinch pepper

STEW

- Pinch saffron threads, crumbled
- 2 teaspoons extra-virgin olive oil
- 8 ounces curly-leaf spinach, stemmed
- 3 ounces Spanish-style chorizo sausage, chopped fine
- 5 garlic cloves, sliced thin
- 1 tablespoon smoked paprika
- 1 teaspoon ground cumin
  Salt and pepper
- 2 (15-ounce) cans chickpeas
- 1 tablespoon sherry vinegar

1. FOR THE PICADA Adjust oven rack to middle position and heat oven to 375 degrees. Pulse almonds in food processor to fine crumbs, about 20 pulses. Add bread, oil, salt, and pepper and pulse bread to coarse crumbs, about 10 pulses. Spread mixture evenly in rimmed baking sheet and bake, stirring often, until golden brown, about 10 minutes. Set aside to cool.

2. FOR THE STEW Combine 2 tablespoons boiling water and saffron in small bowl and let steep for 5 minutes.

3. Heat 1 teaspoon oil in Dutch oven over medium heat until shimmering. Add spinach and 2 tablespoons water, cover, and cook,

The starchy chickpea canning liquid gives this Spanish chickpea and spinach dish body and flavor.

stirring occasionally, until spinach is wilted but still bright green, about 1 minute. Transfer spinach to colander and gently press to release liquid. Transfer spinach to cutting board and chop coarse. Return to colander and press again.

4. Heat remaining 1 teaspoon oil in now-empty pot over medium heat until shimmering. Add chorizo and cook until lightly browned, about 5 minutes. Stir in garlic, paprika, cumin, and ¼ teaspoon pepper and cook until fragrant, about 30 seconds. Stir in chickpeas and their liquid, 1 cup water, and saffron mixture and bring to simmer. Cook, stirring occasionally, until chickpeas are tender and liquid has thickened slightly, 10 to 15 minutes.

5. Off heat, stir in picada, spinach, and vinegar and let sit until heated through, about 2 minutes. Adjust sauce consistency with hot water as needed. Season with salt and pepper to taste. Serve.

TO MAKE AHEAD

- Picada, spinach, and stew, prepared through step 4, can be refrigerated separately for up to 3 days
- To reheat, bring stew, covered, to gentle simmer, stirring often, and continue with step 5

Italian Vegetable Stew

SERVES 6 TO 8
ACTIVE TIME 50 MINUTES
TOTAL TIME 1 HOUR 45 MINUTES

WHY THIS RECIPE WORKS Italy's *ciambotta* is a ratatouille-like stew, chock-full of veggies, that makes for a hearty one-bowl meal. We wanted to avoid the sorry fate of most recipes—mushy vegetables floating in a weak, one-note broth. To keep the zucchini and peppers from watering down the stew, we precooked them in a skillet to drive off excess moisture before adding them to the pot. To thicken the broth, we embraced the eggplant's natural tendency to fall apart and simmered it until it completely broke down into the tomato-enriched sauce (microwaving it first helped to rid it of its excess moisture). To deepen the flavor of the stew, we browned the eggplant along with the onion and potato, then sautéed some tomato paste to develop lots of flavorful fond before adding the liquid to the pot. Finally, we found that a quick basil and oregano pesto—whirred together in the food processor and stirred into the zucchini and peppers before we added them to the pot—gave the soup a bold, bright herbal flavor. Serve with crusty bread.

PESTO

⅓ cup chopped fresh basil
⅓ cup fresh oregano leaves
6 garlic cloves, minced
2 tablespoons extra-virgin olive oil
¼ teaspoon red pepper flakes

STEW

12 ounces eggplant, peeled and cut into ½-inch pieces
Salt
¼ cup extra-virgin olive oil
1 large onion, chopped
1 pound russet potatoes, peeled and cut into ½-inch pieces
2 tablespoons tomato paste
2¼ cups water
1 (28-ounce) can whole peeled tomatoes, drained with juice reserved, chopped coarse
2 zucchini, halved lengthwise, seeded, and cut into ½-inch pieces
2 red or yellow bell peppers, stemmed, seeded, and cut into ½-inch pieces
1 cup shredded fresh basil

1. **FOR THE PESTO** Process all ingredients in food processor until finely ground, about 1 minute, scraping down sides of bowl as needed.

2. **FOR THE STEW** Toss eggplant with 1½ teaspoons salt in bowl. Line surface of large plate with double layer of coffee filters and lightly spray with vegetable oil spray. Spread eggplant evenly over coffee filters and microwave until eggplant is dry to touch and slightly shriveled, 8 to 12 minutes, tossing halfway through cooking.

3. Heat 2 tablespoons oil in Dutch oven over high heat until shimmering. Add eggplant, onion, and potatoes, and cook, stirring frequently, until eggplant browns, about 2 minutes.

4. Push vegetables to sides of pot. Add 1 tablespoon oil and tomato paste to clearing and cook, stirring often, until brown fond develops on bottom of pot, about 2 minutes. Stir in 2 cups water and tomatoes and their juice, scraping up any browned bits. Bring to boil. Reduce heat to medium, cover, and gently simmer until eggplant is completely broken down and potatoes are tender, 20 to 25 minutes.

5. Meanwhile, heat remaining 1 tablespoon oil in 12-inch skillet over high heat until just smoking. Add zucchini, bell peppers, and ½ teaspoon salt and cook, stirring occasionally, until vegetables are browned and tender, 10 to 12 minutes. Push vegetables to sides of skillet. Add pesto to clearing and cook until fragrant, about 1 minute. Stir pesto into vegetables and transfer to bowl. Off heat, add remaining ¼ cup water to skillet and scrape up any browned bits.

6. Remove Dutch oven from heat and stir in vegetable mixture and water from skillet. Cover and let stew stand for 20 minutes to let flavors blend.

7. Stir in basil and season with salt to taste. Serve.

> **TO MAKE AHEAD**
>
> - Stew, prepared through step 6, can be refrigerated for up to 3 days
> - To reheat, bring stew, covered, to gentle simmer, stirring often; adjust consistency with hot water as needed and continue with step 7

SEEDING ZUCCHINI

Halve zucchini lengthwise, then gently scrape out seeds using soupspoon.

For a chunky and rich sauce in our ground beef chili, we use canned diced tomatoes with their juice and tomato puree.

All-American Beef Chili

SERVES 6 TO 8   `FREEZE IT`
ACTIVE TIME 45 MINUTES
TOTAL TIME 2 HOURS 20 MINUTES

WHY THIS RECIPE WORKS With the goal of developing a no-fuss chili that would taste far better than the sum of its parts, we knew that adding the spices with the aromatics would boost their potency. Commercial chili powder, backed by cumin, coriander, cayenne, oregano, and red pepper flakes, provided plenty of spice notes and heat. For the meat, 85 percent lean ground beef gave us full, deep flavor. Using both diced tomatoes and tomato puree provided chunks of tomato and a rich, thick sauce. Adding the beans with the tomatoes ensured that they cooked enough to absorb flavor but not so much that they fell apart. Finally, cooking the chili with the lid on for only half the simmering time resulted in a rich, thick consistency. Note that chilis made of mostly beef (and a few vegetables) tend to freeze well. Serve with lime wedges, chopped cilantro, sliced scallions, minced onion, diced avocado, shredded cheddar or Monterey Jack cheese, and/or sour cream.

¼ cup chili powder
1 tablespoon ground cumin
2 teaspoons ground coriander
1 teaspoon red pepper flakes
1 teaspoon dried oregano
½ teaspoon cayenne pepper
  Salt
2 tablespoons vegetable oil
2 onions, chopped fine
1 red bell pepper, stemmed, seeded, and cut into ½-inch pieces
6 garlic cloves, minced
2 pounds 85 percent lean ground beef
2 (15-ounce) cans dark red kidney beans, rinsed
1 (28-ounce) can diced tomatoes
1 (28-ounce) can tomato puree

1. Combine chili powder, cumin, coriander, pepper flakes, oregano, cayenne, and 1 teaspoon salt in bowl.

2. Heat oil in Dutch oven over medium heat until shimmering. Add onions and bell pepper and cook until softened, 8 to 10 minutes. Stir in garlic and cook until fragrant, about 30 seconds. Stir in spice mixture and cook, stirring constantly, until fragrant, about 1 minute.

3. Stir in half of beef. Increase heat to medium-high and cook, breaking up meat with spoon, until no longer pink, 3 to 5 minutes. Add remaining beef and cook until no longer pink, about 3 minutes. Stir in beans, diced tomatoes with their juice, and tomato puree and bring to simmer. Cover, reduce heat to gentle simmer, and cook, stirring occasionally, for 1 hour.

4. Uncover and continue to simmer gently until beef is tender and sauce is dark, rich, and slightly thickened, about 45 minutes longer. (If chili begins to stick to bottom of pot or looks too thick, stir in water as needed.) Season with salt to taste. Serve.

> **TO MAKE AHEAD**
> - Chili can be refrigerated for up to 3 days or frozen for up to 1 month; if frozen, thaw completely in refrigerator
> - To reheat, bring chili, covered, to gentle simmer, stirring often; adjust consistency with hot water as needed

Ultimate Beef Chili

SERVES 6 TO 8 **FREEZE IT**

ACTIVE TIME 1 HOUR 30 MINUTES

TOTAL TIME 4 HOURS 30 MINUTES TO 5 HOURS

WHY THIS RECIPE WORKS To create a deeply flavorful and beefy chili, we turned to meaty blade steaks for the base, as they were easy to cut into pieces, cooked up tender and stayed in big chunks, and had great flavor. For complex chili flavor, we skipped supermarket chili powder in favor of making our own with a combination of fruity ancho and fiery árbol chiles; for a grassy heat, we added fresh jalapeños. Adding cornmeal to our chili powder gave it a welcome thickening power. Dried beans, quick-brined before cooking, were a must so they would stay creamy for the duration of cooking. To finish the chili with even greater depth of flavor, we relied on a trio of secret ingredients: lager, unsweetened cocoa, and molasses. A 4-pound chuck-eye roast, well trimmed of fat, can be substituted for the steak. Because much of the chili flavor is held in the fat of this dish, refrain from skimming fat from the surface. Wear gloves when working with both dried and fresh chiles. Dried New Mexican or guajillo chiles make a good substitute for the anchos; 1/8 teaspoon cayenne may be substituted for each dried árbol. Good choices for toppings include diced avocado, chopped red onion, chopped cilantro, lime wedges, sour cream, and shredded Monterey Jack or cheddar cheese.

8 ounces (1¼ cups) dried pinto beans, rinsed and picked over
  Salt
6 dried ancho chiles (about 1¾ ounces), stemmed, seeded, and torn into 1-inch pieces
2–4 dried árbol chiles, stemmed, pods split, and seeded
3 tablespoons cornmeal
2 teaspoons dried oregano
2 teaspoons ground cumin
2 teaspoons unsweetened cocoa powder
2½ cups chicken broth
2 onions, cut into ¾-inch pieces (about 2 cups)
3 small jalapeño chiles, stemmed, seeded, and cut into ½-inch pieces
3 tablespoons vegetable oil
4 garlic cloves, minced
1 (14.5-ounce) can diced tomatoes
2 teaspoons molasses
3½ pounds blade steak, ¾ inch thick, trimmed and cut into ¾-inch pieces
1½ cups mild-flavored lager, such as Budweiser

1. Combine 4 quarts water, beans, and 3 tablespoons salt in Dutch oven and bring to boil over high heat. Remove pot from heat, cover, and let stand for 1 hour. Drain and rinse well.

2. Adjust oven rack to lower-middle position and heat oven to 300 degrees. Place ancho chiles in 12-inch skillet over medium-high heat; toast, stirring frequently, until flesh is fragrant, 4 to 6 minutes, reducing heat if chiles begin to smoke. Transfer to bowl of food processor and cool. Do not wash out skillet.

3. Add árbol chiles, cornmeal, oregano, cumin, cocoa, and ½ teaspoon salt to food processor with toasted ancho chiles; process until finely ground, about 2 minutes. With processor running, very slowly add ½ cup broth until smooth paste forms, about 45 seconds, scraping down sides of bowl as necessary. Transfer paste to small bowl. Place onions in now-empty processor bowl and pulse until roughly chopped, about 4 pulses. Add jalapeños and pulse until consistency of chunky salsa, about 4 pulses, scraping down bowl as necessary.

4. Heat 1 tablespoon oil in large Dutch oven over medium-high heat. Add onion mixture and cook, stirring occasionally, until moisture has evaporated and vegetables are softened, 7 to 9 minutes. Add garlic and cook until fragrant, about 1 minute. Add chili paste, tomatoes and their juice, and molasses; stir until chili paste is thoroughly combined. Add remaining 2 cups broth and beans; bring to boil, then reduce heat to simmer.

5. Meanwhile, heat 1 tablespoon oil in 12-inch skillet over medium-high heat until shimmering. Pat beef dry with paper towels and sprinkle with 1 teaspoon salt. Add half of beef and cook until browned on all sides, about 10 minutes. Transfer meat to Dutch oven. Add half of lager to skillet, scraping up any browned bits, and bring to simmer. Transfer lager to Dutch oven. Repeat with remaining 1 tablespoon oil, steak, and lager. Once last addition of lager has been added to Dutch oven, stir to combine and return mixture to simmer.

6. Cover pot and transfer to oven. Cook until meat and beans are fully tender, 1½ to 2 hours. Let chili stand, uncovered, 10 minutes.

7. Stir well and season to taste with salt before serving.

TO MAKE AHEAD

- Chili can be refrigerated for up to 3 days or frozen for up to 1 month; if frozen, thaw completely in refrigerator
- To reheat, bring chili, covered, to gentle simmer, stirring often; adjust consistency with hot water as needed

Our chili gets silky texture and a hint of corn flavor from the addition of convenient corn muffin mix.

Easier Chili con Carne

SERVES 6 TO 8 **FREEZE IT**

ACTIVE TIME 1 HOUR 15 MINUTES

TOTAL TIME 3 HOURS

WHY THIS RECIPE WORKS Many chili con carne recipes call for toasting and grinding whole chiles. We wanted to create a simpler but nevertheless still authentic-tasting version. For the meat, we settled on beef chuck, our favorite cut for stews because its substantial marbling provides rich flavor and tender texture after prolonged cooking. To add a smoky meatiness to our chili, we browned the beef in bacon fat instead of oil. We added a jalapeño for brightness and heat and minced chipotle for smoky, spicy depth. A few tablespoons of convenient corn muffin mix, in place of masa harina (corn flour), helped thicken our chili and give it a silky texture. If the bacon does not render a full 3 tablespoons of fat in step 1, supplement it with vegetable oil. Serve with diced avocado, chopped red onion, lime wedges, and/or shredded Monterey Jack or cheddar cheese.

1 (14.5-ounce) can diced tomatoes

2 teaspoons minced canned chipotle chile in adobo sauce

4 slices bacon, chopped fine

4 pounds boneless beef chuck-eye roast, pulled apart at seams, trimmed, and cut into 1-inch pieces
Salt and pepper

1 onion, chopped fine

1 jalapeño chile, stemmed, seeded, and chopped fine

3 tablespoons chili powder

4 garlic cloves, minced

1½ teaspoons ground cumin

½ teaspoon dried oregano

4 cups water

1 tablespoon packed brown sugar

2 tablespoons yellow corn muffin mix

1. Process tomatoes and their juice and chipotle in food processor until smooth, about 30 seconds. Cook bacon in Dutch oven over medium heat until crisp, about 8 minutes; transfer to paper towel–lined plate. Pour off and reserve 3 tablespoons bacon fat.

2. Pat beef dry with paper towels and season with salt and pepper. Heat 1 tablespoon reserved bacon fat in now-empty pot over medium-high heat until just smoking. Brown half of beef well on all sides, about 8 minutes; transfer to bowl. Repeat with 1 tablespoon bacon fat and remaining beef.

3. Add remaining 1 tablespoon bacon fat, onion, and jalapeño to fat left in pot and cook over medium heat until softened, about 5 minutes. Stir in chili powder, garlic, cumin, and oregano and cook until fragrant, about 30 seconds. Stir in water, pureed tomato mixture, bacon, sugar, and browned beef and any accumulated juices. Bring to boil, then reduce heat to low and simmer, covered, for 1 hour.

4. Uncover and skim excess fat from surface of stew using large spoon. Continue to simmer, uncovered, until meat is tender, 30 to 45 minutes.

5. Ladle 1 cup chili liquid into medium bowl and stir in muffin mix; cover and microwave until mixture is thickened, about 1 minute. Slowly whisk mixture into chili and simmer until chili is slightly thickened, 5 to 10 minutes. Season with salt to taste, and serve.

TO MAKE AHEAD

- Chili, prepared through step 4, can be refrigerated for up to 3 days or frozen for up to 1 month; if frozen, thaw completely in refrigerator
- To reheat, bring chili, covered, to gentle simmer, stirring often; adjust consistency with hot water as needed and continue with step 5

Hearty Beef Chili with Sweet Potatoes and Black Beans

SERVES 6 TO 8

ACTIVE TIME 1 HOUR

TOTAL TIME 3 HOURS 15 MINUTES

WHY THIS RECIPE WORKS For a hearty beef and vegetable chili greater than the sum of its parts, we started with well-marbled, inexpensive beef chuck-eye for its ability to become meltingly tender. We browned it for rich flavor and then stewed it until it was fork-tender. An aromatic base of garlic, cumin, chipotle, and chili powder gave our stew depth and some heat. The heat balanced out the sweetness of the potatoes and bell pepper, and mild beer added further complexity. We added some sweet potatoes in the beginning, knowing that they would break down to thicken our stew, and stirred in the beans with the tomatoes so that they cooked enough to absorb flavor but not so much that they fell apart. Once the meat was tender, we added the rest of the potatoes and bell pepper, cooking them until tender but firm. Serve with lime wedges, sliced avocado, cilantro leaves, sour cream, and shredded Monterey Jack or cheddar cheese.

3½ pounds boneless beef chuck-eye roast, pulled apart at seams, trimmed, and cut into 1-inch pieces
Salt and pepper
3 tablespoons vegetable oil
1 onion, chopped
1½ pounds sweet potatoes, peeled and cut into ½-inch pieces
3 garlic cloves, minced
1 tablespoon ground cumin
1 tablespoon minced canned chipotle chile in adobo sauce
2 teaspoons chili powder
1 (28-ounce) can diced tomatoes
1½ cups mild-flavored lager, such as Budweiser
2 (15-ounce) cans black beans, rinsed
1 red bell pepper, stemmed, seeded, and cut into ½-inch pieces
4 scallions, sliced thin

1. Adjust oven rack to middle position and heat oven to 300 degrees. Pat beef dry with paper towels and season with salt and pepper. Heat 1 tablespoon oil in Dutch oven over medium heat until shimmering. Add half of beef and brown on all sides, 6 to 8 minutes; transfer to large bowl. Repeat with 1 tablespoon oil and remaining beef.

2. Add remaining 1 tablespoon oil to now-empty pot and heat until shimmering. Add onion and ¾ cup sweet potatoes and cook until just beginning to brown, 5 to 7 minutes. Stir in garlic,

We cook some of the sweet potatoes for a longer time so that they break down and thicken the stew.

cumin, chipotle, chili powder, and 1 teaspoon salt and cook until fragrant, about 30 seconds. Add tomatoes and their juice, beer, beans, and browned beef and any accumulated juices, scraping up any browned bits.

3. Bring chili to simmer. Cover, transfer pot to oven, and cook, stirring occasionally, until sweet potatoes are broken down and beef is just tender, about 1 hour 40 minutes.

4. Stir in remaining sweet potatoes and bell pepper and continue to cook until meat and sweet potatoes are tender, about 20 minutes. Remove pot from oven, uncover, and let chili stand until thickened slightly, about 15 minutes.

5. Season with salt to taste. Serve, sprinkling individual portions with scallions.

> **TO MAKE AHEAD**
> - Chili, prepared through step 4, can be refrigerated for up to 2 days
> - To reheat, bring chili, covered, to gentle simmer, stirring often; adjust consistency with hot water as needed and continue with step 5

Colorado Green Chili

SERVES 6 · FREEZE IT

ACTIVE TIME 1 HOUR 40 MINUTES
TOTAL TIME 2 HOURS 30 MINUTES

WHY THIS RECIPE WORKS This Colorado chili is based on pork and lots of green Hatch chiles. Since real Hatch chiles can be hard to find, we approximated the flavor with Anaheims and jalapeños. We halved the Anaheims before roasting, which meant no tedious flipping, and pureed half of the chiles (as well as the diced tomatoes), chopping the other half by hand to create texture. Pork butt is rich and meaty, and starting it in a covered pan with water until the fat rendered let us brown it all in one batch. Using the oven to cook the chili provided gentle heat—and hands-off cooking—and we finished the stew with the chopped roasted jalapeños to add a fresh hit of heat. Serve with sour cream and minced fresh cilantro.

3 pounds boneless pork butt roast, pulled apart at seams, trimmed, and cut into 1-inch pieces
Salt
2 pounds (10 to 12) Anaheim chiles, stemmed, halved lengthwise, and seeded
3 jalapeño chiles
1 (14.5-ounce) can diced tomatoes
1 tablespoon vegetable oil
2 onions, chopped fine
8 garlic cloves, minced
1 tablespoon ground cumin
¼ cup all-purpose flour
4 cups chicken broth
Cayenne pepper
Lime wedges

1. Combine pork, ½ cup water, and ½ teaspoon salt in Dutch oven. Cover and cook over medium heat, stirring occasionally, for 20 minutes. Uncover and increase heat to medium-high. Cook, stirring often, until liquid evaporates and pork browns in its own fat, 15 to 20 minutes; transfer to bowl.

2. Meanwhile, adjust 1 oven rack to lowest position and second rack 6 inches from broiler element. Heat broiler. Line rimmed baking sheet with aluminum foil and spray with vegetable oil spray. Arrange Anaheims, skin side up, and jalapeños in single layer on prepared sheet. Broil chiles on upper rack until mostly blackened and soft, 15 to 20 minutes, flipping jalapeños halfway through broiling. Place Anaheims in large bowl, cover with plastic wrap, and let skins steam loose for 5 minutes. Set aside jalapeños. Heat oven to 325 degrees. (Chiles can be refrigerated for up to 1 day.)

3. Remove skins from Anaheims. Chop half of Anaheims into ½-inch pieces; transfer to bowl. Process remaining Anaheims in food processor until smooth, about 10 seconds; transfer to bowl with chopped Anaheims. Pulse tomatoes and their juice in now-empty food processor until coarsely ground, about 4 pulses.

4. Heat oil in now-empty Dutch oven over medium heat until shimmering. Add onions and cook until lightly browned, 5 to 7 minutes. Stir in garlic and cumin and cook until fragrant, about 30 seconds. Stir in flour and cook for 1 minute. Stir in broth, Anaheims, tomatoes, and pork and any accumulated juices. Bring to simmer, scraping up any browned bits. Cover, transfer to lower oven rack, and cook until pork is tender, 1 to 1¼ hours.

5. Stem, seed, and finely chop jalapeños (do not peel), and stir into chili. Season chili with salt and cayenne to taste. Serve with lime wedges.

TO MAKE AHEAD

- Chili can be refrigerated for up to 3 days or frozen for up to 1 month; if frozen, thaw completely in refrigerator
- To reheat, bring chili, covered, to gentle simmer, stirring often; adjust consistency with hot water as needed

---

NOTES FROM THE TEST KITCHEN

Using Fresh Chile Peppers

Chiles get their heat from chemical compounds called capsaicinoids, the best known being capsaicin. If you like a lot of heat, you can use the entire chile when cooking. If you prefer a milder dish, remove the ribs and seeds. Here are the fresh chiles we reach for most in the test kitchen.

JALAPEÑO Perhaps the best-known chile, jalapeños are moderately hot and have a bright, grassy flavor similar to a green bell pepper. They can be dark green or scarlet red.

POBLANO These chiles are very dark green in color. When ripe, they turn a reddish brown. They have a fruity, subtly spicy flavor. Thanks to their large size, they are also ideal for stuffing. Poblanos can be found in Latin markets and many supermarkets.

ANAHEIM With their acidic, lemony flavor, mild spiciness, and crisp texture, these popular chiles can be eaten raw, roasted, or fried; they are also frequently stuffed or used in salsa. Anaheim chiles are medium green in color and have a long, tapered shape.

A trio of fresh chiles makes this Southwestern-style chicken and bean chili a light and bright alternative to beef chili.

White Chicken Chili

SERVES 4 TO 6
ACTIVE TIME 1 HOUR
TOTAL TIME 1 HOUR 25 MINUTES

WHY THIS RECIPE WORKS White chicken chili promises a lighter, fresher alternative to the tomato-based kind. To ensure that the chicken in our chili stayed moist and tender, we started with bone-in chicken breasts. We browned them to develop fond (the flavorful bits on the bottom of the pot) and render their fat, which we used to sauté the aromatics. Then we gently poached the chicken until it was just cooked through and shredded it into easy-to-eat (and reheat) bite-size pieces. A trio of jalapeño, poblano, and Anaheim chiles brought the perfect balance of flavor, complexity, and modest heat to our chili. For more heat, include the jalapeño seeds and ribs. If you can't find Anaheim chiles, substitute an additional poblano and an additional jalapeño. Serve with sour cream, tortilla chips, and lime wedges.

1 onion, chopped
2 jalapeño chiles, stemmed, seeded, and chopped
2 poblano chiles, stemmed, seeded, and chopped
2 Anaheim chiles, stemmed, seeded, and chopped
2 pounds bone-in split chicken breasts, trimmed
  Salt and pepper
1 tablespoon vegetable oil
4 garlic cloves, minced
2 teaspoons ground cumin
1 teaspoon ground coriander
2 (15-ounce) cans cannellini beans, rinsed
3 cups chicken broth
3 tablespoons minced fresh cilantro
3 scallions, sliced thin
2 tablespoons lime juice

1. Pulse onion and 1 jalapeño together in food processor to consistency of chunky salsa, about 12 pulses. Transfer mixture to medium bowl. Pulse poblanos and Anaheims together in now-empty food processor to consistency of chunky salsa, about 12 pulses; transfer to bowl with onion and jalapeño.

2. Pat chicken dry with paper towels and season with salt and pepper. Heat oil in Dutch oven over medium-high heat until just smoking. Brown chicken well on all sides, 7 to 10 minutes; transfer to plate.

3. Pour off all but 1 tablespoon fat from pot, add chile-onion mixture, garlic, cumin, coriander, and 1 teaspoon salt, cover, and cook over medium heat until vegetables are softened, 8 to 10 minutes.

4. Remove pot from heat and transfer 1 cup cooked vegetables to now-empty food processor. Add 1 cup beans and ½ cup broth to food processor and process mixture until smooth, about 20 seconds. Stir processed bean mixture and remaining 2½ cups broth into pot, scraping up any browned bits, and bring to simmer over medium heat. Nestle chicken into pot along with any accumulated juices and bring to simmer. Cover, reduce heat to low, and gently simmer until chicken registers 160 degrees, about 20 minutes.

5. Remove pot from heat, transfer chicken to cutting board, let cool slightly, then shred into bite-size pieces using 2 forks, discarding skin and bones.

6. Stir shredded chicken into pot, along with remaining beans, remaining jalapeno, cilantro, scallions, and lime juice. Season with salt to taste, and serve.

TO MAKE AHEAD

- Chili, shredded chicken, remaining beans, and remaining jalapeño, prepared through step 5, can be refrigerated separately for up to 3 days
- To reheat, bring chili, covered, to gentle simmer, stirring often; adjust consistency with hot water as needed and continue with step 6

The tequila adds a noticeable pleasing zing to this tomatoey ground turkey and pinto bean chili.

Tequila-Lime Turkey Chili

SERVES 6 TO 8   FREEZE IT

ACTIVE TIME 45 MINUTES

TOTAL TIME 2 HOURS 30 MINUTES

WHY THIS RECIPE WORKS For a no-fuss flavorful turkey chili, we found that the type of turkey we used and when we added it were key. Ground turkey that was 93 percent lean remained moist and had enough fat to flavor our chili. Adding half of the meat in the beginning allowed time for its flavor to infuse the chili. For improved texture and moister meat, we pinched the remaining turkey into small pieces and stirred them in toward the end. A can each of diced and crushed tomatoes added enough liquid without making the chili too thin. Tequila and a bit of honey added complex flavor. Be sure to use ground turkey, not ground turkey breast (also labeled 99 percent fat-free). Serve with your favorite toppings.

1 tablespoon vegetable oil
2 onions, chopped fine
1 red bell pepper, stemmed, seeded, and cut into ½-inch pieces
¼ cup chili powder

6 garlic cloves, minced
1 tablespoon ground cumin
2 teaspoons ground coriander
1 teaspoon red pepper flakes
1 teaspoon dried oregano
½ teaspoon cayenne pepper
2 pounds 93 percent lean ground turkey
2 (15-ounce) cans pinto beans, rinsed
1 (28-ounce) can diced tomatoes
1 (28-ounce) can crushed tomatoes
2 cups chicken broth
¼ cup tequila
1 tablespoon honey
Water, as needed
Salt

1. Heat oil in Dutch oven over medium heat until shimmering. Add onions, bell pepper, chili powder, garlic, cumin, coriander, pepper flakes, oregano, and cayenne and cook, stirring often, until vegetables are softened, about 10 minutes.

2. Add 1 pound turkey, increase heat to medium-high, and cook, breaking up meat with wooden spoon, until no longer pink, about 4 minutes. Stir in beans, diced tomatoes and their juice, crushed tomatoes, and broth and bring to simmer. Reduce heat to medium-low and simmer until chili has begun to thicken, about 1 hour.

3. Pat remaining 1 pound turkey together into ball, then pinch off teaspoon-size pieces of meat and stir into chili, along with tequila and honey. Continue to simmer, stirring occasionally, until turkey is tender and chili is slightly thickened, about 40 minutes. (If chili begins to stick to bottom of pot or looks too thick, stir in water as needed.) Season with salt to taste, and serve.

TO MAKE AHEAD

- Chili can be refrigerated for up to 3 days or frozen for up to 1 month; if frozen, thaw completely in refrigerator
- To reheat, bring chili, covered, to gentle simmer, stirring often; adjust consistency with hot water as needed

Ultimate Vegetarian Chili

SERVES 6 TO 8   FREEZE IT

ACTIVE TIME 1 HOUR 25 MINUTES

TOTAL TIME 4 HOURS (PLUS 8 HOURS TO SOAK BEANS)

WHY THIS RECIPE WORKS To develop a vegetarian version of classic chili so flavorful and satisfying that even meat lovers would enjoy it, we used two kinds of beans and bulgur to give it a substantial texture. A combination of umami-rich ingredients— soy sauce, dried shiitake mushrooms, and tomatoes—added deep, savory flavor. When we ground walnuts and stirred them in, they contributed even more savoriness plus richness and body. For the chiles, we chose a combination of dried ancho and New Mexican chiles, toasted them in the oven until fragrant, and then ground them and added them in. To substitute chili powder for the dried chiles, grind the shiitakes and oregano and add them to the pot with ¼ cup of chili powder in step 4. We recommend a mix of at least two types of beans, one creamy (such as cannellini or navy) and one earthy (such as pinto, black, or red kidney). For more information on salt-soaking beans, see page 314. For a spicier chili, use both jalapeños. Serve the chili with lime wedges, sour cream, diced avocado, chopped red onion, and/or shredded Monterey Jack or cheddar cheese, if desired.

A mix of dried beans and homemade chili powder plus bulgur and walnuts make for a rich and flavorful veg chili.

Salt
1 pound (2½ cups) assorted dried beans, picked over and rinsed
2 dried ancho chiles
2 dried New Mexican chiles
½ ounce dried shiitake mushrooms, chopped coarse
4 teaspoons dried oregano
½ cup walnuts, toasted
1 (28-ounce) can diced tomatoes, drained with juice reserved
3 tablespoons tomato paste
3 tablespoons soy sauce
1–2 jalapeño chiles, stemmed and chopped coarse
6 garlic cloves, minced
¼ cup vegetable oil
2 pounds onions, chopped fine
1 tablespoon ground cumin
⅔ cup medium-grind bulgur
¼ cup minced fresh cilantro

1. Dissolve 3 tablespoons salt in 4 quarts cold water in large container. Add beans and soak at room temperature for at least 8 hours or up to 24 hours. Drain and rinse well.

2. Adjust oven rack to middle position and heat oven to 300 degrees. Arrange ancho and New Mexican chiles on rimmed baking sheet and toast until fragrant and puffed, about 8 minutes. Transfer to plate, let cool for 5 minutes, then remove stems and seeds. Working in batches, grind toasted chiles, mushrooms, and oregano in spice grinder until finely ground.

3. Process walnuts in food processor until finely ground, about 30 seconds; transfer to bowl. Process drained tomatoes, tomato paste, soy sauce, jalapeño, and garlic in food processor until tomatoes are finely chopped, about 45 seconds.

4. Heat oil in Dutch oven over medium-high heat until shimmering. Add onions and 1¼ teaspoons salt and cook, stirring occasionally, until onions begin to brown, 8 to 10 minutes. Reduce heat to medium, add ground chile mixture and cumin, and cook, stirring constantly, until fragrant, about 1 minute. Stir in beans and 7 cups water and bring to boil. Cover pot, transfer to oven, and cook for 45 minutes.

5. Stir in bulgur, ground walnuts, tomato mixture, and reserved tomato juice and continue to cook in oven, covered, until beans are fully tender, about 2 hours. Remove pot from oven, stir well, and let stand, uncovered, for 20 minutes.

6. Stir in cilantro and season with salt to taste before serving.

TO MAKE AHEAD

- Chili, prepared through step 5, can be refrigerated for up to 3 days or frozen for up to 1 month; if frozen, thaw completely in refrigerator
- To reheat, bring chili, covered, to gentle simmer, stirring often; adjust consistency with hot water as needed and continue with step 6

Black Bean Chili

SERVES 6 TO 8
ACTIVE TIME 35 MINUTES
TOTAL TIME 2 HOURS 40 MINUTES

WHY THIS RECIPE WORKS Black bean chili should be primarily about the beans—they should be creamy, tender, and well seasoned. Knowing that dried beans supply superior texture, we looked for ways to boost the meaty flavor of the chili. The answer was white mushrooms, which also lent plenty of body. Whole cumin seeds and minced chipotles added depth and smokiness, and a surprise addition, toasted mustard seeds, provided more complexity. Served with a spritz of lime and a sprinkle of minced cilantro, this rich, hearty chili was so satisfying that no one missed the meat. We strongly prefer the texture and flavor of mustard seeds and cumin seeds in this chili; however, ground cumin and dry mustard can be substituted—add ½ teaspoon ground cumin and/or ½ teaspoon dry mustard to the pot with the chili powder in step 3. Serve with sour cream, shredded cheddar or Monterey Jack cheese, chopped tomatoes, and/or minced onion.

Chopped white mushrooms and two chopped red bell peppers give our black bean chili a hearty texture.

- 1 pound white mushrooms, trimmed and broken into rough pieces
- 1 tablespoon mustard seeds
- 2 teaspoons cumin seeds
- 3 tablespoons vegetable oil
- 1 onion, chopped fine
- 9 garlic cloves, minced
- 1 tablespoon minced canned chipotle chile in adobo sauce
- 3 tablespoons chili powder
- 2½ cups vegetable broth
- 2½ cups water, plus extra as needed
- 1 pound (2½ cups) dried black beans, picked over and rinsed
- 1 tablespoon packed light brown sugar
- ⅛ teaspoon baking soda
- 2 bay leaves
- 1 (28-ounce) can crushed tomatoes
- 2 red bell peppers, stemmed, seeded, and cut into ½-inch pieces
- ½ cup minced fresh cilantro
  Salt
  Lime wedges

1. Adjust oven rack to lower-middle position and heat oven to 325 degrees. Pulse mushrooms in food processor until uniformly coarsely chopped, about 10 pulses.

2. Toast mustard seeds and cumin seeds in Dutch oven over medium heat, stirring constantly, until fragrant, about 1 minute. Stir in oil, onion, and processed mushrooms, cover, and cook until vegetables have released their liquid, about 5 minutes. Uncover and continue to cook until vegetables are browned, 5 to 10 minutes.

3. Stir in garlic and chipotle and cook until fragrant, about 30 seconds. Stir in chili powder and cook, stirring constantly, until fragrant, about 1 minute. Stir in broth, water, beans, sugar, baking soda, and bay leaves and bring to simmer, skimming as needed. Cover, transfer to oven, and cook for 1 hour.

4. Stir in crushed tomatoes and bell peppers and continue to cook in oven, covered, until beans are fully tender, about 1 hour longer. (If chili begins to stick to bottom of pot or is too thick, add water as needed.) Remove pot from oven and discard bay leaves.

5. Stir in cilantro, season with salt to taste, and serve with lime wedges.

TO MAKE AHEAD

- Chili, prepared through step 4, can be refrigerated for up to 3 days
- To reheat, bring chili, covered, to gentle simmer, stirring often; adjust consistency with hot water as needed and continue with step 5

Butternut Squash Chili with Quinoa

SERVES 6

ACTIVE TIME 50 MINUTES

TOTAL TIME 1 HOUR 50 MINUTES

WHY THIS RECIPE WORKS This stick-to-your-ribs African-style butternut squash chili features bold spices, a hefty amount of garlic and ginger, and aromatic coconut milk. We roasted the squash with chopped onions until both the squash and the onions started to brown at the edges, giving the soup a strong backbone of flavor. We pureed a portion of the roasted vegetables with dry-roasted peanuts for a rich, smooth base to our soup. We sautéed sweet bell pepper and spicy jalapeño and briefly bloomed a trio of warm spices before adding in the liquid. A combination of diced tomatoes and coconut milk made a creamy but bright broth, and nutty quinoa added heartiness and a subtle pop of texture. If you buy unwashed quinoa (or if you are unsure whether it's washed), be sure to rinse it before cooking to remove its bitter protective coating (called saponin). For more spice, include the ribs and seeds from the jalapeño. Serve with hot sauce.

- 3 pounds butternut squash, peeled, seeded, and cut into ½-inch pieces (9 cups)
- 2 onions, cut into ½-inch pieces
- 6 tablespoons vegetable oil
  Salt and pepper
- 5 cups water, plus extra as needed
- ¾ cup salted dry-roasted peanuts, chopped
- 1 large red bell pepper, stemmed, seeded, and cut into ½-inch pieces
- 1 jalapeño chile, stemmed, seeded, and minced
- 2 tablespoons grated fresh ginger
- 3 garlic cloves, minced
- ¾ teaspoon ground cinnamon
- ¾ teaspoon ground coriander
- ½ teaspoon cayenne pepper
- 1 (14.5-ounce) can diced tomatoes
- 1 (13.5-ounce) can coconut milk
- 1 cup prewashed white quinoa
- ¼ cup minced fresh cilantro or parsley

1. Adjust oven racks to upper-middle and lower-middle positions and heat oven to 450 degrees. Toss squash, onions, ¼ cup oil, 1 teaspoon salt, and ½ teaspoon pepper together in bowl. Spread vegetables out in even layer over 2 rimmed baking sheets. Roast vegetables, stirring occasionally, until tender, 45 to 50 minutes, switching and rotating sheets halfway through roasting.

2. In food processor, process ½ cup roasted vegetables, 2 cups water, and ¼ cup peanuts until smooth, about 1 minute.

Blending peanuts with some of the roasted squash gives this chili silky body and intense sweet, nutty flavor.

3. Heat remaining 2 tablespoons oil in Dutch oven over medium-high heat until shimmering. Add bell pepper, jalapeño, and 2 teaspoons salt and cook until peppers start to soften, about 5 minutes. Stir in ginger, garlic, cinnamon, coriander, cayenne, and ¾ teaspoon pepper, and cook until fragrant, about 30 seconds. Stir in remaining 3 cups water, tomatoes and their juice, remaining roasted vegetables, and pureed vegetable mixture, scraping up any browned bits.

4. Add coconut milk and quinoa and bring to boil. Reduce heat to low and simmer, stirring occasionally, until quinoa is tender, about 15 minutes.

5. Season chili with salt and pepper to taste. Adjust consistency with additional hot water as needed. Sprinkle individual portions with cilantro and remaining ½ cup peanuts and serve.

TO MAKE AHEAD

- Chili, prepared through step 3, can be refrigerated for up to 3 days
- To reheat, bring chili, covered, to gentle simmer, stirring often, and continue with step 4

Salads

■ EASY (30 minutes or less active time)   ■ FREEZE IT
Photo: Wheat Berry Salad with Orange and Carrots

Classic Caesar Salad

SERVES 4 TO 6 `EASY`

ACTIVE TIME 30 MINUTES

TOTAL TIME 1 HOUR

WHY THIS RECIPE WORKS The appeal of a well-made Caesar salad is undeniable, but it is often out of reach on a busy weeknight because making the dressing involves a few steps more than your usual salad; plus, there are the homemade croutons. Luckily both the dressing and croutons can be made ahead and stored. For our Caesar salad, we wanted crisp-tender romaine lettuce napped with a creamy, garlicky dressing boasting a pleasing salty undertone, with crunchy, savory croutons strewn throughout. To start, we cut the extra-virgin olive oil in the dressing with canola oil, which made for a milder flavor, and we used egg yolks instead of a whole egg to add richness. For a robust, though not aggressive, garlic flavor we minced the garlic into a pulp and then steeped it in lemon juice. Incorporating a portion of the Parmesan into the dressing while saving some to serve over the salad provided a double layer of cheese flavor. Tossed with slices of crisp romaine and paired with classic croutons, our Caesar is better than ever. A quarter-cup of Egg Beaters may be substituted for the egg yolks. Since anchovy fillets vary in size, more than six fillets may be necessary to yield 1 tablespoon of minced anchovies. A rasp-style grater makes quick work of turning the garlic into a paste.

2 tablespoons lemon juice, plus extra for seasoning
¾ teaspoon garlic, minced to paste
2 large egg yolks
6 anchovy fillets, rinsed, patted dry, minced, and mashed to paste with fork (1 tablespoon)
½ teaspoon Worcestershire sauce
5 tablespoons canola oil
5 teaspoons extra-virgin olive oil
1½ ounces Parmesan cheese, grated fine (¾ cup)
Pepper
2 romaine lettuce hearts (12 ounces), cut into ¾-inch pieces (8 cups)
1 recipe Croutons for Caesar Salad (recipe follows)

1. Whisk lemon juice and garlic paste together in large bowl. Let stand for 10 minutes.

2. Whisk egg yolks, anchovies, and Worcestershire into garlic mixture. While whisking constantly, drizzle canola oil and olive oil into bowl in slow, steady stream until fully emulsified. Add ½ cup Parmesan and pepper to taste; whisk until incorporated.

3. Add romaine to dressing and toss to coat. Add croutons and mix gently until evenly distributed. Season with extra lemon juice to taste. Serve immediately, passing remaining ¼ cup Parmesan separately.

`TO MAKE AHEAD`

- Dressing, prepared through step 2, can be refrigerated for up to 2 days
- To serve, whisk dressing to loosen and continue with step 3

CROUTONS FOR CAESAR SALAD

MAKES 3 CUPS `EASY`

ACTIVE TIME 10 MINUTES

TOTAL TIME 30 MINUTES (PLUS COOLING TIME)

3 ounces baguette, cut into ¾-inch cubes (3 cups)
2 tablespoons extra-virgin olive oil
¼ teaspoon pepper
⅛ teaspoon salt

Adjust oven rack to middle position and heat oven to 350 degrees. Toss all ingredients together in bowl. Bake on rimmed baking sheet until golden and crisp, about 15 minutes. Let croutons cool completely on sheet. Serve.

`TO MAKE AHEAD`

Croutons can be stored at room temperature for up to 24 hours

---

Kale Caesar Salad

SERVES 4 TO 6

ACTIVE TIME 45 MINUTES

TOTAL TIME 1 HOUR 30 MINUTES

WHY THIS RECIPE WORKS Kale offers the make-ahead cook a great option for a salad. Because kale is notoriously tough and fibrous, it actually benefits from being prepared ahead. In fact it may be the only leafy green salad you can dress hours in advance. In order to soften the leaves and make them more palatable, we soaked them in a warm water bath for 10 minutes. Next we tossed the kale with the Caesar salad dressing, letting it marinate in the refrigerator for at least 20 minutes; this gave the salad time to cool back down and allowed the flavors to meld together. To balance the strong flavor of kale, our dressing is extra-potent, with extra Worcestershire sauce and a splash of white wine vinegar and Dijon mustard for kick. The kale leaves must be dressed at least

Soaking fibrous kale leaves in a warm water bath easily softens them for a more tender salad.

20 minutes (or up to 6 hours) before serving. We like to use curly kale in this salad because its curly edges help to hold on to the dressing.

SALAD

- 12 ounces curly kale, stemmed and cut into 1-inch pieces (16 cups)
- 1 ounce Parmesan cheese, grated (½ cup)
- 1 recipe Croutons for Caesar Salad (page 82)

DRESSING

- ½ cup mayonnaise
- ¼ cup grated Parmesan cheese
- 2 tablespoons lemon juice
- 1 tablespoon white wine vinegar
- 1 tablespoon Worcestershire sauce
- 1 tablespoon Dijon mustard
- 3 anchovy fillets, rinsed
- 1 garlic clove, minced
- ½ teaspoon salt
- ½ teaspoon pepper
- ¼ cup extra-virgin olive oil

1. FOR THE SALAD Place kale in large bowl and cover with warm tap water (110 to 115 degrees). Swish kale around to remove grit. Let kale sit in warm water bath for 10 minutes. Remove kale from water and spin dry in salad spinner in multiple batches. Pat leaves dry with paper towels if still wet.

2. FOR THE DRESSING Process mayonnaise, Parmesan, lemon juice, vinegar, Worcestershire, mustard, anchovies, garlic, salt, and pepper in blender until pureed, about 30 seconds. With blender running, slowly add oil until emulsified.

3. Toss kale with ¾ cup dressing in large bowl. Refrigerate dressed kale for 20 minutes.

4. Toss Parmesan and croutons with dressed kale. Serve, passing remaining ¼ cup dressing at table.

TO MAKE AHEAD

- Dressed kale and remaining ¼ cup dressing, prepared through step 3, can be refrigerated separately for up to 6 hours
- To serve, whisk dressing to loosen and continue with step 4

NOTES FROM THE TEST KITCHEN

Types of Kale

Kale comes in several different varieties, and they each have a unique flavor and texture. We use different types in different recipes.

TUSCAN KALE Tuscan kale is also called black, dinosaur, cavolo nero, or Lacinato. It has a sweet, mineral-y flavor and a tender texture when eaten raw, and becomes robust and rich when braised.

CURLY KALE Also called Scottish or green, curly kale has a pungent grassy flavor when raw that becomes nutty when braised.

RED KALE We don't use red kale (also called Russian Red or Winter Red), because we find its texture to be leathery and tough even when it's braised.

BABY KALE Tender baby kale doesn't require any soaking or massaging to be eaten raw, and it won't hold up to braising.

SIMPLE GREEN SALADS AND VINAIGRETTES

Green salads don't immediately sound like great candidates for making ahead, but if you store them properly you can keep a simple mix of veggies or a more elaborate fruit, cheese, and nut salad crisp and fresh until you're ready to eat, saving you valuable chopping time and kitchen space later. We layer heartier fruits and vegetables at the bottom of the bowl, and separate wet ingredients, such as soft cheese, away from ingredients that need to stay crisp and dry, like toasted nuts and aged cheese. Delicate fresh herbs are best sprinkled on top. Toss with ¼ cup of one of our make-ahead vinaigrettes just before serving and you'll have (almost) instant salad.

SPINACH AND FRISÉE WITH BLUEBERRIES, FETA, AND ALMONDS

SERVES 4 TO 6   EASY
ACTIVE TIME 15 MINUTES
TOTAL TIME 15 MINUTES

- 1 cup blueberries
- 1 medium head frisée, torn into 2-inch pieces
- 6 ounces (6 cups) baby spinach
- ¼ cup vinaigrette
  Salt and pepper
- 4 ounces feta cheese, cut into small chunks (1 cup)
- ½ cup sliced almonds, toasted

Toss blueberries, frisée, and spinach together in large bowl. Drizzle dressing over top and gently toss to combine. Season with salt and pepper to taste. Sprinkle with feta and almonds, and serve.

TO MAKE AHEAD ▸

Layer blueberries at bottom of large bowl, followed by frisée, feta, and spinach, then top with almonds; assembled salad can be refrigerated up to 24 hours before dressing and serving

ARUGULA SALAD WITH FENNEL AND PARMESAN

SERVES 4 TO 6   EASY
ACTIVE TIME 10 MINUTES
TOTAL TIME 10 MINUTES

- ½ small fennel bulb, fronds minced, stalks discarded, bulb halved, cored, and sliced thin
- 6 ounces (6 cups) baby arugula
- ¼ cup vinaigrette
  Salt and pepper
- 2 ounces Parmesan, shaved

Toss sliced fennel, fennel fronds, and arugula together in large bowl. Drizzle vinaigrette over top and gently toss to combine. Season with salt and pepper to taste, sprinkle with Parmesan, and serve.

TO MAKE AHEAD ▸

Layer sliced fennel at bottom of large bowl, followed by arugula and fennel fronds, then top with Parmesan; assembled salad can be refrigerated up to 24 hours before dressing and serving

MIXED GREENS WITH ASPARAGUS AND SHREDDED CARROTS

SERVES 4 TO 6   EASY
ACTIVE TIME 10 MINUTES
TOTAL TIME 10 MINUTES

- 2 large carrots, peeled and grated
- 1 pound asparagus, tips cut into ¾-inch-long pieces, stalks cut on bias into 2-inch lengths
- 6 ounces (6 cups) mesclun greens
- ¼ cup vinaigrette
  Salt and pepper

Toss carrots, asparagus, and lettuce together in large bowl. Drizzle vinaigrette over top and gently toss to combine Season with salt and pepper to taste, and serve.

TO MAKE AHEAD ▸

Layer carrots at bottom of large bowl, followed by asparagus, then lettuce; assembled salad can be refrigerated up to 24 hours before dressing and serving

MAKE-AHEAD VINAIGRETTE

MAKES ABOUT 1 CUP   `EASY`
ACTIVE TIME 15 MINUTES
TOTAL TIME 15 MINUTES

WHY THIS RECIPE WORKS When you want to make a vinaigrette to stash in your fridge for the week, this is the recipe that will stay fresh and emulsified. In addition to oil and vinegar (or lemon juice), we make our vinaigrette with a combination of emulsifiers (mustard and mayonnaise) and a stabilizer (molasses), which help the emulsion form and hold for several days. We also use a 2:1 ratio of extra-virgin olive oil to vegetable oil, which prevents the oil molecules from bonding together and solidifying in the refrigerator while still allowing the distinct flavor of the olive oil to come through. The dressing template is adaptable to a variety of oils and acids, as well as aromatics and fresh herbs. Regular or light mayonnaise can be used in this recipe. Do not use blackstrap molasses. You can substitute toasted hazelnut or walnut oil for the extra-virgin olive oil.

> 1 tablespoon mayonnaise
> 1 tablespoon molasses
> 1 tablespoon Dijon mustard
> ½ teaspoon salt
> ¼ cup wine vinegar
> ½ cup extra-virgin olive oil
> ¼ cup vegetable oil

1. Combine mayonnaise, molasses, mustard, and salt in 2-cup jar with tight-fitting lid. Stir with fork until mixture is milky in appearance and no lumps of mayonnaise or molasses remain. Add vinegar, seal jar, and shake until smooth, about 10 seconds.

2. Add ¼ cup olive oil, seal jar, and shake vigorously until thoroughly combined, about 10 seconds. Repeat, adding remaining ¼ cup olive oil and vegetable oil in 2 additions, shaking vigorously until thoroughly combined after each addition. (After third addition, vinaigrette should be glossy and lightly thickened, with no pools of oil on its surface.) Serve.

VARIATIONS

MAKE-AHEAD SHERRY-SHALLOT VINAIGRETTE   `EASY`

Substitute sherry vinegar for wine vinegar. Add 2 teaspoons finely minced shallot and 2 teaspoons minced fresh thyme to jar with mayonnaise, mustard, and molasses.

MAKE-AHEAD LEMON, GARLIC AND CHIVE VINAIGRETTE   `EASY`

Substitute lemon juice for wine vinegar. Add 2 teaspoons grated lemon zest, 2 teaspoons minced fresh chives, and 1 finely minced garlic clove to jar with mayonnaise, mustard, and molasses.

TO MAKE AHEAD

- Vinaigrette can be refrigerated for up to 1 week
- To serve, shake briefly to recombine

Buying Salad Greens

Not only is there a dizzying array of greens available at the supermarket now, but in a good market you can buy the same greens more than one way: full heads, prewashed in a bag, in a clamshell, and loose in bulk bins. Which is the right choice for you? A sturdy lettuce like romaine can be washed and stored for up to a week, making it a good option for many nights' worth of salads. Bags of pre-washed baby spinach, arugula, and mesclun mix offer great convenience, but be sure to turn over the bags and inspect the greens as closely as you can; the sell-by date alone doesn't ensure quality, so if you see moisture in the bag or hints of blackened leaf edges, move on.

Don't buy bags of already-cut lettuce that you can otherwise buy as whole heads, like romaine, Bibb or red leaf. Precut lettuce will be inferior in quality because the leaves begin to spoil once they are cut (bagged hearts of romaine are fine but stay away from bags of cut romaine). Endive and radicchio are always sold in heads, and because they are sturdy and will last a while, they are nice to have on hand to complement other greens or to add more interest to a salad. And when a special salad is planned for company, buy the greens either the day of the party or the day before for the best results.

Caramelized sweet potatoes and a bright pomegranate vinaigrette are the perfect complement to earthy kale.

Kale Salad with Roasted Sweet Potatoes and Pomegranate Vinaigrette

SERVES 6 TO 8 · EASY

ACTIVE TIME 30 MINUTES
TOTAL TIME 1 HOUR 30 MINUTES

WHY THIS RECIPE WORKS Here we pair earthy, hearty kale with roasted sweet potatoes for an entrée-worthy salad. As with our Kale Caesar Salad (page 82), we found that the tough texture of raw kale benefitted from a 10-minute soak in warm water and then time to marinate in the dressing. Caramelized roasted potatoes, shredded radicchio, crunchy pecans, a sprinkling of Parmesan cheese, and a sweet pomegranate vinaigrette turned our salad into a main course. If you can't find pomegranate molasses, substitute 2 tablespoons of lemon juice, 2 teaspoons of mild molasses, and 1 teaspoon of honey. Tuscan kale (also known as dinosaur or Lacinato kale) is more tender than curly kale and red kale; do not use baby kale.

SALAD

- 1½ pounds sweet potatoes, peeled, and cut into ½-inch pieces
- 2 teaspoons extra-virgin olive oil
  Salt and pepper
- 12 ounces Tuscan kale, stemmed and sliced crosswise into ½-inch-wide strips (7 cups)
- ½ head radicchio (5 ounces), cored and sliced thin
- ⅓ cup pecans, toasted and chopped
  Shaved Parmesan cheese

VINAIGRETTE

- 2 tablespoons water
- 1½ tablespoons pomegranate molasses
- 1 small shallot, minced
- 1 tablespoon honey
- 1 tablespoon cider vinegar
  Salt and pepper
- ¼ cup extra-virgin olive oil

1. FOR THE SALAD Adjust oven rack to middle position and heat oven to 400 degrees. Toss sweet potatoes with oil and season with salt and pepper. Arrange potatoes in single layer in rimmed baking sheet and roast until browned, 25 to 30 minutes, flipping potatoes halfway through roasting. Transfer to plate and let cool for 20 minutes.

2. Meanwhile, place kale in large bowl and cover with warm tap water (110 to 115 degrees). Swish kale around to remove grit. Let kale sit in warm water bath for 10 minutes. Remove kale from water and spin dry in salad spinner in multiple batches. Pat leaves dry with paper towels if still wet.

3. FOR THE VINAIGRETTE Whisk water, pomegranate molasses, shallot, honey, vinegar, ¼ teaspoon salt, and ¼ teaspoon pepper together in bowl. Whisking constantly, slowly drizzle in oil.

4. Toss kale, roasted potatoes, and radicchio with ⅓ cup vinaigrette in large bowl, cover, and refrigerate for 20 minutes.

5. Drizzle remaining vinaigrette over kale mixture, season with salt and pepper to taste, and toss to combine. Sprinkle with pecans and shaved Parmesan. Serve.

> **TO MAKE AHEAD**
> - Dressed kale-vegetable mixture and remaining vinaigrette, prepared through step 4, can be refrigerated separately for up to 24 hours
> - To serve, bring kale-vegetable mixture and remaining vinaigrette to room temperature, whisk dressing to recombine, and continue with step 5

STEMMING KALE

A. Hold leaf at base of stem and use knife to slash leafy portion from either side of stem.

B. Alternatively, fold each leaf in half and cut along edge of rib to remove thickest part of rib and stem.

Chopped Salad

SERVES 6 `EASY`

ACTIVE TIME 30 MINUTES

TOTAL TIME 1 HOUR 25 MINUTES

WHY THIS RECIPE WORKS We liked the idea of a salad that could be assembled in advance, with all the ingredients attractively layered and covered with a creamy dressing, put in the fridge for a night, and simply tossed and served the next day. But our early attempts produced overdressed salads with soggy vegetables—until we got the ingredients and proportions just right. We tried several varieties of lettuce, but iceberg retained the best crunch after sitting with the dressing for a day. Salting the lettuce pulled moisture out, helping it to keep its crunch; we used the released moisture to thin our creamy dressing to the perfect consistency. Soft ingredients such as mushrooms and spinach wilted into mush, but crunchy vegetables like celery, bell peppers, and cucumbers stayed crisp in the salad overnight. To make this salad hearty enough for dinner, we crisped a whole pound of bacon and crumbled it over the top along with a generous amount of tangy blue cheese. For a creamy dressing with a subtle kick, we thinned mayonnaise with a little cider vinegar and spiked it with hot sauce. Frank's RedHot is our favorite brand of hot sauce. If using a hotter brand, such as Tabasco, reduce the amount to 1 tablespoon.

1 pound bacon
1 head iceberg lettuce (9 ounces), cored and chopped coarse
 Salt and pepper
½ red onion, sliced thin

1 recipe Easy-Peel Hard-Cooked Eggs (page 88), chopped
1½ cups frozen peas
4 celery ribs, sliced thin
1 red bell pepper, stemmed, seeded, and chopped
1 cucumber, halved lengthwise, seeded, and sliced thin
6 ounces blue cheese, crumbled (1½ cups)
1½ cups mayonnaise
3 tablespoons cider vinegar
2 tablespoons hot sauce
2 teaspoons sugar

1. Cook half of bacon in 12-inch skillet over medium-high heat until crisp, about 10 minutes. Transfer to paper towel–lined plate. Repeat with remaining bacon and let cool. Crumble bacon into bite-size pieces; set aside.

2. Place half of lettuce in large serving bowl and sprinkle with ½ teaspoon salt. Rinse onion under cold water; pat dry with paper towels. Layer onion, eggs, peas, celery, bell pepper, and cucumber over lettuce. Add remaining lettuce to bowl, sprinkle with ½ teaspoon salt, and top with bacon and cheese.

> **NOTES FROM THE TEST KITCHEN**
>
> ### Storing Salad Greens
> Here's the best way to store the most common lettuces.
>
> | LETTUCE TYPE | HOW TO STORE |
> | --- | --- |
> | Crisp heads, such as iceberg and romaine | Core lettuce, wrap in moist paper towels, and refrigerate in plastic produce bag or zipper-lock bag left slightly open. |
> | Leafy greens, such as arugula, baby spinach, and mesclun | If prewashed, store in original plastic container or bag. If not prewashed, wash and dry thoroughly in salad spinner and store directly in spinner between layers of paper towels, or lightly roll in paper towels and store in zipper-lock bag left slightly open. |
> | Tender heads, such as Boston and Bibb lettuce | If lettuce comes with root attached, leave lettuce portion attached to root and store in original plastic container, plastic produce bag, or zipper-lock bag left slightly open. If lettuce is without root, wrap in moist paper towels and refrigerate in plastic produce bag or zipper-lock bag left slightly open. |

3. Combine mayonnaise, vinegar, hot sauce, sugar, and 1½ teaspoons pepper in bowl, then spread evenly over top of salad.

4. Toss until salad is evenly coated with dressing and season with salt and pepper to taste. Serve.

TO MAKE AHEAD

Assembled salad, prepared through step 3, can be refrigerated for up to 24 hours

---

EASY-PEEL HARD-COOKED EGGS

MAKES 6 EGGS   **EASY**
ACTIVE TIME 5 MINUTES
TOTAL TIME 35 MINUTES

Be sure to use large eggs that have no cracks and are cold from the refrigerator. If you don't have a steamer basket, use a spoon or tongs to gently place the eggs in the water. It does not matter if the eggs are above the water or partially submerged. You can use this method for fewer than six eggs without altering the timing. You can also double this recipe as long as you use a pot and steamer basket large enough to hold the eggs in a single layer. There's no need to peel the eggs right away. They can be stored in their shells and peeled when needed.

6 large eggs

1. Bring 1 inch water to rolling boil in medium saucepan over high heat. Place eggs in steamer basket. Transfer basket to saucepan. Cover, reduce heat to medium-low, and cook eggs for 13 minutes.

2. When eggs are almost finished cooking, combine 2 cups ice cubes and 2 cups cold water in medium bowl. Using tongs or spoon, transfer eggs to ice bath; let sit for 15 minutes. Peel before using.

TO MAKE AHEAD

Unpeeled hard-cooked eggs can be refrigerated for up to 1 week

The thinly sliced raw Brussels sprouts in this fresh salad sit in a lemony dressing that softens and seasons them.

Brussels Sprout Salad with Pecorino and Pine Nuts

SERVES 8   **EASY**
ACTIVE TIME 25 MINUTES
TOTAL TIME 55 MINUTES

WHY THIS RECIPE WORKS To make Brussels sprouts shine in a salad, we found that preparing them ahead of time was a great way to get rid of some of their vegetal rawness. Rather than cooking the sprouts, we sliced them very thin and then marinated them in a bright vinaigrette made with lemon juice and Dijon mustard. The 30-minute soak in the acidic dressing softened and seasoned the sprouts, bringing out and balancing their flavor. Stirring toasted pine nuts and shredded Pecorino Romano into our salad just before serving added a layer of crunch and nutty richness. Slice the sprouts as thin as possible. Shred the Pecorino Romano on a coarse grater.

3 tablespoons lemon juice

2 tablespoons Dijon mustard

1 small shallot, minced

1 garlic clove, minced

  Salt and pepper

6 tablespoons extra-virgin olive oil

2 pounds Brussels sprouts, trimmed, halved, and sliced very thin

3 ounces Pecorino Romano cheese, shredded (1 cup)

½ cup pine nuts, toasted

1. Whisk lemon juice, mustard, shallot, garlic, and ½ teaspoon salt together in large bowl. Whisking constantly, drizzle in oil.

2. Add Brussels sprouts, toss to combine, and let sit for 30 minutes.

3. Stir in Pecorino and pine nuts and season with salt and pepper to taste. Serve.

TO MAKE AHEAD

- Vinaigrette and sliced Brussels sprouts can be refrigerated separately for up to 3 days
- To serve, bring vinaigrette to room temperature, whisk to recombine, and continue with step 2
- Dressed salad can be held for up to 2 hours before serving

SHREDDING BRUSSELS SPROUTS FOR SALAD

1. Peel off any loose or discolored leaves and slice off bottom of stem end, leaving leaves attached.

2. Halve Brussels sprouts through stem end, then slice very thin.

Quickly blanching broccoli helps it keep its bright color and crunch for up to three days before assembling the salad.

Broccoli Salad with Raisins and Walnuts

SERVES 4 TO 6 **EASY**

ACTIVE TIME 25 MINUTES

TOTAL TIME 35 MINUTES

WHY THIS RECIPE WORKS Most recipes for this potluck classic leave the broccoli raw, but we found that cooking it briefly in boiling water improved both its flavor and its appearance. Adding the hardier stems to the cooking water before the florets leveled the playing field, so both became tender at the same time. Drying the broccoli in a salad spinner rid it of excess moisture, so the dressing—a tangy mayo-and-vinegar mixture—wouldn't get watered down. As an added benefit, when treated this way, the broccoli retained its color, flavor, and crunch for a few days, allowing us to prepare it well in advance of assembling the salad. We brought crunch and salty-sweet balance to this salad by adding toasted walnuts and golden raisins. When prepping the broccoli, keep the stems and florets separate. If you don't own a salad spinner, lay the broccoli on a clean dish towel to dry in step 2.

½ cup golden raisins

1½ pounds broccoli, florets cut into 1-inch pieces, stalks peeled and sliced ¼ inch thick

½ cup mayonnaise

1 tablespoon balsamic vinegar

Salt and pepper

½ cup walnuts, toasted and chopped coarse

1 large shallot, minced

1. Bring 3 quarts water to boil in Dutch oven. Fill large bowl halfway with ice and water. Combine ½ cup of boiling water and raisins in small bowl, cover, and let sit for 5 minutes; drain.

2. Meanwhile, add broccoli stalks to pot of boiling water and cook for 1 minute. Add florets and cook until slightly tender, about 1 minute. Drain broccoli, then transfer to bowl of ice water and let sit until chilled, about 5 minutes. Drain again, transfer broccoli to salad spinner, and spin dry.

3. Whisk mayonnaise, vinegar, ½ teaspoon salt, and ¼ teaspoon pepper together in large bowl.

4. Add broccoli, raisins, walnuts, and shallot to bowl with dressing and toss to combine. Season with salt and pepper to taste, and serve.

TO MAKE AHEAD ▸

- Blanched broccoli, plumped raisins, and dressing, prepared through step 3, can be refrigerated separately for up to 3 days
- Dressed salad can be refrigerated for up to 2 hours before serving

Braised Beet Salad with Lemon and Almonds

SERVES 4 TO 6   **EASY**

ACTIVE TIME 30 MINUTES

TOTAL TIME 1 HOUR

WHY THIS RECIPE WORKS For a flavorful beet salad that maximized the sweet, earthy flavor of the beets, we decided to braise the beets in a minimal amount of water instead of roasting them. Halving the beets cut down on the cooking time; in just 45 minutes, the beets were tender and their skins slipped off easily. To further amplify their flavor, we reduced the braising liquid and added brown sugar and vinegar to make a glossy sauce. For flavor and contrast, we added toasted nuts (or pepitas), fresh herbs, and citrus zest. To ensure even cooking, we recommend using beets of similar size—roughly 2 to 3 inches in diameter.

1½ pounds beets, trimmed and halved horizontally

1¼ cups water

Salt and pepper

3 tablespoons distilled white vinegar

1 tablespoon packed light brown sugar

1 shallot, sliced thin

1 teaspoon grated lemon zest

½ cup whole almonds, toasted and chopped

2 tablespoons minced fresh mint

1 teaspoon minced fresh thyme

1. Place beets, cut side down, in 11-inch straight-sided sauté pan or Dutch oven. Add water and ¼ teaspoon salt and bring to simmer over high heat. Reduce heat to low, cover, and simmer until beets are tender and tip of paring knife inserted into beets meets no resistance, 45 to 50 minutes.

2. Transfer beets to cutting board and let cool. Increase heat to medium-high and reduce cooking liquid, stirring occasionally, until pan is almost dry, 5 to 6 minutes. Add vinegar and sugar, return to boil, and cook, stirring constantly with heat-resistant spatula, until spatula leaves wide trail when dragged through glaze, 1 to 2 minutes. Remove pan from heat.

3. When beets are cool, rub off skins with paper towel and cut into ½-inch wedges. Add beets, shallot, lemon zest, ½ teaspoon salt, and ¼ teaspoon pepper to glaze and toss to coat.

4. Transfer beets to serving dish and sprinkle with almonds, mint, and thyme. Serve.

VARIATIONS

Braised Beet Salad with Lime and Pepitas **EASY**

Omit thyme. Substitute lime zest for lemon zest, toasted pepitas for almonds, and cilantro for mint.

Braised Beet Salad with Orange and Walnuts **EASY**

Substitute orange zest for lemon zest, toasted and chopped walnuts for almonds, and parsley for mint.

TO MAKE AHEAD ▸

- Dressed beet mixture, prepared through step 3, can be refrigerated for up to 24 hours
- To serve, bring beets to room temperature, season with vinegar, salt, and pepper to taste, and continue with step 4

We season roasted butternut squash with a bold blend of Middle Eastern spices for a salad with complex flavor.

Roasted Butternut Squash Salad with Za'atar and Parsley

SERVES 4 TO 6 **EASY**

ACTIVE TIME 30 MINUTES

TOTAL TIME 1 HOUR

WHY THIS RECIPE WORKS The sweet, nutty flavor of roasted butternut squash pairs best with flavors that are bold enough to balance that sweetness. To fill this role in our roasted butternut squash salad, we chose the traditional Middle Eastern spice blend za'atar (a pungent combination of toasted sesame seeds, thyme, marjoram, and sumac). We found that using high heat and placing the rack in the lowest position produced squash that retained a firm-tender texture even after being dressed and held for several days. Dusting the za'atar over the hot squash worked much like toasting the spice, boosting its flavor. For a foil to the tender squash, we added crunchy pepitas. Pomegranate seeds added a burst of tartness and color. Pepitas, or pumpkin seeds, are available at most supermarkets and natural foods stores. You can substitute chopped red grapes or small blueberries for the pomegranate seeds. We prefer to use our homemade Za'atar (page 180) but you can substitute store-bought if you wish, though flavor can vary by brand.

3 pounds butternut squash, peeled, seeded, and cut into ½-inch pieces (8 cups)
3 tablespoons extra-virgin olive oil
  Salt and pepper
1 teaspoon za'atar
1 small shallot, minced
1½ tablespoons lemon juice
1½ tablespoons honey
¾ cup fresh parsley leaves
⅓ cup unsalted pepitas, toasted
½ cup pomegranate seeds

1. Adjust oven rack to lowest position and heat oven to 500 degrees. Toss squash with 1 tablespoon oil in bowl and season with salt and pepper. Lay squash in single layer on rimmed baking sheet and roast until and tender but still firm, 15 to 20 minutes, stirring halfway through roasting. Remove squash from oven, sprinkle with za'atar, and let cool for 15 minutes.

2. Whisk shallot, lemon juice, honey, and ¼ teaspoon salt together in large bowl. Whisking constantly, drizzle in remaining 2 tablespoons oil. Add squash and toss to combine.

3. Add parsley and pepitas and toss gently to combine. Sprinkle with pomegranate seeds and serve.

TO MAKE AHEAD

- Dressed squash, prepared through step 2, can be refrigerated for up to 3 days
- To serve, bring squash to room temperature, season with lemon juice, salt, and pepper to taste, and continue with step 3

Celery Root Salad with Apple and Parsley

SERVES 4 TO 6 **EASY**

ACTIVE TIME 25 MINUTES

TOTAL TIME 25 MINUTES (PLUS 30 MINUTES CHILLING TIME)

WHY THIS RECIPE WORKS Unlike cooked celery root purees or gratins, a celery root salad maintains the vegetable's pristine white appearance, its crunchy, coleslaw-like texture, and (most important) its refreshing herbal flavor. For easy peeling, we removed the top and bottom from the celery root and then used a paring knife to remove the outer layer of flesh. For thin pieces of celery root that would retain their crunch, we grated it coarse. We dressed the celery root with a vinaigrette finished with sour cream, which lent the salad creamy, tangy richness. Tart Granny Smith apple complemented the celery root nicely, and we freshened it up with sliced scallions and a combination of fresh parsley and tarragon. Add a teaspoon or so more oil to the dressed salad if it seems a bit dry.

2 tablespoons lemon juice
1½ tablespoons Dijon mustard
1 teaspoon honey
Salt and pepper
3 tablespoons vegetable oil
3 tablespoons sour cream
1 celery root (14 ounces), peeled
½ Granny Smith apple, peeled and cored
2 scallions, sliced thin
2 teaspoons minced fresh parsley
2 teaspoons minced fresh tarragon (optional)

1. Whisk lemon juice, mustard, honey, and ½ teaspoon salt together in medium bowl. Whisking constantly, drizzle in oil. Whisk in sour cream.

2. Grate celery root and apple using food processor fitted with shredding disk or coarse grater, then immediately stir into dressing (to prevent browning). Season with salt and pepper to taste. Cover and refrigerate for at least 30 minutes.

3. Stir in scallions, parsley, and tarragon, if using, and serve.

VARIATION

Celery Root Salad with Red Onion, Mint, Orange, and Fennel Seeds EASY

Add ½ teaspoon grated orange zest and 1 teaspoon fennel seeds to dressing. Substitute 2 tablespoons finely chopped red onion for scallion and mint for tarragon.

TO MAKE AHEAD

- Dressed celery root mixture, prepared through step 2, can be refrigerated for up to 24 hours
- To serve, season with lemon juice, salt, and pepper to taste and continue with step 3

PEELING CELERY ROOT

1. Cut ½ inch from both root end and opposite end.

2. To peel, cut from top to bottom, rotating celery root.

Raw fennel stays cool and crunchy in this citrus salad that can be dressed and refrigerated up to 24 hours in advance.

Algerian-Style Fennel, Orange, and Olive Salad

SERVES 4 TO 6 EASY
ACTIVE TIME 25 MINUTES
TOTAL TIME 25 MINUTES

WHY THIS RECIPE WORKS In Algeria, raw fennel is used as a distinctive base for crisp, light salads. We liked the fennel best when it was sliced as thin as possible; this kept the texture from being too tough or chewy. Sweet, juicy oranges were a perfect match for the fennel. To ensure they were evenly distributed in the salad, we cut the oranges into bite-size pieces and tossed the salad gently to keep the segments from falling apart. To finish off the salad, we added some oil-cured black olives, fresh mint, and lemon juice. Because this dish is so simple, using high-quality ingredients is essential. Blood oranges are traditional; navel oranges, tangelos, or Cara Caras can also be used, but since they are larger, you'll need just three of them.

4 blood oranges
2 fennel bulbs, stalks discarded, bulbs halved, cored, and sliced thin

½ cup pitted oil-cured black olives, sliced thin

 2 tablespoons lemon juice

Salt and pepper

¼ cup extra-virgin olive oil

¼ cup chopped fresh mint

1. Cut away peel and pith from oranges. Quarter oranges, then slice each quarter crosswise into ¼-inch-thick pieces. Combine oranges, fennel, and olives in large bowl.

2. In small bowl, whisk lemon juice, ¼ teaspoon salt, and ⅛ teaspoon pepper together. Whisking constantly, drizzle in oil. Drizzle dressing over salad and toss gently to coat.

3. Sprinkle with mint, season with salt and pepper to taste, and serve.

TO MAKE AHEAD

- Dressed salad, prepared through step 2, can be refrigerated for up to 24 hours
- To serve, bring to room temperature, season with lemon juice to taste, and continue with step 3

PREPARING FENNEL

1. After cutting off stalks and feathery fronds, cut thin slice from base of fennel bulb and remove any tough or blemished layers.

2. Cut bulb in half vertically through base, then use small knife to remove pyramid-shaped core.

3. Slice each half into thin slices to ensure best texture.

Toasting the grains of couscous in butter keeps them from getting mushy and adds flavor.

Couscous Salad with Lemon and Parsley

SERVES 4 TO 6 **EASY**
ACTIVE TIME 30 MINUTES
TOTAL TIME 40 MINUTES

WHY THIS RECIPE WORKS Couscous, a starch made from durum semolina, the high-protein wheat flour that is also used to make pasta, is one of the fastest side dishes to prepare. We wanted to create a few interesting couscous salad recipes that we could make ahead. First, we borrowed a technique used for rice pilaf to keep the pearls of couscous fluffy and separate and add flavor at the same time: We toasted the grains in butter, stirring the tiny pasta granules until they were lightly browned with a nutty aroma. The toasting set the proteins in the pasta, which helped set the shape of the starch granules and prevented them from absorbing too much water, thus turning to mush. (This was especially important when making this recipe ahead of time; the couscous stayed light and fluffy even after 3 days in the fridge.) We finished cooking the couscous in a combination of water and chicken broth for its savory—but not overwhelming—flavor. For a Mediterranean salad, we dressed the cooked couscous with an olive oil, citrus, and herb vinaigrette and stirred in fresh parsley, scallions, lemon juice, and toasted almonds.

2 tablespoons unsalted butter

2 garlic cloves, minced

2 cups couscous

1 cup water

1 cup chicken broth

Salt and pepper

¼ cup chopped fresh parsley

4 scallions, sliced thin

3 tablespoons lemon juice, plus extra for seasoning

6 tablespoons extra-virgin olive oil

1 cup sliced almonds, toasted

1. Melt butter in medium saucepan over medium-high heat. Stir in garlic and cook until fragrant, about 30 seconds. Add couscous and cook, stirring frequently, until grains begin to brown, about 5 minutes. Add water, broth, and 1 teaspoon salt; stir briefly to combine, cover, and remove pan from heat. Let stand until liquid is absorbed and couscous is tender, about 7 minutes. Uncover and fluff couscous with fork.

2. Whisk parsley, scallions, and lemon juice together in large bowl. Whisking constantly, drizzle in oil.

3. Stir in couscous and almonds until well combined. Season with salt, pepper, and extra lemon juice to taste. Serve.

VARIATIONS

Couscous Salad with Feta and Olives EASY

In step 2, substitute 1 finely chopped small red onion for scallions. Add 1½ cups crumbled feta cheese; 1 cucumber, peeled, seeded, and chopped fine; and 1 cup pitted kalamata olives, chopped coarse, along with couscous in step 3.

Couscous Salad with Cilantro and Pepitas EASY

In step 1, add 2½ teaspoons ground cumin and ½ teaspoon cayenne pepper to couscous with broth. Substitute ½ cup chopped fresh cilantro for parsley; 3 tablespoons lime juice (2 limes) for lemon juice; and pepitas for almonds.

Couscous Salad with Cherries and Goat Cheese EASY

Substitute 1 cup chopped arugula for parsley and 1 cup pecans, toasted and chopped, for almonds. Add 1 cup dried cherries, chopped, and 1 cup crumbled goat cheese along with couscous in step 3.

TO MAKE AHEAD

- Cooked couscous and vinaigrette, prepared through step 2, can be refrigerated separately for up to 3 days
- To serve, bring couscous and vinaigrette to room temperature, whisk vinaigrette to recombine, and continue with step 3
- Dressed salad can be held for up to 2 hours before serving

Toasted pearl couscous becomes perfectly cooked using the absorption method and a measured amount of water.

Pearl Couscous Salad with Radishes and Watercress

SERVES 6
ACTIVE TIME 50 MINUTES
TOTAL TIME 55 MINUTES

WHY THIS RECIPE WORKS Pearl couscous, also known as Israeli couscous, has a chewy texture and toasty flavor. We wanted a foolproof method for cooking pearl couscous to serve as the base for salads. To give the spheres maximum flavor, we toasted them in oil to bring out their nuttiness. Once they turned golden brown, we added a measured amount of water that the pearls soaked up. This absorption method helped produce more evenly cooked results than boiling the couscous like regular pasta. Plus, the covered pot required little attention. Once the water was absorbed, the warm couscous was spread out to cool quickly. We tried storing the assembled salad in the fridge, but after just one day it was dry and clumpy, with muted flavors. Instead, we stored the cooked pasta and dressing separately, and added delicate components like watercress and herbs just before serving. This kept the salad bright, light, and moist. Do not substitute regular couscous in this dish, as it requires a different cooking method and will not work.

¼ cup extra-virgin olive oil

2 cups pearl couscous

2½ cups water

   Salt and pepper

3 tablespoons sherry vinegar, plus extra for seasoning

1 teaspoon Dijon mustard

1 teaspoon smoked paprika

¼ teaspoon sugar

2 ounces (2 cups) watercress, torn into bite-size pieces

6 scallions, sliced thin

6 radishes, trimmed and cut into matchsticks

1½ cups coarsely chopped fresh parsley

½ cup walnuts, toasted and chopped coarse

4 ounces goat cheese, crumbled (1 cup)

1. Cook 1 tablespoon oil and couscous in medium saucepan over medium heat, stirring frequently, until half of grains are golden brown, about 5 minutes. Stir in water and ½ teaspoon salt, increase heat to high, and bring to boil. Reduce heat to medium-low, cover, and simmer, stirring occasionally, until water is absorbed and couscous is tender, 9 to 12 minutes.

2. Off heat, let couscous sit, covered, for 3 minutes. Transfer couscous to rimmed baking sheet and let cool completely, about 15 minutes.

3. Whisk vinegar, mustard, paprika, sugar, and ⅛ teaspoon salt together in large bowl. Whisking constantly, drizzle in remaining 3 tablespoons oil.

4. Add couscous, watercress, scallions, radishes, parsley, and walnuts to vinaigrette and toss to combine. Season with salt, pepper, and extra vinegar to taste. Let sit for 5 minutes. Sprinkle with goat cheese and serve.

VARIATION
Pearl Couscous Salad with Tomatoes, Olives, and Ricotta Salata

SERVES 6

Do not substitute regular couscous in this dish, as it requires a different cooking method and will not work in this recipe. Crumbled feta cheese can be substituted for the ricotta salata.

¼ cup extra-virgin olive oil

2 cups pearl couscous

2½ cups water

   Salt and pepper

3 tablespoons red wine vinegar, plus extra for seasoning

1 teaspoon Dijon mustard

12 ounces grape tomatoes, quartered

2 ounces (2 cups) baby spinach, sliced ¼ inch thick

1½ cups coarsely chopped fresh basil

3 ounces ricotta salata cheese, crumbled (¾ cup)

⅔ cup pitted kalamata olives, sliced

½ cup pine nuts, toasted

¼ cup minced fresh chives

1. Heat 1 tablespoon oil and couscous in medium saucepan over medium heat, stirring frequently, until half of grains are golden brown, about 5 minutes. Stir in water and ½ teaspoon salt, increase heat to high, and bring to boil. Reduce heat to medium-low, cover, and simmer, stirring occasionally, until water is absorbed and couscous is tender, 9 to 12 minutes.

2. Off heat, let couscous sit, covered, for 3 minutes. Transfer couscous to rimmed baking sheet and let cool completely, about 15 minutes.

3. Whisk vinegar, mustard, and ⅛ teaspoon salt together in large bowl. Whisking constantly, drizzle in remaining 3 tablespoons oil.

4. Add couscous, tomatoes, spinach, basil, ricotta salata, olives, pine nuts, and chives to vinaigrette and toss to combine. Season with salt, pepper, and extra vinegar to taste. Let sit for 5 minutes. Serve.

TO MAKE AHEAD

- Cooked couscous and vinaigrette, prepared through step 3, can be refrigerated separately for up to 3 days
- To serve, bring couscous and vinaigrette to room temperature, whisk vinaigrette to recombine, and continue with step 4
- Dressed salad can be held for up to 2 hours before serving

Quinoa, Black Bean, and Mango Salad with Lime Dressing

SERVES 4 TO 6 **EASY**

ACTIVE TIME 30 MINUTES

TOTAL TIME 50 MINUTES

WHY THIS RECIPE WORKS We wanted to feature the delicate texture and nutty flavor of quinoa in a fresh-tasting salad hearty enough for a main course. We started by toasting the quinoa to bring out its flavor before adding liquid to the pan and simmering the grains until nearly tender. We then spread the quinoa over a rimmed baking sheet so that the residual heat would finish cooking it as it sat, giving us perfectly cooked, fluffy grains. Black beans, mango, and red bell pepper lent the salad heartiness, bright flavor, and color. A simple but intense dressing gave this dish

Hearty quinoa is a great choice for a make-ahead salad because its taste and texture keep well in the fridge.

the acidity needed to keep its flavors fresh. We also added scallions and avocado for bite and creaminess. If you buy unwashed quinoa (or if you are unsure if it's washed), rinse it and then spread it out over a clean dish towel to dry for 15 minutes before cooking.

1½ cups prewashed white quinoa
2¼ cups water
    Salt and pepper
5 tablespoons lime juice (3 limes)
½ jalapeño chile, stemmed, seeded, and chopped
¾ teaspoon ground cumin
½ cup extra-virgin olive oil
⅓ cup fresh cilantro leaves
1 red bell pepper, stemmed, seeded, and chopped
1 mango, peeled, pitted, and cut into ¼-inch pieces
1 (15-ounce) can black beans, rinsed
2 scallions, sliced thin
1 avocado, halved, pitted, and sliced thin

1. Toast quinoa in large saucepan over medium-high heat, stirring often, until very fragrant and makes continuous popping sound, 5 to 7 minutes. Stir in water and ½ teaspoon salt and

bring to simmer. Cover, reduce heat to low, and simmer gently until most of water has been absorbed and quinoa is nearly tender, about 15 minutes. Spread quinoa onto rimmed baking sheet and let cool for 20 minutes; transfer to large bowl.

2. Process lime juice, jalapeño, cumin, and 1 teaspoon salt in blender until jalapeño is finely chopped, about 15 seconds. With blender running, add oil and cilantro; continue to process until smooth and emulsified, about 20 seconds.

3. Add bell pepper, mango, black beans, scallions, and lime-jalapeño dressing to cooled quinoa and toss to combine. Season with salt and pepper to taste. Serve, topping individual portions with avocado.

> **TO MAKE AHEAD**
> - Cooked quinoa and vinaigrette, prepared through step 2, can be refrigerated separately for up to 3 days
> - To serve, bring quinoa and vinaigrette to room temperature, whisk vinaigrette to recombine, and continue with step 3
> - Dressed salad can be held for up to 2 hours before serving

Wheat Berry Salad with Orange and Carrots

SERVES 4 TO 6   EASY
ACTIVE TIME 25 MINUTES
TOTAL TIME 1 HOUR 40 MINUTES

WHY THIS RECIPE WORKS Orange and tarragon are a classic pairing, and it's easy to understand why: Sweet-tart orange boosts and brightens tarragon's grassy licorice notes, creating a remarkably vibrant flavor. This combination shone against a backdrop of mildly nutty wheat berries, especially after we added shredded carrots for crunch and orange zest for a deeper citrus flavor. A simple red wine vinaigrette finished off this fresh, crowd-pleasing salad with a sophisticated mix of flavors. Do not add more than 1½ teaspoons of salt when cooking the wheat berries; adding more will prevent the grains from softening. If using quick-cooking or presteamed wheat berries (read the ingredient list on the package to determine this), you will need to decrease the wheat berry cooking time in step 1.

1½ cups wheat berries
    Salt and pepper
1 orange
3 tablespoons red wine vinegar, plus extra for seasoning
1½ tablespoons Dijon mustard
1 small shallot, minced
1 garlic clove, minced

⅛ teaspoon grated orange zest

1½ teaspoons honey

2 tablespoons extra-virgin olive oil

3 carrots, peeled and shredded

1 tablespoon minced fresh tarragon

1. Bring 4 quarts water to boil in Dutch oven. Add wheat berries and 1½ teaspoons salt, return to boil, and cook until tender but still chewy, 1 hour to 1 hour 10 minutes. Drain wheat berries, spread in rimmed baking sheet, and let cool completely, about 15 minutes.

2. Whisk vinegar, mustard, shallot, garlic, orange zest, honey, and ¼ teaspoon salt together in large bowl until combined. Whisking constantly, slowly drizzle in oil.

3. Cut away peel and pith from orange. Quarter orange, then slice crosswise into ¼-inch-thick pieces and add to dressing. Add wheat berries, carrots, and tarragon and gently toss to coat. Season with salt, pepper, and extra vinegar to taste. Serve.

TO MAKE AHEAD

- Cooked wheat berries and vinaigrette, prepared through step 2, can be refrigerated separately for up to 3 days
- To serve, bring wheat berries and vinaigrette to room temperature, whisk vinaigrette to recombine, and continue with step 3
- Dressed salad can be held for up to 2 hours before serving

Farro Salad with Butternut Squash, Radicchio, and Blue Cheese

SERVES 6 EASY

ACTIVE TIME 30 MINUTES

TOTAL TIME 1 HOUR

WHY THIS RECIPE WORKS For this appealing farro salad we turned to ingredients that could hold their own with this nutty grain, namely roasted butternut squash, assertive chopped radicchio, and tangy blue cheese. To cook the farro, we wondered if we could bypass the traditional step of soaking the grains overnight and then cooking them slowly for over an hour in favor of a simpler, quicker method. After testing out a few cooking techniques, we learned that boiling the grains in plenty of salted water and then draining them yielded nicely firm but tender farro—no soaking necessary. While the farro cooked, we roasted butternut squash and assembled a hearty dressing. We prefer the flavor and texture of whole farro, in which the grain's germ and bran have been retained. Pearled farro can be used, but the texture may be softer. Do not use quick-cooking or presteamed farro (read the ingredient list on the package to determine this)

in this recipe. The cooking time for farro can vary greatly among different brands, so we recommend beginning to check for doneness after 10 minutes.

2 pounds butternut squash, peeled, seeded, and cut into ½-inch pieces (3⅓ cups)

¼ cup extra-virgin olive oil

Salt and pepper

1½ cups whole farro, rinsed

2 tablespoons cider vinegar, plus extra for seasoning

2 tablespoons minced shallot

1 teaspoon Dijon mustard

Pinch cayenne pepper

1 cup chopped radicchio

½ cup chopped fresh parsley

2 ounces blue cheese, crumbled (½ cup)

1. Adjust oven rack to lowest position and heat oven to 500 degrees. Toss squash with 1 tablespoon oil and ½ teaspoon salt. Spread squash in even layer on rimmed baking sheet and roast until tender, 20 to 22 minutes. Push squash to 1 side of sheet and transfer to wire rack to cool.

2. While squash roasts, bring 2 quarts water to boil in large saucepan. Stir in farro and 1 tablespoon salt. Return to boil and cook until grains are tender with slight chew, 15 to 30 minutes. Drain well. Spread on empty side of sheet with squash and let cool for 15 minutes.

3. Whisk remaining 3 tablespoons oil, vinegar, shallot, mustard, cayenne, and ¼ teaspoon salt together in large bowl.

4. Add cooled farro and squash, radicchio, parsley, and blue cheese to dressing and toss to combine. Season with salt, pepper, and extra vinegar to taste. Serve.

VARIATION

Farro Salad with Asparagus, Snap Peas, Tomatoes, and Feta

SERVES 4 TO 6 EASY

6 ounces asparagus, trimmed and cut into 1-inch lengths

6 ounces sugar snap peas, strings removed, cut into 1-inch lengths

Salt and pepper

1½ cups whole farro, rinsed

3 tablespoons extra-virgin olive oil

2 tablespoons lemon juice, plus extra for seasoning

2 tablespoons minced shallot

1 teaspoon Dijon mustard

6 ounces cherry tomatoes, halved

2 ounces feta cheese, crumbled (½ cup)

3 tablespoons chopped fresh dill

1. Bring 4 quarts water to boil in Dutch oven. Add asparagus, snap peas, and 1 tablespoon salt and cook until crisp-tender, about 3 minutes. Fill large bowl halfway with ice and water. Using slotted spoon, transfer vegetables to ice water to cool. Drain and set aside.

2. Add farro to boiling water, return to boil, and cook until grains are tender with slight chew, 15 to 30 minutes. Drain well, spread in rimmed baking sheet, and let cool for 15 minutes.

3. Whisk oil, lemon juice, shallot, mustard, ¼ teaspoon salt, and ¼ teaspoon pepper together in large bowl.

4. Add cooked vegetables, farro, tomatoes, feta, and dill to dressing and toss gently to combine. Season with salt, pepper, and extra lemon juice to taste. Serve.

TO MAKE AHEAD ▶

- Cooked farro, cooked vegetables, and vinaigrette, prepared through step 3, can be refrigerated separately for up to 3 days
- To serve, bring farro, vegetables, and vinaigrette to room temperature, whisk vinaigrette to recombine, and continue with step 4
- Dressed salad can be held for up to 2 hours before serving

Egyptian Barley Salad

SERVES 6 TO 8 **EASY**

ACTIVE TIME 30 MINUTES
TOTAL TIME 40 MINUTES

WHY THIS RECIPE WORKS We set out to create a vibrant pearl barley salad with a balance of sweetness, tang, and nuttiness. First, we had to find a consistent cooking method for the barley. We turned to what we call the "pasta method," in which we simply boil the grains until tender. Inspired by the flavors of Egypt, we incorporated toasty pistachios, tangy pomegranate molasses, and bright cilantro, all balanced by warm spices and golden raisins. Salty feta cheese, pungent scallions, and pomegranate seeds adorned the dish for a colorful composed salad with dynamic flavors and textures. But when making this salad's dressing ahead, we found that the pomegranate molasses's brightness was muted a bit. So, we made a little more dressing than we would typically need for this salad; the extra dressing gave us leeway to dress more heavily when reviving the salad from refrigerator storage. If you can't find pomegranate molasses, substitute 2 tablespoons of lemon juice, 2 teaspoons of mild molasses, and 1 teaspoon of honey. Do not substitute hulled barley or hull-less barley in this recipe. If using quick-cooking or presteamed barley (read the ingredient list on the package to determine this), you will need to decrease the barley cooking time in step 1.

Boiling nutty pearl barley like pasta ensures its grains become tender and stay separate.

1½ cups pearl barley
Salt and pepper
3 tablespoons extra-virgin olive oil, plus extra for serving
2 tablespoons pomegranate molasses
1 teaspoon lemon juice
½ teaspoon ground cinnamon
¼ teaspoon ground cumin
½ cup coarsely chopped fresh cilantro
⅓ cup golden raisins
¼ cup shelled pistachios, toasted and chopped coarse
3 ounces feta cheese, cut into ½-inch cubes (¾ cup)
6 scallions, green parts only, sliced thin
½ cup pomegranate seeds

1. Bring 4 quarts water to boil in Dutch oven. Add barley and 1 tablespoon salt, return to boil, and cook until tender, 20 to 40 minutes. Drain barley, spread in rimmed baking sheet, and let cool for 15 minutes.

2. Whisk oil, pomegranate molasses, lemon juice, cinnamon, cumin, and ½ teaspoon salt together in large bowl.

3. Add barley, cilantro, raisins, and pistachios and gently toss to combine. Season with salt, and pepper to taste. Spread barley salad evenly on serving platter and arrange feta, scallions, and pomegranate seeds in separate diagonal rows on top. Drizzle with extra oil and serve.

TO MAKE AHEAD

- Cooked barley and vinaigrette, prepared through step 2, can be refrigerated separately for up to 3 days
- To serve, bring barley and vinaigrette to room temperature, whisk vinaigrette to recombine, and continue with step 3, seasoning with lemon juice to taste
- Dressed salad can be held for up to 2 hours before serving

Bulgur Salad with Grapes and Feta

SERVES 4 **EASY**

ACTIVE TIME 20 MINUTES

TOTAL TIME 1 HOUR 35 MINUTES

WHY THIS RECIPE WORKS This fresh and flavorful bulgur salad showcases sweet grapes and tangy feta cheese. We softened the bulgur in water, lemon juice, and salt. Once the bulgur was tender, we tossed it with more fresh lemon juice, cumin, and cayenne for depth of flavor, along with the grapes and feta. Quartering the grapes ensured we got some sweetness in every bite. Scallions and mint gave the salad plenty of bright, fresh flavor. Finally, for textural contrast, we added crunchy toasted almonds. When making this salad ahead, we found that the delicate ingredients (grapes, almonds, feta, and herbs) mushed and dulled in flavor after sitting overnight. Instead, we opted to leave these items out until just before serving to keep everything fresh and crisp. When shopping, don't confuse bulgur with cracked wheat, which has a much longer cooking time and will not work in this recipe.

1½ cups medium-grind bulgur, rinsed
  1 cup water
  5 tablespoons lemon juice (2 lemons), plus extra
     for seasoning
     Salt and pepper
¼ cup extra-virgin olive oil
¼ teaspoon ground cumin
     Pinch cayenne pepper
  6 ounces seedless red grapes, quartered (1 cup)
½ cup slivered almonds, toasted
  2 ounces feta cheese, crumbled (½ cup)
  2 scallions, sliced thin
¼ cup chopped fresh mint

We soften the bulgur for this salad in water and lemon juice to make it tender and to add flavor.

1. Combine bulgur, water, ¼ cup lemon juice, and ¼ teaspoon salt in bowl. Cover and let sit at room temperature until grains are softened, about 1½ hours.

2. Whisk oil, cumin, cayenne, ¼ teaspoon salt, and remaining 1 tablespoon lemon juice together in large bowl.

3. Add soaked bulgur, grapes, almonds, feta, scallions, and mint to dressing and toss to combine. Season with salt, pepper, and extra lemon juice to taste. Serve.

TO MAKE AHEAD

- Soaked bulgur and vinaigrette, prepared through step 2, can be refrigerated separately for up to 3 days
- To serve, bring bulgur and vinaigrette to room temperature, whisk vinaigrette to recombine, and continue with step 3
- Dressed salad can be held for up to 2 hours before serving

For creamy but firm lentils we brine them in warm salt water to soften their skins before cooking them in the oven.

Lentil Salad with Olives, Mint, and Feta

SERVES 4 TO 6 **EASY**

ACTIVE TIME 20 MINUTES

TOTAL TIME 1 HOUR 45 MINUTES

WHY THIS RECIPE WORKS The main challenge in making a lentil salad is cooking the lentils so that they maintain their shape and firm-tender bite. We found this required two key steps: salt-soaking the lentils, which softened their skins, leading to fewer blowouts, and cooking the lentils in the oven, which heated them gently. Then we paired the earthy beans with a tart vinaigrette and bold mix-ins. We mixed bright white wine vinegar with extra-virgin olive oil, then added fresh mint, minced shallot, and kalamata olives. A sprinkle of rich feta finished the dish. French green lentils, or *lentilles du Puy*, are our preferred choice for this recipe, but it works with any type of lentil except red or yellow. Salt-soaking helps keep the lentils intact, but if you don't have time, they'll still taste good. You will need an ovensafe medium saucepan for this recipe. The salad can be served warm or at room temperature.

Salt and pepper
1 cup lentilles du Puy, picked over and rinsed
5 garlic cloves, lightly crushed and peeled
1 bay leaf
5 tablespoons extra-virgin olive oil
3 tablespoons white wine vinegar
½ cup pitted kalamata olives, chopped coarse
1 large shallot, minced
½ cup chopped fresh mint
1 ounce feta cheese, crumbled (¼ cup)

1. Dissolve 1 teaspoon salt in 4 cups warm water (about 110 degrees) in bowl. Add lentils and soak at room temperature for 1 hour. Drain well.

2. Adjust oven rack to middle position and heat oven to 325 degrees. Combine lentils, 4 cups water, garlic, bay leaf, and ½ teaspoon salt in medium ovensafe saucepan. Cover, transfer saucepan to oven, and cook until lentils are tender but remain intact, 40 minutes to 1 hour.

3. Drain lentils well, discarding garlic and bay leaf. In large bowl, whisk oil and vinegar together. Add lentils, olives, and shallot and toss to combine. Season with salt and pepper to taste.

4. Transfer to serving dish, gently stir in mint, and sprinkle with feta. Serve warm or at room temperature.

VARIATIONS

Lentil Salad with Hazelnuts and Goat Cheese **EASY**
Substitute 3 tablespoons red wine vinegar for white wine vinegar and add 2 teaspoons Dijon mustard to dressing. Omit olives and substitute ¼ cup chopped fresh parsley for mint. Substitute ¼ cup crumbled goat cheese for feta and sprinkle salad with ¼ cup coarsely chopped toasted hazelnuts before serving.

Lentil Salad with Carrots and Cilantro **EASY**
Omit shallot and feta. Toss 2 carrots, peeled and cut into 2-inch-long matchsticks, with 1 teaspoon ground cumin, ½ teaspoon ground cinnamon, and ⅛ teaspoon cayenne pepper in bowl; cover and microwave until carrots are tender but still crisp, 2 to 4 minutes. Substitute 3 tablespoons lemon juice for white wine vinegar, carrots for olives, and ¼ cup chopped fresh cilantro for mint.

TO MAKE AHEAD

- Dressed lentil mixture, prepared through step 3, can be refrigerated for up to 3 days
- To serve, bring lentils to room temperature, season with vinegar, salt, and pepper to taste, and continue with step 4
- Dressed salad can be held for up to 2 hours before serving

Black-Eyed Peas with Walnuts and Pomegranate

SERVES 4 TO 6   `EASY`

ACTIVE TIME 20 MINUTES

TOTAL TIME 20 MINUTES

WHY THIS RECIPE WORKS Black-eyed peas are a pantry staple, and their delicate skins, creamy interiors, and fairly mild flavor make them a great base for a tart dressing and crunchy additions. To simplify preparation, we used canned black-eyed peas, which have great flavor and texture. To make a bright salad with complex flavor, we turned to walnuts and pomegranate seeds along with scallions and parsley for fresh notes. We created a punchy dressing by using lemon juice and pomegranate molasses, which offered balanced acidity and tang. Finally, we incorporated dukkah, a nut and seed blend used as a seasoning across North Africa. The dukkah added a bit more textural contrast as well as a final hit of bold and earthy flavor. We prefer to use our homemade Dukkah (recipe follows); you can substitute store-bought dukkah if you wish, but flavor can vary greatly by brand. If you can't find pomegranate molasses, substitute 2 tablespoons of lemon juice, 2 teaspoons of mild molasses, and 1 teaspoon of honey.

- 3 tablespoons extra-virgin olive oil
- 3 tablespoons dukkah
- 2 tablespoons lemon juice
- 2 tablespoons pomegranate molasses
  Salt and pepper
- 2 (15-ounce) cans black-eyed peas, rinsed
- ½ cup pomegranate seeds
- ½ cup walnuts, toasted and chopped
- ½ cup minced fresh parsley
- 4 scallions, sliced thin

1. Whisk oil, 2 tablespoons dukkah, lemon juice, pomegranate molasses, ¼ teaspoon salt, and ⅛ teaspoon pepper in large bowl until smooth. Add peas and pomegranate seeds and toss well to combine.

2. Stir in walnuts, parsley, and scallions, season with salt and pepper to taste, and sprinkle with remaining 1 tablespoon dukkah. Serve.

◤ TO MAKE AHEAD ◥

- Dressed black-eyed pea mixture, prepared through step 1, can be refrigerated for up to 3 days
- To serve, bring to room temperature, season with lemon juice, salt, and pepper to taste, and continue with step 2
- Dressed salad can be held for up to 2 hours before serving

◤ NOTES FROM THE TEST KITCHEN ◥

Toasting Nuts and Seeds

Toasting nuts and seeds maximizes their flavor and crunch. For less than 1 cup of nuts or seeds, put them in a dry skillet over medium heat. Shake the skillet occasionally to prevent scorching and toast until they are lightly browned and fragrant, 3 to 8 minutes. Watch them closely since they can go from golden to burnt very quickly.

DUKKAH

MAKES 2 CUPS

ACTIVE TIME 1 HOUR

TOTAL TIME 1 HOUR 15 MINUTES

Dukkah is a North African blend that contains spices, nuts, and seeds. It's traditionally sprinkled on olive oil as a dip for bread, but it also makes a great crunchy coating for goat cheese, a garnish for soup, or a topping for grain and bean salads.

- 1 (15-ounce) can chickpeas, rinsed
- 1 teaspoon extra-virgin olive oil
- ½ cup shelled pistachios, toasted
- ⅓ cup black sesame seeds, toasted
- 2½ tablespoons coriander seeds, toasted
- 1 tablespoon cumin seeds, toasted
- 2 teaspoons fennel seeds, toasted
- 1½ teaspoons pepper
- 1¼ teaspoons salt

1. Adjust oven rack to middle position and heat oven to 400 degrees. Pat chickpeas dry with paper towels and toss with oil. Spread chickpeas into single layer in rimmed baking sheet and roast until browned and crisp, 40 to 45 minutes, stirring every 5 to 10 minutes; let cool completely.

2. Process chickpeas in food processor until coarsely ground, about 10 seconds; transfer to medium bowl. Pulse pistachios and sesame seeds in now-empty food processor until coarsely ground, about 15 pulses; transfer to bowl with chickpeas. Process coriander, cumin, and fennel seeds in again-empty food processor until finely ground, 2 to 3 minutes; transfer to bowl with chickpeas. Add pepper and salt and whisk until mixture is well combined.

◤ TO MAKE AHEAD ◥

Dukkah can be refrigerated for up to 1 month

Warming canned chickpeas helps them to absorb more of the flavorful salad dressing.

Chickpea Salad with Carrots, Arugula, and Olives

SERVES 4 TO 6 `EASY`
ACTIVE TIME 15 MINUTES
TOTAL TIME 35 MINUTES

WHY THIS RECIPE WORKS Canned chickpeas are an ideal ingredient for a salad because they can absorb flavors easily and provide texture. Here a flavorful pairing of sweet carrots, peppery arugula, and briny olives transforms bland canned chickpeas into a bright and savory salad. We found that heating the chickpeas in the microwave briefly softened them just enough to allow them to quickly soak up the tangy vinaigrette. We prefer Pastene Chickpeas. Shred the carrots on the large holes of a box grater or use a food processor fitted with the shredding disk.

2 (15-ounce) cans chickpeas, rinsed
¼ cup extra-virgin olive oil
2 tablespoons lemon juice
  Salt and pepper
  Pinch cayenne pepper

3 carrots, peeled and shredded
½ cup pitted kalamata olives, chopped coarse
1 ounce (1 cup) baby arugula, chopped coarse

1. Microwave chickpeas in medium bowl until hot, about 1½ minutes. Stir in oil, lemon juice, ¾ teaspoon salt, ½ teaspoon pepper, and cayenne and let sit for 30 minutes. Add carrots and olives and toss to combine.

2. Add arugula, gently toss to combine, and season with salt and pepper to taste. Serve.

VARIATIONS
Chickpea Salad with Fennel and Arugula `EASY`
Substitute 1 fennel bulb, stalks discarded, bulb halved, cored, and cut into ¼-inch pieces, for carrots and olives.

Chickpea Salad with Carrots, Raisins, and Almonds `EASY`
Substitute lime juice for lemon juice and ½ cup golden raisins, ¼ cup chopped fresh mint, and ¼ cup toasted sliced almonds for arugula and olives.

TO MAKE AHEAD
- Dressed chickpea mixture, prepared through step 1, can be refrigerated for up to 2 days
- To serve, bring to room temperature, and continue with step 2
- Dressed salad can be held for up to 2 hours before serving

White Bean Salad

SERVES 4 TO 6 `EASY`
ACTIVE TIME 20 MINUTES
TOTAL TIME 1 HOUR

WHY THIS RECIPE WORKS One of our favorite recipes using white beans is a simple salad preparation that allows the creamy, sweet beans to shine. This well-balanced, superflavorful white bean salad is the perfect way to add some protein and substance to a meal; we used classic Spanish flavors and ingredients to give the salad an identity. Cannellini beans worked perfectly, since they have a savory, buttery flavor. We steeped the beans in a garlicky broth, which infused them with more flavor. While the beans sat, we had enough time to rid our shallots of any harshness by briefly marinating them in sherry vinegar. Red bell pepper offered sweetness and crunch, parsley provided an herbal presence, and chives gave the salad some subtle onion notes, rounding out the dish nicely. Our ultrasimple and versatile salad ended up with a surprisingly complex flavor profile.

¼ cup extra-virgin olive oil
3 garlic cloves, peeled and smashed
2 (15-ounce) cans cannellini beans, rinsed
  Salt and pepper
1 tablespoon sherry vinegar
1 small shallot, minced
1 red bell pepper, stemmed, seeded, and cut into
  ¼-inch pieces
¼ cup chopped fresh parsley
2 teaspoons chopped fresh chives

1. Cook 1 tablespoon oil and garlic in medium saucepan over medium heat, stirring often, until garlic turns golden but not brown, about 3 minutes. Add beans, 2 cups water, and 1 teaspoon salt and bring to simmer. Remove from heat, cover, and let sit for 20 minutes.

2. Meanwhile, combine vinegar and shallot in large bowl and let sit for 20 minutes. Drain beans and discard garlic. Add beans, bell pepper, and remaining 3 tablespoons oil to shallot mixture and gently toss to combine. Let sit for 20 minutes.

3. Stir in parsley and chives and season with salt and pepper to taste. Serve.

VARIATION

White Bean Salad with Tomatoes and Olives EASY
Substitute 1 cup quartered cherry tomatoes for bell pepper and ½ cup chopped fresh basil for parsley and chives. Add ⅓ cup chopped kalamata olives to salad before tossing to combine.

TO MAKE AHEAD
- Dressed white bean mixture, prepared through step 2, can be refrigerated for up to 3 days
- To serve, bring to room temperature, season with vinegar, salt, and pepper to taste, and continue with step 3
- Dressed salad can be held for up to 2 hours before serving

Buttermilk Coleslaw
SERVES 4 EASY
ACTIVE TIME 20 MINUTES
TOTAL TIME 1 HOUR 10 MINUTES (PLUS 30 MINUTES CHILLING TIME)

WHY THIS RECIPE WORKS We wanted our coleslaw recipe to produce crisp, evenly cut pieces of cabbage lightly coated with a flavorful buttermilk dressing that would cling to the cabbage instead of collecting in the bottom of the bowl. We found that salting and draining the cabbage removed excess water and wilted it to a pickle-crisp texture. For a dressing that was both hefty and tangy, we combined buttermilk, mayonnaise, and sour cream.

½ medium head red or green cabbage, cored, quartered,
  and shredded (6 cups)
  Salt and pepper
1 carrot, peeled and shredded
½ cup buttermilk
2 tablespoons mayonnaise
2 tablespoons sour cream
1 small shallot, minced
2 tablespoons minced fresh parsley
½ teaspoon cider vinegar
½ teaspoon sugar
¼ teaspoon Dijon mustard

1. Toss shredded cabbage and 1 teaspoon salt in colander set over large bowl and let sit until wilted, at least 1 hour or up to 4 hours. Rinse cabbage under cold running water. Press, but do not squeeze, to drain, and blot dry with paper towels.

2. Combine wilted cabbage and carrot in large bowl. In separate bowl, whisk buttermilk, mayonnaise, sour cream, shallot, parsley, vinegar, sugar, mustard, ¼ teaspoon salt, and ⅛ teaspoon pepper together. Pour dressing over cabbage and toss to combine. Refrigerate until chilled, about 30 minutes. Serve.

VARIATIONS

Buttermilk Coleslaw with Scallions and Cilantro EASY
Omit mustard. Substitute 1 tablespoon minced fresh cilantro for parsley and 1 teaspoon lime juice for cider vinegar. Add 2 thinly sliced scallions to dressing.

Lemony Buttermilk Coleslaw EASY
Substitute 1 teaspoon lemon juice for cider vinegar. Add 1 teaspoon minced fresh thyme and 1 tablespoon minced fresh chives to dressing.

TO MAKE AHEAD
- Coleslaw can be refrigerated for up to 3 days
- To serve, season with vinegar, salt, and pepper to taste

Classic Potato Salad

SERVES 4 TO 6
ACTIVE TIME 40 MINUTES
TOTAL TIME 1 HOUR (PLUS 1 HOUR CHILLING TIME)

WHY THIS RECIPE WORKS Potato salad is arguably the ultimate make-ahead salad in part because it needs to chill and because doing the prep work ahead of time means you won't be scrambling at the last minute before a picnic. We were looking for a salad worth the time and the wait with flavorful, tender potatoes punctuated by crunchy bits of onion and celery. We found that seasoning the potatoes while they're hot maximizes flavor, so we tossed hot russet potatoes with white vinegar. In the crunch department, celery is a must, and one rib was just enough. Among scallions, shallots, and onions, red onion was the winner for its bright color and taste. For a pickled flavor, we decided on pickle relish, which required no preparation and gave the potato salad a subtle sweetness. Note that this recipe calls for celery seeds (which add complexity of flavor), not celery salt; if only celery salt is available, use the same amount but omit the salt in the dressing. When testing the potatoes for doneness, simply taste a piece; do not overcook the potatoes or they will become mealy and will break apart. The potatoes must be just warm, or even fully cooled, when you add the dressing. If the potato salad seems a little dry, add up to 2 tablespoons more mayonnaise. See page 88 for our Easy-Peel Hard-Cooked Eggs.

3 pounds russet potatoes, peeled and cut into ¾-inch cubes
  Salt
2 tablespoons distilled white vinegar
½ cup mayonnaise
3 tablespoons sweet pickle relish
1 celery rib, chopped fine
2 tablespoons finely chopped red onion
2 tablespoons minced fresh parsley
¾ teaspoon dry mustard
¾ teaspoon celery seeds
¼ teaspoon pepper
2 large hard-cooked eggs, peeled and cut into ¼-inch cubes (optional)

1. Place potatoes in large saucepan and add water to cover by 1 inch. Bring to boil over medium-high heat. Add 1 tablespoon salt, reduce heat to medium, and simmer, stirring occasionally, until potatoes are tender, about 8 minutes.

2. Drain potatoes and transfer to large bowl. Add vinegar and toss gently to combine using rubber spatula. Let stand until potatoes are just warm, about 20 minutes.

Starting cubes of russet potatoes in cold water is the key to potatoes that hold their shape in our potato salad.

3. Meanwhile, combine mayonnaise, relish, celery, onion, parsley, mustard, celery seeds, pepper, and ½ teaspoon salt in small bowl. Using rubber spatula, gently fold mayonnaise mixture and eggs, if using, into potatoes. Refrigerate until chilled, about 1 hour. Serve.

TO MAKE AHEAD
- Salad can be refrigerated for up to 24 hours
- To serve, season with vinegar, salt, and pepper to taste

Classic Chicken Salad

SERVES 4 TO 6 **EASY**
ACTIVE TIME 20 MINUTES
TOTAL TIME 1 HOUR

WHY THIS RECIPE WORKS Recipes for chicken salad are only as good as the chicken. If the chicken is dry or flavorless, no amount of dressing or add-ins will camouflage it. To ensure juicy, flavorful chicken, we used a method based on *sous vide* cooking (submerging vacuum-sealed foods in a temperature-controlled water bath).

Our ideal formula was four chicken breasts and 6 cups of cold water heated to 170 degrees and then removed from the heat, covered, and left to stand for about 15 minutes. Incomparably moist, this chicken was perfect for our salad. To ensure that the chicken cooks through, don't use breasts that weigh more than 8 ounces or are thicker than 1 inch. Make sure to start with cold water in step 1. This salad can be served in a sandwich or spooned over leafy greens.

Salt and pepper
4 (6- to 8-ounce) boneless, skinless chicken breasts, trimmed and pounded to 1-inch thickness
½ cup mayonnaise
2 tablespoons lemon juice
1 teaspoon Dijon mustard
2 celery ribs, minced
1 shallot, minced
1 tablespoon minced fresh parsley
1 tablespoon minced fresh tarragon

1. Dissolve 2 tablespoons salt in 6 cups cold water in Dutch oven. Submerge chicken in water. Heat pot over medium heat until water registers 170 degrees. Remove from heat, cover pot, and let stand until chicken registers 165 degrees, 15 to 17 minutes. Transfer chicken to paper towel–lined rimmed baking sheet and refrigerate until cool, about 30 minutes.

2. Whisk mayonnaise, lemon juice, mustard, and ¼ teaspoon pepper together in large bowl. Pat chicken dry with paper towels and cut into ½-inch pieces. Add chicken, celery, shallot, parsley, and tarragon to mayonnaise mixture and toss to combine. Season with salt and pepper to taste. Serve.

VARIATIONS
Curried Chicken Salad with Cashews
SERVES 4 TO 6   EASY

Salt and pepper
4 (6- to 8-ounce) boneless, skinless chicken breasts, trimmed and pounded to 1-inch thickness
1 teaspoon vegetable oil
1 teaspoon curry powder
⅛ teaspoon cayenne pepper
½ cup mayonnaise
2 tablespoons lime juice
1 teaspoon grated fresh ginger
2 celery ribs, minced
1 shallot, minced
½ cup raw cashews, toasted and chopped coarse
⅓ cup golden raisins
2 tablespoons minced fresh cilantro

1. Dissolve 2 tablespoons salt in 6 cups cold water in Dutch oven. Submerge chicken in water. Heat pot over medium heat until water registers 170 degrees. Remove from heat, cover pot, and let stand until chicken registers 165 degrees, 15 to 17 minutes. Transfer chicken to paper towel–lined rimmed baking sheet and refrigerate until cool, about 30 minutes.

2. Microwave vegetable oil, curry powder, and cayenne in bowl until oil is hot, about 30 seconds. Whisk mayonnaise, lime juice, ginger, and curry mixture together in large bowl.

3. Pat chicken dry with paper towels and cut into ½-inch pieces. Add chicken, celery, shallot, cashews, raisins, and cilantro to mayonnaise mixture and toss to combine. Season with salt and pepper to taste. Serve.

Chicken Salad with Red Grapes and Smoked Almonds
SERVES 4 TO 6   EASY

Salt and pepper
4 (6- to 8-ounce) boneless, skinless chicken breasts, trimmed and pounded to 1-inch thickness
½ cup mayonnaise
1 teaspoon Dijon mustard
¼ teaspoon grated lemon zest plus 2 tablespoons juice
6 ounces seedless red grapes, quartered (1 cup)
2 celery ribs, minced
½ cup smoked almonds, chopped coarse
1 shallot, minced
1 tablespoon minced fresh parsley
1 teaspoon minced fresh rosemary

1. Dissolve 2 tablespoons salt in 6 cups cold water in Dutch oven. Submerge chicken in water. Heat pot over medium heat until water registers 170 degrees. Remove from heat, cover pot, and let stand until chicken registers 165 degrees, 15 to 17 minutes. Transfer chicken to paper towel–lined rimmed baking sheet and refrigerate until cool, about 30 minutes.

2. Whisk mayonnaise, mustard, lemon zest and juice, and ¼ teaspoon pepper together in large bowl. Pat chicken dry with paper towels and cut into ½-inch pieces. Add chicken, grapes, celery, almonds, shallot, parsley, and rosemary to mayonnaise mixture and toss to combine. Season with salt and pepper to taste. Serve.

TO MAKE AHEAD ▶
- Salad can be refrigerated for up to 2 days
- To serve, season with lemon or lime juice, salt, and pepper to taste

Draining the tuna and patting it dry removes excess moisture and prevents watery tuna salad.

Tuna Salad

SERVES 4 TO 6   EASY
ACTIVE TIME 15 MINUTES
TOTAL TIME 25 MINUTES

WHY THIS RECIPE WORKS Even a simple tuna salad has its problems. It can be simultaneously watery, flavorless, drowning in mayonnaise, and overpowered by raw onion. There are nearly as many tuna choices at the supermarket as there are fish in the sea. Canned solid white tuna can be somewhat chalky and dry, so we pressed the tuna dry, then marinated it in oil for 10 minutes. Adding the oil and seasonings to the tuna before stirring in the mayo really infused the tuna with flavor. To soften the onion's harshness, the easiest solution was microwaving it in the oil for a couple of minutes before adding it to the tuna. To finish, all our tuna salad needed was some celery for crunch. Do not use chunk light tuna in this recipe. Our favorite brand of canned tuna is Wild Planet Wild Albacore Tuna. If you can't find it, use canned solid white albacore tuna packed in water.

¼ cup finely chopped onion
2 tablespoons olive oil
3 (5-ounce) cans solid white albacore tuna
2 teaspoons lemon juice
  Salt and pepper
½ teaspoon sugar
½ cup plus 2 tablespoons mayonnaise
1 celery rib, chopped fine

1. Microwave onion and oil in bowl until onion begins to soften, about 2 minutes. Let cool slightly, about 5 minutes.

2. Meanwhile, place tuna in fine-mesh strainer and press dry with paper towels. Transfer tuna to medium bowl and mash with fork until finely flaked. Stir in onion mixture, lemon juice, ½ teaspoon salt, ½ teaspoon pepper, and sugar, and let sit for 10 minutes.

3. Stir in mayonnaise and celery and season with salt and pepper to taste. Serve.

VARIATIONS
Tuna Salad with Roasted Red Peppers and Capers   EASY
Add ¼ cup jarred roasted red peppers, patted dry and chopped, and 2 tablespoons rinsed and minced capers to tuna with onion mixture.

Tuna Salad with Lemon and Dill   EASY
Increase lemon juice to 1 tablespoon. Add ½ teaspoon grated lemon zest and 1 tablespoon minced fresh dill to tuna with onion mixture.

TO MAKE AHEAD
- Salad can be refrigerated for up to 24 hours
- To serve, season with lemon juice, salt, and pepper to taste

Egg Salad

SERVES 4 TO 6   EASY
ACTIVE TIME 20 MINUTES
TOTAL TIME 50 MINUTES

WHY THIS RECIPE WORKS For creamy, flavorful egg salad with perfectly cooked eggs and just the right amount of crunch, we followed a few simple steps. First, we relied on our Easy-Peel Hard-Cooked Eggs (page 88), which yield eggs with creamy yolks, tender whites, and no green ring. We diced the eggs and then combined them with mayonnaise (our tasters dismissed cottage cheese, sour cream, and cream cheese), lemon juice, Dijon mustard, red onion, celery, and parsley. Be sure to use red onion; yellow onion is too harsh.

    1 recipe Easy-Peel Hard-Cooked Eggs (page 88)
    ¼ cup mayonnaise
    2 tablespoons minced red onion
    1 tablespoon minced fresh parsley
    ½ celery rib, minced
    2 teaspoons Dijon mustard
    2 teaspoons lemon juice
      Salt and pepper

    1. Peel and dice eggs.
    2. Mix eggs with mayonnaise, onion, parsley, celery, mustard, and lemon juice in bowl and season with salt and pepper to taste. Serve.

    VARIATIONS
    ### Egg Salad with Radishes, Scallion, and Dill   EASY
    Substitute minced fresh dill for parsley and 1 thinly sliced scallion for red onion. Add 3 minced radishes.

    ### Curried Egg Salad   EASY
    Substitute minced fresh cilantro for parsley and add 1½ teaspoons curry powder.

    TO MAKE AHEAD
    • Salad can be refrigerated for up to 24 hours
    • To serve, season with lemon juice, salt, and pepper to taste

    # Shrimp Salad
    SERVES 4
    ACTIVE TIME 45 MINUTES
    TOTAL TIME 50 MINUTES

    WHY THIS RECIPE WORKS Great shrimp salad should possess firm and tender shrimp and a perfect deli-style dressing that doesn't mask the flavor of the shrimp or drown out the other ingredients. We started by adding the raw shrimp to cold court bouillon and then we heated everything to a near-simmer to cook the shrimp gently. We kept the traditional mayonnaise in our shrimp salad recipe, but limited the amount to ¼ cup per pound

For foolproof tender cooked shrimp, we start them in a cold poaching liquid where they absorb flavor as they heat.

of shrimp. We preferred milder minced shallot over onion, and minced celery for its subtle flavor and crunch. This recipe can also be prepared with large shrimp (26 to 30 per pound); the cooking time will be 1 to 2 minutes less. The recipe can be easily doubled; cook the shrimp in a 7-quart Dutch oven and increase the cooking time to 12 to 14 minutes. Serve the salad over greens or on toasted, buttered buns.

    1 pound extra-large shrimp (21 to 25 per pound), peeled, deveined, and tails removed
    5 tablespoons lemon juice (2 lemons), spent halves reserved
    5 sprigs fresh parsley plus 1 teaspoon minced
    3 sprigs fresh tarragon plus 1 teaspoon minced
    1 tablespoon sugar
    1 teaspoon black peppercorns
      Salt and pepper
    ¼ cup mayonnaise
    1 small shallot, minced
    1 small celery rib, minced

1. Combine shrimp, ¼ cup lemon juice, reserved lemon halves, parsley sprigs, tarragon sprigs, sugar, peppercorns, and 1 teaspoon salt with 2 cups cold water in medium saucepan. Cook over medium heat, stirring often, until shrimp are pink and firm to touch, and centers are no longer translucent, 8 to 10 minutes (water should be just bubbling around edge of pan and should register 165 degrees).

2. Remove pan from heat, cover, and let shrimp sit in broth for 2 minutes. Meanwhile, fill bowl with ice and water. Drain shrimp, discarding lemon halves, herbs, and peppercorns, and plunge immediately into ice water to stop cooking. Let sit until chilled, about 3 minutes. Remove shrimp from ice water and pat dry with paper towels.

3. Whisk mayonnaise, shallot, celery, remaining 1 tablespoon lemon juice, minced parsley, and minced tarragon together in medium bowl. Cut shrimp in half lengthwise and then cut each half into thirds. Add shrimp to mayonnaise mixture and toss to combine. Season with salt and pepper to taste. Serve.

TO MAKE AHEAD ▶

- Cooked and chilled shrimp, prepared through step 2, can be refrigerated for up to 24 hours
- Dressed salad can be refrigerated for up to 12 hours before serving

Moroccan Chicken Salad with Apricots and Almonds

SERVES 4 TO 6
ACTIVE TIME 45 MINUTES
TOTAL TIME 1 HOUR

WHY THIS RECIPE WORKS For a creative chicken salad, we were inspired by the flavors of Morocco: apricots, lemon, and warm spices. To give our dressing complex flavor, we reached for garam masala, a traditional spice blend of coriander, cumin, ginger, cinnamon, and black pepper. We also added a little more coriander, honey, and smoked paprika for depth. Blooming the spices in the microwave deepened their flavors for an even bolder dressing. Chickpeas further echoed the Moroccan theme and lent heartiness, and crisp romaine combined with slightly bitter watercress made the perfect bed of greens for our toppings. Reserving a bit of the dressing to drizzle on just before serving made the flavors pop.

1½ pounds boneless, skinless chicken breasts, trimmed
    Salt and pepper
¾ cup extra-virgin olive oil

Marinating cooked chicken, chickpeas, and dried apricots in a bold dressing infuses them with flavor.

1 teaspoon garam masala
½ teaspoon ground coriander
    Pinch smoked paprika
¼ cup lemon juice (2 lemons)
1 tablespoon honey
1 (15-ounce) can chickpeas, rinsed
¾ cup dried apricots, chopped coarse
1 shallot, sliced thin
2 tablespoons minced fresh parsley
2 romaine lettuce hearts (12 ounces), cut into 1-inch pieces
4 ounces (4 cups) watercress
½ cup whole almonds, toasted and chopped coarse

1. Pat chicken dry with paper towels and season with salt and pepper. Heat 1 tablespoon oil in 12-inch skillet over medium-high heat until just smoking. Brown chicken well on first side, 6 to 8 minutes. Flip chicken, add ½ cup water, and cover. Reduce heat to medium-low and continue to cook until chicken registers 160 degrees, 5 to 7 minutes. Transfer chicken to cutting board, let cool slightly, then slice ½ inch thick on bias. Let cool to room temperature, about 15 minutes.

2. Meanwhile, microwave 1 tablespoon oil, garam masala, coriander, and paprika in medium bowl until oil is hot and fragrant, about 30 seconds. Whisk 3 tablespoons lemon juice, honey, ¼ teaspoon salt, and ¼ teaspoon pepper into spice mixture. Whisking constantly, drizzle in remaining oil.

3. In large bowl, combine cooled chicken, chickpeas, apricots, shallot, parsley, and half of dressing and toss to coat. Let mixture sit for 15 to 30 minutes. Whisk remaining 1 tablespoon lemon juice into remaining dressing.

4. Toss romaine, watercress, and almonds together in serving bowl, drizzle remaining dressing over top, and toss to combine. Season with salt and pepper to taste. Top with chicken mixture and serve.

TO MAKE AHEAD

- Dressed chicken mixture and remaining vinaigrette, prepared through step 3, can be refrigerated separately for up to 2 days
- To serve, bring chicken mixture and vinaigrette to room temperature, whisk vinaigrette to recombine, and continue with step 4

Tofu Salad with Vegetables

SERVES 4 TO 6
ACTIVE TIME 1 HOUR
TOTAL TIME 1 HOUR 10 MINUTES

WHY THIS RECIPE WORKS Our goal for this recipe was a light and easy Asian-flavored salad that boasted plenty of vegetables in a bright vinaigrette. First we sought out a mix of vegetables that, along with tofu, would give our salad heft. We settled on napa cabbage, snow peas, red bell pepper, bean sprouts, and carrots. Next we considered the tofu. We preferred soft tofu here for its creamy, custard-like texture, and we pan-fried it to give it a slightly crispy outside. Draining the tofu before cooking helped to create a light golden crust. Lime juice, fish sauce, fresh ginger, sesame oil, and Sriracha gave our vinaigrette plenty of punch. A sprinkling of cilantro and toasted sesame seeds provided the perfect accents. Firm or extra-firm tofu will also work here, but will have a drier texture.

28 ounces soft tofu, cut into ¾-inch cubes
    Salt and pepper
3 tablespoons lime juice (2 limes)
3 tablespoons honey
2 tablespoons rice vinegar
2 tablespoons fish sauce, plus extra for seasoning
1 tablespoon grated fresh ginger
1½ teaspoons Sriracha sauce
6 tablespoons vegetable oil
3 tablespoons toasted sesame oil
4 cups shredded napa cabbage
6 ounces snow peas, strings removed, cut in half lengthwise
2 carrots, peeled and shredded
1 red bell pepper, stemmed, seeded, and cut into ½-inch pieces
1 cup bean sprouts
2 scallions, sliced thin on bias
3 tablespoons minced fresh cilantro
1 tablespoon sesame seeds, toasted

1. Spread tofu over paper towel–lined baking sheet, let drain for 20 minutes, then gently press dry with paper towels. Season with salt and pepper. Meanwhile, whisk lime juice, honey, vinegar, fish sauce, ginger, and Sriracha together in medium bowl. Whisking constantly, drizzle in ¼ cup vegetable oil and sesame oil. Measure out and reserve ¼ cup dressing separately for salad.

2. Heat 1 tablespoon vegetable oil in 12-inch nonstick skillet over medium-high heat until shimmering. Add half of tofu and brown lightly on all sides, about 5 minutes; transfer to bowl with remaining dressing. Repeat with remaining 1 tablespoon vegetable oil and remaining tofu. Gently toss tofu to coat with dressing, then let cool to room temperature, about 10 minutes.

3. Combine cabbage, snow peas, carrots, bell pepper, bean sprouts, and scallions in separate large bowl.

4. Drizzle vegetables with reserved dressing and toss to combine. Add tofu mixture and toss gently to combine. Season with fish sauce to taste. Sprinkle with cilantro and sesame seeds and serve.

TO MAKE AHEAD

- Dressed tofu, remaining vinaigrette, and vegetable mixture, prepared through step 3, can be refrigerated separately for up to 24 hours
- To serve, bring tofu, vegetables, and vinaigrette to room temperature, whisk vinaigrette to recombine, and continue with step 4

CHAPTER 4

Pasta and Pizza

■ EASY (30 minutes or less active time)   ■ FREEZE IT

Photo: Penne with Garden Vegetable Sauce

We use whole peeled tomatoes in our marinara but we break them up first and remove the seeds for the best texture.

Classic Spaghetti Marinara

SERVES 4 TO 6   **FREEZE IT**

ACTIVE TIME 1 HOUR

TOTAL TIME 1 HOUR

WHY THIS RECIPE WORKS For the best, most robustly flavored marinara sauce, we started by picking the right tomatoes. Canned whole tomatoes provide great flavor and texture year-round; using our hands to remove the hard core and seeds was easy. For a sauce with intense tomato flavor, we sautéed the tomatoes until they glazed the bottom of the pan and then we added the reserved juice. Using a skillet provided more surface area and encouraged faster evaporation and flavor concentration, while red wine added depth. Adding a portion of uncooked tomatoes, along with chopped basil and a drizzle of olive oil, just before serving gave our sauce a bright, fresh finish. If you prefer a chunkier sauce, give it just three or four pulses in the food processor in step 4.

2 (28-ounce) cans whole peeled tomatoes
3 tablespoons extra-virgin olive oil
1 onion, chopped fine
2 garlic cloves, minced
2 teaspoons minced fresh oregano or ½ teaspoon dried
⅓ cup dry red wine
3 tablespoons chopped fresh basil
  Salt and pepper
  Sugar
1 pound spaghetti
  Grated Parmesan cheese

1. Drain tomatoes in fine-mesh strainer set over large bowl. Open tomatoes with your hands and remove and discard seeds and fibrous cores; let tomatoes drain, about 5 minutes. Measure out and reserve ¾ cup tomatoes separately. Reserve 2½ cups drained tomato juice; discard extra juice.

2. Heat 2 tablespoons oil in 12-inch skillet over medium heat until shimmering. Add onion and cook until softened and lightly browned, 5 to 7 minutes. Stir in garlic and oregano and cook until fragrant, about 30 seconds. Stir in remaining drained tomatoes and increase heat to medium-high. Cook, stirring often, until liquid has evaporated and tomatoes begin to brown and stick to skillet, 10 to 12 minutes.

3. Stir in wine and cook until thick and syrupy, about 1 minute. Stir in reserved tomato juice, scraping up any browned bits. Bring to simmer and cook, stirring occasionally, until sauce is thickened, 8 to 10 minutes.

4. Transfer sauce to food processor, add reserved ¾ cup tomatoes, and pulse until slightly chunky, about 8 pulses.

5. Return sauce to now-empty skillet and stir in basil and remaining 1 tablespoon oil. Season with salt, pepper, and sugar to taste.

6. Meanwhile, bring 4 quarts water to boil in large pot. Add pasta and 1 tablespoon salt and cook, stirring often, until al dente. Reserve ½ cup cooking water, then drain pasta and return it to pot. Add sauce and toss to combine. Season with salt and pepper to taste, and add reserved cooking water as needed to adjust consistency. Serve with Parmesan.

TO MAKE AHEAD

- Sauce, prepared through step 4, can be refrigerated for up to 3 days or frozen for up to 1 month; if frozen, thaw completely in refrigerator
- To reheat, bring sauce, covered, to gentle simmer, stirring often, and continue with step 5

Pasta with Easy Meat Sauce

SERVES 4 TO 6 **FREEZE IT**

ACTIVE TIME 45 MINUTES

TOTAL TIME 45 MINUTES

WHY THIS RECIPE WORKS Most quick meat sauces involve nothing more than throwing ground beef, aromatics, and canned tomatoes into a pot and simmering it all for half an hour. We wanted an easy version that would taste as if it had been simmered all day. In our quest for such a sauce, we discovered a few tricks. Browning the meat can dry it out and toughen it, so we skipped this step. Instead, we browned a small amount of white mushrooms, which we had ground in the food processor. Cooking the mushrooms for about 10 minutes left browned bits on the bottom of the pan that instilled our sauce with deep, savory flavor. To further ensure that the meat stayed tender, we blended it with a panade (a mixture of bread and milk) before cooking it just until it lost its color. Finally, for good tomato flavor, we added tomato paste to the browned vegetables and deglazed the pan with a little tomato juice before adding the canned tomatoes. Using two varieties of canned tomatoes struck a nice balance; diced tomatoes lent a chunky texture, and tomato sauce provided a smooth foundation.

  2 ounces white mushrooms, trimmed and halved
  1 slice hearty white sandwich bread, torn into quarters
  2 tablespoons whole milk
    Salt and pepper
  8 ounces 85 percent lean ground beef
  1 tablespoon extra-virgin olive oil
  ½ onion, chopped fine
  3 garlic cloves, minced
  1 tablespoon tomato paste
  ⅛ teaspoon red pepper flakes
  1 (14.5-ounce) can diced tomatoes, drained with ¼ cup juice reserved
  1½ teaspoons minced fresh oregano or ½ teaspoon dried
  1 (15-ounce) can tomato sauce
  ¼ cup grated Parmesan cheese, plus extra for serving
  1 pound spaghetti

1. Pulse mushrooms in food processor until finely chopped, about 4 pulses; transfer to bowl. Pulse bread, milk, ½ teaspoon salt, and ½ teaspoon pepper in now-empty food processor until paste forms, about 4 pulses. Add ground beef and pulse until well combined, about 3 pulses.

Buying Canned Tomatoes

Since canned tomatoes are processed at the height of freshness, they deliver more flavor than off-season fresh tomatoes. But with all the options lining supermarket shelves, it's not always clear what you should buy. We tested a variety of canned tomato products to determine the best uses for each.

WHOLE TOMATOES Whole tomatoes are peeled tomatoes packed in their own juice or puree. They are best when fresh tomato flavor is a must. Whole tomatoes are quite soft and break down quickly when cooked. Those packed in juice have a livelier flavor than those in puree.

DICED TOMATOES Diced tomatoes are peeled, machine-diced, and packed in their own juice or puree. Many brands contain calcium chloride, a firming agent that helps the chunks maintain their shape. Diced tomatoes are best for rustic tomato sauces with a chunky texture, and in long-cooked stews and soups where you want the tomatoes to hold their shape. We favor diced tomatoes packed in juice because they have a fresher flavor than those packed in puree.

CRUSHED TOMATOES Crushed tomatoes are whole tomatoes ground very finely, then enriched with tomato puree. They work well in smoother sauces, and their thicker consistency makes them ideal when you want to make a sauce quickly. You can also crush your own canned diced tomatoes in a food processor.

TOMATO PUREE AND TOMATO SAUCE Tomato puree and tomato sauce are both cooked and strained to remove the seeds. These products are best suited to long-cooked dishes where a thick, even texture is important. Tomato puree provides deep, hearty flavor to long-simmered braises and sauces; in sauces where the focus is more on the tomatoes, tomato sauce is a better choice.

TOMATO PASTE Tomato paste is tomato puree that has been cooked to remove almost all moisture. Because it's naturally full of glutamates, tomato paste brings out savory notes. We use it in a variety of recipes, including both long-simmered sauces and quicker-cooking dishes, to lend a deep, well-rounded tomato flavor and color.

2. Heat oil in large saucepan over medium-high heat until shimmering. Add onion and processed mushrooms and cook until softened and lightly browned, about 5 minutes. Stir in garlic, tomato paste, and pepper flakes and cook until fragrant, about 30 seconds. Stir in reserved tomato juice and 1 teaspoon fresh oregano (if using dried, add full amount), scraping up any browned bits. Stir in meat mixture and cook, breaking up meat with wooden spoon, until no longer pink, about 3 minutes.

3. Stir in diced tomatoes and tomato sauce, bring to gentle simmer, and cook until sauce has thickened and flavors meld, about 10 minutes.

4. Stir in Parmesan and remaining ½ teaspoon fresh oregano, and season with salt and pepper to taste.

5. Meanwhile, bring 4 quarts water to boil in large pot. Add pasta and 1 tablespoon salt and cook, stirring often, until al dente. Reserve ½ cup cooking water, then drain pasta and return it to pot. Add sauce and toss to combine. Season with salt and pepper to taste, and add reserved cooking water as needed to adjust consistency. Serve with extra Parmesan.

TO MAKE AHEAD ▶

- Sauce, prepared through step 3, can be refrigerated for up to 3 days or frozen for up to 1 month; if frozen, thaw completely in refrigerator
- To reheat, bring sauce, covered, to gentle simmer, stirring often, and continue with step 4

A combination of sweet Italian sausage and ground beef gives our meatballs hearty flavor and a sturdy texture.

Spaghetti with Meatballs and Marinara

SERVES 8 TO 10   **FREEZE IT**

ACTIVE TIME 1 HOUR 30 MINUTES

TOTAL TIME 2 HOURS

WHY THIS RECIPE WORKS Tender, flavorful meatballs served over pasta with a long-simmered marinara sauce make a great dinner for company or for family. To build a sauce with a long-simmered flavor, we started by sautéing onions and then added a healthy dose of garlic, oregano, and red pepper flakes. Reserving half of this mixture to season the meatballs streamlined our recipe. With tomato paste for richness and red wine to deglaze the pan, we had a strong flavor foundation for our sauce. Next, we decided to use canned crushed tomatoes for their ease and for their packing liquid, which prevented the sauce from over-reducing during the reheat. For hearty meatballs, we combined 80 percent lean ground beef with boldly flavored sweet Italian sausage. This lean mixture held its shape well, but to compensate for the decreased amount of fat, we added a panade of sandwich bread and milk. This kept the meat moist and prevented it from getting tough. To boost the flavor further, a good dose of Parmesan and parsley did the trick. A couple eggs were also important for texture and flavor; their rich fats and emulsifiers added moistness, richness, and structure to our meatballs. For a golden-brown crust without the hassle of frying, we baked our meatballs on baking sheets in a superhot oven.

SAUCE

¼ cup extra-virgin olive oil

3 onions, chopped fine

8 garlic cloves, minced

1 tablespoon dried oregano

½ teaspoon red pepper flakes

1 (6-ounce) can tomato paste

1 cup dry red wine

1 cup water

4 (28-ounce) cans crushed tomatoes

1 ounce Parmesan cheese, grated (½ cup)

¼ cup chopped fresh basil
   Salt and pepper

MEATBALLS AND PASTA

4 slices hearty white sandwich bread, torn into pieces
¾ cup milk
½ pound sweet Italian sausage, casings removed
2 ounces Parmesan cheese, grated (1 cup)
½ cup minced fresh parsley
2 large eggs
2 garlic cloves, minced
1½ teaspoons salt
2½ pounds 80 percent lean ground chuck
2 pounds spaghetti

1. FOR THE SAUCE Heat oil in Dutch oven over medium-high heat until shimmering. Add onions and cook until golden, 10 to 15 minutes. Stir in garlic, oregano, and pepper flakes and cook until fragrant, about 30 seconds. Transfer half of onion mixture to bowl; set aside for meatballs.

2. Stir tomato paste into onion mixture left in pot and cook over medium-high heat until fragrant, about 1 minute. Stir in wine and cook until thickened slightly, about 2 minutes. Stir in water and tomatoes and simmer over low heat until sauce is no longer watery, 45 minutes to 1 hour.

3. FOR THE MEATBALLS AND PASTA Meanwhile, line 2 rimmed baking sheets with aluminum foil and spray with vegetable oil spray. Adjust oven racks to upper-middle and lower-middle positions and heat oven to 475 degrees. Mash bread and milk together in large bowl until smooth. Mix in reserved onion mixture, sausage, Parmesan, parsley, eggs, garlic, and salt. Add beef and knead with your hands until well combined. Shape meat mixture into 30 meatballs (about ¼ cup each) and place on prepared sheets, spaced evenly apart.

4. Roast meatballs until well browned, about 20 minutes, switching and rotating sheets halfway through baking. Transfer meatballs to pot with sauce and simmer for 15 minutes.

5. Stir in Parmesan and basil and season with salt and pepper to taste.

6. Meanwhile, bring 8 quarts water to boil in 12-quart pot. Add pasta and 2 tablespoons salt and cook, stirring often, until al dente. Reserve ½ cup cooking water, then drain pasta and return it to pot. Add several spoonfuls of sauce (without meatballs) and toss to combine. Add reserved cooking water as needed to adjust consistency. Serve pasta with remaining sauce and meatballs.

> **TO MAKE AHEAD**
>
> - Sauce and shaped meatballs, prepared through step 3, can be refrigerated separately for up to 24 hours; reshape meatballs and continue with step 4
> - Alternatively, cooked meatballs in sauce, prepared through step 4, can be refrigerated for up to 3 days or frozen for up to 1 month; if frozen, thaw completely in refrigerator; to reheat, bring sauce, covered, to gentle simmer, stirring often, and continue with step 5

Pasta with Classic Bolognese Sauce

SERVES 4 TO 6   `FREEZE IT`
ACTIVE TIME 1 HOUR
TOTAL TIME 4 HOURS

WHY THIS RECIPE WORKS A good Bolognese sauce should be thick and smooth with rich, complex flavor. The meat should be first and foremost, but there should be sweet, salty, and acidic flavors in the background. To get this complexity, we built our Bolognese in layers, starting with just onion, carrot, and celery sautéed in butter. Then we added meatloaf mix (a combination of ground beef, veal, and pork). For dairy, we used milk, which complemented the meat flavor without adding too much richness.

MAKING MEATBALLS

1. Crumble sausage into bowl with onion mixture and add Parmesan, parsley, eggs, garlic, and salt.

2. Using your hands, gently work ground beef into sausage mixture.

3. Gently roll mixture into thirty 2½-inch meatballs and place them on 2 rimmed baking sheets.

4. Bake meatballs until well browned, then transfer them to marinara sauce to finish cooking.

For just the right texture and deep flavor, we simmer our Bolognese sauce for 3 hours.

Once the milk was reduced, we added white wine to the pot for a more robust sauce, followed by chopped whole canned tomatoes. A long, slow simmer produced a luxuriously rich sauce with layers of flavor and tender meat. If you can't find meatloaf mix, use 6 ounces (85 percent lean) ground beef and 6 ounces ground pork.

- 5 tablespoons unsalted butter
- 2 tablespoons finely chopped onion
- 2 tablespoons minced carrot
- 2 tablespoons minced celery
  Salt and pepper
- 12 ounces meatloaf mix
- 1 cup whole milk
- 1 cup dry white wine
- 1 (28-ounce) can whole peeled tomatoes, drained with juice reserved, tomatoes chopped fine
- 1 pound fettuccine or linguini
  Grated Parmesan cheese

1. Melt 3 tablespoons butter in Dutch oven over medium heat. Add onion, carrot, celery, and ½ teaspoon salt and cook until softened, about 5 minutes. Add meatloaf mix and cook, breaking up meat with wooden spoon, until no longer pink, about 5 minutes.

2. Stir in milk and simmer until liquid evaporates and only fat remains, 10 to 15 minutes. Stir in wine, bring to simmer, and cook until wine evaporates, 10 to 15 minutes.

3. Stir in tomatoes and reserved tomato juice and bring to simmer. Reduce heat to low so that sauce continues to simmer just barely, with occasional bubble or two at surface, until liquid has evaporated, about 3 hours. Season with salt and pepper to taste.

4. Meanwhile, bring 4 quarts water to boil in large pot. Add pasta and 1 tablespoon salt and cook, stirring often, until al dente. Reserve ½ cup cooking water, then drain pasta and return it to pot. Add sauce and remaining 2 tablespoons butter and toss to combine. Season with salt and pepper to taste, and add reserved cooking water as needed to adjust consistency. Serve with Parmesan.

TO MAKE AHEAD

- Sauce, prepared through step 3, can be refrigerated for up to 3 days or frozen for up to 1 month; if frozen, thaw completely in refrigerator
- To reheat, bring sauce, covered, to gentle simmer, stirring often, and continue with step 4

Pasta with Mushroom Bolognese Sauce

SERVES 4 TO 6   **FREEZE IT**
ACTIVE TIME 1 HOUR
TOTAL TIME 1 HOUR

WHY THIS RECIPE WORKS For a vegetarian pasta sauce that mimicked the rich, long-cooked flavor and hearty texture of Bolognese, we turned to two types of mushrooms to replicate that complexity: Dried porcini delivered depth of flavor while 2 pounds of fresh cremini gave the sauce a satisfying, substantial texture. To further round out the sauce's savory flavor, we added two umami-rich ingredients: soy sauce and tomato paste. A dash of heavy cream at the end rounded out the sauce and gave it a decadent silkiness.

- 2 pounds cremini mushrooms, trimmed and quartered
- 1 carrot, peeled and chopped
- 1 small onion, chopped
- 1 (28-ounce) can whole peeled tomatoes

3 tablespoons unsalted butter
½ ounce dried porcini mushrooms, rinsed and minced
3 garlic cloves, minced
1 teaspoon sugar
2 tablespoons tomato paste
1 cup dry red wine
½ cup vegetable broth
1 tablespoon soy sauce
  Salt and pepper
3 tablespoons heavy cream
1 pound fettuccine or linguini
  Grated Parmesan cheese

1. Working in batches, pulse cremini mushrooms in food processor until pieces are no larger than ½ inch, 5 to 7 pulses; transfer to large bowl. Pulse carrot and onion in now-empty processor until chopped fine, 5 to 7 pulses; transfer to bowl with mushrooms. Pulse tomatoes and their juice in now-empty processor until chopped fine, 6 to 8 pulses; set aside separately.

2. Melt butter in Dutch oven over medium heat. Add processed vegetables and porcini mushrooms, cover, and cook, stirring occasionally, until they release their liquid, about 5 minutes. Uncover, increase heat to medium-high, and cook until liquid has evaporated and vegetables begin to brown, 12 to 15 minutes.

3. Stir in garlic and sugar and cook until fragrant, about 30 seconds. Stir in tomato paste and cook for 1 minute. Stir in wine and simmer until nearly evaporated, about 5 minutes.

4. Stir in processed tomatoes, broth, soy sauce, ½ teaspoon salt, and ¼ teaspoon pepper, and bring to simmer. Reduce heat to medium-low and simmer until sauce has thickened but is still moist, 8 to 10 minutes. Off heat, stir in cream and season with salt and pepper to taste.

5. Meanwhile, bring 4 quarts water to boil in large pot. Add pasta and 1 tablespoon salt and cook, stirring often, until al dente. Reserve ⅔ cup cooking water, then drain pasta and return it to pot. Add sauce and toss to combine. Season with salt and pepper to taste, and adjust consistency with reserved cooking water as needed. Serve with Parmesan.

TO MAKE AHEAD

- Sauce, prepared through step 4, can be refrigerated for up to 3 days or frozen for up to 1 month; if frozen, thaw completely in refrigerator
- To reheat, bring sauce, covered, to gentle simmer, stirring often, and continue with step 5

NOTES FROM THE TEST KITCHEN

Cooking Pasta 101

Cooking pasta seems simple, but perfect pasta takes some finesse. Here's how we do it in the test kitchen.

USE PLENTY OF WATER To prevent sticking, you'll need 4 quarts of water to cook up to 1 pound of dried pasta. Pasta leaches starch as it cooks; without plenty of water to dilute it, the starch will coat the noodles and they will stick. Use a pot with at least a 6-quart capacity so that the water won't boil over.

SALT THE WATER Adding salt to the pasta cooking water is essential; it seasons and adds flavor to the pasta. Add 1 tablespoon of salt per 4 quarts of water. Be sure to add the salt with the pasta, not before, so it will dissolve and not stain the pot.

SKIP THE OIL It's a myth that adding oil to pasta cooking water prevents the pasta from sticking together as it cooks. Adding oil to cooking water just creates a slick on the surface of the water, doing nothing for the pasta. To prevent pasta from sticking, simply stir the pasta for a minute or two when you add it to the boiling water and then stir occasionally while it's cooking.

CHECK OFTEN FOR DONENESS The timing instructions given on the box are almost always too long and will result in mushy, overcooked pasta. Tasting is the best way to check for doneness. We typically prefer pasta cooked al dente, when it still has a little bite left in the center.

RESERVE SOME WATER Reserve about ½ cup cooking water before draining the pasta—the water is flavorful and can help loosen a thick sauce.

DON'T RINSE We generally don't rinse pasta after draining; it washes away the starch and makes the pasta taste watery. However, we make an exception for pasta salads that need to chill before serving, where the extra starch would make the pasta too sticky.

KEEP IT HOT If you're using a large serving bowl for the pasta, place it under the colander while draining the pasta. The hot water heats up the bowl, which keeps the pasta warm longer.

BIG-BATCH SLOW-COOKER PASTA SAUCES

When it comes to making big batches of pasta sauce to stash in your freezer, your slow cooker is a great helping hand because sauces can simmer away untended for hours while they develop deep flavor. **Note** All these recipes make enough sauce for 3 pounds of pasta. You will need a 5- to 7-quart slow-cooker for these recipes.

TO MAKE AHEAD

Pasta sauces can be refrigerated for up to 3 days or frozen for up to 1 month; if frozen, thaw completely in refrigerator before reheating

SLOW-COOKER FARM STAND TOMATO SAUCE

MAKES 9 CUPS   EASY   FREEZE IT

COOKING TIME 10 TO 11 HOURS ON LOW OR 7 TO 8 HOURS ON HIGH

- 2 onions, chopped fine
- ¼ cup tomato paste
- 2 tablespoons extra-virgin olive oil, plus extra for seasoning
- 6 garlic cloves, minced
- 1 tablespoon chopped fresh oregano or 1 teaspoon dried
- ½ cup dry red wine
- ¼ cup instant tapioca
- 2 bay leaves
- 7 pounds tomatoes, cored and peeled
- ¼ cup chopped fresh basil
  Salt and pepper

1. Microwave onions, tomato paste, oil, garlic, and oregano in bowl, stirring occasionally, until onions are softened, about 5 minutes; transfer to slow cooker. Stir wine, tapioca, and bay leaves into slow cooker.

2. Add tomatoes, cover, and cook until tomatoes are very soft and beginning to disintegrate, 10 to 11 hours on low or 7 to 8 hours on high.

3. Discard bay leaves. Mash tomatoes with potato masher until mostly smooth. Transfer sauce to Dutch oven, bring to simmer over medium-high heat, and cook until thickened, about 20 minutes. Stir in basil and season with salt, pepper, and extra oil to taste. Serve.

SLOW-COOKER MARINARA SAUCE

MAKES 9 CUPS   EASY   FREEZE IT

COOKING TIME 10 TO 11 HOURS ON LOW OR 7 TO 8 HOURS ON HIGH

- 2 tablespoons extra-virgin olive oil
- 2 onions, chopped fine
- 6 garlic cloves, minced
- 2 tablespoons tomato paste
- 2 tablespoons minced fresh oregano or 2 teaspoons dried
- 2 anchovy fillets, rinsed and minced
  Pinch red pepper flakes
- 1 cup dry red wine
- 1 (28-ounce) can crushed tomatoes
- 1 (28-ounce) can diced tomatoes, drained
- 1 (28-ounce) can tomato sauce
- 2 tablespoons soy sauce
- 2 teaspoons sugar, plus extra as needed
  Salt and pepper

1. Heat oil in 12-inch skillet over medium-high heat until shimmering. Add onions and cook until softened and lightly browned, 8 to 10 minutes. Stir in garlic, tomato paste, oregano, anchovies, and red pepper flakes and cook until fragrant, about 1 minute. Stir in wine, scraping up any browned bits. Bring to simmer and cook until thickened, about 5 minutes; transfer to slow cooker.

2. Stir in crushed and diced tomatoes, tomato sauce, and soy sauce. Cover and cook until sauce is deeply flavored, 10 to 11 hours on low or 7 to 8 hours on high. Stir in sugar and season with salt, pepper, and extra sugar to taste. Serve.

SLOW-COOKER MEATY TOMATO SAUCE

MAKES 12 CUPS   EASY   FREEZE IT

COOKING TIME 9 TO 10 HOURS ON LOW OR 6 TO 7 HOURS ON HIGH

Boneless pork butt roast is often labeled Boston butt in the supermarket.

- 2 onions, chopped
- 12 garlic cloves, minced
- ¼ cup tomato paste
- 2 tablespoons extra-virgin olive oil
- 2 tablespoons minced fresh oregano or 2 teaspoons dried
- ¼ teaspoon red pepper flakes
- 1 (28-ounce) can diced tomatoes, drained
- 1 (28-ounce) can tomato puree
- ¾ cup dry red wine
- ⅓ cup soy sauce
- 2 bay leaves
- 1 (3-pound) boneless pork butt roast, trimmed and quartered
  Salt and pepper
- ¼ cup minced fresh parsley

1. Microwave onions, garlic, tomato paste, oil, oregano, and pepper flakes in bowl, stirring occasionally, until onions are softened, about 5 minutes; transfer to slow cooker. Stir in diced tomatoes, tomato puree, wine, soy sauce, and bay leaves. Season pork with salt and pepper and nestle into slow cooker.

2. Cover and cook until pork is tender, 9 to 10 hours on low or 6 to 7 hours on high.

3. Discard bay leaves. Using large spoon, skim excess fat from surface of sauce. Break pork into bite-size pieces with tongs. Stir in parsley and season with salt and pepper to taste. Serve.

SLOW-COOKER SHORT RIBS AND RED WINE SAUCE

MAKES 12 CUPS `EASY` `FREEZE IT`

COOKING TIME 9 TO 10 HOURS ON LOW OR 6 TO 7 HOURS ON HIGH

- 2 tablespoons extra-virgin olive oil
- 2 onions, chopped fine
- 2 carrots, peeled and cut into ¼-inch pieces
- 1 celery rib, minced
- ¼ cup tomato paste
- 6 garlic cloves, minced
- 1½ cups dry red wine
- 1 (28-ounce) can diced tomatoes, drained
- 1 (28-ounce) can tomato puree
- 2 bay leaves
- 3 pounds boneless short ribs, trimmed and cut into 1½-inch pieces
- Salt and pepper
- ½ cup minced fresh parsley

1. Heat oil in 12-inch skillet over medium-high heat until shimmering. Add onions, carrots, and celery and cook until vegetables are softened and lightly browned, 8 to 10 minutes. Stir in tomato paste and garlic and cook until fragrant, about 1 minute. Stir in wine, scraping up any browned bits, and simmer until thickened, about 6 minutes; transfer to slow cooker.

2. Stir in diced tomatoes, tomato puree, and bay leaves. Season beef with salt and pepper and nestle into slow cooker. Cover and cook until beef is tender, 9 to 10 hours on low or 6 to 7 hours on high.

3. Discard bay leaves. Using large spoon, skim excess fat from surface of sauce. Break beef into bite-size pieces with tongs. Stir in parsley and season with salt and pepper to taste. Serve.

SLOW-COOKER SPICY SAUSAGE RAGU WITH RED PEPPERS

MAKES 12 CUPS `EASY` `FREEZE IT`

COOKING TIME 9 TO 10 HOURS ON LOW OR 6 TO 7 HOURS ON HIGH

- 2 tablespoons extra-virgin olive oil
- 2 pounds hot Italian sausage, casings removed
- 2 onions, chopped
- 6 garlic cloves, minced
- 2 tablespoons tomato paste
- 2 tablespoons minced fresh oregano or 2 teaspoons dried
- 1 teaspoon red pepper flakes
- 1 cup dry red wine
- 1 (28-ounce) can crushed tomatoes
- 1 (28-ounce) can diced tomatoes, drained
- 1 (28-ounce) can tomato sauce
- 2 red bell peppers, stemmed, seeded, and cut into ½-inch pieces
- ½ cup minced fresh parsley
- Salt and pepper

1. Heat 1 tablespoon oil in 12-inch skillet over medium-high heat until just smoking. Brown sausage well, breaking up large pieces with wooden spoon, about 5 minutes; transfer to slow cooker.

2. Pour off all but 2 tablespoons fat from skillet, add onions, and cook over medium heat until softened and lightly browned, 8 to 10 minutes. Stir in garlic, tomato paste, oregano, and pepper flakes and cook until fragrant, about 1 minute. Stir in wine, scraping up any browned bits, and simmer until thickened, about 5 minutes; transfer to slow cooker.

3. Stir in crushed tomatoes, diced tomatoes, and tomato sauce. Cover and cook until sauce is deeply flavored, 9 to 10 hours on low or 6 to 7 hours on high.

4. Microwave bell peppers with remaining 1 tablespoon oil in bowl, stirring occasionally, until tender, about 5 minutes. Using large spoon, skim excess fat from surface of sauce. Stir in bell peppers and parsley and season with salt and pepper to taste. Serve.

To ensure all the vegetables in this fresh sauce have the right texture, we cook them in batches, adding the zucchini last.

Penne with Garden Vegetable Sauce

SERVES 4 TO 6
ACTIVE TIME 45 MINUTES
TOTAL TIME 45 MINUTES

WHY THIS RECIPE WORKS A fresh summer vegetable pasta sauce sounds easy, but it's actually more difficult than you'd think. The trick was figuring out how to get distinct pieces of crisp-tender vegetables with a saucy, flavorful base. We gathered a variety of veggies—zucchini, cherry tomatoes, carrots, and bell peppers—and started sautéing. However, the flavors became too homogeneous and the vegetables cooked at different rates; some were mushy, while others were too crisp. We had better luck when we cooked the vegetables in batches. First, we sautéed the tomatoes, onion, carrots, and bell peppers until the tomatoes started to break down and created a pasta-clinging sauciness that enveloped the just-tender carrots and peppers. Porcini mushrooms, tomato paste, garlic, oregano, and just a little bit of red pepper flakes gave depth to the sauce without overwhelming the delicate vegetable flavors. We added the zucchini towards the very end to keep them from overcooking and turning mushy. A hefty portion of chopped basil, added just before serving, ensured that our dinner tasted—and looked—like it was fresh from the garden.

¼ cup extra-virgin olive oil
1 pound cherry tomatoes, halved
2 yellow bell peppers, stemmed, seeded, and chopped
1 onion, chopped
2 carrots, peeled and shredded
Salt and pepper
½ ounce dried porcini mushrooms, rinsed and minced
3 tablespoons tomato paste
4 garlic cloves, minced
1 tablespoon minced fresh oregano or 1 teaspoon dried
⅛ teaspoon red pepper flakes
½ cup vegetable broth
2 zucchini, quartered lengthwise and sliced ¼ inch thick
1 pound penne
¼ cup chopped fresh basil
Grated Parmesan cheese

1. Heat oil in Dutch oven over medium heat until shimmering. Add tomatoes, bell peppers, onion, carrots, 1½ teaspoons salt, and ½ teaspoon pepper and cook, stirring occasionally, until vegetables are softened and tomatoes are broken down, 8 to 10 minutes.

2. Stir in mushrooms, tomato paste, garlic, oregano, and pepper flakes and cook until fragrant, about 1 minute. Stir in broth and bring to simmer. Stir in zucchini and cook until zucchini is just tender, about 4 minutes.

3. Meanwhile, bring 4 quarts water to boil in large pot. Add pasta and 1 tablespoon salt and cook, stirring often, until al dente. Reserve ½ cup cooking water, then drain pasta and return it to pot. Add sauce and toss to combine. Stir in basil and season with salt and pepper to taste. Add reserved cooking water as needed to adjust consistency. Serve with Parmesan.

TO MAKE AHEAD

- Sauce, prepared through step 2, can be refrigerated for up to 3 days
- To reheat, bring sauce, covered, to gentle simmer, stirring often, and continue with step 3

A béchamel sauce binds our macaroni and cheese casserole while toasted bread crumbs make a nice, crunchy topping.

Baked Macaroni and Cheese

SERVES 6 ‖ FREEZE IT

ACTIVE TIME 50 MINUTES
TOTAL TIME 2 HOURS

WHY THIS RECIPE WORKS For a classic home-style macaroni and cheese that would appeal to adults and kids alike, we kept things simple, staying away from pungent cheeses and an overly rich sauce made with eggs and cream. Instead, we started with a béchamel sauce (butter, flour, and milk), adding chicken broth both for a savory flavor and to keep the sauce from becoming too thick in the oven. Adding a combination of extra-sharp cheddar and Colby to the sauce gave it both ultracheesy flavor and an incredibly creamy texture. Once the cheese was incorporated, we stirred in our macaroni (cooked until nearly tender) and moved it all to a baking dish. For a crunchy topping, we toasted some panko bread crumbs with melted butter, sprinkled them over the casserole, and baked the dish until it was bubbling and golden on top.

1 cup panko bread crumbs
2 tablespoons unsalted butter, melted, plus 6 tablespoons unsalted butter
Salt and pepper
1 pound elbow macaroni or small shells
1 garlic clove, minced
1 teaspoon dry mustard
¼ teaspoon cayenne pepper
6 tablespoons all-purpose flour
3½ cups whole milk
2¼ cups chicken broth
1 pound Colby cheese, shredded (4 cups)
8 ounces extra-sharp cheddar cheese, shredded (2 cups)

1. Adjust oven rack to middle position and heat oven to 350 degrees. Toss panko with melted butter and season with salt and pepper. Spread evenly in aluminum foil–lined rimmed baking sheet and bake, stirring occasionally, until golden brown, about 10 minutes; let cool to room temperature. Increase oven temperature to 400 degrees.

2. Bring 4 quarts water to boil in large pot. Add macaroni and 1 tablespoon salt and cook, stirring often, until just starting to soften, about 5 minutes. Drain macaroni and set aside.

3. Dry now-empty pot, add remaining 6 tablespoons butter, and melt over medium heat. Stir in garlic, mustard, and cayenne and cook until fragrant, about 30 seconds. Add flour and cook, stirring constantly, until golden, about 1 minute. Slowly whisk in milk and broth until smooth. Bring to gentle simmer and cook, whisking often, until thickened, about 15 minutes.

4. Off heat, gradually whisk in Colby and cheddar until melted and smooth. Season with salt and pepper to taste. Stir in macaroni, breaking up any clumps. Transfer macaroni mixture to 13 by 9-inch baking dish and sprinkle with panko mixture.

5. Place dish on clean foil-lined rimmed baking sheet and bake until bubbling around edges, 25 to 35 minutes. Let casserole cool for 20 minutes. Serve.

TO MAKE AHEAD ▶

- Casserole, prepared through step 4, can be wrapped tightly in plastic wrap, covered with aluminum foil, and refrigerated for up to 24 hours or frozen for up to 1 month; if frozen, thaw completely in refrigerator
- To bake, unwrap casserole, cover with greased aluminum foil, and bake on foil-lined sheet in 400-degree oven until hot throughout, 20 to 25 minutes; remove foil and continue to bake until crumbs are crisp, 15 to 20 minutes

Four kinds of cheese give this classic casserole the requisite creamy richness.

Creamy Baked Four-Cheese Pasta

SERVES 6

ACTIVE TIME 35 MINUTES

TOTAL TIME 1 HOUR 40 MINUTES

WHY THIS RECIPE WORKS This classic Italian iteration of macaroni and cheese, *pasta ai quattro formaggi*, is made with four cheeses and heavy cream. We wanted ours to have a rich, creamy sauce, properly cooked pasta, and a crisp bread-crumb topping. For the best cheese flavor and texture, we used Italian fontina, Gorgonzola, Pecorino Romano, and Parmesan cheeses. We started with a classic roux-based béchamel—cooking butter with flour and then adding cream. However, with an eye towards making the dish ahead of time, we realized that the amount of cream we needed to keep the sauce creamy for reheating left the dish too rich and dense. Instead, we swapped out most of the cream for evaporated milk, which delivered a silky texture without being too heavy. Knowing the pasta would spend some time in the oven, we cooked it just shy of al dente. This allowed it to turn perfectly tender as it baked in the sauce. Topped with toasted panko bread crumbs and a little more Parmesan, our pasta dinner was rich but not heavy.

1 cup panko bread crumbs
2 tablespoons unsalted butter, melted, plus 4 tablespoons unsalted butter
Salt and pepper
1½ ounces Parmesan cheese, grated (¾ cup)
1 pound penne
1 tablespoon extra-virgin olive oil
2 tablespoons all-purpose flour
2 (12-ounce) cans evaporated milk
1 cup heavy cream
6 ounces fontina cheese, shredded (1½ cups)
4 ounces Gorgonzola cheese, crumbled (1 cup)
1½ ounces Pecorino Romano cheese, grated (¾ cup)

1. Adjust oven rack to middle position and heat oven to 350 degrees. Toss panko with melted butter and season with salt and pepper. Spread evenly in aluminum foil–lined rimmed baking sheet and bake, stirring occasionally, until golden brown, about 10 minutes; let cool to room temperature. Combine cooled panko mixture and ¼ cup Parmesan. Increase oven temperature to 400 degrees.

2. Bring 4 quarts water to boil in large pot. Add pasta and 1 tablespoon salt and cook, stirring often, until just starting to soften, about 5 minutes. Drain pasta in colander and toss with oil; leave in colander and set aside.

3. Dry now-empty pot, add remaining 4 tablespoons butter, and melt over medium-low heat. Add flour and cook, stirring constantly, until golden, about 1 minute. Slowly whisk in evaporated milk, cream, ¼ teaspoon salt, and ¼ teaspoon pepper until smooth and bring to gentle simmer.

4. Off heat, gradually whisk in fontina, Gorgonzola, Pecorino, and remaining ½ cup Parmesan until melted and smooth. Stir in pasta, breaking up any clumps. Transfer pasta mixture to 13 by 9-inch baking dish.

5. Sprinkle with panko mixture. Place dish on foil-lined rimmed baking sheet and bake until golden and bubbling around edges, 25 to 35 minutes. Let casserole cool for 20 minutes. Serve.

> **TO MAKE AHEAD**
> - Casserole, prepared through step 4, can be refrigerated for up to 24 hours
> - To bake, stir well, cover with greased aluminum foil and bake on foil-lined sheet in 300-degree oven until hot throughout, about 30 minutes, stirring every 10 minutes; remove foil, stir, sprinkle with panko mixture, and continue to bake until crumbs are crisp, about 5 minutes

A combo of fresh corn and cherry tomatoes adds freshness to this creamy casserole.

Creamy Corn and Tomato Pasta Bake

SERVES 8

ACTIVE TIME 45 MINUTES

TOTAL TIME 1 HOUR 30 MINUTES

WHY THIS RECIPE WORKS Most baked pasta casseroles result in mushy noodles and flavorless vegetables in a thick, overly rich sauce. To solve this issue, we parcooked the pasta until it was just beginning to soften so that it wouldn't overcook when baked or reheated. A combination of cream, vegetable broth, and white wine formed the basis of a simple flour-thickened sauce. Leaving the sauce a bit loose ensured that there was enough liquid to finish cooking the pasta during baking or reheating. For the vegetables, we chose a fresh combination of corn and tomatoes. Sprinkling additional cheese over the top before baking protected the pasta and ensured it cooked through evenly.

1 pound penne
  Salt and pepper
2 tablespoons extra-virgin olive oil
1 onion, chopped
3 garlic cloves, minced
1 tablespoon minced fresh thyme or 1 teaspoon dried
⅛ teaspoon red pepper flakes
¼ cup all-purpose flour
2 cups vegetable broth
2 cups heavy cream
½ cup dry white wine
4 ears of corn, kernels cut from cobs
8 ounces fontina cheese, shredded (2 cups)
2 ounces Parmesan cheese, grated (1 cup)
1 pound cherry tomatoes, halved
1 tablespoon chopped fresh basil, parsley, or tarragon

1. Bring 4 quarts water to boil in large pot. Add pasta and 1 tablespoon salt cook, stirring often, until just beginning to soften, about 5 minutes. Drain pasta in colander and toss with 1 tablespoon oil; set aside.

2. Adjust oven rack to middle position and heat oven to 400 degrees. Dry now-empty pot and heat remaining 1 tablespoon oil over medium heat until shimmering. Add onion, 1 teaspoon salt, and ½ teaspoon pepper and cook until softened, about 5 minutes. Stir in garlic, thyme, and pepper flakes and cook until fragrant, about 30 seconds. Add flour and cook, stirring constantly, until golden, about 1 minute. Slowly whisk in broth, cream, and wine, smoothing out any lumps. Stir in corn and bring to simmer.

3. Off heat, gradually whisk in 1 cup fontina and ½ cup Parmesan into sauce until cheese is melted and sauce is smooth. Stir in tomatoes and pasta, breaking up any clumps. Transfer pasta mixture to 13 by 9-inch baking dish and sprinkle with remaining 1 cup fontina and ½ cup Parmesan.

4. Place baking dish on aluminum foil–lined rimmed baking sheet and bake until golden and bubbling around edges, 25 to 35 minutes. Let casserole cool for 20 minutes. Sprinkle with basil and serve.

> **TO MAKE AHEAD** ▶
>
> - Casserole, prepared through step 3, can be refrigerated for up to 24 hours
> - To bake, cover with greased aluminum foil and bake on foil-lined sheet in 400-degree oven until hot throughout, about 35 minutes; remove foil and continue to bake until cheese is golden, 25 to 35 minutes, before garnishing as directed

Chicken and Wild Mushroom Penne Bake

SERVES 8 `EASY`

ACTIVE TIME 25 MINUTES

TOTAL TIME 1 HOUR

WHY THIS RECIPE WORKS To create a comforting and updated version of baked pasta with chicken and mushrooms, we started by highlighting a variety of mixed wild mushrooms. Their distinct earthy notes provided the perfect deep background flavor for our casserole. A bit of dried porcini mushrooms provided extra oomph and reinforced the fresh mushroom flavor. We wanted a rich, gooey sauce, so we made a classic cream sauce enriched with white wine, thyme, a splash of sherry vinegar and both Gruyère and Parmesan cheeses. We boiled the pasta for just 5 minutes to ensure it wouldn't overcook and become mushy while baking. We found it easiest to use boneless, skinless chicken breasts; by poaching the breasts whole in our sauce, then shredding them, we could guarantee juicy, tender chicken each time. We finished off our casserole with a little more Gruyère and Parmesan to create a perfect cheesy, crusty layer on top and a flourish of minced chives after baking for a bright, clean bite. Any mix of wild mushrooms can be used here.

1 pound penne
  Salt and pepper
2 tablespoons extra-virgin olive oil
1½ pounds chanterelle, cremini, oyster, and shiitake mushrooms, stemmed and sliced thin
1 onion, chopped fine
½ ounce dried porcini mushrooms, rinsed and minced
8 garlic cloves, minced
1 tablespoon minced fresh thyme or 1 teaspoon dried
¼ cup all-purpose flour
2 cups chicken broth
1 cup dry white wine
2 pounds boneless, skinless chicken breasts, trimmed
1 cup heavy cream
6 ounces Gruyère cheese, shredded (1½ cups)
2 ounces Parmesan cheese, grated (1 cup)
2 tablespoons sherry vinegar
2 tablespoons minced fresh chives

1. Bring 4 quarts of water to boil in large pot. Add pasta and 1 tablespoon salt and cook, stirring often, until just starting to soften, about 5 minutes. Drain pasta in colander and toss with 1 tablespoon oil; leave in colander and set aside.

2. Dry now-empty pot and heat remaining 1 tablespoon oil over medium heat until shimmering. Add mixed mushrooms, onion, porcini mushrooms, and 1 teaspoon salt. Cover and cook, stirring often, until mushrooms have released their liquid, about 10 minutes. Uncover, increase heat to medium-high, and continue to cook until mushrooms are dry and browned, 5 to 10 minutes.

3. Stir in garlic and thyme and cook until fragrant, about 30 seconds. Add flour and cook, stirring constantly, until golden, about 1 minute. Slowly whisk in broth and wine and bring to simmer. Season chicken with salt and pepper and nestle into pot. Reduce heat to low, cover, and simmer gently until chicken registers 160 degrees, about 15 minutes. Transfer chicken to cutting board, let cool slightly, then shred into bite-size pieces using 2 forks

4. Adjust oven rack to middle position and heat oven to 400 degrees. Off heat, gradually whisk cream, 1 cup Gruyère, ½ cup Parmesan, and vinegar into sauce until cheese is melted and sauce is smooth. Stir in shredded chicken and pasta, breaking up any clumps. Season with salt and pepper to taste. Transfer pasta mixture to 13 by 9-inch baking dish and sprinkle with remaining ½ cup Gruyère and ½ cup Parmesan.

5. Place baking dish on aluminum foil–lined rimmed baking sheet and bake until golden and bubbling around edges, 25 to 35 minutes. Let casserole cool 20 minutes. Sprinkle with chives and serve.

TO MAKE AHEAD

- Casserole, prepared through step 4, can be refrigerated for up to 24 hours
- To bake, cover with greased aluminum foil and bake on foil-lined sheet in 400-degree oven until hot throughout, about 35 minutes; remove foil and continue to bake until cheese is golden, 25 to 35 minutes, before garnishing as directed

All About Mushrooms

With their substantial, meaty texture and deep flavor, mushrooms are a great way to add complex meatiness to pasta dishes, soups, sauces, stir-fries, and stuffings. We also enjoy them simply sautéed, stuffed, marinated, or grilled on their own. Here's everything you need to know about buying, storing, and preparing mushrooms.

BUYING MUSHROOMS There are many varieties of fresh mushrooms available at the supermarket now: the humble white button mushroom, as well as cremini, shiitake, oyster, and portobello mushrooms, for starters. We find cremini mushrooms to be firmer and more flavorful than less-expensive white mushrooms, but the two are interchangeable in any recipe. If possible, always buy mushrooms loose so that you can inspect their quality. When buying white or cremini mushrooms, look for mushrooms with whole, intact caps; avoid those with discoloration or dry, shriveled patches. Pick mushrooms with large caps and minimal stems.

TYPES OF MUSHROOMS

In addition to the most common white mushroom, here are four varieties of mushrooms we like to use in the test kitchen to add flavor and textural interest to dishes.

CHANTERELLE mushrooms are bright yellow to pale orange in color and grow under oak trees. Tasters found them nutty and fruity.

CREMINI mushrooms have the same shape as white mushrooms but are brown in color and more intensely flavored than their pale cousins. Tasters described them as rich and sweet, like a caramelized white mushroom.

OYSTER mushrooms are beige, cream, or gray in color. They are delicate and best cooked only briefly. Tasters described them as redolent of fried oysters, delicate and briny.

SHIITAKE mushrooms, which are tan to dark brown in color, are esteemed in Japan and China. Tasters described them as woody, earthy, savory, and meaty.

STORING MUSHROOMS Because of their high moisture content, mushrooms are very perishable; most mushrooms can be kept fresh for only a few days. To extend their shelf life as long as possible, store loose mushrooms in the crisper drawer in a partially open zipper-lock bag. Store packaged mushrooms in their original containers, as these are designed to "breathe," maximizing the life of the mushrooms. Once the package has been opened, simply rewrap it with plastic wrap.

CLEANING MUSHROOMS When it comes to cleaning, you can ignore the advice against washing mushrooms, which exaggerates their ability to absorb water. As long as they are washed before they are cut, we found that 6 ounces of mushrooms gain only about ¼ ounce of water. However, rinsing can cause discoloration, so don't wash mushrooms that will be eaten raw; simply brush dirt away with a soft pastry brush or cloth. If you are cooking the mushrooms, rinse away dirt and grit with cold water just before using and then spin them dry in a salad spinner.

BUYING AND PREPARING DRIED PORCINI We often turn to dried porcini to add potent savory flavor to dishes. Because the mushrooms are dried, their flavor is concentrated and they are conveniently shelf-stable. When buying dried porcini, always inspect the mushrooms. Avoid those with small holes, which indicate the mushrooms may have been subjected to pinworms. Look for large, smooth porcini free of holes, dust, and grit. Because porcini mushrooms are foraged, not farmed, they vary in cleanliness. Always remove any grit before using; we like to swish them in a bowl of water to loosen dirt, then rinse them.

PREPARING MUSHROOMS

For mushrooms with tender stems, such as white and cremini, trim stems, then prep and cook stems alongside caps.

For mushrooms with tough, woody stems, such as shiitakes and portobellos, stems should be removed.

Blanching and shocking the broccoli rabe tames its assertive bitterness and ensures it stays brightly colored.

Baked Ziti with Sausage and Broccoli Rabe

SERVES 8

ACTIVE TIME 55 MINUTES

TOTAL TIME 1 HOUR 45 MINUTES

WHY THIS RECIPE WORKS In Italy, pasta with broccoli rabe and sausage is a popular dish. We transformed these classic flavors into an easy, yet elegant, cassero le. Our flavor choices were traditional: sweet Italian sausage, red pepper flakes, lemon zest, and a bit of anchovy for an umami backbone. A rich, creamy sauce with two cheeses was the perfect way to round out our dish. Broccoli cut into 1½-inch pieces can be substituted for the broccoli rabe.

1 pound broccoli rabe, trimmed and cut into 1½-inch pieces
   Salt and pepper
1 pound ziti
2 tablespoons extra-virgin olive oil
1 pound sweet or hot Italian sausage, casings removed
1 onion, chopped fine
8 garlic cloves, sliced thin
2 anchovy fillets, rinsed and minced

2 teaspoons lemon zest plus 2 tablespoons juice
1 teaspoon red pepper flakes
⅓ cup all-purpose flour
2 cups chicken broth
1½ cups heavy cream
½ cup dry white wine
8 ounces fontina cheese, shredded (2 cups)
2 ounces Parmesan cheese, grated (1 cup)

1. Bring 4 quarts water to boil in large pot. Fill large bowl halfway with ice and water. Add broccoli rabe and 1 tablespoon salt to boiling water and cook until crisp-tender, about 1 minute. Using slotted spoon, transfer broccoli rabe to ice water and let cool, about 2 minutes; drain and pat dry.

2. Return pot of water to boil, add pasta, and cook, stirring often, until just starting to soften, about 5 minutes. Drain pasta in colander and toss with 1 tablespoon oil; leave in colander and set aside.

3. Adjust oven rack to middle position and heat oven to 400 degrees. Dry now-empty pot and heat remaining 1 tablespoon oil over medium heat until shimmering. Add sausage and cook, breaking up meat with wooden spoon, until no longer pink, about 3 minutes. Using slotted spoon, transfer sausage to paper towel-lined plate.

4. Pour off all but 1 tablespoon fat from pot, add onion and ½ teaspoon salt, and cook until softened and lightly browned, 5 to 7 minutes. Stir in garlic, anchovies, lemon zest, and pepper flakes and cook until fragrant, about 30 seconds. Add flour and cook, stirring constantly, until golden, about 1 minute. Slowly whisk in broth, cream, and wine, scraping up any browned bits and smoothing out any lumps. Bring to simmer and cook until thickened slightly, about 2 minutes.

5. Off heat, gradually whisk 1 cup fontina and ½ cup Parmesan into sauce until cheese is melted and sauce in smooth. Stir in lemon juice, broccoli rabe, pasta, and sausage, breaking up any clumps. Season with salt and pepper to taste. Transfer pasta mixture to 13 by 9-inch baking dish and sprinkle with remaining 1 cup fontina and remaining ½ cup Parmesan.

6. Place baking dish on aluminum foil–lined rimmed baking sheet and bake until golden and bubbling around edges, 25 to 35 minutes. Let casserole cool for 20 minutes before serving.

TO MAKE AHEAD

• Casserole, prepared through step 5, can be refrigerated for up to 24 hours

• To bake, cover with greased aluminum foil and bake on foil-lined sheet in 400-degree oven until hot throughout, about 35 minutes; remove foil and continue to bake until cheese is golden, 25 to 35 minutes

We dollop creamy ricotta between two layers of sauced pasta for the ultimate baked ziti.

Baked Ziti with Ricotta Cheese

SERVES 8   FREEZE IT

ACTIVE TIME 45 MINUTES

TOTAL TIME 1 HOUR 45 MINUTES

WHY THIS RECIPE WORKS For an inspired baked ziti, we focused on perfecting every element of this family favorite. Sautéed garlic and red pepper flakes provided a savory foundation to our easy sauce, and two big cans of crushed tomatoes added rich, long-simmered flavor in short order. Stirring some of the pasta cooking water into the briefly simmered sauce provided further insurance against dryness. A middle layer of ricotta promised creamy pockets of cheese, while a topping of shredded mozzarella and grated Parmesan gave the ziti a nicely browned crust. Finishing with chopped basil kept our perfect baked ziti fresh-looking and bright-tasting.

12 ounces (1½ cups) whole-milk or part-skim ricotta cheese

¼ cup extra-virgin olive oil
    Salt and pepper

12 ounces whole-milk mozzarella cheese, shredded (3 cups)

3 ounces Parmesan cheese, grated (1½ cups)

1½ pounds ziti

3 garlic cloves, minced

½ teaspoon red pepper flakes

2 (28-ounce) cans crushed tomatoes

¼ cup chopped fresh basil

1. Adjust oven rack to middle position and heat oven to 400 degrees. Mix ricotta, 2 tablespoons oil, ½ teaspoon salt, and ½ teaspoon pepper together in bowl. In separate bowl, combine mozzarella and Parmesan.

2. Bring 6 quarts water to boil in large pot. Add pasta and 1½ tablespoons salt and cook, stirring often, until just beginning to soften, about 5 minutes. Reserve 1½ cups cooking water, then drain pasta and set aside.

3. Dry now-empty pot, add remaining 2 tablespoons oil, garlic, and pepper flakes and cook over medium heat until fragrant but not brown, about 2 minutes. Stir in tomatoes, bring to simmer, and cook until thickened slightly, about 15 minutes. Season with salt and pepper to taste.

4. Stir pasta and reserved cooking water into sauce. Transfer half of pasta mixture to 13 by 9-inch baking dish. Dollop large spoonfuls of ricotta mixture evenly over pasta, then spread remaining pasta mixture evenly over ricotta. Sprinkle with mozzarella mixture.

5. Place baking dish on aluminum foil–lined rimmed baking sheet and bake until spotty brown and bubbling around edges, 25 to 35 minutes. Let casserole cool for 20 minutes. Sprinkle with basil and serve.

VARIATION

Baked Ziti with Italian Sausage   FREEZE IT

Add 1 pound sweet or hot Italian sausage, casings removed, to pot before adding oil, garlic, and pepper flakes in step 3; cook sausage, breaking up meat with wooden spoon, until no longer pink, about 5 minutes. Stir in oil, garlic, and pepper flakes, and cook until fragrant, about 30 seconds, before adding tomatoes. Continue with recipe as directed.

TO MAKE AHEAD

- Casserole, prepared through step 4, can be wrapped tightly in plastic wrap, covered with aluminum foil, and refrigerated for up to 24 hours or frozen for up to 1 month; if frozen, thaw completely in refrigerator

- To bake, unwrap casserole, cover with greased aluminum foil, and bake on foil-lined sheet in 400-degree oven until hot throughout, 20 to 25 minutes; remove foil and continue to bake until cheese is golden, about 20 minutes, before garnishing as directed

Our easy-to-make meaty tomato sauce helps to create a hearty lasagna without a lot of work.

Hearty Meat Lasagna

SERVES 8 **FREEZE IT**

ACTIVE TIME 1 HOUR

TOTAL TIME 1 HOUR 50 MINUTES

WHY THIS RECIPE WORKS We wanted a rich, ultrameaty lasagna that would impress the whole family at the next get-together—but we didn't want to spend all day making it. Determined to create a flavorful lasagna in 2 hours or less, we came up with several short-cuts. First, we made a quick meat sauce with meatloaf mix (ground beef, pork, and veal), tomatoes, and cream. For the cheese layer, we stuck with tradition and sprinkled mozzarella over a mixture of ricotta, Parmesan, fresh basil, and an egg, which helped thicken and bind the mixture. No-boil lasagna noodles eliminated the process of boiling and draining conventional lasagna noodles. Covering the lasagna with aluminum foil for the first part of baking helped the noodles soften; removing the foil for the last 25 minutes guaranteed a perfect golden-brown cheese layer on top. If you can't find meatloaf mix, use 8 ounces (85 percent lean) ground beef and 8 ounces ground pork.

SAUCE

2 tablespoons extra-virgin olive oil
1 onion, chopped fine
Salt and pepper
6 garlic cloves, minced
1 pound meatloaf mix
¼ cup heavy cream
1 (28-ounce) can tomato puree
1 (28-ounce) can diced tomatoes, drained
¼ cup chopped fresh basil

LASAGNA

24 ounces (3 cups) whole-milk or part-skim ricotta cheese
3 ounces Parmesan cheese, grated (1½ cups)
¼ cup chopped fresh basil
1 large egg, lightly beaten
½ teaspoon salt
½ teaspoon pepper
12 no-boil lasagna noodles
1 pound whole-milk mozzarella cheese, shredded (4 cups)

1. FOR THE SAUCE Heat oil in Dutch oven over medium heat until shimmering. Add onion, 1 teaspoon salt, and 1 teaspoon pepper and cook until softened, about 5 minutes. Stir in garlic and cook until fragrant, about 30 seconds. Add meatloaf mix and cook, breaking up meat with wooden spoon, until no longer pink, about 5 minutes. Stir in cream and simmer until liquid evaporates and only fat remains, about 4 minutes. Stir in tomato puree and tomatoes, bring to simmer, and cook until flavors meld, about 5 minutes. Off heat, stir in basil and season with salt and pepper to taste.

2. FOR THE LASAGNA Adjust oven rack to middle position and heat oven to 400 degrees. Combine ricotta, 1 cup Parmesan, basil, egg, salt, and pepper in bowl.

NOTES FROM THE TEST KITCHEN

No-Boil Noodles

No-boil (also called oven-ready) lasagna noodles are precooked at the factory; during baking, the moisture from the sauce softens, or rehydrates them. The most common no-boil noodle measures 7 inches long and 3½ inches wide; 3 noodles fit perfectly in a 13 by 9-inch dish, and 2 noodles fit nicely in an 8-inch square dish. Note that some no-boil lasagna noodle packages contain only 12 noodles; be sure to check the recipe for how many noodles are required. Our favorite brand is Barilla No-Boil Lasagne; we found these delicate, flat noodles closely resembled fresh pasta in texture.

3. Spread 1 cup sauce over bottom of 13 by 9-inch baking dish (avoiding large chunks of meat). Lay 3 noodles in dish, spread ⅓ cup ricotta mixture over each noodle, then top with 1 cup mozzarella and 1 cup sauce (in that order). Repeat layering process 2 more times. Top with remaining 3 noodles, remaining sauce, remaining 1 cup mozzarella, and remaining ½ cup Parmesan.

4. Cover dish tightly with greased aluminum foil, place on foil-lined rimmed baking sheet, and bake for 15 minutes. Uncover, and continue to bake until spotty brown and bubbling around edges, 25 to 35 minutes. Let casserole cool for 10 minutes before serving.

▶ TO MAKE AHEAD

- Lasagna, prepared through step 3, can be wrapped tightly in plastic wrap, covered with aluminum foil, and refrigerated for up to 24 hours or frozen for up to 1 month; if frozen, thaw completely in refrigerator
- To bake, unwrap lasagna, cover with greased aluminum foil, and bake on foil-lined sheet in 400-degree oven until hot throughout, about 1 hour; remove foil and continue to bake until cheese is golden, about 10 minutes

We leave the broccoli rabe crunchy so that it bakes to the perfect texture in our sausage lasagna.

Sausage and Broccoli Rabe Lasagna

SERVES 8 **FREEZE IT**

ACTIVE TIME 1 HOUR

TOTAL TIME 1 HOUR 50 MINUTES

WHY THIS RECIPE WORKS For an ultraflavorful take on our classic Hearty Meat Lasagna (page 128), we replaced the meatloaf mix with savory Italian sausage and added broccoli rabe. We sautéed the sausage briefly with the aromatics, but didn't let it brown to avoid an unpleasant pebbly texture in the finished lasagna. Our major challenge was to find a way to prevent the broccoli rabe from turning army green and mushy. To resolve this, we cut the parboiling time in half, from 2 minutes to 1 minute, leaving us with still-crunchy broccoli rabe that then cooked to an ideal texture when we baked the lasagna. Broccoli cut into 1-inch pieces can be substituted for the broccoli rabe.

SAUCE

 1 pound broccoli rabe, trimmed and cut into 1-inch pieces
   Salt and pepper
 2 tablespoons extra-virgin olive oil
 1 onion, chopped fine
 6 garlic cloves, minced
 1½ pounds hot or sweet Italian sausage, casings removed
 1 (28-ounce) can tomato puree
 1 (28-ounce) can diced tomatoes, drained

LASAGNA

 24 ounces (3 cups) whole-milk or part-skim ricotta cheese
 3 ounces Parmesan cheese, grated (1½ cups)
 ½ cup chopped fresh basil
 1 large egg, lightly beaten
 ½ teaspoon salt
 ½ teaspoon pepper
 12 no-boil lasagna noodles
 1 pound whole-milk mozzarella cheese, shredded (4 cups)

1. FOR THE SAUCE Bring 2 quarts water to boil in large pot. Fill large bowl halfway with ice and water. Add broccoli rabe and 1 tablespoon salt to boiling water and cook until crisp-tender, about 1 minute. Using slotted spoon, transfer broccoli rabe to ice water and let cool, about 2 minutes; drain and pat dry.

2. Dry now-empty pot, add oil, and heat over medium heat until shimmering. Add onion, 1 teaspoon salt, and 1 teaspoon pepper and cook until softened, about 5 minutes. Stir in garlic and cook until fragrant, about 30 seconds. Add sausage and cook, breaking up meat with wooden spoon, until no longer pink, about

5 minutes. Stir in broccoli rabe, tomato puree, and tomatoes, bring to simmer, and cook until flavors meld, about 5 minutes. Season with salt and pepper to taste.

3. FOR THE LASAGNA Adjust oven rack to middle position and heat oven to 400 degrees. Combine ricotta, 1 cup Parmesan, basil, egg, salt, and pepper in bowl.

4. Spread 1 cup sauce over bottom of 13 by 9-inch baking dish (avoiding large chunks of meat). Lay 3 noodles in dish, spread ⅓ cup ricotta mixture over each noodle, then top with 1 cup mozzarella and 1 cup sauce (in that order). Repeat layering process 2 more times. Top with remaining 3 noodles, remaining sauce, remaining 1 cup mozzarella, and remaining ½ cup Parmesan.

5. Cover dish tightly with greased aluminum foil, place on foil-lined rimmed baking sheet, and bake for 15 minutes. Uncover, and continue to bake until spotty brown and bubbling around edges, 25 to 35 minutes. Let casserole cool for 10 minutes before serving.

> **TO MAKE AHEAD**
>
> • Lasagna, prepared through step 4, can be wrapped tightly in plastic wrap, covered with aluminum foil, and refrigerated for up to 24 hours or frozen for up to 1 month; if frozen, thaw completely in refrigerator
> • To bake, unwrap lasagna, cover with greased aluminum foil, and bake on foil-lined sheet in 400-degree oven until hot throughout, about 1 hour; remove foil and continue to bake until cheese is golden, about 10 minutes

Roasted Zucchini and Eggplant Lasagna

SERVES 8

ACTIVE TIME 1 HOUR

TOTAL TIME 2 HOURS

WHY THIS RECIPE WORKS Vegetable lasagna recipes are often filled with watery, tasteless vegetables and weighed down by excess cheese. We wanted a flavorful vegetable lasagna that didn't fall into any of the usual traps. Eggplant and zucchini are easy to prep, making them excellent choices. Roasting the vegetables not only drove off excess liquid that would otherwise water down the sauce, but it also caramelized the vegetables, adding savory depth. Ricotta cheese is traditional in lasagna, but we found that it muted the roasted vegetable flavor, so we layered our lasagna with only mozzarella and Parmesan, which lent plenty of rich cheese flavor and gooey texture. No-boil noodles made quick work of the assembly. Be sure to grease the baking sheets before spreading the vegetables so they don't stick during roasting.

Omitting the ricotta from this hearty vegetable lasagna lets the flavor of the roasted vegetables shine.

SAUCE

1½ pounds zucchini, cut into ½-inch pieces

1½ pounds eggplant, cut into ½-inch pieces

5 tablespoons extra-virgin olive oil

9 garlic cloves, minced

   Salt and pepper

1 onion, chopped fine

1 (28-ounce) can crushed tomatoes

1 (28-ounce) can diced tomatoes

2 tablespoons chopped fresh basil

LASAGNA

12 no-boil lasagna noodles

12 ounces whole-milk mozzarella cheese, shredded (3 cups)

4 ounces Parmesan cheese, grated (2 cups)

1. FOR THE SAUCE Adjust oven racks to upper-middle and lower-middle positions and heat oven to 400 degrees. Toss zucchini and eggplant with 3 tablespoons oil, two-thirds of garlic, 1 teaspoon salt, and 1 teaspoon pepper. Spread vegetables in 2 greased rimmed baking sheets and bake, stirring occasionally, until softened and golden brown, 35 to 45 minutes; set aside.

2. Heat remaining 2 tablespoons oil in large saucepan over medium heat until shimmering. Add onion and cook until softened, about 5 minutes. Stir in remaining garlic and cook until fragrant, about 30 seconds. Stir in crushed tomatoes and diced tomatoes with their juice, bring to simmer, and cook until flavors meld, about 5 minutes. Off heat, stir in basil and season with salt and pepper to taste. (You should have 7 cups sauce. Add water as needed to reach 7 cups.)

3. FOR THE LASAGNA Spread 1 cup sauce over bottom of 13 by 9-inch baking dish. Lay 3 noodles in dish, spread one-quarter of vegetables over noodles, then top with 1 cup sauce, ⅔ cup mozzarella, and ½ cup Parmesan (in that order). Repeat layering process 2 more times. Top with remaining 3 noodles, remaining vegetables, remaining sauce, remaining 1 cup mozzarella, and remaining ½ cup Parmesan.

4. Cover dish tightly with greased aluminum foil, place on foil-lined rimmed baking sheet, and bake for 15 minutes. Uncover, and continue to bake until spotty brown and bubbling around edges, 25 to 35 minutes. Let casserole cool for 10 minutes before serving.

▶ TO MAKE AHEAD ▶

- Lasagna, prepared through step 3, can be refrigerated for up to 24 hours
- To bake, cover with greased aluminum foil and bake on foil-lined sheet in 400-degree oven until hot throughout, about 45 minutes; remove foil, and continue to bake until cheese is golden, about 10 minutes

Stuffed Shells with Amatriciana Sauce

SERVES 8

ACTIVE TIME 1 HOUR 10 MINUTES

TOTAL TIME 2 HOURS

WHY THIS RECIPE WORKS Stuffed shells are a satisfying weeknight pasta dish, so we set out to create a recipe that could be assembled in advance and go from refrigerator to oven without sacrificing flavor or texture. But when we reheated a batch of basic stuffed shells with marinara sauce, we found that the ricotta had turned watery, and the flavor of the sauce was washed out. A little Parmesan cheese and two eggs helped to bind the filling and prevent it from getting watery overnight, and mozzarella cheese gave the filling a rich, creamy texture. To amp up the flavor

A boldly flavored Amatriciana sauce with red pepper and pancetta makes these stuffed shells super flavorful.

of our sauce, we were inspired by the bold flavors of Italian Amatriciana sauce, with its smoky pancetta and kick of red pepper flakes. Those few simple ingredients ensured that the sauce was rich and flavorful once the casserole was baked. Crushed tomatoes provided a smooth sauce base with just the right amount of texture. When buying pancetta, ask to have it sliced ¼ inch thick. If you can't find pancetta, you can substitute 6 ounces of thick-cut, or slab, bacon.

SAUCE

    1 tablespoon extra-virgin olive oil
    6 ounces pancetta, cut into 1 by ¼-inch pieces
    1 onion, chopped fine
      Salt and pepper
  ¼ teaspoon red pepper flakes
    2 (28-ounce) cans crushed tomatoes

SHELLS

12 ounces jumbo pasta shells
   Salt
12 ounces (1½ cups) whole-milk or part-skim ricotta cheese
10 ounces whole-milk mozzarella cheese, shredded (2½ cups)
 3 ounces Parmesan cheese, grated (1½ cups)
 2 large eggs, lightly beaten
 6 tablespoons chopped fresh basil
 3 garlic cloves, minced

1. FOR THE SAUCE Heat oil in large saucepan over medium heat until shimmering. Add pancetta and cook until lightly browned and crisp, about 8 minutes. Using slotted spoon, transfer pancetta to paper towel–lined plate.

2. Pour off all but 3 tablespoons fat from saucepan, add onion and ¼ teaspoon salt and cook until softened, about 5 minutes. Stir in pepper flakes and cook until fragrant, about 30 seconds. Stir in tomatoes, bring to simmer, and cook until thickened slightly, about 10 minutes. Stir in pancetta and season with salt and pepper to taste.

3. FOR THE SHELLS Bring 4 quarts water to boil in large pot. Line rimmed baking sheet with clean dish towel. Add pasta and 1 tablespoon salt to boiling water and cook, stirring occasionally, until just beginning to soften, about 8 minutes. Drain pasta and transfer to prepared sheet. Using dinner fork, pry apart any shells that have clung together, discarding any that are badly torn (you should have 30 to 33 good shells).

4. Adjust oven rack to middle position and heat oven to 400 degrees. Combine ricotta, 1½ cups mozzarella, 1 cup Parmesan, eggs, ¼ cup basil, garlic, and ½ teaspoon salt in bowl; transfer to zipper-lock bag. Using scissors, cut off 1 corner of bag and pipe 1 tablespoon filling into each shell.

5. Spread 2 cups sauce over bottom of 13 by 9-inch baking dish. Arrange filled shells seam side down in dish. Spread remaining sauce over shells, then top with remaining 1 cup mozzarella and remaining ½ cup Parmesan.

FILLING SHELLS

Transfer ricotta mixture to zipper-lock bag and snip off 1 corner of bag. Pipe 1 tablespoon filling into each shell.

6. Cover dish tightly with greased aluminum foil, place on foil-lined rimmed baking sheet, and bake for 15 minutes. Uncover, and continue to bake until spotty brown and bubbling around edges, 25 to 35 minutes. Let casserole cool for 10 minutes. Sprinkle with remaining 2 tablespoons basil and serve.

TO MAKE AHEAD

- Casserole, prepared through step 5, can be refrigerated for up to 24 hours
- To bake, cover with greased aluminum foil and bake on foil-lined sheet in 400-degree oven until hot throughout, 25 to 35 minutes; remove foil and continue to bake until cheese is golden, about 10 minutes, before garnishing as directed

Baked Manicotti with Cheese Filling

SERVES 6 TO 8   **FREEZE IT**
ACTIVE TIME 1 HOUR
TOTAL TIME 1 HOUR 40 MINUTES

WHY THIS RECIPE WORKS Manicotti may look homey, but blanching and stuffing pasta tubes is a tedious chore, and the ricotta filling can be uninspired and watery. We wanted a simpler, better recipe that had all of the comforting, cheesy flavor but none of the fuss. We did away with the slippery pasta tubes and instead spread the filling onto no-boil lasagna noodles that we had briefly soaked in hot water to make them pliable enough to roll up easily. After baking the manicotti, we broiled the dish for a few minutes to give it a nicely bronzed crown. Note that some no-boil lasagna noodle packages contain only 12 noodles; this recipe requires 16 noodles.

SAUCE

 2 tablespoons extra-virgin olive oil
 3 garlic cloves, minced
 ½ teaspoon red pepper flakes (optional)
 2 (28-ounce) cans crushed tomatoes
 2 tablespoons chopped fresh basil
   Salt and pepper

MANICOTTI

1½ pounds (3 cups) whole-milk or part-skim ricotta cheese
 8 ounces whole-milk mozzarella cheese, shredded (2 cups)
 4 ounces Parmesan cheese, grated (2 cups)
 2 large eggs, lightly beaten
 2 tablespoons minced fresh parsley
 2 tablespoons chopped fresh basil
 ¾ teaspoon salt

No need to struggle with stuffing pasta tubes, as our recipe relies on soaked, no-boil noodles wrapped around the filling.

½   teaspoon pepper
16   no-boil lasagna noodles

1. FOR THE SAUCE Cook oil, garlic, and pepper flakes, if using, in large saucepan over medium heat until fragrant but not brown, about 2 minutes. Stir in tomatoes, bring to simmer, and cook until thickened slightly, about 15 minutes. Off heat, stir in basil and season with salt and pepper to taste.

2. FOR THE MANICOTTI Combine ricotta, mozzarella, 1 cup Parmesan, eggs, parsley, basil, salt, and pepper in bowl.

3. Pour 1 inch of boiling water into 13 by 9-inch broiler-safe baking dish. Slip noodles into water, 1 at a time. Let noodles soak, separating them with tip of knife to prevent sticking, until pliable, about 5 minutes. Remove noodles from water and place in single layer on clean dish towels. Discard water and dry baking dish.

4. Adjust oven rack to middle position and heat oven to 400 degrees. Spread 1½ cups sauce over bottom of now-empty dish. Working with several noodles at a time, spread ¼ cup ricotta mixture evenly over bottom three-quarters of each noodle. Roll noodles up around filling, then arrange seam side down in dish. Spread remaining sauce over manicotti.

5. Sprinkle manicotti with remaining 1 cup Parmesan, cover dish tightly with greased aluminum foil, place on foil-lined rimmed baking sheet, and bake until bubbling, about 40 minutes. Remove baking dish from oven. Adjust oven rack 6 inches from broiler element and heat broiler. Uncover dish and broil until Parmesan is spotty brown, 4 to 6 minutes. Let casserole cool for 10 minutes before serving.

VARIATIONS
Baked Manicotti with Prosciutto `FREEZE IT`
Arrange 1 piece of very thinly sliced prosciutto (you will need 16 slices, about 8 ounces total) on each noodle before spreading cheese filling and rolling manicotti.

Baked Manicotti Puttanesca `FREEZE IT`
Add 3 rinsed and minced anchovy fillets to saucepan with garlic. Add ¼ cup pitted and chopped kalamata olives and 2 tablespoons rinsed and minced capers to ricotta mixture.

TO MAKE AHEAD
- Casserole, prepared through step 4, can be wrapped tightly in plastic wrap, covered with aluminum foil, and refrigerated for up to 24 hours or frozen for up to 1 month; if frozen, thaw completely in refrigerator
- To bake, cover with greased aluminum foil and bake on foil-lined sheet in 375-degree oven until hot throughout, about 1 hour; remove foil and broil as directed in step 5

ASSEMBLING MANICOTTI

1. Working with several soaked noodles at a time, spread ¼ cup ricotta mixture evenly over bottom three-quarters of each noodle.

2. Roll noodles up around filling, then lay them seam side down in baking dish.

Pasta Salad with Pesto

SERVES 8 TO 10

ACTIVE TIME 45 MINUTES

TOTAL TIME 1 HOUR 15 MINUTES

WHY THIS RECIPE WORKS More light and refreshing than a cream-based sauce or a chunky ragu, pesto makes for an excellent accompaniment to pasta during the hot summer months. It couldn't be simpler to make; just process fresh basil, garlic, pine nuts, salty Parmesan cheese, and extra-virgin olive oil together in a food processor. However, a few challenges arose when we tried to transform the simple sauce into a cold pasta salad topping. When we tossed the pesto directly with hot pasta the sauce became separated and greasy as the pasta cooled. We found that spreading the pasta on a baking sheet for about half an hour before adding the pesto was enough to adequately combat the problem. To help prevent the pesto from turning dark over time we added a handful of baby spinach, which set the bright green color, but was mild enough in flavor to let the basil shine. Finally we found that adding some mayonnaise was the perfect way to give our pesto the clingy, thick texture ideal for a pasta salad. We finished off our salad by reserving some of the toasted pine nuts to add a nice nutty crunch and tossed in sweet cherry tomatoes for a bright burst of freshness. Other pasta shapes can be substituted for the farfalle.

This sturdy pesto pasta salad, with its combination of basil and spinach, stays fresh and brightly colored for days.

2	garlic cloves, unpeeled
1	pound farfalle
	Salt and pepper
5	tablespoons extra-virgin olive oil
3	cups fresh basil leaves, lightly bruised
1	cup baby spinach
¾	cup pine nuts, toasted
2	tablespoons lemon juice
1½	ounces Parmesan cheese, grated (¾ cup), plus extra for serving
6	tablespoons mayonnaise
12	ounces cherry tomatoes, quartered

1. Bring 4 quarts water to boil in large pot. Add garlic and cook for 1 minute. Remove garlic with slotted spoon and rinse under cold water to stop cooking. Let garlic cool slightly, then peel and chop fine; set aside.

2. Meanwhile, add pasta and 1 tablespoon salt to boiling water and cook, stirring often, until tender. Reserve ¼ cup cooking water. Drain pasta, toss with 1 tablespoon oil, and spread in single layer on rimmed baking sheet. Let pasta and cooking water cool to room temperature, about 30 minutes.

3. Process basil, spinach, ¼ cup pine nuts, lemon juice, garlic, and 1 teaspoon salt in food processor until smooth, about 30 seconds, scraping down sides of bowl as needed. Add Parmesan, mayonnaise, and remaining ¼ cup oil and process until thoroughly combined; transfer to large bowl.

4. Toss cooled pasta with pesto, adding reserved cooking water, 1 tablespoon at a time, until pesto evenly coats pasta.

5. Fold in remaining ½ cup pine nuts and tomatoes. Season with salt and pepper to taste. Serve.

TO MAKE AHEAD

- Cooled pasta can be tossed with half of pesto and refrigerated for up to 3 days; refrigerate remaining pesto separately, covered with 1 tablespoon extra-virgin olive oil
- To serve, microwave pasta to remove chill, 1 to 2 minutes, then toss pasta with reserved pesto, adding hot water as needed, 1 tablespoon at a time, until pasta is evenly coated, and continue with step 5

Cool and Creamy Macaroni Salad

SERVES 8 TO 10
ACTIVE TIME 45 MINUTES
TOTAL TIME 45 MINUTES

WHY THIS RECIPE WORKS Our creamy macaroni salad wraps pasta elbows and chopped celery and onion in a creamy dressing. We cooked the pasta until tender—not just al dente—and left a little moisture on it. The pasta absorbed the water rather than our creamy dressing (which could have left our salad dry and bland). We added a fair amount of lemon juice to the salad to balance the richness of the mayonnaise. This was one of the rare occasions in which we preferred garlic powder to fresh garlic because the flavor wasn't as sharp and the powder dissolved into the smooth dressing. Cooking the pasta until it is completely tender and leaving it slightly wet after rinsing are important for the texture of the finished salad.

  1 pound elbow macaroni
    Salt and pepper
  ½ cup finely chopped red onion
  1 celery rib, minced
  ¼ cup minced fresh parsley
  2 tablespoons lemon juice
  1 tablespoon Dijon mustard
  ⅛ teaspoon garlic powder
    Pinch cayenne pepper
1½ cups mayonnaise

1. Bring 4 quarts water to boil in large pot. Add macaroni and 1 tablespoon salt and cook, stirring often, until tender. Drain macaroni, rinse with cold water, and drain again, leaving macaroni slightly wet.

2. Toss macaroni, onion, celery, parsley, lemon juice, mustard, garlic powder, and cayenne together in large bowl and let sit until flavors are absorbed, about 2 minutes. Stir in mayonnaise and let sit until salad is no longer watery, 5 to 10 minutes. Season with salt and pepper to taste. Serve.

VARIATIONS
Cool and Creamy Macaroni Salad with Curry, Apple, and Golden Raisins
Increase cayenne to ¼ teaspoon and add 1 Granny Smith apple, cored and chopped, 1 cup golden raisins, ½ cup mango chutney, and 2 teaspoons curry powder to macaroni with onion and other flavorings.

We drain and then rinse macaroni, leaving it slightly wet, for a salad with the perfect texture.

Cool and Creamy Macaroni Salad with Sharp Cheddar and Chipotle
Add 1½ cups shredded extra-sharp cheddar cheese and 2 tablespoons minced canned chipotle chile in adobo sauce to macaroni with onion and other flavorings.

Cool and Creamy Macaroni Salad with Roasted Red Peppers and Capers
Add 1 cup jarred roasted red peppers, chopped, and 6 tablespoons drained capers, chopped, to macaroni with onion and other flavorings.

> **TO MAKE AHEAD**
> - Salad can be refrigerated for up to 2 days
> - To serve, toss salad with hot water as needed, 1 tablespoon at a time, until creamy; season with salt and pepper to taste

PESTO SAUCES

Flavorful pestos can be made with lots of different ingredients—from parsley and arugula to sun-dried tomatoes, cherry tomatoes, roasted red peppers, and more. Keeping pesto on hand in your fridge or freezer makes it easy to dress up plain pasta in a pinch. A good pesto has two basic requirements: You should use a high-quality extra-virgin olive oil (because its flavor will really shine through), and you should toast the garlic (to help tame its fiery, raw flavor). Note that the flavor and texture of these pestos vary quite a bit, which means that the amount you need to coat your pasta adequately will vary. **Note** All these recipes make enough pesto to sauce at least 1 pound of pasta.

TO MAKE PESTO Process all ingredients except oil and cheese in food processor until smooth, scraping down bowl as needed. With processor running, slowly add oil until incorporated. Transfer pesto to bowl, stir in cheese(s), and season with salt to taste. When tossing pesto with cooked pasta, add some of pasta cooking water as needed (up to ½ cup) to loosen consistency of pesto.

TO MAKE AHEAD

Pesto can be refrigerated for up to 3 days or frozen for up to 3 months; to prevent browning, press plastic wrap flush to surface, or top with thin layer of extra-virgin olive oil

CLASSIC BASIL PESTO
MAKES ¾ CUP **EASY** **FREEZE IT**
ACTIVE TIME 20 MINUTES
TOTAL TIME 20 MINUTES

Pounding the basil briefly before processing the pesto helps bring out its flavorful oils. To bruise the basil, place it in a large zipper-lock bag and pound lightly with a rolling pin or meat pounder. The optional parsley helps give the pesto a vibrant green hue. For sharper flavor, substitute Pecorino Romano for the Parmesan.

- 2 cups fresh basil leaves, lightly bruised
- 2 tablespoons fresh parsley leaves (optional)
- ¼ cup pine nuts, toasted
- 3 garlic cloves, toasted and minced
- 7 tablespoons extra-virgin olive oil
- ¼ cup grated Parmesan cheese

PARSLEY AND TOASTED NUT PESTO
MAKES 1½ CUPS **EASY** **FREEZE IT**
ACTIVE TIME 20 MINUTES
TOTAL TIME 20 MINUTES

Though basil is the go-to herb when making a green pesto, parsley makes a surprisingly delicious substitute. To balance out the grassy, heartier flavor of parsley, we found it necessary to ramp up the nut flavor. Pecans have a more pronounced flavor than pine nuts. You can substitute walnuts, blanched almonds, skinned hazelnuts, or any combination thereof for the pecans.

- 1 cup pecans, toasted
- ¼ cup fresh parsley leaves
- 3 garlic cloves, toasted and minced
- 7 tablespoons extra-virgin olive oil
- ¼ cup grated Parmesan cheese

ROASTED RED PEPPER PESTO
MAKES 1½ CUPS **EASY** **FREEZE IT**
ACTIVE TIME 20 MINUTES
TOTAL TIME 20 MINUTES

This pesto tastes great when made with homemade roasted red peppers, but jarred roasted red peppers work fine in this recipe. The pesto made with jarred peppers will have a more acidic flavor, so before using them be sure to rinse and dry the jarred peppers well.

- 2 roasted red bell peppers, peeled and chopped (1 cup)
- ¼ cup fresh parsley leaves
- 3 garlic cloves, toasted and minced
- 1 shallot, chopped
- 1 tablespoon fresh thyme leaves
- ½ cup extra-virgin olive oil
- ¼ cup grated Parmesan cheese

GREEN OLIVE AND ORANGE PESTO

MAKES 1½ CUPS `EASY` `FREEZE IT`

ACTIVE TIME 20 MINUTES

TOTAL TIME 20 MINUTES

Using high-quality green olives is crucial to the success of this pesto. Look for fresh green olives (packed in brine) in the supermarket's refrigerated section or at the salad bar.

1½ cups fresh parsley leaves
½ cup pitted green olives
½ cup slivered almonds, toasted
2 garlic cloves, toasted and minced
½ teaspoon grated orange zest plus 2 tablespoons juice
½ cup extra-virgin olive oil
1½ ounces Parmesan cheese, grated (¾ cup)

SUN-DRIED TOMATO PESTO

MAKES 1½ CUPS `EASY` `FREEZE IT`

ACTIVE TIME 20 MINUTES

TOTAL TIME 20 MINUTES

We prefer sun-dried tomatoes packed in oil over those that are packaged dried.

1 cup oil-packed sun-dried tomatoes, patted dry and chopped
¼ cup walnuts, toasted
3 garlic cloves, toasted and minced
½ cup extra-virgin olive oil
1 ounce Parmesan cheese, grated (½ cup)

TOASTING GARLIC

Toast unpeeled cloves in 8-inch skillet over medium heat, shaking pan occasionally, until color of cloves deepens slightly, about 7 minutes. Let toasted garlic cool slightly, then peel and mince.

KALE AND SUNFLOWER SEED PESTO

MAKES 1½ CUPS `EASY` `FREEZE IT`

ACTIVE TIME 20 MINUTES

TOTAL TIME 20 MINUTES

Kale, with its earthy, slightly bitter flavor, and sunflower seeds, with their strong flavor, are well matched here.

2 cups chopped kale leaves
1 cup fresh basil leaves
½ cup raw sunflower seeds, toasted
2 garlic cloves, toasted and minced
1 teaspoon red pepper flakes (optional)
½ cup extra-virgin olive oil
1½ ounces Parmesan cheese, grated (¾ cup)

PARSLEY, ARUGULA, AND RICOTTA PESTO

MAKES 1½ CUPS `EASY` `FREEZE IT`

ACTIVE TIME 20 MINUTES

TOTAL TIME 20 MINUTES

Do not use nonfat ricotta or the pesto will be dry and gummy.

1 cup fresh parsley leaves
1 cup baby arugula
¼ cup pine nuts, toasted
3 garlic cloves, toasted and minced
7 tablespoons extra-virgin olive oil
⅓ cup (3 ounces) whole-milk or part-skim ricotta cheese
2 tablespoons grated Parmesan cheese

Making the Most of Pesto

Sure, pesto tastes terrific on pasta, but don't sell it short; its robust, concentrated flavor can jazz up just about anything, from sandwiches and omelets to soups and salads. Because a few tablespoons can transform a dish from boring to best in show, it's always nice to have some pesto on hand. Here are some of our favorite ways to use pesto.

- Stir pesto into mashed potatoes for a simple twist on this classic comfort food
- Dollop pesto onto soups for a heady, herbal aroma
- Brush pesto on fish or chicken after roasting or grilling for a quick flavor boost
- Toss warm steamed veggies with pesto for an interesting riff on the weeknight side dish
- Use pesto in place of mayonnaise or mustard on deli sandwiches
- Thin pesto with lemon juice to make a quick vinaigrette
- Drizzle pesto over slices of pizza or calzones
- Use pesto to flavor fresh cheeses such as mozzarella or ricotta
- Use a few tablespoons of pesto as an easy marinade for chicken or fish
- Stir a couple of tablespoons of pesto into equal parts mayonnaise and sour cream for a quick dipping sauce
- Serve with veggies or chips

A bright vinaigrette rather than mayonnaise is the key to a make-ahead pasta salad with lots of fresh appeal.

Tortellini Salad with Asparagus and Fresh Basil Vinaigrette

SERVES 4 TO 6 **EASY**

ACTIVE TIME 30 MINUTES
TOTAL TIME 45 MINUTES

WHY THIS RECIPE WORKS For a super-easy pasta salad that would impress any picnic crowd, we paired convenient store-bought cheese tortellini with crisp asparagus and a dressing inspired by the flavors of classic pesto. First, we blanched the asparagus in the same water we later used to cook the tortellini, which instilled the pasta with the asparagus's delicate flavor. Once the tortellini were cooked, we tossed them in a bold dressing of extra-virgin olive oil, lemon juice, shallot, and garlic. To finish the salad, we tossed in some bright, juicy cherry tomatoes, fresh basil, grated Parmesan, and toasted pine nuts along with the blanched asparagus just before serving. Cooking the tortellini until it is completely tender and leaving it slightly wet after rinsing are important for the texture of the finished salad.

  1 pound thin asparagus, trimmed and cut into 1-inch lengths
    Salt and pepper

  1 pound dried cheese tortellini
  3 tablespoons lemon juice, plus extra for seasoning
  1 shallot, minced
  2 garlic cloves, minced
  ½ cup extra-virgin olive oil
  12 ounces cherry tomatoes, halved
  1 ounce Parmesan cheese, grated (½ cup)
  ¾ cup chopped fresh basil, mint, or parsley
  ¼ cup pine nuts, toasted

1. Bring 4 quarts water to boil in large pot. Fill large bowl halfway with ice and water. Add asparagus and 1 tablespoon salt to boiling water and cook until crisp-tender, about 2 minutes. Using slotted spoon, transfer asparagus to ice water and let cool, about 2 minutes; drain and pat dry.

2. Return pot of water to boil. Add tortellini and cook, stirring often, until tender. Drain tortellini, rinse with cold water, and drain again, leaving tortellini slightly wet.

3. Whisk lemon juice, shallot, garlic, 1 teaspoon salt, and ¾ teaspoon pepper together in large bowl. Whisking constantly, drizzle in oil. Add tortellini and toss to combine.

4. Add asparagus, tomatoes, Parmesan, basil, and pine nuts and gently toss to combine. Season with salt, pepper, and extra lemon juice to taste. Serve.

TO MAKE AHEAD

- Cooled tortellini can be tossed with half of vinaigrette; refrigerate tortellini mixture, cooked asparagus, and remaining vinaigrette separately for up to 2 days
- To serve, bring tortellini mixture, asparagus, and vinaigrette to room temperature; whisk vinaigrette to recombine, then stir ¼ cup boiling water and vinaigrette into tortellini mixture to refresh and continue with step 4

TRIMMING ASPARAGUS SPEARS

1. Remove 1 stalk of asparagus from bunch and bend it at thicker end until it snaps.

2. Using chef's knife, trim ends of remaining asparagus with broken asparagus as guide.

Slices of deli meat and cheese make this fusilli salad hearty enough for a main course.

Fusilli Salad with Salami, Provolone, and Sun-Dried Tomato Vinaigrette

SERVES 4   EASY

ACTIVE TIME 20 MINUTES
TOTAL TIME 30 MINUTES

WHY THIS RECIPE WORKS Pasta salad from the deli counter might be convenient, but that's about all it has going for it—the heavy dose of mayo, mushy pasta, and dull, overcooked vegetables translate into a disappointing dish. For a bold and satisfying pasta salad that wouldn't taste like a last-ditch dinner, we were inspired by traditional antipasto flavors. Thickly cut salami and provolone added a salty, savory bite and richness, and a handful of sliced kalamata olives added a brininess that helped to punch up the flavor. With several rich ingredients already in the mix, a mayonnaise-based dressing was overkill, so we swapped it out in favor of a bright olive oil–based vinaigrette accented with tangy sun-dried tomatoes, red wine vinegar, garlic, and basil. When left to marinate for a day or two, the pasta took on even more flavor; to loosen the dressing and quickly take the chill off the pasta, we stirred in a little boiling water. Chopped baby spinach added just before serving lent extra color and freshness. Other pasta shapes can be substituted for the fusilli.

> 8 ounces fusilli
>   Salt and pepper
> ¾ cup oil-packed sun-dried tomatoes, rinsed, patted dry, and minced, plus 2 tablespoons packing oil
> ¼ cup red wine vinegar, plus extra for seasoning
> 2 tablespoons chopped fresh basil or parsley
> 1 garlic clove, minced
> ¼ cup extra-virgin olive oil
> 4 (¼-inch-thick) slices deli salami or pepperoni (8 ounces), cut into 1-inch-long matchsticks
> 4 (¼-inch-thick) slices deli provolone (8 ounces), cut into 1-inch-long matchsticks
> ½ cup pitted kalamata olives, sliced
> 2 ounces (2 cups) baby spinach, chopped

1. Bring 4 quarts water to boil in large pot. Add pasta and 1 tablespoon salt and cook, stirring often, until tender. Drain pasta, rinse with cold water, and drain again, leaving pasta slightly wet.

2. Whisk sun-dried tomatoes, vinegar, basil, garlic, ¾ teaspoon salt, and ¾ teaspoon pepper together in large bowl. Whisking constantly, drizzle in olive oil and sun-dried tomato packing oil. Add pasta, salami, cheese, and olives and toss to combine.

3. Add spinach and gently toss to combine. Season with salt, pepper, and extra vinegar to taste. Serve.

> **TO MAKE AHEAD** ▶
> - Cooled fusilli can be tossed with salami, cheese, olives, and half of vinaigrette; refrigerate fusilli mixture and remaining vinaigrette separately for up to 2 days
> - To serve, bring fusilli mixture and vinaigrette to room temperature; whisk vinaigrette to recombine, then stir ¼ cup boiling water and vinaigrette into fusilli mixture to refresh and continue with step 3

With its vibrant mix of textures and flavors, this orzo salad makes a stunning side dish.

Orzo Salad with Broccoli and Radicchio

SERVES 4

ACTIVE TIME 45 MINUTES

TOTAL TIME 45 MINUTES

WHY THIS RECIPE WORKS To give this fresh orzo salad a variety of balanced flavors, we included broccoli, bitter radicchio, salty sun-dried tomatoes, and crunchy pine nuts. Cooking the orzo in the same water that we used to quickly blanch the broccoli imparted a delicate vegetal flavor throughout the dish and helped streamline the recipe. To ensure that the orzo was tender even when served cold, we cooked it al dente. To bring together all the flavors of the dish, we made a bold dressing with balsamic vinegar and honey. Toasting the pine nuts intensified their nutty flavor and brought further dimension to the orzo. Sharp Parmesan added the perfect salty accent, and a hefty dose of chopped basil

gave us a fresh finish to lighten this hearty dish. Cooking the pasta until it is completely tender and leaving it slightly wet after rinsing are important for the texture of the finished salad.

12 ounces broccoli florets, cut into 1-inch pieces
    Salt and pepper
1⅓ cups orzo
½ cup oil-packed sun-dried tomatoes, rinsed, patted dry, and minced, plus 3 tablespoons packing oil
¼ cup balsamic vinegar, plus extra for seasoning
1 garlic clove, minced
1 teaspoon honey
3 tablespoons extra-virgin olive oil
1 head radicchio (10 ounces), cored and chopped fine
2 ounces Parmesan cheese, grated (1 cup)
½ cup pine nuts, toasted
½ cup chopped fresh basil

1. Bring 4 quarts water to boil in large pot. Fill large bowl halfway with ice and water. Add broccoli and 1 tablespoon salt to boiling water and cook until crisp-tender, about 2 minutes. Using slotted spoon, transfer broccoli to ice water and let cool, about 2 minutes; drain and pat dry.

2. Return pot of water to boil. Add orzo and cook, stirring often, until tender. Drain orzo, rinse with cold water, and drain again, leaving orzo slightly wet.

3. Whisk sun-dried tomatoes, vinegar, garlic, honey, and 1 teaspoon salt together in large bowl. Whisking constantly, drizzle in olive oil and tomato packing oil. Add orzo and radicchio and toss to combine.

4. Add broccoli, Parmesan, pine nuts, and basil and gently toss to combine. Season with salt, pepper, and extra vinegar to taste. Serve.

TO MAKE AHEAD

- Cooled orzo can be tossed with radicchio and half of vinaigrette; refrigerate orzo mixture, cooked broccoli, and remaining vinaigrette separately for up to 2 days
- To serve, bring orzo mixture, broccoli, and vinaigrette to room temperature; whisk vinaigrette to recombine, then stir ¼ cup boiling water and vinaigrette into orzo mixture to refresh and continue with step 4

When making this easy soba noodle salad ahead, simply refresh it with hot water and extra oil before serving.

Cold Soba Noodle Salad

SERVES 4 **EASY**

ACTIVE TIME 30 MINUTES
TOTAL TIME 30 MINUTES

WHY THIS RECIPE WORKS Cold soba noodles are traditionally served with a dipping sauce that offers a delicate balance of Japanese flavors. For a fork-friendly take on this simple yet satisfying dish, we decided to turn the dipping sauce into a dressing. Soy sauce, mirin, and wasabi provided a flavorful base. Ginger added some heat, and thin slices of nori (dried seaweed) sprinkled over the top offered subtly briny, grassy notes. Peppery radishes and thinly sliced scallions added freshness and crunch. To prevent the cooked soba noodles from sticking together while we prepped the dressing, we tossed them with vegetable oil. To give this salad more heat, add additional wasabi paste to taste. Nori can be found in the international aisle at the supermarket or at an Asian market or a natural foods market. Do not substitute other types of noodles for the soba noodles here. Cooking the noodles until completely tender and leaving them slightly wet after rinsing are important for the texture of the finished salad.

14 ounces dried soba noodles
  Salt
 1 tablespoon vegetable oil
¼ cup soy sauce
 3 tablespoons mirin
½ teaspoon sugar
½ teaspoon grated fresh ginger
¼ teaspoon wasabi paste or powder
 4 radishes, trimmed and shredded
 2 scallions, sliced thin on bias
 1 (8 by 2½-inch) piece nori, cut into matchsticks
  with scissors

1. Bring 4 quarts water to boil in large pot. Add noodles and 1 tablespoon salt and cook, stirring often, until tender. Drain noodles, rinse with cold water, and drain again, leaving noodles slightly wet. Transfer noodles to large bowl and toss with oil.

2. Whisk soy sauce, mirin, sugar, ginger, and wasabi together in bowl, then pour over noodles. Add radishes and scallions and gently toss to combine. Sprinkle individual portions with nori before serving.

TO MAKE AHEAD

- Salad (without nori) can be refrigerated for up to 24 hours
- To serve, toss salad with hot water as needed, 1 tablespoon at a time, drizzle with oil, and sprinkle with nori

Sesame Noodles with Chicken

SERVES 4

ACTIVE TIME 45 MINUTES
TOTAL TIME 45 MINUTES

WHY THIS RECIPE WORKS For easy, authentic-tasting sesame noodles, we turned to everyday pantry staples to deliver the same addictive flavor. Grinding chunky peanut butter and toasted sesame seeds together made the perfect stand-in for hard-to-find Asian sesame paste. Garlic, ginger, soy sauce, rice vinegar, hot sauce, and brown sugar rounded out the sauce. For flavorful, tender chicken, we browned and then poached boneless, skinless chicken breasts, then shredded them. Scallions, shredded carrot, and red bell pepper lent the dish fresh flavor, color, and crunch. We prefer the flavor and texture of chunky peanut butter here; however, creamy peanut butter can be used. If you cannot find fresh Chinese egg noodles, substitute 12 ounces dried spaghetti or linguine. Cooking the noodles until completely tender and leaving them slightly wet after rinsing are important for the texture of the finished salad.

Grinding up crunchy peanut butter and toasted sesame seeds forms the base for the sauce that coats the noodles.

SAUCE

- 5 tablespoons soy sauce
- ¼ cup chunky peanut butter
- 3 tablespoons sesame seeds, toasted
- 2 tablespoons rice vinegar
- 2 tablespoons packed light brown sugar
- 1 tablespoon grated fresh ginger
- 2 garlic cloves, minced
- 1 teaspoon hot sauce
- ½ cup hot tap water

NOODLES

- 1½ pounds boneless, skinless chicken breasts, trimmed
  Salt and pepper
- 1 tablespoon vegetable oil
- 1 pound fresh Chinese noodles
- 1 tablespoon salt
- 2 tablespoons toasted sesame oil
- 4 scallions, sliced thin on bias

- 1 carrot, peeled and shredded
- 1 red bell pepper, stemmed, seeded, and cut into ½-inch pieces
- 2 tablespoons minced fresh cilantro
- 1 tablespoon sesame seeds, toasted

1. FOR THE SAUCE Process all ingredients except water in blender until smooth, about 30 seconds. With blender running, add hot water, 1 tablespoon at a time, until sauce has consistency of heavy cream (you may not need all of water).

2. FOR THE NOODLES Pat chicken dry with paper towels and season with salt and pepper. Heat vegetable oil in 12-inch skillet over medium-high heat until just smoking. Brown chicken well on first side, 6 to 8 minutes. Flip chicken, add ½ cup water, and cover. Reduce heat to medium-low and cook until chicken registers 160 degrees, 5 to 7 minutes. Transfer chicken to cutting board, let cool slightly, then shred into bite-size pieces using 2 forks; set aside.

3. Meanwhile, bring 4 quarts water to boil in large pot. Add noodles and salt and cook, stirring often, until tender. Drain noodles, rinse with cold water, and drain again, leaving noodles slightly wet. Transfer noodles to large bowl and toss with sesame oil.

4. Add sauce, shredded chicken, scallions, carrot, and bell pepper and gently toss to combine. Season with salt and pepper to taste. Sprinkle individual portions with cilantro and sesame seeds before serving.

TO MAKE AHEAD

- Sauce, cooled chicken, and noodle mixture, prepared through step 3, can be refrigerated separately for up to 2 days
- To serve, bring sauce, chicken, and noodle mixture to room temperature; stir ¼ cup boiling water into sauce to loosen, and continue with step 4

Simple Skillet Pizza

MAKES TWO 11-INCH PIZZAS
ACTIVE TIME 1 HOUR
TOTAL TIME 1 HOUR 25 MINUTES (PLUS 1 TO 1½ HOURS RISING TIME)

WHY THIS RECIPE WORKS Many recipes for homemade pizza require a serious time investment and call for specialized equipment like a baking stone or a pizza peel. We set out to develop a simpler, less time-consuming recipe. To avoid having to wait for a baking stone to heat up in the oven, we simply used a 12-inch skillet. The trick was to assemble the pizza in the skillet and start cooking it on the stovetop. This both heated up the skillet and started to cook the bottom crust. Once the bottom crust began to brown we simply slid the skillet into a very hot oven to finish cooking the pizza through and melt the cheese. We prefer to use our Easy Pizza Sauce (page 145) and homemade dough, but if you're pressed for time, you can substitute your favorite jarred sauce and 1 pound of premade dough from the supermarket or your local pizzeria. Feel free to sprinkle simple toppings over the pizza before baking, such as pepperoni, sautéed mushrooms, or browned sausage, but keep the toppings light or they may weigh down the thin crust and make it soggy.

DOUGH

2 cups plus 2 tablespoons (11⅔ ounces) bread flour
1⅛ teaspoons instant or rapid-rise yeast
¾ teaspoon salt
1 tablespoon olive oil
¾ cup warm water (110 degrees)

PIZZA

¼ cup extra-virgin olive oil
1 cup Easy Pizza Sauce (page 145)
¼ cup grated Parmesan cheese
6 ounces mozzarella cheese shredded (1½ cups)

1. FOR THE DOUGH Pulse flour, yeast, and salt together in food processor to combine, about 5 pulses. With processor running, add oil, then water, and process until rough ball forms, 30 to 40 seconds. Let dough rest for 2 minutes, then process for 30 seconds longer. (If after 30 seconds dough is very sticky and clings to blade, add extra flour as needed.)

2. Transfer dough to lightly floured counter and knead until smooth, about 1 minute. Shape dough into tight ball, place in large, lightly oiled bowl, and cover tightly with plastic wrap.

3. Place in warm spot and let dough rise until doubled in size, 1 to 1½ hours.

4. FOR THE PIZZA Adjust oven rack to upper-middle position and heat oven to 500 degrees. Grease 12-inch ovensafe skillet with 2 tablespoons oil.

5. Place dough on lightly floured counter, divide in half, and cover with greased plastic wrap. Working with 1 piece of dough at a time (keep other piece covered), use rolling pin to flatten dough into 11-inch round. Transfer dough to prepared skillet and reshape as needed. Using back of spoon, spread ½ cup sauce evenly over dough, leaving ½-inch border. Sprinkle 2 tablespoons Parmesan and ¾ cup mozzarella over sauce.

6. Set skillet over high heat and cook until outside edge of dough is set, pizza is lightly puffed, and bottom crust is spotty brown when gently lifted with spatula, about 3 minutes.

7. Transfer skillet to oven and bake pizza until edges are brown and cheese is melted and spotty brown, 7 to 10 minutes. Using potholders (skillet handle will be hot), remove skillet from oven and slide pizza onto wire rack. Let pizza cool for 5 minutes, then slice and serve. Wipe out skillet with paper towels and let cool slightly, then repeat with remaining ingredients to make second pizza.

TO MAKE AHEAD

Pizza dough, prepared through step 2, can be refrigerated for up to 16 hours; to bake, let sit at room temperature for 30 minutes and continue with step 4 (omitting step 3)

MAKING SKILLET PIZZA

1. Place dough on lightly floured counter, divide in half, and cover with greased plastic wrap. Roll 1 piece of dough into 11-inch round.

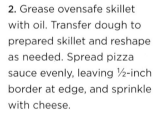

2. Grease ovensafe skillet with oil. Transfer dough to prepared skillet and reshape as needed. Spread pizza sauce evenly, leaving ½-inch border at edge, and sprinkle with cheese.

3. Set skillet over high heat and cook pizza until outside edge is set and bottom crust is spotty brown, about 3 minutes. Transfer skillet to oven and bake until edges are brown and cheese is melted and spotty brown.

Ultimate Thin-Crust Pizza

MAKES TWO 13-INCH PIZZAS **FREEZE IT**

ACTIVE TIME 1 HOUR

TOTAL TIME 1 HOUR 25 MINUTES (PLUS 25 HOURS RISING AND RESTING TIME)

WHY THIS RECIPE WORKS Although our Simple Skillet Pizza (page 142) is easy and tastes great, when we want authentic, parlor-quality pizza with long-fermented flavor, we turn to an overnight dough baked on a pizza stone. This recipe requires a bit of time to complete, and although much of that time is hands-off, we wanted to make sure our time investment was worthwhile so we set out to perfect our crust. We opted for high-protein bread flour, which resulted in a chewy, nicely tanned crust. The right proportions of flour, water, and yeast gave us dough that would stretch and would retain moisture as it baked. We kneaded the dough quickly in a food processor and then let it proof in the refrigerator for at least a day to develop its flavors. After we shaped and topped the pizza, it went onto a blazing-hot baking stone to cook. Placing the stone near the top of the oven allowed the top as well as the bottom of the pizza to brown. We recommend King Arthur brand bread flour. Some baking stones can crack under the intense heat of the broiler; be sure to check the manufacturer's website. It is important to use ice water in the dough to prevent it from overheating in the food processor. Shape the second dough ball while the first pizza bakes, but don't top the pizza until right before you bake it. If you add more toppings, keep them light or they may weigh down the thin crust.

DOUGH

- 3 cups (16½ ounces) bread flour
- 2 tablespoons sugar
- ½ teaspoon instant or rapid-rise yeast
- 1⅓ cups ice water
- 1 tablespoon vegetable oil
- 1½ teaspoons salt

PIZZA

- 1 cup Easy Pizza Sauce (recipe follows)
- 1 ounce Parmesan cheese, grated fine (½ cup)
- 8 ounces whole-milk mozzarella cheese, shredded (2 cups)

1. FOR THE DOUGH Pulse flour, sugar, and yeast in food processor until combined, about 5 pulses. With processor running, slowly add ice water and process until dough is just combined

Letting the pizza dough proof for 24 hours in the refrigerator adds flavor and prevents it from puffing up in the oven.

and no dry flour remains, about 10 seconds. Let dough rest for 10 minutes.

2. Add oil and salt to dough and process until dough forms satiny, sticky ball that clears sides of bowl, 30 to 60 seconds. Transfer dough to lightly oiled counter and knead by hand to form smooth, round ball, about 30 seconds. Place dough seam side down in lightly greased large bowl or container, cover tightly with plastic wrap, and refrigerate for at least 24 hours.

3. FOR THE PIZZA One hour before baking, adjust oven rack 4 inches from broiler element, set baking stone on rack, and heat oven to 500 degrees. Press down on dough to deflate. Transfer dough to clean counter, divide in half, and cover loosely with greased plastic. Pat 1 piece of dough (keep remaining piece covered) into 4-inch round. Working around circumference of dough, fold edges toward center until ball forms.

4. Flip ball seam side down and, using your cupped hands, drag in small circles on counter until dough feels taut and round and all seams are secured on underside. (If dough sticks to your hands, lightly dust top of dough with flour.) Repeat with remaining piece of dough. Space dough balls 3 inches apart, cover loosely with greased plastic, and let rest for 1 hour.

5. Heat broiler for 10 minutes. Meanwhile, coat 1 dough ball generously with flour and place on well-floured counter. Using your fingertips, gently flatten into 8-inch round, leaving 1 inch of outer edge slightly thicker than center. Using your hands, gently stretch dough into 12-inch round, working along edge and giving disk quarter turns.

6. Transfer dough to well-floured pizza peel and stretch into 13-inch round. Using back of spoon or ladle, spread ½ cup tomato sauce in even layer over surface of dough, leaving ¼-inch border around edge. Sprinkle ¼ cup Parmesan evenly over sauce, followed by 1 cup mozzarella.

7. Slide pizza carefully onto baking stone and return oven to 500 degrees. Bake until crust is well browned and cheese is bubbly and partially browned, 8 to 10 minutes, rotating pizza halfway through baking. Transfer pizza to wire rack and let cool for 5 minutes before slicing and serving. Heat broiler for 10 minutes. Repeat with remaining dough, sauce, and toppings, returning oven to 500 degrees when pizza is placed on stone.

TO MAKE AHEAD

- Pizza dough, prepared through step 2, can be refrigerated for up to 3 days
- Pizza dough balls, prepared through step 4 (minus the 1 hour rest), can be frozen for up to 2 weeks; thaw completely in refrigerator before continuing with step 5

EASY PIZZA SAUCE

MAKES 2 CUPS **EASY** **FREEZE IT**
ACTIVE TIME 10 MINUTES
TOTAL TIME 10 MINUTES

While it is convenient to use jarred pizza sauce, we think it is almost as easy (and a lot tastier) to whip up your own. This recipe will yield more than is needed in our Simple Skillet Pizza (page 142) or our Ultimate Thin-Crust Pizza (page 144) but the extra freezes well.

1 (28-ounce) can whole peeled tomatoes drained with juice reserved
1 tablespoon extra-virgin olive oil
1 teaspoon red wine vinegar
2 garlic cloves minced
1 teaspoon dried oregano
½ teaspoon salt
¼ teaspoon pepper

Process drained tomatoes with oil, vinegar, garlic, oregano, salt, and pepper in food processor until smooth, about 30 seconds. Transfer mixture to liquid measuring cup and add reserved tomato juice until sauce measures 2 cups.

TO MAKE AHEAD

Sauce can be refrigerated for up to 1 week or frozen for up to 1 month; if frozen, thaw completely in refrigerator

SHAPING AND BAKING THIN CRUST PIZZA DOUGH

1. Flip each ball of dough seam side down and drag in circles on counter until dough feels taut and seams are secured.

2. After dough rests, coat with flour, place on floured counter, flatten into 8-inch round, then and stretch into 12-inch round.

3. Transfer dough to floured pizza peel and stretch into 13-inch round. Spread ½ cup tomato sauce in even layer over dough and add cheese.

4. Slide pizza onto baking stone and return oven to 500 degrees. Bake 8 to 10 minutes, rotating pizza halfway through baking.

■ EASY (30 minutes or less active time)   ■ FREEZE IT
Photo: Curried Chicken and Coconut Rice Casserole with Lime-Yogurt Sauce

Toasted bread and hazelnuts thicken a romesco sauce made with jarred roasted red peppers, smoked paprika, and honey.

Pan-Seared Chicken Breasts with Romesco Sauce

SERVES 4

ACTIVE TIME 40 MINUTES

TOTAL TIME 1 HOUR

WHY THIS RECIPE WORKS Looking to create a simple sauce that would provide a boost in flavor and richness to quick-cooking chicken breasts, we found inspiration in the classic Spanish sauce, romesco. To keep things simple, we used a combination of boldly flavored jarred and no-cook ingredients to build our sauce. Our version was a thick, coarse mixture of roasted red peppers, toasted hazelnuts and cubed bread, sherry vinegar, olive oil, smoked paprika, and garlic that we whirled together in the food processor. The roasted red peppers and paprika provided a sweet smokiness, the sherry vinegar gave the sauce an acidic punch, and the under-pinning of nuts and bread lent texture and body, as well as brought all the other ingredients together. A teaspoon of honey helped bring all the flavors into focus. Best of all, this complex, flavorful sauce came together in no time. Sprinkling the chicken breasts with an ultrasimple mixture of paprika, salt, and pepper seasoned

them nicely and didn't steal attention from the sauce. After just a few minutes in the skillet, the chicken was juicy and cooked through. You will need at least a 12-ounce jar of roasted red peppers for this recipe.

SAUCE

- ½ slice hearty white sandwich bread, cut into ½-inch pieces
- ¼ cup hazelnuts, skinned
- 2 tablespoons extra-virgin olive oil
- 2 garlic cloves, sliced thin
- 1 cup jarred roasted red peppers, rinsed and patted dry
- 1½ tablespoons sherry vinegar
- 1 teaspoon honey
- ½ teaspoon smoked paprika
- ½ teaspoon salt
  Pinch cayenne pepper

CHICKEN

- ½ teaspoon smoked paprika
- ½ teaspoon salt
- ¼ teaspoon pepper
- 4 (6- to 8-ounce) boneless, skinless chicken breasts, trimmed
- 2 tablespoons vegetable oil

1. FOR THE SAUCE Cook bread, hazelnuts, and 1 tablespoon oil in 12-inch skillet over medium heat, stirring constantly, until bread and hazelnuts are lightly toasted, about 3 minutes. Add garlic and cook, stirring constantly, until fragrant, about 30 seconds. Transfer mixture to food processor and pulse until coarsely chopped, about 5 pulses. Add red peppers, vinegar, honey, paprika, salt, cayenne, and remaining 1 tablespoon oil to processor and pulse until finely chopped, 5 to 8 pulses. Transfer sauce to bowl and set aside for serving.

2. FOR THE CHICKEN Combine paprika, salt, and pepper in bowl. Pat chicken dry with paper towels and sprinkle spice mixture evenly over chicken; let sit for at least 20 minutes.

3. Heat oil in 12-inch nonstick skillet over medium-high heat until just smoking. Add chicken and cook until golden and registers 160 degrees, about 6 minutes per side. Transfer chicken to carving board, tent with foil, and let rest for 5 minutes. Serve with sauce.

> **TO MAKE AHEAD**
> - Sauce can be refrigerated for up to 2 days
> - Seasoned chicken, prepared through step 2, can be refrigerated for up to 24 hours
> - To cook, bring sauce to room temperature, pat chicken dry with paper towels, and continue with step 3

Pan-Seared Chicken Breasts with Sun-Dried Tomato Sauce

Omit honey, smoked paprika, and cayenne. Substitute ¼ cup pine nuts for hazelnuts, 1 small tomato, cored and cut into ½-inch pieces, and ½ cup oil-packed sun-dried tomatoes for red peppers, and 2 tablespoons balsamic vinegar for sherry vinegar. Add 2 table-spoons chopped fresh basil to food processor with tomato.

Pan-Seared Chicken Breasts with Olive-Orange Sauce

Omit smoked paprika and cayenne. Cut away peel and pith from 1 orange. Quarter orange, then slice crosswise into ½-inch-thick pieces. Substitute ¼ cup slivered almonds for hazelnuts; orange pieces and ¾ cup pitted kalamata olives for red peppers; and 1½ tablespoons red wine vinegar for sherry vinegar. Add ¼ teaspoon fennel seeds to skillet with garlic and 2 tablespoons chopped fresh mint to food processor with orange.

Pan-Seared Chicken Breasts with Chickpea Salad

SERVES 4 **EASY**

ACTIVE TIME 30 MINUTES
TOTAL TIME 55 MINUTES

WHY THIS RECIPE WORKS For an updated version of a quick and easy seared chicken breast dinner we turned to the flavors of the Mediterranean, pairing boneless, skinless chicken breasts with a flavorful and easy-to-prepare chickpea salad. A robust dressing of fruity extra-virgin olive oil, tangy lemon juice, and floral honey enhanced with smoked paprika and cumin was the perfect complement to the slightly nutty chickpeas and did double duty a reserved amount made an excellent marinade for our chicken. A quick stovetop sear produced golden brown, juicy chicken that we served whole atop our salad. We found that soaking and cooking the chickpeas from scratch was unnecessary and overly time-consuming, so we opted for canned chickpeas to simplify the dish. Adding thinly sliced red onion to the salad provided a subtle heat and nice crunch. Finally, a sprinkle of freshly torn mint leaves lent a bright, herbal finish and pop of green color to this quick, flavor-packed dish.

 6 tablespoons extra-virgin olive oil
 2 teaspoons honey
1½ teaspoon smoked paprika
 1 teaspoon ground cumin
   Salt and pepper
 4 (6- to 8-ounce) boneless, skinless chicken breasts, trimmed
 ¼ cup lemon juice (2 lemons)

Our simple marinade infuses mild chicken breasts with flavor and also acts as a dressing base for the chickpea salad.

 2 (15-ounce) cans chickpeas, rinsed
 ½ red onion, sliced thin
 ¼ cup torn fresh mint

1. Whisk 5 tablespoons oil, honey, paprika, cumin, ½ teaspoon salt, and ½ teaspoon pepper together in bowl. Transfer 2 table-spoons oil mixture into large bowl, add chicken, and toss to coat; let sit for at least 20 minutes. Whisk lemon juice into remaining oil mixture in bowl, then stir in chickpeas and onion.

2. Pat chicken dry with paper towels. Heat remaining 1 table-spoon oil in 12-inch nonstick skillet over medium-high heat until just smoking. Add chicken and cook until golden and registers 160 degrees, about 6 minutes per side. Transfer chicken to carving board, tent with foil, and let rest for 5 minutes.

3. Stir mint into chickpea mixture and season with salt and pepper to taste. Serve with chicken.

TO MAKE AHEAD

Seasoned chicken and chickpea mixture, prepared through step 1, can be refrigerated separately for up to 24 hours

Chicken Baked in Foil with Sweet Potatoes and Radishes

SERVES 4

ACTIVE TIME 45 MINUTES

TOTAL TIME 1 HOUR 10 MINUTES

WHY THIS RECIPE WORKS Despite its reputation for delivering bland, boring food, steaming in a pouch (we use aluminum foil) is actually an excellent way to cook delicate boneless, skinless chicken breasts. Besides being healthy, this method is fast and convenient, it keeps food moist, and the packets are easy to store in the fridge, making them an ideal prep-ahead dinner. We solved the bland problem by adding flavorful ingredients like sweet potatoes, celery, and radishes. The hardy sweet potatoes protected the delicate chicken from the hot baking sheet and absorbed flavor from the chicken as it cooked. The crunch of celery and the bright, peppery flavor of the radishes were a nice complement to the earthy sweet potatoes. Nutty sesame oil, sliced garlic, and red onion provided an aromatic flavor base. Fresh ginger and spicy red pepper flakes gave the dish bold flavor. A couple of tablespoons of rice vinegar and cilantro added just before serving contributed brightness to round out this dish. To ensure even cooking, buy chicken breasts of the same size. If using table salt, use only ⅛ teaspoon for each entire breast.

¼ cup extra-virgin olive oil

6 garlic cloves, sliced thin

1 tablespoon grated fresh ginger

1 teaspoon toasted sesame oil

¼ teaspoon red pepper flakes

12 ounces sweet potatoes, peeled and sliced crosswise ¼ inch thick

4 radishes, trimmed and quartered

2 celery ribs, quartered lengthwise and cut into 2-inch lengths

½ large red onion, sliced ½ inch thick, layers separated Kosher salt and pepper

4 (6- to 8-ounce) boneless, skinless chicken breasts, trimmed

2 tablespoons rice vinegar

2 tablespoons minced fresh cilantro

1. Adjust oven rack to lowest position and heat oven to 475 degrees. Spray centers of four 20 by 12-inch sheets of aluminum foil with vegetable oil spray. Microwave olive oil, garlic, ginger, sesame oil, and pepper flakes in small bowl until garlic begins to brown, about 1 minute. Combine potatoes, radishes, celery, onion, ½ teaspoon salt, and garlic oil in large bowl.

For Chicken Baked in Foil with Potatoes and Carrots, hardy potatoes protect the chicken breasts from overcooking.

2. Pat chicken dry with paper towels. Sprinkle each side of each chicken breast with ⅛ teaspoon salt, then season with pepper. Position 1 piece of prepared foil with long side parallel to edge of counter. In center of foil, arrange one-quarter of potato slices in 2 rows perpendicular to edge of counter. Lay 1 chicken breast on top of potato slices. Place one-quarter of vegetables around chicken. Repeat with remaining prepared foil, remaining potato slices, remaining chicken, and remaining vegetables. Drizzle any remaining oil mixture from bowl over chicken.

3. Bring short sides of foil together and crimp to seal tightly. Crimp remaining open ends of packets, leaving as much headroom as possible inside packets.

4. Place packets on rimmed baking sheet and bake until chicken registers 160 degrees, 18 to 23 minutes. (To check temperature, poke thermometer through foil of 1 packet and into chicken.) Let chicken rest in packets for 3 minutes.

5. Transfer chicken packets to individual serving plates, open carefully (steam will escape), and slide contents onto plates. Drizzle rice vinegar over chicken and vegetables and sprinkle with cilantro. Serve.

VARIATION

Chicken Baked in Foil with Potatoes and Carrots

Substitute 12 ounces Yukon Gold potatoes (unpeeled, sliced ¼ inch thick) and 2 carrots (peeled, quartered lengthwise and cut into 2-inch lengths), for sweet potatoes, radishes, and celery; substitute lemon juice for rice vinegar. Substitute 1 teaspoon minced fresh thyme for ginger and 2 tablespoons minced fresh chives for cilantro.

TO MAKE AHEAD ▶

Chicken packets, prepared through step 3, can be refrigerated for up to 24 hours

MAKING A FOIL PACKET

1. Arrange one-quarter of potato slices in 2 rows.

2. Lay 1 chicken breast on top of potato slices and arrange one-quarter of vegetables around chicken.

3. Bring short sides of foil together and crimp edges to seal.

4. Crimp open edges at either end of packet together to seal, leaving as much headroom as possible.

All of the prep work for this flavorful stir-fry can be done ahead of time to create a ready-to-cook meal.

Stir-Fried Chicken with Snap Peas and Shiitakes

SERVES 4
ACTIVE TIME 40 MINUTES
TOTAL TIME 1 HOUR

WHY THIS RECIPE WORKS In order for our stir-fry to be make-ahead friendly, we needed to choose our ingredients carefully. We tested several vegetables, and ultimately decided on the combination of rich, meaty shiitake mushrooms and crisp, fresh sugar snap peas. Both the mushrooms and snap peas stood up well to being prepped and stored; plus, they cooked at a similar rate. We made a flavorful, umami-packed sauce from soy sauce, sherry, brown sugar, ginger, garlic, and orange zest. "Velveting" the chicken, or marinating in a combination of cornstarch and oil (we used sesame oil for flavor), helped prevent stringiness and encouraged the sauce to cling to the meat. We found that we could boost the flavor of our chicken even further by mixing a small amount of our sauce with our velveting mixture. We were happy to find that letting

POULTRY   151

the chicken sit in the mixture overnight had no adverse effects. We topped our stir-fry with peanuts for crunch and thinly sliced scallions for a fresh onion bite. Serve with rice.

¼ cup soy sauce

¼ cup dry sherry

¼ cup packed brown sugar

1 tablespoon toasted sesame oil

1 (2-inch) piece fresh ginger, peeled and grated

2 garlic cloves, minced

1 teaspoon grated orange zest plus ¼ cup juice

1 pound boneless, skinless chicken breasts, trimmed, halved lengthwise, then sliced thin crosswise

3 tablespoons cornstarch

3 tablespoons vegetable oil

8 ounces shiitake mushrooms, stemmed and sliced ¼ inch thick

8 ounces sugar snap peas, strings removed and halved crosswise on bias

¼ cup dry-roasted peanuts, chopped

2 scallions, sliced thin on bias

1. Combine soy sauce, sherry, sugar, sesame oil, ginger, garlic, and orange zest in bowl. Transfer 3 tablespoons soy sauce mixture to second bowl, add chicken and cornstarch, and toss to coat; let sit for 20 minutes. Whisk orange juice into remaining soy sauce mixture.

2. Heat 1 tablespoon vegetable oil in 12-inch nonstick skillet over high heat until just smoking. Add half of chicken, breaking up any clumps, and cook without stirring for 1 minute. Stir chicken and continue to cook until lightly browned, about 30 seconds; transfer to clean bowl. Repeat with 1 tablespoon vegetable oil and remaining chicken.

3. Heat remaining 1 tablespoon vegetable oil in now-empty skillet over high heat until just smoking. Add mushrooms and snap peas and cook, stirring occasionally, until mushrooms are softened and snap peas are spotty brown, about 4 minutes.

4. Return chicken to skillet with vegetables, whisk sauce to recombine, then add to skillet. Cook, tossing constantly, until sauce is thickened, about 1 minute. Off heat, sprinkle with peanuts and scallions. Serve.

TO MAKE AHEAD

Marinated chicken and sauce, prepared through step 1, and prepped vegetables can be refrigerated separately for up to 24 hours

Using plenty of salt in our marinade helps to keep the small pieces of chicken moist over the intense heat of the grill.

Grilled Chicken Kebabs

SERVES 4 TO 6
ACTIVE TIME 50 MINUTES
TOTAL TIME 2 HOURS

WHY THIS RECIPE WORKS Grilled chicken kebabs should feature chunks of juicy chicken with lightly charred exteriors, but often they turn out dry. We thought an overnight marinade would be the perfect solution to this problem. We knew we wanted a salty base that would act like a brine, seasoning the chicken and encouraging juiciness, and we wanted to include ingredients that would boost the chicken's mild flavor. We turned to a combination of fresh herbs, shallot, and a small amount of sugar, which we combined in a food processor to eliminate tedious chopping. While we didn't want the marinade to be overly sweet, we found that a little sugar encouraged the chicken to brown during its short time on the grill, and the sweetness also helped to temper the flavor of the raw shallot. We reserved some of the marinade to pour over the cooked kebabs to reinforce their flavor, and we found that adding a little lemon juice did wonders to brighten up the finished dish. You will need eight 12-inch metal skewers for this recipe.

½ cup plus 1 tablespoon extra-virgin olive oil

½ cup water

¼ cup fresh parsley leaves

2 tablespoons fresh thyme leaves

1 shallot, chopped

1 tablespoon sugar

1 teaspoon salt

¼ teaspoon pepper

1 tablespoon lemon juice

1 large red onion, halved through root end, core discarded, each half cut into 4 wedges, and each wedge cut crosswise into thirds

2 pounds boneless, skinless chicken breasts, trimmed and cut into 1½-inch pieces

2 red bell peppers, stemmed, seeded, and cut into 1-inch pieces

1. Process ½ cup oil, water, parsley, thyme, shallot, sugar, salt, and pepper in food processor until smooth, about 20 seconds. Transfer ¼ cup marinade to small bowl and stir in lemon juice; set aside.

2. Gently toss onion pieces with remaining 1 tablespoon oil in separate bowl. Microwave, covered, until just tender, 3 to 5 minutes. Thread chicken, onion, and bell peppers evenly onto eight 12-inch metal skewers. Arrange skewers in 13 by 9-inch baking dish, pour remaining marinade over top, and turn to coat. Cover and refrigerate kebabs for at least 1 hour, turning occasionally to coat evenly.

3A. FOR A CHARCOAL GRILL Open bottom vent completely. Light large chimney starter half filled with charcoal briquettes (3 quarts). When top coals are partially covered with ash, pour evenly over grill. Set cooking grate in place, cover, and open lid vent completely. Heat grill until hot, about 5 minutes.

3B. FOR A GAS GRILL Turn all burners to high, cover, and heat grill until hot, about 15 minutes. Turn all burners to medium.

4. Meanwhile, pat kebabs dry with paper towels. Clean and oil cooking grate. Place kebabs on grill and cook (covered if using gas), turning often, until kebabs are well browned on all sides and chicken registers 160 degrees, 14 to 18 minutes.

5. Transfer kebabs to serving platter. Stir reserved marinade to recombine, then drizzle over kebabs. Tent with aluminum foil and let rest for 5 to 10 minutes. Serve.

TO MAKE AHEAD

- Kebabs and reserved lemon-oil mixture, prepared through step 2, can be refrigerated separately for up to 24 hours
- To cook, bring reserved lemon-oil mixture to room temperature and continue with step 3

NOTES FROM THE TEST KITCHEN

Buying Chicken

Here's what you need to know when buying chicken.

DECIPHERING LABELS A lot of labeling doesn't (necessarily) mean much. Companies can exploit loopholes to qualify for "Natural/All-Natural," "Hormone-Free," and "Vegetarian Diet/Fed" labeling. "USDA Organic," however, isn't all hype: The chickens must eat all organic feed without animal by-products, be raised without antibiotics, and have access to the outdoors.

PAY ATTENTION TO PROCESSING Our research showed that processing is the major player in chicken's texture and flavor. We found that brands labeled "water-chilled" (soaked in a water bath in which they absorb up to 14 percent of their weight in water, which you pay for since chicken is sold by the pound) or "enhanced" (injected with broth and flavoring) are unnaturally spongy and are best avoided. Labeling law says water gain must be shown on the product label, so these should be easily identifiable. When buying whole chickens or chicken parts, look for those that are labeled "air-chilled." Without the excess water weight, these brands are less spongy (but still plenty juicy) and have more chicken flavor.

BONELESS, SKINLESS BREASTS AND CUTLETS Try to pick a package with breasts of similar size, and pound them to an even thickness so they will cook at the same rate. You can buy cutlets ready to go at the grocery store, but we don't recommend it. These cutlets are usually ragged and of various sizes; it's better to cut your own cutlets from breasts.

BONE-IN PARTS You can buy a whole chicken or chicken parts at the supermarket, but sometimes it's hard to tell by looking at the package if it's been properly butchered. If you have a few minutes of extra time, consider buying a whole chicken and butchering it yourself.

WHOLE CHICKENS Whole chickens come in various sizes. Broilers and fryers are younger chickens that weigh 2½ to 4½ pounds. A roaster (or "oven-stuffer roaster") is an older chicken and usually weighs between 5 and 7 pounds. Stewing chickens, which are older laying hens, are best used for stews since the meat is tougher and more stringy. A 3½- to 4-pound bird will feed three or four people.

Boneless chicken thighs give this traditional taco filling better flavor than the typical breasts.

Shredded Chicken Tacos

SERVES 6   **FREEZE IT**

ACTIVE TIME 1 HOUR 15 MINUTES
TOTAL TIME 1 HOUR 30 MINUTES

WHY THIS RECIPE WORKS *Tinga de pollo* is a traditional taco filling that typically combines shredded chicken breast meat with a flavorful tomato-chipotle sauce. For deeper flavor, we chose boneless thighs and cooked them directly in the sauce. Fire-roasted tomatoes increased smokiness, and a little brown sugar and lime juice and zest further boosted the complexity. Simmering the cooked shredded chicken in the sauce before serving allowed the sauce to thicken and the flavors to meld and penetrate the meat. If you can't find Cotija cheese, use farmer's cheese or feta instead.

CHICKEN
2 pounds boneless, skinless chicken thighs, trimmed
  Salt and pepper
2 tablespoons vegetable oil
1 onion, halved and sliced thin
3 garlic cloves, minced
1 teaspoon ground cumin

¼ teaspoon ground cinnamon
1 (14.5-ounce) can fire-roasted diced tomatoes
½ cup chicken broth
2 tablespoons minced canned chipotle chile in adobo sauce plus 2 teaspoons adobo sauce
½ teaspoon brown sugar
1 teaspoon grated lime zest plus 2 tablespoons juice

TACOS
12 (6-inch) corn tortillas, warmed
1 avocado, halved, pitted, and cut into ½-inch pieces
2 ounces Cotija cheese, crumbled (½ cup)
6 scallions, minced
  Fresh cilantro leaves
  Lime wedges

1. FOR THE CHICKEN Pat chicken dry with paper towels and season with salt and pepper. Heat 1 tablespoon oil in Dutch oven over medium-high heat until shimmering. Add half of chicken and brown on both sides, 3 to 4 minutes per side. Transfer to large plate and repeat with remaining chicken.

2. Reduce heat to medium, add remaining 1 tablespoon oil to now-empty pot, and heat until shimmering. Add onion and cook, stirring frequently, until softened, about 5 minutes. Add garlic, cumin, and cinnamon and cook until fragrant, about 1 minute. Add tomatoes and their juice, broth, chipotle and adobo sauce, and sugar and bring to boil, scraping up any browned bits.

3. Return chicken and any accumulated juices to pot, reduce heat to medium-low, cover, and simmer until meat registers 195 degrees, 15 to 20 minutes, flipping chicken after 5 minutes. Transfer chicken to cutting board.

4. Transfer cooking liquid to blender and process until smooth, 15 to 30 seconds. Return sauce to pot. When cool enough to handle, shred chicken into bite-size pieces using 2 forks. Return chicken to pot with sauce. Cook over medium heat, stirring frequently, until sauce is thickened and clings to chicken, about 10 minutes. Stir in lime zest and juice and season with salt and pepper to taste.

5. FOR THE TACOS Spoon chicken into center of each warm tortilla and serve, passing avocado, Cotija, scallions, cilantro, and lime wedges separately.

TO MAKE AHEAD ▸

- Shredded chicken, prepared through step 4, can be refrigerated for up to 3 days or frozen for up to 1 month; if frozen, thaw completely in refrigerator
- To reheat, bring chicken mixture, covered, to gentle simmer, stirring often and adjusting consistency with hot water, and continue with step 5

To achieve perfectly cooked chicken and rice in this classic casserole, we cook them one at a time in the creamy sauce.

Creamy Chicken and Rice Casserole with Peas, Carrots, and Cheddar

SERVES 8

ACTIVE TIME 50 MINUTES

TOTAL TIME 1 HOUR 10 MINUTES

WHY THIS RECIPE WORKS We wanted to develop a hearty chicken and rice casserole that would appeal to kids and adults alike, and we wanted to be able to make this weeknight workhorse ahead of time. We started by replacing the typical cream soup with a flour-thickened sauce enhanced with some aromatics. But we quickly found that cooking chicken and rice together can be tricky, and cooking them separately required dirtying another pot. By poaching the chicken breasts in the sauce first, we found it easy to remove them once cooked, then stir in the rice. This two-step method worked like a charm; both elements cooked evenly and each absorbed the sauce's flavor while lending their own key attributes to the sauce. We were also happy to find that chicken cooked this way tasted juicier and maintained its texture better,

even when held overnight. To boost the sauce's flavor, we used chicken broth and some cream for richness; a small amount of flour thickened the sauce nicely. The final components of the casserole were shredded cheddar cheese, which added a pleasant bite; easy-to-use frozen peas and carrots; and a bit of fresh lemon juice to brighten everything up. Fresh bread crumbs added great crunch and held up nicely in the fridge or freezer. After adding the rice, be sure to stir the sauce often for the first few minutes, using a heatproof rubber spatula; this is when the rice is most likely to clump and stick to the bottom of the pot. Serve with lemon wedges, if desired.

4 slices hearty white sandwich bread, torn into quarters
4 tablespoons unsalted butter plus 2 tablespoons melted
5 tablespoons minced fresh parsley
  Salt and pepper
1 onion, chopped fine
3 garlic cloves, minced
⅛ teaspoon cayenne pepper
¼ cup all-purpose flour
6 cups chicken broth
1 cup heavy cream
2 pounds boneless, skinless chicken breasts, trimmed
1½ cups long-grain white rice
1 (1-pound) bag frozen peas and carrots (3 cups)
8 ounces sharp cheddar cheese, shredded (2 cups)
2 tablespoons lemon juice

1. Adjust oven rack to middle position and heat oven to 300 degrees. Pulse bread and 2 tablespoons melted butter in food processor to coarse crumbs, about 6 pulses. Spread crumbs evenly over rimmed baking sheet and bake, stirring occasionally, until light golden and dry, 20 to 30 minutes. Let crumbs cool completely, about 20 minutes, then toss with 2 tablespoons parsley and season with salt and pepper to taste; set aside.

2. Increase oven temperature to 400 degrees. Melt remaining 4 tablespoons butter in Dutch oven over medium heat. Add onion and 1 teaspoon salt and cook until softened and lightly browned, 5 to 7 minutes. Stir in garlic and cayenne and cook until fragrant, about 30 seconds. Stir in flour and cook, stirring constantly, until golden, about 1 minute. Slowly whisk in broth and cream.

3. Add chicken and bring to simmer. Reduce heat to low, cover, and cook until chicken registers 160 degrees, 10 to 15 minutes. Transfer chicken to cutting board.

4. Stir rice into liquid in pot, cover, and cook over low heat, stirring often, until rice has absorbed much of liquid and is just tender, 15 to 20 minutes.

5. When chicken is cool enough to handle, shred into bite-size pieces using 2 forks. Off heat, stir in shredded chicken and any accumulated juices, peas and carrots, cheddar, and lemon juice and season with salt and pepper to taste. Pour mixture into 13 by 9-inch baking dish and sprinkle evenly with crumb topping.

6. Bake until sauce is bubbling and hot throughout, 10 to 15 minutes. Sprinkle with remaining 3 tablespoons parsley before serving.

TO MAKE AHEAD

- Casserole, prepared through step 5, can be refrigerated for up to 2 days
- To bake, cover with greased aluminum foil and bake in 400-degree oven until hot throughout, 40 to 50 minutes; remove foil and continue to bake until crumbs are crisp, 10 to 20 minutes, before garnishing as directed

Curried Chicken and Coconut Rice Casserole with Lime-Yogurt Sauce

SERVES 8

ACTIVE TIME 1 HOUR

TOTAL TIME 1 HOUR 45 MINUTES

WHY THIS RECIPE WORKS Classic chicken and rice is always a favorite, but we wanted to develop a version of this dish with a bit more pizzazz. To liven things up, we looked to the warm, complex flavors associated with Indian curries. We built a flavorful poaching liquid—chicken broth, onion, curry powder, and minced garlic—and used it to gently cook the chicken through, infusing the meat with flavor. We then removed the chicken and added our rice and coconut milk. While the rice cooked, we shredded the chicken into bite-size pieces. Tasters liked a combination of cauliflower florets and sweet red bell peppers (cut into small pieces so they would tenderize when baked). Once the casserole was baked, we decided to add a few simple accompaniments to give the dish more of the complex flavor we were looking for. We whisked up a light and tangy yogurt sauce seasoned with tart lime zest and juice and cilantro. A sprinkle of scallions provided a fresh, savory bite, and toasted almonds provided a crunchy contrast to the tender rice. We prefer to use whole-milk yogurt in this recipe; however, low-fat or nonfat yogurt will also work.

Cooking the rice in curry powder–enhanced broth and coconut milk infuses it with bold flavor.

1	cup plain yogurt
2	tablespoons minced fresh cilantro or mint
1	teaspoon grated lime zest plus 1 tablespoon juice
	Salt and pepper
2	tablespoons extra-virgin olive oil
1	onion, chopped fine
1	tablespoon curry powder
2	garlic cloves, minced
2½	cups chicken broth
1	cup water
2	pounds boneless, skinless chicken breasts, trimmed
1½	cups long-grain white rice
1	cup canned coconut milk
½	head cauliflower (1 pound), cored and cut into ½-inch florets (3 cups)
1	red bell pepper, stemmed, seeded, and cut into ¼-inch pieces
⅓	cup sliced almonds, toasted
2	scallions, sliced thin

1. Adjust oven rack to middle position and heat oven to 400 degrees. Combine yogurt, cilantro, lime zest and juice, and ¼ teaspoon salt in bowl; set aside. Heat oil in Dutch oven over medium heat until shimmering. Add onion and 1½ teaspoons salt and cook until softened, about 5 minutes. Stir in curry powder, garlic, and ¼ teaspoon pepper and cook until fragrant, about 30 seconds. Whisk in broth and water.

2. Add chicken and bring to simmer. Reduce heat to low, cover, and cook until chicken registers 160 degrees, 10 to 15 minutes. Transfer chicken to cutting board.

3. Stir rice and coconut milk into pot with broth, cover, and cook, stirring often, until rice has absorbed much of liquid and is just tender, 15 to 20 minutes. When chicken is cool enough to handle, shred into bite-size pieces using 2 forks. Off heat, stir in shredded chicken and any accumulated juices, cauliflower florets, and bell pepper. Pour mixture into 13 by 9-inch baking dish.

4. Bake until liquid is absorbed and rice is tender, 20 to 30 minutes, stirring halfway through cooking. Fluff rice with fork and sprinkle with almonds and scallions. Serve with yogurt sauce.

TO MAKE AHEAD

- Yogurt sauce can be refrigerated for up to 2 days
- Casserole, prepared through step 3, can be refrigerated for up to 2 days
- To bake, cover with greased aluminum foil and bake in 400-degree oven until hot throughout, about 1 hour, before garnishing as directed

Breaded Chicken Cutlets

SERVES 4   EASY   FREEZE IT

ACTIVE TIME 30 MINUTES
TOTAL TIME 35 MINUTES

WHY THIS RECIPE WORKS Basic breaded chicken cutlets are an easy starting point for a multitude of delicious meals. We wanted to create a straightforward staple recipe that produced golden brown and juicy cutlets that we could cook right away or freeze for a future busy night. By removing the tenderloin and pounding out our chicken breasts to an even half-inch thickness we ensured uniform cooking. To eliminate the need to make bread crumbs and to achieve a supercrispy crust, we used store-bought panko bread crumbs. The dry, jagged edges of panko crisped up beautifully and provided a perfect crunchy exterior for our cutlets. A shallow fry on the stovetop made for quick cooking and a brief rest on a paper towel–lined plate helped to wick away excess moisture and prevented the cutlets from becoming soggy.

¾ cup all-purpose flour
2 large eggs
¾ cup panko bread crumbs
4 (6- to 8-ounce) boneless, skinless chicken breasts, trimmed and pounded ½ inch thick
Salt and pepper
¾ cup vegetable oil
Lemon wedges

1. Spread flour in shallow dish. Lightly beat eggs in second shallow dish. Place panko in third shallow dish. Pat chicken dry with paper towels and season with salt and pepper.

2. Working with 1 cutlet at a time, dredge in flour, shaking off excess; dip in egg mixture, allowing excess to drip off; and coat with panko, pressing gently to adhere. Transfer to plate and let sit for 5 minutes.

3. Heat oil in 12-inch nonstick skillet over medium-high heat until shimmering. Place 2 cutlets in skillet and cook until deep golden brown and crisp and chicken registers 160 degrees, about 2½ minutes per side, gently pressing on cutlets with spatula for even browning. Transfer to clean paper towel–lined plate and repeat with remaining 2 cutlets.

4. Serve with lemon wedges.

TO MAKE AHEAD

- Breaded chicken, prepared through step 2, can be refrigerated for up to 24 hours
- Alternatively, cooked chicken, prepared through step 3, can be frozen for up to 1 month; to reheat, place frozen cutlets on wire rack set in rimmed baking sheet and bake in 400-degree oven on middle rack until crisp and hot throughout, 20 to 30 minutes

POUNDING CHICKEN BREASTS

To create chicken breasts of even thickness, simply pound the thicker ends of the breasts until they are all of uniform thickness. Though some breasts will still be larger in size, at least they will cook at the same rate.

We keep the coating on our breaded chicken cutlets crisp by replacing some of the bread crumbs with Parmesan cheese.

SAUCE

- 2 tablespoons extra-virgin olive oil
- 2 garlic cloves, minced
  Kosher salt and pepper
- ¼ teaspoon dried oregano
  Pinch red pepper flakes
- 1 (28-ounce) can crushed tomatoes
- ¼ teaspoon sugar
- 2 tablespoons chopped fresh basil

CHICKEN

- 2 (6- to 8-ounce) boneless, skinless chicken breasts, trimmed, halved horizontally, and pounded ½ inch thick
- 1 teaspoon kosher salt
- 2 ounces whole-milk mozzarella cheese, shredded (½ cup)
- 2 ounces fontina cheese, shredded (½ cup)
- 1 large egg
- 1 tablespoon all-purpose flour
- 1½ ounces Parmesan cheese, grated (¾ cup)
- ½ cup panko bread crumbs
- ½ teaspoon garlic powder
- ¼ teaspoon dried oregano
- ¼ teaspoon pepper
- ⅓ cup vegetable oil
- ¼ cup torn fresh basil

Best Chicken Parmesan

SERVES 4   **FREEZE IT**

ACTIVE TIME 1 HOUR

TOTAL TIME 1 HOUR 30 MINUTES

WHY THIS RECIPE WORKS Traditional chicken Parmesan is a minefield of potential problems: dry meat, soggy crust, and a chewy blanket of mozzarella. To keep the meat moist, we salted the cutlets for 20 minutes, and to keep the exterior crunchy, we replaced more than half of the bread crumbs with grated Parmesan cheese. Mixing the usual shredded mozzarella with creamy fontina helped ensure that the cheese stayed smooth and melty, not congealed, and we placed the mixture directly on the fried cutlet so that it formed a waterproof layer between the crust and the sauce. A simple homemade sauce made with plenty of aromatics and fresh basil was the perfect finishing touch to this improved classic. This recipe makes enough sauce to top the cutlets as well as four servings of pasta.

1. FOR THE SAUCE Heat 1 tablespoon oil in medium saucepan over medium heat until shimmering. Stir in garlic, ¾ teaspoon salt, oregano, and pepper flakes and cook until fragrant, about 30 seconds. Stir in tomatoes and sugar, increase heat to high, and bring to simmer. Reduce heat to medium-low and simmer until thickened, about 20 minutes. Off heat, stir in basil and remaining 1 tablespoon oil. Season with salt and pepper to taste, and cover to keep warm.

2. FOR THE CHICKEN Sprinkle each side of each cutlet with ⅛ teaspoon salt and let stand at room temperature for 20 minutes. Combine mozzarella and fontina in bowl and set aside.

3. Adjust oven rack 4 inches from broiler element and heat broiler. Whisk egg and flour together in shallow dish until smooth. Combine Parmesan, panko, garlic powder, oregano, and pepper in second shallow dish. Pat chicken dry with paper towels. Working with 1 cutlet at a time, dredge in egg mixture, allowing excess to drip off, then coat with Parmesan mixture, pressing gently to adhere; transfer to large plate.

4. Heat oil in 10-inch nonstick skillet over medium-high heat until shimmering. Carefully place 2 cutlets in skillet and cook until crispy and deep golden, 1½ to 2 minutes per side. Transfer to paper towel–lined plate and repeat with remaining 2 cutlets.

5. Place cutlets on rimmed baking sheet and sprinkle cheese mixture evenly over top. Broil until cheese is melted and beginning to brown, 2 to 4 minutes.

6. Transfer chicken to serving platter and top each cutlet with 2 tablespoons sauce. Sprinkle with basil and serve immediately, passing remaining sauce separately.

TO MAKE AHEAD

- Sauce can be refrigerated for up to 3 days or frozen for up to 1 month; if frozen, thaw completely in refrigerator
- Breaded chicken, prepared through step 3, can be refrigerated for up to 24 hours
- Alternatively, cooked chicken, prepared through step 4, can be frozen for up to 1 month; to reheat, place frozen cutlets on wire rack set in rimmed baking sheet, top with cheese, bake in 400-degree oven on middle rack until crisp and hot throughout, 20 to 30 minutes, and continue with step 6

Chicken Nuggets with Honey Mustard Sauce

SERVES 4 TO 6   **FREEZE IT**

ACTIVE TIME 40 MINUTES

TOTAL TIME 1 HOUR 20 MINUTES

WHY THIS RECIPE WORKS Store-bought chicken nuggets are convenient, but their mushy texture and bland flavor can't compare to homemade versions. We wanted a straightforward recipe for nuggets we would be happy to have on hand. Brining the chicken prevented it from drying out and seasoned the bland breast meat. We cut the brining time in half by slicing the meat into nuggets beforehand. Ground-up panko bread crumbs combined with flour and a pinch of baking soda encouraged a crispy browned exterior on our nuggets. Using whole eggs to help the coating adhere made the nuggets too eggy, but the whites alone didn't have as much binding power. We found that using egg whites and resting the nuggets before frying solved the problem. Don't brine the chicken longer than 30 minutes or it will be too salty. If using kosher chicken, do not brine in step 1. To crush the panko, place it inside a zipper-lock bag and lightly beat it with a rolling pin. This recipe can easily be doubled.

½ cup yellow mustard
⅓ cup honey
    Salt and pepper
2 tablespoons Worcestershire sauce
4 (6- to 8-ounce) boneless, skinless chicken
    breasts, trimmed

A pinch of baking soda encourages the crunchy panko coating on our homemade chicken nuggets to brown.

3 large egg whites
1 cup all-purpose flour
1 cup panko bread crumbs, crushed
2 teaspoons onion powder
½ teaspoon garlic powder
½ teaspoon baking soda
1 quart peanut or vegetable oil

1. Whisk mustard and honey together in bowl and season with salt and pepper to taste; set aside. Whisk 2 cups cold water, 1 tablespoon salt, and Worcestershire together in large bowl to dissolve salt. Cut each chicken breast diagonally into thirds, then cut each third diagonally into ½-inch-thick pieces. Add chicken to brine and refrigerate, covered, for 30 minutes.

2. Remove chicken from brine and pat dry with paper towels. Lightly beat egg whites in shallow dish until foamy. Combine flour, panko, onion powder, ½ teaspoon salt, ¾ teaspoon pepper, garlic powder, and baking soda in second shallow dish.

3. Working with a few chicken pieces at a time, dip in egg whites, allowing excess to drip off, then coat with flour mixture, pressing gently to adhere. Transfer to plate and let sit for 10 minutes (do not discard remaining flour mixture). Working in batches, return chicken to dish with flour mixture, turning to coat and pressing gently to adhere.

4. Meanwhile, heat oil in large Dutch oven over medium-high heat to 350 degrees. Fry half of chicken until golden brown, 3 to 5 minutes, adjusting burner if necessary to maintain oil temperature between 300 and 325 degrees. Transfer to paper towel-lined rack, return oil to 350 degrees and repeat with remaining chicken.

5. Serve with honey mustard sauce.

TO MAKE AHEAD ▶

- Sauce can be refrigerated for up to 5 days
- Breaded chicken, prepared through step 3, can be refrigerated for up to 24 hours
- Alternatively, cooked chicken, prepared through step 4, can be frozen for up to 1 month; to reheat, place frozen nuggets on wire rack set in rimmed baking sheet and bake in 400-degree oven on middle rack until crisp and hot throughout, 10 to 15 minutes, flipping once halfway through baking

CUTTING CHICKEN INTO NUGGETS

1. Using chef's knife, cut each chicken breast on bias into thirds.

2. Working with largest piece, turn cut end toward you and slice into ½-inch-thick pieces.

3. With knife almost parallel to cutting board, cut 2 smaller thirds into pieces.

To make fried chicken taste just as good the next day, we recrisp it in a hot 400-degree oven.

Batter Fried Chicken

SERVES 4 TO 6
ACTIVE TIME 1 HOUR 15 MINUTES
TOTAL TIME 2 HOURS TO 2 HOURS 30 MINUTES

WHY THIS RECIPE WORKS Perfectly fried chicken is an unbeatable crowd-pleaser, but most recipes disappoint, with bland meat and soggy coatings that fall far short of the ide al. The old-fashioned method of dipping chicken in a batter (not unlike pancake batter) before frying promises a delicate, crunchy coating and is easier than the typical messy flour-egg-flour preparation. To foolproof and modernize this unusual technique, we started by brining chicken pieces to ensure moist and seasoned meat. We found that using equal parts cornstarch and flour in the batter produced an ultracrisp crust on the chicken, while baking powder added lift and lightness without doughiness. Black pepper, paprika, and cayenne gave the batter simple but unambiguous flavor. Best of all, this chicken can be recrisped to its original glory in a hot oven even a full day after frying. You will need at least a 6-quart Dutch oven for this recipe. If using kosher chicken, do not brine and instead season with salt in step 4 after patting the chicken dry.

¼ cup sugar
Salt and pepper
4 pounds bone-in chicken pieces (split breasts cut in half, drumsticks, and/or thighs)
1 cup all-purpose flour
1 cup cornstarch
2 teaspoons baking powder
1 teaspoon paprika
½ teaspoon cayenne pepper
3 quarts peanut or vegetable oil

1. Whisk 1 quart cold water, sugar, and ¼ cup salt together in large bowl to dissolve. Add chicken, cover, and refrigerate for 30 minutes to 1 hour.

2. Whisk flour, cornstarch, baking powder, paprika, cayenne, 1 teaspoon salt, and 5 teaspoons pepper together in large bowl. Whisk in 1¾ cups water until smooth. Refrigerate until needed (but no longer than 1 hour).

3. Adjust oven rack to middle position and heat oven to 200 degrees; set wire rack in rimmed baking sheet. Heat oil in large Dutch oven over medium-high heat to 350 degrees.

4. Remove chicken from brine and pat dry with paper towels. Whisk batter to recombine. Add one-third of chicken to batter and toss to coat thoroughly. Remove chicken from batter, allowing excess to drip back into bowl, and add to hot oil.

5. Fry chicken until deep golden and breasts register 160 degrees and drumsticks/thighs register 175 degrees, adjusting burner, if necessary, to maintain oil temperature between 300 and 325 degrees, 12 to 15 minutes. Transfer chicken to prepared baking sheet and keep warm in oven.

6. Return oil to 350 degrees and repeat with remaining chicken and batter in 2 batches, transferring batches to oven to keep warm. Serve.

TO MAKE AHEAD

- Fried chicken can be refrigerated for up to 24 hours
- To reheat, place chicken on wire rack set in baking sheet, let sit at room temperature for 30 minutes, then reheat in 400-degree oven until hot, 10 to 15 minutes

NOTES FROM THE TEST KITCHEN

Poultry Safety and Handling

It's important to follow some basic safety procedures when storing, handling, and cooking chicken, turkey, and other poultry.

REFRIGERATING Keep poultry refrigerated until just before cooking. Bacteria thrive at temperatures between 40 and 140 degrees. This means leftovers should also be promptly refrigerated.

FREEZING AND THAWING Poultry can be frozen in its original packaging or after repackaging. If you are freezing it for longer than two months, rewrap (or wrap over packaging) with foil or plastic wrap, or place inside a zipper-lock bag. You can keep poultry frozen for several months, but after two months the texture and flavor will suffer. Don't thaw frozen poultry on the counter; this puts it at risk of growing bacteria. Thaw it in its packaging in the refrigerator (in a container to catch its juices), or in the sink under cold running water. Count on one day of defrosting in the refrigerator for every 4 pounds of bird.

HANDLING RAW POULTRY When handling raw poultry, make sure to wash hands, knives, cutting boards, and counters (and anything else that has come into contact with the raw bird, its juices, or your hands) with hot, soapy water. Be careful not to let the poultry, its juices, or your unwashed hands touch foods that will be eaten raw. When seasoning raw poultry, touching the salt-shaker or pepper mill can lead to cross-contamination. To avoid this, set aside the necessary salt and pepper before handling the poultry.

RINSING The U.S. Department of Agriculture advises against washing poultry. Rinsing poultry will not remove or kill much bacteria, and the splashing of water around the sink can spread the bacteria found in raw poultry.

COOKING AND LEFTOVERS Poultry should be cooked to an internal temperature of 160 degrees to ensure any bacteria have been killed (however, we prefer the flavor and texture of thigh meat cooked to at least 175 degrees). Leftover cooked poultry should be refrigerated and consumed within three days.

Adding lemon juice to the sauce instead of the marinade adds brightness and prevents the chicken from becoming mushy.

Baked Chicken with Spring Vegetables, Capers, and Lemon

SERVES 4 **EASY**

ACTIVE TIME 30 MINUTES

TOTAL TIME 1 HOUR 45 MINUTES

WHY THIS RECIPE WORKS Baked chicken is an old standby, but it can be a little ho-hum. We wanted to turn simple baked chicken into a full make-ahead meal, complete with tender, flavorful vegetables and a zesty sauce to accompany the moist, well-seasoned meat. Using bone-in chicken breasts prevented them from drying out in the oven. We marinated the chicken in an aromatic oil-based mixture, forgoing any acidic elements to avoid making the chicken mushy. For vegetables, we chose cherry tomatoes, jarred artichokes, and asparagus, all of which required minimal prep work. Adding the asparagus at the end of cooking ensured that it stayed crisp-tender. A handful of capers and a few fresh lemon slices added brightness to the mix. To give the finished dish extra flavor, we reserved a bit of the marinade and enhanced it with fresh lemon juice to serve with the chicken after cooking.

GARLIC AND HERB MARINADE

½ cup extra-virgin olive oil

¼ cup fresh parsley, tarragon, or basil leaves

1 shallot, chopped

6 garlic cloves, minced

1 teaspoon salt

¼ teaspoon pepper

2 tablespoons lemon juice

CHICKEN

1½ cups jarred whole artichoke hearts packed in water, drained and patted dry

8 ounces cherry tomatoes

¼ cup capers, rinsed

½ lemon, trimmed and sliced into ¼-inch-thick rounds

½ teaspoon salt

¼ teaspoon pepper

4 (10- to 12-ounce) bone-in split chicken breasts, trimmed

8 ounces thin asparagus, trimmed and halved crosswise

2 tablespoons chopped fresh tarragon

1. FOR THE MARINADE Process oil, parsley, shallot, garlic, salt, and pepper in food processor until smooth, about 20 seconds, scraping down sides of bowl as needed. Transfer ¼ cup marinade to bowl and stir in lemon juice; set dressing aside for serving.

2. FOR THE CHICKEN In large bowl toss 2 tablespoons marinade with artichokes, tomatoes, capers, lemon slices, salt, and pepper. In separate bowl, toss chicken with remaining marinade. Refrigerate vegetables and chicken for at least 30 minutes.

3. Adjust oven rack to middle position and heat oven to 450 degrees. Transfer vegetables to 13 by 9-inch baking dish and lay chicken on top, skin side up. Bake until chicken registers 160 degrees, about 45 minutes.

4. Transfer chicken to cutting board, tent loosely with aluminum foil, and let rest for 10 minutes. Meanwhile, stir asparagus into vegetables in dish and bake until asparagus is crisp-tender, about 10 minutes.

5. Place chicken on top of vegetables in dish. Whisk reserved dressing to recombine, then pour over top of chicken and vegetables. Sprinkle with tarragon, and serve.

TO MAKE AHEAD

- Marinated vegetables, chicken, and dressing, prepared through step 2, can be refrigerated separately for up to 2 days
- To bake, bring dressing to room temperature and continue with step 3

Bone-in, skin-on chicken breasts are easy to stuff with a cheesy filling without the hassle of rolling and tying.

Lemon–Goat Cheese Stuffed Chicken Breasts

SERVES 4   **EASY**

ACTIVE TIME 25 MINUTES
TOTAL TIME 1 HOUR

WHY THIS RECIPE WORKS It's hard to beat a juicy chicken breast stuffed with a flavorful cheesy filling. We wanted an easy make-ahead version of this classic, without the fuss of butterflying, pounding, rolling, and tying the chicken. Boneless, skinless chicken breasts were a nonstarter; they required too much knife work and didn't guarantee stellar results. Bone-in, skin-on chicken breasts, on the other hand, proved to be the right choice. To create a pocket for a dollop of our creamy, flavorful filling, all we needed to do was gently separate the skin from the meat. So far, so good—except for the flabby, inedible skin we were left with after baking. Cranking the oven up to 450 degrees solved that problem; this round of chicken baked up golden and crispy.

4 (10- to 12-ounce) bone-in split chicken breasts, trimmed and halved crosswise
Salt and pepper
3 ounces goat cheese, softened
2 ounces cream cheese, softened
2 teaspoons minced fresh thyme
1 garlic clove, minced
¼ teaspoon grated lemon zest
1 tablespoon extra-virgin olive oil

1. Adjust oven rack to middle position and heat oven to 450 degrees. Set wire rack in aluminum foil–lined rimmed baking sheet. Pat chicken dry with paper towels and season with salt and pepper. Stir goat cheese, cream cheese, thyme, garlic, lemon zest, ⅛ teaspoon salt, and ⅛ teaspoon pepper in bowl until combined.

2. Using your fingers, carefully loosen center portion of skin covering each breast. Place about 1½ tablespoons cheese mixture under skin, directly on meat in center of each breast half.

3. Brush chicken skin with oil, then place breasts skin side up on prepared rack. Bake until chicken registers 160 degrees, 35 to 40 minutes. Let rest for 5 to 10 minutes before serving.

TO MAKE AHEAD

Stuffed chicken, prepared through step 2, can be refrigerated for up to 24 hours

NOTES FROM THE TEST KITCHEN

Buying Goat Cheese

Produced in many countries in numerous forms, goat cheese (sometimes labeled chèvre) can be aged or fresh, soft or firm, musky or mild, etc. That said, most of what you can buy in American supermarkets (and the variety we favor in our recipes) is relatively young cheese packaged in a log shape; it has a creamy, slightly grainy texture and a tangy, milky flavor. When shopping for goat cheese, avoid precrumbled cheeses—they tend to be dry and chalky. Our favorite goat cheese is Laura Chenel's Fresh Chèvre Log. Once opened, goat cheese should be wrapped in parchment or waxed paper and can be stored in the refrigerator for up to two weeks.

A two-level grill fire helps the chicken cook through without charring and also enables us to crisp the skin.

Grilled Tandoori-Style Chicken with Yogurt Sauce

SERVES 4 **EASY**

ACTIVE TIME 25 MINUTES

TOTAL TIME 1 HOUR 20 MINUTES

WHY THIS RECIPE WORKS Tandoori chicken achieves its hallmark charred, crispy skin and juicy, flavorful meat from a combination of a three-day marinade and a superheated tandoori oven. We wanted to develop a grilled chicken dish inspired by this Indian classic. First we focused on the marinade; we chose a variety of traditional Indian spices and added oil to bloom them, as well as a good amount of salt so that the marinade would have the effect of a brine, guaranteeing juicy meat. For the grilling method, we spread the coals over just half of the grill to create both a hotter and a cooler zone; this allowed us to cook the chicken gently on the cooler side before transferring it to the hot side to sear and char the skin. To reinforce the flavors of the marinade, we created a quick yogurt sauce, mixing in a few tablespoons of marinade and adding fresh cilantro and lime juice.

½ cup vegetable oil

¼ cup water

1 tablespoon grated fresh ginger

1 tablespoon ground coriander

1½ teaspoons ground cumin

1½ teaspoons salt

1 teaspoon ground turmeric

½ teaspoon ground cinnamon

¼ teaspoon cayenne pepper

¼ cup plain yogurt

2 tablespoons minced fresh cilantro

2 teaspoons lime juice

4 (10- to 12-ounce) bone-in split chicken breasts, trimmed and halved crosswise

1. Process oil, water, ginger, coriander, cumin, salt, turmeric, cinnamon, and cayenne in food processor until smooth, about 20 seconds. In small bowl, combine yogurt, cilantro, lime juice, and 2 tablespoons oil-spice mixture; set aside.

2. Combine chicken and remaining oil-spice mixture in large bowl, tossing to coat. Cover with plastic wrap and refrigerate for at least 1 hour.

3A. FOR A CHARCOAL GRILL Open bottom vent completely. Light large chimney starter filled with charcoal briquettes (6 quarts). When top coals are partially covered with ash, pour evenly over half of grill. Set cooking grate in place, cover, and open lid vent completely. Heat grill until hot, about 5 minutes.

3B. FOR A GAS GRILL Turn all burners to high, cover, and heat grill until hot, about 15 minutes. Turn primary burner to medium-high and turn off other burner(s).

4. Clean and oil cooking grate. Place chicken skin side down on cooler side of grill with thicker ends of breasts facing hotter side of grill. Cook, covered, until chicken registers 145 to 150 degrees, 20 to 30 minutes. Slide chicken to hotter side of grill and cook, turning as needed, until chicken is browned and registers 160 degrees, about 10 minutes.

5. Transfer chicken to serving platter. Stir yogurt-marinade mixture to recombine, then drizzle over chicken. Tent with aluminum foil and let rest for 5 to 10 minutes. Serve.

TO MAKE AHEAD

- Chicken and yogurt sauce, prepared through step 2, can be refrigerated separately for up to 24 hours
- To cook, bring sauce to room temperature and continue with step 3

Cutting chicken breasts in half ensures that the vegetables won't be smothered underneath them and steam.

One-Pan Roast Chicken Breasts with Butternut Squash and Kale

SERVES 4 **EASY**

ACTIVE TIME 30 MINUTES

TOTAL TIME 1 HOUR

WHY THIS RECIPE WORKS Recipes that use a single sheet pan to cook chicken and vegetables together promise a full meal, simple prep, and minimal cleanup. However, this method often leads to unevenly cooked meat and vegetables. To get the chicken and vegetables to cook at the same rate, we used bone-in split chicken breasts, which contain less fat than a whole chicken and don't run the risk of smothering the vegetables underneath, causing them to steam. Halving the breasts further assisted in even cooking. We selected hearty, autumnal vegetables to pair with our chicken: butternut squash, kale, and shallots. A sprinkling of dried cranberries added a sweet-tart chew to the mix and a simple sage marinade worked to season both the chicken and vegetables. Because we used only breast meat, we were able to drastically shorten our cooking time (compared to a whole chicken) to just 25 minutes, plenty of time to achieve crispy chicken skin, tender

but not mushy squash, and fully cooked and lightly crisped kale. We topped our chicken with a drizzle of light, creamy yogurt sauce accented with orange zest and garlic to bring the whole dish into harmony. Both curly and Lacinato kale will work in this recipe.

½ cup extra-virgin olive oil
2 tablespoons minced fresh sage
2 teaspoons honey
  Salt and pepper
¾ cup plain whole milk yogurt
1 tablespoon water
7 garlic cloves, peeled (6 whole, 1 minced)
1 teaspoon grated orange zest
8 ounces kale, stemmed and cut into 2-inch pieces
2 pounds butternut squash, peeled, seeded, and cut into 1-inch pieces, (6 cups)
8 shallots, peeled and halved
½ cup dried cranberries
2 teaspoons paprika
4 (10- to 12-ounce) bone-in split chicken breasts, trimmed and halved crosswise

1. Adjust oven rack to upper-middle position and heat oven to 475 degrees. Whisk oil, sage, honey, 1 teaspoon salt, and ½ teaspoon pepper in large bowl until well combined. In separate bowl whisk yogurt, water, minced garlic, orange zest, and 1 tablespoon oil mixture together; set yogurt sauce aside for serving.

2. Vigorously squeeze and massage kale with hands in large bowl until leaves are uniformly darkened and slightly wilted, about 1 minute. Add squash, shallots, cranberries, whole garlic cloves, and ¼ cup oil mixture and toss to combine. Whisk paprika into remaining oil mixture, then add chicken and toss to coat.

3. Spread vegetables in single layer on rimmed baking sheet, then place chicken, skin side up, on top of vegetables. Bake until chicken registers 160 degrees, 25 to 35 minutes, rotating sheet halfway through baking.

4. Transfer chicken to serving platter, tent with aluminum foil, and let rest for 5 to 10 minutes. Toss vegetables with any

MASSAGING KALE

Vigorously squeeze and massage kale with hands on counter or in large bowl until leaves are uniformly darkened and slightly wilted, about 1 minute for flat-leaf kale (or 5 minutes for curly-leaf or red kale).

accumulated chicken juices and transfer to platter with chicken. Drizzle ¼ cup yogurt sauce over chicken and serve, passing remaining yogurt sauce separately.

TO MAKE AHEAD ▸

Yogurt sauce, marinated vegetables, and marinated chicken, prepared through step 2, can be refrigerated separately for up to 24 hours

One-Pan Roast Chicken with Root Vegetables

SERVES 4 **EASY**
ACTIVE TIME 30 MINUTES
TOTAL TIME 1 HOUR 10 MINUTES

WHY THIS RECIPE WORKS For a different take on an easy, one-pan dinner, we decided to use chicken parts along with flavorful root vegetables and Brussels sprouts. To ensure even cooking, we were careful not to smother the vegetables underneath the chicken. But using chicken parts complicated things slightly: By the time the dark meat was cooked through, the delicate white meat was overcooked and dry. We solved this problem by placing the breasts in the center of the pan, and putting the thighs and drumsticks around the perimeter where the heat was more intense. A similar treatment for the vegetables—leafy Brussels sprouts in the middle, hardier potatoes and carrots on the outside—also proved effective. Use Brussels sprouts no bigger than golf balls, as larger ones are often tough and woody.

12 ounces red potatoes, unpeeled, cut into 1-inch pieces
12 ounces Brussels sprouts, trimmed and halved
 8 shallots, peeled and halved
 4 carrots, peeled, cut into 2-inch pieces, thick ends halved lengthwise
¼ cup vegetable oil
 6 garlic cloves, peeled
 4 teaspoons minced fresh thyme or 1½ teaspoons dried
 2 teaspoons minced fresh rosemary or ½ teaspoon dried
3½ pounds bone-in chicken pieces (2 split breasts cut in half crosswise, 2 drumsticks, and 2 thighs), trimmed
Salt and pepper
 1 teaspoon sugar

1. Adjust oven rack to upper-middle position and heat oven to 475 degrees. Combine potatoes, Brussels sprouts, shallots, carrots, 2 tablespoons oil, garlic, 2 teaspoons thyme, and 1 teaspoon rosemary in bowl, tossing to coat.

Carefully arranging the chicken and vegetables on the pan is the key to getting everything to cook at the same rate.

2. In separate bowl, combine chicken, remaining 2 tablespoons oil, remaining 2 teaspoons thyme, remaining 1 teaspoon rosemary, ¼ teaspoon salt, and ⅛ teaspoon pepper, tossing to coat.

3. Spread vegetables in single layer in rimmed baking sheet, discarding any excess liquid and arranging Brussels sprouts in center. Season vegetables with sugar, ½ teaspoon salt, and ¼ teaspoon pepper.

4. Place chicken skin side up on top of vegetables, arranging breast pieces in center and leg and thigh pieces around perimeter of sheet. Bake until breasts register 160 degrees and drumsticks/thighs register 175 degrees, 35 to 40 minutes, rotating sheet halfway through baking.

5. Transfer chicken to serving platter, tent with aluminum foil, and let rest for 5 to 10 minutes. Return vegetables to oven and continue to bake until lightly browned, 5 to 10 minutes. Toss vegetables with any accumulated chicken juices and transfer to platter with chicken. Serve.

TO MAKE AHEAD ▸

Marinated vegetables and chicken, prepared through step 2, can be refrigerated separately for up to 24 hours

Chicken Provençal

SERVES 4 **FREEZE IT**

ACTIVE TIME 1 HOUR 10 MINUTES
TOTAL TIME 2 HOURS 25 MINUTES

WHY THIS RECIPE WORKS Chicken Provençal represents the best of rustic peasant food—bone-in chicken simmered all day in a tomatoey, garlicky herb broth flavorful enough to mop up with crusty bread. We started with bone-in chicken thighs and browned them in oil to develop rich flavor and create fond. To keep the sauce from becoming greasy, we poured off most of the fat left behind before sautéing the mushrooms and onion. Diced tomatoes, white wine, and chicken broth also went into the sauce before we braised the browned chicken; minced anchovy made the dish taste richer and fuller. We used fresh parsley in addition to the traditional herbes de Provence, and we finished with grated lemon zest and pitted niçoise olives for a chicken Provençal with authentic, long-simmered flavor. This dish is often served with rice or slices of crusty bread, but soft polenta is also a good accompaniment.

8 (5- to 7-ounce) bone-in chicken thighs, trimmed
Salt and pepper
1 tablespoon vegetable oil
12 ounces white mushrooms, trimmed, halved if small or medium, quartered if large
1 large onion, chopped fine
4 garlic cloves, minced
1 anchovy fillet, rinsed and minced
¾ teaspoon herbes de Provence
4 teaspoons tomato paste
1 tablespoon all-purpose flour
¼ cup dry white wine
1¾ cups chicken broth
1 (14.5-ounce) can diced tomatoes, drained
2 bay leaves
½ cup pitted niçoise olives, chopped
2 tablespoons minced fresh parsley
½ teaspoon grated lemon zest

1. Adjust oven rack to lower-middle position and heat oven to 300 degrees. Pat chicken dry with paper towels and season with salt and pepper. Heat oil in Dutch oven over medium-high heat until just smoking. Brown half of chicken well on both sides, about 10 minutes; transfer to plate. Pour off all but 1 tablespoon fat left in pot and repeat with remaining chicken.

2. Pour off all but 1 tablespoon fat left in pot and stir in mushrooms, onion, and ¼ teaspoon salt. Cover and cook over medium heat, stirring often, until mushrooms have released their liquid, about 5 minutes. Uncover and cook, stirring often, until mushrooms are browned, about 10 minutes.

Browning bone-in chicken before braising in a flavorful mixture of canned tomatoes, wine, and broth builds deep flavor.

3. Stir in garlic, anchovy, and herbes de Provence and cook until fragrant, about 30 seconds. Stir in tomato paste and flour and cook for 1 minute. Stir in wine, scraping up any browned bits. Slowly stir in broth, smoothing out any lumps, then add tomatoes and bay leaves.

4. Discard skin from chicken, then nestle into pot along with any accumulated juices. Increase heat to high and bring to simmer. Cover, transfer pot to oven, and cook until chicken registers 195 degrees, about 1¼ hours. Remove pot from oven and discard bay leaves.

5. Stir in olives, cover, and let sit for 5 minutes. Stir in parsley and lemon zest, season with salt and pepper to taste, and serve.

TO MAKE AHEAD

- Braised chicken, prepared through step 4, can be refrigerated for up to 2 days or frozen for up to 1 month; if frozen, thaw completely in refrigerator
- To reheat, bring chicken, covered, to gentle simmer, and cook until chicken is hot throughout, adjusting consistency with hot water as needed, and continue with step 5

After coating the chicken with a spicy yogurt mixture, we broil the breasts whole so they don't dry out.

Chicken Tikka Masala

SERVES 4 TO 6
ACTIVE TIME 1 HOUR 10 MINUTES
TOTAL TIME 2 HOURS TO 2 HOURS 30 MINUTES

WHY THIS RECIPE WORKS To create an approachable method for producing moist, tender chunks of chicken in a rich, lightly spiced tomato sauce, we began by coating the chicken in a yogurt mixture seasoned with cumin, coriander, and cayenne. Baking the chicken breasts was quick and worked well, but the additional char we achieved with the broiler was better and required no extra time. The basic combination of garam masala, fresh ginger, and fresh cilantro gave our masala sauce an authentic Indian taste. Serve with rice.

CHICKEN TIKKA
  1 teaspoon salt
  ½ teaspoon ground cumin
  ½ teaspoon ground coriander
  ¼ teaspoon cayenne pepper

  2 pounds boneless, skinless chicken breasts, trimmed
  1 cup plain yogurt
  2 tablespoons vegetable oil
  1 tablespoon grated fresh ginger
  2 garlic cloves, minced

MASALA SAUCE
  3 tablespoons vegetable oil
  1 onion, chopped fine
  1 serrano chile, stemmed, seeded, and minced
  1 tablespoon tomato paste
  1 tablespoon garam masala
  2 garlic cloves, minced
  2 teaspoons grated fresh ginger
  1 (28-ounce) can crushed tomatoes
  2 teaspoons sugar
    Salt
  ⅔ cup heavy cream
  ¼ cup chopped fresh cilantro

1. FOR THE CHICKEN Combine salt, cumin, coriander, and cayenne in bowl. Sprinkle both sides of chicken with spice mixture, pressing gently to adhere. Place chicken on plate, cover with plastic wrap, and refrigerate for 30 minutes to 1 hour. In large bowl, whisk yogurt, oil, ginger, and garlic together; set aside.

2. FOR THE MASALA SAUCE Heat oil in Dutch oven over medium heat until shimmering. Add onion and cook, stirring frequently, until light golden, 8 to 10 minutes. Stir in serrano, tomato paste, garam masala, garlic, and ginger and cook until fragrant, about 3 minutes. Add crushed tomatoes, sugar, and ½ teaspoon salt and bring to boil. Reduce heat to medium-low, cover, and simmer for 15 minutes, stirring occasionally. Stir in cream and return to simmer. Remove pan from heat and cover to keep warm.

3. Meanwhile, adjust oven rack 6 inches from broiler element and heat broiler. Coat chicken in yogurt mixture and place on wire rack set in aluminum foil–lined rimmed baking sheet. Broil until chicken registers 160 degrees and is lightly charred in spots, 10 to 18 minutes, flipping chicken halfway through cooking.

4. Let chicken rest for 5 minutes, then cut into 1-inch chunks and stir into warm sauce (do not simmer chicken in sauce). Stir in cilantro, season with salt to taste, and serve.

TO MAKE AHEAD
- Seasoned chicken, yogurt sauce, and masala sauce, prepared through step 2, can be refrigerated separately for up to 24 hours
- To cook, bring sauce, covered, to gentle simmer, stirring often, and continue with step 3

Chicken Tagine with Chickpeas and Apricots

SERVES 4 TO 6
ACTIVE TIME 1 HOUR
TOTAL TIME 1 HOUR 30 MINUTES

WHY THIS RECIPE WORKS Tagines are a North African specialty: exotically spiced, assertively flavored stews slow-cooked in earthenware vessels of the same name. Traditional recipes usually require a time-consuming cooking method, a special pot (the tagine), and hard-to-find ingredients; we wanted to make tagines more accessible. First off, we found that a Dutch oven was a serviceable substitute for a tagine. Almost all of the recipes we collected called for a whole chicken, cut into pieces, but we found thighs alone to be juicier and more tender; plus, their uniform size meant they cooked evenly. Chickpeas, carrots, onion, and garlic rounded out the stew, and dried apricots lent pops of sweetness. Since the spice blend for tagines can contain upward of 30 spices, we experimented until we landed on a blend that was short on ingredients but long on flavor. Cumin and ginger lent depth, cinnamon brought warmth, and citrusy coriander boosted the stew's lemon flavor (as did a couple of broad ribbons of lemon zest). Serve with couscous or rice.

We fill our chicken tagine with heady North African spices but temper them with sweet honey and dried apricots.

- 8 (5- to 7-ounce) bone-in chicken thighs, trimmed
  Salt and pepper
- 2 tablespoons extra-virgin olive oil
- 1 large onion, halved and sliced ¼ inch thick
- 3 (2-inch) strips lemon zest plus 3 tablespoons juice
- 5 garlic cloves, minced
- 1¼ teaspoons paprika
- ½ teaspoon ground cumin
- ¼ teaspoon cayenne pepper
- ¼ teaspoon ground cinnamon
- ¼ teaspoon ground coriander
- ¼ teaspoon ground ginger
- 2 cups chicken broth
- 2 carrots, peeled, halved lengthwise, and sliced ½ inch thick
- 1 (15-ounce) can chickpeas, rinsed
- 1 tablespoon honey
- 1 cup dried apricots, halved
- 2 tablespoons chopped fresh cilantro

1. Pat chicken dry with paper towels and season with salt and pepper. Heat oil in Dutch oven over medium-high heat until just smoking. Add thighs and brown on both sides, about 5 minutes per side. Transfer to plate and discard skin. Pour off all but 1 tablespoon fat from pot.

2. Add onion and 2 strips lemon zest to now-empty pot and cook over medium heat until softened, about 5 minutes. Stir in 4 teaspoons garlic, paprika, cumin, cayenne, cinnamon, coriander, and ginger and cook until fragrant, about 1 minute. Stir in broth, carrots, chickpeas, and honey, scraping up any browned bits. Nestle thighs into pot along with any accumulated juices and bring to simmer. Reduce heat to medium-low, cover, and cook until thighs register 195 degrees, 30 to 40 minutes.

3. Transfer chicken to plate and discard lemon zest. Using large spoon, skim excess fat from surface of sauce. Return chicken and any accumulated juices to pot.

4. Stir in apricots, bring to simmer over medium heat, and cook until apricots are warmed through, about 5 minutes. Mince remaining 1 strip lemon zest and add to pot, along with lemon juice, remaining garlic, and cilantro. Season with salt and pepper to taste, and serve.

> **TO MAKE AHEAD**
> - Tagine, prepared through step 3, can be refrigerated for up to 3 days
> - To reheat, bring chicken, covered, to gentle simmer, cook until chicken is hot throughout, and continue with step 4

The rich flavor and consistency of this classic Spanish dish comes from a sherry-based sauce thickened with almonds.

Spanish Braised Chicken with Sherry and Saffron

SERVES 4 **FREEZE IT**

ACTIVE TIME 1 HOUR 10 MINUTES
TOTAL TIME 2 HOURS

WHY THIS RECIPE WORKS To make *pollo en pepitoria* that was rich but balanced, we brightened the lush nut- and egg yolk–thickened sauce with canned tomatoes (more consistent year-round than fresh tomatoes) and a little lemon juice. We added some of the braising liquid to the nut mixture when we blended it to make the sauce; this helped it puree thoroughly but still retain a pleasantly coarse consistency. Chicken thighs are fully cooked when they reach 175 degrees, but we purposely overcooked them—and did it slowly—which allowed collagen in the meat to break down into gelatin, making the meat more tender and juicy. We were happy to find that we could also make this rich braise well in advance and keep it in the freezer. See page 88 for our recipe for Easy-Peel Hard-Cooked Eggs.

8 (5- to 7-ounce) bone-in chicken thighs, trimmed
    Salt and pepper

1 tablespoon extra-virgin olive oil
1 onion, chopped fine
3 garlic cloves, minced
1 bay leaf
¼ teaspoon ground cinnamon
⅔ cup dry sherry
1 (14.5-ounce) can whole peeled tomatoes, drained and chopped fine
1 cup chicken broth
2 hard-cooked eggs, peeled, yolks and whites separated, whites minced
½ cup slivered blanched almonds, toasted
    Pinch saffron threads, crumbled
2 tablespoons chopped fresh parsley
1½ teaspoons lemon juice

1. Adjust oven rack to middle position and heat oven to 300 degrees. Pat chicken dry with paper towels and season with salt and pepper. Heat oil in 12-inch skillet over high heat until just smoking. Add thighs and brown on both sides, 10 to 12 minutes. Transfer thighs to large plate, discard skin, and pour off all but 2 teaspoons fat from skillet.

2. Return skillet to medium heat, add onion and ¼ teaspoon salt and cook, stirring frequently, until just softened, about 3 minutes. Add 2 teaspoons garlic, bay leaf, and cinnamon and cook until fragrant, about 1 minute. Add sherry and cook, scraping up any browned bits, until beginning to thicken, about 2 minutes. Stir in tomatoes and broth and bring to simmer. Return thighs to skillet, cover, transfer to oven, and cook until chicken registers 195 degrees, 45 to 50 minutes. Transfer thighs to serving platter and cover loosely with aluminum foil to keep warm.

3. Discard bay leaf. Transfer ¾ cup chicken cooking liquid, egg yolks, almonds, saffron, and remaining garlic to blender jar. Process until smooth, about 2 minutes, scraping down jar as needed. Return almond mixture to skillet. Add 1 tablespoon parsley and lemon juice and bring to simmer over medium heat. Cook, whisking frequently, until thickened, 3 to 5 minutes. Season with salt and pepper to taste.

4. Pour sauce over chicken, sprinkle with remaining 1 tablespoon parsley and egg whites, and serve.

TO MAKE AHEAD

- Braised chicken and sauce, prepared through step 3, can be refrigerated together for up to 3 days or frozen for up to 1 month; if frozen, thaw completely in refrigerator
- To reheat, bring sauce and chicken, covered, to gentle simmer, cook until chicken is hot throughout, and continue with step 4

We brush on our flavorful homemade barbecue sauce in stages so that its flavor comes through after grilling.

Sweet and Tangy Grilled Barbecue Chicken

SERVES 6 TO 8
ACTIVE TIME 1 HOUR
TOTAL TIME 2 HOURS (PLUS 6 HOURS SALTING TIME)

WHY THIS RECIPE WORKS Barbecued chicken falls victim to numerous pitfalls: The chicken cooks unevenly, frequent flare-ups cause the skin to blacken, and the sauce is usually too thick and cloyingly sweet. We set out to foolproof this American classic. For chicken that was well seasoned all the way to the bone, we applied a rub: Salt, onion and garlic powders, paprika, a touch of cayenne, and some brown sugar maintained a bold presence even after grilling. Placing a disposable aluminum pan opposite the coals in our grill setup and filling the pan partially with water lowered the temperature inside the grill, which ensured that all the chicken pieces cooked at a slow, steady rate. We smartened the typical ketchup-based barbecue sauce with molasses, while cider vinegar, Worcestershire sauce, and Dijon mustard kept the sweetness in check. We waited to apply the sauce until after searing the chicken, which prevented the sauce from burning and gave the chicken skin a chance to develop color first. Applying the sauce in stages, rather than all at once, ensured that its bright tanginess wasn't lost. When browning the chicken over the hotter side of the grill, move it away from any flare-ups.

CHICKEN
- 2 tablespoons packed dark brown sugar
- 1½ tablespoons kosher salt
- 1½ teaspoons garlic powder
- 1½ teaspoons onion powder
- 1½ teaspoons paprika
- ¼ teaspoon cayenne pepper
- 6 pounds bone-in chicken pieces (split breasts and/or leg quarters), trimmed

SAUCE
- 1 cup ketchup
- 5 tablespoons molasses
- 3 tablespoons cider vinegar
- 2 tablespoons Worcestershire sauce
- 2 tablespoons Dijon mustard
- ¼ teaspoon pepper
- 2 tablespoons vegetable oil
- ⅓ cup grated onion
- 1 garlic clove, minced
- 1 teaspoon chili powder
- ¼ teaspoon cayenne pepper
- 1 large disposable aluminum roasting pan (if using charcoal) or 2 disposable aluminum pie plates (if using gas)

1. FOR THE CHICKEN Combine sugar, salt, garlic powder, onion powder, paprika, and cayenne in bowl. Arrange chicken on rimmed baking sheet and sprinkle both sides evenly with spice rub. Cover with plastic wrap and refrigerate for at least 6 hours.

2. FOR THE SAUCE Whisk ketchup, molasses, vinegar, Worcestershire, mustard, and pepper together in bowl. Heat oil in medium saucepan over medium heat until shimmering. Add onion and garlic and cook until softened, 2 to 4 minutes. Add chili powder and cayenne and cook until fragrant, about 30 seconds. Whisk in ketchup mixture and bring to boil. Reduce heat to medium-low and simmer gently for 5 minutes. Set aside ⅔ cup sauce to baste chicken and reserve remaining sauce for serving.

3A. FOR A CHARCOAL GRILL Open bottom vent halfway and place disposable pan filled with 3 cups water on 1 side of grill. Light large chimney starter filled with charcoal briquettes (6 quarts). When top coals are partially covered with ash, pour evenly over other half of grill (opposite disposable pan). Set cooking grate in place, cover, and open lid vent halfway. Heat grill until hot, about 5 minutes.

3B. FOR A GAS GRILL Place 2 disposable pie plates, each filled with 1½ cups water, directly on 1 burner of gas grill (opposite primary burner). Turn all burners to high, cover, and heat grill until hot, about 15 minutes. Turn primary burner to medium-high and turn off other burner(s). (Adjust primary burner as needed to maintain grill temperature of 325 to 350 degrees.)

4. Clean and oil cooking grate. Place chicken, skin side down, on hotter side of grill and cook until browned and blistered in spots, 2 to 5 minutes. Flip chicken and cook until second side is browned, 4 to 6 minutes. Move chicken to cooler side and brush both sides with ⅓ cup sauce. Arrange chicken, skin side up, with leg quarters closest to fire and breasts farthest away. Cover (positioning lid vent over chicken if using charcoal) and cook for 25 minutes.

5. Brush both sides of chicken with remaining ⅓ cup sauce and continue to cook, covered, until breasts register 160 degrees and leg quarters register 175 degrees, 25 to 35 minutes longer.

6. Transfer chicken to serving platter, tent with aluminum foil, and let rest for 10 minutes. Serve, passing reserved sauce separately.

TO MAKE AHEAD

- Seasoned chicken, prepared through step 1, can be refrigerated for up to 24 hours
- Sauce can be refrigerated for up to 1 week

Lemon zest and aromatics help tame the heat of black pepper and red pepper flakes in our spicy grilled chicken.

Grilled Chicken Diavolo

SERVES 4 **EASY**
ACTIVE TIME 30 MINUTES
TOTAL TIME 1 HOUR 20 MINUTES

WHY THIS RECIPE WORKS Chicken diavolo is characterized by its spicy heat, which is typically provided by plenty of black and/or dried red pepper. We started by testing a handful of recipes that used a range of different flavors and cooking techniques and came away most impressed by those that were grilled. Pieces were easier to handle than a whole bird, and a potent mixture of oil, lemon zest, aromatics, and a generous dose of red pepper flakes and black pepper pulled double duty as both a marinade and a sauce base. A two-level grill fire ensured that the chicken cooked through and browned nicely but didn't char, and adding a packet of wood chips to the grill lent complementary smoky flavor to our spicy chicken. To use wood chunks on a charcoal grill, substitute one medium wood chunk, soaked in water for 1 hour, for the wood chip packet.

3 pounds bone-in chicken pieces (split breasts cut in half, drumsticks, and/or thighs), trimmed
½ cup extra-virgin olive oil
4 garlic cloves, minced
1 tablespoon chopped fresh rosemary
2 teaspoons grated lemon zest plus 4 teaspoons juice
2 teaspoons red pepper flakes
1 teaspoon sugar
Salt and pepper
½ teaspoon paprika
1 cup wood chips

1. Pat chicken dry with paper towels. Whisk oil, garlic, rosemary, lemon zest, pepper flakes, sugar, 1 teaspoon pepper, and paprika in large bowl until combined. Measure out ¼ cup oil mixture and set aside. Whisk 2¼ teaspoons salt into remaining oil mixture. Add chicken, turn to coat, and refrigerate for at least 1 hour.

2. Just before grilling, soak wood chips in water for 15 minutes, then drain. Using large piece of heavy-duty aluminum foil, wrap soaked chips in 8 by 4 ½-inch foil packet. (Make sure chips do not poke holes in sides or bottom of packet.) Cut 2 evenly spaced 2-inch slits in top of packet.

3A. FOR A CHARCOAL GRILL Open bottom vent halfway. Light large chimney starter filled with charcoal briquettes (6 quarts). When top coals are partially covered with ash, pour two-thirds evenly over half of grill, then pour remaining coals over other half of grill. Place wood chip packet on larger pile of coals. Set cooking grate in place, cover, and open lid vent halfway. Heat grill until hot and wood chips are smoking, about 5 minutes.

3B. FOR A GAS GRILL Place wood chip packet over primary burner. Turn all burners to high, cover, and heat grill until hot and wood chips are smoking, about 15 minutes. Turn primary burner to medium and turn other burner(s) to low. (Adjust primary burner as needed to maintain grill temperature of 400 to 425 degrees.)

4. Meanwhile, remove chicken from marinade and pat dry with paper towels. Clean and oil cooking grate. Place chicken, skin side up, on cooler side of grill. Cover and cook until lightly browned, 8 to 12 minutes. Flip chicken, cover, and cook until breasts register 155 degrees and drumsticks/thighs register 170 degrees, 7 to 10 minutes.

5. Transfer chicken, skin side down, to hotter side of grill and cook (covered if using gas) until well browned, about 3 minutes. Flip and continue to cook (covered if using gas) until breasts register 160 degrees and drumsticks/thighs register 175 degrees, 1 to 3 minutes. Transfer chicken to platter, tent loosely with foil, and let rest for 5 to 10 minutes.

6. Meanwhile, heat reserved oil mixture in small saucepan over low heat until fragrant and garlic begins to brown, 3 to 5 minutes. Off heat, whisk in lemon juice and ¼ teaspoon salt. Spoon sauce over chicken. Serve.

TO MAKE AHEAD

Marinated chicken and sauce, prepared through step 1, can be refrigerated separately for up to 24 hours

MAKING A WOOD CHIP PACKET

Drain soaked wood chips and spread them in center of large piece of heavy-duty aluminum foil. Fold to seal edges; then cut two slits in foil packet to allow smoke to escape.

A looser sauce is key to getting the texture of the filling right when making pot pies to store in the freezer.

Individual Chicken Pot Pies for the Freezer

SERVES 6   **FREEZE IT**

ACTIVE TIME 1 HOUR 35 MINUTES

TOTAL TIME 2 HOURS 40 MINUTES (PLUS FREEZING TIME)

WHY THIS RECIPE WORKS Chicken pot pie is the ultimate comfort food, so we sought a way to streamline this classic dish and make individual pot pies that we could pull out of the freezer and bake any time. There are many challenges that arise in making a pot pie with a beautiful flaky crust, tender and flavorful chicken and vegetables, and a creamy sauce; when we added "freezer-friendly" to the list of requirements, this recipe became an even taller order. First, we decided to use small disposable loaf pans, which would make storage and reheating easy and allow us to serve only the number we needed (without all our ramekins being tied up in the freezer). Browning boneless, skinless breasts before cooking them in broth gave our pie the deepest chicken flavor (without the hassle of roasting). A bit of thyme and lemon juice brightened up the creamy filling, and a bit of extra liquid ensured that the filling didn't dry out in the freezer. As for the topping, we opted to skip the homemade pie dough in favor of store-bought, which was easy to use and kept the process more streamlined. To make the crusts sturdy enough to hold up on top of the filling, we made a double-thick crust by gluing two crusts together with water. To make sure that the crusts didn't overbrown in the time it took the filling to warm through, we covered the pies for part of the baking time. To preserve their color, don't thaw the peas before adding them to the filling in step 6. Depending on how many people you are feeding, you can bake all six pies at once or bake one or two at time. Be aware that ready-made store-bought pie dough rounds typically come two to a box.

1½ pounds boneless, skinless chicken breasts, trimmed
    Salt and pepper
  2 tablespoons vegetable oil
5½ cups chicken broth
  2 tablespoons unsalted butter
  3 carrots, peeled and cut into ½-inch pieces
  1 onion, chopped fine
  1 celery rib, minced
  ½ cup all-purpose flour
  ¼ cup whole milk
  2 teaspoons minced fresh thyme or ¾ teaspoon dried
  2 tablespoons lemon juice
  4 (9-inch) store-bought pie dough rounds
1½ cups frozen peas
  6 2-cup disposable aluminum loaf pans
  1 large egg, beaten

1. Pat chicken dry with paper towels and season with salt and pepper. Heat 1 tablespoon oil in Dutch oven over medium-high heat until just smoking. Add chicken and cook until well browned, about 2½ minutes per side. Add broth and bring to simmer. Reduce heat to low, cover, and cook until chicken registers 160 degrees, 6 to 8 minutes. Transfer chicken to cutting board and broth to large bowl.

2. Melt butter with remaining 1 tablespoon oil in now-empty pot over medium-high heat. Add carrots, onion, celery, and ¼ teaspoon salt and cook until lightly browned and softened, 8 to 10 minutes. Reduce heat to medium, add flour, and cook for 1 minute. Whisk in milk, thyme, and reserved broth and bring to simmer. Cook, whisking often, until sauce thickens, about 10 minutes.

3. Shred chicken into bite-size pieces using 2 forks. Off heat, stir in lemon juice and shredded chicken and season with salt and pepper to taste. Transfer filling to bowl and let cool completely. Cover bowl with plastic wrap and refrigerate until well chilled, about 1 hour.

4. Place 2 dough rounds on lightly floured counter. Brush surface of each round with water, then place remaining 2 dough rounds on moistened rounds, pressing gently to adhere.

5. Position 1 inverted loaf pan on 1 layered dough round. Using sharp paring knife, cut out piece of dough using pan as template. Repeat twice more for total of 3 dough pieces, then repeat process on second layered dough round. Discard excess dough.

6. Stir peas into chilled filling, then evenly divide filling among loaf pans. Top each pan with 1 dough piece, then use fork to seal edges. Using paring knife, cut 3 steam vents in each pot pie. Tightly wrap each loaf pan in 2 layers of plastic and 1 layer of aluminum foil, then freeze pot pies completely.

7. Adjust oven rack to middle position and heat oven to 400 degrees. Unwrap frozen pot pies and arrange on rimmed baking sheet. Brush each pot pie with egg and cover with foil. Bake until filling is starting to bubble, about 40 minutes. Uncover pot pies and bake until crusts are golden brown, about 35 minutes. Let pot pies rest for 10 minutes before serving.

▶ TO MAKE AHEAD ▶

Pot pies, prepared through step 6, can be frozen for up to 1 month

Classic Chicken Pot Pie
SERVES 6 TO 8　**FREEZE IT**
ACTIVE TIME 1 HOUR 30 MINUTES
TOTAL TIME 2 HOURS 30 MINUTES

WHY THIS RECIPE WORKS For a streamlined chicken pot pie, we started by poaching boneless, skinless chicken breasts in broth. This made for tender chicken that could be shredded into bite-size pieces that the sauce could cling to. For the sauce, we sautéed our aromatics and vegetables before adding flour to make a roux. Whisking in the reserved chicken poaching liquid along with milk built rich flavor. A bit of sherry brightened up the filling. We stirred in the shredded chicken, peas, and parsley just before topping the pie to ensure that these delicate ingredients didn't overcook in the oven. You can use store-bought pie dough in place of homemade in this recipe.

1½ pounds boneless, skinless chicken breasts, trimmed
  2 cups chicken broth
  4 tablespoons unsalted butter
  1 onion, chopped fine
  3 carrots, peeled and sliced ¼ inch thick
  2 celery ribs, sliced ¼ inch thick
    Salt and pepper
  2 garlic cloves, minced
  2 teaspoons minced fresh thyme or ½ teaspoon dried
  ½ cup all-purpose flour

Poaching the chicken for our pot pie in broth enhances the chickeny flavor of the filling and ensures tender meat.

1½ cups milk
¼ cup dry sherry
1 cup frozen peas
3 tablespoons minced fresh parsley
1 recipe Foolproof Double-Crust Pie Dough (page 371)
1 egg, lightly beaten with 1 teaspoon water

1. Adjust oven rack to lower-middle position and heat oven to 400 degrees. Bring chicken and broth to simmer in Dutch oven over medium heat. Reduce heat to low, cover, and cook until chicken registers 160 degrees, 10 to 15 minutes. Transfer chicken to cutting board and broth to bowl.

2. Melt butter in now-empty pot over medium heat. Add onion, carrots, celery, and 1 teaspoon salt and cook until softened, about 5 minutes. Stir in garlic and thyme and cook until fragrant, about 30 seconds. Stir in flour and cook for 1 minute. Whisk in reserved broth and milk, scraping up any browned bits and smoothing out any lumps. Bring to simmer and cook until sauce is thickened, about 3 minutes. Season with salt and pepper to taste, then stir in sherry.

3. Once chicken is cool enough to handle, shred into bite-size pieces using 2 forks, then add to sauce, along with any accumulated juices, peas, and parsley. Transfer to 13 by 9-inch baking dish.

4. Roll each disk dough into 9-inch round on well-floured counter, then overlap by half, brushing with water where dough overlaps. Roll together to seal, then roll into 16 by 12-inch rectangle. Loosely roll dough around rolling pin and gently unroll it over filling in dish, letting excess dough hang over edge. Trim dough to ½ inch beyond lip of dish, then tuck overhang under itself; folded edge should be flush with edge of dish. Crimp dough evenly around edge of dish using your fingers. Cut five 2-inch slits in top of dough.

5. Brush surface with egg wash and bake until topping is golden and filling is bubbling, about 30 minutes, rotating dish halfway through cooking. Let cool for 20 minutes before serving.

▶ TO MAKE AHEAD

- Pot pie, prepared through step 4, can be refrigerated for up to 24 hours; to bake, continue with step 5, increasing cooking time to 40 to 50 minutes
- Alternatively, pot pie filling, prepared through step 3, can be frozen for up to 1 month; to bake, thaw completely in refrigerator, then bring to gentle simmer, covered, stirring often, before transferring to baking dish and continuing with step 4

Chicken and Dumplings

SERVES 6 TO 8
ACTIVE TIME 1 HOUR 15 MINUTES
TOTAL TIME 2 HOURS

WHY THIS RECIPE WORKS Chicken and dumplings is a cornerstone of American comfort food, but many recipes require several hours of work. We wanted a quicker version that would taste just as good. Replacing the whole chicken (which must be cut up into parts) with boneless, skinless breasts was a good start. To ensure that the meat stayed moist, we poached the breasts in broth and then removed them while we built the rest of the stew. This had the added benefit of enhancing the flavor of the broth. Tasters liked a mix of carrots and onion and welcomed the fresh pop of peas stirred in at the end. Dry sherry, garlic, thyme and bay leaves added flavor. Flour helped to thicken the stew base nicely, and cream added richness. Dropped biscuit-style dumplings were easier to make than rolled, noodle-style dumplings, and using a full tablespoon of baking powder ensured that the dumplings were fluffy and not dense. For tender dumplings, the dough should be gently mixed right before the dumplings are dropped onto the stew.

We use a full tablespoon of baking powder in our dropped biscuit-style dumplings so they turn out light and fluffy.

STEW

5 cups chicken broth
2 pounds boneless, skinless chicken breasts, trimmed
5 tablespoons unsalted butter
4 carrots, peeled and sliced ¼ inch thick
1 large onion, chopped fine
1 teaspoon salt
3 garlic cloves, minced
6 tablespoons all-purpose flour
¾ cup dry sherry
⅓ cup heavy cream
2 bay leaves
½ teaspoon dried thyme
½ teaspoon pepper
1½ cups frozen peas
¼ cup minced fresh parsley

DUMPLINGS

2 cups all-purpose flour
1 tablespoon baking powder
½ teaspoon salt
1⅓ cups heavy cream

1. FOR THE STEW Bring broth to simmer in Dutch oven over high heat. Add chicken and return to simmer. Reduce heat to low, cover, and cook until chicken registers 160 degrees, 10 to 15 minutes. Transfer chicken to cutting board and broth to bowl.

2. Melt butter in now-empty Dutch oven over medium-high heat. Add carrots, onion, and salt and cook until softened, about 7 minutes. Stir in garlic and cook until fragrant, about 30 seconds. Stir in flour and cook, stirring frequently, for 1 minute. Stir in sherry, scraping up browned bits. Stir in reserved broth, cream, bay leaves, thyme, and pepper and bring to boil. Cover, reduce heat to low, and simmer until stew thickens, about 20 minutes.

3. FOR THE DUMPLINGS Whisk flour, baking powder, and salt together in large bowl. Stir in cream until incorporated (dough will be very thick and shaggy).

4. Discard bay leaves and return stew to rapid simmer. Shred chicken into bite-size pieces using 2 forks and add to stew along with any accumulated juices, peas, and 3 tablespoons parsley. Using 2 large soupspoons, drop golf ball–size dumplings onto stew about ¼ inch apart (you should have 16 to 18 dumplings). Reduce heat to low, cover, and cook until dumplings have doubled in size, 15 to 18 minutes. Sprinkle with remaining 1 tablespoon parsley and serve.

TO MAKE AHEAD

- Stew and poached chicken, prepared through step 2, can be refrigerated separately for up to 24 hours
- To cook, bring stew, covered, to gentle simmer, stirring often, and continue with step 3

Chicken Enchiladas

SERVES 4 TO 6 **FREEZE IT**
ACTIVE TIME 1 HOUR 10 MINUTES
TOTAL TIME 2 HOURS

WHY THIS RECIPE WORKS Making enchiladas is quite an undertaking, from preparing the sauce and the filling to assembling and baking everything. We wanted a make-ahead version of this popular casserole, and we hoped to streamline the process a little, too. We tried making the enchiladas with straight-from-the-package tortillas but the result was a mushy and lackluster casserole. To solve this, we prepped the tortillas, brushing both sides with vegetable oil and warming them in the microwave. The warmed tortillas were easy to fill and roll, and the oil sealed the surface of the tortillas, preventing them from becoming soggy so they held up during storage and baking. When making the casserole ahead, we found it best to store the enchiladas separately from the sauce so that we could bake the enchiladas partway through before adding the sauce, giving the top of the casserole

Oiling and microwaving the tortillas before assembling the casserole helps our enchiladas hold up when stored overnight.

a chance to crisp and brown. For the sauce, we used canned tomato sauce as a convenient base. Then, to punch up the flavor of the sauce, we bloomed a full 3 tablespoons of chili powder in oil along with garlic, cumin, and coriander. If you prefer, Monterey Jack cheese can be used instead of cheddar, or, for a mellower flavor and creamier texture, try substituting an equal amount of *queso fresco*. Serve with sour cream, diced avocado, shredded romaine lettuce, and/or lime wedges.

¼ cup vegetable oil
1 onion, chopped fine
3 tablespoons chili powder
3 garlic cloves, minced
2 teaspoons ground coriander
2 teaspoons ground cumin
2 teaspoons sugar
½ teaspoon salt
1 pound boneless, skinless chicken thighs, trimmed and cut into ¼-inch-wide strips
2 (8-ounce) cans tomato sauce
⅓ cup water
½ cup minced fresh cilantro

⅓ cup jarred jalapeños, rinsed, patted dry, and chopped
10 ounces sharp cheddar cheese, shredded (2½ cups)
12 (6-inch) corn tortillas
Vegetable oil spray

1. Adjust oven rack to middle position and heat oven to 400 degrees. Heat 2 tablespoons oil in large saucepan over medium heat until shimmering. Add onion and cook until softened and lightly browned, 5 to 7 minutes. Stir in chili powder, garlic, coriander, cumin, sugar, and salt and cook until fragrant, about 30 seconds. Stir in chicken, tomato sauce, and water and bring to gentle simmer. Cook, stirring occasionally, until chicken is tender and flavors blend, 8 to 10 minutes.

2. Pour mixture through fine-mesh strainer into bowl, pressing on strained chicken mixture to extract as much sauce as possible; set sauce aside. Transfer chicken mixture to bowl, refrigerate for 20 minutes to chill, then stir in cilantro, jalapeños, and 2 cups cheddar.

3. Brush both sides of tortillas with remaining 2 tablespoons oil. Stack tortillas, wrap in damp dish towel, and place on plate; microwave until warm and pliable, about 1 minute. Working with 1 warm tortilla at a time, spread ⅓ cup chicken filling across center of tortilla, roll tortilla tightly around filling, and place seam side down in greased 13 by 9-inch baking dish; arrange enchiladas in 2 columns across width of dish.

4. Spray top of enchiladas with oil spray and bake uncovered until lightly toasted on top, 10 to 15 minutes. Pour sauce over enchiladas, covering tortillas completely, then sprinkle remaining ½ cup cheddar across center of enchiladas. Cover dish tightly with greased aluminum foil and bake until enchiladas are hot throughout, bubbling around edges, and cheese is melted, 20 to 25 minutes. Serve immediately.

TO MAKE AHEAD ▶

Enchiladas, wrapped tightly in plastic wrap and covered with aluminum foil, and sauce, prepared through step 3, can be refrigerated separately for up to 24 hours or frozen for up to 1 month; if frozen, thaw completely in refrigerator

ARRANGING ENCHILADAS

In order to fit 12 enchiladas in a 13 by 9-inch casserole dish, you need to arrange them widthwise in the pan, in two rows of six enchiladas.

Ground turkey cooks quickly and works perfectly as a meaty backdrop for classic Mexican flavors.

Mexican Lasagna with Turkey

SERVES 6 TO 8
ACTIVE TIME 1 HOUR 10 MINUTES
TOTAL TIME 2 HOURS 25 MINUTES

WHY THIS RECIPE WORKS For a comfort food classic that marries the best qualities of two international favorites, we set out to create a hearty, make-ahead Mexican lasagna. Mild-flavored and convenient ground turkey made a good base for our filling; it paired well with all the ingredients and flavors of the dish and provided a meaty backbone for the green enchilada sauce and the smoky chipotle. Plus, it could be cooked in minutes along with the aromatics, keeping things easy. We added corn and pinto beans to make this dish feel satisfying. For the layers of cheese, we used Monterey Jack, which melted beautifully. To form the layers, we used corn tortillas; brushing them with oil and heating them briefly in the microwave kept them from turning to mush as the lasagna cooked. We added a bit of flour to thicken the sauce, which made it harder for the tortillas to soak up liquid if stored overnight. Be sure to use ground turkey, not ground turkey breast

(also labeled 99 percent fat-free), in this recipe. Serve with salsa, diced avocado, sour cream, scallions, and/or lime wedges.

¼ cup vegetable oil
4 scallions, sliced thin
4 garlic cloves, minced
4 teaspoons minced canned chipotle chile in adobo sauce
½ teaspoon salt
¼ teaspoon pepper
1½ pounds ground turkey
3 tablespoons all-purpose flour
2 cups chicken broth
1 (15-ounce) can pinto beans, rinsed
1 (10-ounce) can green enchilada sauce
2 cups frozen corn, thawed
⅓ cup plus 2 tablespoons minced fresh cilantro
18 (6-inch) corn tortillas
12 ounces Monterey Jack cheese, shredded (3 cups)

1. Adjust oven rack to middle position and heat oven to 400 degrees. Heat 2 tablespoons oil in Dutch oven over medium heat until shimmering. Add scallions, garlic, chipotle, salt, and pepper and cook until fragrant, about 1 minute. Add turkey and cook, breaking up meat with wooden spoon, until no longer pink, 3 to 5 minutes. Stir in flour and cook for 1 minute.

2. Stir in broth, beans, and enchilada sauce. Bring to simmer and cook until mixture is slightly thickened and flavors blend, about 10 minutes. Stir in corn and ⅓ cup cilantro and let cool to room temperature, about 30 minutes.

3. Brush both sides of tortillas with remaining 2 tablespoons oil. Stack tortillas, wrap in damp dish towel, and place on plate; microwave until warm and pliable, about 1 minute.

4. Spread one-third of cooled turkey mixture on bottom of 13 by 9-inch baking dish. Arrange 6 tortillas on top of filling, overlapping as needed, and sprinkle with 1 cup Monterey Jack. Repeat layering of filling, tortillas, and Monterey Jack once more. Spread remaining filling in dish. Cut remaining 6 tortillas into quarters and scatter over filling. Sprinkle with remaining 1 cup Monterey Jack.

5. Cover dish tightly with greased aluminum foil and bake until hot throughout and bubbling around edges, about 30 minutes. Remove foil and continue to bake until topping is golden brown, about 15 minutes. Let cool for 10 minutes. Sprinkle with remaining 2 tablespoons cilantro and serve.

TO MAKE AHEAD

Lasagna, prepared through step 4, can be refrigerated for up to 24 hours

We rub chicken with a mixture of salt and baking soda to guarantee moist, flavorful meat and the crispest skin.

Never-Fail Crispy Roast Chicken

SERVES 3 TO 4 EASY

ACTIVE TIME 20 MINUTES

TOTAL TIME 1 HOUR 30 MINUTES (PLUS 12 HOURS SALTING TIME)

WHY THIS RECIPE WORKS A well-seasoned, juicy roast chicken with crispy, flavorful skin is as good as it gets, but for all its simplicity, really good roast chicken is tough to get right. Brining can help guarantee moist and flavorful meat, but it's usually at the expense of crispy skin. To overcome this challenge, we turned to a combination of salt and baking powder. A salt rub makes meat juicy in a process similar to brining, but unlike brining, it doesn't prevent the skin from crisping. And the lengthy rest that salting requires made it the perfect method for make-ahead roast chicken. Adding baking powder to the rub not only sped up the dehydration process that salting encourages (which is the cornerstone of crispy skin), it also accelerated browning during roasting, making for even crisper, more flavorful skin. Separating the skin from the meat and poking the fat deposits with a skewer allowed the rendered fat to flow freely from the roasting chicken and prevented the skin from becoming soggy. In search of the best roasting method, we found that placing the chicken breast side up in a preheated skillet gave the thighs a jump start on cooking, and turning the oven off while the chicken finished cooking slowed the evaporation of juices, ensuring moist, tender meat.

1½ teaspoons salt
⅛ teaspoon vegetable oil
1 teaspoon baking powder
½ teaspoon pepper
1 (3½- to 4-pound) whole chicken, giblets discarded

1. Combine salt and oil in small bowl and stir until salt is evenly coated with oil. Stir in baking powder and pepper until thoroughly combined. Pat chicken dry with paper towels. Using your fingers, gently loosen skin covering breast and thighs. Using metal skewer or tip of paring knife, poke 15 to 20 holes in fat deposits on top of breasts and thighs.

2. Rub salt–baking powder mixture evenly over surface of chicken. Tie legs together with twine and tuck wingtips behind back. Set chicken breast side up on wire rack set in rimmed baking sheet. Refrigerate chicken, uncovered, for at least 12 hours.

3. Adjust oven rack to middle position, place 12-inch skillet on rack, and heat oven to 450 degrees. Carefully transfer chicken breast side up to preheated skillet in oven (skillet handle will be hot). Roast chicken until breasts register 120 degrees and thighs register 135 degrees, 25 to 35 minutes. Turn off oven and leave chicken in oven until breasts register 160 degrees and thighs register 175 degrees, 25 to 35 minutes.

4. Transfer chicken to carving board and let rest, uncovered, for 20 minutes. Carve chicken and serve.

> **TO MAKE AHEAD**
>
> Salted chicken, prepared through step 2, can be refrigerated for up to 24 hours

A layer of the Middle Eastern spice blend *za'atar* adds a flavorful crust to simple roast chicken.

Za'atar-Rubbed Butterflied Chicken with Preserved Lemon Vinaigrette

SERVES 3 TO 4

ACTIVE TIME 1 HOUR

TOTAL TIME 1 HOUR 20 MINUTES (PLUS 6 HOURS SALTING TIME)

WHY THIS RECIPE WORKS For an easy, but impressive, weeknight dinner, we turned to a simple dish of chicken rubbed with *za'atar*. Za'atar is the Arabic name for wild thyme, but now commonly denotes an addictive spice mixture of thyme, sumac, and sesame. Using olive oil to form a paste, we spread za'atar and salt underneath the chicken skin and let it rest, which had the same effect as brining the chicken. To cook the chicken, we borrowed an Italian technique of cooking under a brick (or a pot in this case). Once we had crisp skin, we brushed on additional za'atar and olive oil paste. Finishing the chicken breast side up in a hot oven turned the paste into a crisp crust. While the chicken cooked, we created a zesty vinaigrette that brightened up the finished dish.

We prefer to use our homemade Za'atar (recipe follows); you can substitute store-bought za'atar if you wish, though flavor can vary by brand. If you can't find preserved lemons, you can microwave four 2-inch strips lemon zest, minced, 1 teaspoon lemon juice, ½ teaspoon water, ¼ teaspoon sugar, and ¼ teaspoon salt at 50 percent power until the liquid evaporates, about 1½ minutes, stirring and mashing the lemon with the back of a spoon every 30 seconds.

> 5 tablespoons plus 1 teaspoon extra-virgin olive oil
> 2 tablespoons za'atar
>   Salt and pepper
> 1 (3½- to 4-pound) whole chicken, giblets discarded
> 1 tablespoon minced fresh mint
> ¼ preserved lemon, pulp and white pith removed, rind rinsed and minced (1 tablespoon)
> 2 teaspoons white wine vinegar
> ½ teaspoon Dijon mustard

1. Combine 1 tablespoon oil, 1 tablespoon za'atar, and 1 teaspoon salt in small bowl. With chicken breast side down, use kitchen shears to cut through bones on either side of backbone. Discard backbone and trim any excess fat or skin at neck. Flip chicken and tuck wingtips behind back. Press firmly on breastbone to flatten, then pound breast to be same thickness as leg and thigh. Pat chicken dry with paper towels and, using your fingers, gently loosen skin covering breast and thighs. Rub za'atar-oil paste evenly under skin. Transfer chicken to large plate and refrigerate for at least 6 hours.

ZA'ATAR

MAKES ½ CUP   **EASY**

ACTIVE TIME 5 MINUTES

TOTAL TIME 5 MINUTES

Za'atar is an aromatic Middle Eastern spice blend that is used as both a seasoning and a condiment. Try sprinkling it in olive oil as a dip for bread, or use it in grain dishes or as a flavorful topping for hummus or other dips.

> ½ cup dried thyme, ground
> 2 tablespoons sesame seeds, toasted
> 1½ tablespoons ground sumac

Combine all ingredients in bowl.

TO MAKE AHEAD

Za'atar can be stored at room temperature in airtight container for up to 1 year

---

2. Adjust oven rack to lowest position and heat oven to 450 degrees. Pat chicken dry with paper towels and season with salt and pepper. Combine 1 tablespoon oil and remaining 1 tablespoon za'atar in small bowl. Heat 1 teaspoon oil in 12-inch skillet over medium-high heat until just smoking. Place chicken skin side down in skillet, reduce heat to medium, and place heavy pot on chicken to press flat. Cook chicken until skin is crisp and browned, 20 to 25 minutes. (If chicken is not crisp after 20 minutes, increase heat to medium-high).

3. Off heat, remove pot and carefully flip chicken. Brush skin with za'atar mixture, transfer skillet to oven, and roast until breast registers 160 degrees and thighs register 175 degrees, 10 to 20 minutes.

4. Transfer chicken to carving board and let rest for 10 minutes. Meanwhile, whisk mint, lemon, vinegar, mustard, ⅛ teaspoon salt, and ⅛ teaspoon pepper together in bowl until combined. Whisking constantly, slowly drizzle in remaining 3 tablespoons oil until emulsified. Carve chicken and serve with dressing.

▶ TO MAKE AHEAD ▶

Chicken, prepared through step 1, can be refrigerated for up to 24 hours

BUTTERFLYING A CHICKEN

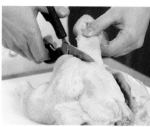

1. Cut through bones on either side of backbone and trim any excess fat and skin around neck. Discard backbone.

2. Flip chicken over and use heel of your hand to flatten breastbone.

3. Cover chicken with plastic wrap and pound breast to be same thickness as legs and thighs.

A simple grill setup produces results similar to the traditional rotisserie cooking method for huli huli chicken.

Huli Huli Chicken

SERVES 4 TO 6
ACTIVE TIME 1 HOUR 15 MINUTES
TOTAL TIME 2 HOURS 30 MINUTES

WHY THIS RECIPE WORKS Authentic Hawaiian huli huli chicken is typically something home cooks buy instead of make. The birds are continually basted with a sticky-sweet glaze and "huli"-ed, which means "turned" in Hawaiian. To adapt this recipe for an achievable homemade option, we had to change both the sauce and the technique. For the teriyaki-like glaze, we developed a version with soy sauce, rice vinegar, ginger, garlic, chili-garlic sauce, ketchup, brown sugar, and lots and lots of pineapple juice. We reduced the sauce until it was thick, glossy, and sweet to get the same effect as constantly basting without having to babysit the chicken on the grill. To mimic a Hawaiian rotisserie, we spread the coals in a single layer. The direct heat rendered the fat and crisped the skin, but the chicken was far enough from the coals to avoid burning. When basting the chicken with the glaze in step 4, be careful not to drip too much of it onto the coals, as this could cause flare ups.

To use wood chunks instead of wood chips when using a charcoal grill, substitute two medium wood chunks, soaked in water for 1 hour, for the wood chip packet.

CHICKEN

- 2 (3½- to 4-pound) whole chickens, giblets discarded
- 2 cups soy sauce
- 1 tablespoon vegetable oil
- 6 garlic cloves, minced
- 1 tablespoon grated fresh ginger

GLAZE

- 3 (6-ounce) cans pineapple juice
- ¼ cup packed light brown sugar
- ¼ cup soy sauce
- ¼ cup ketchup
- ¼ cup rice vinegar
- 2 tablespoons grated fresh ginger
- 4 garlic cloves, minced
- 2 teaspoons Asian chili-garlic sauce

- 2 cups wood chips

1. FOR THE CHICKEN With 1 chicken breast side down, use kitchen shears to cut through bones on either side of backbone. Discard backbone and trim any excess fat or skin at neck. Flip chicken over and, using chef's knife, cut through breastbone to separate chicken into halves. Tuck wingtips behind back. Repeat with second chicken. Combine soy sauce and 2 quarts cold water in large container. Heat oil in large saucepan over medium-high heat until shimmering. Add garlic and ginger and cook until fragrant, about 30 seconds. Stir into soy sauce mixture. Add chicken and refrigerate, covered, for at least 1 hour.

2. FOR THE GLAZE Combine pineapple juice, sugar, soy sauce, ketchup, vinegar, ginger, garlic, and chili-garlic sauce in now-empty saucepan and bring to boil. Reduce heat to medium and simmer until thick and syrupy (you should have about 1 cup), 20 to 25 minutes. Soak wood chips in water for 15 minutes, then drain. Using large piece of heavy-duty aluminum foil, wrap soaked chips in 8 by 4½-inch foil packet. (Make sure chips do not poke holes in sides or bottom of packet.) Cut 2 evenly spaced 2-inch slits in top of packet.

3A. FOR A CHARCOAL GRILL Open bottom vent halfway. Light large chimney starter three-quarters filled with charcoal briquettes (4½ quarts). When top coals are partially covered with ash, pour evenly over grill. Place foil packet on coals. Set cooking grate in place, cover, and open lid vent open halfway. Heat grill until hot and wood chips are smoking, about 5 minutes.

3B. FOR A GAS GRILL Remove cooking grate and place wood chip packet directly on primary burner. Set grate in place, turn all burners to high, cover, and heat grill until hot and wood chips are smoking, about 15 minutes. Turn all burners to medium-low. (Adjust burners as needed to maintain grill temperature around 350 degrees.)

4. Clean and oil cooking grate. Remove chicken from brine and pat dry with paper towels. Place chicken skin side up on grill (do not place chicken directly above foil packet). Cover and cook chicken until well browned on bottom and thighs register 120 degrees, 25 to 30 minutes. Flip chicken skin side down and continue to cook, covered, until skin is well browned and crisp, breasts register 160 degrees, and thighs register 175 degrees, 20 to 25 minutes longer. Transfer chicken to platter, brush with half of glaze, and let rest for 5 minutes. Serve, passing remaining glaze at table.

TO MAKE AHEAD

- Chicken, prepared through step 1, can be refrigerated for up to 8 hours
- Glaze, prepared through step 2, can be refrigerated for up to 3 days

SPLITTING CHICKENS

1. Place chicken, breast side down, on cutting board. Use kitchen shears to cut through bones on either side of backbone; remove backbone.

2. Flip chicken and use your hand to flatten. Using chef's knife, cut lengthwise through breastbone to separate chicken into halves.

Halving Cornish game hens before broiling creates a more even surface for browning.

Roasted Cornish Game Hens

SERVES 4

ACTIVE TIME 50 MINUTES

TOTAL TIME 1 HOUR 10 MINUTES (PLUS 4 HOURS SALTING TIME)

WHY THIS RECIPE WORKS Cornish game hens offer crisp skin and delicate meat and are an elegant alternative to chicken. But these small hens do present one significant challenge: By the time the skin is crisp and golden, the meat is dry and overcooked, and while brining encourages juicy meat, the added moisture prevents the skin from ever getting crisp. Our solution was to use a dry brining technique; this involved applying a salt rub on the skin and letting the meat rest to draw moisture from the surface of the hens to the meat inside. Adding some baking powder to the rub further dehydrated the skin, and poking holes in the fat on the breasts and thighs helped the fat to render. These hens came out moist and juicy, but even when we baked them in a hot oven on a preheated baking sheet, the skin still didn't get crisp. Typically we look to the broiler to achieve browning in a flash, but because of the hens' irregular shape, the broiler gave us uneven results. Instead, we decided to remove the backbone of the birds and split them in half, creating an even surface for the broiler to brown and crisp. After a brief 10 minutes in a hot oven, we turned on the broiler, and in 5 minutes more we had perfectly juicy hens with crisp, golden-brown skin. The required salting time and quick cooking time make this a natural choice for a company-worthy make-ahead main. If your hens weigh 1½ to 2 pounds, cook three instead of four, and extend the initial cooking time in step 4 to 15 minutes.

4 (1¼- to 1½-pound) Cornish game hens, giblets discarded
   Kosher salt and pepper
3¼ teaspoons vegetable oil
1 teaspoon baking powder

1. Working with 1 hen at a time, use kitchen shears to cut through bones on either side of backbone; discard backbone. Lay hen skin side up and flatten by pressing firmly on breastbone. Using sharp chef's knife, cut through center of breast to make 2 halves.

2. Combine 1 tablespoon salt and ¼ teaspoon oil in small bowl and stir until salt is evenly coated with oil. Stir in baking powder until thoroughly combined. Pat hens dry with paper towels. Using your fingers, gently loosen skin covering breast and thighs. Using metal skewer or tip of paring knife, poke 10 to 15 holes in fat deposits on top of breast halves and thighs. Tuck wingtips underneath hens.

3. Sprinkle 1 tablespoon salt on underside (bone side) of hens. Turn hens skin side up and rub salt–baking powder mixture evenly over surface. Transfer hens, skin side up, to wire rack set in rimmed baking sheet. Refrigerate hens, uncovered, for at least 4 hours.

4. Adjust oven racks to upper-middle and lowest positions, place clean rimmed baking sheet on lower rack, and heat oven to 500 degrees. Brush skin of hens with remaining 1 tablespoon oil and season with pepper. Carefully transfer hens, skin side down, to hot sheet and bake for 10 minutes.

5. Remove hens from oven and heat broiler. While broiler heats, flip hens skin side up. Transfer baking sheet with hens to upper rack and broil until well browned and breasts register 160 degrees and thighs register 175 degrees, about 5 minutes, rotating as necessary to promote even browning. Let rest for 5 to 10 minutes before serving.

TO MAKE AHEAD

Salted hens, prepared through step 3, can be refrigerated for up to 24 hours

We sear our turkey breast in a Dutch oven to crisp the skin and then gently roast it in a moderate oven.

Spice-Rubbed Turkey Breast with Sour Orange Sauce

SERVES 8 TO 10

ACTIVE TIME 1 HOUR 15 MINUTES

TOTAL TIME 3 HOURS (PLUS 6 HOURS SALTING TIME)

WHY THIS RECIPE WORKS A roasted turkey breast can easily feed a small group and is a great backdrop for a flavorful sauce, but getting moist, juicy meat and crisp skin can be a challenge. To accomplish this, we used a technique that incorporated both high-temperature searing for crisp skin and roasting at a lower temperature to ensure moist meat. We started by searing the turkey breast in a large Dutch oven to get some flavorful browning and then transferred the pot to a 325-degree oven to let the breast cook through. The addition of a potent spice paste gave this mild cut mellow heat and deep flavor. Rubbing the mixture under the skin and over the exterior of the turkey ensured big flavor in every bite. Lifting the skin to apply the spice rub had the added advantage of creating pockets of air that made it easier for the fat to render and the skin to crisp. A simple yet potent sauce made

with aromatics, fresh orange juice, and a bit of tarragon was the perfect finishing touch. Many supermarkets are now selling "hotel-cut" turkey breasts, which still have the wings and rib cage attached. If this is the only type of breast you can find, you will need to remove the wings and cut away the rib cage with kitchen shears before proceeding with the recipe.

TURKEY

Salt and pepper

2 tablespoons vegetable oil

2 teaspoons five-spice powder

1½ teaspoons ground cumin

1 teaspoon garlic powder

¼ teaspoon cayenne pepper

¼ teaspoon ground cardamom

1 (6- to 7-pound) bone-in whole turkey breast, trimmed

SOUR ORANGE SAUCE

1 tablespoon vegetable oil

1 shallot, minced

1 garlic clove, minced

2 cups chicken broth

2 cups orange juice (4 oranges)

2 tablespoons white wine vinegar, plus extra for seasoning

1 tablespoon cornstarch

1 tablespoon water

2 teaspoons fresh chopped tarragon

1. FOR THE TURKEY Combine 1 tablespoon salt, 1 teaspoon pepper, 1 tablespoon oil, five-spice powder, cumin, garlic powder, cayenne, and cardamom in bowl. Using your fingers, gently loosen skin covering breast. Rub paste evenly over and under skin. Place turkey on large plate, cover with plastic wrap, and refrigerate for at least 6 hours.

2. FOR THE SOUR ORANGE SAUCE Heat oil in large saucepan over medium heat until shimmering. Add shallot and cook until softened, about 3 minutes. Add garlic and cook until fragrant, about 30 seconds. Stir in broth, orange juice, and vinegar, increase heat to high, and bring to boil. Cook, stirring occasionally, until sauce is reduced to 1¼ cups, about 20 minutes. Whisk cornstarch and water together in small bowl. Whisk slurry into sauce and cook until thickened, about 1 minute; remove from heat and cover to keep warm.

3. Adjust oven rack to middle position and heat oven to 325 degrees. Heat remaining 1 tablespoon oil in Dutch oven over medium heat until just smoking. Place turkey, skin side down, in Dutch oven and cook, turning breast on its sides as needed, until lightly browned, 8 to 10 minutes.

4. Rotate turkey skin side up and transfer pot to oven. Roast until turkey registers 160 degrees, about 1½ hours. Transfer turkey to carving board, tent with foil, and let rest for 20 minutes.

5. Stir 1 tablespoon turkey pan drippings and tarragon into orange sauce and season with salt, pepper, and additional vinegar to taste. Carve turkey and serve with sauce.

TO MAKE AHEAD

- Seasoned turkey and sauce, prepared through step 2, can be refrigerated separately for up to 24 hours
- To cook, bring sauce, covered, to gentle simmer, stirring often, and continue with step 3

Turkey Burgers with Feta and Herbs
SERVES 4 **EASY**
ACTIVE TIME 30 MINUTES
TOTAL TIME 35 MINUTES

WHY THIS RECIPE WORKS Lean, mild turkey burgers are well suited to being dressed up with flavorful add-ins. But the added work can make them seem like a hassle for a busy weeknight, so we wanted a make-ahead version that we could grab from the fridge and throw into a skillet. We set out to create a turkey burger with a crisp, browned outside and a full-flavored, moist interior. Since getting moist and flavorful meat was crucial, we first tried grinding our own turkey thighs. But while this provided great flavor, it was more work than we wanted for this quick recipe. Luckily, we discovered that store-bought ground turkey enriched with a little ricotta cheese made an excellent burger. The cheese kept the burgers moist without adding a lot of extra fat. To achieve a nicely browned, crusty exterior, we tried searing the burgers over high heat, but this resulted in an overbrowned crust and raw interior. To cook the burgers to a safe temperature without burning them or drying out the meat, we briefly seared them, then partially covered the pan and turned the heat down to gently cook them through. Finally, to elevate our basic turkey burger to company-worthy fare, we added fresh parsley and chives plus crumbled feta cheese. Ricotta cheese can burn easily, so keep a close watch on the burgers as they cook. Be sure to use ground turkey, not ground turkey breast (also labeled 99 percent fat-free) in this recipe. Serve with your favorite burger toppings.

1½ pounds ground turkey
4 ounces (½ cup) part-skim ricotta cheese
2 tablespoons minced fresh chives
1 tablespoon minced fresh parsley
¾ teaspoon salt
¼ teaspoon pepper

We discovered that the key to moist, flavorful turkey burgers is adding a bit of ricotta cheese.

2 ounces feta cheese, crumbled (½ cup)
1 tablespoon vegetable oil
4 hamburger buns

1. Break turkey into small pieces in bowl, then add ricotta, chives, parsley, salt, and pepper. Using your hands, knead mixture until thoroughly combined. Gently mix in feta until just combined. Divide meat mixture into 4 equal portions. Form each into loose ball, then pat lightly into ¾-inch-thick burger.

2. Heat oil in 12-inch nonstick skillet over medium heat until just smoking. Lay burgers in skillet and cook until crisp and lightly browned on first side, 2 to 4 minutes. Flip burgers and continue to cook until lightly browned on second side, 2 to 4 minutes.

3. Reduce heat to low, partially cover, and continue to cook, flipping as needed, until burgers register 160 degrees, 14 to 18 minutes. Transfer burgers to serving platter and let rest for 5 minutes. Serve on hamburger buns.

TO MAKE AHEAD

Burgers, prepared through step 1, can be refrigerated for up to 24 hours

■ EASY (30 minutes or less active time)   ■ FREEZE IT
Photo: Spice-Rubbed Flank Steak with Toasted Corn and Black Bean Salad

A marinade with soy sauce and sugar ensures deeply seasoned and nicely charred grilled steak tips.

Grilled Teriyaki Steak Tips

SERVES 4 TO 6 **EASY**

ACTIVE TIME 30 MINUTES

TOTAL TIME 1 HOUR 50 MINUTES

WHY THIS RECIPE WORKS Marinating is an easy way to transform steak that's headed for the grill, lending bold flavor, keeping the meat moist, and seasoning it throughout. Traditionally, marinades contain an acidic ingredient like lemon juice or vinegar; this is thought to tenderize the meat, but we've found that acids can wreak havoc on the texture of the meat, turning it spongy and discolored. Instead, a high concentration of salt in a marinade is the real key to getting flavorful, tender meat because it acts like a brine and is also a flavor booster. With this in mind, we turned to a teriyaki marinade with a base of salty soy sauce to give our grilled steak tips great flavor. Along with the soy sauce, we added a good amount of oil to help coat the meat and bloom the spices. Some sugar brought our marinade into balance and encouraged great char on the grill. A small amount of reserved marinade poured over the cooked steak tips refreshed their flavor, and a

couple of teaspoons of mirin, a sweet rice wine, added a hint of brightness. Sirloin steak tips, also known as flap meat, are sold as whole steaks, cubes, and strips. To ensure uniform pieces that cook evenly, we prefer to purchase whole steak tips and cut them ourselves. We found these steak tips to be more tender when cooked to medium, but if you prefer them more or less done, see our guidelines on page 189.

½ cup vegetable oil
⅓ cup soy sauce
⅓ cup sugar
¼ cup water
2 scallions, chopped
2 tablespoons grated fresh ginger
2 garlic cloves, minced
⅛ teaspoon red pepper flakes
2 teaspoons mirin
2 pounds sirloin steak tips, trimmed

1. Process oil, soy sauce, sugar, water, scallions, ginger, garlic, and pepper flakes in food processor until smooth, about 20 seconds. Transfer ¼ cup marinade to small bowl and stir in mirin; set aside for serving.

2. Pat beef dry with paper towels, prick all over with fork, then cut into 2½-inch pieces. Combine beef and remaining marinade in separate bowl; toss to coat. Refrigerate beef and mirin mixture separately for at least 1 hour.

3. Before grilling, remove reserved marinade from refrigerator and let sit at room temperature. Pat beef dry with paper towels.

4A. FOR A CHARCOAL GRILL Open bottom vent completely. Light large chimney starter filled with charcoal briquettes (6 quarts). When top coals are partially covered with ash, pour evenly over grill. Set cooking grate in place, cover, and open lid vent completely. Heat grill until hot, about 5 minutes.

4B. FOR A GAS GRILL Turn all burners to high, cover, and heat grill until hot, about 15 minutes. Leave all burners on high.

5. Clean and oil cooking grate. Lay beef on grill and cook (covered if using gas), turning as needed, until well browned on all sides, charred at edges, and registers 130 to 135 degrees (for medium), 8 to 10 minutes. Transfer beef to platter. Stir mirin mixture to recombine, then drizzle over beef. Tent with aluminum foil and let rest for 5 to 10 minutes. Serve.

TO MAKE AHEAD

Marinated steak and reserved mirin mixture, prepared through step 2, can be refrigerated separately for up 24 hours

Spice-Rubbed Flank Steak with Toasted Corn and Black Bean Salad

SERVES 4

ACTIVE TIME 40 MINUTES
TOTAL TIME 1 HOUR 50 MINUTES

WHY THIS RECIPE WORKS The big, beefy flavor of flank steak is well suited to the grill, but to keep this recipe convenient for a weeknight, we set out to find a method for bringing it indoors with equally flavorful results. Broiling gave us a nicely browned crust, but it overcooked the meat. Roasting allowed us to turn out a perfect medium-rare steak, but it never developed a flavorful crust. In our search for the perfect sear, we browned the steak on the stovetop and then moved it to the oven to roast. To enhance the flavor of the steak, we wanted a spice rub that developed flavor as it sat; a combination of chili powder, cumin, coriander, cinnamon, and red pepper flakes added just the right amount of heat and complexity. A bright black bean and corn salad complemented the steak. To bring out the corn's sweet flavor, we browned it in the skillet while the steak rested. Be sure to use fresh corn here; canned or frozen corn will not brown well. For a spicier salad, use the larger amount of chipotle. We prefer this steak cooked to medium-rare, but if you prefer it more or less done, see our guidelines.

1½ teaspoons chili powder
1½ teaspoons ground cumin
1½ teaspoons packed dark brown sugar
¾ teaspoon ground coriander
 Salt and pepper
 Pinch ground cinnamon
 Pinch red pepper flakes
1 (1½- to 2-pound) flank steak, trimmed
3 tablespoons plus 1 teaspoon vegetable oil
2 tablespoons lime juice
2 scallions, sliced thin
1–2 teaspoons minced canned chipotle chile in adobo sauce
1 (15-ounce) can black beans, rinsed
1 red bell pepper, stemmed, seeded, and chopped fine
¼ cup minced fresh cilantro
3 ears corn, kernels cut from cobs

1. Combine chili powder, cumin, sugar, coriander, ½ teaspoon salt, ½ teaspoon pepper, cinnamon, and pepper flakes in bowl. Rub steak with spice mixture, cover with plastic wrap, and refrigerate for at least 1 hour.

2. Meanwhile, whisk 2 tablespoons oil, lime juice, scallions, and chipotle together in large bowl. Stir in beans, bell pepper, and cilantro; set aside.

Taking the Temperature of Meat

Since the temperature of beef, lamb, and pork will continue to rise as the meat rests—an effect called carryover cooking—they should be removed from the oven, grill, or pan when they are 5 to 10 degrees below the desired serving temperature. The following temperatures should be used to determine when to stop the cooking process.

FOR THIS INGREDIENT	COOK TO THIS TEMPERATURE
BEEF/LAMB	
Rare	115 to 120 degrees (120 to 125 degrees after resting)
Medium-Rare	120 to 125 degrees (125 to 130 degrees after resting)
Medium	130 to 135 degrees (135 to 140 degrees after resting)
Medium-Well	140 to 145 degrees (145 to 150 degrees after resting)
Well-Done	150 to 155 degrees (155 to 160 degrees after resting)
PORK	
Chops and Tenderloin	145 degrees (150 degrees after resting)
Loin Roasts	140 degrees (145 degrees after resting)

3. Adjust oven rack to middle position and heat oven to 450 degrees. Pat steak dry with paper towels. Heat 1 tablespoon oil in 12-inch ovensafe skillet over medium-high heat until just smoking. Place steak in skillet and cook until well browned on first side, 3 to 4 minutes. Flip steak, transfer skillet to oven, and roast until steak is browned on second side and registers 120 to 125 degrees (for medium-rare), 4 to 5 minutes.

4. Carefully remove skillet from oven (skillet handle will be hot). Transfer steak to carving board, tent with aluminum foil, and let rest for 5 to 10 minutes.

5. Being careful of hot skillet handle, wipe out skillet using paper towels. Add remaining 1 teaspoon oil and heat over medium heat until shimmering. Add corn and cook, without stirring, until

well browned and toasted, 5 to 7 minutes. Stir toasted corn into bean salad and season with salt and pepper to taste. Slice steak thin against grain and serve with corn-bean salad.

TO MAKE AHEAD ▶

Spice-rubbed steak and bean salad, prepared through step 2, can be refrigerated separately for up 24 hours

Grilled Sugar Steak

SERVES 4 TO 6 **EASY**
ACTIVE TIME 20 MINUTES
TOTAL TIME 1 HOUR 40 MINUTES

WHY THIS RECIPE WORKS Sugar steak may sound odd, but this unique dish has serious appeal: Juicy, medium-rare strip steak is coated with a delicate sugar crust, delivering a fleeting moment of sweetness followed by a flood of meaty, savory flavor. But simply rubbing sugar and salt on a steak and grilling it didn't work—the sugar caused moisture to collect on the surface of the steaks and they steamed on the grill, leaving no trace of the crisp crust we were hoping for. Instead, we found that if we let the steaks rest for at least an hour, we could use the moisture to our advantage: When we rubbed on more of the salt-sugar mixture just before grilling, the moisture actually helped the mixture adhere to the meat. Finally, we kept the steaks moving on the grill to ensure that the sugar crust formed but didn't burn. Be sure to use kosher salt here, as the crystal size of table salt is very different and this recipe depends on accurate measurements. Note that you will have some sugar mixture left over after seasoning the steaks. If your steaks are more than 1 inch thick, pound them to 1 inch. We prefer this steak cooked to medium-rare, but if you prefer it more or less done, see our guidelines on page 189.

¼ cup sugar
Kosher salt and pepper
4 (9- to 11-ounce) boneless strip steaks, 1 inch thick, trimmed

1. Mix sugar and 3 tablespoons salt together in bowl. Pat steaks dry with paper towels and place in 13 by 9-inch baking dish. Evenly sprinkle 1½ teaspoons sugar mixture over top of each steak. Flip steaks and sprinkle second side of each steak with 1½ teaspoons sugar mixture. Cover with plastic wrap and let sit at room temperature for 1 hour.

2. Before grilling, sprinkle steaks with 1 teaspoon sugar mixture on each side, then season with pepper (steaks will be wet; do not pat dry).

To get a crisp sugar crust on steak, we let the sugar- and salt-rubbed meat rest and apply more of the rub before grilling.

3A. FOR A CHARCOAL GRILL Open bottom vent completely. Light large chimney starter mounded with charcoal briquettes (7 quarts). When top coals are partially covered with ash, pour evenly over half of grill. Set cooking grate in place, cover, and open lid vent completely. Heat grill until hot, about 5 minutes.

3B. FOR A GAS GRILL Turn all burners to high, cover, and heat grill until hot, about 15 minutes. Leave all burners on high.

4. Clean and oil cooking grate. Place steaks on hotter side of grill (if using charcoal) and cook (covered if using gas) until evenly charred on first side, 3 to 5 minutes, rotating and switching positions for even cooking. Flip steaks and continue to cook until meat registers 120 to 125 degrees (for medium-rare), 3 to 5 minutes, rotating and switching positions for even cooking.

5. Transfer steaks to wire rack set in rimmed baking sheet and let rest for 5 minutes. Slice and serve.

TO MAKE AHEAD ▶

Sugar-salt rubbed steak, prepared through step 1, can be refrigerated for up 24 hours

Skirt Steak with Pinto Bean Salad

SERVES 4 EASY

ACTIVE TIME 25 MINUTES

TOTAL TIME 30 MINUTES

WHY THIS RECIPE WORKS Because skirt steak is thin, it's an ideal cut for a quick weeknight meal. For a southwestern-inspired flavor profile, we rubbed the steak with paprika, salt, and pepper, and paired it with a simple pinto bean salad. Lime juice brightened up the pinto bean salad, and chipotle in adobo provided subtle spicy and smoky notes. Even better, we found that we preferred both the steak and the pinto bean salad when made a day ahead, as the salt and spices penetrated the meat and kept it juicy, and the flavors of the salad melded overnight. We prefer this steak cooked to medium-rare, but if you prefer it more or less done, see our guidelines on page 189. Be sure to slice the steak thin against the grain or it will be very chewy. Serve with lime wedges.

2 (15-ounce) cans pinto beans, rinsed
½ cup finely chopped red onion
2 tablespoons lime juice
2 tablespoons vegetable oil
2 teaspoons minced canned chipotle chile in adobo sauce
  Salt and pepper
1 teaspoon paprika
1 (1-pound) skirt steak, trimmed and cut into thirds
¼ cup chopped fresh cilantro

1. Combine beans, onion, lime juice, 1 tablespoon oil, chipotle, ½ teaspoon salt, and ½ teaspoon pepper in bowl.

2. Combine paprika, ½ teaspoon salt, and ¼ teaspoon pepper in separate bowl. Pat steak dry with paper towels and rub evenly with paprika mixture.

3. Heat remaining 1 tablespoon oil in 12-inch skillet over medium-high heat until just smoking. Cook steak until well browned and meat registers 120 to 125 degrees (for medium-rare), about 2 minutes per side. Transfer steak to carving board, tent loosely with foil, and let rest for 5 minutes.

4. Transfer bean salad to platter and sprinkle with cilantro. Slice steak thin against grain and arrange on top of bean salad. Serve.

▶ TO MAKE AHEAD ▶

- Bean salad and spice-rubbed steak, prepared through step 2, can be refrigerated separately for up to 24 hours
- To cook, bring bean salad to room temperature, season with lime juice, salt, and pepper to taste, and continue with step 3

Grilled Beef Kebabs

SERVES 4 TO 6

ACTIVE TIME 35 MINUTES

TOTAL TIME 1 HOUR 55 MINUTES

WHY THIS RECIPE WORKS Kebabs packed with juicy beef and fresh vegetables make great summertime fare. The problem is that they can take quite a bit of time to put together, from prepping to marinating. Make-ahead beef kebabs seemed like the perfect solution. Trimming and cutting all the meat and vegetables and refrigerating them overnight didn't affect the finished product, and sitting for an hour or more in the marinade gave the kebabs time to absorb as much flavor as possible. We turned to the food processor to make quick work of the marinade, combining soy sauce, Worcestershire sauce, garlic, brown sugar, and chives for an easy steak sauce that packed a lot of flavor. Kebabs cook in minutes on the grill, and while the red bell pepper softened in the time it took for the beef to cook through, the red onion pieces still tasted raw. Microwaving the red onion with oil before skewering proved to be the best solution; the microwave parcooked the onion so that after a short stint on the grill, it was tender and charred. To finish, we reserved ¼ cup of the marinade to pour over the kebabs to give them a bright hit of flavor. You will need eight 12-inch metal skewers for this recipe. We found the kebab meat to be more tender when cooked to medium, but if you prefer it more or less done, see our guidelines on page 189.

½ cup soy sauce
⅓ cup plus 1 tablespoon extra-virgin olive oil
¼ cup Worcestershire sauce
2 tablespoons packed dark brown sugar
2 tablespoons minced fresh chives
4 garlic cloves, minced
1½ teaspoons pepper
1 large red onion, halved through root end, core discarded, each half cut into 4 wedges and each wedge cut crosswise into thirds
2 pounds blade steaks, trimmed and cut into 1½-inch pieces
2 red bell peppers, stemmed, seeded, and cut into 1-inch pieces

1. Process soy sauce, ⅓ cup oil, Worcestershire, sugar, chives, garlic, and pepper in food processor until smooth, about 20 seconds. Transfer ¼ cup marinade to bowl; set aside for serving.

2. Gently toss onion pieces with remaining 1 tablespoon oil in bowl, cover, and microwave until just tender, 3 to 5 minutes. Thread beef, onion, and bell peppers evenly onto eight 12-inch metal skewers. Arrange skewers in 13 by 9-inch baking dish, pour remaining marinade over top, and turn to coat. Cover and refrigerate kebabs for at least 1 hour.

3. Before grilling, pat kebabs dry with paper towels.

4A. FOR A CHARCOAL GRILL Open bottom vent completely. Light large chimney starter filled with charcoal briquettes (6 quarts). When top coals are partially covered with ash, pour evenly over half of grill. Set cooking grate in place, cover, and open lid vent completely. Heat grill until hot, about 5 minutes.

4B. FOR A GAS GRILL Turn all burners to high, cover, and heat grill until hot, about 15 minutes. Leave all burners on high.

5. Clean and oil cooking grate. Grill kebabs (covered if using gas), turning often, until well browned on all sides and beef registers 130 to 135 degrees (for medium), 8 to 12 minutes. Transfer kebabs to platter. Stir reserved marinade to recombine, then drizzle over kebabs. Tent with aluminum foil and let rest for 5 to 10 minutes. Serve.

> **TO MAKE AHEAD**
> • Marinated kebabs and reserved marinade, prepared through step 2, can be refrigerated separately for up to 24 hours; turn kebabs occasionally to ensure even marinating
> • To cook, bring reserved marinade to room temperature and continue with step 3

TRIMMING BLADE STEAKS

1. Halve each steak lengthwise, leaving center line of gristle attached to 1 half.

2. Slice away gristle from half to which it is still attached.

Steak Tacos

SERVES 4 TO 6
ACTIVE TIME 40 MINUTES
TOTAL TIME 1 HOUR 15 MINUTES

WHY THIS RECIPE WORKS To develop an indoor steak taco recipe that yielded meat as tender, juicy, and rich-tasting as grilled, we chose flank steak, which is beefy and tender when sliced thin across the grain. Pan searing gave us the browned exterior and crisp,

brittle edges characteristic of grilled meat. A paste of oil, cilantro, scallions, garlic, and jalapeño, which we applied to the meat and then scraped off just before cooking, gave our steak taco recipe a flavor boost without sacrificing browning. We prefer this steak cooked slightly above medium-rare, but if you prefer it more or less done, see our guidelines on page 189. For a less spicy dish, remove some or all of the ribs and seeds from the jalapeños before chopping them for the marinade. In addition to the toppings suggested below, try serving the tacos with salsa, pickled onions, or thinly sliced radishes or cucumber.

HERB PASTE
½ cup packed fresh cilantro leaves
3 scallions, chopped coarse
1 jalapeño chile, stemmed, seeded, and chopped coarse
3 garlic cloves, chopped coarse
½ teaspoon ground cumin
¼ cup vegetable oil
1 tablespoon lime juice

STEAK
1 (1½- to 1¾-pound) flank steak, cut lengthwise (with grain) into 4 equal pieces
Salt
½ teaspoon sugar
½ teaspoon pepper
2 tablespoons vegetable oil

TACOS
12 (6-inch) corn tortillas, warmed
Fresh cilantro leaves
Minced white onion
Lime wedges

1. FOR THE HERB PASTE Pulse cilantro, scallions, jalapeño, garlic, and cumin in food processor until finely chopped, 10 to 12 pulses, scraping down sides as necessary. Add oil and process until mixture is smooth and resembles pesto, about 15 seconds. Transfer 2 tablespoons herb paste to bowl and whisk in lime juice; set aside for serving.

2. FOR THE STEAK Using dinner fork, poke each piece of steak 10 to 12 times on each side. Place in large baking dish, rub all sides of steak with 1½ teaspoons salt, then coat with remaining herb paste. Cover with plastic wrap and refrigerate for at least 30 minutes.

3. Scrape herb paste off steak and sprinkle all sides of pieces evenly with sugar and pepper. Heat oil in 12-inch nonstick skillet over medium-high heat until just smoking. Place steak in skillet and cook until well browned, about 3 minutes. Flip steak and

To achieve a crisp, browned exterior on the flank steak for our indoor taco recipe, we pan-sear the meat in four pieces.

sear until second side is well browned, 2 to 3 minutes. Using tongs, stand each piece on cut side and cook, turning as necessary, until all cut sides are well browned and meat registers 125 to 130 degrees, 2 to 7 minutes. Transfer steak to cutting board and let rest for 5 minutes.

4. FOR THE TACOS Using sharp chef's knife or carving knife, slice steak pieces against grain into ⅛-inch-thick pieces. Transfer sliced steak to bowl with herb paste–lime juice mixture and toss to coat. Season with salt. Spoon small amount of sliced steak into center of each warm tortilla and serve immediately, passing toppings separately.

TO MAKE AHEAD

- Marinated steak and reserved herb paste, prepared through step 2, can be refrigerated separately for up to 24 hours
- To cook, bring reserved herb paste to room temperature and continue with step 3

Beef Stir-Fry with Bell Peppers and Black Pepper Sauce

SERVES 4

ACTIVE TIME 45 MINUTES

TOTAL TIME 1 HOUR

WHY THIS RECIPE WORKS We discovered that in order to produce a stir-fry with velvety, tender beef normally only found in Chinese restaurants, we needed to choose the right cut of meat and treat it correctly. Flank steak, cut across the grain into bite-size pieces, delivered great beef flavor and a moderate chew. Adding some cornstarch to the marinade before flash searing the meat in a very hot pan finished the job of delivering supertender, restaurant-quality stir-fried beef. Crisp-tender red and green bell peppers complemented the beef with bright flavor, and scallions gave the dish a fresh, oniony bite. Bathing the dish in a Cantonese-style black pepper sauce tied all of the flavors together, balancing sweetness with a subtle heat. By marinating the beef, making the sauce, and slicing the vegetables in advance, this became a perfect weeknight meal that was in and out of the pan in under 15 minutes. When preparing the beef, freezing the steak for 15 minutes makes it easier to slice thin.

- 3 tablespoons soy sauce
- 3 tablespoons dry sherry or Chinese rice wine
- 1 tablespoon cornstarch
- 2½ teaspoons packed light brown sugar
- 1 pound flank steak, trimmed, cut into 2- to 2½-inch strips with grain, each strip cut crosswise against grain into ¼-inch-thick slices
- ¼ cup water
- 3 garlic cloves, minced
- 1 tablespoon grated fresh ginger
- 1 tablespoon oyster sauce
- 2 teaspoons rice vinegar
- 2 teaspoons coarsely ground pepper
- 1½ teaspoons toasted sesame oil
- 3 tablespoons plus 1 teaspoon vegetable oil
- 1 red bell pepper, stemmed, seeded, and cut into ¼-inch-wide strips
- 1 green bell pepper, stemmed, seeded, and cut into ¼-inch-wide strips
- 6 scallions, white parts sliced thin on bias, green parts cut into 2-inch pieces

1. Whisk 1 tablespoon soy sauce, 1 tablespoon sherry, 1½ teaspoons cornstarch, and ½ teaspoon sugar together in large bowl. Add beef to soy sauce mixture, stir to coat, and let sit at room temperature for 15 minutes.

2. Whisk water, garlic, ginger, oyster sauce, vinegar, pepper, sesame oil, remaining 2 tablespoons soy sauce, remaining 2 tablespoons sherry, remaining 1½ teaspoons cornstarch, and remaining 2 teaspoons sugar together in second bowl.

3. Heat 2 teaspoons vegetable oil in 12-inch nonstick skillet over high heat until just smoking. Add half of beef in single layer. Cook without stirring for 1 minute. Continue to cook, stirring occasionally, until spotty brown on both sides, 1 to 2 minutes longer. Transfer to bowl. Repeat with 2 teaspoons vegetable oil and remaining beef.

4. Return now-empty skillet to high heat, add 2 teaspoons vegetable oil, and heat until just beginning to smoke. Add bell peppers and scallion greens and cook, stirring occasionally, until vegetables are spotty brown and crisp-tender, about 4 minutes. Transfer vegetables to bowl with beef.

5. Return now-empty skillet to medium-high heat and add remaining 4 teaspoons vegetable oil and scallion whites. Cook, stirring frequently, until lightly browned, about 30 seconds. Return beef and vegetables to skillet and stir to combine.

6. Whisk sauce to recombine. Add to skillet and cook, stirring constantly, until sauce has thickened, about 30 seconds. Serve immediately.

TO MAKE AHEAD

Marinated beef and sauce, prepared through step 2, can be refrigerated separately for up to 24 hours

CUTTING UP FLANK STEAK FOR STIR-FRY

1. To make slicing flank steak easier, freeze it until firm, about 15 minutes. Slice meat lengthwise (with the grain) into 2-inch-wide strips.

2. Slice each 2-inch strip thin (against grain) into ¼-inch-thick slices.

Herbed Roast Beef

SERVES 6 TO 8
ACTIVE TIME 35 MINUTES
TOTAL TIME 2 HOURS 50 MINUTES TO 3 HOURS 20 MINUTES

WHY THIS RECIPE WORKS For a roast beef dressed to impress without much effort, we turned to a swirl of herbs and mustard. To start, we combined fresh herbs with the mustard, butterflied the roast, and spread the herbs over the interior of the meat before folding it back together and securing it with twine. A simple herb butter, spread over the resting roast, melted and mingled with the natural juices of the meat, creating a flavorful sauce without the need to dirty another pan.

⅓ cup chopped fresh parsley
1 shallot, minced
2 tablespoons minced fresh thyme
2 tablespoons olive oil
1 tablespoon Dijon mustard
4 tablespoons unsalted butter, softened
1 (4-pound) top sirloin roast, fat trimmed to ¼ inch thick
1 tablespoon salt
1 tablespoon pepper

1. Combine parsley, shallot, and thyme in bowl. Transfer 2 tablespoons herb mixture to separate bowl and stir in 1 tablespoon oil and mustard. Add softened butter to remaining herb mixture and mash with fork to combine; set aside for serving.

2. Using sharp knife, slice roast horizontally through middle, leaving ½ inch of meat intact at end. Open roast up, sprinkle with salt and pepper, then spread evenly with herb-mustard mixture. Fold meat back to its original position, then tie securely at 1-inch intervals with kitchen twine. Refrigerate for at least 1 hour.

3. Adjust oven rack to middle position and heat oven to 275 degrees. Place V-rack inside roasting pan. Pat roast dry with paper towels. Heat remaining 1 tablespoon oil in large skillet over medium-high heat until just smoking. Brown roast on all sides, 8 to 12 minutes, then transfer to V-rack. Roast beef until it registers 120 to 125 degrees (for medium-rare), 1½ to 2 hours.

4. Transfer roast to carving board, spread with herb-butter mixture, tent with foil, and let rest for 20 minutes. Remove kitchen twine. Slice roast crosswise against grain into ¼-inch-thick slices. Serve.

TO MAKE AHEAD

Beef roast and herbed butter, prepared through step 2, can be refrigerated separately for up to 24 hours

Splitting a chuck-eye roast into two pieces allows us to remove stubborn knobs of fat and shorten the cooking time.

Classic Beef Pot Roast

SERVES 6 TO 8 ACTIVE TIME 1 HOUR
TOTAL TIME 4 HOURS 30 MINUTES TO 5 HOURS

WHY THIS RECIPE WORKS The ideal make-ahead dish is one that improves in flavor and texture from one day to the next. We found exactly that with our Classic Beef Pot Roast. While the roast tasted great when served right away, chilling it overnight not only made the roast moister and easier to slice, but it also brought out deeper, beefier flavor in the meat and the gravy. To start, we separated a boneless chuck-eye roast into two pieces, which allowed us to remove the knobs of fat that stubbornly refused to render and shortened the cooking time by about an hour. Next, we built a flavorful base with a *mirepoix* of onions, carrot, and celery plus garlic, tomato paste, red wine, thyme, and a bay leaf. Some recipes use water as the primary cooking liquid, but when we tried this, the gravy turned out as you'd expect—watery. We had better luck with beef broth. The resulting gravy boasted a rich, complex character.

Sealing the pot with aluminum foil before securing the lid and moving the pot to the oven concentrated the steam for an even simmer and fork-tender meat. To make the gravy, we blended all of the flavorful braising ingredients, not wasting an ounce of what went into the pot with the meat. The result: a meltingly tender roast sauced in a savory, full-bodied gravy. Use a Dutch oven that holds 7 quarts or more for this recipe.

1 (4-pound) boneless beef chuck-eye roast, pulled into 2 pieces at natural seam and trimmed of large pieces of fat
  Salt and pepper
2 tablespoons unsalted butter
2 onions, halved and sliced thin
1 large carrot, peeled and chopped
1 celery rib, chopped
2 garlic cloves, minced
1 cup beef broth, plus extra as needed
¾ cup dry red wine
1 tablespoon tomato paste
1 sprig fresh thyme
1 bay leaf
1 tablespoon balsamic vinegar

1. Adjust oven rack to middle position and heat oven to 300 degrees. Tie roasts crosswise with kitchen twine at 1-inch intervals. Pat dry with paper towels and season with salt and pepper.

2. Melt butter in Dutch oven over medium heat. Add onions and cook, stirring occasionally, until softened and beginning to brown, 8 to 10 minutes. Stir in carrot and celery and cook for 5 minutes. Stir in garlic and cook until fragrant, about 30 seconds. Stir in broth, ½ cup wine, tomato paste, thyme sprig, and bay leaf and bring to simmer.

3. Nestle roasts on top of vegetables. Cover pot tightly with large piece of aluminum foil, then cover with lid. Transfer pot to oven and cook until fork easily slips in and out of meat, 3½ to 4 hours, turning roasts over several times during cooking.

4. Remove pot from oven. Transfer roasts to carving board, tent with foil, and let rest while finishing sauce. Strain liquid through fine-mesh strainer into 4-cup liquid measuring cup. Discard bay leaf and thyme sprig; reserve vegetables. Let liquid settle for 5 minutes, then skim excess fat from surface. Add extra broth to defatted liquid as needed to total 3 cups.

5. Process liquid and vegetables in blender until smooth, about 2 minutes. Transfer sauce to medium saucepan and bring to simmer over medium heat. Stir in remaining ¼ cup wine and vinegar and season with salt and pepper to taste. Slice meat against grain into ½-inch-thick slices and arrange on platter. Spoon half of sauce over meat and serve with remaining sauce.

> **TO MAKE AHEAD**

- Pot roast with 3 cups liquid and reserved vegetables, prepared through step 4, can be refrigerated for up to 2 days
- To reheat, transfer meat to cutting board, slice into ½-inch-thick slices, arrange in 13 by 9-inch baking dish, cover with foil, reheat in 325-degree oven for 45 minutes, and continue with step 5

Beef Braised in Barolo

SERVES 6
ACTIVE TIME 1 HOUR 30 MINUTES
TOTAL TIME 4 HOURS 45 MINUTES

WHY THIS RECIPE WORKS The Italian version of pot roast is an inexpensive cut of beef braised in wine. But what a difference that wine makes. Full-bodied Barolo has been called the "wine of kings" and can be somewhat expensive, so this pot roast has to be special. We wanted moist, tender meat in a rich, savory sauce that would do justice to the regal wine. A chuck-eye roast won't dry out after a long braise, but it has a line of fat in the middle that we felt was out of place in this refined dish. Separating the roast into two smaller ones enabled us to discard most of this fat before cooking the meat, and the two roasts cooked more quickly than one larger one. We tied each roast to hold their shape and then browned them in the fat rendered from pancetta, which added rich flavor. Next, we browned some aromatics and poured a whole bottle of wine into the pot. Barolo has such a bold flavor that we needed something in the braising liquid to temper it, and that proved to be a can of diced tomatoes. When the meat was done, we removed it from the pot, reduced the sauce, and strained out the vegetables. Dark, full-flavored, and lustrous, this sauce bestowed nobility on our humble cut of meat. Purchase pancetta that is cut to order, about ¼ inch thick. If pancetta is not available, substitute an equal amount of salt pork (find the meatiest piece possible), cut it into ¼-inch cubes, and boil it in 3 cups of water for about 2 minutes to remove excess salt. After draining, use it as you would pancetta. Use a Dutch oven that holds 7 quarts or more for this recipe.

1 (3½-pound) boneless beef chuck-eye roast, pulled into 2 pieces at natural seam and trimmed of large pieces of fat
   Salt and pepper
4 ounces pancetta, cut into ¼-inch cubes

This elegant take on pot roast relies on canned diced tomatoes to temper the bold red wine sauce.

2 onions, chopped
2 carrots, chopped
2 celery ribs, chopped
1 tablespoon tomato paste
3 garlic cloves, minced
1 tablespoon all-purpose flour
½ teaspoon sugar
1 (750-ml) bottle Barolo wine
1 (14.5-ounce) can diced tomatoes, drained
1 sprig fresh thyme, plus 1 teaspoon minced
1 sprig fresh rosemary
10 sprigs fresh parsley

1. Adjust oven rack to middle position and heat oven to 300 degrees. Tie roasts crosswise with kitchen twine at 1-inch intervals. Pat dry with paper towels and season with salt and pepper. Cook pancetta in Dutch oven over medium heat, stirring occasionally, until browned and crisp, about 8 minutes. Using slotted spoon, transfer pancetta to paper towel–lined plate. Pour off all but 2 tablespoons fat left in pot and place over medium-high heat until just smoking. Brown beef well on all sides, about 8 minutes; transfer to plate.

2. Add onions, carrots, celery, and tomato paste to fat left in pot and cook over medium heat until softened and browned, about 6 minutes. Stir in garlic, flour, sugar, and reserved pancetta and cook until fragrant, about 30 seconds. Stir in wine and tomatoes, scraping up any browned bits. Add thyme sprig, rosemary sprig, and parsley sprigs.

3. Return roasts and any accumulated juices to pot. Increase heat to high, bring to boil, then place large sheet of aluminum foil over pot and cover tightly with lid. Transfer pot to oven and cook until fork easily slips in and out of meat, about 3 hours, turning roasts over several times during cooking.

4. Transfer beef to carving board and tent with foil to keep warm. Let liquid settle for 5 minutes, then skim excess fat from surface. Stir in minced thyme, bring to boil over high heat, and cook, whisking vigorously, until vegetables have broken down and thickened sauce measures about 3½ cups, about 18 minutes.

5. Strain liquid through large fine-mesh strainer, pressing on solids with spatula to extract as much liquid as possible; discard solids. (You should have 1½ cups strained sauce; if necessary, return sauce to Dutch oven and reduce to 1½ cups). Season sauce with salt and pepper to taste.

6. Remove kitchen twine from meat and discard. Slice meat against grain into ½-inch-thick slices and arrange on platter. Spoon some sauce over meat and serve with remaining sauce.

> **TO MAKE AHEAD**
>
> - Beef with sauce, prepared through step 5, can be refrigerated for up to 2 days
> - To reheat, transfer meat to carving board, slice into ½-inch-thick pieces, arrange in 13 by 9-inch baking dish, cover with foil, and reheat in 325-degree oven for 45 minutes; reheat sauce and continue with step 6

TYING A POT ROAST

We divide chuck-eye roast into two pieces so we can trim away the interior fat. Then we secure the roasts with twine at 1-inch intervals to promote even cooking.

We use gelatin to give the sauce for our boneless short ribs extra body and a luxurious, supple texture.

Braised Beef Short Ribs

SERVES 6   **FREEZE IT**

ACTIVE TIME 1 HOUR 20 MINUTES

TOTAL TIME 3 HOURS 20 MINUTES TO 3 HOURS 50 MINUTES

WHY THIS RECIPE WORKS To develop a recipe for fork-tender short ribs in a silky, grease-free sauce that would cook in just a few hours, we chose boneless ribs, which are significantly less fatty than ribs with bones. We missed the body that the bones' connective tissue contributed, so we added some gelatin to the sauce for suppleness. To ramp up the richness of our relatively quick recipe, we reduced wine with some browned aromatics before using it to cook the meat. Make sure that the ribs are at least 4 inches long and 1 inch thick. If boneless ribs are unavailable, substitute 7 pounds of bone-in beef short ribs, at least 4 inches long with 1 inch of meat above the bone, and remove the bones yourself. We recommend a bold red wine such as Cabernet Sauvignon or Côtes du Rhône. Serve with egg noodles, mashed potatoes, or roasted potatoes. Use a Dutch oven that holds 7 quarts or more for this recipe.

3½ pounds boneless short ribs, trimmed
    Salt and pepper
2 tablespoons vegetable oil
2 large onions, sliced thin (about 4 cups)
1 tablespoon tomato paste
6 garlic cloves, peeled
2 cups red wine
1 cup beef broth
4 large carrots, peeled and cut into 2-inch pieces
4 sprigs fresh thyme
1 bay leaf
¼ cup cold water
½ teaspoon unflavored gelatin

1. Adjust oven rack to lower-middle position and heat oven to 300 degrees. Pat beef dry with paper towels and season with salt and pepper. Heat 1 tablespoon oil in Dutch oven over medium-high heat until smoking. Add half of beef and cook until well browned on all sides, 8 to 12 minutes; transfer to bowl. Repeat with remaining 1 tablespoon oil and remaining beef.

2. Add onions to fat left in pot and cook over medium heat, stirring occasionally, until softened and beginning to brown, 12 to 15 minutes. (If onions begin to darken too quickly, add 1 to 2 tablespoons water to pot.) Stir in tomato paste and cook, stirring constantly, until bottom of pan is well browned, about 2 minutes. Stir in garlic and cook until fragrant, about 30 seconds. Stir in wine, scraping up any browned bits. Increase heat to medium-high and simmer until reduced by half, 8 to 10 minutes.

3. Stir in broth, carrots, thyme, and bay leaf. Add browned beef and any accumulated juices and bring to simmer. Cover, transfer pot to oven, and cook until fork slips easily in and out of meat, 2 to 2½ hours, turning meat over several times during cooking.

4. Place water in small bowl and sprinkle gelatin on top; let stand at least 5 minutes. Transfer meat and carrots to platter and tent with foil. Pour braising liquid through fine-mesh strainer into fat separator and let settle for 5 minutes. Return defatted juices to now-empty Dutch oven and cook over medium heat until reduced to 1 cup, 5 to 10 minutes. Off heat, stir in gelatin mixture and season with salt and pepper to taste. Pour sauce over meat and serve.

> **TO MAKE AHEAD**
>
> - Short ribs, prepared through step 3, can be refrigerated for up to 3 days or frozen for up to 1 month; if frozen, thaw completely in refrigerator
> - To reheat, skim off and discard any congealed fat, bring short ribs, covered, to gentle simmer, cook until hot throughout, and continue with step 4

Refrigerating the meat in its sauce overnight keeps it moist and makes it easier to slice the next day.

Onion-Braised Beef Brisket

SERVES 6 TO 8
ACTIVE TIME 1 HOUR 15 MINUTES
TOTAL TIME 5 HOURS 45 MINUTES TO 6 HOURS 15 MINUTES

WHY THIS RECIPE WORKS Brisket is the ideal cut for braising, as it takes hours of slow cooking to soften this otherwise tough-as-leather cut. Sadly, this patience is often rewarded with shreds of dry, chewy meat in dull, greasy sauce. For this recipe, we decided to make a flavor-packed braising liquid with onions, brown sugar, wine, and aromatics that would later act as a savory serving sauce. Browning the brisket before braising it gave it deeper, meatier flavor, and sealing the brisket with the sauce into a foil packet while cooking produced beautifully moist meat. We also found that we could easily make this dish ahead of time with excellent results: After braising the brisket, we let the meat stand overnight in the refrigerator in the braising liquid, which helped to keep the brisket moist and flavorful by allowing it to reabsorb some of the sauce. As an added benefit, when the sauce cooled, the excess fat separated from it and solidified on top, making it a cinch to remove the next day. The overnight refrigeration also made slicing the brisket simple. If you prefer a spicy sauce, increase the amount of cayenne to ¼ teaspoon. You will need 18-inch-wide heavy-duty foil for this recipe. Serve over mashed potatoes or buttered egg noodles.

1 (4- to 5-pound) beef brisket, flat cut preferred, fat trimmed to ¼ inch
Salt and pepper
1 teaspoon vegetable oil
3 large onions, halved and sliced ½ inch thick
1 tablespoon packed brown sugar
1 tablespoon tomato paste
3 garlic cloves, minced
1 tablespoon paprika
⅛ teaspoon cayenne pepper
2 tablespoons all-purpose flour
1 cup chicken broth
1 cup dry red wine
3 sprigs fresh thyme
3 bay leaves
2 teaspoons cider vinegar

1. Adjust oven rack to lower-middle position and heat oven to 300 degrees. Line 13 by 9-inch baking dish with two 24-inch by 18-inch pieces heavy-duty aluminum foil, positioning them perpendicular to each other and allowing excess to hang over edge of dish. Pat brisket dry with paper towels and place fat side up on cutting board. Using dinner fork, poke holes in meat through fat layer about 1 inch apart. Season both sides of brisket with salt and pepper.

2. Heat oil in 12-inch skillet over medium-high heat until just smoking. Place brisket fat side up in skillet; brisket may ride up sides of pan, but will shrink as it cooks. Weight brisket with heavy Dutch oven or cast-iron skillet and cook until well browned, about 7 minutes. Remove Dutch oven, flip brisket, and cook on second side, without weight, until well browned, about 7 minutes. Transfer brisket to platter.

3. Pour off all but 1 tablespoon fat left in skillet, add onions, sugar, and ¼ teaspoon salt, and cook over medium-high heat, stirring occasionally, until softened and golden, 10 to 12 minutes. Stir in tomato paste and cook, stirring constantly, until paste browns, about 2 minutes. Stir in garlic, paprika, and cayenne and cook until fragrant, about 30 seconds. Sprinkle flour over onions and stir until well combined. Stir in broth, wine, thyme sprigs, and bay leaves, scraping up any browned bits. Bring mixture to simmer and cook until fully thickened, about 5 minutes.

4. Pour sauce and onions into prepared baking dish. Nestle brisket fat side up in into dish. Fold foil extensions over and crimp to seal. Transfer to oven and cook until brisket is tender and fork slips easily in and out of meat, 3½ to 4 hours; to test for doneness, open foil with caution and watch for steam.

5. Remove brisket from oven and let sit at room temperature, still wrapped in foil, for 1 hour. Carefully open foil and transfer brisket to carving board. Pour braising liquid through fine-mesh strainer into fat separator and let settle for 5 minutes. Discard bay leaves and thyme sprigs from strained onions; reserve onions.

6. Pour defatted juices into medium saucepan and simmer until slightly thickened and measures 2 cups, 5 to 10 minutes. Stir onions and vinegar into sauce and season with salt and pepper to taste. Slice brisket against grain into ¼-inch-thick slices, arrange in 13 by 9-inch baking dish, and pour sauce over top. Serve.

> **TO MAKE AHEAD**
> - Reserved onions and brisket with sauce, prepared through step 5, can be refrigerated separately for up to 2 days
> - To reheat, transfer meat to cutting board, scrape congealed sauce into saucepan, and continue with step 6; then, cover dish with foil and reheat in 350-degree oven for 30 minutes

Corned Beef and Cabbage
SERVES 6 TO 8
ACTIVE TIME 40 MINUTES
TOTAL TIME 4 HOURS 10 MINUTES TO 4 HOURS 40 MINUTES (PLUS 6 DAYS SALTING TIME)

WHY THIS RECIPE WORKS Our home-corned beef is perfectly seasoned and balanced, with complex flavor thanks to the presence of aromatics and spices. Although the process takes several days, it's almost entirely hands-off. We cured the meat (a flat-cut brisket was best) in a brine made with both table salt and pink salt, which was well worth the special order as it improved both the flavor and the color of the final product. We let the brisket cook through in the gentle, even heat of the oven and then used the flavorful braising liquid to cook potatoes, carrots, and cabbage on the stove. Pink curing salt #1, which can be purchased online or in stores specializing in meat curing, is a mixture of table salt and nitrites; it is also called Prague Powder #1, Insta Cure #1, or DQ Curing Salt #1. In addition to the pink salt, we use table salt here. If using Diamond Crystal kosher salt, increase the salt to 1½ cups; if using Morton kosher salt, increase to 1⅛ cups. This recipe requires six days to corn the beef, and you will need cheesecloth. Look for a uniformly thick brisket to ensure that the beef cures evenly. The brisket will look gray after curing but will turn pink once cooked. Use a Dutch oven that holds 7 quarts or more for this recipe.

Pink curing salt is essential to getting the best flavor and color for our home-corned beef.

CORNED BEEF

1 (4½- to 5-pound) beef brisket, flat cut
¾ cup salt
½ cup packed brown sugar
2 teaspoons pink curing salt #1
6 garlic cloves, peeled
6 bay leaves
5 allspice berries
2 tablespoons peppercorns
1 tablespoon coriander seeds

VEGETABLES

6 carrots, peeled, halved crosswise, thick ends halved lengthwise
1½ pounds small red potatoes, unpeeled
1 head green cabbage (2 pounds), uncored, cut into 8 wedges

1. FOR THE CORNED BEEF Trim fat on surface of brisket to ⅛ inch. Dissolve salt, sugar, and curing salt in 4 quarts water in large container. Add brisket, 3 garlic cloves, 4 bay leaves, allspice

berries, 1 tablespoon peppercorns, and coriander seeds. Weigh brisket down with plate, cover, and refrigerate for 6 days.

2. Adjust oven rack to middle position and heat oven to 275 degrees. Remove brisket from brine, rinse, and pat dry with paper towels. Cut 8-inch square triple thickness of cheesecloth. Place remaining 3 garlic cloves, remaining 2 bay leaves, and remaining 1 tablespoon peppercorns in center of cheesecloth and tie into bundle with kitchen twine. Place brisket, spice bundle, and 2 quarts water in Dutch oven. (Brisket may not lie flat but will shrink as it cooks.)

3. Bring to simmer over high heat, cover, and transfer to oven. Cook until meat is tender and fork slips easily in and out of meat, 2½ to 3 hours.

4. Remove pot from oven and turn off oven. Transfer brisket to large ovensafe platter, ladle 1 cup of cooking liquid over meat, cover, and return to oven to keep warm.

5. FOR THE VEGETABLES Add carrots and potatoes to pot and bring to simmer over high heat. Reduce heat to medium-low, cover, and simmer until vegetables begin to soften, 7 to 10 minutes. Add cabbage to pot, increase heat to high, and return to simmer. Reduce heat to low, cover, and simmer until all vegetables are tender, 12 to 15 minutes.

6. While vegetables cook, transfer beef to cutting board and slice against grain into ¼-inch-thick pieces. Return beef to platter. Using slotted spoon, transfer vegetables to platter with beef. Moisten with additional broth and serve.

> **TO MAKE AHEAD**
>
> - Corned beef, prepared through step 3, can be refrigerated for up to 3 days
> - To reheat, transfer meat to cutting board, slice into ¼-inch-thick pieces, arrange in 13 by 9-inch baking dish, pour 1 cup liquid over meat, cover with foil, and reheat in 350-degree oven for 30 minutes; bring remaining cooking liquid to simmer and continue with step 5

Shepherd's Pie

SERVES 6 TO 8 **FREEZE IT**
ACTIVE TIME 1 HOUR
TOTAL TIME 2 HOURS 15 MINUTES

WHY THIS RECIPE WORKS Traditional shepherd's pie, with slow-cooked stewed lamb and gravy topped with mashed potatoes, is delicious but time-consuming to make. We wanted a streamlined recipe with flavorful meat. The most common shortcut is to use ground meat, so we began by swapping the lamb for ground beef. To keep the meat tender even if the pie was frozen and reheated, we skipped browning it and just cooked it until no longer pink. To replace the missing flavor from the browned meat, we sautéed the onions, carrots, and tomato paste to create a flavorful fond in the pot. We deglazed the pot with red wine and boosted the filling's flavor with thyme and Worcestershire sauce. The Worcestershire lent the gravy depth, color, and a subtle savory note. We also added chicken broth to the filling to make sure it stayed moist and saucy. For the mashed potato topping, we used enough cream and butter so that the topping could be frozen and reheated without becoming gluey and dry. To achieve a beautiful golden-brown top on our pie, we broiled the casserole for a few minutes at the end of baking. Be sure to buy 93 percent lean ground beef or the finished casserole will be too greasy.

To keep the ground beef in our shepherd's pie nice and tender, we sauté it until it's just cooked through but not brown.

 1 tablespoon vegetable oil
 2 onions, chopped fine
 5 carrots, peeled and sliced ¼ inch thick
   Salt and pepper
 2 pounds 93 percent lean ground beef
 4 garlic cloves, minced
 4 teaspoons tomato paste
 ⅓ cup all-purpose flour
 ½ cup dry red wine
 2 cups chicken broth
 2 teaspoons minced fresh thyme or ½ teaspoon dried
 ¾ teaspoon Worcestershire sauce
 3 pounds russet potatoes, peeled and cut into 1-inch pieces
 ¾ cup heavy cream, warmed
 4 tablespoons unsalted butter, softened
 ⅔ cup frozen peas

1. Adjust oven rack to upper-middle position and heat oven to 400 degrees. Heat oil in Dutch oven over medium heat until shimmering. Add onions, carrots, 1 teaspoon salt, and ½ teaspoon pepper and cook until softened, 8 to 10 minutes. Add ground beef, breaking up meat with wooden spoon, and cook until no longer pink, about 5 minutes. Stir in garlic and tomato paste and cook until fragrant, about 30 seconds. Stir in flour and cook for 2 minutes.

2. Slowly stir in wine and cook until slightly reduced, about 2 minutes. Stir in broth, thyme, and Worcestershire, scraping up any browned bits. Bring to simmer and cook, stirring occasionally, until mixture is slightly thickened, 6 to 8 minutes. Season with salt and pepper to taste, and spread evenly into broiler-safe 13 by 9-inch baking dish.

3. Meanwhile, place potatoes and 1 tablespoon salt in large saucepan and add water to cover by 1 inch. Bring to boil, then reduce to simmer and cook until potatoes are tender, about 20 minutes; drain potatoes. Return potatoes to now-empty saucepan and

cook over low heat until dry, about 1 minute. Off heat, mash potatoes smooth with potato masher. Stir in cream, followed by butter, and season with salt and pepper to taste.

4. Sprinkle peas evenly over filling, gently pressing them into dish. Dollop potatoes evenly over top, spreading it right to pan edges.

5. Drag fork across top of potatoes to make ridges. Bake casserole on aluminum foil–lined rimmed baking sheet until hot throughout, about 35 to 40 minutes. Remove casserole from oven and heat broiler. Broil casserole until potatoes are spotty brown, 5 to 10 minutes, rotating dish halfway through broiling. Let cool for 10 minutes before serving.

TO MAKE AHEAD
- Casserole, prepared through step 4, can be refrigerated for up to 2 days or frozen for up to 1 month; if frozen, thaw completely in refrigerator
- To bake, cover with foil, place on foil-lined rimmed baking sheet, and continue with step 5, increasing baking time to 1½ hours; uncover and broil as directed

Beef Tamale Pie

SERVES 6 TO 8 **FREEZE IT**

ACTIVE TIME 45 MINUTES

TOTAL TIME 1 HOUR 30 MINUTES

WHY THIS RECIPE WORKS Tamale pie—lightly seasoned, tomatoey ground beef with a cornbread topping—is easy to prepare and makes a satisfying supper. But in many recipes, the filling either tastes bland and one-dimensional or turns heavy. As for the cornbread topping, it's usually from a mix and tastes like it. We wanted a tamale pie with a rich, well-seasoned filling and a cornbread topping with real corn flavor. We found that 85 percent lean ground beef gave us a good balance of richness and flavor. We started by browning onion and jalapeño and then added the beef, cooking it until it was no longer pink. For seasoning, we used a generous amount of chili powder along with extra cumin and some minced garlic, which we added to the aromatics in the Dutch oven to "bloom," or intensify, their flavors. The addition of canned black beans and frozen corn was a simple way to make our pie heartier, and canned crushed tomatoes contributed additional flavor and texture. Monterey Jack cheese stirred into the mixture enriched the filling and also helped thicken it. And to finish our pie, we made a simple buttermilk-enhanced cornbread batter, which we spread over the filling and baked. The rich and lightly sweet cornbread beautifully complemented the slightly spicy filling. Serve with lime wedges.

Our tamale pie features a rich ground beef, black bean, and corn filling enriched with shredded cheese.

FILLING

- 1 tablespoon vegetable oil
- 1 onion, chopped fine
- 1 jalapeño chile, stemmed, seeded, and minced
  Salt and pepper
- 1½ pounds 85 percent lean ground beef
- 2 tablespoons chili powder
- 4 garlic cloves, minced
- 1 teaspoon ground cumin
- 1 (28-ounce) can crushed tomatoes
- 1 (15-ounce) can black beans, rinsed
- 1½ cups frozen corn
- 8 ounces Monterey Jack cheese, shredded (2 cups)
- ¼ cup minced fresh cilantro

CORNBREAD

- 1½ cups (7½ ounces) all-purpose flour
- 1 cup (5 ounces) cornmeal
- ¼ cup (1¾ ounces) sugar
- 2 teaspoons baking powder
- ¼ teaspoon baking soda
- ¾ teaspoon salt
- 1 cup buttermilk
- 8 tablespoons unsalted butter, melted and cooled
- 2 large eggs, lightly beaten

1. FOR THE FILLING Adjust oven rack to middle position and heat oven to 375 degrees. Heat oil in Dutch oven over medium heat until shimmering. Add onion, jalapeño, and 1 teaspoon salt and cook until softened and lightly browned, 5 to 7 minutes. Add ground beef, breaking up meat with wooden spoon, and cook until no longer pink, 3 to 5 minutes.

2. Stir in chili powder, garlic, and cumin and cook until fragrant, about 30 seconds. Stir in tomatoes, scraping up any browned bits. Off heat, stir in beans, corn, Monterey Jack, and cilantro. Season with salt and pepper to taste, and spread evenly into 13 by 9-inch baking dish.

3. FOR THE CORNBREAD Whisk flour, cornmeal, sugar, baking powder, baking soda, and salt together in large bowl. In separate bowl, whisk buttermilk, melted butter, and eggs together until butter forms small clumps. Stir buttermilk mixture into flour mixture with rubber spatula until combined. Spread batter evenly over filling, spreading it right to edges of dish.

4. Bake until filling is bubbly and crust is baked through and golden, about 45 minutes. Let cool slightly before serving.

A generous amount of chili powder and a can of Ro-tel tomatoes gives our taco bake multilayered heat.

> **TO MAKE AHEAD** ▶
>
> - Casserole, prepared through step 3, can be refrigerated for up to 2 days; to bake, continue with step 4, increasing baking time to about 1 hour
> - Alternatively, casserole, prepared through step 3, can be frozen for up to 1 month; to bake, cover with foil and bake for 30 minutes, then uncover and continue to bake until filling is bubbly and crust is baked through, about 1 hour

Spicy Beef Taco Bake

SERVES 6

ACTIVE TIME 40 MINUTES

TOTAL TIME 50 MINUTES

WHY THIS RECIPE WORKS Our spicy beef taco bake packs all the great texture and flavor of taco night into an easy one-dish meal that could easily be prepped ahead of time. We used 93 percent lean ground beef instead of the usual 90 percent because we found that excess grease pooled on the bottom of the dish if stored overnight. We flavored the beef with onion, garlic, chili powder, and oregano, blooming the seasonings in oil to bring out their complex flavors. Both the chili powder and some Ro-tel tomatoes gave this dish multilayered heat. Layers of Colby Jack cheese helped to bind the beans and the meat. Taco shells broken into pieces and even more cheese made the perfect topping. If you can't find Ro-tel tomatoes, substitute one 14.5-ounce can diced tomatoes, drained, and one 4-ounce can chopped green chiles, drained, reserving 6 tablespoons of the tomato juice and 2 tablespoons of the chile juice. Colby Jack cheese is also known as CoJack; if unavailable, substitute Monterey Jack cheese. Be sure to buy 93 percent lean ground beef or the finished casserole will be too greasy. Serve with sour cream, chopped red onion, shredded lettuce, and/or salsa.

1 tablespoon vegetable oil
1 onion, chopped fine
  Salt and pepper
3 tablespoons chili powder
4 garlic cloves, minced
2 teaspoons minced fresh oregano or ½ teaspoon dried
1½ pounds 93 percent lean ground beef
2 (10-ounce) cans Ro-tel Diced Tomatoes & Green Chilies, drained with ½ cup juice reserved
2 teaspoons cider vinegar
1 teaspoon packed brown sugar
1 (16-ounce) can refried beans
¼ cup minced fresh cilantro
6 ounces Colby Jack cheese, shredded (1½ cups)
12 taco shells, broken into 1-inch pieces
2 scallions, sliced thin

1. Adjust oven rack to middle position and heat oven to 400 degrees. Heat oil in 12-inch skillet over medium heat until shimmering. Add onion and ½ teaspoon salt and cook until softened, about 5 minutes. Stir in chili powder, garlic, and oregano and cook until fragrant, about 1 minute. Add ground beef and cook, breaking up meat with wooden spoon, until no longer pink, 3 to 5 minutes.

2. Stir in half of tomatoes, reserved tomato juice, vinegar, and sugar. Bring to simmer and cook until mixture is very thick, about 5 minutes. Season with salt and pepper to taste.

3. Meanwhile, combine remaining tomatoes, refried beans, and cilantro and spread evenly into 13 by 9-inch baking dish. Sprinkle ½ cup Colby Jack over top. Spread beef mixture into baking dish and sprinkle with ½ cup Colby Jack. Scatter taco shell pieces over top, then sprinkle with remaining ½ cup Colby Jack.

4. Bake until filling is bubbling and top is spotty brown, about 10 minutes. Let casserole cool slightly, sprinkle with scallions, and serve.

TO MAKE AHEAD ▸

• Casserole, prepared through step 3, can be refrigerated for up to 24 hours
• To bake, cover with greased foil, bake in 400-degree oven for 25 minutes, then uncover and continue to bake for 10 minutes

All-American Meatloaf

SERVES 6 TO 8
ACTIVE TIME 45 MINUTES
TOTAL TIME 1 HOUR 30 MINUTES

WHY THIS RECIPE WORKS There is something comforting about having a meatloaf ready to go into the oven after a long day. But assembling a good meatloaf is more than throwing ingredients together; it requires some time to prepare and assemble. We wanted to do all of the work ahead of time so that we could simply bake the meatloaf when we wanted it. Meatloaf mix made the juiciest and most flavorful meatloaf. Combining flavorful mix-ins like Dijon mustard, Worcestershire sauce, and aromatics before adding the meat gave the loaf the most cohesive, tender structure. A panade of milk and saltines along with two eggs added moisture and gave the loaf a nice texture. For easy cleanup, we baked the loaf on a sheet of aluminum foil. Poking holes in the foil and placing it on a wire rack set in a rimmed baking sheet allowed excess grease to drain away as the loaf baked. If you are using round saltines, use 19 instead of 17. Place the saltines in a zipper-lock bag and use a rolling pin to crush them. Meatloaf mix is a prepackaged mix of ground beef, pork, and veal; if it's unavailable, use 1 pound each of ground pork and 85 percent lean ground beef.

½ cup ketchup
¼ cup packed light brown sugar
4 teaspoons cider vinegar
1 tablespoon vegetable oil
1 onion, chopped fine
2 garlic cloves, minced
2 teaspoons minced fresh thyme or ½ teaspoon dried
½ cup milk
17 square saltines, crushed (⅔ cup)
⅓ cup minced fresh parsley
2 large eggs, lightly beaten
2 teaspoons Dijon mustard
2 teaspoons Worcestershire sauce
1 teaspoon salt
½ teaspoon pepper
¼ teaspoon hot sauce
2 pounds meatloaf mix

1. Adjust oven rack to middle position and heat oven to 350 degrees. Fold sheet of heavy-duty aluminum foil to form 10 by 6-inch rectangle. Center foil on wire rack set in rimmed baking sheet. Poke holes in foil with skewer (about ½ inch apart). Spray foil with vegetable oil spray. Combine ketchup, sugar, and vinegar in bowl.

2. Heat oil in 8-inch skillet over medium heat until shimmering. Add onion and cook until softened, about 5 minutes. Stir in garlic and thyme and cook until fragrant, about 30 seconds; transfer to large bowl and let cool slightly.

3. Add milk and saltines to cooled onion mixture and mash with fork until chunky paste forms. Stir in parsley, eggs, mustard, Worcestershire, salt, pepper, and hot sauce until combined. Add meatloaf mix and knead with your hands until thoroughly combined. Transfer meat mixture to foil rectangle and shape into 9 by 5-inch loaf using your wet hands.

4. Brush top and sides of meatloaf with half of glaze and bake for 1 hour. Brush loaf with remaining glaze and bake until it registers 160 degrees, 20 to 30 minutes. Let cool for 20 minutes before slicing and serving.

TO MAKE AHEAD ▸

Meatloaf and glaze, prepared through step 3, can be refrigerated separately for up to 24 hours

MAKING ALL-AMERICAN MEATLOAF

1. Fold sheet of heavy-duty aluminum foil to form 10 by 6-inch rectangle. Center foil on wire rack set in rimmed baking sheet. Poke holes in foil with skewer (about ½ inch apart).

2. Transfer meat mixture to foil rectangle and shape into 9 by 5-inch loaf using your wet hands.

Mashing half the beans for the filling gives these freezer-friendly burritos a creamy consistency.

Beef and Bean Burritos

MAKES 8 BURRITOS   **FREEZE IT**

ACTIVE TIME 1 HOUR

TOTAL TIME 1 HOUR 40 MINUTES

WHY THIS RECIPE WORKS Whether as a quick lunch on the go or an easy dinner when the refrigerator is bare, frozen burritos may satisfy our hunger pangs, but not much else. We set out to create flavorful burritos that could withstand being stored in the freezer. To streamline our filling, we swapped the traditional stewed and shredded meat for easy ground beef. Mashing half of the beans gave our filling a creamy consistency, and a generous amount of spices contributed bold flavor. White rice, cooked in chicken broth with garlic, along with a good amount of fresh cilantro and sharp cheddar cheese rounded out our flavorful filling. Reheating the burritos was as simple as microwaving them for a few minutes, and a quick run under the broiler melted and browned the cheesy topping. Serve with hot sauce and sour cream.

2⅔ cups chicken broth

  1 cup long-grain white rice

  8 garlic cloves, minced

    Salt

⅓ cup minced fresh cilantro

  1 (15-ounce) can pinto beans, rinsed

  1 tablespoon vegetable oil

  1 onion, chopped fine

¼ cup tomato paste

  1 tablespoon ground cumin

  1 teaspoon dried oregano

  1 teaspoon chipotle chile powder

  1 pound 90 percent lean ground beef

  4 teaspoons lime juice

  8 (10-inch) flour tortillas

12 ounces sharp cheddar cheese, shredded (3 cups)

1. Bring 2 cups broth, rice, half of garlic, and 1 teaspoon salt to boil in small saucepan over medium-high heat. Reduce heat to low, cover, and cook until rice is tender and all liquid has been absorbed, about 20 minutes. Off heat, let sit, covered, for 10 minutes. Add cilantro, fluff rice with fork, and set aside to cool.

2. Meanwhile, using potato masher, coarsely mash half of beans with remaining ⅔ cup broth in medium bowl. Heat oil in 12-inch nonstick skillet over medium heat until shimmering. Add onion and cook until softened, about 5 minutes. Stir in tomato paste, cumin, oregano, chile powder, and remaining garlic and cook until fragrant, about 1 minute. Add ground beef and cook, breaking up meat with wooden spoon, until no longer pink, 8 to 10 minutes.

3. Add mashed bean mixture and cook, stirring constantly, until combined, about 1 minute. Stir in lime juice, 1 teaspoon salt, and remaining whole beans. Let filling cool to room temperature, about 20 minutes.

4. Adjust oven rack to middle position and heat broiler. Line rimmed baking sheet with foil. Wrap tortillas in clean dish towel; microwave until soft and pliable, about 90 seconds.

5. Arrange tortillas on counter. Divide rice, beef-and-bean filling, and 2 cups cheddar evenly over bottom halves of tortillas, leaving 1- to 2-inch border at edge. Fold sides of each tortilla over filling, fold bottom of tortilla over sides and filling, and roll tightly into burrito.

6. Transfer burritos to prepared baking sheet and sprinkle tops with remaining 1 cup cheese. Broil until cheese is melted and starting to brown, 3 to 5 minutes, rotating sheet halfway through broiling. Serve.

TO MAKE AHEAD ▶

- Burritos, prepared through step 5, can be refrigerated for up to 24 hours or frozen for up to 1 month
- To reheat, microwave burrito(s) until softened and hot throughout, 3 to 5 minutes, and continue with step 6

COOK-ALL-DAY ENTRÉES FROM THE SLOW COOKER

A recipe that can cook all day in the slow cooker is the ultimate trick for making dinner ahead. A bit of up-front work allows you to come home to a hot, home-cooked meal that requires only a few minutes of attention to get on the table. Large, well-marbled cuts of meat are perfectly suited to all-day cooking, and they make enough for a couple of meals. You will need a 5- to 7-quart slow cooker for these recipes.

SLOW-COOKER CLASSIC POT ROAST

SERVES 8

COOKING TIME 9 TO 10 HOURS ON LOW OR 6 TO 7 HOURS ON HIGH

If potatoes are larger than 1 to 2 inches in diameter, cut them into 1-inch pieces.

- 1 (5- to 6-pound) boneless beef chuck-eye roast, pulled into 2 pieces at natural seam and trimmed
  Salt and pepper
- 2 tablespoons vegetable oil
- 1 onion, chopped
- 2 celery ribs, chopped
- 2 tablespoons all-purpose flour
- 1 tablespoon tomato paste
- 3 garlic cloves, minced
- 1 teaspoon minced fresh thyme or ¼ teaspoon dried
- ½ cup dry red wine
- 2 pounds small Yukon Gold potatoes, unpeeled
- 1 pound carrots, peeled and halved crosswise, thick ends halved lengthwise
- ½ cup beef broth
- 2 bay leaves
- 2 tablespoons minced fresh parsley

1. Pat beef dry with paper towels and season with salt and pepper. Tie 3 pieces of kitchen twine around each piece of beef to create 2 evenly shaped roasts. Heat oil in 12-inch skillet over medium-high heat until just smoking. Brown roasts on all sides, 7 to 10 minutes; transfer to large plate.

2. Add onion, celery, ½ teaspoon salt, and ¼ teaspoon pepper to fat left in skillet and cook until softened and lightly browned, 8 to 10 minutes. Stir in flour, tomato paste, garlic, and thyme and cook until fragrant, about 1 minute. Slowly whisk in wine, scraping up any browned bits and smoothing out any lumps; transfer to slow cooker.

3. Stir potatoes, carrots, broth, and bay leaves into slow cooker. Nestle roasts into slow cooker along with any accumulated juices, cover, and cook until beef is tender and fork slips easily in and out of meat, 9 to 10 hours on low or 6 to 7 hours on high.

4. Transfer roasts to carving board, tent with aluminum foil, and let rest for 15 minutes. Discard bay leaves. Using slotted spoon, transfer vegetables to serving dish. Strain sauce into fat separator and let sit for 5 minutes; discard solids. Pour defatted sauce into bowl and season with salt and pepper to taste; discard fat.

5. Remove twine from roasts, slice meat against grain into ½-inch-thick slices, and arrange on serving platter. Spoon 1 cup sauce over meat and serve with remaining sauce and vegetables.

> **TO MAKE AHEAD**
>
> - Pot roast with defatted sauce and vegetables, prepared through step 4, can be refrigerated separately for up to 2 days
> - To reheat, transfer meat to carving board, slice into ½-inch-thick slices, arrange in 13 by 9-inch baking dish, cover with foil, and reheat in 325-degree oven for 1 hour; reheat sauce, defat with large spoon, and continue with step 5

SLOW-COOKER CUBAN-STYLE PORK ROAST WITH MOJO SAUCE

SERVES 8

COOKING TIME 9 TO 10 HOURS ON LOW OR 6 TO 7 HOURS ON HIGH

Boneless pork butt roast is often labeled Boston butt in the supermarket. Serve with rice.

- 1 (5- to 6- pound) boneless pork butt roast, trimmed and halved
  Salt and pepper
- 5 tablespoons extra-virgin olive oil
- 1 onion, chopped
- 2 teaspoons dried oregano
- 1½ teaspoons ground cumin
- 6 garlic cloves, minced
- ½ cup water
- 1 tablespoon grated orange zest plus ½ cup juice
- 1 tablespoon minced canned chipotle chile in adobo sauce
- ¼ cup distilled white vinegar

1. Pat pork dry with paper towels and season with salt and pepper. Tie 3 pieces of kitchen twine around each piece of pork to create 2 evenly shaped roasts. Heat 1 tablespoon oil in 12-inch skillet over medium-high heat until just smoking. Brown roasts on all sides, 7 to 10 minutes; transfer to large plate.

2. Add onion, 1 teaspoon salt, and 1 teaspoon pepper to fat left in skillet and cook over medium heat until softened and lightly browned, 5 to 7 minutes. Stir in oregano, cumin, and two-thirds of garlic and cook until fragrant, about 30 seconds. Stir in water, scraping up any browned bits; transfer to slow cooker.

3. Stir orange zest and ¼ cup juice and chipotle into slow cooker. Nestle roasts into slow cooker along with any accumulated juices, cover, and cook until pork is tender and fork slips easily in and out of meat, 9 to 10 hours on low or 6 to 7 hours on high.

4. Transfer roasts to carving board, tent with aluminum foil, and let rest for 20 minutes. Strain cooking liquid into fat separator and let sit for 5 minutes; discard solids. Pour ¼ cup defatted liquid into medium bowl; discard fat and remaining liquid. Whisk in vinegar, remaining ¼ cup oil, remaining garlic, remaining ¼ cup orange juice, ¼ teaspoon salt, and ¼ teaspoon pepper.

5. Remove twine from roasts, slice meat against grain into ½-inch-thick slices, and arrange on serving platter. Serve with sauce.

TO MAKE AHEAD

- Pork with sauce, prepared through step 3, can be refrigerated for up to 2 days
- To reheat, transfer meat to carving board, slice into ½-inch-thick slices, arrange in 13 by 9-inch baking dish, cover with foil, and reheat in 325-degree oven for 1 hour; reheat sauce, defat with large spoon, and continue with step 4

SLOW-COOKER BRAISED BRISKET AND ONIONS

SERVES 8

COOKING TIME 9 TO 10 HOURS ON LOW OR 6 TO 7 HOURS ON HIGH

- 1 tablespoon paprika
- 2 teaspoons onion powder
  Salt and pepper
- 1 teaspoon garlic powder
- ⅛ teaspoon cayenne pepper
- 1 (5-pound) beef brisket, flat cut, fat trimmed to ¼ inch
- 1 tablespoon vegetable oil
- 3 onions, halved and sliced ½ inch thick
- 1 tablespoon packed brown sugar
- 1 tablespoon tomato paste
- 3 garlic cloves, minced
- 3 tablespoons all-purpose flour
- 1 cup chicken broth
- 2 tablespoons plus 1 teaspoon red wine vinegar
- 3 sprigs fresh thyme
- 3 bay leaves

1. Combine paprika, onion powder, 1 teaspoon salt, garlic powder, and cayenne in bowl. Using fork, prick brisket all over. Rub spice mixture over brisket, wrap tightly in plastic wrap, and refrigerate for at least 8 hours. Unwrap brisket and place in slow cooker.

2. Heat oil in 12-inch skillet over medium heat until shimmering. Add onions, sugar, tomato paste, and garlic and cook until onions are softened and lightly browned, 8 to 10 minutes. Stir in flour and cook for 1 minute. Slowly stir in broth, scraping up any browned bits and smoothing out any lumps; transfer to slow cooker.

3. Stir 2 tablespoons vinegar, thyme sprigs, and bay leaves into slow cooker. Cover and cook until brisket is tender and fork slips easily in and out of meat, 9 to 10 hours on low or 6 to 7 hours on high.

4. Transfer brisket to carving board, tent with aluminum foil, and let rest for 20 minutes. Discard thyme sprigs and bay leaves. Using large spoon, skim fat from surface of sauce. Stir in remaining 1 teaspoon vinegar and season with salt and pepper to taste.

5. Slice brisket ½ inch thick against grain and arrange on serving platter. Spoon 1 cup sauce over meat and serve, passing remaining sauce separately.

TO MAKE AHEAD

- Brisket, prepared through step 1, can be refrigerated for up to 24 hours
- Brisket with sauce, prepared through step 3, can be refrigerated for up to 2 days
- To reheat, transfer meat to carving board, slice into ½-inch-thick slices, arrange in 13 by 9-inch baking dish, cover with foil, and reheat in 325-degree oven for 1 hour; reheat sauce with onions (discarding thyme sprigs and bay leaves and defatting liquid with large spoon) and continue with step 5

A coating of cornstarch and cornflake crumbs becomes ultracrisp when pan-fried, even after 24 hours in the fridge.

Breaded Pork Chops

SERVES 4
ACTIVE TIME 50 MINUTES
TOTAL TIME 1 HOUR 50 MINUTES

WHY THIS RECIPE WORKS Crispy pan-fried pork chops are delicious but time-consuming to make; usually they are coated first in flour, then in egg, then in bread crumbs before being pan-fried. We wanted to do all the prep work ahead so we could simply drop the pork chops into a hot skillet the next day, but when we tried to store the breaded chops overnight, the breading turned soggy and limp as the flour and bread crumbs absorbed moisture from the meat and the egg. Switching from flour to cornstarch helped to lighten and crisp our coating. To help the coating stick, we swapped the egg for buttermilk, which created a tacky layer that more effectively bound the crust to the chops. For added insurance, we made shallow cuts in the chops to release juices and sticky meat proteins, further encouraging the coating to adhere. Bread crumbs also absorb moisture quickly, so we swapped them for crushed corn flakes; tossed with additional cornstarch, they

stayed crisp even after sitting overnight in the refrigerator. You can substitute 1 cup of store-bought cornflake crumbs for the whole cornflakes; omit the processing step and mix the crumbs with the cornstarch, salt, and pepper. Be sure to buy chops of equal thickness to ensure they all cook at the same rate.

⅔ cup cornstarch
1 cup buttermilk
2 tablespoons Dijon mustard
1 garlic clove, minced
4 cups (4 ounces) cornflakes
Salt and pepper
8 (3- to 4-ounce) boneless pork chops, ½ to ¾ inch thick, trimmed
⅔ cup vegetable oil
Lemon wedges

1. Place ⅓ cup cornstarch in shallow dish. In second shallow dish, whisk buttermilk, mustard, and garlic until combined. Process cornflakes, ½ teaspoon salt, ½ teaspoon pepper, and remaining ⅓ cup cornstarch in food processor until cornflakes are finely ground, about 10 seconds; transfer mixture to third shallow dish.

2. Pat chops dry with paper towels. Using sharp knife, cut 2 slits, about 2 inches apart, through outer layer of fat and silverskin. Then, cut 1/16-inch-deep slits on both sides of chops, spaced ½ inch apart, in crosshatch pattern. Season chops with salt and pepper. Working with 1 chop at a time, dredge in cornstarch, dip in buttermilk mixture, then coat with cornflake mixture, pressing gently to adhere. Transfer coated chops to large plate and refrigerate for at least 1 hour.

3. Set wire rack in rimmed baking sheet. Adjust oven rack to middle position, place prepared sheet on oven rack, and heat oven to 200 degrees. Line large plate with triple layer of paper towels. Heat ⅓ cup oil in 12-inch nonstick skillet over medium-high heat until shimmering. Place 4 chops in skillet and cook until golden brown and crispy, 2 to 5 minutes.

4. Carefully flip chops and continue to cook until second side is golden brown and crispy and pork registers 145 degrees, 2 to 5 minutes. Transfer chops to paper towel–lined plate, let drain for 30 seconds on each side, then transfer to rack in oven. Discard oil in skillet, clean with paper towels, and repeat with remaining ⅓ cup oil and remaining chops. Serve with lemon wedges.

TO MAKE AHEAD

Breaded chops, prepared through step 2, can be refrigerated for up to 24 hours

Thick-Cut Pork Chops with Spicy Red Pepper Relish

SERVES 4

ACTIVE TIME 40 MINUTES

TOTAL TIME 2 HOURS

WHY THIS RECIPE WORKS For thick-cut pork chops that boasted both a juicy interior and a nicely caramelized exterior, we started the chops in a low oven and slowly roasted them until they were nearly cooked through. Then we transferred them to a hot skillet and seared them until we had a good crust and the interior was cooked to perfection. We paired our chops with a simple yet potent red pepper relish made with sweet bell peppers and spicy jalapeños, along with onion, garlic, and mustard seeds in a sweet and sour base of sugar and vinegar. Be sure to buy chops of equal thickness to ensure they all cook at the same rate.

RELISH

1 large red bell pepper, stemmed, seeded, and cut into 1-inch pieces

1 jalapeño chile, stemmed, seeded, and cut into 1-inch pieces

½ small onion, chopped

2 garlic cloves, peeled

¼ cup distilled white vinegar

¼ cup sugar

½ teaspoon yellow mustard seeds

½ teaspoon salt

PORK CHOPS

1 tablespoon salt

1 teaspoon garlic powder

1 teaspoon ground coriander

¼ teaspoon pepper

4 (12-ounce) bone-in pork rib chops, 1½ inches thick

1–2 tablespoons vegetable oil

1. FOR THE RELISH Pulse bell pepper, jalapeño, onion, and garlic in food processor until chopped into ¼-inch pieces, 8 to 10 pulses. Bring vinegar, sugar, mustard seeds, and salt to boil in large saucepan over medium-high heat. Add processed vegetables, reduce heat to medium, and simmer until mixture has thickened, 15 to 18 minutes. Transfer to serving bowl and let cool.

2. FOR THE PORK CHOPS Combine salt, garlic powder, coriander, and pepper in bowl. Pat chops dry with paper towels. Using sharp knife, cut 2 slits, about 2 inches apart, through outer layer of fat and silverskin. Rub chops evenly with spice mixture.

3. Place chops on wire rack set in rimmed baking sheet and let stand at room temperature for 45 minutes.

Roasting and then pan-searing thick-cut pork chops ensures juicy interiors and caramelized exteriors.

4. Adjust oven rack to middle position and heat oven to 275 degrees. Transfer chops to oven and roast until pork registers 120 to 125 degrees, 30 to 45 minutes.

5. Heat 1 tablespoon oil in 12-inch skillet over high heat until just smoking. Place 2 chops in skillet and sear, lifting chops periodically to prevent sticking, until well browned, 3½ to 6 minutes, flipping chops halfway through cooking. (Reduce heat if browned bits in pan bottom start to burn.) Transfer chops to plate and repeat with remaining 2 chops, adding extra 1 tablespoon oil if pan is dry.

6. Reduce heat to medium. Use tongs to stand 2 pork chops on their sides. Holding chops together with tongs, return to skillet and sear sides of chops (with exception of bone side) until browned and chops register 145 degrees, about 1½ minutes. Repeat with remaining 2 chops. Let chops rest, tented with foil, for 10 minutes. Serve with relish.

TO MAKE AHEAD

- Relish, prepared through step 1, can be refrigerated for up to 1 week; bring to room temperature before serving
- Spice-rubbed pork chops, prepared through step 2, can be refrigerated for up to 24 hours

Apple cider, apple butter, and apple cider vinegar give our braised pork chops layers of apple flavor.

Cider-Braised Pork Chops

SERVES 4 **FREEZE IT**

ACTIVE TIME 1 HOUR

TOTAL TIME 2 HOURS 30 MINUTES TO 3 HOURS

WHY THIS RECIPE WORKS Pork and apples are a tried-and-true pairing, but the apple flavor in cider-braised pork chops can be fleeting, and recipes often skimp on the time necessary for the pork to become fall-off-the-bone tender. We wanted tender, juicy chops infused with deep apple flavor. Patting the chops dry before adding them to the hot oil helped them to develop a flavorful crust. To boost the apple flavor, we supplemented the cider with apple butter, which thickened the sauce and made it rich and glossy. Garlic and thyme offered savory aromatic notes. To further reinforce the apple flavor and brighten the sauce at the end of cooking, we whisked in more apple butter and some cider vinegar just before serving. Be sure to buy chops of equal thickness to ensure they all cook at the same rate.

4 (10- to 12-ounce) bone-in blade-cut pork chops, about
  1 inch thick, trimmed
  Salt and pepper

2 tablespoons vegetable oil
1 onion, chopped
¼ cup apple butter
2 tablespoons all-purpose flour
3 garlic cloves, minced
1 cup apple cider
1 sprig fresh thyme
1 tablespoon cider vinegar
1 tablespoon minced fresh parsley

1. Adjust oven rack to lower-middle position and heat oven to 300 degrees. Cut 2 slits, about 2 inches apart, through outer layer of fat and silverskin on each chop. Pat chops dry with paper towels and season with salt and pepper. Heat 1 tablespoon oil in Dutch oven over medium-high heat until just smoking. Brown 2 chops well on 1 side, about 4 minutes; transfer to plate. Repeat with remaining 1 tablespoon oil and remaining 2 chops.

2. Pour off all but 1 tablespoon fat left in pot, add onion, and cook over medium heat until softened, about 5 minutes. Stir in 2 tablespoons apple butter, flour, and garlic and cook until fragrant, about 1 minute. Stir in cider and thyme sprig, scraping up any browned bits, and bring to boil.

3. Nestle chops into pot along with any accumulated juices, cover, and transfer to oven. Cook until chops are completely tender, 1½ to 2 hours.

4. Transfer chops to serving platter. Strain sauce, let liquid settle for 5 minutes, then skim excess fat from surface. Whisk in vinegar, parsley, and remaining 2 tablespoons apple butter and season with salt and pepper to taste. Serve.

TO MAKE AHEAD

- Braised pork chops, prepared through step 3, can be refrigerated for up to 3 days or frozen for up to 1 month; if frozen, thaw completely in refrigerator
- To reheat, bring chops, covered, to gentle simmer and cook until hot throughout, adjusting consistency with hot water or cider as needed, and continue with step 4

PREVENTING CURLED PORK CHOPS

To prevent pork chops from buckling and curling when cooked, cut 2 small slits, about 2 inches apart, through outer layer of fat and silverskin on each chop.

We brown and then braise flavorful Italian sausages on top of hearty greens and beans in this rustic dish.

Sausage and White Beans with Mustard Greens

SERVES 4

ACTIVE TIME 1 HOUR

TOTAL TIME 1 HOUR 25 MINUTES

WHY THIS RECIPE WORKS This rich, stew-like dish combines meaty sausage, creamy white beans, and fresh greens. Sweet Italian sausage, which is very flavorful and easy to get, was a good starting point. Browning the sausage deepened its flavor and rendered the fat, which we used to sauté onion, garlic, and thyme. We added a healthy splash of white wine before adding the chicken broth, tomatoes, and beans. Using canned cannellini beans eliminated an overnight soak. For the greens, we enjoyed the peppery spice of mustard greens, which we gently wilted before braising them. To finish, a sprinkle of cheesy bread crumbs and parsley added pleasant crunch and freshness. You can substitute kale for the mustard greens.

2 slices hearty white sandwich bread

¼ cup extra-virgin olive oil

¼ cup grated Parmesan cheese

Salt and pepper

1 pound hot or sweet Italian sausage

1 onion, chopped fine

2 tablespoons minced fresh thyme or 2 teaspoons dried

6 garlic cloves, minced

½ cup dry white wine

1 (14.5-ounce) can diced tomatoes, drained with juice reserved

1½ cups chicken broth

1 (15-ounce) can cannellini beans, rinsed

12 ounces mustard greens, stemmed and cut into 2-inch pieces

2 tablespoons minced fresh parsley

1. Pulse bread in food processor until finely ground, 10 to 15 pulses. Heat 2 tablespoons oil in 12-inch nonstick skillet over medium heat until shimmering. Add bread crumbs and cook, stirring constantly, until crumbs begin to brown, 3 to 5 minutes. Add Parmesan and cook, stirring constantly, until crumbs are golden brown, 1 to 2 minutes. Transfer to bowl and season with salt and pepper to taste.

2. Prick sausages with fork in several places. Heat 1 tablespoon oil in Dutch oven over medium-high heat until just smoking. Brown sausages well on all sides, about 8 minutes; transfer to plate.

3. Heat remaining 1 tablespoon oil in now-empty pot over medium heat until shimmering. Add onion and ¼ teaspoon salt and cook until softened and lightly browned, 5 to 7 minutes. Stir in thyme and garlic and cook until fragrant, about 30 seconds. Stir in wine and reserved tomato juice, scraping up any browned bits, and cook until nearly evaporated, about 5 minutes. Stir in broth, beans, and tomatoes and bring to simmer.

4. Stir in mustard greens and cook until slightly wilted, about 1 minute. Place sausages on top of greens. Reduce heat to low, cover, and cook until greens are wilted and reduced in volume by about half, about 10 minutes. Uncover, increase heat to medium-low, and continue to cook, stirring occasionally, until sausages are cooked through and greens are tender, about 15 minutes.

5. Off heat, mash portion of beans against side of pot with back of spoon to thicken sauce. Serve, sprinkling individual portions with bread crumbs and parsley.

TO MAKE AHEAD

- Parmesan bread crumbs, prepared through step 1, can be stored at room temperature for up to 2 weeks
- Sausage, white beans, and mustard greens, prepared through step 4, can be refrigerated for up to 2 days
- To reheat, bring mixture to gentle simmer, cook until sausage is hot throughout, and continue with step 5

Rubbing pork tenderloins with crushed herbes de Provence gives them great flavor without any fuss.

Provençal Pork Tenderloin with Apples and Shallots

SERVES 4 TO 6
ACTIVE TIME 40 MINUTES
TOTAL TIME 1 HOUR 50 MINUTES

WHY THIS RECIPE WORKS Pork tenderloins are a great week-night dinner option because they adapt well to many different flavors and they cook relatively fast. To make this dinner even easier, we came up with a version that could be prepped ahead of time and cooked a day later. We started by rubbing the tenderloins with herbes de Provence, which was a simple way to provide a nice blend of flavors. Crumbling the herbs helped them to coat the pork more evenly. A hearty combination of apples and shallots nicely complemented the rich pork. With the flavors established, we turned to the cooking method. We seared the pork in a skillet to brown it, then transferred it to a plate while we browned the apples and shallots in the same pan, flavoring them with the fond from the pork. Then we nestled the browned pork into the apples and shallots to finish cooking gently in the oven. While the pork rested, we added butter to the apples and shallots for some extra richness.

You can find herbes de Provence in most large grocery stores; however, 1 teaspoon each of dried thyme, dried rosemary, and dried marjoram can be substituted.

- 2 (1-pound) pork tenderloins, trimmed
- 1 tablespoon herbes de Provence, crumbled
  Salt and pepper
- 6 shallots, sliced ½ inch thick
- 3 Golden Delicious apples, peeled, cored, and cut into ½-inch-thick wedges
- ¼ cup vegetable oil
- ½ teaspoon sugar
- 1 tablespoon unsalted butter

1. Season pork with herbes de Provence, salt, and pepper, wrap with plastic wrap, and refrigerate for at least 1 hour. Meanwhile, toss shallots, apples, 2 tablespoons oil, and sugar together in bowl.

2. Adjust oven rack to lowest position and heat oven to 350 degrees. Pat pork dry with paper towels. Heat remaining 2 tablespoons oil in 12-inch ovensafe skillet over medium-high heat until just smoking. Place both pork tenderloins in skillet, spaced 1 inch apart, and brown well on all sides, 8 to 10 minutes; transfer to plate.

3. Add apple mixture to now-empty skillet, discarding any excess liquid. Cook until shallots and apples begin to soften and brown lightly, 10 to 12 minutes. Off heat, nestle tenderloins and any accumulated juices into apple mixture, alternating thicker end to thinner end. Transfer skillet to oven and roast pork until it registers 145 degrees, 15 to 20 minutes.

4. Carefully remove skillet from oven (skillet handle will be hot). Transfer pork to carving board, tent with aluminum foil, and let rest for 5 to 10 minutes. Stir butter into apple mixture, season with salt and pepper to taste, and cover to keep warm. Slice pork into ½-inch-thick slices and serve with apple mixture.

TO MAKE AHEAD

Spice-rubbed pork and apple mixture, prepared through step 1, can be refrigerated separately for up to 24 hours

REMOVING PORK SILVERSKIN

Silverskin is a swath of connective tissue located between the meat and the fat that covers its surface. To remove silverskin, simply slip a knife under it, angle knife slightly upward, and use a gentle back-and-forth motion.

Grilled Stuffed Pork Tenderloin with Piquillo Pepper and Manchego Stuffing

SERVES 6

ACTIVE TIME 40 MINUTES

TOTAL TIME 1 HOUR 40 MINUTES

WHY THIS RECIPE WORKS Though pork tenderloin is sublimely tender, it is also prone to drying out and often lacking flavor. We wanted a grilled tenderloin packed with flavor—in a stuffing—so we worked on creating potent complementary combinations for our pork. We drew inspiration from the Mediterranean with a Spanish-inspired smoked paprika, Manchego cheese, and piquillo pepper stuffing and an Italian-inspired porcini mushroom, pine nut, and artichoke variation. To fit plenty of flavor inside this skinny cut, we pounded the tenderloin thin and rolled it around the filling, opting for a thick paste whose richness countered the leanness of our meat. A layer of slightly bitter spinach added further balance and complexity. Indirect heat on the grill allowed the stuffing to heat through before the exterior of the pork overcooked, and a brown sugar rub caramelized nicely, giving the pork a deep amber hue. Stuffing and rolling the pork in advance made it a breeze on serving day. We prefer natural to enhanced pork (pork that has been injected with a salt solution to increase moistness and flavor) for this recipe; enhanced pork will turn the stuffing soggy.

STUFFING

- 1 slice hearty white sandwich bread, torn into ½-inch pieces
- ¾ cup jarred piquillo peppers, rinsed and patted dry
- 2 ounces Manchego cheese, shredded (½ cup)
- ¼ cup pine nuts, toasted
- 2 garlic cloves, minced
- 1 teaspoon minced fresh thyme
- ½ teaspoon smoked paprika
  Salt and pepper

PORK

- 2 (1¼- to 1½-pound) pork tenderloins, trimmed
  Salt and pepper
- 1 cup baby spinach
- 4 teaspoons packed dark brown sugar
- 2 tablespoons extra-virgin olive oil

1. FOR THE STUFFING Pulse all ingredients in food processor until coarsely chopped, 5 to 10 pulses. Season with salt and pepper to taste.

2. FOR THE PORK Cut each tenderloin in half horizontally, stopping ½ inch from edge so halves remain attached. Open up tenderloins, cover with plastic wrap, and pound to ¼-inch thickness. Trim any ragged edges to create rough rectangle about 10 inches by 6 inches. Season interior of pork with salt and pepper.

3. With long side of pork facing you, spread half of stuffing mixture over bottom half of pork followed by ½ cup of spinach. Roll away from you into tight cylinder, taking care not to squeeze stuffing out ends. Position tenderloin seam side down, evenly space 5 pieces kitchen twine underneath, and tie. Repeat with remaining tenderloin, stuffing, and spinach.

4. Before grilling, combine sugar, 1 teaspoon salt, and 1 teaspoon pepper in bowl. Coat pork with oil, then rub entire surface with brown sugar mixture.

5A. FOR A CHARCOAL GRILL Open bottom vent completely. Light large chimney starter filled with charcoal briquettes (6 quarts). When top coals are partially covered with ash, pour evenly over half of grill. Set cooking grate in place, cover, and open lid vent completely. Heat grill until hot, about 5 minutes.

5B. FOR A GAS GRILL Turn all burners to high, cover, and heat grill until hot, about 15 minutes. Leave primary burner on high and turn off other burner(s). (Adjust primary burner as needed during cooking to maintain grill temperature between 325 and 350 degrees.)

6. Clean and oil cooking grate. Place pork on cooler side of grill, cover, and cook until meat registers 140 degrees, 25 to 30 minutes, rotating pork halfway through cooking. Transfer pork to carving board, tent with aluminum foil, and let rest for 20 minutes. Remove twine, slice pork into ½-inch-thick slices, and serve.

STUFFING A PORK TENDERLOIN

1. Cut each tenderloin in half horizontally, stopping ½ inch from edge so halves remain attached. Open up tenderloins, cover with plastic wrap, and pound to ¼-inch thickness.

2. With long side of pork facing you, spread half of stuffing mixture over bottom half of pork followed by ½ cup of spinach. Roll away from you into tight cylinder, taking care not to squeeze stuffing out ends.

Grilled Stuffed Pork Tenderloin with Artichoke and Porcini Stuffing

Substitute following mixture for stuffing: Pulse ½ ounce dried porcini mushrooms, rinsed and minced, ¾ cup canned artichoke hearts, patted dry, ½ cup grated Parmesan cheese, ¼ cup oil-packed sun-dried tomatoes, rinsed and chopped, ¼ cup fresh parsley leaves, 2 tablespoons toasted pine nuts, 2 minced garlic cloves, 1 teaspoon grated lemon zest and 2 teaspoons lemon juice in food processor until coarsely chopped, 5 to 10 pulses. Season with salt and pepper to taste.

TO MAKE AHEAD

Stuffed pork, prepared through step 3, can be refrigerated for up to 24 hours

Roasted Pork Loin with Potatoes and Mustard Sauce

SERVES 6 **EASY**

ACTIVE TIME 30 MINUTES

TOTAL TIME 2 HOURS 30 MINUTES

WHY THIS RECIPE WORKS For a complete pork loin dinner, we wanted a savory rub, an easy side dish, and a fragrant sauce—and we wanted to be able to prep everything ahead of time. We rubbed our meat with savory spices and salt to infuse it with flavor, and then we gently roasted the pork at a relatively low temperature to keep it from drying out. This gave us tender, juicy pork, but we were looking for a crisper crust. Broiling the pork for just 5 minutes added the nicely browned exterior that was missing. To round out our meal, we wanted an accompaniment that could hold up to being stored overnight and bake alongside the pork. Small red potatoes seemed like a good choice since we could roast them in the same amount of time as the pork. To lend them some additional flavor, we tossed them with bacon pieces. To prevent the potatoes from oxidizing as they sat, we added some oil. A quick mustard vinaigrette was an easy finishing touch. Use small red potatoes measuring 1 to 2 inches in diameter.

1½ teaspoons garlic powder
1½ teaspoons dried oregano
1½ teaspoons ground coriander
1½ teaspoons ground cumin
   Salt and pepper
1 (2½- to 3-pound) boneless pork loin roast, trimmed
2½ pounds small red potatoes, unpeeled, halved
4 slices bacon, cut into ½-inch pieces
7 tablespoons extra-virgin olive oil

Small red potatoes cook through at the same rate as a pork loin roast, allowing us to make an entrée and a side at once.

¼ cup minced fresh parsley
1 shallot, minced
2 tablespoons whole-grain mustard
1½ tablespoons white wine vinegar
   Pinch sugar

1. Combine garlic, oregano, coriander, cumin, ½ teaspoon salt, and ½ teaspoon pepper in bowl. Rub pork evenly with spice mixture, wrap with plastic wrap, and refrigerate for at least 1 hour. Meanwhile, toss potatoes, bacon, and 2 tablespoons oil together in bowl. In separate bowl, combine ¼ cup oil, parsley, shallot, mustard, vinegar, and sugar.

2. Adjust oven rack to upper-middle position and heat oven to 325 degrees. Line rimmed baking sheet with aluminum foil and brush with remaining 1 tablespoon oil. Pat pork dry with paper towels and place fat side up in center of prepared sheet. Place bacon and potatoes, cut side down, on sheet around roast and season with salt and pepper.

3. Roast pork and potatoes until pork registers 130 degrees, 40 minutes to 1 hour, rotating sheet halfway through roasting. Remove pork and potatoes from oven, adjust oven rack 6 inches from broiler element, and heat broiler. Broil until pork is spotty brown and registers 140 degrees, 3 to 5 minutes.

4. Transfer pork to carving board, tent with foil, and let rest for 15 to 20 minutes. Return potatoes to oven and continue to broil until lightly browned, 5 to 10 minutes. Slice pork into ½-inch-thick slices. Whisk sauce to recombine and serve with pork and potatoes.

TO MAKE AHEAD ▶

- Spice-rubbed pork, potato-bacon mixture, and sauce, prepared through step 1, can be refrigerated separately for up to 24 hours
- To cook, bring sauce to room temperature and continue with step 2

Roasted Spice-Stuffed Pork Loin

SERVES 6
ACTIVE TIME 40 MINUTES
TOTAL TIME 2 HOURS 40 MINUTES

WHY THIS RECIPE WORKS A roast pork loin can be a delicious dinner, but not if it comes out of the oven with so-so flavor and dry, tough meat. Rubbing the roast with sugar and salt and letting it rest for at least an hour gave the roast a flavorful crust and seasoned it throughout so it came out of the oven juicy and tender. To add even more flavor to our roast, we butterflied the loin and applied a spice rub to the inside before rolling it back up and rubbing the outside with our salt rub. This gave our meat bold flavor throughout; plus, we were able to use the same flavors to make a quick glaze: After searing the roast in a skillet, we added maple syrup and more of the warm spices to the pan so the glaze would pick up the flavorful fond. We used the glaze to coat the pork as it roasted. Finally, while the pork rested, we added a little chicken broth and vinegar to the glaze to make a luscious sauce to serve alongside our pork.

 2 tablespoons packed brown sugar
 Salt and pepper
 2 tablespoons vegetable oil
 1 tablespoon paprika
 ¾ teaspoon ground cinnamon
 Cayenne pepper
 1 (2½- to 3-pound) boneless pork loin roast, trimmed
 ⅓ cup maple syrup
 ⅓ cup chicken broth
 1 teaspoon cider vinegar

Butterflying a pork roast and then rolling it around a flavorful spice rub seasons the meat from edge to center.

1. Combine sugar, 2 teaspoons salt, and 1½ teaspoons pepper in bowl. In separate bowl, microwave 1 tablespoon oil, paprika, 1 teaspoon salt, ¼ teaspoon cinnamon, and pinch cayenne until fragrant, about 30 seconds; let cool slightly.

2. With roast fat side up, cut horizontally through meat, one-third of way up from bottom, stopping ½ inch from edge. Open roast and press flat; 1 side will be twice as thick. Continue cutting thicker side of roast in half, stopping ½ inch from edge. Open roast, cover with plastic wrap, and gently pound flat.

3. Rub cooled oil mixture on cut surface of meat, leaving ½-inch border on all sides. Starting from short side, roll roast into tight cylinder and tie with kitchen twine at 1-inch intervals. Rub roast with sugar mixture, wrap with plastic wrap, and refrigerate for at least 1 hour.

4. Adjust oven rack to lower-middle position and heat oven to 325 degrees. Combine maple syrup, remaining ½ teaspoon cinnamon, and pinch cayenne in bowl. Pat pork dry with paper towels. Heat remaining 1 tablespoon oil in 12-inch ovensafe skillet over medium-high heat until just smoking. Brown roast on all sides, about 6 minutes; transfer to plate. Pour off fat from skillet.

5. Add maple syrup mixture to now-empty skillet and cook over medium heat, scraping up any browned bits, until fragrant, about 1 minute. Off heat, return roast to skillet along with any accumulated juices and turn to coat. Turn roast fat side up, transfer skillet to oven, and roast until pork registers 140 degrees, 45 minutes to 1 hour, turning roast to coat with glaze twice during roasting.

6. Carefully remove skillet from oven (skillet handle will be hot). Transfer pork to carving board, tent with aluminum foil, and let rest for 15 to 20 minutes.

PREPARING A ROASTED SPICE-STUFFED PORK LOIN

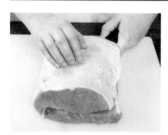

1. With roast fat side up, cut horizontally through meat, one-third of way up from bottom, stopping ½ inch from edge.

2. Open roast and press flat; 1 side will be twice as thick. Continue cutting thicker side of roast in half, stopping ½ inch from edge.

3. Open roast, cover with plastic wrap, and gently pound flat.

4. Rub cooled oil mixture on cut surface of meat, leaving ½-inch border on all sides. Starting from short side, roll roast into tight cylinder and tie with kitchen twine at 1-inch intervals

7. Meanwhile, being careful of hot skillet handle, skim foam from surface of pan juices using large spoon. Transfer skillet to stovetop, whisk in broth and vinegar, and simmer over medium heat until slightly thickened, about 3 minutes. Season with salt and pepper to taste. Discard twine, slice pork into ½-inch-thick slices and serve with glaze.

TO MAKE AHEAD ▶

Stuffed pork, prepared through step 3, can be refrigerated for up to 24 hours

Shredded Pork Tostadas

SERVES 4 TO 6
ACTIVE TIME 1 HOUR 20 MINUTES
TOTAL TIME 2 HOURS 25 MINUTES

WHY THIS RECIPE WORKS We wanted our pork tostadas to have the crisp texture and smoky tomato flavor of traditional Mexican shredded pork (called *tinga*). To achieve this, we simmered cubed pork butt roast in water flavored with aromatics and then shredded and fried the meat to make it crisp. Canned tomato sauce and chipotle chile powder contributed to a deep and complex sauce. The trimmed pork should weigh about 1½ pounds. Pork butt roast is often labeled Boston butt in the supermarket. Tinga is traditionally served on tostadas (crisp fried corn tortillas), but you can also use the meat in tacos and burritos. Make sure to buy tortillas made only with corn, lime, and salt—preservatives will compromise quality. Our winning brand of ready-made tostadas, Mission, is also an excellent choice. We prefer the flavor of chipotle powder, but two minced canned chipotle chiles can be used in its place.

  2 pounds boneless pork butt roast, trimmed and cut into 1-inch pieces
  2 onions (1 quartered, 1 chopped fine)
  5 garlic cloves (3 peeled and smashed, 2 minced)
  4 sprigs fresh thyme
     Salt
 ¾ cup vegetable oil
 12 (6-inch) corn tortillas
  2 tablespoons olive oil
 ½ teaspoon dried oregano
  1 (14.5-ounce) can tomato sauce
  1 tablespoon chipotle chile powder
  2 bay leaves
     Queso fresco
     Fresh cilantro leaves
     Diced avocado
     Lime wedges

1. Bring pork, quartered onion, smashed garlic cloves, thyme sprigs, 1 teaspoon salt, and 6 cups water to simmer in large saucepan over medium-high heat, skimming off any foam that rises to surface. Reduce heat to medium-low, partially cover, and cook until pork is tender, about 1½ hours.

2. Meanwhile, line baking sheet with triple layer paper towels. Heat vegetable oil in 8-inch skillet over medium heat to 350 degrees. Using fork, poke center of each tortilla 3 or 4 times (to prevent puffing). Working with 1 tortilla at a time, fry until crisp and lightly browned, 45 to 60 seconds, using potato masher to keep submerged in oil. Transfer to prepared sheet and season with salt to taste.

3. Drain pork, reserving 1 cup cooking liquid. Discard onion, garlic, and thyme sprigs. Return pork to saucepan and, using potato masher, mash until shredded into rough ½-inch pieces.

4. Heat olive oil in 12-inch nonstick skillet over medium-high heat until shimmering. Add shredded pork, chopped onion, and oregano and cook, stirring often, until pork is well browned and crisp, 7 to 10 minutes. Stir in minced garlic and cook until fragrant, about 30 seconds. Stir in tomato sauce, chile powder, bay leaves, and reserved cooking liquid and simmer until nearly evaporated, 5 to 7 minutes. Discard bay leaves and season with salt to taste.

5. Spoon small amount of shredded pork onto center of each tostada. Serve with queso fresco, cilantro, avocado, and lime wedges.

TO MAKE AHEAD

- Braised pork, prepared through step 1, can be refrigerated for up to 2 days
- Tostadas, prepared through step 2, can be stored at room temperature for up to 24 hours
- To finish cooking, bring pork in cooking liquid, covered, to gentle simmer, cook until hot throughout, and continue with step 3; warm tostadas in 300-degree oven for 10 minutes

MAKING TOSTADAS

Working with 1 tortilla at a time, fry until crisp and lightly browned, 45 to 60 seconds, using potato masher to keep tortilla submerged in oil.

Storing Meat Safely

Proper storage is the best way to prolong the shelf life of meat and prevent waste.

REFRIGERATING MEAT Raw meat should be refrigerated well wrapped and never on shelves that are above other food. Check regularly to make sure that your refrigerator's temperature is between 35 and 40 degrees. Most raw and cooked meat will keep for two to three days in the refrigerator. Raw ground meat and raw poultry will keep for two days, while smoked ham and bacon will keep for up to two weeks.

FREEZING MEAT In general, meat tastes best when it hasn't been frozen. The slow process of freezing that occurs in a home freezer (as compared with a commercial freezer) causes large ice crystals to form. The crystals rupture the cell walls of the meat, permitting the release of juices during cooking, resulting in drier meat. If you're going to freeze meat, wrap it well in plastic wrap and then place the meat in a zipper-lock bag and squeeze out excess air. Label the bag and use the meat within a few months.

THAWING MEAT All meat can be thawed safely on a plate or rimmed baking sheet in the refrigerator (and this is the only safe method for large cuts like whole chickens). Never thaw meat on the counter, where bacteria will rapidly multiply. According to the U.S. Department of Agriculture, frozen food that is properly thawed is safe to refreeze. However, a second freeze-thaw cycle aggravates moisture loss, reducing the quality of the meat, so we don't recommend it.

QUICK THAW FOR SMALL CUTS Flat cuts like chicken breasts, pork chops, and steaks will thaw more quickly when left on a metal surface rather than on a wood or a plastic one, because metal can transfer ambient heat much more quickly. To thaw frozen wrapped steaks, chops, and ground meat (flattened to 1 inch thick before freezing), place in a skillet (heavy steel and cast-iron skillets work best) in a single layer. Flip the meat every half-hour until it's thawed. Small cuts can also be sealed in zipper-lock bags and submerged in hot (140-degree) water—this method will safely thaw chicken breasts, steaks, and chops in under 15 minutes.

Cooking country-style ribs to the right temperature is essential to achieving perfectly tender light and dark meat.

Sweet and Tangy Grilled Country-Style Ribs

SERVES 4 TO 6   **EASY**

ACTIVE TIME 25 MINUTES

TOTAL TIME 1 HOUR 35 MINUTES

WHY THIS RECIPE WORKS Country-style ribs are less like baby back ribs or spareribs and more like well-marbled pork chops. They contain both lean loin meat and a section of dark shoulder meat. The trick to cooking these on the grill was getting both parts to cook evenly. We started with a simple dry rub of chili powder, cayenne, salt, and brown sugar, which encouraged browning while adding a complex sweetness. We cooked the ribs to 150 degrees, at which point both the light and the dark meat were nicely tender. We started the ribs over the hotter side of the grill for excellent browning and finished them on the cooler side, where it was easy to baste the ribs with barbecue sauce and allow it to slowly caramelize without burning. When purchasing bone-in country-style ribs, look for those that are approximately 1 inch thick and that contain a large proportion of dark meat. Be sure to carefully trim the pork to reduce the number of flare-ups on the grill.

  4 teaspoons packed brown sugar
1½ teaspoons salt
  1 tablespoon chili powder
  ⅛ teaspoon cayenne pepper
  4 pounds bone-in country-style pork ribs, trimmed
  ½ cup barbecue sauce, plus extra for serving

1. Combine sugar, salt, chili powder, and cayenne in bowl. Rub ribs evenly with spice mixture, wrap in plastic wrap, and refrigerate for at least 1 hour.

2A. FOR A CHARCOAL GRILL Open bottom vent halfway. Light large chimney starter filled with charcoal briquettes (6 quarts). When top coals are partially covered with ash, pour evenly over half of grill. Set cooking grate in place, cover, and open lid vent halfway. Heat grill until hot, about 5 minutes.

2B. FOR A GAS GRILL Turn all burners to high, cover, and heat grill until hot, about 15 minutes. Leave primary burner on high and turn off other burners to maintain grill temperature around 350 degrees.

3. Clean and oil cooking grate. Place ribs on hotter side of grill. Cover and cook until well browned on both sides, 4 to 7 minutes total. Move ribs to cooler side of grill and brush with ¼ cup sauce. Cover and cook for 6 minutes.

4. Flip ribs and brush with remaining ¼ cup sauce. Cover and continue to cook until pork registers 150 degrees, 5 to 10 minutes longer. Transfer ribs to platter, tent with aluminum foil, and let rest for 10 minutes. Serve with extra sauce.

TO MAKE AHEAD

Spice-rubbed ribs, prepared through step 1, can be refrigerated for up to 24 hours

Indoor Barbecue Ribs

SERVES 4 TO 6

ACTIVE TIME 50 MINUTES

TOTAL TIME 6 HOURS 30 MINUTES TO 7 HOURS

WHY THIS RECIPE WORKS Barbecued ribs get their uniquely complex character from the slow mingling of flavors in meat, sauce, and smoke. We wanted to develop a recipe for indoor ribs that allowed these flavors to build without having to fire up the grill. We found that we could achieve great flavor and fall-off-the-bone tenderness by first rubbing the ribs in a mixture of salt, pepper, brown sugar, smoked paprika, and a bit of cayenne and then slow-roasting them in a moderate oven for about 5 hours. During the first 2 hours in the oven we simply roasted the ribs to allow the spice rub to cook into the meat, and during the final stint in the oven, we built up layers of "bark" by painting the ribs with barbecue sauce. We tried different styles of sauce and found we got the most authentic barbecue flavor when we incorporated espresso powder, mustard, and liquid smoke into the traditional base of vinegar, ketchup, and molasses. Look for liquid smoke that contains no salt or additional flavorings.

BARBECUE SAUCE

- 1 tablespoon vegetable oil
- 1 onion, chopped fine
  Salt and pepper
- 1 tablespoon smoked paprika
- 1½ cups chicken broth
- ¾ cup cider vinegar
- ¾ cup dark corn syrup
- ¾ cup ketchup
- ½ cup molasses
- 2 tablespoons brown mustard
- 1 tablespoon hot sauce
- 1 tablespoon instant espresso powder
- ½ teaspoon liquid smoke

RIBS

- 3 tablespoons smoked paprika
- 2 tablespoons packed brown sugar
- 1 tablespoon salt
- 1 teaspoon pepper
- ¼ teaspoon cayenne pepper
- 2 (2½ to 3-pound) racks St. Louis-style spareribs, trimmed, membrane removed

1. FOR THE BARBECUE SAUCE Heat oil in large saucepan over medium heat until shimmering. Add onion and ¼ teaspoon salt and cook until softened, about 5 minutes. Stir in paprika and cook until fragrant, about 30 seconds. Whisk in broth, vinegar, corn syrup, ketchup, molasses, mustard, hot sauce, and espresso powder and bring to simmer. Reduce heat to medium-low and simmer, stirring occasionally, until thickened and reduced to 2 cups, 50 minutes to 1 hour. Off heat, stir in liquid smoke and season with salt and pepper to taste. Measure out ½ cup sauce and set aside for serving.

2. FOR THE RIBS Combine paprika, sugar, salt, pepper, and cayenne in bowl. Pat ribs dry with paper towels. Rub evenly with spice mixture, wrap in plastic wrap, and refrigerate for at least 1 hour.

3. Adjust oven rack to middle position and heat oven to 275 degrees. Set wire rack in aluminum foil–lined rimmed baking sheet. Place ribs, meat side up, on prepared sheet and bake for 2 hours.

We amp up a classic barbecue sauce with espresso powder and liquid smoke to give our indoor ribs authentic flavor.

4. Remove ribs from oven and brush top of each rack with ¼ cup barbecue sauce. Return ribs to oven and bake until tender and fork inserted into meat meets no resistance, 2½ to 3 hours longer, brushing with additional barbecue sauce every hour.

5. Remove ribs from oven, tent with foil, and let rest for 20 minutes. Slice meat between bones to separate ribs, and serve with reserved sauce.

TO MAKE AHEAD

- Barbecue sauce, prepared through step 1, can be refrigerated for up to 1 week; bring to room temperature before serving
- Spice-rubbed ribs, prepared through step 2, can be refrigerated for up to 24 hours
- Alternatively, cooked ribs, prepared through step 4, can be refrigerated for up to 3 days; to reheat, place ribs on wire rack set in foil-lined rimmed baking sheet and let sit at room temperature for 30 minutes, then cover ribs with foil and reheat in 400-degree oven for 15 minutes, uncover, and continue to cook until edges of meat begin to sizzle, 5 to 10 minutes, and continue with step 5

Pine nuts lend richness and keep our lamb *kofte* from becoming tough; gelatin keeps the meat moist.

Lamb Kofte

SERVES 4 TO 6

ACTIVE TIME 35 MINUTES

TOTAL TIME 2 HOURS

WHY THIS RECIPE WORKS Middle Eastern *kofte* are lamb kebabs made from ground lamb mixed with lots of warm spices and fresh herbs. The seasoned meat is shaped into logs, skewered, and refrigerated for up to a day to develop the flavors. This refrigerated resting period makes grilling easier, as it helps the meat to firm up and stick to the skewer—and it made this recipe a natural fit for make-ahead cooking. Swapping out a handful of spices for garam masala helped to streamline our recipe without sacrificing the overall flavor. Pine nuts are a typical addition: They lend great flavor and keep the kofte from becoming overly tough or springy. Surprisingly, we discovered that a small amount of gelatin helped keep the meat moist and tender; since gelatin holds up to 10 times its weight in water, the juices released during cooking were simply reabsorbed. A cool yogurt sauce made a perfect serving accompaniment. You will need eight 12-inch metal skewers for this recipe. If

grilling over charcoal, you will need a 13 by 9-inch disposable aluminum roasting pan. Serve with rice pilaf or make sandwiches with warm pita bread, sliced red onion, and chopped fresh mint.

YOGURT-GARLIC SAUCE

- 1 cup plain whole-milk yogurt
- 2 tablespoons lemon juice
- 2 tablespoons tahini
- 1 garlic clove, minced
- ½ teaspoon salt

KOFTE

- ½ cup pine nuts
- 4 garlic cloves, peeled
- 2 teaspoons garam masala
- 1½ teaspoons hot smoked paprika
- 1 teaspoon salt
- ½ teaspoon pepper
- 1½ pounds ground lamb
- ½ cup grated onion, drained
- ⅓ cup minced fresh mint
- ⅓ cup minced fresh parsley
- 1½ teaspoons unflavored gelatin

1. FOR THE YOGURT-GARLIC SAUCE Whisk all ingredients together in bowl, cover, and refrigerate for at least 1 hour.

2. FOR THE KOFTE Process pine nuts, garlic, garam masala, paprika, salt, and pepper in food processor until coarse paste forms, 30 to 45 seconds. Transfer mixture to large bowl. Add lamb, onion, mint, parsley, and gelatin and knead with your hands until thoroughly combined and mixture feels slightly sticky, about 2 minutes.

3. Divide mixture into 8 equal portions. Shape each portion into 5-inch-long cylinder about 1 inch in diameter. Using eight 12-inch metal skewers, thread 1 cylinder onto each skewer, pressing gently to adhere, then transfer to lightly greased rimmed baking sheet. Cover and refrigerate for at least 1 hour.

4A. FOR A BROILER Adjust oven rack 8 inches from broiler element and heat broiler. Set wire rack in clean, aluminum foil–lined rimmed baking sheet and spray with vegetable oil spray. Arrange skewers evenly on prepared rack. Broil until browned and meat registers 160 degrees, 15 to 20 minutes, turning skewers halfway through broiling.

4B. FOR A CHARCOAL GRILL Using skewer, poke 12 holes in bottom of disposable pan. Open bottom vent completely and place pan in center of grill. Light large chimney starter two-thirds filled with charcoal briquettes (4 quarts). When top coals are partially covered with ash, pour into pan. Set cooking grate in place, cover, and open lid vent completely. Heat grill until hot, about 5 minutes. Clean and oil cooking grate. Place skewers directly over coals at

45-degree angle to bars. Cook until browned on first side and meat easily releases from grill, 4 to 7 minutes. Flip skewers and continue to cook until browned on second side and meat registers 160 degrees, about 6 minutes.

4C. FOR A GAS GRILL Turn all burners to high, cover, and heat grill until hot, about 15 minutes. Leave all burners on high. Clean and oil cooking grate. Place skewers at 45-degree angle to bars. Cover and cook until browned on first side and meat easily releases from grill, 4 to 7 minutes. Flip skewers and continue to cook, covered, until browned on second side and meat registers 160 degrees, about 6 minutes.

5. Transfer skewers to platter and serve with yogurt-garlic sauce.

> **TO MAKE AHEAD**
> - Sauce, prepared through step 1, can be refrigerated for up to 24 hours; bring to room temperature before serving
> - Kofte, prepared through step 3, can be refrigerated for up to 24 hours

Greek-Style Lamb Pita Sandwiches with Tzatziki Sauce

SERVES 4   **FREEZE IT**

ACTIVE TIME 1 HOUR

TOTAL TIME 1 HOUR 10 MINUTES

WHY THIS RECIPE WORKS Greek gyros are classic sandwiches of seasoned, marinated lamb, tomato, lettuce, and cucumber-yogurt tzatziki sauce stuffed inside a soft pita. The traditional method for cooking the meat employs an electric vertical rotisserie on which layers of sliced and marinated leg of lamb are stacked. After cooking for hours, the meat is shaved with a long slicing knife, creating pieces with crisp exteriors and moist interiors infused with garlic and oregano. We wanted to translate this recipe for the home kitchen. Surprisingly, using ground lamb—which we formed into patties—was easy and came close to reproducing the texture of rotisserie lamb. A modified panade, or wet binder, of pita bread crumbs, lemon juice, and garlic gave our patties a sturdier structure and fuller, more savory flavor. For a crisp outside and moist inside, we browned our patties in a skillet until a crust formed on each side. Although we prefer the richness of plain whole-milk yogurt for the sauce, low-fat yogurt can be substituted. If using pocketless pitas, do not cut off the tops in step 4; instead, use a portion of a fifth pita to create crumbs. The skillet may appear crowded when you begin cooking the patties, but they will shrink slightly as they cook.

To replicate the flavor and texture of lamb cooked on a traditional vertical rotisserie, we simply pan-fry lamb patties.

TZATZIKI SAUCE

- 1 cup plain whole-milk yogurt
- ½ medium cucumber, peeled, seeded, and diced fine (½ cup)
- 1 tablespoon lemon juice
- ¼ teaspoon salt
- 1 tablespoon minced fresh mint or dill
- 1 small garlic clove, minced

SANDWICHES

- 4 (8-inch) pita breads
- ½ onion, chopped coarse
- 4 teaspoons fresh lemon juice
- 1 tablespoon minced fresh oregano or 1 teaspoon dried
- 2 garlic cloves, minced
- ½ teaspoon salt
- ¼ teaspoon ground black pepper
- 1 pound ground lamb
- 2 teaspoons vegetable oil
- 1 large tomato, sliced thin
- 2 cups shredded iceberg lettuce
- 2 ounces feta cheese, crumbled (½ cup)

1. **FOR THE TZATZIKI SAUCE** Line fine-mesh strainer set over deep container or bowl with 3 paper coffee filters or triple layer of paper towels. Spoon yogurt into lined strainer, cover, and refrigerate for 30 minutes.

2. Meanwhile, combine cucumber, lemon juice and ⅛ teaspoon salt in colander set over bowl and let stand for 30 minutes.

3. Discard drained liquid from yogurt. Combine thickened yogurt, drained cucumber, remaining ⅛ teaspoon salt, mint, and garlic in clean bowl.

4. **FOR THE SANDWICHES** Adjust oven rack to middle position and heat oven to 350 degrees. Cut top quarter off each pita bread. Tear quarters into 1-inch pieces. (You should have ¾ cup pita pieces.) Stack pitas and tightly wrap with aluminum foil. Process onion, lemon juice, oregano, garlic, salt, pepper, and pita bread pieces in food processor until smooth paste forms, about 30 seconds. Transfer onion mixture to large bowl; add lamb and gently mix with your hands until thoroughly combined. Divide mixture into 12 equal pieces and roll into balls. Gently flatten balls into round disks, about ½ inch thick and 2½ inches in diameter.

5. Place foil-wrapped pitas directly on oven rack and heat for 10 minutes. Meanwhile, heat oil in 12-inch nonstick skillet over medium-high heat until just smoking. Add patties and cook until well browned and crust forms, 3 to 4 minutes. Flip patties, reduce heat to medium, and cook until well browned and crust forms on second side, about 5 minutes longer. Transfer patties to paper towel–lined plate.

6. Using spoon, spread ¼ cup tzatziki sauce inside each pita. Divide patties evenly among pitas; top each sandwich with tomato slices, ½ cup shredded lettuce, and 2 tablespoons feta. Serve immediately.

TO MAKE AHEAD ▶

- Sauce can be refrigerated for up to 24 hours; season with salt and pepper to taste before serving
- Lamb patties, prepared through step 4, can be refrigerated for up to 24 hours or frozen for up to 1 month; if frozen, thaw completely in refrigerator

TRIMMING PITA

Using sharp chef's knife, cut top quarter off each pita and reserve trimmed pieces to use as binder in lamb patties.

Marinating chunks of lamb and vegetables in an aromatic oil-based mixture infuses them with lots of flavor.

Grilled Lamb Shish Kebabs

SERVES 4 TO 6
ACTIVE TIME 1 HOUR
TOTAL TIME 2 HOURS

WHY THIS RECIPE WORKS When done right, lamb shish kebabs pair well-browned, tender meat with crisp vegetables. For our recipe, we opted to use a boneless leg of lamb; it's inexpensive and cooks up tender in minutes. Marinating the lamb ensured that it stayed moist throughout cooking. You will need six 12-inch metal skewers for this recipe. If you have long, thin pieces of meat, roll or fold them into approximate 2-inch cubes before skewering. We prefer these kebabs cooked to medium-rare, but if you prefer them more or less done, see our guidelines on page 189.

MARINADE

- 6 tablespoons extra-virgin olive oil
- 7 large fresh mint leaves
- 2 teaspoons chopped fresh rosemary
- 2 garlic cloves, peeled
- 1 teaspoon salt

½ teaspoon grated lemon zest plus 2 tablespoons juice

¼ teaspoon pepper

KEBABS

2 pounds boneless leg of lamb, pulled apart at seams, trimmed, and cut into 2-inch pieces

2 zucchini or yellow summer squash, halved lengthwise and sliced 1 inch thick

2 red or green bell peppers, stemmed, seeded, and cut into 1½-inch pieces

2 red onions, cut into 1-inch pieces, 3 layers thick

1. FOR THE MARINADE Process all ingredients in food processor until smooth, about 1 minute, scraping down sides of bowl as needed. Transfer 3 tablespoons marinade to large bowl and reserve for vegetables.

2. FOR THE KEBABS Toss remaining marinade with lamb in bowl, cover, and refrigerate for 1 hour. In separate bowl, toss zucchini, bell peppers, and onions with reserved 3 tablespoons marinade, cover, and let sit at room temperature for at least 30 minutes.

3. Before grilling, pat lamb dry with paper towels and thread tightly onto two 12-inch metal skewers. Thread vegetables, separately, onto four 12-inch metal skewers, in alternating pattern of zucchini, bell pepper, and onion.

4A. FOR A CHARCOAL GRILL Open bottom vent completely. Light large chimney starter mounded with charcoal briquettes (7 quarts). When top coals are partially covered with ash, pour evenly over center of grill, leaving 2-inch gap between grill wall and charcoal. Set cooking grate in place, cover, and open lid vent completely. Heat grill until hot, about 5 minutes.

4B. FOR A GAS GRILL Turn all burners to high, cover, and heat grill until hot, about 15 minutes. Leave primary burner on high and turn other burner(s) to medium-low.

5. Clean and oil cooking grate. Place lamb skewers on grill (directly over coals if using charcoal or over hotter side of grill if using gas). Place vegetable skewers on grill (near edge of coals but still over coals if using charcoal or on cooler side of grill if using gas). Cook (covered if using gas), turning skewers every 3 to 4 minutes, until lamb is well browned and registers 120 to 125 degrees (for medium-rare), 10 to 15 minutes.

6. Transfer lamb skewers to platter, tent with aluminum foil, and let rest while finishing vegetables. Continue to cook vegetable skewers until tender and lightly charred, 5 to 7 minutes; transfer to platter. Using tongs, slide lamb and vegetables off skewers onto platter. Serve.

TO MAKE AHEAD

Marinated lamb and vegetables, prepared through step 2, can be refrigerated separately for up to 24 hours

We discovered that cooking lamb shoulder chops to medium gives them the best texture.

Grilled Lamb Shoulder Chops with Salsa Verde

SERVES 4 **EASY**

ACTIVE TIME 25 MINUTES

TOTAL TIME 1 HOUR 10 MINUTES

WHY THIS RECIPE WORKS Lamb shoulder chops are significantly less expensive than rib or loin chops, and their flavor is much more complex due to their delicate networks of fat and collagen-rich connective tissue—an appealing option, we thought, for a quick, economical, anytime-meal from the grill. We marinated them in a simple mix of garlic, oil, oregano, and salt and pepper and cooked them medium-rare. While we liked the flavor, they turned out to be a little too chewy. Simply cooking them for a little longer had the desired effect—the extra time on the grill allowed more of the fat to render and the connective tissue to break down. Our chops were great straight from a 30-minute marinade but we found that leaving them overnight resulted in even better flavor, and the salt helped keep the meat juicy. The bold, charred flavor of the lamb paired nicely with a fresh, herb-packed salsa verde. Capers and white wine vinegar added briny brightness to the sauce, while a couple of anchovy fillets boosted umami flavor without adding fishiness. We prefer the texture of these chops cooked to medium and do not recommend cooking them less; see our guidelines on page 189.

½ cup extra-virgin olive oil
2 garlic cloves, minced
2 teaspoons minced fresh oregano
Salt and pepper
4 (8- to 12-ounce) lamb shoulder chops (blade or round bone), ¾ to 1 inch thick, trimmed
1½ cups fresh parsley leaves
½ cup fresh tarragon leaves
4 teaspoons white wine vinegar
1 tablespoon capers, rinsed
2 anchovy fillets, rinsed

1. Whisk ¼ cup oil, 1½ teaspoons garlic, oregano, ¾ teaspoon salt, and ½ teaspoon pepper together in large bowl, add chops, and turn to coat. Cover and refrigerate for at least 30 minutes.

2. Meanwhile, pulse parsley, tarragon, vinegar, capers, anchovies, ⅛ teaspoon salt, ⅛ teaspoon pepper, remaining ¼ cup oil, and remaining garlic in food processor until finely chopped (mixture should not be smooth), about 10 pulses, scraping down sides of bowl as needed. Transfer to serving bowl and let sit for 30 minutes.

3. Before grilling, brush any extra marinade off lamb chops with paper towels.

4A. FOR A CHARCOAL GRILL Open bottom vent completely. Light large chimney starter filled with charcoal briquettes (6 quarts). When top coals are partially covered with ash, pour evenly over grill. Set cooking grate in place, cover, and open lid vent completely. Heat grill until hot, about 5 minutes.

4B. FOR A GAS GRILL Turn all burners to high, cover, and heat grill until hot, about 15 minutes. Leave all burners on high.

5. Clean and oil cooking grate. Place chops on grill (covered if using gas) and cook until well browned and meat registers 130 to 135 degrees (for medium), 4 to 6 minutes per side. Transfer chops to serving platter, tent with aluminum foil, and let rest for 5 minutes. Drizzle salsa verde over lamb and serve.

> **TO MAKE AHEAD** ▶
> - Marinated lamb and salsa verde, prepared through step 2, can be refrigerated separately for up to 24 hours
> - To cook, bring salsa verde to room temperature and continue with step 3

Cooking racks of lamb in a low oven guarantees beautifully rosy meat; browning them in a skillet offers a crisp crust.

Rack of Lamb with Mint-Almond Relish

SERVES 4 TO 6 **EASY**
ACTIVE TIME 30 MINUTES
TOTAL TIME 2 HOURS 15 MINUTES

WHY THIS RECIPE WORKS If you're going to spend the money on rack of lamb, you want to be sure you cook it right—as with other simple dishes, there's no disguising imperfection. We wanted to develop a foolproof recipe that produced perfectly pink and juicy meat encased in an intensely brown, crisp shell. To prepare the racks, we frenched them (cleaned the rib bones of meat and fat), and also discovered that we needed to remove a second layer of internal fat (along with a thin strip of meat) to avoid a greasy finished dish. We slowly roasted the lamb in a low oven to ensure a uniformly rosy, juicy interior. To crisp the exterior, we quickly seared the racks after roasting. A spiced salt nicely complemented the flavor of the lamb, and a simple stir-together relish was enough to dress up this company-worthy dish. We found we could eliminate much of the hands-on work on serving day by making the relish and preparing the racks in advance. We prefer the milder taste and bigger size of domestic lamb, but you may substitute imported lamb from New Zealand and Australia. Since imported racks are generally smaller, in step 1 season each rack with ½ teaspoon of the salt mixture and reduce the cooking time to 50 minutes to 1 hour 10 minutes. We prefer these racks cooked to medium, but if you prefer them more or less done, see our guidelines on page 189.

RELISH

- ½ cup minced fresh mint
- ¼ cup sliced almonds, toasted and chopped fine
- ¼ cup extra-virgin olive oil
- 2 tablespoons red currant jelly
- 4 teaspoons red wine vinegar
- 2 teaspoons Dijon mustard
- Salt and pepper

LAMB

- 2 (1¾- to 2-pound) racks of lamb, fat trimmed to ⅛ to ¼ inch and rib bones frenched
- Kosher salt
- 1 teaspoon ground anise or ground fennel
- 1 teaspoon vegetable oil

TRIMMING AND FRENCHING A RACK OF LAMB

1. If rack has fat cap, peel back thick outer layer of fat from racks, along with thin flap of meat underneath it. Use boning knife to cut any tissue connecting fat cap to rack.

2. Using boning or paring knife, trim remaining thin layer of fat that covers loin, leaving strip of fat that separates the loin and small eye of meat directly above it.

3. Make straight cut along top side of bones, 1 inch up from small eye of meat. Remove any fat above this line and scrape any remaining meat or fat from exposed bones.

1. FOR THE RELISH Combine all ingredients in bowl and season with salt and pepper to taste; let sit for 1 hour.

2. FOR THE LAMB Adjust oven rack to middle position and heat oven to 250 degrees. Using sharp knife, cut slits in fat cap, spaced ½ inch apart, in crosshatch pattern, being careful to cut down to but not into meat. Combine 2 tablespoons salt and anise in bowl. Rub each rack evenly with ¾ teaspoon salt mixture, rubbing seasoning into slits. Reserve remaining salt mixture.

3. Place racks, bone side down, on wire rack set in rimmed baking sheet. Roast until meat registers 130 to 135 degrees (for medium), about 1 hour and 25 minutes.

4. Heat oil in 12-inch skillet over high heat until just smoking. Place 1 rack, bone side up, in skillet and cook until well browned, 1 to 2 minutes. Transfer to carving board. Pour off all but 1 teaspoon fat from skillet and repeat browning with second rack.

5. Tent racks with aluminum foil and let rest for 20 minutes. Cut between ribs to separate chops and sprinkle cut side with ½ teaspoon salt mixture. Serve, passing relish and remaining salt mixture separately.

TO MAKE AHEAD ▶

- Relish, prepared through step 1, can be refrigerated for up to 24 hours; bring to room temperature before serving
- Spice-rubbed lamb, prepared through step 2, can be refrigerated for up to 24 hours; store remaining salt mixture at room temperature

Roast Butterflied Leg of Lamb with Coriander, Cumin, and Mustard Seeds

SERVES 6 TO 8
ACTIVE TIME 40 MINUTES
TOTAL TIME 2 HOURS 30 MINUTES

WHY THIS RECIPE WORKS Swapping in a butterflied leg of lamb for the usual bone-in or boned, rolled, and tied leg options provided us with a number of benefits: thorough seasoning, a great ratio of crust to meat, and faster, more even cooking. By first roasting the lamb in a 250-degree oven, we were able to keep the meat juicy, while a final blast under the broiler was all it took to crisp and brown the exterior. We ditched the usual spice rub (which had a tendency to scorch under the broiler) in favor of a slow-cooked spice-infused oil that both seasoned the lamb during cooking and provided the basis for a quick sauce. When we salted and placed it on its bed of roasted spices 24 hours in advance, we found the lamb even juicier, more buttery, and more deeply flavored, making this an easy and delicious recipe to prepare in advance for a larger gathering. We prefer the subtler flavor and larger size of lamb

A spice-infused oil does double duty by flavoring the lamb as it cooks and acting as a flavorful sauce base.

labeled "domestic" or "American" for this recipe. The amount of salt (1½ tablespoons) in step 2 is for a 4- to 4½-pound leg. If using a larger leg, add an additional teaspoon of salt for every pound. We prefer this lamb cooked to medium-rare, but if you prefer it more or less done, see our guidelines on page 189.

LAMB

- ⅓ cup vegetable oil
- 3 shallots, sliced thin
- 4 garlic cloves, peeled and smashed
- 1 (1-inch) piece ginger, sliced into ½-inch-thick rounds and smashed
- 1 tablespoon coriander seeds
- 1 tablespoon cumin seeds
- 1 tablespoon mustard seeds
- 3 bay leaves
- 2 (2-inch) strips lemon zest
- 1 (4- to 4½-pound) butterflied leg of lamb
  Kosher salt

SAUCE

- ⅓ cup chopped fresh mint
- ⅓ cup chopped fresh cilantro
- 1 shallot, minced
- 2 tablespoons lemon juice
  Salt and pepper

1. FOR THE LAMB Adjust 1 oven rack to lower-middle position and second rack 4 to 5 inches from broiler element. Heat oven to 250 degrees. Stir together oil, shallots, garlic, ginger, coriander seeds, cumin seeds, mustard seeds, bay leaves, and lemon zest on rimmed baking sheet and bake on lower rack until spices are softened and fragrant and shallots and garlic turn golden, about 1 hour. Remove sheet from oven, discard bay leaves, and let cool.

2. Meanwhile, place lamb on cutting board with fat cap facing down. Using sharp knife, trim any pockets of fat and connective tissue from underside of lamb. Flip lamb over, trim fat cap so it's between ⅛ and ¼ inch thick, and pound roast to even 1-inch thickness. Cut slits, spaced ½ inch apart, in fat cap in crosshatch pattern, being careful to cut down to but not into meat. Rub 1½ tablespoons salt over entire roast and into slits. Let stand, uncovered, at room for 1 hour. Thoroughly pat lamb dry with paper towels and transfer, fat side up, to sheet (directly on top of spices).

3. Roast on lower rack until lamb registers 120 degrees, 30 to 40 minutes. Remove sheet from oven and heat broiler. Broil lamb on upper rack until surface is well browned and charred in spots and lamb registers 120 to 125 degrees (for medium-rare), 3 to 8 minutes.

4. Remove sheet from oven and, using 2 pairs of tongs, transfer lamb to carving board (some spices will cling to bottom of roast); tent with aluminum foil and let rest for 20 minutes.

5. FOR THE SAUCE Meanwhile, carefully pour pan juices through fine-mesh strainer into medium bowl, pressing on solids to extract as much liquid as possible; discard solids. Stir in mint, cilantro, shallot, and lemon juice. Add any accumulated lamb juices to sauce and season with salt and pepper to taste.

6. With long side facing you, slice lamb with grain into 3 equal pieces. Turn each piece and slice against grain into ¼-inch-thick slices. Serve with sauce. (Briefly warm sauce in microwave if it has cooled and thickened.)

TO MAKE AHEAD

Lamb and spices, prepared through step 2, can be refrigerated for up to 24 hours

The flavor of our braised lamb shanks improves with an overnight rest in the fridge.

Braised Lamb Shanks

SERVES 8
ACTIVE TIME 40 MINUTES
TOTAL TIME 3 HOURS 40 MINUTES TO 4 HOURS 10 MINUTES

WHY THIS RECIPE WORKS Rich and hearty, these braised lamb shanks are the perfect centerpiece for a winter meal. The key was to build a flavorful braising sauce that would ultimately be strained and served with the meltingly tender shanks. We started by sautéing a traditional *mirepoix* (onion, celery, and carrot), adding garlic and herbs, and then adding flour and tomato paste for meaty depth. After deglazing the pan with wine and broth, we had a flavorful sauce to add to the roasting pan. We found we could skip the step of browning the lamb shanks because it made them tough and they browned enough in the heat of the oven. Best of all, the flavors of the lamb and sauce were even better upon reheating, making this a great make-ahead entrée. Make sure the shanks are well trimmed and all large pockets of fat have been removed.

8   (12- to 16-ounce) lamb shanks, trimmed
    Salt and pepper
3   tablespoons olive oil
2   onions, chopped fine
2   celery ribs, minced
1   carrot, peeled and cut into 2-inch pieces
5   garlic cloves, minced
2   teaspoons minced fresh thyme
2   teaspoons minced fresh rosemary
½   cup all-purpose flour
2   tablespoons tomato paste
2½ cups dry red wine
3½ cups chicken broth, plus extra as needed

1. Adjust oven rack to lower-middle position and heat oven to 325 degrees. Pat lamb shanks dry with paper towels and season with salt and pepper.

2. Heat oil in Dutch oven over medium heat until shimmering. Add onions, celery, carrot, and ¼ teaspoon salt and cook, stirring often, until softened and lightly browned, 8 to 10 minutes. Stir in garlic, thyme, and rosemary and cook until fragrant, about 30 seconds. Stir in flour and tomato paste and cook, stirring constantly, for 1 minute. Slowly whisk in wine, scraping up any browned bits. Whisk in broth until smooth and bring to simmer. Carefully transfer liquid to large roasting pan.

3. Nestle shanks into pan, cover pan with aluminum foil, and transfer to oven. Cook until shanks are very tender and fork slips easily in and out of meat, but meat is not falling off bone, 3 to 3½ hours, turning shanks over once during cooking.

4. Transfer shanks to platter and tent with foil. Strain cooking liquid through fine-mesh strainer into fat separator, pressing on solids to extract as much liquid as possible; discard solids. Let liquid settle for 5 minutes, then pour defatted liquid into liquid measuring cup and season with salt and pepper to taste. Portion shanks into individual shallow bowls, pour liquid over top, and serve.

TO MAKE AHEAD

- Braised lamb shanks, prepared through step 3, can be refrigerated for up to 3 days
- To reheat, cook in covered Dutch oven in 375-degree oven for 1½ hours, turning shanks occasionally to keep moist, and continue with step 4

CHAPTER 7

Fish and Seafood

■ EASY (30 minutes or less active time)   ■ FREEZE IT
Photo: Maryland Corn and Crab Cakes with Rémoulade

We rub a potent spice mixture on only one side of our salmon fillets so that the spices don't burn as the skin crisps.

Blackened Salmon

SERVES 4 EASY
ACTIVE TIME 30 MINUTES
TOTAL TIME 30 MINUTES

WHY THIS RECIPE WORKS When we envisioned our ideal version of blackened salmon, we set the bar high: We wanted a flavorful rub, perfectly medium-rare center, a deeply seared—but not burnt—crust, and crispy skin. We quickly found that many of the pitfalls that plague this dish have to do with the spice rub. Most rubs we tried were too mild to stand up to rich, oily salmon; plus, they scorched quickly, leaving us with a burnt exterior and a raw center. To address these issues, we created an assertive blend with smoky-sweet paprika, coriander, fennel, clove, and cayenne, and rubbed it onto the fish. The flavor was good, but by the time the skin had crisped, the spices on the skin had charred. We solved this problem by rubbing our spice mixture only on the flesh, allowing the skin to cook more slowly without fear of burning the spices. The best way to ensure uniformity is to buy a 1½- to 2-pound whole center-cut fillet and cut it into four pieces. It is important to keep the skin on during cooking; remove it afterward if you prefer not to serve it.

4 (6-to 8-ounce) skin-on salmon fillets
1½ teaspoons smoked paprika
½ teaspoon ground coriander
½ teaspoon ground fennel
 Salt and pepper
¼ teaspoon cayenne pepper
⅛ teaspoon cloves
1 teaspoon vegetable oil
 Lemon wedges

1. Using sharp knife, make 3 or 4 shallow slashes about 1 inch apart on skin side of each fillet, being careful not to cut into flesh. Combine paprika, coriander, fennel, ½ teaspoon salt, ¼ teaspoon pepper, cayenne, and cloves in bowl. Pat salmon dry with paper towels and rub flesh side evenly with spice mixture; season skin side with salt and pepper.

2. Heat oil in 12-inch nonstick skillet over medium heat until shimmering. Place salmon flesh side down in skillet and cook until dark brown, 3 to 5 minutes. Gently flip salmon, reduce heat to medium-low, and continue to cook until center is still translucent when checked with tip of paring knife and registers 125 degrees (for medium-rare), 9 to 12 minutes longer. Serve with lemon wedges.

> **TO MAKE AHEAD** ▶
> - Spice-rubbed salmon, prepared through step 1, can be refrigerated for up to 24 hours
> - To cook, pat salmon dry with paper towels and continue with step 2

Grill-Smoked Salmon

SERVES 6 EASY
ACTIVE TIME 20 MINUTES
TOTAL TIME 2 HOURS

WHY THIS RECIPE WORKS To produce silky, smoky salmon fillets worthy of being a dinner entrée, we rubbed individual fillets with sugar and salt and cooked them over a moderate grill fire, which allowed them to spend plenty of time absorbing flavor without overcooking. The best way to ensure uniformity is to buy a 2¼- to 3-pound whole center-cut fillet and cut it into six pieces. It is important to keep the skin on during cooking; remove it afterward if you prefer not to serve it. Do use mesquite wood in this recipe. If you'd like to use wood chunks instead of wood chips when using a charcoal grill, substitute two medium wood chunks, soaked in water for 15 minutes, for the wood chip packet. Serve the salmon with lemon wedges or "Smoked Salmon Platter" Sauce.

Our grill-smoked salmon relies on a salt and sugar rub for thorough seasoning and a silky texture.

2 tablespoons sugar
1 tablespoon kosher salt
6 (6- to 8-ounce) skin-on salmon fillets
2 cups wood chips, 1 cup soaked in water for 15 minutes and drained

1. Combine sugar and salt in bowl. Set salmon, skin side down, on wire rack set in rimmed baking sheet and sprinkle flesh side evenly with sugar mixture. Refrigerate, uncovered, for 1 hour. Brush any excess salt and sugar from salmon using paper towels and blot salmon dry. Return fish to wire rack and refrigerate, uncovered, until ready to cook.

2. Meanwhile, using large piece of heavy-duty aluminum foil, wrap soaked chips and unsoaked chips together in 8 by 4½-inch foil packet. (Make sure chips do not poke holes in sides or bottom of packet.) Cut 2 evenly spaced 2-inch slits in top of packet. Fold piece of heavy-duty foil into 18 by 6-inch rectangle.

3A. FOR A CHARCOAL GRILL Open bottom vent halfway. Light large chimney starter one-third filled with charcoal briquettes (2 quarts). When top coals are partially covered with ash, pour into steeply banked pile against side of grill. Place wood chip packet on coals. Set cooking grate in place, cover, and open lid vent halfway. Heat grill until hot and wood chips are smoking, about 5 minutes.

3B. FOR A GAS GRILL Remove cooking grate and place wood chip packet directly on primary burner. Set cooking grate in place and turn primary burner to high (leave other burner[s] off). Cover and heat grill until hot and wood chips begin to smoke, 15 to 25 minutes. Turn primary burner to medium. (Adjust primary burner as needed to maintain grill temperature between 275 to 300 degrees.)

4. Clean and oil cooking grate. Place foil rectangle on cooler side of grill and place salmon fillets on foil, spaced at least ½ inch apart. Cover (position lid vent over fish if using charcoal) and cook until center of salmon is still translucent when checked with tip of paring knife and registers 125 degrees (for medium-rare), 30 to 40 minutes. Transfer to platter. Serve warm or at room temperature.

▶ TO MAKE AHEAD

- Salt-rubbed salmon, prepared through step 1, can be refrigerated for up to 24 hours
- To cook, pat salmon dry with paper towels and continue with step 2

"SMOKED SALMON PLATTER" SAUCE
MAKES 1½ CUPS **EASY**
ACTIVE TIME 15 MINUTES
TOTAL TIME 15 MINUTES

1 large egg yolk, plus 1 hard-cooked large egg, chopped fine
2 teaspoons Dijon mustard
2 teaspoons sherry vinegar
½ cup vegetable oil
2 tablespoons capers, rinsed, plus 1 teaspoon caper brine
2 tablespoons minced shallot
2 tablespoons minced fresh dill

Whisk egg yolk, mustard, and vinegar together in medium bowl. Whisking constantly, slowly drizzle in oil until emulsified, about 1 minute. Gently fold in hard- cooked egg, capers and brine, shallot, and dill.

▶ TO MAKE AHEAD

- Sauce can be refrigerated for up to 24 hours
- To serve, bring to room temperature and stir to recombine

Marinating salmon in a combination of miso, sugar, sake, and mirin for 6 hours gives it a pleasantly firm, dense texture.

Miso-Marinated Salmon

SERVES 4 | **EASY**

ACTIVE TIME 20 MINUTES
TOTAL TIME 20 MINUTES (PLUS 6 HOURS MARINATING TIME)

WHY THIS RECIPE WORKS The Japanese technique of marinating fish in miso started as a way to preserve a fresh catch without refrigeration during its long journey inland. In the last few years, however, it has become a popular restaurant preparation in this country. The technique itself is quite simple. Miso is combined with sugar, sake, and mirin (sweet Japanese rice wine) to make a marinade. This miso-based marinade works much like a typical curing technique. The miso (a paste made by fermenting soybeans and sometimes other grains with salt and a grain- or bean-based starter called koji), sugar, and alcohol all work to season and pull moisture out of the flesh, resulting in a firmer, denser texture. Miso also adds flavor benefits: sweetness, acidity, and water-soluble compounds such as glutamic acid that, over time, penetrate the proteins and lend them deeply complex flavor. The fish is then scraped clean and broiled, producing meaty-textured, well-seasoned fillets with a lacquered savory-sweet glaze. Note that the fish needs to marinate for at least 6 hours before cooking. The best way to ensure

uniformity is to buy a 1½- to 2-pound whole center-cut fillet and cut it into four pieces. It is important to keep the skin on during cooking; remove it afterward if you prefer not to serve it. Yellow, red, or brown miso paste can be used instead of white.

- ½ cup white miso paste
- ¼ cup sugar
- 3 tablespoons sake
- 3 tablespoons mirin
- 4 (6- to 8-ounce) skin-on salmon fillets
  Lemon wedges

1. Whisk miso, sugar, sake, and mirin together in medium bowl until sugar and miso are dissolved (mixture will be thick). Dip each fillet into miso mixture to evenly coat all flesh sides. Place salmon skin side down in baking dish and pour any remaining miso mixture over fillets. Cover with plastic wrap and refrigerate for at least 6 hours.

2. Adjust oven rack 8 inches from broiler element and heat broiler. Place wire rack in rimmed baking sheet and cover with aluminum foil. Using your fingers, scrape miso mixture from fillets (do not rinse) and place salmon skin side down on foil, leaving 1 inch between fillets.

3. Broil salmon until deeply browned and center of salmon is still translucent when checked with tip of paring knife and registers 125 degrees (for medium-rare), 8 to 12 minutes, rotating sheet halfway through cooking and shielding edges of fillets with foil if necessary. Transfer to platter and serve with lemon wedges.

TO MAKE AHEAD ▶

Salmon, prepared through step 1, can be refrigerated for up to 24 hours

REMOVING PINBONES

A. For large side of salmon, drape fish over inverted bowl. Grasp protruding pinbones with needle-nose pliers or tweezers and pull to remove.

B. For fillets, run your fingers over surface to locate pinbones. (They will feel like tiny bumps.) Remove and discard.

A simple mixture of extra-virgin olive oil, herbs, and lemon zest infuses salmon with flavor as it cooks and as it chills.

Herb-Poached Salmon with Cucumber and Dill Salad

SERVES 4 **EASY**

ACTIVE TIME 25 MINUTES
TOTAL TIME 1 HOUR 40 MINUTES

WHY THIS RECIPE WORKS Chilled poached salmon is an easy make-ahead dinner, and our simple hands-off oven-poaching method delivered salmon with an ultrasilky texture. Wrapped in a foil packet, the fish slowly steamed in a little lemon juice and the moisture from the salmon itself, keeping the fish moist and tender when chilled. This method gave us rich salmon flavor that wasn't washed out by poaching liquid. Because the gently cooked fish can appear to have a semi-translucent orange hue, like that of smoked salmon, even though it is fully cooked (the normal opaque color returns after it is chilled), taking its temperature through the foil was the best way to determine when the salmon was perfectly cooked. A simple paste of extra-virgin olive oil, fresh herbs, and lemon zest infused the salmon with flavor as it sat. A fresh cucumber-dill salad dressed with tangy Greek yogurt was the perfect light counterpart to our rich and meaty salmon. The best way to ensure uniformity

is to buy a 1½- to 2-pound whole center-cut fillet and cut it into four pieces. It is important to keep the skin on during cooking; remove it afterward if you prefer not to serve it.

¼ cup minced fresh dill
 1 tablespoon minced fresh parsley
 1 tablespoon extra-virgin olive oil
 1 teaspoon grated lemon zest plus 2 tablespoons juice
   Salt and pepper
 4 (6- to 8-ounce) skin-on salmon fillets
¼ cup plain Greek yogurt
 2 tablespoons mayonnaise
 2 cucumbers, peeled, halved lengthwise, seeded, and sliced thin
   Lemon wedges

1. Adjust oven rack to middle position and heat oven to 250 degrees. Spray center of 18-inch square sheet of heavy-duty aluminum foil with vegetable oil spray. Combine 2 teaspoons dill, parsley, oil, lemon zest, ¼ teaspoon salt, and ¼ teaspoon pepper in small bowl.

2. Pat salmon dry with paper towels and season both sides with salt. Arrange fillets, skin side down, side by side in center of foil. Sprinkle salmon with 1 tablespoon lemon juice and spread herb mixture over top. Bring opposite sides of foil together and crimp to seal tightly. Crimp remaining open ends of packet, leaving as much headroom as possible inside packet, then place in 13 by 9-inch baking dish.

3. Cook until color of flesh has turned from pink to orange and thickest part of fillet registers 135 to 140 degrees, 45 minutes to 1 hour. (To check temperature, poke thermometer through foil of packet and into salmon.) Transfer foil packet to large plate. Carefully open foil packet (steam will escape) and let salmon cool to room temperature on foil, about 30 minutes.

4. Meanwhile, whisk yogurt, mayonnaise, remaining 1 tablespoon lemon juice, and remaining 2 tablespoons dill together in bowl.

5. Pour off any accumulated liquid from foil packet, and carefully transfer salmon to serving platter. Stir cucumbers into yogurt mixture and toss to combine. Season with salt and pepper to taste. Serve salmon with cucumber-dill salad and lemon wedges.

> **TO MAKE AHEAD**
> - Salmon and yogurt mixture, prepared through step 4, can be refrigerated separately for up to 2 days
> - To serve, bring salmon and yogurt mixture to room temperature, brush away any solidified poaching liquid from salmon, and continue with step 5

Buying Salmon

FRESH VERSUS FARMED In season, we prefer the more pronounced flavor of wild-caught salmon to farmed Atlantic salmon. If you're going to spend the extra money for wild salmon, make sure it looks and smells fresh, and realize that high-quality salmon is available only from late spring through the end of summer.

CUTS OF SALMON There are many ways to buy salmon. Our preference is for thick center-cut fillets, which can be poached, steamed, pan-seared, roasted, or grilled. Cut from the head end or center, these fillets are the prime cut of the fish. They are thick enough to sear nicely without overcooking. Buy the total amount you need in one piece and cut the individual fillets yourself. Stay away from thin fillets, which are cut from the tail end and cook so fast that it is impossible to get a nice sear before the fish is overcooked—plus one end is very, very thin while the other is always much thicker.

SKIN-ON OR BONE-IN Some recipes benefit from using skin-on salmon; for recipes that call for skinless salmon, you can remove it yourself or ask your fishmonger to do it. Bone-in steaks are an excellent choice for pan-searing, grilling, or roasting, but they should not be poached. You may see boneless steaks rolled and tied into a circular shape; these are as versatile as the bone-in steaks.

Oven-Poached Side of Salmon

SERVES 8 TO 10   `EASY`
ACTIVE TIME 20 MINUTES
TOTAL TIME 1 HOUR 30 MINUTES

WHY THIS RECIPE WORKS A side of salmon is an elegant choice when entertaining. We wanted a method for cooking a side of salmon that didn't require a poacher. To do this, we decided to get rid of the water and steam the salmon in its own moisture. We wrapped the seasoned fish in heavy-duty foil and placed it directly on the oven rack, which offered more even cooking than using a baking sheet. Cooking the salmon low and slow gave the best results—moist, rich fish. If serving a big crowd, you can oven-poach two individually wrapped sides of salmon in the same oven (on the upper-middle and lower-middle racks) without altering the cooking time. White wine vinegar can be substituted for the cider vinegar.

Cooking salmon in foil in a low oven allows it to poach gently in its own juices, resulting in a supremely supple texture.

 1 (4-pound) skin-on side of salmon, pinbones removed
   Salt
 2 tablespoons cider vinegar
 6 sprigs fresh tarragon or dill, plus 2 tablespoons minced
 2 lemons, sliced thin, plus lemon wedges for serving

1. Adjust oven rack to middle position and heat oven to 250 degrees. Cut 3 pieces of heavy-duty aluminum foil to be 1 foot longer than side of salmon. Working with 2 pieces of foil, fold up 1 long side of each by 3 inches. Lay sheets side by side with folded sides touching, fold edges together to create secure seam, and press seam flat. Center third sheet of foil over seam. Spray foil with vegetable oil spray.

2. Pat salmon dry with paper towels and season with salt. Lay salmon, skin side down, in center of foil. Sprinkle with vinegar, then top with tarragon sprigs and lemon slices. Fold foil up over salmon to create seam on top and gently fold foil edges together to secure; do not crimp too tightly.

3. Lay foil-wrapped salmon directly on oven rack (without baking sheet). Cook until color of salmon has turned from pink to orange and thickest part registers 135 to 140 degrees, 45 minutes to 1 hour.

4. Remove salmon from oven and open foil. Let salmon cool at room temperature for 30 minutes. Pour off any accumulated liquid, then reseal salmon in foil and refrigerate until cold, at least 1 hour.

5. To serve, unwrap salmon and brush away lemon slices, tarragon sprigs, and any solidified poaching liquid. Transfer fish to serving platter, sprinkle with minced tarragon, and serve with lemon wedges.

TO MAKE AHEAD

- Salmon, prepared through step 4, can be refrigerated for up to 2 days
- To serve, bring to room temperature and continue with step 5

Crispy Breaded Cod Fillets

SERVES 4   EASY

ACTIVE TIME 30 MINUTES
TOTAL TIME 2 HOURS 25 MINUTES

WHY THIS RECIPE WORKS Baked fish with a crispy, flavorful crumb topping is a satisfying and delicious meal. But could it be convenient, too? We wanted a recipe that would deliver fish with a crunchy crumb topping that actually stuck to the fish, and we wanted to be able to make it up to a day in advance. Keeping these lofty goals in mind, we began from the top: the breading. Toasting panko bread crumbs on the stovetop with melted butter ensured the crunchiest texture; even a day later, the toasted topping was crispy. Since we already had the skillet out to toast the panko, we decided to add aromatics to the skillet to bump up the breading's flavor. To get it to stick to the fillets, we spread a mixture of mayonnaise, egg yolk, and lemon zest on top of the fish fillets before pressing on the crumbs, which boosted flavor as well as sticking power. Halibut and haddock are good substitutes for the cod.

- 3 tablespoons unsalted butter
- 1 large shallot, minced
  Salt and pepper
- 1 garlic clove, minced
- 1 teaspoon minced fresh thyme or ¼ teaspoon dried
- ¾ cup panko bread crumbs
- 2 tablespoons minced fresh parsley
- 2 tablespoons mayonnaise
- 1 large egg yolk
- ½ teaspoon grated lemon zest
- 4 (6- to 8-ounce) skinless cod fillets, 1 to 1¼ inches thick

1. Melt butter in 12-inch skillet over medium heat. Add shallot and ½ teaspoon salt and cook until softened, about 3 minutes.

Toasting panko crumbs in butter guarantees a crisp coating for our breaded cod fillets, even after being stored in the fridge.

Stir in garlic and thyme and cook until fragrant, about 30 seconds. Add panko and ¼ teaspoon pepper and cook, stirring constantly, until evenly browned, about 4 minutes. Transfer panko mixture to shallow dish and let cool for 10 minutes. Stir in parsley.

2. Whisk mayonnaise, egg yolk, lemon zest, and ¼ teaspoon pepper together in bowl. Pat cod dry with paper towels. Brush tops of fillets evenly with mayonnaise mixture. Working with 1 fillet at a time, dredge coated side in panko mixture, pressing gently to adhere. Place fillets, crumb side up, on large plate. Cover and refrigerate cod for at least 1 hour.

3. Adjust oven rack to middle position and heat oven to 300 degrees. Set wire rack in rimmed baking sheet and spray with vegetable oil spray. Transfer cod to prepared rack and bake until fish flakes apart when gently prodded with paring knife and registers 140 degrees, 45 to 55 minutes, rotating sheet halfway through baking. Season with salt and pepper to taste and serve.

TO MAKE AHEAD

Breaded cod, prepared through step 2, can be refrigerated for up to 24 hours

Choosing the right fish is essential to making fish sticks with a firm, meaty texture and good flavor.

Oven-Fried Fish Sticks with Old Bay Dipping Sauce

SERVES 4 **EASY** **FREEZE IT**

ACTIVE TIME 30 MINUTES
TOTAL TIME 40 MINUTES

WHY THIS RECIPE WORKS Store-bought frozen fish sticks are too often bland, dried out, and uninspiring. But we knew that these freezer staples would be easy to make at home using fresh fish and a flavorful breaded coating that would appeal to kids and adults alike. We started our quest for a better fish stick with the fish. Firm, meaty haddock stood up to a substantial crunchy coating and held its shape during cooking. We made sure our fish was well seasoned by enhancing our flour dredge with Old Bay. A mixture of eggs, mayonnaise and mustard offered richness and helped the crumbs to stick. We ensured our fish sticks wouldn't suffer from a soggy coating by toasting panko bread crumbs. A simple stir-together Old Bay dipping sauce was a great finishing touch. Best of all, these fish sticks can be kept in the fridge or freezer for a convenient weeknight crowd-pleaser. Halibut and cod are good substitutes for the haddock.

DIPPING SAUCE
½ cup plain Greek yogurt
¼ cup mayonnaise
1 tablespoon Dijon mustard
1½ teaspoons Old Bay seasoning
 Salt and pepper

FISH STICKS
1 cup plus 2 tablespoons all-purpose flour
1½ tablespoons Old Bay seasoning
 Salt and pepper
3 large eggs
⅓ cup mayonnaise
3 tablespoons Dijon mustard
3 cups panko bread crumbs
3 tablespoons vegetable oil
2 pounds skinless haddock fillets, 1 inch thick, sliced crosswise into 1-inch-wide strips

1. FOR THE DIPPING SAUCE Whisk all ingredients together in bowl. Season with salt and pepper to taste; set aside.

2. FOR THE FISH STICKS Adjust oven rack to middle position and heat oven to 450 degrees. Set wire rack in rimmed baking sheet and spray with vegetable oil spray. Combine ¾ cup flour, Old Bay, ½ teaspoon salt, and ¼ teaspoon pepper in shallow dish. Whisk remaining 6 tablespoons flour, eggs, mayonnaise, and mustard together in second shallow dish. Combine panko and oil in 12-inch skillet and toast over medium-high heat until lightly browned, about 5 minutes. Transfer toasted panko to third shallow dish. Pat haddock dry with paper towels.

3. Working with 1 piece at a time, dredge haddock in flour mixture, dip in egg mixture, then coat with panko, pressing gently to adhere; transfer to prepared wire rack.

4. Bake until crumbs are golden and fish flakes apart when gently prodded with paring knife and registers 140 degrees, 10 to 12 minutes. Season with salt and pepper to taste, and serve with dipping sauce.

TO MAKE AHEAD

- Breaded fish sticks, prepared through step 3, can be refrigerated for up to 24 hours or frozen for up to 1 month
- To bake, continue with step 4; if frozen, brush off any ice crystals that may have formed, and increase baking time to 18 to 22 minutes

Letting the halibut finish cooking off the heat in our boldly flavored braising liquid ensures perfectly tender fish.

Sicilian-Style Braised Halibut

SERVES 4

ACTIVE TIME 1 HOUR

TOTAL TIME 1 HOUR 10 MINUTES

WHY THIS RECIPE WORKS For an elegant Sicilian-inspired dinner, we developed a recipe for braised halibut in a vibrant, dynamic sauce. Although easy to prepare, this dish requires carefully balancing all of the sweet, sour, and salty flavors. First, we worked on creating a fragrant and flavorful braising liquid. We started with onion, garlic, thyme, and pepper flakes, which brought the flavors into focus. We simmered these aromatics with white wine, whole peeled tomatoes, and clam juice, which gave the sauce a pleasant brininess. The addition of golden raisins and capers added sweet and tangy pops of flavor, while a sprinkling of mint added another layer of complexity and herbal depth. Orange zest and coriander offered citrusy notes, while pine nuts provided nice textural contrast. We chose halibut, a hearty yet tender and flaky white fish, because it stood up to the bold flavors of the braise. Best of all, making this dish ahead was as simple as putting the sauce

together in advance and then poaching the fish the day we wanted to eat it. Cod, sea bass, and red snapper are good substitutes for the halibut. Serve with crusty bread and lemon wedges.

   2 tablespoons extra-virgin olive oil
   1 onion, chopped fine
     Salt and pepper
   2 garlic cloves, minced
   ½ teaspoon minced fresh thyme or ⅛ teaspoon dried
     Pinch red pepper flakes
   1 (14-ounce) can whole peeled tomatoes, drained with juice reserved, chopped coarse
   ¼ cup dry white wine
   1 (8-ounce) bottle clam juice
   2 tablespoons golden raisins
   1 tablespoon capers, rinsed
   4 (6-to 8-ounce) skinless halibut fillets, 1 to 1¼ inches thick
   1 teaspoon ground coriander
   1 teaspoon grated orange zest
   2 tablespoons pine nuts, toasted
   2 tablespoons chopped fresh mint

1. Heat oil in 12-inch skillet over medium heat until shimmering. Add onion, ½ teaspoon salt, and ¼ teaspoon pepper and cook until softened, about 5 minutes. Stir in garlic, thyme, and pepper flakes and cook until fragrant, about 30 seconds.

2. Stir in reserved tomato juice and wine, bring to boil, and cook until reduced by half, about 4 minutes. Stir in tomatoes, clam juice, raisins, and capers and bring to simmer. Reduce heat to medium-low, and gently simmer until thickened slightly and flavors meld, about 15 minutes.

3. Pat fish dry with paper towels and sprinkle with coriander, ½ teaspoon salt, and ¼ teaspoon pepper. Stir orange zest into sauce, then nestle fish into skillet. Return to gentle simmer, cover, and cook until exterior of fish is opaque, 5 to 7 minutes. Flip fish, remove skillet from heat, and let sit covered until fish flakes apart when gently prodded with paring knife and registers 140 degrees, 5 to 7 minutes.

4. Season with salt and pepper to taste. Serve, sprinkling individual portions with pine nuts and mint.

> **TO MAKE AHEAD**
> - Braising sauce, prepared through step 2, can be refrigerated for up to 24 hours
> - To cook, bring braising sauce, covered, to gentle simmer, stirring often, and continue with step 3

Cod Baked in Foil with Leeks and Carrots

SERVES 4 `EASY`

ACTIVE TIME 25 MINUTES
TOTAL TIME 45 MINUTES

WHY THIS RECIPE WORKS Cooking fish *en papillote*, or folded in a pouch, is a classic French technique that, in addition to being incredibly easy, allows the fish to steam in its own juices and thus emerge moist and flavorful. We found that foil was easier to work with than parchment. Placing the packets on the oven's lower-middle rack concentrated the exuded liquid and deepened the flavor. Carrots and leeks, cut into matchsticks, cooked at the same rate as the fish. A flavorful compound butter added richness and flavor without weighing down the fresh ingredients. Haddock and halibut are good substitutes for the cod, as long as they are 1 to 1¼ inches thick. Open each packet promptly after baking to prevent overcooking. Zest the lemon before cutting it into wedges.

- 4 tablespoons unsalted butter, softened
- 1 teaspoon minced fresh thyme
- 2 garlic cloves, minced
- 1¼ teaspoons grated lemon zest, plus lemon wedges for serving
  Salt and pepper
- 2 tablespoons minced fresh parsley
- 2 carrots, peeled and cut into matchsticks
- 1 pound leeks, white and light green parts only, halved lengthwise, washed thoroughly, and cut into matchsticks
- ¼ cup dry vermouth or dry white wine
- 4 (6- to 8-ounce) skinless cod fillets, 1 to 1¼ inches thick

1. Adjust oven rack to lower-middle position and heat oven to 450 degrees. Mash butter, thyme, half of garlic, ¼ teaspoon lemon zest, ¼ teaspoon salt, and ⅛ teaspoon pepper in bowl. In separate bowl, combine parsley, remaining garlic, and remaining 1 teaspoon lemon zest. In third bowl, combine carrots and leeks and season with salt and pepper.

2. Cut eight 12-inch sheets of aluminum foil; arrange 4 flat on counter. Divide vegetable mixture among foil sheets, mounding it in center, and sprinkle with vermouth. Pat cod dry with paper towels, season with salt and pepper, and place on top of vegetables. Spread butter mixture over fish.

3. Place second square of foil on top of cod. Press edges of foil together and fold over several times until packet is well sealed and measures about 7 inches. Place packets on rimmed baking sheet, overlapping as needed.

4. Bake packets for 15 minutes. Carefully open foil, allowing steam to escape away from you. Using thin metal spatula, gently slide cod and vegetables, and any accumulated juices, onto plate. Sprinkle with parsley mixture and serve with lemon wedges.

For a summery take on Cod Baked in Foil, we make a base of salted zucchini slices and top it with a fresh tomato relish.

VARIATION

Cod Baked in Foil with Zucchini and Tomatoes

SERVES 4 `EASY`

- 1 pound zucchini, sliced ¼ inch thick
  Salt and pepper
- 2 plum tomatoes, cored, seeded, and chopped
- 2 tablespoons extra-virgin olive oil
- 2 garlic cloves, minced
- 1 teaspoon minced fresh oregano
- ⅛ teaspoon red pepper flakes
- ¼ cup dry vermouth or dry white wine
- 4 (6- to 8-ounce) skinless cod fillets, 1 to 1¼ inches thick
- ¼ cup chopped fresh basil
  Lemon wedges

1. Toss zucchini with ½ teaspoon salt in bowl, transfer to colander, and let sit for 30 minutes. Pat zucchini dry thoroughly with paper towels, pressing firmly on each slice to remove as much liquid as possible. Meanwhile, combine tomatoes, oil, garlic, oregano, pepper flakes, ¼ teaspoon salt, and ⅛ teaspoon pepper in bowl.

2. Adjust oven rack to lower-middle position and heat oven to 450 degrees. Cut eight 12-inch sheets of aluminum foil; arrange 4 flat on counter. Shingle zucchini in center of foil sheets and sprinkle with vermouth. Pat cod dry with paper towels, season with salt and pepper, and place on top of zucchini. Spread tomato mixture over fish.

3. Place second square of foil on top of cod. Press edges of foil together and fold over several times until packet is well sealed and measures about 7 inches. Place packets on rimmed baking sheet, overlapping as needed.

4. Bake packets for 15 minutes. Carefully open foil, allowing steam to escape away from you. Using thin metal spatula, gently slide cod and vegetables, and any accumulated juices, onto plate. Sprinkle with basil and serve with lemon wedges.

> **TO MAKE AHEAD** ▶
>
> Cod packets, prepared through step 3, can be refrigerated for up to 3 hours; if refrigerated for longer than 30 minutes, increase cooking time to 17 minutes

ASSEMBLING COD IN FOIL PACKETS

1. Cut eight 12-inch sheets of foil; arrange 4 flat on counter. Place vegetables in center of foil sheets and sprinkle with vermouth.

2. Pat cod dry with paper towels, season with salt and pepper, and place on top of vegetables. Spread butter mixture (or relish) on top of fish.

3. Place second square of foil on top of fish. Press edges of foil together and fold over several times until packet is well sealed and measures about 7 inches.

Reserving some of our creamy coconut sauce to drizzle on after cooking prevents the couscous from becoming mushy.

Thai-Style Fish and Creamy Coconut Couscous Packets

SERVES 4 **EASY**
ACTIVE TIME 30 MINUTES
TOTAL TIME 1 HOUR 10 MINUTES

WHY THIS RECIPE WORKS For a fresh and modern spin on the simple technique of cooking fish in a packet, we decided to cook halibut fillets on a bed of fluffy couscous with a flavorful, Thai-inspired sauce. We mixed coconut milk, ginger, fish sauce, a little cilantro for a fresh herbal touch, and red pepper flakes for a subtle hint of heat. The bold sauce transformed the couscous into a rich and creamy side and infused the fish with flavor. We found that if we used too much sauce during cooking, the couscous soaked up all of the liquid and ended up gummy while the fish tasted bland. So we reserved some of the sauce to drizzle over the fish before serving. Cod, seabass, and red snapper are good substitutes for the halibut. For an accurate measurement of boiling water, bring a full kettle of water to a boil and then measure out the desired amount.

1½ cups couscous
2 cups boiling water plus ¼ cup room-temperature water
  Salt and pepper
1 cup canned coconut milk
¼ cup chopped fresh cilantro
2 tablespoons fish sauce
1 tablespoon grated fresh ginger
3 garlic cloves, minced
⅛ teaspoon red pepper flakes
4 (6- to 8-ounce) skinless halibut fillets, 1 to 1½ inches thick
2 tablespoons rice vinegar

1. Adjust oven rack to middle position and heat oven to 400 degrees. Combine couscous and boiling water in medium bowl. Immediately cover with plastic wrap and let sit until liquid is absorbed and couscous is tender, about 5 minutes. Fluff couscous with fork and season with salt and pepper to taste. Let cool completely, about 20 minutes.

2. Combine room-temperature water, coconut milk, cilantro, fish sauce, ginger, garlic, and pepper flakes in small bowl.

3. Spray centers of four 14 by 12-inch sheets of heavy-duty aluminum foil with vegetable oil spray. Pat halibut dry with paper towels. Divide couscous evenly among foil pieces, mounding it in center of each piece. Place 1 fillet on top of each couscous mound and spoon 1 tablespoon sauce over top. Reserve remaining coconut sauce.

4. Bring short sides of foil together and crimp to seal tightly. Crimp remaining open ends of packets, leaving as much headroom as possible inside packets.

5. Place packets on rimmed baking sheet and bake until fish flakes apart when gently prodded with paring knife and registers 140 degrees, 15 to 18 minutes. (To check temperature, poke thermometer through foil of 1 packet and into fish.) Let halibut rest in packets for 3 minutes.

6. Microwave coconut sauce until warmed through, about 1 minute. Stir in rice vinegar. Transfer fish packets to individual serving plates, open carefully (steam will escape), and slide contents onto plates. Drizzle warm sauce over fish and couscous. Serve.

TO MAKE AHEAD

- Fish packets and remaining coconut sauce, prepared through step 4, can be refrigerated for up to 24 hours
- To bake, continue with step 5, increasing cooking time to 18 to 20 minutes

NOTES FROM THE TEST KITCHEN

Buying and Storing Fish

WHAT TO LOOK FOR Make sure the fish you buy is fresh. Always buy fish from a trusted source (preferably one with high volume to help ensure freshness). The store, and the fish in it, should smell like the sea, not fishy or sour. All the fish should be on ice or properly refrigerated. Fillets and steaks should look bright, shiny, and firm, not dull or mushy. Whole fish should have moist, taut skin, clear eyes, and bright red gills.

WHAT TO ASK FOR It is always better to have your fishmonger slice steaks and fillets to order rather than buying precut pieces that may have been sitting around. Don't be afraid to be picky at the seafood counter; a ragged piece of fish will be difficult to cook properly. It is important to keep your fish cold, so if you have a long ride home, ask your fishmonger for a bag of ice.

BUYING FROZEN FISH If you have to buy your fish frozen, choose thin fillets like flounder and sole. These freeze quickly, minimizing moisture loss. Firm fillets like halibut, snapper, tilapia, and salmon are acceptable to buy frozen if cooked beyond medium-rare, but at lower degrees of doneness they will have a dry, stringy texture. Make sure frozen fish is frozen solid, with no signs of freezer burn or excessive crystallization around the edges and no blood in the packaging. The ingredients should include only the name of the fish you are buying.

DEFROSTING FISH To defrost fish in the refrigerator overnight, remove the fish from its packaging, place it in a single layer on a rimmed plate or dish (to catch any water), and cover it with plastic wrap. You can also do a "quick thaw" by leaving the vacuum-sealed bags under cool running tap water for 30 minutes. Do not use a microwave to defrost fish; it will alter the texture of the fish or, worse, partially cook it. Dry the fish thoroughly with paper towels before seasoning and cooking it.

HOW TO STORE IT If you're not using fish the same day you buy it, it's important to store it properly: Unwrap the fish, pat it dry, put it in a zipper-lock bag, press out the air, and seal the bag. Set the fish on a bed of ice in a bowl or container (that can hold the water once the ice melts), and place it in the back of the fridge, where it is coldest. If the ice melts before you use the fish, replenish it. The fish should keep for one day.

A dual pan-searing and oven-roasting method produces swordfish that is well browned but not dry.

Pan-Roasted Swordfish with Chermoula

SERVES 4 **EASY**

ACTIVE TIME 25 MINUTES
TOTAL TIME 30 MINUTES

WHY THIS RECIPE WORKS Swordfish is a great fish for pan-roasting since its sturdy flesh takes well to flavorful browning, but it can be a challenge to keep the fish from drying out. We didn't want to compromise on either texture or flavor, so we set out to develop a technique for cooking swordfish that would produce perfectly cooked and tender fish with good browning. A combination of pan-searing and oven-roasting proved best. To be sure the swordfish steaks wouldn't overcook, we seared one side in a hot skillet, then turned the steaks over before placing them in the oven to finish cooking. When they were done, the steaks were browned but still moist inside. To take our fish to the next level, we needed a flavorful sauce that could stand up to the meaty fish. For inspiration, we turned to Moroccan *chermoula*, a traditional marinade or sauce made with hefty amounts of cilantro, lemon, and garlic that packs a big flavor punch. To make ours, we simply tossed our ingredients in a food processor and whirred everything together until smooth. If swordfish isn't available, you can substitute four 6- to 8-ounce halibut steaks, 1 to 1½ inches thick; be sure to adjust the cooking time in step 2 as needed. You will need a 12-inch ovensafe nonstick skillet for this recipe.

CHERMOULA

- ¾ cup fresh cilantro leaves
- ¼ cup extra-virgin olive oil
- 2 tablespoons lemon juice
- 4 garlic cloves, minced
- ½ teaspoon ground cumin
- ½ teaspoon paprika
- ¼ teaspoon salt
- ⅛ teaspoon cayenne pepper

FISH

- 4 (6- to 8-ounce) skinless swordfish steaks, 1¼ to 1½ inches thick
- ½ teaspoon ground cumin
  Salt and pepper
- 2 tablespoons extra-virgin olive oil

1. FOR THE CHERMOULA Process all ingredients in food processor until smooth, about 1 minute, scraping down sides of bowl as needed; set aside for serving.

2. FOR THE FISH Adjust oven rack to middle position and heat oven to 325 degrees. Pat swordfish dry with paper towels, sprinkle with cumin, and season with salt and pepper.

3. Heat oil in 12-inch ovensafe nonstick skillet over medium-high heat until just smoking. Place swordfish in skillet and cook until well browned on first side, about 5 minutes.

4. Gently flip swordfish using 2 spatulas and transfer skillet to oven. Roast until fish flakes apart when gently prodded with paring knife and registers 140 degrees, 5 to 8 minutes. Serve with chermoula.

TO MAKE AHEAD

- Chermoula sauce can be refrigerated for up to 2 days; to serve, bring to room temperature and season with salt and lemon juice to taste
- Seasoned fish, prepared through step 2, can be refrigerated for up to 24 hours

We rub chunks of swordfish with coriander and grill them alongside the ingredients for our smoky caponata.

Grilled Swordfish Skewers with Caponata

SERVES 4 TO 6
ACTIVE TIME 35 MINUTES
TOTAL TIME 35 MINUTES

WHY THIS RECIPE WORKS Swordfish has a robust taste all its own and needs costarring ingredients with just as much oomph. We decided to put the smoky flavor of the grill to work, threading swordfish pieces onto skewers and pairing them with a Sicilian-inspired grilled caponata—a saucy mix of eggplant and tomatoes with a sweet-and-sour profile. As a base for the caponata, we grilled eggplant, cherry tomatoes, lemons, and scallions alongside the swordfish and added an aromatic blend of warm spices for a potent sauce to complement the fish. Once grilled, the lemons transformed from tart and acidic to sweet and rich. Rubbing the swordfish with a bit of ground coriander, salt, and pepper added complexity and provided flavor that popped with the tomato, scallions, and a final sprinkling of fresh basil. If swordfish isn't available, you can substitute halibut. You will need six 12-inch metal skewers for this recipe.

¼ cup extra-virgin olive oil
1½ tablespoons honey
1 tablespoon grated lemon zest, plus 2 lemons, halved
5 teaspoons ground coriander
2 garlic cloves, minced
1 teaspoon ground cumin
Salt and pepper
¼ teaspoon ground cinnamon
⅛ teaspoon ground nutmeg
1½ pounds skinless swordfish steaks, 1¼ to 1½ inches thick, cut into 1¼-inch pieces
12 ounces cherry tomatoes
1 small eggplant (12 ounces), cut crosswise on bias into ½-inch-thick ovals
6 scallions, trimmed
¼ cup pitted kalamata olives, chopped
2 tablespoons chopped fresh basil

1. Whisk 2 tablespoons oil, honey, lemon zest, 2 teaspoons coriander, garlic, cumin, ¾ teaspoon salt, ¼ teaspoon pepper, cinnamon, and nutmeg together in large bowl. Microwave, stirring occasionally, until fragrant, about 1 minute; set aside.

2. Pat swordfish dry with paper towels, rub with remaining 1 tablespoon coriander, and season with salt and pepper. Thread fish onto three 12-inch metal skewers. Thread tomatoes onto three 12-inch metal skewers. Brush swordfish, tomatoes, eggplant, and scallions with remaining 2 tablespoons oil.

3A. FOR A CHARCOAL GRILL Open bottom vent completely. Light large chimney starter filled with charcoal briquettes (6 quarts). When top coals are partially covered with ash, pour evenly over grill. Set cooking grate in place, cover, and open lid vent completely. Heat grill until hot, about 5 minutes.

3B. FOR A GAS GRILL Turn all burners to high, cover, and heat grill until hot, about 15 minutes. Leave all burners on high.

4. Clean cooking grate, then repeatedly brush grate with well-oiled paper towels until black and glossy, 5 to 10 times. Place swordfish, tomatoes, eggplant, scallions, and lemon halves on grill. Cook (covered if using gas), turning as needed, until swordfish flakes apart when gently prodded with paring knife and registers 140 degrees and tomatoes, eggplant, scallions, and lemon halves are softened and lightly charred, 5 to 15 minutes. Transfer items to serving platter as they finish grilling and tent with aluminum foil. Let swordfish rest while finishing caponata.

5. Once lemons are cool enough to handle, squeeze into fine-mesh strainer set over bowl, extracting as much juice as possible. Add juice to spiced oil-honey mixture; whisk to combine and stir in olives.

6. Using tongs, slide tomatoes off skewers onto cutting board. Chop tomatoes, eggplant, and scallions coarse; transfer to bowl with caponata; and gently toss to combine. Season with salt and pepper to taste. Remove swordfish from skewers, sprinkle with basil, and serve with caponata.

TO MAKE AHEAD
- Honey-oil mixture and skewers, prepared through step 2, can be refrigerated separately for up to 24 hours
- To cook, bring honey-oil mixture to room temperature and continue with step 3

Grilled Tuna Steaks with Lime-Ginger Vinaigrette

SERVES 4 **EASY**

ACTIVE TIME 25 MINUTES

TOTAL TIME 1 HOUR 25 MINUTES

WHY THIS RECIPE WORKS Tuna steaks are a treat, and the intense heat of the grill is perfect for getting a good sear on the outside while keeping the inside tender, moist, and pleasantly pink. We wanted a foolproof method for grilling tuna to perfection, and we decided to make a vinaigrette that would complement the fish but not overshadow it. We found that marinating the fish before grilling worked to season it throughout and ensure remarkably moist grilled fish; a bit of ginger and five-spice powder proved a simple way to boost the flavor of our oil-based marinade. We found we could let the steaks marinate for up to 24 hours, making our recipe more flexible. As for the grilling method, we built a hot, concentrated fire by pouring the coals over only half the grill, which encouraged the exteriors of the steaks to cook quickly before the interiors could overcook. To accompany the steaks, we made a lime-ginger vinaigrette and gave it more aromatic depth with coriander seeds, fresh cilantro, and fresh basil. A bit of fish sauce offered some umami notes.

VINAIGRETTE

2 tablespoons lime juice

1½ teaspoons grated fresh ginger

1 teaspoon coriander seeds, crushed

¼ teaspoon red pepper flakes

1 tablespoon fish sauce

1 tablespoon chopped fresh basil

1 tablespoon chopped fresh cilantro leaves

⅓ cup canola oil

Salt and pepper

A hot, concentrated grill fire sears the outside of the tuna steaks before the interiors have a chance to overcook.

FISH

3 tablespoons extra-virgin olive oil

½ teaspoon grated fresh ginger

½ teaspoon five-spice powder

Salt and pepper

4 (6- to 8-ounce) tuna steaks

1. FOR THE VINAIGRETTE Whisk lime juice, ginger, coriander, pepper flakes, fish sauce, basil and cilantro in bowl until well combined. Whisking constantly, drizzle in oil. Season with salt and pepper to taste, and set aside.

2. FOR THE FISH Combine oil, ginger, five spice, ½ teaspoon salt, and ¼ teaspoon pepper in 1-gallon zipper-lock plastic bag; add tuna, seal bag, toss to coat, and refrigerate for at least 1 hour.

3A. FOR A CHARCOAL GRILL Open bottom vent completely. Light large chimney starter filled with charcoal briquettes (6 quarts). When top coals are partially covered with ash, pour evenly over half of grill. Set cooking grate in place, cover, and open lid vent completely. Heat grill until hot, about 5 minutes.

3B. FOR A GAS GRILL Turn all burners to high, cover, and heat grill until hot, about 15 minutes. Leave all burners on high.

4. Clean cooking grate, then repeatedly brush grate with well-oiled paper towels until grate is black and glossy, 5 to 10 times.

5. Remove tuna from oil, place on grill (on hotter side if using charcoal), and cook (covered if using gas) until grill marks form and bottom surface is opaque, 1 to 3 minutes.

6. Flip tuna and cook until opaque at perimeter and translucent red at center when checked with tip of paring knife and registers 110 degrees (for rare), about 1½ minutes, or until opaque at perimeter and reddish pink at center when checked with tip of paring knife and registers 125 degrees (for medium-rare), about 3 minutes. Serve with vinaigrette.

TO MAKE AHEAD ▶

Vinaigrette and marinated tuna, prepared through step 2, can be refrigerated separately for up to 24 hours

Spicy Grilled Fish Tacos
SERVES 6
ACTIVE TIME 45 MINUTES
TOTAL TIME 1 HOUR 15 MINUTES

WHY THIS RECIPE WORKS Grilled fish tacos are a perfect summer meal, and we found that choosing the right fish was key. Swordfish held up well on the grill; when rubbed with a bold spice blend, the moist fillets charred beautifully, giving them even more depth of flavor. As an added bonus, the marinated fish could not only be held overnight, but actually improved in flavor when cooked the next day. A salsa made with grilled pineapple and crunchy raw bell peppers added great flavor and texture. Mahi-mahi, tuna, and halibut fillets are all good substitutes for the swordfish, but to ensure the best results buy 1-inch-thick fillets and cut them in a similar fashion to the swordfish.

- 3 tablespoons vegetable oil
- 1 tablespoon ancho chile powder
- 2 teaspoons chipotle chile powder
- 2 garlic cloves, minced
- 1 teaspoon dried oregano
- 1 teaspoon ground coriander
  Salt
- 2 pounds skinless swordfish steaks, 1 inch thick, cut lengthwise into 1-inch-wide strips
- 1 pineapple, peeled, quartered lengthwise, cored, and each quarter halved lengthwise
- 1 jalapeño chile
- 18 (6-inch) corn tortillas
- 1 red bell pepper, stemmed, seeded, and cut into ¼-inch pieces

For the deepest flavor, we marinate chunks of swordfish with bold spices for up to 24 hours before grilling.

- 2 tablespoons minced fresh cilantro, plus extra for serving
- 4 tablespoons lime juice (2 limes), plus lime wedges for serving
- ½ head iceberg lettuce, cored and sliced thin (3 cups)
- 1 avocado, halved, pitted, and sliced thin

1. Mix 2 tablespoons oil, ancho chile powder, chipotle chile powder, garlic, oregano, coriander, and 1 teaspoon salt in large bowl.

2. Add swordfish to bowl with chile mixture, and stir gently with rubber spatula to coat fish. Cover and refrigerate for at least 30 minutes.

3A. FOR A CHARCOAL GRILL Open bottom vent completely. Light large chimney starter mounded with charcoal briquettes (7 quarts). When top coals are partially covered with ash, pour evenly over grill. Set cooking grate in place, cover, and open lid vent completely. Heat grill until hot, about 5 minutes.

3B. FOR A GAS GRILL Turn all burners to high, cover, and heat grill until hot, about 15 minutes. Turn all burners to medium-high.

4. Clean cooking grate, then repeatedly brush grate with well-oiled paper towels until grate is black and glossy, 5 to 10 times. Brush both sides of pineapple with remaining 1 tablespoon oil.

Place swordfish on half of grill. Place pineapple and jalapeño on other half. Cover and cook until fish, pineapple, and jalapeño have begun to brown, 3 to 5 minutes. Using thin spatula, flip swordfish, pineapple, and jalapeño. Cover and continue to cook until second sides of pineapple and jalapeño are browned and swordfish registers 140 degrees, 3 to 5 minutes. Transfer swordfish to large platter, flake into pieces, and tent with aluminum foil. Transfer pineapple and jalapeño to cutting board.

5. Clean cooking grate. Place half of tortillas on grill. Grill until softened and speckled with brown spots, 30 to 45 seconds per side. Wrap tortillas in dish towel or foil to keep warm. Repeat with remaining tortillas.

6. When cool enough to handle, finely chop pineapple and jalapeño. Transfer to medium bowl and stir in bell pepper, cilantro, and lime juice. Season with salt to taste. Top tortillas with flaked fish, salsa, lettuce, and avocado. Serve with lime wedges and extra cilantro.

> **TO MAKE AHEAD** ▸
> Marinated swordfish, prepared through step 2, can be refrigerated for up to 24 hours

California Fish Tacos

SERVES 6
ACTIVE TIME 50 MINUTES
TOTAL TIME 1 HOUR 15 MINUTES

WHY THIS RECIPE WORKS Classic California-style tacos combine delicate fried whitefish, crunchy cabbage, spicy pickled onions, and creamy white sauce piled onto a corn tortilla (or two) to deliver an irresistibly dynamic combination of colors, textures, and flavors. When it came to the batter coating, we liked the yeasty, slightly bitter flavor that beer imparted. But all too often, beer batter coatings are thick and heavy, obscuring the delicate fish. A combination of flour, cornstarch, and baking powder transformed our batter into an ethereally thin, light, and crispy coating. Once the fish was fried, we found that the exterior stayed crisp and the interior juicy and tender for an hour in a warm oven, making this party-worthy entrée easier to prepare for company. Plus, the taco accompaniments could be made two days in advance, so all we had to do on serving day was fry the fish. Use a Dutch oven that holds 6 quarts or more for this recipe. Note that the pickled onions become spicier over time. Light-bodied American lagers, such as Budweiser, work best here. Halibut and haddock are good substitutes for the cod. Cut the fish on a slight bias if your fillets aren't quite 4 inches wide. You should end up with about 24 pieces of fish. Serve with green salsa, if desired.

We lighten up a beer batter coating for fish with flour, cornstarch, and baking powder.

PICKLED ONIONS
1 small red onion, halved and sliced thin
2 jalapeño chiles, stemmed and sliced into thin rings
1 cup white wine vinegar
2 tablespoons lime juice
1 tablespoon sugar
1 teaspoon salt

CABBAGE SLAW
3 cups shredded green cabbage
¼ cup pickling liquid from pickled onions
½ teaspoon salt
½ teaspoon pepper

WHITE SAUCE
½ cup mayonnaise
½ cup sour cream
2 tablespoons lime juice
2 tablespoons milk

FISH

2 pounds skinless cod fillets, cut crosswise into 4 by
  1-inch strips
  Salt and pepper
¾ cup all-purpose flour
¼ cup cornstarch
1 teaspoon baking powder
1 cup beer
1 quart peanut or vegetable oil
18 (6-inch) corn tortillas, warmed
1 cup fresh cilantro leaves

1. FOR THE PICKLED ONIONS Combine onion and jalapeños in medium bowl. Bring vinegar, lime juice, sugar, and salt to boil in small saucepan. Pour vinegar mixture over onion mixture and let sit for at least 30 minutes.

2. FOR THE CABBAGE SLAW Toss all ingredients together in bowl.

3. FOR THE WHITE SAUCE Whisk all ingredients together in bowl.

4. FOR THE FISH Adjust oven rack to middle position and heat oven to 200 degrees. Set wire rack in rimmed baking sheet. Pat cod dry with paper towels and season with salt and pepper. Whisk flour, cornstarch, baking powder, and 1 teaspoon salt together in large bowl. Add beer and whisk until smooth. Transfer cod to batter and toss until evenly coated.

5. Add oil to large Dutch oven until it measures about ¾ inch deep and heat over medium-high heat to 350 degrees. Working with 5 or 6 pieces at a time, remove fish from batter, allowing excess to drip back into bowl, and add to hot oil, briefly dragging cod along surface of oil to prevent sticking. Adjust burner, if necessary, to maintain oil temperature between 325 and 350 degrees. Fry cod, stirring gently to prevent pieces from sticking together, until golden brown and crispy, about 2 minutes per side. Transfer cod to prepared wire rack and place in oven to keep warm. Return oil to 350 degrees and repeat with remaining fish.

6. Divide fish evenly among tortillas. Top with pickled onions, cabbage, white sauce, and cilantro. Serve.

> **TO MAKE AHEAD**

- Pickled onions, cabbage slaw, and white sauce, prepared through step 3, can be refrigerated separately for up to 2 days; bring to room temperature before serving
- Fried fish can be kept warm in 200-degree oven for up to 1 hour before serving

Cream enhanced with lemon juice, salt, and pepper makes a supereasy sauce for our classic stuffed sole.

Stuffed Sole Fillets

SERVES 4 TO 6 **EASY**
ACTIVE TIME 25 MINUTES
TOTAL TIME 40 MINUTES

WHY THIS RECIPE WORKS When it comes to a classic dish like stuffed fillets of sole, the trick is to keep it simple. We set out to get back to basics, honoring the mild flavor and delicate silky texture of sole with a simple stuffing and sauce and proper cooking technique for an elegant weeknight meal. For our stuffing, we used homemade bread crumbs with mayonnaise, butter, chives, garlic, lemon zest, and a bit of Dijon mustard to make a flavorful, comforting mix that wouldn't overwhelm the fish. Instead of fussing with a separate serving sauce, we found that a mixture of lemon juice and cream poured over the bundles thickened into a perfect accompaniment as they cooked, as well as protected our delicate fillets. A hearty white sandwich bread like Arnold's Country Classic or Pepperidge Farm Farmhouse made the best bread crumbs. Store-bought bread crumbs weren't worth buying. To check the doneness of the fish, use the tip of a paring knife to prod the fish gently—the flesh should be opaque and flaky, but still juicy.

4 slices hearty white sandwich bread, torn into pieces

½ cup mayonnaise

3 tablespoons unsalted butter, melted

3 tablespoons finely chopped fresh chives

1 tablespoon Dijon mustard

2 garlic cloves minced

2 teaspoons grated lemon zest plus 1 tablespoon juice
  Salt and pepper

8 (3- to 4-ounce) skinless sole fillets

¾ cup heavy cream

1. Adjust oven rack to middle position and heat oven to 475 degrees. Grease 13 by 9-inch baking dish. Pulse bread in food processor to coarse crumbs, about 10 pulses. Transfer crumbs to large bowl and microwave, stirring occasionally, until golden and crisp, 4 to 8 minutes. Add mayonnaise, melted butter, 2 tablespoons chives, mustard, garlic, lemon zest, ¼ teaspoon salt and ⅛ teaspoon pepper and stir until combined.

2. Pat fish dry with paper towels. Place sole, skinned-side up, on clean counter. Mound ¼ cup filling in middle of each fillet. Fold tapered end of sole tightly over filling and then fold thicker end of fish over top to make tidy bundle. Arrange sole bundles in baking dish, seam side down, leaving small space between bundles.

3. Combine cream, lemon juice, ¼ teaspoon salt, and ⅛ teaspoon pepper in bowl. Pour cream mixture over fish. Bake until fish flakes apart when gently prodded with paring knife and filling is hot, 12 to 16 minutes. Sprinkle with remaining 1 tablespoon chives. Season with salt and pepper to taste, and serve.

TO MAKE AHEAD

Sole bundles, prepared through step 2, can be refrigerated for up to 24 hours

Sole Florentine

SERVES 4 TO 6
ACTIVE TIME 40 MINUTES
TOTAL TIME 55 MINUTES

WHY THIS RECIPE WORKS Sole Florentine features sweet fillets of sole wrapped around a rich spinach filling. Add a creamy sauce and a topping of buttery cracker crumbs and it is easy to understand why this dish has long been a restaurant favorite. We built the base of the sauce by sautéing shallot, thyme, and garlic, and then whisking in cream. To thicken it, a simple slurry made with cream and cornstarch worked perfectly. For the filling we turned to frozen spinach, adding Parmesan to bind it and a little of the sauce for

We use convenient frozen spinach, Parmesan, and a bit of our cream sauce in a simple stuffing for Sole Florentine.

richness. After assembling the stuffed fillets, we simply added the sauce and sprinkled crushed Ritz crackers on top for crunch before baking. Try to buy fish fillets of equal size to ensure even cooking. Be sure to squeeze out as much moisture as possible from the thawed spinach or it will water down the sauce. To check the doneness of the fish, use the tip of a paring knife to prod the fish gently—the flesh should be opaque and flaky, but still juicy.

2 tablespoons unsalted butter

1 shallot, minced

2 teaspoons minced fresh thyme

1 small garlic clove, minced

2 cups heavy cream

4 teaspoons cornstarch
  Salt and pepper

20 ounces frozen spinach, thawed and squeezed dry

1 ounce Parmesan cheese, grated (½ cup)

8 (6-ounce) skinless sole fillets, ¼ to ½ inch thick

15 Ritz crackers, crushed fine
  Lemon wedges

1. Melt 1 tablespoon butter in medium saucepan over medium-high heat. Add shallot and cook until softened, about 2 minutes. Stir in thyme and garlic and cook until fragrant, about 30 seconds. Stir in 1¾ cups cream and bring to simmer. Whisk remaining ¼ cup cream and cornstarch together in bowl, then whisk mixture into saucepan and simmer until sauce is thickened, about 2 minutes. Season with salt and pepper to taste. Set aside to cool.

2. Adjust oven rack to middle position and heat oven to 475 degrees. Combine 1 cup sauce, spinach, and Parmesan in bowl and season with salt and pepper to taste. Pat sole dry with paper towels. Grease 13 by 9-inch baking dish with remaining 1 tablespoon butter.

3. Place sole, skinned-side up, on clean counter. Divide spinach filling equally among sole fillets, mounding it in middle of each fillet. Fold tapered end of sole tightly over filling and then fold thicker end of fish over top to make tidy bundle. Arrange sole bundles in baking dish, seam side down, leaving small space between bundles, and press lightly to flatten. Pour remaining sauce over top.

4. Sprinkle cracker crumbs over fish and bake until fish flakes apart when gently prodded with paring knife and filling is hot, 12 to 15 minutes. Season with salt and pepper to taste; serve with lemon wedges.

> **TO MAKE AHEAD** ▶
> Sole bundles, prepared through step 3, can be refrigerated for up to 24 hours

MAKING FISH BUNDLES

1. Place sole smooth side down. Divide spinach equally among fillets, mounding in middle of each. Fold tapered end of sole tightly over filling, then fold thicker end over top to make tidy bundle.

2. Arrange sole bundles in baking dish, seam side down and evenly spaced apart, and press lightly to flatten. Pour remaining sauce over top and sprinkle with Ritz crumbs.

We use a disposable pan to grill the ingredients for a sauce alongside shrimp skewers and then slide the shrimp right in.

Grilled Shrimp Skewers with Cilantro–Red Pepper Sauce

SERVES 4 TO 6 **EASY**
ACTIVE TIME 30 MINUTES
TOTAL TIME 45 MINUTES

WHY THIS RECIPE WORKS Grilling shrimp in their shells protects the delicate flesh, but seasonings are peeled away at the table. To deliver tender, juicy, boldly flavored shrimp without the shells, we crammed peeled shrimp onto skewers, which prevented overcooking. We set the skewers over a hot fire, and after only a few minutes, they had picked up attractive grill marks. We cooked the ingredients for a flavorful spiced red pepper sauce in a pan alongside the shrimp, then slid the shrimp into the sauce after cooking, adding fresh cilantro and lemon juice to brighten things up. You will need four 12-inch metal skewers for this recipe.

SHRIMP
2 pounds extra-large shrimp (21 to 25 per pound), peeled and deveined
2 tablespoons extra-virgin olive oil
½ teaspoon ground cumin

½ teaspoon paprika
Salt and pepper
½ teaspoon sugar

SAUCE

1 small red bell pepper, stemmed, seeded, and
chopped fine
⅓ cup finely chopped red onion
¼ cup extra-virgin olive oil
3 garlic cloves, minced
1 teaspoon paprika
½ teaspoon ground cumin
¼ teaspoon cayenne pepper
⅛ teaspoon salt
1 (10-inch) disposable aluminum pan
⅓ cup minced fresh cilantro
2 tablespoons lemon juice, plus lemon wedges for serving

1. FOR THE SHRIMP Pat shrimp dry with paper towels. Thread shrimp tightly onto four 12-inch metal skewers, alternating direction of heads and tails. Brush shrimp with oil and sprinkle with paprika and cumin and season with salt and pepper. Sprinkle one side of each skewer with sugar.

2. FOR THE SAUCE Combine bell pepper, onion, oil, garlic, paprika, cumin, cayenne, and salt in disposable aluminum pan.

3A. FOR A CHARCOAL GRILL Open bottom grill vent completely. Light large chimney starter mounded with charcoal briquettes (7 quarts). When top coals are partially covered with ash, pour evenly over grill. Set cooking grate in place, cover, and open lid vent completely. Heat grill until hot, about 5 minutes.

3B. FOR A GAS GRILL Turn all burners to high, cover, and heat grill until hot, about 15 minutes. Leave all burners on high.

4. Clean and oil cooking grate. Place shrimp skewers, sugared side down, on one half of grill and sauce in aluminum pan on other half of grill. Use tongs to push shrimp together on skewers if they have separated. Grill (covered if using gas) until shrimp are lightly charred, about 5 minutes. Flip shrimp skewers and continue to grill (covered if using gas) until second side is pink, about 2 minutes longer.

5. Remove skewers and sauce from grill, and gently slide shrimp off skewers into sauce. Stir in cilantro and lemon juice. Serve immediately with lemon wedges.

TO MAKE AHEAD

- Shrimp skewers and sauce, prepared through step 2, can be refrigerated separately for up to 24 hours
- To cook, continue with step 3, increasing grilling time to 3 minutes on second side of shrimp

Shrimp Burgers

SERVES 4   **FREEZE IT**

ACTIVE TIME 40 MINUTES
TOTAL TIME 40 MINUTES

WHY THIS RECIPE WORKS The best shrimp burgers should put the sweet shrimp flavor front and center. We wanted to make burgers with clean shrimp taste and a crisp crust. We created the patty's meaty texture by finely chopping a third of the shrimp in a food processor and coarsely chopping the remaining shrimp. This step also made our shrimp slightly sticky for easy binding, aided further by some cayenne-seasoned mayonnaise. Chopped scallions gave our burgers extra fresh flavor. For a crunchy coating ready to crisp up in the skillet, we dredged the patties in panko bread crumbs. Although shrimp burgers are often deep-fried, we opted to pan-fry ours until they emerged crisp and brown. We put the finishing touches on our shrimp burgers by serving them on a soft bun with a smear of homemade tartar sauce. We prefer untreated shrimp—those without added sodium or preservatives like sodium tripolyphosphate (STPP). Most frozen shrimp have been treated (the ingredient list should tell you). If you're using treated shrimp, decrease the amount of salt to ⅛ teaspoon. If you're purchasing shell-on shrimp, you should buy about 1½ pounds. If you find that the bread crumbs are browning too quickly in step 4, reduce the heat.

TARTAR SAUCE

¾ cup mayonnaise
3 tablespoons finely chopped dill pickles plus
1 teaspoon brine
1 small shallot, minced
1 tablespoon capers, rinsed and chopped fine
¼ teaspoon pepper

BURGERS

1 cup panko bread crumbs
1¼ pounds peeled and deveined large shrimp (26 to
30 per pound), tails removed
2 tablespoons mayonnaise
¼ teaspoon pepper
½ teaspoon salt
⅛ teaspoon cayenne pepper
3 scallions, chopped fine
3 tablespoons vegetable oil
4 hamburger buns
4 leaves Bibb lettuce

1. FOR THE TARTAR SAUCE Combine all ingredients in bowl and refrigerate until needed.

2. FOR THE BURGERS Place panko in shallow dish. Place one-third of shrimp (1 cup), mayonnaise, pepper, salt, and cayenne in food processor and pulse until shrimp are finely chopped, about 8 pulses. Add remaining two-thirds of shrimp (2 cups) to shrimp mixture in processor and pulse until coarsely chopped, about 4 pulses, scraping down sides of bowl as needed. Transfer shrimp mixture to bowl and stir in scallions.

3. Divide shrimp mixture into 4 equal portions and pack into 3½-inch-wide patties. Working with one patty at a time, dredge both sides of patties in panko, pressing lightly to adhere, and transfer to plate.

4. Heat oil in 12-inch nonstick skillet over medium heat until shimmering. Place patties in skillet and cook until golden brown on first side, 3 to 5 minutes. Carefully flip and continue to cook until shrimp registers 140 to 145 degrees and second side is golden brown, 3 to 5 minutes longer. Transfer burgers to paper towel–lined plate and let drain, about 30 seconds per side. Spread tartar sauce on bun bottoms, then place burgers and lettuce on top. Cover with bun tops. Serve.

TO MAKE AHEAD

- Tartar sauce can be refrigerated for up to 3 days
- Shrimp burgers, prepared through step 3, can be refrigerated for up to 24 hours; to cook, continue with step 4, increasing cooking time to about 6 minutes per side
- Alternatively, shrimp burgers, prepared through step 3, can be frozen for up to 1 month; to cook, continue with step 4, browning burgers for about 3 minutes per side; then transfer burgers to wire rack set in rimmed baking sheet and bake in 400-degree oven on middle rack until burgers register 140 to 145 degrees, 15 to 20 minutes

PEELING AND DEVEINING SHRIMP

1. Break shell under swimming legs, which will come off as shell is removed. Leave tail intact if desired, or tug tail to remove shell.

2. Use paring knife to make shallow cut along back of shrimp to expose vein. Use tip of knife to lift out vein. Discard vein by wiping blade against paper towel.

A moderate amount of mayonnaise and fresh homemade bread crumbs hold our salmon cakes together.

Salmon Cakes

SERVES 4   **EASY**   **FREEZE IT**

ACTIVE TIME 30 MINUTES
TOTAL TIME 1 HOUR 30 MINUTES

WHY THIS RECIPE WORKS We wanted moist, flavorful salmon cakes that tasted foremost like salmon for a quick and delicious dinner. Many salmon cake recipes use canned salmon, but since the salmon is the star of this dish, we found that it was well worth the additional modest expense and effort required to make our cakes with fresh salmon. Cakes made with canned salmon were lackluster (to say the least) and mushy, while those made with fresh salmon were moist and full of flavor, with an appealing, chunky texture. A food processor made quick work of chopping the salmon into pieces. To keep the cakes together in the skillet, we used a light binder of mayonnaise and bread crumbs. Store-bought bread crumbs muddled the flavor of the salmon, so we made our own fresh crumbs from white sandwich bread. Minced shallot added aromatic depth, and some Dijon mustard provided moistness and a bit of heat; we finished the mixture with a little parsley

for fresh herb flavor and finally had a bright and meaty salmon cake that truly tasted like salmon. Be sure to process the fish in three separate batches and for no more than four pulses, or it will turn to paste and be impossible to shape. If you don't have a food processor, salmon is easy to chop by hand; to make it even easier, put the salmon in the freezer for 10 minutes before chopping. If you find that the bread crumbs are browning too quickly in step 3, reduce the heat.

1½ slices hearty white sandwich bread, torn into 1-inch pieces
1 pound skinless salmon, cut into 1-inch pieces
1 shallot, minced
3 tablespoons mayonnaise
2 tablespoons minced fresh parsley
2 teaspoons Dijon mustard
⅛ teaspoon salt
⅛ teaspoon pepper
1 tablespoon vegetable oil
Lemon wedges

1. Pulse bread in food processor to coarse crumbs, about 4 pulses; transfer to large bowl. Working in 3 batches, pulse salmon in now-empty processor until coarsely chopped into ¼-inch pieces, about 2 pulses, transferring each batch to bowl with bread crumbs. Gently mix until thoroughly combined.

2. Whisk shallot, mayonnaise, parsley, mustard, salt, and pepper together in separate bowl, then gently fold into salmon mixture until just combined. Divide salmon mixture into 4 equal portions and pack into 3-inch-wide cakes. Cover and refrigerate cakes for at least 1 hour.

3. Heat oil in 12-inch nonstick skillet over medium heat until shimmering. Gently lay cakes in skillet and cook until crisp and well browned on first side, 4 to 5 minutes. Gently flip cakes and continue to cook until golden brown on second side and cakes register 125 to 130 degrees, about 4 minutes. Serve with lemon wedges.

TO MAKE AHEAD

- Salmon cakes, prepared through step 2, can be refrigerated for up to 24 hours
- Alternatively, salmon cakes, prepared through step 2, can be frozen for up to 1 month; to cook, continue with step 3, browning cakes for about 3 minutes per side; then, transfer cakes to wire rack set in rimmed baking sheet and bake in 400-degree oven on middle rack until cakes register 125 to 130 degrees, 10 to 12 minutes

Dredging our cod cakes in panko before pan-frying them creates a crisp, golden crust.

Cod Cakes with Garlic-Basil Aïoli

SERVES 4 `EASY` `FREEZE IT`

ACTIVE TIME 25 MINUTES

TOTAL TIME 25 MINUTES

WHY THIS RECIPE WORKS Fish cakes are fast to make in the food processor, but many recipes add so much filler that they taste more like bread crumbs than fish. We used fresh cod in this recipe, and processed the cod in two batches to avoid overworking the fish, which would give the cakes a pasty texture. To hold the cakes together, we used an egg along with just enough crunchy panko. A light dredging in more panko created a crisp crust that turned golden once cooked. A quick garlicky aïoli dressed up the fish cakes, and we also used a few tablespoons of the aïoli to add a touch more binding power as well as flavor to the cakes. We found that we could successfully freeze the cod cakes for up to a month,

making them a great ready-to-cook dinner option. Halibut and haddock are good substitutes for the cod. Be careful not to over-process the cod in step 2. If you find that the bread crumbs are browning too quickly in step 3, reduce the heat.

½ cup mayonnaise
¼ cup chopped fresh basil
2 tablespoons lemon juice
1 garlic clove, minced
  Salt and pepper
1½ cups panko bread crumbs
1 pound skinless cod fillets, cut into 1-inch pieces
1 large egg, lightly beaten
2 scallions, chopped fine
¼ cup extra-virgin olive oil

1. Process mayonnaise, basil, lemon juice, and garlic in food processor until smooth and pale green, about 20 seconds; transfer to bowl and season with salt and pepper to taste. Spread ¾ cup panko in shallow dish.

2. Working in 2 batches, pulse cod in food processor until some is finely minced and some is coarsely chopped, about 3 pulses; transfer to large bowl. Gently fold in remaining ¾ cup panko, egg, scallions, 3 tablespoons garlic-basil aïoli, ½ teaspoon salt, and ¼ teaspoon pepper. Divide cod mixture into 4 equal portions and pack into 3½-inch-wide cakes. Dredge patties in panko, pressing gently to adhere.

3. Heat oil in 12-inch nonstick skillet over medium heat until shimmering. Lay patties in skillet and cook until golden on both sides, about 3 minutes per side. Serve with remaining aïoli.

`TO MAKE AHEAD`

- Aïoli can be refrigerated for up to 3 days
- Cod cakes, prepared through step 2, can be refrigerated for up to 24 hours; to cook, continue with step 3, increasing cooking time to about 5 minutes per side
- Alternatively, cod cakes, prepared through step 2, can be frozen for up to 1 month; to cook, continue with step 3, browning cakes for about 4 minutes per side; then, transfer cakes to wire rack set in rimmed baking sheet and bake in 400-degree oven on middle rack until cakes register 140 degrees, 13 to 15 minutes

Broiling instead of pan-frying our corn and crab cakes eliminates the need for flipping.

Maryland Corn and Crab Cakes with Rémoulade

SERVES 4 **EASY**

ACTIVE TIME 30 MINUTES
TOTAL TIME 1 HOUR 45 MINUTES

WHY THIS RECIPE WORKS We wanted to combine two of our favorite summer pleasures by incorporating corn into a crab cake packed with sweet crabmeat, the barest breading, and just enough binder to hold the cake together. After forming the cakes, we chilled them in the fridge for up to 24 hours, which allowed them to set up and the crumbs to absorb moisture. Even with this convenient make-ahead option, our real fuss-reducing breakthrough was to forgo messy pan-frying for broiling. Broiled in one batch on a baking sheet, the crab cakes required no flipping, so they remained intact and moist with a flavorful, golden crust. (Dunking one side of each crab cake in extra saltine crumbs prevented the bottom from becoming soggy.) The flavor and texture of these crab cakes depends on the type of crabmeat you buy; we strongly prefer to use fresh jumbo lump crabmeat. Rémoulade sauce is a classic complement to seafood dishes. You can substitute 1 tablespoon chopped bread-and-butter pickles for the sweet pickle relish.

RÉMOULADE SAUCE

½ cup mayonnaise
1½ teaspoons sweet pickle relish
1 teaspoon hot sauce
1 teaspoon lemon juice
1 teaspoon minced fresh parsley
½ teaspoon capers, rinsed and chopped fine
½ teaspoon Dijon mustard
½ teaspoon minced garlic
Salt and pepper

CRAB AND CORN CAKES

14 square saltines
1 pound jumbo lump crabmeat, picked over for shells
1 ear corn, kernels cut from cob
3 scallions, minced
¼ cup mayonnaise
2 tablespoons unsalted butter, melted
1 large egg yolk
1 tablespoon Dijon mustard
2 teaspoons hot sauce
1 teaspoon Old Bay seasoning
Lemon wedges

1. FOR THE RÉMOULADE SAUCE Whisk all ingredients together in small bowl and season with salt and pepper to taste; refrigerate until ready to serve.

2. FOR THE CRAB AND CORN CAKES Process saltines in food processor until finely ground, about 15 seconds. Pat crabmeat dry with paper towels. Using rubber spatula, gently combine crabmeat, ¼ cup ground saltines, corn, scallions, mayonnaise, melted butter, egg yolk, mustard, hot sauce, and Old Bay in large bowl.

3. Divide mixture into 4 equal portions and pack into 3-inch-wide cakes. Press top of each cake in remaining ground saltine crumbs. Transfer crab cakes, crumb side down, to large plate, cover, and refrigerate for at least 1 hour.

4. Adjust oven rack 8 inches from broiler element and heat broiler. Line rimmed baking sheet with aluminum foil and spray with vegetable oil spray. Transfer crab cakes to prepared sheet, crumb side down. Broil until crab cakes are golden brown, 12 to 15 minutes. Let crab cakes rest for 2 minutes, then serve with lemon wedges and rémoulade sauce.

TO MAKE AHEAD

- Rémoulade sauce can be refrigerated for up to 3 days
- Crab cakes, prepared through step 3, can be refrigerated for up to 24 hours

CHAPTER 8

Vegetarian Mains

■ EASY (30 minutes or less active time)   ■ FREEZE IT
Photo: Eggplant Involtini

For ultraflavorful quinoa patties, we add sun-dried tomatoes and use some of the packing oil to bloom our aromatics.

Quinoa Patties

SERVES 4

ACTIVE TIME 1 HOUR

TOTAL TIME 2 HOURS 40 MINUTES

WHY THIS RECIPE WORKS For appealing quinoa patties, we used white quinoa, which softened enough for us to shape. An egg plus a yolk and some fresh bread crumbs bound the grains together; chilling the patties for at least an hour further ensured that they stayed together in the pan. Sun-dried tomatoes, scallions, baby spinach, and a little lemon zest and juice rounded out the patties' flavor. We like the convenience of prewashed quinoa; rinsing removes the quinoa's bitter protective coating (called saponin). If you buy unwashed quinoa (or if you are unsure whether it's washed), rinse it before cooking. Serve these patties with one of the sauces on page 260.

½ cup oil-packed sun-dried tomatoes, chopped coarse, plus 1 tablespoon packing oil

4 scallions, chopped fine

4 garlic cloves, minced

2 cups water

1 cup prewashed white quinoa

1 teaspoon salt

2 slices hearty white sandwich bread

1 large egg plus 1 large yolk, beaten

½ teaspoon grated lemon zest plus 2 teaspoons juice

2 ounces (2 cups) baby spinach, chopped

2 ounces Parmesan cheese, grated (1 cup)

2 tablespoons vegetable oil

1. Line rimmed baking sheet with parchment paper. Heat tomato oil in large saucepan over medium heat until shimmering. Add scallions and cook until softened, 3 to 5 minutes. Stir in garlic and cook until fragrant, about 30 seconds. Stir in water, quinoa, and salt and bring to simmer. Cover, reduce heat to medium-low, and simmer until quinoa is tender, 16 to 18 minutes.

2. Off heat, let quinoa sit, covered, until liquid is fully absorbed, about 10 minutes. Transfer quinoa to large bowl and let cool for 15 minutes.

3. Pulse bread in food processor until coarsely ground, about 10 pulses. Add egg and yolk and lemon zest and pulse until mixture comes together, about 5 pulses. Stir bread mixture, tomatoes, lemon juice, spinach, and Parmesan into cooled quinoa until combined. Divide mixture into 8 equal portions, pack firmly into ½-inch-thick patties, and place on prepared sheet. Cover and refrigerate patties for 1 hour.

4. Heat 1 tablespoon vegetable oil in 12-inch nonstick skillet over medium-low heat until shimmering. Gently lay 4 patties in skillet and cook until well browned on first side, 5 to 7 minutes. Gently flip patties and cook until golden brown on second side, 5 to 7 minutes. Transfer patties to serving platter and tent with aluminum foil. Return now-empty skillet to medium-low heat and repeat with remaining 1 tablespoon vegetable oil and remaining patties. Serve.

TO MAKE AHEAD

Quinoa patties, prepared through step 3, can be refrigerated for up to 24 hours

Chickpea Cakes

SERVES 4

ACTIVE TIME 1 HOUR

TOTAL TIME 2 HOURS 15 MINUTES

WHY THIS RECIPE WORKS Buttery, nutty chickpeas make a great foundation for a light yet filling vegetarian patty. They are protein-rich and just as satisfying as a beef burger, and they can be mixed and formed ahead of time and stored overnight for a quick dinner.

To keep our recipe easy, we decided to use canned beans rather than dried, which would require an overnight soak before we could prep and form the patties. Pulsing the chickpeas in the food processor was quick and gave us just the right coarse texture for cohesive cakes. For the flavors, we started with the fragrant Indian spice mix garam masala. Tasters liked the aromatic flavor of onion, but it released moisture as it sat, making the cakes gummy. Swapping the onion for scallions fixed the problem, lending a nice onion flavor without excess moisture. Fresh cilantro added a bright complexity. For a cool, creamy counterpoint, we made a simple cucumber-yogurt sauce to top the cakes. Be careful to avoid overprocessing the bean mixture, as it will cause the cakes to become mealy in texture.

    2 (15-ounce) cans chickpeas, rinsed
    ½ cup plain Greek yogurt
    2 large eggs
    6 tablespoons extra-virgin olive oil
    1 teaspoon garam masala
    ¼ teaspoon salt
    ⅛ teaspoon cayenne pepper
    1 cup panko bread crumbs
    5 scallions, sliced thin
    3 tablespoons minced fresh cilantro
    1 shallot, minced
    1 recipe Cucumber-Yogurt Sauce (page 260)

1. Line rimmed baking sheet with parchment paper. Pulse chickpeas in food processor to coarse puree with few large pieces remaining, about 8 pulses.

2. In medium bowl, whisk yogurt, eggs, 2 tablespoons oil, garam masala, salt, and cayenne together. Stir in processed chickpeas, panko, scallions, cilantro, and shallot until combined. Divide mixture into 8 equal portions, pack firmly into 1-inch-thick patties, and place on prepared sheet. Cover and refrigerate patties for 1 hour.

3. Heat 2 tablespoons oil in 12-inch nonstick skillet over medium heat until shimmering. Gently lay 4 patties in skillet and cook until well browned on first side, 6 to 8 minutes. Gently flip patties and cook until golden brown on second side, 6 to 8 minutes. Transfer patties to serving platter and tent with aluminum foil. Return now-empty skillet to medium heat and repeat with remaining 2 tablespoons oil and remaining patties. Serve with Cucumber-Yogurt Sauce.

TO MAKE AHEAD
Chickpea cakes, prepared through step 2, can be refrigerated for up to 24 hours

Brining dried chickpeas is essential to creating sturdy falafel with moist and tender interiors.

Falafel

SERVES 6 to 8   **FREEZE IT**
ACTIVE TIME 45 MINUTES
TOTAL TIME 45 MINUTES (PLUS 8 HOURS TO SOAK CHICKPEAS)

WHY THIS RECIPE WORKS Falafel, savory fried chickpea patties, should have a moist, light interior and a well-browned, crisp crust. Starting with dried chickpeas was essential; falafel made with canned chickpeas were mushy and wouldn't hold their shape. We soaked the dried chickpeas overnight in salted water, which softened them slightly. We then ground the soaked chickpeas with lots of fresh herbs and warm spices. Shaping the falafel into small disks ensured that the exteriors developed a crunchy, golden-brown crust while the interiors stayed moist. Shallow frying worked nicely and required far less oil than deep frying. The recipe worked perfectly when made ahead, as most of the work could be done in advance and the patties could be cooked straight from the fridge or freezer. The chickpeas in this recipe must be soaked overnight; you cannot substitute canned or quick-soaked chickpeas. Serve the falafel in lavash or pita bread with lettuce, chopped tomatoes or cucumbers, and Tahini-Yogurt Sauce (page 260).

Salt and pepper
12　ounces (2 cups) dried chickpeas, picked over and rinsed
10　scallions, chopped coarse
　1　cup fresh parsley leaves
　1　cup fresh cilantro leaves
　6　garlic cloves, minced
　½　teaspoon ground cumin
　⅛　teaspoon ground cinnamon
　2　cups vegetable oil

1. Dissolve 3 tablespoons salt in 4 quarts cold water in large container. Add chickpeas and soak at room temperature for 8 hours.

2. Drain and rinse chickpeas. Process chickpeas, scallions, parsley, cilantro, garlic, 1 teaspoon salt, 1 teaspoon pepper, cumin, and cinnamon in food processor until smooth, about 1 minute, scraping down sides of bowl as needed.

3. Line rimmed baking sheet with parchment paper. Pinch off and shape chickpea mixture into 2-tablespoon-size disks, about 1½ inches wide and 1 inch thick, and place on prepared sheet.

4. Adjust oven rack to middle position and heat oven to 200 degrees. Set wire rack in rimmed baking sheet. Heat oil in 12-inch skillet over medium-high heat to 375 degrees. Fry half of falafel until deep golden brown, 2 to 5 minutes per side, adjusting burner as needed to maintain oil temperature of 375 degrees. Using slotted spoon, transfer falafel to wire rack and keep warm in oven. Return oil to 375 degrees and repeat with remaining falafel. Serve.

TO MAKE AHEAD ▶
- Chickpeas, prepared through step 1, can be soaked for up to 24 hours
- Falafel, prepared through step 3, can be refrigerated for up to 3 days or frozen for up to 1 month; do not thaw before cooking

Black Bean Burgers
SERVES 6　**FREEZE IT**
ACTIVE TIME 45 MINUTES
TOTAL TIME 1 HOUR 45 MINUTES

WHY THIS RECIPE WORKS As with many meatless patties, black bean burgers often get their structure from fillers that rob them of their black bean flavor. We wanted burgers that featured earthy bean flavor at their heart with just enough seasoning and mix-ins to give them a little zest and intrigue. We also wanted patties that weren't wet or gluey but rather just cohesive enough to hold together when flipped in the pan, with a little textural contrast from chunks of beans and a nice crust. For convenient and reliable

Ground tortilla chips help to hold our black bean burgers together while keeping the bean flavor front and center.

beans, we turned to canned, and pulsed them in the food processor to ensure the best texture. Eggs, flour, and an unorthodox ingredient—tortilla chips—bound the patties together without over-whelming the beans' flavor. Refrigerating the mixture before forming patties allowed it to firm up so the patties would better hold their shape when cooked. Our favorite canned black beans are Bush's Best. When forming the patties, it is important to pack them firmly together. Serve these burgers with one of the sauces on page 260.

　2　(15-ounce) cans black beans, rinsed
　2　large eggs
　2　tablespoons all-purpose flour
　4　scallions, minced
　3　tablespoons minced fresh cilantro
　2　garlic cloves, minced
　1　teaspoon hot sauce
　1　teaspoon ground cumin
　½　teaspoon ground coriander
　¼　teaspoon salt
　¼　teaspoon pepper

1 ounce tortilla chips, crushed coarse (½ cup)
8 teaspoons vegetable oil
6 hamburger buns

1. Spread beans onto rimmed baking sheet lined with triple layer of paper towels and let drain for 15 minutes. In large bowl, whisk eggs and flour together into uniform paste, then stir in scallions, cilantro, garlic, hot sauce, cumin, coriander, salt, and pepper.

2. Process tortilla chips in food processor until finely ground, about 30 seconds. Add black beans and pulse until beans are roughly broken down, about 5 pulses. Stir processed bean mixture into egg mixture until well combined. Cover and refrigerate for 1 hour.

3. Adjust oven rack to middle position and heat oven to 200 degrees. Set wire rack in rimmed baking sheet. Divide bean mixture into 6 equal portions. Firmly pack each portion into tight ball, then flatten to 3½-inch-diameter patty and place on rimmed baking sheet.

4. Heat 2 teaspoons oil in 10-inch nonstick skillet over medium heat until shimmering. Carefully lay 3 patties in skillet and cook until bottoms are well browned and crisp, about 5 minutes. Flip patties, add 2 teaspoons oil to skillet, and cook until well browned and crisp on second side, 3 to 5 minutes.

5. Transfer burgers to wire rack and keep warm in oven. Repeat with remaining 4 teaspoons oil and remaining patties. Place burgers on buns and serve.

> **TO MAKE AHEAD**
> - Burger mixture, prepared through step 2, can be refrigerated for up to 24 hours
> - Patties, prepared through step 3, can be frozen for up to 1 month; thaw completely before cooking

Beet and Pinto Bean Burgers

SERVES 8   **FREEZE IT**

ACTIVE TIME 45 MINUTES
TOTAL TIME 1 HOUR 10 MINUTES

WHY THIS RECIPE WORKS Looking for a modern twist on the typical bean burger, we combined pinto beans with vibrant shredded beets, and we also packed in a generous amount of basil leaves. The result was a substantial but fresh-tasting burger with some sweetness from the beets and the bright, complementary aroma of basil. We incorporated bulgur for heft and ground nuts for meaty richness. Garlic and mustard deepened the savory flavors. While the bulgur cooked, we pulsed the other ingredients in the food processor to just the right consistency. To bind the burgers, we turned to a surprising ingredient: carrot baby food. The carrot added tackiness and its subtle sweetness heightened that of the shredded beets; plus, it was already conveniently puréed. Panko bread crumbs further bound the mixture and helped the patties sear up with a crisp crust. Do not use fine-grind, coarse-grind, or cracked-wheat bulgur in this recipe; they will not work. Serve these burgers with one of the sauces on page 260.

Salt and pepper
⅔ cup medium-grind bulgur, rinsed
1 large beet (9 ounces), peeled and shredded
¾ cup walnuts
½ cup fresh basil leaves
2 garlic cloves, minced
1 (15-ounce) can pinto beans, rinsed
1 (4-ounce) jar carrot baby food
1 tablespoon whole-grain mustard
1½ cups panko bread crumbs
6 tablespoons vegetable oil, plus extra as needed
8 hamburger buns

1. Bring 1½ cups water and ½ teaspoon salt to boil in small saucepan. Off heat, stir in bulgur, cover, and let stand until tender, 15 to 20 minutes. Drain bulgur, pressing with rubber spatula to remove excess moisture, and spread onto rimmed baking sheet; let cool slightly.

2. Meanwhile, pulse beet, walnuts, basil, and garlic in food processor until finely chopped, about 12 pulses, scraping down sides of bowl as needed. Add beans, carrot baby food, 2 tablespoons water, mustard, 1½ teaspoons salt, and ½ teaspoon pepper and pulse until well combined, about 8 pulses. Transfer mixture to large bowl and stir in panko and cooled bulgur.

3. Adjust oven rack to middle position and heat oven to 200 degrees. Set wire rack in rimmed baking sheet. Divide mixture into 8 equal portions and pack into 3½-inch-wide patties.

4. Heat 3 tablespoons oil in 12-inch nonstick skillet over medium-high heat until shimmering. Gently lay 4 patties in skillet and cook until crisp and well browned on first side, about 4 minutes. Gently flip patties and cook until crisp and well browned on second side, about 4 minutes, adding extra oil if skillet looks dry.

5. Transfer burgers to wire rack and keep warm in oven. Repeat with remaining 3 tablespoons oil and remaining patties. Place burgers on buns and serve.

> **TO MAKE AHEAD**
> - Burgers, prepared through step 3, can be frozen for up to 1 month
> - To cook, brown frozen patties on both sides, then bake in 350-degree oven until warmed through, about 10 minutes

SAUCES FOR BURGERS, FRITTERS, AND MORE

These simple, versatile sauces and toppings are an easy way to add a little extra flavor, texture, or brightness to dishes. They're perfect as toppings for vegetable cakes and fritters or drizzled over rice bowls or curries.

CUCUMBER-YOGURT SAUCE

MAKES ABOUT 2½ CUPS   **EASY**
ACTIVE TIME 5 MINUTES
TOTAL TIME 20 MINUTES

Cilantro, mint, parsley, or tarragon can be substituted for the dill if desired.

- 1 cucumber, peeled, halved lengthwise, seeded, and shredded
  Salt and pepper
- 1 cup plain Greek yogurt
- 2 tablespoons extra-virgin olive oil
- 2 tablespoons minced fresh dill
- 1 garlic clove, minced

Toss cucumber with ½ teaspoon salt in fine-mesh strainer and let drain for 15 minutes. Combine drained cucumber with yogurt, oil, dill, and garlic and season with salt and pepper to taste.

TO MAKE AHEAD

Sauce can be refrigerated for up to 1 day

EASY CHERRY TOMATO SALSA

MAKES ABOUT 1 CUP   **EASY**
ACTIVE TIME 5 MINUTES
TOTAL TIME 5 MINUTES

- 6 ounces cherry tomatoes, quartered
- 1 tablespoon extra-virgin olive oil
- 1 tablespoon minced fresh cilantro
- 1½ teaspoons lime juice
  Salt and pepper

Combine all ingredients in bowl and season with salt and pepper to taste.

TO MAKE AHEAD

Salsa can be refrigerated for up to 1 day

TAHINI-YOGURT SAUCE

MAKES ABOUT 1 CUP   **EASY**
ACTIVE TIME 5 MINUTES
TOTAL TIME 35 MINUTES

- ⅓ cup tahini
- ⅓ cup plain Greek yogurt
- ¼ cup water
- 3 tablespoons lemon juice
- 1 garlic clove, minced
  Salt and pepper

Whisk tahini, yogurt, water, lemon juice, garlic, and ¾ teaspoon salt together in bowl. Let sit until flavors meld, about 30 minutes. Season with salt and pepper to taste.

TO MAKE AHEAD

Sauce can be refrigerated for up to 4 days

CILANTRO-MINT CHUTNEY

MAKES ABOUT 1 CUP   **EASY**
ACTIVE TIME 10 MINUTES
TOTAL TIME 10 MINUTES

- 2 cups packed fresh cilantro leaves
- 1 cup packed fresh mint leaves
- ⅓ cup plain yogurt
- ¼ cup finely chopped onion
- 1 tablespoon lime juice
- 1½ teaspoons sugar
- ½ teaspoon ground cumin
- ¼ teaspoon salt

Process all ingredients in food processor until smooth, about 20 seconds, stopping to scrape down bowl as needed.

TO MAKE AHEAD

Chutney can be refrigerated for up to 1 day

ROASTED TOMATO–ORANGE JAM

MAKES ABOUT 1 CUP   **EASY**
ACTIVE TIME 15 MINUTES
TOTAL TIME 30 MINUTES

Line the baking sheet with foil for easy cleanup.

- 12 ounces cherry tomatoes, halved
- 1 shallot, sliced thin
- 1 tablespoon extra-virgin olive oil
- ¼ teaspoon salt
- ⅛ teaspoon ground cinnamon
- 2 tablespoons orange marmalade

Adjust oven rack to middle position and heat oven to 425 degrees. Toss tomatoes, shallot, oil, salt, and cinnamon together in bowl. Spread mixture onto aluminum foil–lined rimmed baking sheet and roast until edges of tomatoes are well browned, 15 to 20 minutes; let cool slightly. Transfer mixture to food processor, add marmalade, and process until smooth, about 10 seconds.

TO MAKE AHEAD

Jam can be refrigerated for up to 1 week

Ultimate Veggie Burgers

SERVES 12   **FREEZE IT**

ACTIVE TIME 1 HOUR
TOTAL TIME 2 HOURS

WHY THIS RECIPE WORKS Store-bought veggie burgers are convenient but notoriously inedible. We wanted to develop a homemade version that was more than worth the trouble, with complex savory flavor and a satisfying texture. We tried a variety of soy products, but none had a texture that we liked in a burger. When we turned to a more traditional base for veggie burgers we had better luck. Lentils had the best flavor, and bulgur and panko further bulked up our burgers; plus, they absorbed the excess moisture the lentils retained even after thorough drying. Adding aromatic vegetables was a no-brainer; onions, celery, leek, and garlic provided great depth of flavor without being overwhelming. We knew that cremini mushrooms would give our burgers a meaty flavor, but we were surprised to find that adding ground cashews took them to the next level. Pulsing everything together in the food processor made for a more cohesive and even-textured mix, and mayonnaise provided the necessary fat and binding qualities. After forming the mixture into patties, we simply seared them in a skillet to give them a crunchy, browned exterior. Do not use fine-grind, coarse-grind, or cracked-wheat bulgur in this recipe; they will not work. Cremini mushrooms are also known as baby bella mushrooms. Serve these burgers with one of the sauces at left.

Cremini mushrooms and cashews give our lentil-based veggie burgers savory depth of flavor.

¾ cup dried brown lentils, picked over and rinsed
    Salt and pepper
¾ cup medium-grind bulgur, rinsed
½ cup vegetable oil
2 onions, chopped fine
1 celery rib, chopped fine
1 small leek, white and light green parts only, halved lengthwise, chopped fine, and washed thoroughly
2 garlic cloves, minced
1 pound cremini or white mushrooms, trimmed and sliced ¼ inch thick
1 cup raw cashews
⅓ cup mayonnaise
2 cups panko bread crumbs
12 hamburger buns

1. Bring 3 cups water, lentils, and 1 teaspoon salt to boil in medium saucepan over high heat. Reduce heat to medium-low and simmer gently, stirring occasionally, until lentils are just beginning to fall apart, about 25 minutes. Drain lentils, spread out over paper towel–lined baking sheet, andw pat dry; let cool to room temperature.

2. Meanwhile, bring 2 cups water and ½ teaspoon salt to boil in small saucepan. Off heat, stir in bulgur, cover, and let stand until tender, 15 to 20 minutes. Drain bulgur, pressing with rubber spatula to remove excess moisture, and transfer to large bowl; let cool slightly.

3. Heat 1 tablespoon oil in 12-inch nonstick skillet over medium-high heat until shimmering. Add onions, celery, leek, and garlic and cook, stirring occasionally, until vegetables begin to brown, about 10 minutes. Spread vegetable mixture onto second baking sheet.

4. Heat 1 tablespoon oil in now-empty skillet over high heat until shimmering. Add mushrooms and cook, stirring occasionally, until golden brown, about 12 minutes; add to baking sheet with other vegetables and let cool to room temperature, about 20 minutes.

5. Pulse cashews in food processor until finely chopped, about 15 pulses. Stir cashews into bulgur, then stir in cooled lentils, vegetable-mushroom mixture, and mayonnaise. Working in 2 batches, pulse mixture in now-empty food processor until coarsely chopped, 15 to 20 pulses (mixture should be cohesive but roughly textured); transfer to clean bowl.

6. Stir in panko and 1 teaspoon salt and season with pepper to taste. Divide mixture into 12 portions, about ½ cup each, shaping each into tightly packed patty about 4 inches in diameter and ½ inch thick. Place patties on paper towel–lined baking sheet.

7. Heat 2 tablespoons oil in 12-inch nonstick skillet over medium-high heat until shimmering. Place 4 burgers in skillet and cook until well browned on both sides, about 4 minutes per side; transfer to plate. Repeat with remaining 4 tablespoons oil and remaining burgers. Place burgers on buns and serve.

TO MAKE AHEAD

- Burgers, prepared through step 6, can be refrigerated for up to 3 days
- Burgers, prepared through step 6, can be frozen for up to 1 month; to cook, brown frozen patties on both sides, then bake in 350-degree oven until warmed through, about 10 minutes

Barley with Lentils, Mushrooms, and Tahini-Yogurt Sauce

SERVES 4
ACTIVE TIME 45 MINUTES
TOTAL TIME 1 HOUR 40 MINUTES

WHY THIS RECIPE WORKS This superhearty barley-based dish makes a substantial side or a satisfying vegetarian main, and a creamy sauce makes it extra rich. To balance the grains, we decided to use robust lentils and earthy mushrooms. We tested all types of lentils and found that tasters favored black lentils for their nutty flavor and their ability to hold their shape once cooked. We were happy to find that we could cook the barley and lentils together in one pot, since the sturdy black lentils held their shape as the barley cooked through. Hoping to keep our recipe streamlined, we set the cooked barley and lentils aside and attempted to brown the mushrooms in the same pot. Unfortunately, the mushrooms were too crowded in the pot, which caused them to steam and overcook. Switching to a large nonstick skillet to cook the mushrooms resulted in more browning and faster cooking, since the increased surface area allowed the mushrooms more contact with the pan. We tested many varieties of mushrooms, including white mushrooms, cremini, porcini, and portobellos; we liked the combination of meaty, plump portobellos along with savory, flavor-rich rehydrated dried porcini. Our tangy Tahini-Yogurt Sauce worked perfectly to balance these hearty flavors, and fresh dill and strips of lemon peel brightened and balanced the earthy notes of the

barley and lentils. Do not substitute hulled, hull-less, quick-cooking, or presteamed barley (read the ingredient list on the package to determine this) in this recipe. While we prefer black lentils here, *lentilles du Puy*, brown lentils, or green lentils can be substituted.

½ ounce dried porcini mushrooms, rinsed
1 cup pearl barley
½ cup black lentils, picked over and rinsed
Salt and pepper
2 tablespoons extra-virgin olive oil
1 onion, chopped fine
2 large portobello mushroom caps, cut into 1-inch pieces
3 (2-inch) strips lemon zest, sliced thin lengthwise
¾ teaspoon ground coriander
2 tablespoons chopped fresh dill
1 recipe Tahini-Yogurt Sauce (page 260)

1. Microwave 1½ cups water and porcini mushrooms in covered bowl until steaming, about 1 minute. Let sit until softened, about 5 minutes. Drain porcini in fine-mesh strainer lined with coffee filter, reserving soaking liquid, and chop porcini.

2. Bring 4 quarts water to boil in Dutch oven. Add barley, lentils, and 1 tablespoon salt, return to boil, and cook until tender, 20 to 40 minutes. Drain barley and lentils, return to now-empty pot, and cover to keep warm.

3. Meanwhile, heat oil in 12-inch nonstick skillet over medium heat until shimmering. Add onion and cook until softened, about 5 minutes. Stir in portobello mushrooms, cover, and cook until portobellos have released their liquid and begin to brown, about 4 minutes.

4. Uncover, stir in lemon zest, coriander, ½ teaspoon salt, and ¼ teaspoon pepper, and cook until fragrant, about 30 seconds. Stir in porcini and porcini soaking liquid, bring to boil, and cook, stirring occasionally, until liquid is thickened slightly and reduced to ½ cup, about 5 minutes.

5. Stir portobello mixture and dill into barley-lentil mixture and season with salt and pepper to taste. Serve with tahini-yogurt sauce.

TO MAKE AHEAD

- Barely-lentil mixture and portobello mixture, prepared through step 4, can be refrigerated separately for up to 3 days
- To reheat, combine barley-lentil mixture and mushroom mixture in Dutch oven and cook over medium-low heat until hot throughout, adding water if pot is very dry

To give our vegetarian red beans deep flavor, we use chipotle chile in adobo along with some smoked paprika.

Red Beans and Rice

SERVES 6 to 8

ACTIVE TIME 40 MINUTES

TOTAL TIME 2 HOURS (PLUS 8 HOURS TO SOAK BEANS)

WHY THIS RECIPE WORKS Red beans and rice is a traditional New Orleans dish. We wanted to make a vegetarian version of this simple, homey dinner using widely available ingredients. We substituted small red beans for the local Camellia-brand dried red beans and replaced the smoky, meaty flavor of tasso (traditional Cajun ham) with a combination of chipotle chile in adobo sauce and smoked paprika. We started by sautéing green pepper, onion, and celery; we then added garlic, thyme, bay leaves, and cayenne pepper to give the beans complex aromatic flavor. In keeping with tradition, we served the saucy beans over white rice to soak up every bit of flavor. In order for the starch from the beans to thicken the cooking liquid, it is important to maintain a vigorous simmer in step 3.

RED BEANS

    Salt and pepper
1 pound (2 cups) small dried red beans, picked over
    and rinsed
3 tablespoons unsalted butter
1 onion, chopped fine
1 green bell pepper, stemmed, seeded, and chopped fine
1 celery rib, chopped fine
3 garlic cloves, minced
2 teaspoons minced canned chipotle chile in adobo sauce
1½ teaspoons smoked paprika
1 teaspoon minced fresh thyme or ¼ teaspoon dried
2 bay leaves
⅛ teaspoon cayenne pepper
1 teaspoon red wine vinegar, plus extra as needed
3 scallions, sliced thin
    Hot sauce

RICE

1 tablespoon unsalted butter
2 cups long-grain white rice, rinsed
3 cups water
1 teaspoon salt

1. FOR THE RED BEANS Dissolve 3 tablespoons salt in 4 quarts cold water in large container. Add beans and soak at room temperature for 8 hours.

2. Drain and rinse beans. Melt 1 tablespoon butter in Dutch oven over medium heat. Add onion, bell pepper, celery, and ½ teaspoon salt and cook, stirring often, until vegetables are softened, 6 to 7 minutes. Stir in garlic, chipotle, paprika, thyme, bay leaves, cayenne, and ¼ teaspoon pepper and cook until fragrant, about 30 seconds.

3. Stir in beans and 9 cups water and bring to boil over high heat. Reduce heat to medium-low and simmer vigorously, stirring occasionally, until beans are just soft and liquid begins to thicken, 45 minutes to 1 hour. Stir in vinegar and 1 teaspoon salt and continue to cook until liquid is thick and beans are fully tender and creamy, about 30 minutes.

4. FOR THE RICE Melt butter in large saucepan over medium heat. Add rice and cook, stirring often, until edges begin to turn translucent, about 2 minutes. Add water and salt and bring to boil. Cover, reduce heat to low, and simmer until liquid is absorbed and rice is tender, about 20 minutes. Remove pot from heat, lay clean folded dish towel underneath lid, and let rice sit for 10 minutes. Fluff rice with fork.

5. Discard bay leaves from beans and stir in remaining 2 tablespoons butter. Season with salt and extra vinegar to taste. Portion rice into individual bowls, top with beans, and sprinkle with scallions. Serve with hot sauce.

TO MAKE AHEAD ▶

- Red beans, prepared through step 1, can be soaked for up to 24 hours
- Cooked beans and rice, prepared through step 4, can be refrigerated separately for up to 3 days
- To reheat, microwave rice in covered bowl until hot throughout, 4 to 6 minutes, fluffing with fork often; reheat beans over medium heat, adjusting consistency with hot water, and continue with step 5

Mushroom Ragout with Farro

SERVES 4

ACTIVE TIME 40 MINUTES

TOTAL TIME 1 HOUR

WHY THIS RECIPE WORKS A mushroom ragout is a rich, intensely flavorful stew made with a variety of wild mushrooms. We wanted a recipe for a simple mushroom ragout with great savory flavor. Meaty, substantial portobellos plus a mix of assorted mushrooms gave the dish balanced mushroom flavor. A small amount of dried porcini added even more complexity, and tomatoes and a splash of dry Madeira wine cut through the richness. To make our ragout hearty, we wanted to include a grain. Delicate quinoa disappeared next to the big bites of mushrooms, and wheat berries took too long to cook, but farro was a hit: Its nutty flavor and chewy texture complemented the mushrooms nicely, and the cooked grains held up well for several days when made in advance. For the best flavor, we prefer to use a combination of white, shiitake, and oyster mushrooms in this recipe; however, you can choose just one or two varieties if you like. The woody stems of shiitakes are unpleasant to eat so be sure to remove them. We prefer the flavor and texture of whole farro; pearled farro can be used, but the texture may be softer. Do not use quick-cooking or presteamed farro (read the ingredient list on the package to determine this) in this recipe. The cooking time for farro can vary greatly among different brands, so we recommend beginning to check for doneness after 10 minutes.

1½ cups whole farro
3½ cups vegetable broth
    Salt and pepper
1 pound portobello mushroom caps, halved and sliced ½ inch wide

We use meaty portobello mushrooms, assorted wild mushrooms, and porcini to give our ragout balanced flavor.

18 ounces assorted mushrooms, trimmed and halved if small or quartered if large
2 tablespoons extra-virgin olive oil
1 onion, chopped fine
½ ounce dried porcini mushrooms, rinsed and minced
3 garlic cloves, minced
1 teaspoon minced fresh thyme or ¼ teaspoon dried
¼ cup dry Madeira
1 (14.5-ounce) can diced tomatoes, drained and chopped
2 tablespoons minced fresh parsley
    Balsamic vinegar

1. Simmer farro and broth in large saucepan over medium heat until farro is tender and creamy, 20 to 25 minutes. Season with salt and pepper to taste; cover and keep warm.

2. Meanwhile, microwave portobello and assorted mushrooms in covered bowl until tender, 6 to 8 minutes. Drain, reserving mushroom juices.

3. Heat oil in Dutch oven over medium-high heat until shimmering. Add onion and porcini and cook until softened and lightly browned, 5 to 7 minutes. Stir in drained mushrooms and cook, stirring often, until mushrooms are dry and lightly browned, about 5 minutes.

4. Stir in garlic and thyme and cook until fragrant, about 30 seconds. Stir in Madeira and reserved mushroom juices, scraping up any browned bits. Stir in tomatoes and simmer gently until sauce is slightly thickened, about 8 minutes.

5. Off heat, stir in parsley and season with salt and pepper to taste. Portion farro into 4 individual serving bowls and top with mushroom mixture. Drizzle with balsamic vinegar to taste. Serve.

TO MAKE AHEAD

- Mushroom ragout and farro, prepared through step 4, can be refrigerated separately for up to 3 days
- To reheat, microwave farro with 1 tablespoon water in covered bowl until hot, 3 to 5 minutes, stirring often; reheat ragout over medium-low heat, adjusting consistency with hot water, and continue with step 5

Indian-Style Vegetable Curry with Potatoes and Cauliflower

SERVES 4 to 6
ACTIVE TIME 55 MINUTES
TOTAL TIME 1 HOUR 15 MINUTES

WHY THIS RECIPE WORKS We wanted a recipe for the ultimate vegetable curry, with a wide variety of perfectly cooked vegetables and a deeply flavorful (but weeknight-friendly) red curry sauce. We started with the sauce. Blooming store-bought curry powder in a bit of oil turned it into a flavor powerhouse, and garam masala added even more spice flavor. To build the rest of our flavor base, we incorporated a generous amount of sautéed onion, garlic, ginger, and fresh chile, as well as tomato paste for sweetness. For the vegetables, we chose hearty potatoes, cauliflower, and peas, plus convenient canned chickpeas. We found that sautéing the spices and main ingredients together enhanced and melded the flavors. Finally, we rounded out our sauce with a combination of water, pureed canned tomatoes, and coconut milk. For more heat, include the chile seeds and ribs when mincing. We prefer the richer flavor of regular coconut milk here; however, light coconut milk can be substituted.

1 (14.5-ounce) can diced tomatoes
3 tablespoons vegetable oil
4 teaspoons curry powder
1½ teaspoons garam masala
2 onions, chopped fine
12 ounces red potatoes, unpeeled, cut into ½-inch chunks

Blooming curry powder and garam masala for the base of our curry makes for a simple yet deeply flavorful dish.

  Salt and pepper
3 garlic cloves, minced
1 serrano chile, stemmed, seeded, and minced
1 tablespoon grated fresh ginger
1 tablespoon tomato paste
½ head cauliflower (1 pound), cored and cut into 1-inch florets
1½ cups water
1 (15-ounce) can chickpeas, rinsed
1½ cups frozen peas
½ cup coconut milk
¼ cup minced fresh cilantro
1 recipe Cilantro-Mint Chutney (page 260)

1. Pulse diced tomatoes with their juice in food processor until nearly smooth with some ¼-inch pieces visible, about 3 pulses.

2. Heat oil in Dutch oven over medium-high heat until shimmering. Add curry powder and garam masala and cook until fragrant, about 10 seconds. Stir in onions, potatoes, and ¼ teaspoon salt and cook, stirring occasionally, until onions are browned and potatoes are golden brown at edges, about 10 minutes.

3. Reduce heat to medium. Stir in garlic, serrano, ginger, and tomato paste and cook until fragrant, about 30 seconds. Add cauliflower florets and cook, stirring constantly, until florets are coated with spices, about 2 minutes.

4. Gradually stir in water, scraping up any browned bits. Stir in chickpeas and processed tomatoes and bring to simmer. Cover, reduce to gentle simmer, and cook until vegetables are tender, 20 to 25 minutes.

5. Stir in peas and coconut milk. Cook, uncovered, over medium-low heat until peas are heated through, 1 to 2 minutes. Off heat, stir in cilantro, season with salt and pepper to taste, and serve with cilantro-mint chutney.

TO MAKE AHEAD ▶

- Curry, prepared through step 4, can be refrigerated for up to 3 days
- To reheat, bring curry to simmer over medium heat, adjusting consistency with hot water, and continue with step 5

Grilled Vegetable Kebabs

SERVES 4

ACTIVE TIME 40 MINUTES

TOTAL TIME 1 HOUR

WHY THIS RECIPE WORKS When it comes to grilled kebabs, vegetables are often an afterthought, typically used as a filler on meat-heavy skewers. But this treatment often leads to mushy, burnt vegetables with no flavor of their own. We wanted to create a recipe that would put the vegetables front and center. We started by choosing the right vegetables. We wanted a good mix of flavors and textures, but we knew that not all veggies would hold up to the high heat of the grill. We started with bell peppers, which sweetened beautifully over the flames, and zucchini, which held its shape nicely and had a satisfying texture. Portobello mushroom caps were the perfect addition to the kebabs; as they released their moisture over the flame, they picked up great char and developed a deep, meaty taste. Tossing grilled vegetables with a bold dressing can amp up their flavor considerably, but for our vegetable kebabs, we took the idea one step further. We tossed the vegetables with half of the dressing before skewering and grilling them, giving them great flavor from the start. We pumped up the complexity and nuance of the remaining dressing with juice from grilled lemons, and tossed it with the cooked vegetables for a punchy, bright finish. You will need eight 12-inch metal skewers for this recipe.

Dressing the vegetables both before and after cooking gives them bold, bright flavor.

¼ cup extra-virgin olive oil
1 teaspoon Dijon mustard
1 teaspoon minced fresh rosemary
1 garlic clove, minced
   Salt and pepper
6 portobello mushroom caps (4 to 5 inches in diameter), quartered
2 zucchini, halved lengthwise and sliced ¾ inch thick
2 red bell peppers, stemmed, seeded, and cut into 1½-inch pieces
2 lemons, quartered

1. Whisk oil, mustard, rosemary, garlic, ½ teaspoon salt, and ¼ teaspoon pepper together in large bowl. Transfer half of dressing to separate bowl and set aside for serving. Toss mushrooms, zucchini, and bell peppers with remaining dressing, then thread in alternating order onto eight 12-inch metal skewers.

2A. FOR A CHARCOAL GRILL Open bottom vent completely. Light large chimney starter half filled with charcoal briquettes (3 quarts). When top coals are partially covered with ash, pour evenly over grill. Set cooking grate in place, cover, and open lid vent completely. Heat grill until hot, about 5 minutes.

2B. FOR A GAS GRILL Turn all burners to high, cover, and heat grill until hot, about 15 minutes. Turn all burners to medium.

3. Clean and oil cooking grate. Place kebabs and lemons on grill. Cook (covered if using gas), turning as needed, until vegetables are tender and well browned, 16 to 18 minutes. Transfer kebabs and lemons to serving platter. Juice 2 lemon quarters into reserved dressing and whisk to combine. Pour dressing over kebabs and serve with remaining lemons.

> **TO MAKE AHEAD**
> - Vegetables and reserved dressing, prepared through step 1, can be refrigerated separately for up to 24 hours
> - To cook, bring dressing to room temperature and continue with step 2, increasing cooking time to 20 to 24 minutes

Grilled Soy-Ginger Glazed Tofu

SERVES 4 to 6
ACTIVE TIME 35 MINUTES
TOTAL TIME 1 HOUR 20 MINUTES

WHY THIS RECIPE WORKS Tofu has a soft, silky texture that contrasts nicely with the crisp, browned crust that results from a quick stint on the grill. A mirin-soy marinade boosted its mild flavor and helped us achieve a darker, crisper crust. Then we made a sweet-savory Asian-style glaze by simmering soy sauce, sugar, mirin, fresh ginger, garlic, and chili-garlic sauce. Some cornstarch helped to thicken the sauce so it would cling to the tofu. We found that the key to successfully grilled tofu was cutting it into the right shape and handling it carefully on the grill. We tried grilling tofu that had been cut into planks, strips, and cubes, and found that tofu cut lengthwise into 1-inch-thick planks fared best. This shape maximized surface contact, and the larger pieces were easier to turn. Using two spatulas provided the best leverage for flipping the delicate tofu. You can use either firm or extra-firm tofu in this recipe. Be sure to handle the tofu gently on the grill, or it may break apart.

28 ounces firm tofu, sliced lengthwise into 1-inch-thick planks
 6 tablespoons mirin
 5 tablespoons soy sauce
 6 tablespoons water
⅓ cup sugar
 1 tablespoon grated fresh ginger
 2 garlic cloves, minced
 2 teaspoons cornstarch
 1 teaspoon Asian chili-garlic sauce
 2 tablespoons vegetable oil
¼ cup minced fresh cilantro

We marinate planks of tofu with mirin and soy sauce to encourage deep browning and a crisp crust when grilled.

1. Spread tofu on paper towel–lined baking sheet, let drain for 20 minutes, then gently press dry with paper towels.

2. Combine tofu, 2 tablespoons mirin, and 1 tablespoon soy sauce in 1-gallon zipper-lock bag and toss to coat; press out as much air as possible and seal bag. Refrigerate for 30 minutes, flipping bag halfway through marinating.

3. Meanwhile, simmer water, sugar, ginger, garlic, cornstarch, chili-garlic sauce, remaining ¼ cup mirin, and remaining ¼ cup soy sauce in small saucepan over medium-high heat until thickened and measures ¾ cup, 5 to 7 minutes; transfer to bowl.

4. Before grilling, remove tofu from marinade, pat dry, and brush with oil.

5A. FOR A CHARCOAL GRILL Open bottom vent completely. Light large chimney starter filled with charcoal briquettes (6 quarts). When top coals are partially covered with ash, pour two-thirds evenly over half of grill, then pour remaining coals over other half of grill. Set cooking grate in place, cover, and open lid vent completely. Heat grill until hot, about 5 minutes.

5B. FOR A GAS GRILL Turn all burners to high, cover, and heat grill until hot, about 15 minutes. Leave all burners on high.

6. Clean and oil cooking grate. Gently place tofu on grill (on hotter part of grill if using charcoal) and cook (covered if using gas) until browned on both sides, 5 to 9 minutes, gently flipping tofu halfway through cooking using 2 spatulas.

7. Slide tofu to cooler part of grill if using charcoal, or turn all burners to medium if using gas. Brush tofu with ¼ cup glaze, flip, and cook until well browned, 1 to 2 minutes. Brush second side of tofu with ¼ cup glaze, flip, and cook until well browned, 1 to 2 minutes. Transfer tofu to platter, brush with remaining glaze, and sprinkle with cilantro. Serve.

TO MAKE AHEAD

Marinated tofu and glaze, prepared through step 3, can be refrigerated separately for up to 24 hours

Barbecued Tempeh Skewers

SERVES 4 **EASY**

ACTIVE TIME 30 MINUTES
TOTAL TIME 1 HOUR 45 MINUTES

WHY THIS RECIPE WORKS Made from whole fermented soybeans and sometimes a mix of grains, tempeh has a firmer, chewier texture than tofu, but it is just as good at soaking up flavor. For an easy grilled tempeh recipe, we cubed and skewered the tempeh. The tempeh cubes took on great char and stayed intact on the grill. We paired the tempeh with a tangy, molasses-y pantry sauce, which tempered its slightly bitter flavor. Firm, sweet red bell peppers and juicy, savory mushrooms turned out to be great contrasting companions. We thinned a portion of our sauce with oil and water for a simple marinade that infused the tempeh with barbecue flavor and made it pleasingly soft and moist. After we got good char on our skewers, we brushed on some sauce as they cooked for a syrupy glaze and applied another coat when they were hot off the grill. You will need eight 12-inch metal skewers for this recipe.

- 2 cups ketchup
- 6 tablespoons molasses
- 2 tablespoons cider vinegar
- 2 teaspoons hot sauce
- ¼ teaspoon liquid smoke (optional)
- ¼ cup vegetable oil
- ¼ cup water
- 1 pound tempeh, cut into 1½-inch-thick pieces
- 1 pound cremini mushrooms, trimmed
- 2 red bell peppers, stemmed, seeded, and cut into 1½-inch pieces

Cubing and skewering hearty, nutty tempeh allows it to hold together on the grill while picking up plenty of char.

1. Whisk ketchup, molasses, vinegar, hot sauce, and liquid smoke, if using, together in bowl. Measure 1 cup sauce into second bowl, whisk in oil and water, then transfer to 1-gallon zipper-lock bag. Add tempeh, mushrooms, and bell peppers to bag, press out air, seal, and toss to coat. Refrigerate for at least 1 hour, flipping bag occasionally.

2. Remove tempeh and vegetables from marinade and thread in alternating order onto eight 12-inch metal skewers. Pat dry with paper towels.

3A. FOR A CHARCOAL GRILL Open bottom vent completely. Light large chimney starter filled with charcoal briquettes (6 quarts). When top coals are partially covered with ash, pour evenly over grill. Set cooking grate in place, cover, and open lid vent completely. Heat grill until hot, about 5 minutes.

3B. FOR A GAS GRILL Turn all burners to high, cover, and heat grill until hot, about 15 minutes. Leave all burners on high.

4. Clean and oil cooking grate. Place skewers on grill and cook (covered if using gas), turning as needed, until tempeh is well browned and vegetables are tender and slightly charred, 8 to 12 minutes.

5. Brush skewers with ¼ cup reserved sauce, flip, and cook until sizzling and well browned, about 1 minute. Brush second side of skewers with ¼ cup sauce, flip, and cook until well browned, about 1 minute. Transfer skewers to platter and brush with ¼ cup sauce. Serve with remaining sauce.

TO MAKE AHEAD

Marinated tempeh and remaining sauce, prepared through step 1, can be refrigerated separately for up to 24 hours

Pan-Seared Tempeh Steaks with Chimichurri

SERVES 4 **EASY**
ACTIVE TIME 30 MINUTES
TOTAL TIME 1 HOUR 30 MINUTES

WHY THIS RECIPE WORKS To put versatile, earthy tempeh at the center of a vegetarian dinner, we gave it a similar treatment to steak. Marinating the tempeh in a highly seasoned base infused it with flavor. Patting the tempeh dry and pan-searing it created a crispy edge and made the texture more cohesive. Next, we wanted to balance the tempeh's earthy flavor by serving it with a bright herb sauce. Chimichurri sauce is a traditional condiment for steak that combines parsley, wine vinegar, oil, lots of garlic, oregano, and a good dose of red pepper flakes. It paired perfectly with our tempeh, lending bright flavor and richness to the seared "steaks."

¼ cup water
6 tablespoons red wine vinegar
6 garlic cloves, minced
2 teaspoons dried oregano
½ teaspoon red pepper flakes
1 pound tempeh, cut into 3½-inch-long by
  ⅜-inch-thick slabs
1 cup fresh parsley leaves
¾ cup extra-virgin olive oil
  Salt and pepper

1. Combine water, ¼ cup vinegar, 1 tablespoon garlic, 1 teaspoon oregano, and ¼ teaspoon pepper flakes in 1-gallon zipper-lock bag. Add tempeh, press out air, seal, and toss to coat. Refrigerate tempeh for at least 1 hour, flipping bag occasionally.

2. Pulse parsley, ½ cup oil, remaining 2 tablespoons vinegar, remaining garlic, remaining 1 teaspoon oregano, remaining ¼ teaspoon pepper flakes, and ½ teaspoon salt in food processor until coarsely chopped, about 10 pulses. Transfer to bowl and season with salt and pepper to taste.

3. Remove tempeh from marinade and pat dry with paper towels. Heat 2 tablespoons oil in 12-inch nonstick skillet over medium heat until shimmering. Add 4 pieces tempeh and cook until golden brown on first side, 2 to 4 minutes.

4. Flip tempeh, reduce heat to medium-low, and continue to cook until golden brown on second side, 2 to 4 minutes; transfer to platter. Wipe out skillet with paper towels and repeat with remaining 2 tablespoons oil and remaining tempeh. Serve with chimichurri sauce.

TO MAKE AHEAD

Marinated tempeh and chimichurri, prepared through step 2, can be refrigerated separately for up to 24 hours

NOTES FROM THE TEST KITCHEN

Tempeh

While tofu has hit the mainstream, its relative, tempeh, might not be as familiar. Tempeh is made by fermenting cooked soybeans and forming a firm, dense cake. (Some versions of tempeh also contain beans, grains, and flavorings.) Because it holds its shape better than tofu when cooked, it serves as a good meat substitute and is a mainstay of many vegetarian diets (and is particularly popular in Southeast Asia). Although it has a strong, almost nutty flavor, it tends to absorb the flavors of any foods or sauces to which it is added, making it a versatile choice for many sorts of dishes from chilis to tacos. Tempeh is sold in most supermarkets and can be found with different grain combinations and flavorings. We prefer to use five-grain tempeh in our recipes, but any tempeh variety will work.

Stir-Fried Tempeh, Napa Cabbage, and Carrots

SERVES 4
ACTIVE TIME 50 MINUTES
TOTAL TIME 1 HOUR 50 MINUTES

WHY THIS RECIPE WORKS For a vegetarian stir-fry redolent with bold Asian flavors, we decided on a combination of tempeh, carrots, and napa cabbage. First we perfected the tempeh, searing it in a hot skillet to give it a crisp brown crust. A simple marinade of orange juice, vinegar, and soy sauce made the seared tempeh even more flavorful. Carrots offered a crunchy, sweet element, and cranking the heat to high ensured good caramelization. Napa cabbage can go from crisp-tender to limp and watery in a matter of seconds, so we cooked it just until it achieved a little

Stir-frying the tempeh and vegetables separately ensures that every ingredient is cooked to perfection.

browning and was heated through. Pairing these ingredients with the right sauce took some experimentation. While we knew we wanted the sauce to have an orange flavor, many orange stir-fry sauces were too light to stand up to the heartiness of the tempeh. Full-flavored and full-bodied orange sweet-and-sour sauce tamed the tempeh's slight bitterness. And the sauce's bright acidity complemented the sweet carrots and mild cabbage. Serve with rice.

½ cup orange juice
½ cup red wine vinegar
2 tablespoons soy sauce
12 ounces tempeh, cut into ½-inch pieces
6 tablespoons sugar
4 scallions, white and green parts separated and sliced thin on bias
3 tablespoons ketchup
3 garlic cloves, minced
1 tablespoon grated fresh ginger
1 teaspoon cornstarch
½ teaspoon red pepper flakes

½ teaspoon salt
3 tablespoons vegetable oil
3 carrots, peeled and sliced on bias ¼ inch thick
½ head napa cabbage (about 1 pound), cored and cut into 1½-inch pieces

1. Whisk 2 tablespoons orange juice, 2 tablespoons vinegar, and soy sauce together in bowl. Add tempeh and toss to coat. Cover and refrigerate for 1 hour.

2. In separate bowl, whisk sugar, scallion whites, ketchup, garlic, ginger, cornstarch, pepper flakes, salt, remaining 6 tablespoons orange juice, and remaining 6 tablespoons vinegar together.

3. Remove tempeh from marinade and pat dry with paper towels. Heat 2 tablespoons oil in 12-inch nonstick skillet over high heat until just smoking. Add tempeh and cook, stirring occasionally, until well browned, 4 to 6 minutes; transfer to plate.

4. Heat remaining 1 tablespoon oil in now-empty skillet over high heat until shimmering. Add carrots and cook until spotty brown, about 4 minutes. Stir in cabbage and cook until vegetables are crisp-tender, about 4 minutes.

5. Add browned tempeh and stir to combine. Whisk sauce to recombine, then add to skillet and cook, stirring constantly, until sauce is thickened, about 2 minutes. Transfer to platter, sprinkle with scallion greens, and serve.

TO MAKE AHEAD

Marinated tempeh and sauce, prepared through step 2, can be refrigerated separately for up to 24 hours

Eggplant Involtini
SERVES 4 to 6
ACTIVE TIME 1 HOUR 15 MINUTES
TOTAL TIME 1 HOUR 45 MINUTES

WHY THIS RECIPE WORKS Eggplant involtini is like a lighter and more summery version of eggplant Parmesan, with the flavorful eggplant planks rolled around a creamy ricotta filling. Traditional recipes require a multistep process of salting the eggplant and then breading and frying it before rolling it around a cheesy filling. We decided to skip the breading and instead incorporate the bread crumbs right into the filling. This method allowed the eggplant's flavor and meaty texture to take center stage in the dish, and it let us sidestep the salting and draining step;

without a coating to turn soggy, we could simply bake the eggplant until its excess moisture evaporated. Adding some bold, flavorful Pecorino Romano to the ricotta meant we could use less filling without sacrificing flavor. Lastly, we threw together a simple but bright tomato sauce in a skillet, added the eggplant bundles to it, and finished the dish under the broiler so we could skip dirtying a casserole dish. Select shorter, wider eggplants for this recipe. We like whole-milk ricotta in this recipe, but part-skim may be used. Do not use fat-free ricotta.

2 large eggplants (1½ pounds each), peeled and sliced lengthwise into ½-inch-thick planks (12 planks), end pieces trimmed to lie flat
6 tablespoons vegetable oil
 Kosher salt and pepper
2 garlic cloves, minced
¼ teaspoon dried oregano
 Pinch red pepper flakes
1 (28-ounce) can whole peeled tomatoes, drained, juice reserved, and tomatoes chopped coarse
1 slice hearty white sandwich bread, torn into 1-inch pieces
8 ounces (1 cup) whole-milk ricotta cheese
1½ ounces Pecorino Romano cheese, grated (¾ cup)
¼ cup plus 1 tablespoon chopped fresh basil
1 tablespoon lemon juice

1. Adjust 1 oven rack to lower-middle position and second rack 8 inches from broiler element. Heat oven to 375 degrees. Line 2 rimmed baking sheets with parchment paper and spray generously with vegetable oil spray. Brush both sides of eggplant slices with 2½ tablespoons oil, then season with ½ teaspoon salt and ¼ teaspoon pepper. Flip slices over and repeat on second side with another 2½ tablespoons oil, ½ teaspoon salt, and ¼ teaspoon pepper. Arrange eggplant slices in single layer on prepared baking sheets. Bake until tender and lightly browned, 30 to 35 minutes, switching and rotating sheets halfway through baking. Let eggplant cool for 5 minutes, then flip each slice over using thin spatula.

2. Meanwhile, heat remaining 1 tablespoon oil in 12-inch broiler-safe skillet over medium-low heat until just shimmering. Add garlic, oregano, pepper flakes, and ½ teaspoon salt and cook until fragrant, about 30 seconds. Stir in tomatoes and their juice, increase heat to high, and bring to simmer. Reduce heat to medium-low and simmer until thickened, about 15 minutes. Remove from heat and cover to keep warm.

3. Pulse bread in food processor until finely ground, 10 to 15 pulses. Combine bread crumbs, ricotta, ½ cup Pecorino, ¼ cup basil, lemon juice, and ½ teaspoon salt in bowl.

4. With widest short side of eggplant facing you, spoon about 3 tablespoons ricotta mixture over bottom third of each eggplant slice (use slightly more filling for larger slices and slightly less for smaller slices). Gently roll up each eggplant slice.

5. Heat broiler. Place eggplant rolls seam side down in tomato sauce in skillet. Bring sauce to simmer over medium heat and cook for 5 minutes. Transfer skillet to oven and broil until eggplant is well browned and cheese is heated through, 5 to 10 minutes. Remove from broiler. Sprinkle with remaining ¼ cup Pecorino and let stand 5 minutes. Sprinkle with remaining 1 tablespoon basil and serve.

TO MAKE AHEAD ▶

Cooked sauce and stuffed eggplant, prepared through step 4, can be refrigerated separately for up to 24 hours

PREPARING EGGPLANT INVOLTINI

1. Peel eggplant and slice lengthwise into ½-inch-thick planks.

2. Arrange eggplant slices in single layer on prepared baking sheets and bake until tender and lightly browned, 30 to 35 minutes.

3. Spoon about 3 tablespoons ricotta mixture over wide end of each eggplant slice and gently roll up each eggplant slice.

Scoring and roasting eggplant halves cut side down on a hot baking sheet prepares them for stuffing.

Stuffed Eggplant with Bulgur

SERVES 4

ACTIVE TIME 45 MINUTES

TOTAL TIME 1 HOUR 30 MINUTES

WHY THIS RECIPE WORKS Italian eggplants are the perfect size for stuffing, and they take on a rich, creamy texture when baked. Roasting the eggplants prior to stuffing was the key to preventing them from turning watery and tasteless. The slight caramelizing effect of roasting them on a preheated baking sheet also added depth of flavor. We then let the eggplants drain briefly on paper towels (which got rid of excess liquid) before adding the stuffing. Hearty, nutty bulgur, which requires only soaking before it's ready to eat, made a perfect filling base. Pecorino Romano cheese added richness while tomatoes lent bright flavor and a bit of moisture. Best of all, the eggplants could be prepared and stuffed a day in advance, so all we had to do the next day was bake them. You can use fine-grind bulgur in this recipe, but do not use coarse-grind or cracked-wheat bulgur. The time it takes for the bulgur to become tender and fluffy in step 3 will depend on the age and type of bulgur used.

4 (10-ounce) Italian eggplants, halved lengthwise
2 tablespoons extra-virgin olive oil
Salt and pepper
½ cup medium-grind bulgur, rinsed
¼ cup water
1 onion, chopped fine
3 garlic cloves, minced
2 teaspoons minced fresh oregano or ½ teaspoon dried
¼ teaspoon ground cinnamon
Pinch cayenne pepper
1 pound plum tomatoes, cored, seeded, and chopped
2 ounces Pecorino Romano cheese, grated (1 cup)
2 tablespoons pine nuts, toasted
2 teaspoons red wine vinegar
2 tablespoons minced fresh parsley

1. Adjust oven racks to upper-middle and lowest positions, place parchment paper–lined rimmed baking sheet on lower rack, and heat oven to 400 degrees.

2. Score flesh of each eggplant half in 1-inch diamond pattern, about 1 inch deep. Brush scored sides of eggplant with 1 tablespoon oil and season with salt and pepper. Lay eggplant, cut side down, on hot baking sheet and roast until flesh is tender, 40 to 50 minutes. Transfer eggplant, cut side down, to paper towel–lined baking sheet and let drain. (Do not wash rimmed baking sheet.)

3. Meanwhile, toss bulgur with water in bowl and let sit until grains are tender and fluffy, 20 to 40 minutes.

4. Heat remaining 1 tablespoon oil in 12-inch skillet over medium heat until shimmering. Add onion and cook until softened, about 5 minutes. Stir in garlic, oregano, cinnamon, cayenne, and ½ teaspoon salt and cook until fragrant, about 30 seconds. Stir in soaked bulgur, tomatoes, ¾ cup Pecorino, pine nuts, and vinegar and let warm through, about 1 minute. Season with salt and pepper to taste.

5. Return eggplant, cut side up, to rimmed baking sheet. Using 2 forks, gently push eggplant flesh to sides to make room for filling. Mound bulgur mixture into eggplant halves and pack lightly with back of spoon. Sprinkle with remaining ¼ cup Pecorino.

6. Bake on upper rack until cheese is melted, 5 to 10 minutes. Sprinkle with parsley and serve.

> **TO MAKE AHEAD**
> - Stuffed eggplant, prepared through step 5, can be refrigerated for up to 24 hours
> - To serve, continue with step 6, increasing cooking time to 10 to 12 minutes

Stuffed Acorn Squash with Barley, Fennel, and Sage

SERVES 4
ACTIVE TIME 45 MINUTES
TOTAL TIME 1 HOUR 30 MINUTES

WHY THIS RECIPE WORKS For a simple but elegant stuffed squash recipe, we started with halved acorn squash. To ensure that we achieved both tender squash and a perfectly cooked filling, we roasted the squash on its own until tender and made an easy filling in the meantime. Hearty pearl barley was an ideal base for the filling. While the barley cooked, we sautéed chopped fennel and onion and then folded this mixture into the barley along with pine nuts, Parmesan, herbs, and a splash of sweet, bright balsamic vinegar. We topped the squash with a sprinkle of additional cheese and baked it for just a few minutes to warm it through. Be sure to look for similar-size squash (1½ pounds each) to ensure even cooking. Do not substitute hulled, hull-less, quick-cooking, or presteamed barley (read the ingredient list on the package to determine this) in this recipe.

Pearl barley enhanced with sautéed fennel, buttery pine nuts, and a splash of balsamic makes a hearty filling for squash.

- 3 tablespoons extra-virgin olive oil
- 2 acorn squashes (1½ pounds each), halved pole to pole and seeded
- Salt and pepper
- ¾ cup pearl barley, rinsed
- 1 onion, chopped fine
- 1 fennel bulb, stalks discarded, bulb halved, cored, and chopped fine
- 6 garlic cloves, minced
- 3 tablespoons minced fresh sage
- 2 ounces Parmesan cheese, grated (1 cup)
- 1 tablespoon unsalted butter
- 1 tablespoon balsamic vinegar
- 2 tablespoons pine nuts, toasted
- 1 tablespoon minced fresh parsley

1. Adjust oven racks to upper-middle and lower-middle positions and heat oven to 400 degrees. Line rimmed baking sheet with aluminum foil and grease with 1 tablespoon oil. Brush cut sides of squash with 1 tablespoon oil, season with salt and pepper, and lay cut side down on prepared baking sheet. Roast on lower rack until tender (paring knife can be slipped into flesh with no resistance), 45 to 55 minutes. Remove squash from oven and increase oven temperature to 450 degrees.

2. Meanwhile, bring 3 quarts water to boil in large saucepan. Stir in barley and ¼ teaspoon salt. Return to boil, then reduce to simmer and cook until barley is tender, 20 to 25 minutes; drain.

3. Wipe now-empty saucepan dry, add remaining 1 tablespoon oil, and heat over medium heat until shimmering. Add onion, fennel, and 1 teaspoon salt and cook until softened, about 10 minutes. Stir in garlic and sage and cook until fragrant, about 30 seconds. Off heat, stir in cooked barley, ¾ cup Parmesan, butter, and vinegar. Season with salt and pepper to taste.

4. Flip roasted squash over and scoop out flesh, leaving ⅛-inch thickness of flesh in each shell. Gently fold squash flesh into barley mixture. Spoon mixture into squash shells, mounding it slightly, and sprinkle with remaining ¼ cup Parmesan.

5. Bake on upper rack until cheese is lightly browned, 5 to 10 minutes. Sprinkle with pine nuts and parsley and serve.

> **TO MAKE AHEAD**
> - Stuffed acorn squash, prepared through step 4, can be refrigerated for up to 24 hours
> - To serve, continue with step 5, increasing cooking time to 15 to 20 minutes

This simplified take on traditional *chiles rellenos* relies on roasted poblanos with a cheesy pinto bean stuffing.

Cheesy Stuffed Poblanos

SERVES 4 to 6
ACTIVE TIME 50 MINUTES
TOTAL TIME 1 HOUR 20 MINUTES

WHY THIS RECIPE WORKS Inspired by the Mexican dish *chiles rellenos*, we set out to make a recipe for cheesy stuffed poblano peppers. Chiles rellenos are traditionally poblano peppers that are stuffed with cheese and then battered and fried. We felt the bright, vegetal flavor of the pepper was lost during frying (not to mention we didn't want to contend with the mess that frying created), and most of the cheese fillings we came across were bland and oozed out of the pepper during cooking. To fix these problems, we first decided to roast the stuffed peppers to deepen their flavor and tenderize the peppers. Stuffing raw poblanos without tearing them was tricky, but after a quick stint in the microwave, they were more pliable. To improve our filling's flavor and to anchor the cheese in the peppers during roasting, we added a couple of cans of pinto beans (half of which we mashed), corn, garlic, onion, and spices to a combination of Monterey Jack and cheddar cheeses.

2 (15-ounce) cans pinto beans, rinsed
1 cup water
1 tablespoon vegetable oil
1 onion, chopped fine
4 garlic cloves, minced
1 tablespoon ground cumin
1 tablespoon minced fresh oregano or 1 teaspoon dried
1 teaspoon chili powder
1 teaspoon grated lime zest plus 1 tablespoon juice
 Salt and pepper
⅛ teaspoon cayenne pepper
2 cups frozen corn
4 ounces Monterey Jack cheese, shredded (1 cup)
4 ounces sharp cheddar cheese, shredded (1 cup)
¼ cup minced fresh cilantro
8 poblano chiles
1 recipe Easy Cherry Tomato Salsa (page 260)

1. Adjust oven racks to upper-middle and lower-middle positions and heat oven to 425 degrees. Line 2 rimmed baking sheets with aluminum foil and set wire rack in each. Using potato masher, mash half of beans and water together in bowl until mostly smooth.

2. Heat oil in 12-inch nonstick skillet over medium heat until shimmering. Add onion and cook until softened, about 5 minutes. Stir in garlic, cumin, oregano, chili powder, lime zest, ½ teaspoon salt, and cayenne and cook until fragrant, about 30 seconds. Stir in mashed bean mixture and cook, stirring constantly, until nearly all liquid has evaporated, 3 to 5 minutes. Stir in remaining beans and corn and cook until warmed through, about 2 minutes. Off heat, stir in Monterey Jack, cheddar, cilantro, and lime juice. Season with salt and pepper to taste.

3. Leaving stem intact, cut slit lengthwise down 1 side of each poblano. Microwave poblanos in covered bowl until just pliable, about 2½ minutes. Gently pry open poblanos, remove seeds, and stuff evenly with bean-cheese mixture.

4. Lay poblanos, stuffed side up, on prepared sheets. Bake until tender, 30 to 40 minutes, switching and rotating sheets halfway through baking. Serve with salsa.

> **TO MAKE AHEAD** ▶
>
> Stuffed poblanos, prepared through step 3, can be refrigerated for up to 24 hours

We use canned tomatillos in our green enchilada sauce to ensure a consistent texture and bright flavor.

Roasted Poblano and Black Bean Enchiladas

SERVES 4 to 6
ACTIVE TIME 1 HOUR
TOTAL TIME 2 HOURS

WHY THIS RECIPE WORKS For truly great vegetarian enchiladas, we wanted a bright, rich green enchilada sauce featuring the sweet-tart flavor of tomatillos. We tried using fresh tomatillos but found that their quality depended largely on the season. Even after roasting, the mealy texture and watery flavor of out-of-season tomatillos was underwhelming. Instead we turned to canned tomatillos, which promised consistent flavor and texture throughout the year without any of the prep work, making our sauce as easy as turning on a food processor. We rounded out the sauce with onion, garlic, cilantro, and lime juice. For the filling, we started with spicy, fruity roasted poblano chiles. Then we smashed some of our canned black beans to create a quick "refried" bean base and stirred in a little of the tomatillo sauce, Monterey Jack cheese, and some classic seasonings, which we bloomed on the stovetop with basic aromatics.

4 poblano chiles
2 (11-ounce) cans tomatillos, drained
2 onions, chopped fine
1 cup fresh cilantro leaves
½ cup vegetable broth
¼ cup vegetable oil
5 garlic cloves, peeled (3 whole, 2 minced)
1 tablespoon lime juice
1 teaspoon sugar
Salt and pepper
1 (15-ounce) can black beans, rinsed
1 teaspoon chili powder
½ teaspoon ground coriander
½ teaspoon ground cumin
8 ounces Monterey Jack cheese, shredded (2 cups)
12 (6-inch) corn tortillas
Vegetable oil spray

1. Adjust oven rack 6 inches from broiler element and heat broiler. Place poblanos on aluminum foil–lined rimmed baking sheet and broil, turning as needed, until skins are charred, 15 to 20 minutes. Transfer poblanos to large bowl, cover with plastic wrap, and let steam for 5 minutes. Remove skins, stems, and seeds, then chop poblanos into ½-inch pieces. Reduce oven temperature to 400 degrees and adjust oven rack to middle position.

2. Process tomatillos, 1 cup onion, ½ cup cilantro, broth, 1 tablespoon oil, 3 whole garlic cloves, lime juice, sugar, and 1 teaspoon salt in food processor until sauce is smooth, about 2 minutes, scraping down sides of bowl as needed. Season with salt and pepper to taste.

3. Mash half of beans in large bowl with potato masher or fork until mostly smooth. Heat 1 tablespoon oil in 12-inch skillet over medium heat until shimmering. Add remaining onion and cook until softened and lightly browned, 5 to 7 minutes. Stir in remaining 2 cloves minced garlic, chili powder, coriander, and cumin and cook until fragrant, about 30 seconds. Stir in chopped poblanos, mashed beans, and remaining whole beans and cook until warmed through, about 2 minutes.

4. Transfer bean mixture to large bowl and stir in 1 cup Monterey Jack and remaining ½ cup cilantro. Season with salt and pepper to taste. Brush both sides of tortillas with remaining 2 tablespoons oil. Stack tortillas, wrap in damp dish towel, and place on plate; microwave until warm and pliable, about 1 minute.

5. Working with 1 warm tortilla at a time, spread ⅓ cup bean-cheese filling across center of tortilla. Roll tortilla tightly around filling and place, seam side down, in greased 13 by 9-inch baking dish; arrange enchiladas in 2 columns across width of dish.

6. Spray top of enchiladas with oil spray and bake uncovered until lightly toasted on top, 10 to 15 minutes. Pour 2 cups sauce evenly over enchiladas, then sprinkle remaining 1 cup Monterey Jack across center of enchiladas. Cover dish tightly with greased aluminum foil and bake until enchiladas are hot throughout, bubbling around edges, and cheese is melted, 20 to 25 minutes. Let cool for 5 minutes. Serve, passing remaining sauce.

TO MAKE AHEAD ▸

- Enchiladas and sauce, prepared through step 5, can be refrigerated separately for up to 24 hours
- To cook, bring sauce to room temperature, whisk well, and continue with step 6

Vegetable Pot Pie

SERVES 4 TO 6
ACTIVE TIME 1 HOUR
TOTAL TIME 1 HOUR 50 MINUTES

WHY THIS RECIPE WORKS We wanted a vegetable pot pie that featured a rich gravy, a tender crust, and a hearty combination of vegetables. Choosing longer-cooking vegetables was important to ensure they didn't overcook; mushrooms, sweet potato, turnip, and Swiss chard worked well. So that each vegetable came out tender, we sautéed the mushrooms, sweet potato, and turnip before stirring in the chard. The vegetables left behind flavorful fond that we incorporated into the sauce, lending it deep, complex flavor. We were glad to find that we could do the work in advance and hold the assembled pot pie in the fridge for up to two days before baking. You can use our homemade Foolproof Single-Crust Pie Dough (page 370) or store-bought pie dough in this recipe. If using store-bought dough, you will still need to roll the dough into a 10-inch circle. Cremini mushrooms are also known as baby bella mushrooms.

- 1 recipe Foolproof Single-Crust Pie Dough (page 370)
- 4 tablespoons unsalted butter
- 1 onion, chopped fine
- 8 ounces cremini mushrooms, trimmed and halved if small or quartered if large
  Salt and pepper
- 1 sweet potato (12 ounces), peeled and cut into ½-inch pieces
- 8 ounces turnips, peeled and cut into ½-inch pieces
- 3 garlic cloves, minced
- ½ teaspoon grated lemon zest plus 1 tablespoon juice
- 8 ounces Swiss chard, stemmed and cut into 1-inch pieces
- 2 tablespoons all-purpose flour
- 2 cups vegetable broth
- 1 ounce Parmesan cheese, grated (½ cup)

- 2 tablespoons minced fresh parsley
- 1 large egg
- 1 teaspoon water

1. Roll dough between 2 large sheets parchment paper into 10-inch circle, flouring as needed. Remove parchment on top of dough. Fold over outer ½-inch edge of dough, then crimp into tidy fluted edge using your fingers. Using paring knife, cut four 2-inch, oval-shaped vents in center. Slide parchment paper with crust onto baking sheet and refrigerate until needed.

2. Meanwhile, adjust oven rack to middle position and heat oven to 400 degrees. Melt 2 tablespoons butter in Dutch oven over medium heat. Add onion, mushrooms, and ½ teaspoon salt and cook until mushrooms have released their liquid, about 5 minutes.

3. Stir in sweet potato and turnips. Reduce heat to medium-low, cover, and cook, stirring occasionally, until potato and turnips begin to soften around edges, 7 to 9 minutes. Stir in garlic and lemon zest and cook until fragrant, about 30 seconds. Stir in chard and cook until wilted, about 2 minutes; transfer to bowl.

4. Melt remaining 2 tablespoons butter in now-empty pot over medium-high heat. Stir in flour and cook for 1 minute. Gradually whisk in broth, scraping up any browned bits and smoothing out any lumps. Bring to simmer and cook until sauce thickens

MAKING A POT PIE CRUST

1. After rolling dough into 10-inch circle, fold over outer ½-inch edge of dough.

2. Crimp edge into tidy fluted edge using your fingers.

3. Using paring knife, cut four 2-inch, oval-shaped vents in center.

slightly, about 1 minute. Off heat, whisk in Parmesan, parsley, lemon juice, and ½ teaspoon salt. Stir in cooked vegetables, along with any accumulated juices, and season with salt and pepper to taste. Transfer filling to 9½-inch deep-dish pie plate set on aluminum foil–lined rimmed baking sheet. Place chilled crust on top.

5. Lightly beat egg, water, and pinch salt together in bowl, then brush over crust. Bake until crust is deep golden brown and filling is bubbling, about 30 minutes. Let cool for 20 minutes before serving.

TO MAKE AHEAD

- Pot pie, prepared through step 4, can be refrigerated for up to 2 days; let filling cool to room temperature in pie plate before topping with chilled crust
- To bake, continue with step 5, increasing baking time to 1 hour; cover loosely with aluminum foil if crust becomes too dark

Vegetable and Bean Tamale Pie

SERVES 6 to 8 **FREEZE IT**

ACTIVE TIME 1 HOUR

TOTAL TIME 2 HOURS

WHY THIS RECIPE WORKS We wanted to develop a vegetarian tamale pie with an ultraflavorful filling and tender cornbread topping. The slightly sweet cornbread was a perfect foil to our spicy filling, and we were happy to find that it held up well to being refrigerated or frozen before being baked. For a hearty and satisfying filling, we turned to a combination of black and kidney beans, fresh zucchini, and corn. Chipotle chiles in adobo sauce added smoky flavor. Stirring the cheese into the filling instead of sprinkling it on top kept it moist and thickened it perfectly. You can substitute two 6.5- to 8.5-ounce packages of cornbread mix for the homemade cornbread topping; mix the batter according to the package instructions and dollop over the pie as directed in step 3. To make the filling spicier, add the larger amount of chipotle.

FILLING

- 3 tablespoons vegetable oil
- 1 onion, chopped fine
  Salt and pepper
- 2 (28-ounce) cans diced tomatoes, drained with 2 cups juice reserved
- 2 teaspoons sugar
- 2 tablespoons chili powder
- 4 garlic cloves, minced
- 2–4 teaspoons minced chipotle chile in adobo sauce
- 2 teaspoons minced fresh oregano or 1 teaspoon dried

A lightly sweet cornbread topping is the perfect complement to our spicy vegetarian tamale pie filling.

- 1 teaspoon ground cumin
- 1 (15-ounce) can black beans, rinsed
- 1 (15-ounce) can kidney or pinto beans, rinsed
- 1½ cups frozen corn
- 1 zucchini, cut into ½-inch cubes
- 8 ounces Monterey Jack cheese, shredded (2 cups)
- ¼ cup minced fresh cilantro
- 4 teaspoons lime juice

CORNBREAD

- 1½ cups (7½ ounces) all-purpose flour
- 1 cup (5 ounces) yellow cornmeal
- 6 tablespoons (2⅔ ounces) sugar
- 2 teaspoons baking powder
- ¼ teaspoon baking soda
- ¾ teaspoon salt
- 1 cup buttermilk
- 8 tablespoons unsalted butter, melted and cooled
- 2 large eggs, lightly beaten

1. FOR THE FILLING Adjust oven rack to middle position and heat oven to 375 degrees. Heat oil in large Dutch oven over medium-high heat until shimmering. Add onion and ½ teaspoon salt and cook until softened and lightly browned, 5 to 7 minutes. Stir in tomatoes and sugar and cook, stirring often, until tomatoes are very dry and browned, 10 to 15 minutes.

2. Stir in chili powder, garlic, chipotle, oregano, and cumin and cook until fragrant, about 1 minute. Stir in reserved tomato juice, scraping up any browned bits. Off heat, stir in black beans, kidney beans, corn, zucchini, Monterey Jack, cilantro, and lime juice and season with salt and pepper to taste. Transfer bean mixture to 13 by 9-inch baking dish.

3. FOR THE CORNBREAD Whisk flour, cornmeal, sugar, baking powder, salt, and baking soda together in large bowl. In separate bowl, whisk buttermilk, butter, and eggs together. Stir buttermilk mixture into flour mixture until uniform. Spread topping evenly over filling, pushing it to edges of baking dish.

4. Bake until filling is bubbly and crust is golden, about 45 minutes. Let cool for 10 minutes before serving.

TO MAKE AHEAD ▶

- Casserole, prepared through step 3, can be refrigerated for up to 2 days; to bake, continue with step 4, increasing baking time 50 to 60 minutes
- Casserole, prepared through step 3, can be frozen for up to 1 month; to bake, unwrap and let sit at room temperature for 30 minutes, cover tightly with aluminum foil and bake for 30 minutes, then remove foil and bake until filling is bubbly and crust is golden, 50 to 60 minutes

Rustic Polenta Casserole with Mushrooms and Swiss Chard

SERVES 6 TO 8
ACTIVE TIME 1 HOUR 15 MINUTES
TOTAL TIME 1 HOUR 40 MINUTES

WHY THIS RECIPE WORKS For a hearty vegetarian polenta casserole, we turned to meaty-tasting mushrooms, which we sautéed until all their liquid evaporated and they were well browned. Garlic and thyme added depth of flavor, and simmering tomatoes with the mushrooms ensured we didn't lose any of the flavorful fond developed while cooking the mushrooms. To bulk up this dish and add a bright vegetal flavor, we used Swiss chard, which we cooked briefly in the skillet to take away its raw bite, counting on the oven to cook the chard the rest of the way. Sprinkled with flavorful fontina cheese to finish, this casserole made a satisfying vegetarian main course.

5 cups water
1⅓ cups whole milk
Salt and pepper

Polenta, a classic comfort food, makes a meal when topped with sautéed vegetables and cheese and baked.

1 cup coarse-ground polenta
2 ounces Parmesan cheese, grated (1 cup)
3 tablespoons unsalted butter
3 tablespoons extra-virgin olive oil
1 onion, chopped fine
1 pound white mushrooms, trimmed and sliced
3 garlic cloves, minced
1 tablespoon minced fresh thyme or 1 teaspoon dried
1 (28-ounce) can diced tomatoes
8 ounces Swiss chard, stemmed and cut into 1-inch pieces
4 ounces fontina cheese, shredded (1 cup)

1. Bring water and milk to boil in large saucepan over medium-high heat. Stir in 1 teaspoon salt, then very slowly pour polenta into boiling liquid while stirring constantly in circular motion with wooden spoon. Reduce to gentle simmer, cover partially, and cook, stirring often and making sure to scrape bottom and sides of pot clean, until polenta no longer has raw cornmeal taste, all liquid has been absorbed, and mixture has uniformly smooth but very loose consistency, 15 to 20 minutes.

2. Off heat, stir in Parmesan and butter and season with salt and pepper to taste. Pour polenta into 13 by 9-inch baking dish and let set up slightly while preparing topping.

3. Adjust oven rack to middle position and heat oven to 400 degrees. Heat oil in 12-inch skillet over medium heat until shimmering. Add onion and ½ teaspoon salt and cook until softened, about 5 minutes. Add mushrooms and cook until mushrooms have released their liquid and are well browned, about 15 minutes. Stir in garlic and thyme and cook until fragrant, about 30 seconds.

4. Stir in tomatoes and their juice, bring to simmer, and cook, stirring occasionally, until sauce has thickened, about 10 minutes. Stir in chard, 1 handful at a time, and cook until wilted, 2 to 4 minutes. Season with salt and pepper to taste. Spread mushroom mixture evenly over polenta.

5. Sprinkle fontina evenly over top. Bake until hot throughout and cheese is melted, about 20 minutes. Let cool for 5 minutes. Serve.

TO MAKE AHEAD ▶

- Casserole, prepared through step 4, can be refrigerated for up to 24 hours
- To bake, cover with aluminum foil and bake in 400-degree oven until bubbling at edges, about 30 minutes, then remove foil, sprinkle with fontina, and bake until cheese melts, 10 to 15 minutes

Farro, White Bean, and Broccoli Rabe Gratin

SERVES 6
ACTIVE TIME 1 HOUR
TOTAL TIME 1 HOUR 10 MINUTES

WHY THIS RECIPE WORKS For this recipe, we set out to create a new kind of casserole, one featuring a whole grain that was both hearty and healthy. We chose Italian flavors, accenting nutty farro with creamy white beans, slightly bitter broccoli rabe, and savory Parmesan. Toasting the farro in the aromatics and oil gave it some extra nuttiness and jump-started the cooking process, making the end result more evenly cooked. We liked small white beans in this dish, as they blended in nicely with the farro while giving it some creaminess and added protein. Blanching the broccoli rabe in salted water tamed its bitterness. We then sautéed it with garlic and pepper flakes for extra flavor. Sun-dried tomatoes gave us the extra pop of flavor we were after. A dusting of Parmesan over the top and a quick stint under the broiler gave this gratin a browned, savory crust. Making this hearty and healthy dinner ahead was

Toasting farro with the aromatics deepens its naturally nutty flavor and jump-starts the cooking process.

simple, as we could assemble the casserole and bake it the next day. We prefer the flavor and texture of whole farro; pearled farro can be used, but the texture may be softer. Do not use quick-cooking or presteamed farro (read the ingredient list on the package to determine this) in this recipe. The cooking time for farro can vary greatly among different brands, so we recommend beginning to check for doneness after 10 minutes.

2 tablespoons extra-virgin olive oil, plus extra for serving
1 onion, chopped fine
   Salt and pepper
1½ cups whole farro, rinsed
2 cups vegetable broth
1½ cups water
4 ounces Parmesan cheese, grated (2 cups)
1 pound broccoli rabe, trimmed and cut into 2-inch lengths
6 garlic cloves, minced
⅛ teaspoon red pepper flakes
1 (15-ounce) can small white beans, rinsed
½ cup oil-packed sun-dried tomatoes, chopped

1. Heat 1 tablespoon oil in large saucepan over medium heat until shimmering. Add onion and ½ teaspoon salt and cook until softened and lightly browned, 5 to 7 minutes. Stir in farro and cook until lightly toasted, about 2 minutes. Stir in broth and water and bring to simmer. Reduce heat to low and continue to simmer, stirring often, until farro is just tender and liquid has thickened into creamy sauce, 20 to 25 minutes. Off heat, stir in 1 cup Parmesan and season with salt and pepper to taste.

2. Meanwhile, bring 4 quarts water to boil in Dutch oven. Add broccoli rabe and 1 tablespoon salt and cook until just tender, about 2 minutes. Drain broccoli rabe and transfer to bowl.

3. Wipe now-empty Dutch oven dry. Add remaining 1 tablespoon oil, garlic, and pepper flakes and cook over medium heat until fragrant and sizzling, 1 to 2 minutes. Stir in drained broccoli rabe and cook until hot and well coated, about 2 minutes. Off heat, stir in beans, sun-dried tomatoes, and farro mixture. Season with salt and pepper to taste. Pour bean-farro mixture into 3-quart broiler-safe casserole dish.

4. Position oven rack 6 inches from broiler element and heat broiler. Sprinkle casserole with remaining 1 cup Parmesan. Broil until lightly browned and hot, 3 to 5 minutes. Let cool for 5 minutes and serve, passing extra oil separately.

> **TO MAKE AHEAD**
> - Gratin, prepared through step 3, can be refrigerated for up to 24 hours
> - To serve, stir ½ cup water into gratin, cover with aluminum foil, and bake in 400-degree oven on upper-middle rack until hot throughout, about 30 minutes, before continuing with step 4

Zucchini Tart

SERVES 4 TO 6 **EASY**

ACTIVE TIME 20 MINUTES

TOTAL TIME 1 HOUR 20 MINUTES

WHY THIS RECIPE WORKS Fresh vegetable tarts sound promising, but often recipes yield soggy crusts and fillings with very little flavor. We set out to develop a simple recipe with a flavorful and foolproof crust, a creamy base, and a topping of perfectly cooked slices of zucchini. To ensure that the zucchini slices didn't leach moisture into the tart, we salted them and let them drain for half an hour on paper towels. We combined a trio of cheeses—Parmesan, ricotta, and mozzarella—with olive oil into a base layer to go under the zucchini. Then all we had to do was spread the cheese mixture over the bottom of the baked tart shell, shingle the zucchini slices on top, and bake the tart until the zucchini was slightly wilted. Drizzling the zucchini with a mixture of olive oil and minced garlic

before baking kept it from drying out and infused it with flavor. We prefer the light flavor of part-skim ricotta here, but whole-milk ricotta can be substituted; do not use fat-free ricotta.

- 1 large zucchini, sliced into ¼-inch-thick rounds
  Salt and pepper
- 4 ounces (½ cup) part-skim ricotta cheese
- 1 ounce Parmesan cheese, grated (½ cup)
- 1 ounce mozzarella cheese, shredded (¼ cup)
- ¼ cup extra-virgin olive oil
- 1 recipe Press-In Tart Dough (page 282), baked and cooled
- 1 garlic clove, minced
- 2 tablespoons chopped fresh basil

1. Spread zucchini out over several layers of paper towels, sprinkle with ½ teaspoon salt, and let drain for 30 minutes. In bowl, combine ricotta, Parmesan, mozzarella, and 1 tablespoon oil, and season with salt and pepper to taste.

2. Adjust oven rack to middle position and heat oven to 425 degrees. Spread ricotta mixture evenly over bottom of tart shell. Blot zucchini dry with paper towels and shingle attractively on top of ricotta in concentric circles.

3. Combine 2 tablespoons oil and garlic in small bowl and brush over zucchini. Bake tart on rimmed baking sheet until bubbling and zucchini is slightly wilted, 20 to 25 minutes, rotating sheet halfway through baking.

4. Let tart cool on baking sheet for at least 10 minutes. To serve, remove outer metal ring of tart pan, slide thin metal spatula between tart and tart pan bottom, and carefully slide tart onto serving platter or cutting board. Sprinkle with basil and drizzle with remaining 1 tablespoon oil before serving.

> **TO MAKE AHEAD**
> - Tart, prepared through step 2, can be refrigerated for up to 24 hours
> - Alternatively, baked tart can be stored at room temperature for up to 4 hours before serving

MAKING A ZUCCHINI TART

Blot zucchini dry with paper towels and shingle attractively on top of ricotta in concentric circles.

Wedges of Camembert cheese are the star of this tart; as the tart bakes, the cheese melts and binds the filling together.

Camembert, Sun-Dried Tomato, and Potato Tart

SERVES 4 TO 6
ACTIVE TIME 40 MINUTES
TOTAL TIME 1 HOUR 15 MINUTES

WHY THIS RECIPE WORKS The inspiration for this tart came from a French dish of cheese, bacon, and potatoes called *tartiflette*. A wheel of soft, melty cheese is the star of this dish. The wheel is sliced through the middle, cut into wedges, then arranged cut side down over the tart. As the tart bakes, the rind forms a crisp crust and the cheese melts out over the filling and into the crevices, binding the potatoes and crust together. We chose creamy, pungent Camembert for the cheese and swapped out the usual bacon for sun-dried tomatoes. Their concentrated, salty-sweet flavor and satisfying texture worked perfectly with the rich cheese and

buttery crust. For the potatoes, we sliced Yukon Gold potatoes and browned them in a skillet before spreading them in the tart shell and topping them with the cheese. If you can't find a wheel of Camembert, look for wedges that you can slice in half. Depending on the ripeness and style of the cheese used, the cheese may melt less and range in mildness of flavor.

2 tablespoons unsalted butter
1 onion, halved and sliced ¼ inch thick
1 pound Yukon Gold potatoes, peeled and sliced ¼ inch thick
2 teaspoons minced fresh thyme
   Salt and pepper
½ cup oil-packed sun-dried tomatoes, rinsed, patted dry, and chopped coarse
1 recipe Press-In Tart Dough (page 282), baked and cooled
1 (8-ounce) wheel Camembert cheese

1. Adjust oven rack to middle position and heat oven to 375 degrees. Melt butter in 12-inch nonstick skillet over medium heat. Add onion and cook, stirring often, until golden brown, about 10 minutes. Stir in potatoes, thyme, 1 teaspoon salt, and ¼ teaspoon pepper and cook, stirring occasionally, until potatoes are completely tender and lightly browned, 8 to 10 minutes. Stir in sun-dried tomatoes.

2. Spread potato mixture evenly into tart shell. Cut Camembert wheel in half horizontally to make 2 thin wheels, then cut each half into 4 wedges. Arrange wedges of cheese, rind side up, over top of tart.

3. Bake tart on rimmed baking sheet until golden and cheese is melted and bubbling, 25 to 35 minutes, rotating sheet halfway through baking.

4. Let tart cool on baking sheet for at least 10 minutes. To serve, remove outer metal ring of tart pan, slide thin metal spatula between tart and tart pan bottom, and carefully slide tart onto serving platter or cutting board. Serve warm.

TO MAKE AHEAD

- Assembled tart, prepared through step 2, can be refrigerated for up to 24 hours
- Alternatively, baked tart can be held at room temperature for 4 hours; to serve, reheat in 400-degree for 5 to 10 minutes

PRESS-IN TART DOUGH

MAKES ENOUGH FOR ONE 9-INCH TART **EASY** **FREEZE IT**
ACTIVE TIME 25 MINUTES
TOTAL TIME 1 HOUR 30 MINUTES

1¼ cups (6¼ ounces) all-purpose flour
 1 tablespoon sugar
 ½ teaspoon salt
 8 tablespoons unsalted butter, cut into ½-inch cubes
   and chilled
2–4 tablespoons ice water

1. Spray 9-inch tart pan with removable bottom with vegetable oil spray. Pulse flour, sugar, and salt in food processor until combined, about 4 pulses. Scatter butter pieces over top and pulse until mixture resembles coarse sand, about 15 pulses. Add 2 tablespoons ice water and continue to process until clumps of dough just begin to form and no powdery bits remain, about 5 seconds. If dough doesn't clump, add remaining ice water, 1 tablespoon at a time, and pulse to incorporate, about 4 pulses.

2. Press two-thirds dough into bottom of prepared pan. Press remaining one-third dough into fluted sides of pan. Lay plastic wrap over dough and smooth out any bumps or shallow areas using your fingertips. Place pan on plate and freeze dough until firm, about 30 minutes. Meanwhile, adjust oven rack to middle position and heat oven to 375 degrees.

3. Place frozen tart shell on rimmed baking sheet. Gently press piece of greased aluminum foil against dough and over edges of tart pan. Fill tart pan with pie weights and bake until top edge of dough just starts to color and surface of dough no longer looks wet, about 30 minutes.

4. Remove sheet from oven and carefully remove foil and weights. Return sheet to oven and continue to bake until tart shell is golden brown, 5 to 10 minutes. Set sheet with tart shell on wire rack and let cool.

▶ TO MAKE AHEAD

- Dough, prepared through step 1, can be refrigerated for up to 2 days or frozen for up to 1 month; let chilled/frozen dough sit on counter until very soft before using
- Unbaked dough-lined tart pan can be frozen for up to 1 month
- Fully baked crust can be held at room temperature for up to 2 days

MAKING A PRESS-IN TART DOUGH

1. Press two-thirds dough into bottom of prepared pan.

2. Press remaining one-third dough into fluted sides of pan.

3. Lay plastic wrap over dough and smooth out any bumps or shallow areas using your fingertips.

Fennel, Olive, and Goat Cheese Tarts

SERVES 4
ACTIVE TIME 45 MINUTES
TOTAL TIME 1 HOUR 10 MINUTES

WHY THIS RECIPE WORKS We wanted to make elegant yet easy tarts inspired by the flavors of the Mediterranean. Using store-bought puff pastry for the tart crust kept the recipe simple. For the filling, fresh fennel and briny cured olives made a light but bold combination. Tangy goat cheese thinned with olive oil and brightened with fresh basil helped bind the vegetables and pastry together. Parbaking the pastry without the weight of the filling allowed it to puff up nicely. To keep the filling firmly in place, we cut a border around the edges of the baked crusts and lightly pressed down on the centers to make neat beds for the cheese and vegetables. To thaw frozen puff pastry, let it sit either in the refrigerator for 24 hours or on the counter for about 1 hour.

1 (9½ by 9-inch) sheet puff pastry, thawed and cut in half
3 tablespoons extra-virgin olive oil
1 large fennel bulb, stalks discarded, bulb halved, cored, and sliced thin

3 garlic cloves, minced
½ cup dry white wine
½ cup pitted oil-cured black olives, chopped
1 teaspoon grated lemon zest plus 1 tablespoon juice
Salt and pepper
8 ounces goat cheese, softened
5 tablespoons chopped fresh basil

1. Adjust oven rack to middle position and heat oven to 425 degrees. Lay puff pastry halves on parchment paper–lined baking sheet and poke all over with fork. Bake pastry until puffed and golden brown, about 15 minutes, rotating baking sheet halfway through baking. Using tip of paring knife, cut ½-inch-wide border around top edge of each pastry, then press centers down with your fingertips.

2. Meanwhile, heat 1 tablespoon oil in 12-inch skillet over medium-high heat until shimmering. Add fennel and cook until softened and browned, about 10 minutes. Stir in garlic and cook until fragrant, 30 seconds. Add wine, cover, and cook for 5 minutes. Uncover and cook until liquid has evaporated and fennel is very soft, 3 to 5 minutes. Off heat, stir in olives and lemon juice and season with salt and pepper to taste.

3. Mix goat cheese, ¼ cup basil, remaining 2 tablespoons oil, lemon zest, and ¼ teaspoon pepper together in bowl, then spread evenly over center of pastry shells. Spoon fennel mixture over top.

4. Bake tarts until cheese is heated through and crust is deep golden, 5 to 7 minutes. Sprinkle with remaining 1 tablespoon basil and serve.

TO MAKE AHEAD
- Baked pastry crust, prepared through step 1, can be stored at room temperature for up to 24 hours
- Assembled tart, prepared through step 3, can be held at room temperature for 2 hours before continuing with step 4

Mushroom and Leek Galette

SERVES 4 to 6 **FREEZE IT**

ACTIVE TIME 1 HOUR 30 MINUTES
TOTAL TIME 4 HOURS

WHY THIS RECIPE WORKS Many free-form vegetable tart recipes simply borrow a standard pastry dough intended for fruit, but vegetables are more prone to leaking liquid into the crust or falling apart when the tart is sliced. We needed a crust that was extra-sturdy and boasted a complex flavor of its own. We also wanted a robust-tasting filling featuring the classic combination of meaty mushrooms and sweet leeks. To give the crust earthy flavor and a hearty crumb, we added some whole-wheat flour. To keep the

A sturdy crust made with whole-wheat flour is the ideal foil for the savory mushrooms and sweet leeks in the filling.

dough tender, we took a hands-off approach to mixing; we just barely mixed the dry and wet ingredients together, and then rested the dough briefly before rolling it out. We gave the dough a series of folds to create numerous layers, which punched up its flaky texture and created more structure. To remove moisture from the vegetables, we microwaved and drained the mushrooms and browned the leeks on the stovetop. Finally, we made a rich binder with crème fraîche, Dijon mustard, and crumbled Gorgonzola. An equal amount of rye flour can be substituted for the whole-wheat flour. Cutting a few small holes in the dough prevents it from lifting off the pan as it bakes. If you do not have a baking stone, you can use a preheated rimless (or inverted) baking sheet.

DOUGH
1¼ cups (6¼ ounces) all-purpose flour
½ cup (2¾ ounces) whole-wheat flour
1 tablespoon sugar
¾ teaspoon salt
10 tablespoons unsalted butter, cut into ½-inch pieces and chilled
7 tablespoons ice water
1 teaspoon distilled white vinegar

FILLING

1¼ pounds shiitake mushrooms, stemmed and sliced thin
5 teaspoons extra-virgin olive oil
1 pound leeks, white and light green parts only, halved lengthwise, sliced ½ inch thick, and washed thoroughly (3 cups)
1 teaspoon minced fresh thyme
2 tablespoons crème fraîche
1 tablespoon Dijon mustard
  Salt and pepper
3 ounces Gorgonzola cheese, crumbled (¾ cup)
1 large egg, lightly beaten
1 tablespoon minced fresh parsley

1. FOR THE DOUGH Pulse all-purpose flour, whole-wheat flour, sugar, and salt in food processor until combined, 2 to 3 pulses. Add butter and pulse until pea-size pieces form, about 10 pulses; transfer to medium bowl. Sprinkle water and vinegar over top. With rubber spatula, use folding motion to mix until loose, shaggy mass forms with some dry flour remaining (do not overwork). Transfer mixture to center of large sheet of plastic wrap, press gently into rough 4-inch square, and wrap tightly. Refrigerate for at least 45 minutes.

2. Transfer dough to lightly floured counter. Roll into 11 by 8-inch rectangle, with short side of rectangle parallel to edge of counter. Using bench scraper, bring bottom third of dough up over middle third, then fold upper third over it, folding like business letter. Turn dough 90 degrees counterclockwise, then roll again into 11 by 8-inch rectangle and fold again into thirds. Turn dough 90 degrees counterclockwise and repeat rolling and folding into thirds. After last fold, fold dough in half to create 4-inch square. Press top of dough gently to seal. Wrap in plastic wrap and refrigerate for at least 45 minutes.

3. FOR THE FILLING Microwave mushrooms in covered bowl until just tender, 3 to 5 minutes. Transfer to colander to drain, then return to bowl. Meanwhile, heat 1 tablespoon oil in 12-inch skillet over medium heat until shimmering. Add leeks and thyme, cover, and cook, stirring occasionally, until leeks are tender and beginning to brown, 5 to 7 minutes. Transfer to bowl with mushrooms. Stir in crème fraîche and mustard and season with salt and pepper to taste. Set aside.

4. Adjust oven rack to lower-middle position, place baking stone on rack, and heat oven to 400 degrees. Remove dough from refrigerator and let stand at room temperature for 15 to 20 minutes. Roll out on generously floured counter to 14-inch circle; trim edges as needed. Transfer dough to parchment paper–lined rimmed baking sheet. Using drinking straw, punch out five ¼-inch circles in dough (one at center and four evenly spaced midway from center to edge of dough). Brush top of dough with 1 teaspoon oil.

5. Spread half of filling evenly over dough, leaving 2-inch border around edge. Sprinkle with half of Gorgonzola, cover with remaining filling, and top with remaining Gorgonzola. Drizzle remaining 1 teaspoon oil over filling. Grasp 1 edge of dough and fold up outer 2 inches over filling. Repeat around circumference of tart, overlapping dough every 2 to 3 inches; gently pinch pleated dough to secure but do not press dough into filling.

6. Brush dough with egg and sprinkle with salt. Lower oven temperature to 375 degrees. Bake until crust is deep golden brown and filling is beginning to brown, 35 to 45 minutes, rotating sheet halfway through baking. Cool tart on baking sheet on wire rack for 10 minutes. Using offset or wide metal spatula, loosen tart from parchment and carefully slide tart off parchment and onto cutting board. Sprinkle with parsley, cut into wedges, and serve.

▶ TO MAKE AHEAD

- Dough, prepared through step 2, can be refrigerated for up to 2 days or frozen for up to 1 month
- Assembled galette, prepared through step 5, can be refrigerated for up to 24 hours; to bake, adjust oven rack to lower-middle position, place baking stone on rack, and heat oven to 400 degrees for 45 minutes before continuing with step 6
- Baked galette can sit at room temperature for up to 4 hours; to serve, reheat in 400-degree oven for 5 to 10 minutes

MAKING GALETTE DOUGH

1. Roll into 11 by 8-inch rectangle, with short side of rectangle parallel to edge of counter.

2. Using bench scraper, bring bottom third of dough up over middle third, then fold upper third over it, folding like business letter. Turn dough 90 degrees. Repeat rolling, folding, and turning dough 90 degrees twice more.

This flavorful baked dish features pureed butternut squash and bulgur flavored with aromatics, spices, and herbs.

Baked Squash Kibbeh

SERVES 4 TO 6
ACTIVE TIME 45 MINUTES
TOTAL TIME 2 HOURS 25 MINUTES

WHY THIS RECIPE WORKS Traditionally, Middle-Eastern kibbeh is a finely ground combination of beef or lamb, bulgur, and onions either formed into balls and deep-fried or pressed into a pan and baked. For a vegetarian version of this flavorful dish, we used butternut squash. We combined the squash with hearty bulgur, spices, and aromatics. To streamline our recipe, we microwaved the prepped squash; in just 15 minutes, it was tender enough to be pureed. We preferred baking our kibbeh over deep-frying, but we swapped the traditional 12-inch baking pan for a 9-inch springform pan, which made slicing and serving the baked kibbeh easier—plus the thicker slices baked up more moist and tender. Because bulgur soaks up a fair amount of liquid as it cooks, the kibbeh initially turned out dry and crumbly when we stirred raw bulgur into the squash. Soaking the bulgur in water for 10 minutes solved this problem. You can use medium-grind bulgur here, but the texture of the kibbeh will be more coarse and moist. Do not use coarse-grind or cracked-wheat bulgur in this recipe; they will not work.

2 pounds butternut squash, peeled, seeded, and cut into ½-inch pieces (6 cups)
3 tablespoons extra-virgin olive oil
1 onion, chopped fine
2 garlic cloves, minced
1 teaspoon ground coriander
¼ teaspoon five-spice powder
1½ cups fine-grind bulgur, rinsed
½ cup all-purpose flour
¼ cup minced fresh cilantro
2 tablespoons minced fresh mint
1 teaspoon salt
½ teaspoon pepper
4 ounces feta cheese, crumbled (1 cup)
2 tablespoons pine nuts, toasted and chopped

1. Adjust oven rack to middle position and heat oven to 400 degrees. Spray 9-inch springform pan with vegetable oil spray. Microwave squash in covered bowl, stirring occasionally, until tender, 15 to 20 minutes. Process cooked squash in food processor until smooth, about 1 minute; set aside.

2. Heat 1 tablespoon oil in 12-inch nonstick skillet over medium heat until shimmering. Add onion and cook until softened, about 5 minutes. Stir in garlic, coriander, and five-spice powder and cook until fragrant, about 30 seconds. Stir in pureed squash and cook until slightly thickened, 2 to 4 minutes; transfer to large bowl and let cool.

3. Meanwhile, place bulgur in separate bowl, add water to cover by 1 inch, and let sit until tender, about 10 minutes. Drain bulgur through fine-mesh strainer, wrap in clean dish towel, and wring tightly to squeeze out as much liquid as possible.

4. Stir bulgur, flour, cilantro, mint, salt, and pepper into cooled squash mixture until well combined. Transfer to prepared pan and press into even layer with your wet hands. Using paring knife, score surface into 8 even wedges, cutting halfway down through mixture.

5. Brush top with remaining 2 tablespoons oil and bake until golden brown and set, about 45 minutes. Sprinkle with feta and pine nuts and continue to bake until cheese is softened and warmed through, about 10 minutes.

6. Let kibbeh cool in pan for 10 minutes. Run thin knife around inside of springform pan ring to loosen, then remove ring. Slice kibbeh into wedges along scored lines and serve.

TO MAKE AHEAD

Assembled kibbeh, prepared through step 4, can be refrigerated for up to 24 hours

■ EASY (30 minutes or less active time)   ■ FREEZE IT
Photo: Roasted Celery Root with Yogurt and Sesame Seeds

Blanched and shocked green beans hold up well in the fridge and reheat perfectly with a quick spin in the microwave.

Green Beans with Bistro Mustard Vinaigrette

SERVES 6 **EASY**

ACTIVE TIME 20 MINUTES
TOTAL TIME 30 MINUTES

WHY THIS RECIPE WORKS When time gets tight while cooking dinner, it's tempting to just microwave a bag of frozen vegetables. We wanted to find a fresh alternative that would be hardy enough to be prepared a day or two ahead of time, requiring only minimal prep work on serving day. Green beans worked perfectly: They held their flavor and texture when blanched (cooked until crisp-tender in rapidly boiling salted water and then chilled in ice water to cool them instantly). They also reheated well in the microwave, eliminating the need to watch the stove at serving time. As for flavoring, tasters liked a slightly sharp mustard vinaigrette, which brought out the best in the beans without overshadowing their mild flavor. The vinaigrette held nicely in the fridge and needed only to be brought to room temperature before being tossed with the beans.

1 pound green beans, ends trimmed
  Salt and pepper
1 tablespoon whole-grain mustard
1½ teaspoons red wine vinegar or sherry vinegar
1 small shallot, minced
1 small garlic clove, minced
½ teaspoon minced fresh thyme
¼ cup extra-virgin olive oil

1. Bring 4 quarts water to boil in large pot over high heat. Fill large bowl halfway with ice and water; set aside. Add beans and 1 tablespoon salt to boiling water and cook until crisp-tender, 2 to 4 minutes.

2. Drain beans, then transfer immediately to ice water. Let beans cool completely, about 5 minutes, then drain and pat dry with paper towels.

3. Whisk mustard, vinegar, shallot, garlic, thyme, ¼ teaspoon salt, and ⅛ teaspoon pepper together in bowl. Whisking constantly, drizzle in oil.

4. Add beans to vinaigrette and toss to combine. Season with salt and pepper to taste, and serve.

> **TO MAKE AHEAD** ▶
> - Blanched beans and vinaigrette, prepared through step 3, can be refrigerated separately for up to 2 days
> - To reheat, bring vinaigrette to room temperature and whisk to recombine; microwave beans in covered bowl until hot and steaming, 4 to 6 minutes, then drain away any accumulated water and continue with step 4

Roasted Brussels Sprouts

SERVES 6 TO 8 **EASY**

ACTIVE TIME 15 MINUTES
TOTAL TIME 40 MINUTES

WHY THIS RECIPE WORKS Roasting is an easy way to produce Brussels sprouts that are caramelized on the outside and tender on the inside. To ensure that we achieved this balance, we started by roasting them covered with foil; tossing them in a little bit of water to create a steamy environment helped cook them through. We then removed the foil and roasted them for another 10 minutes to allow their exteriors to dry out and caramelize. Since Brussels sprouts can take some time to prep, we found that we could prep them in advance so all we needed to do at serving time was toss them on a baking sheet and cook them. If you are buying loose Brussels sprouts, select those that are about 1½ inches long. Quarter Brussels sprouts longer than 2½ inches; don't cut those that are shorter than 1 inch.

Roasting Brussels sprouts cut sides down encourages deeply caramelized exteriors and tender interiors.

2¼ pounds Brussels sprouts, trimmed and halved
 3 tablespoons extra-virgin olive oil
 1 tablespoon water
    Salt and pepper

1. Adjust oven rack to upper-middle position and heat oven to 500 degrees. Toss Brussels sprouts, oil, water, ¾ teaspoon salt, and ¼ teaspoon pepper in bowl until Brussels sprouts are coated.

2. Transfer Brussels sprouts to rimmed baking sheet and arrange so cut sides are facing down. Cover sheet tightly with aluminum foil and roast for 10 minutes. Remove foil and continue to cook until Brussels sprouts are well browned and tender, 10 to 12 minutes. Season with salt and pepper to taste. Serve.

TO MAKE AHEAD

- Brussels sprouts, prepared through step 1 but omitting water, can be refrigerated for up to 24 hours; to bake, sprinkle them with water and continue with step 2
- Roasted Brussels sprouts can be held at room temperature for up to 3 hours; to reheat, bake in 400-degree oven until hot, about 5 minutes

SIMPLE COMPOUND BUTTERS EASY FREEZE IT

Compound butters are a great way to dress up simple vegetable side dishes. Here in the test kitchen, we like to make a double or triple batch, roll it into a log, and store it in the freezer so that flavored butter is always just a slice away. Each of these recipes makes about 8 tablespoons.

TO MAKE COMPOUND BUTTER Whip 8 tablespoons softened unsalted butter with fork until light and fluffy. Mix in any of the ingredient combinations listed below and season with salt and pepper to taste. Wrap in plastic wrap and let rest to blend flavors, about 10 minutes, or roll into log and refrigerate.

PARSLEY-CAPER COMPOUND BUTTER

¼ cup minced fresh parsley
 4 teaspoons capers, rinsed and minced

PARSLEY-LEMON COMPOUND BUTTER

¼ cup minced fresh parsley
 4 teaspoons grated lemon zest

TARRAGON-LIME COMPOUND BUTTER

¼ cup minced scallion
 2 tablespoons minced fresh tarragon
 4 teaspoons lime juice

TAPENADE COMPOUND BUTTER

10 oil-cured black olives, pitted and chopped fine
 1 tablespoon brandy
 2 teaspoons minced fresh thyme
 2 garlic cloves, minced
 1 anchovy fillet, rinsed and minced
¼ teaspoon grated orange zest

CHIPOTLE-CILANTRO COMPOUND BUTTER

 2 teaspoons minced canned chipotle chile in adobo sauce, plus 2 teaspoons adobo sauce
 4 teaspoons minced fresh cilantro
 2 garlic cloves, minced
 2 teaspoons honey
 2 teaspoons grated lime zest

TO MAKE AHEAD

Compound butter can be wrapped tightly in plastic wrap and refrigerated for up to 4 days or frozen for up to 2 months

Roasted Zucchini and Eggplant Medley

SERVES 8 **EASY**

ACTIVE TIME 30 MINUTES
TOTAL TIME 50 MINUTES

WHY THIS RECIPE WORKS We wanted a flavorful roasted vegetable side dish that would be appropriate served alongside a range of main courses, both homey and elegant, and we also wanted to be able to serve it either warm or at room temperature. We quickly learned that paper-thin leafy vegetables such as leeks, radicchio, and Swiss chard don't work because they become slimy when served cold, while root vegetables such as potatoes and parsnips turn starchy and mealy. We had better luck with vegetables like zucchini, eggplant, and tomatoes. After testing a range of cooking methods, broiling turned out to be the best way to achieve plenty of browning on the zucchini and eggplant without overcooking them. Broiling each vegetable separately ensured that they were perfectly done and the pan wasn't too crowded. We quickly sautéed the aromatics to caramelize them and tossed in cherry tomatoes off the heat, which just warmed them through and melded the flavors. A final sprinkle of lemon juice and basil brought welcome brightness. Undercooking the vegetables is crucial; they will continue to cook after they are removed from the oven. Leaving the skins on the eggplant and zucchini helps keep the vegetables from being mushy after they have cooled. Toasted pine nuts also make a nice garnish.

We broil eggplant and zucchini separately to avoid overcrowding the pan and achieve a flavorful char.

- 3 zucchini (about 1½ pounds), quartered lengthwise and sliced crosswise into ¾-inch-wide pieces
- ¼ cup extra-virgin olive oil, plus extra for serving
  Salt and pepper
- 1½ pounds eggplant, cut into 1-inch cubes
- 1 onion, chopped fine
- 1 tablespoon minced fresh thyme or 1 teaspoon dried
- 3 garlic cloves, minced
- 12 ounces cherry tomatoes, quartered
- ¼ cup coarsely chopped fresh basil
- 1 tablespoon lemon juice

1. Adjust oven rack 6 inches from broiler element and heat broiler. Line rimmed baking sheet with aluminum foil and spray with vegetable oil spray.

2. Toss zucchini with 1 tablespoon oil, ¼ teaspoon salt, and pinch pepper. Spread zucchini in even layer on prepared sheet. Broil zucchini, stirring occasionally, until lightly charred around edges but slightly underdone, 7 to 10 minutes; transfer zucchini to shallow serving dish (or casserole dish). Repeat with eggplant, 1 tablespoon oil, and additional salt and pepper; transfer to serving dish.

3. Heat remaining 2 tablespoons oil in 12-inch nonstick skillet over medium heat until shimmering. Add onion, thyme, and ¼ teaspoon salt and cook until lightly browned, about 10 minutes. Stir in garlic and cook until fragrant, about 30 seconds. Off heat, stir in tomatoes. Scatter onion-tomato mixture over broiled vegetables. Cover vegetables and let sit for 10 minutes.

4. Sprinkle with basil, lemon juice, and additional olive oil before serving. (Serve warm or at room temperature.)

VARIATION

Roasted Asparagus and Fennel Medley **EASY**
Thick spears of asparagus work best here.

Substitute 2 medium fennel bulbs (about 1½ pounds), stalks discarded, bulbs halved, cored, and sliced into ¼-inch-thick strips, and 2 pounds thick asparagus, ends trimmed, sliced on bias into 2- to 3-inch lengths, for zucchini and eggplant. Season and broil fennel and asparagus, 1 vegetable at a time, as directed in step 2 (broiling times are the same).

TO MAKE AHEAD ▶

- Vegetables, prepared through step 3, can be refrigerated for up to 2 days
- To reheat, bring vegetables to room temperature (or microwave at 50 percent power for 1 to 2 minutes to serve warm), and continue with step 4

Roasted Celery Root with Yogurt and Sesame Seeds

SERVES 6 EASY
ACTIVE TIME 25 MINUTES
TOTAL TIME 1 HOUR

WHY THIS RECIPE WORKS Celery root, despite its prevalence in supermarkets, is often overlooked as a vegetable side. We wanted to bring this root vegetable to the table and highlight its herbal flavor and pleasant, creamy texture. To unlock the unique flavor of the celery root, we found that roasting was best. By cooking slices on the bottom oven rack at a high temperature, we were able to caramelize the exteriors and concentrate the flavor perfectly. Tangy yogurt brightened with lemon juice and zest complemented the rich and savory celery root. To finish, we sprinkled an aromatic combination of toasted sesame seeds, coriander, and dried thyme over the top before adding whole cilantro leaves to freshen the dish.

- ¼ cup plain yogurt
- ¼ teaspoon grated lemon zest plus 1 teaspoon juice
  Salt and pepper
- 2½ pounds celery root, peeled, halved, and sliced ½ inch thick
- 3 tablespoons extra-virgin olive oil
- 1 teaspoon sesame seeds, toasted
- 1 teaspoon coriander seeds, toasted and crushed
- ¼ teaspoon dried thyme
- ¼ cup fresh cilantro leaves

1. Adjust oven rack to lowest position and heat oven to 425 degrees. Whisk yogurt, lemon zest and juice, and pinch salt together in bowl; set aside. Toss celery root with oil, ½ teaspoon salt, and ¼ teaspoon pepper and arrange in rimmed baking sheet in single layer.

2. Roast celery root until sides touching sheet toward back of oven are well browned, 25 to 30 minutes. Rotate sheet and continue to bake until side touching sheet toward back of oven are well browned, 6 to 10 minutes. Use metal spatula to flip each piece and continue to roast until celery root is very tender and sides touching sheet are browned, 10 to 15 minutes.

3. Transfer celery root to serving platter. Combine sesame seeds, coriander seeds, thyme, and pinch salt. Drizzle celery root with yogurt sauce and sprinkle with seed mixture and cilantro. Serve.

TO MAKE AHEAD ▶

- Yogurt sauce and celery root, prepared through step 1, can be refrigerated separately for up to 24 hours; to bake, season yogurt sauce with salt and pepper to taste, and continue with step 2
- Roasted celery root can be held at room temperature for up to 1 hour; to serve, reheat in 400-degree oven until hot, about 5 minutes

Marinated Eggplant with Capers and Mint

SERVES 4 TO 6 EASY
ACTIVE TIME 20 MINUTES
TOTAL TIME 2 HOURS

WHY THIS RECIPE WORKS Marinated eggplant, a highlight of Greek meze platters, has a surprisingly creamy texture and a deep yet tangy flavor. However, many recipes we tried turned out overly greasy, with accompanying flavors that were either muted and dull or so strong that they overwhelmed the eggplant. We wanted a recipe that would keep the eggplant in the spotlight, with a complementary, brightly flavored marinade. To start, we experimented with cooking techniques: We tried frying but found that the eggplant absorbed too much oil; pan frying in batches required too much time for a simple side dish; and roasting yielded either leathery eggplant skin or undercooked and tough flesh. We found that broiling was perfect; we could achieve flavorful browning on the eggplant and it cooked through nicely. To encourage even more browning, we first salted the eggplant, which drew out excess moisture. As for the marinade, a Greek-inspired combination of extra-virgin olive oil (using only a few tablespoons kept the eggplant from turning greasy), red wine vinegar, capers, lemon zest, oregano, garlic, and mint worked perfectly. When making this dish ahead, we found that the flavor was far better if we brought the eggplant to room temperature before serving. This dish is great as part of an assortment of appetizers or as a vegetable side to any protein. We prefer using kosher salt because residual grains can easily be wiped away from the eggplant; if using table salt, be sure to reduce all of the salt amounts in the recipe by half.

This classic Greek dish features tender eggplant marinated with bold, tangy red wine vinegar.

1½ pounds Italian eggplant, sliced into 1-inch thick rounds
    Kosher salt and pepper
¼ cup extra-virgin olive oil
4 teaspoons red wine vinegar
1 tablespoon capers, rinsed and minced
1 garlic clove, minced
½ teaspoon grated lemon zest
½ teaspoon minced fresh oregano
3 tablespoons minced fresh mint

1. Spread eggplant on paper towel–lined baking sheet, sprinkle both sides with ½ teaspoon salt, and let sit for 30 minutes.

2. Adjust oven rack 4 inches from broiler element and heat broiler. Thoroughly pat eggplant dry with paper towels, arrange on aluminum foil–lined rimmed baking sheet in single layer, and lightly brush both sides with 1 tablespoon oil. Broil eggplant until mahogany brown and lightly charred, 6 to 8 minutes per side.

3. Whisk remaining 3 tablespoons oil, vinegar, capers, garlic, lemon zest, oregano, and ¼ teaspoon pepper together in large bowl. Add eggplant and mint and gently toss to combine.

4. Let eggplant cool to room temperature, about 1 hour. Season with pepper to taste, and serve.

> **TO MAKE AHEAD**
> • Marinated eggplant can be refrigerated for up to 3 days
> • To serve, bring eggplant to room temperature and season with salt and pepper to taste

Grilled Vegetable Salad

SERVES 4 TO 6
ACTIVE TIME 45 MINUTES
TOTAL TIME 55 MINUTES

WHY THIS RECIPE WORKS Grill-charred vegetables flavored with a tangy vinaigrette may sound simple, but small details can make a big difference. The key to grilling vegetables is prepping each one properly for peak performance on the grill. Cutting the zucchini and eggplant in half and then scoring them helped them release excess moisture during grilling, ensuring that our flavorful salad didn't turn soupy and waterlogged. After grilling the vegetables, we chopped them into bite-size pieces and tossed them with a potent vinaigrette. Serve as a side dish to grilled meats and fish; with grilled pita as a salad course; or with hard-cooked eggs, olives, and premium canned tuna as a light lunch.

VINAIGRETTE
1 tablespoon lemon juice
2 teaspoons Dijon mustard
1 garlic clove, minced
¼ teaspoon salt
⅛ teaspoon pepper
3 tablespoons extra-virgin olive oil
2 tablespoons chopped fresh basil, mint, chives, or parsley

VEGETABLES
2 red bell peppers
1 eggplant (14 to 16 ounces), halved lengthwise
1 zucchini (8 to 10 ounces), halved lengthwise
1 red onion, cut into ½-inch-thick rounds
4 plum tomatoes, cored and halved lengthwise
3 tablespoons extra-virgin olive oil
    Salt and pepper
    Lemon wedges

To achieve flavorful char on the vegetables in this grilled salad, we score halved zucchini and eggplant before grilling.

1. FOR THE VINAIGRETTE Whisk lemon juice, mustard, garlic, salt, and pepper together in large bowl. Whisking constantly, slowly drizzle in oil. Whisk in basil and set aside.

2. FOR THE VEGETABLES Slice ¼ inch off tops and bottoms of bell peppers and remove cores. Make slit down 1 side of each bell pepper and then press flat into 1 long strip, removing ribs and remaining seeds with knife as needed. Cut strips in half crosswise (you should have 4 bell pepper pieces).

3. Using sharp paring knife, cut ½-inch crosshatch pattern in flesh of eggplant and zucchini, being careful to cut down to but not through skin. Push toothpick horizontally through each onion slice to keep rings intact while grilling. Brush tomatoes, peppers, zucchini, and onion all over with oil, then brush eggplant with remaining oil. Season vegetables with salt and pepper.

4A. FOR A CHARCOAL GRILL Open bottom vent completely. Light large chimney starter filled with charcoal briquettes (6 quarts). When top coals are partially covered with ash, pour evenly over grill. Set cooking grate in place, cover, and open lid vent completely. Heat grill until hot, about 5 minutes.

4B. FOR A GAS GRILL Turn all burners to high, cover, and heat grill until hot, about 15 minutes. Turn all burners to medium-high.

5. Clean and oil cooking grate. Grill vegetables, starting cut sides down for eggplant and zucchini, until tender and well browned and skins of bell peppers, eggplant, and tomatoes are charred, 8 to 16 minutes, turning and moving vegetables as necessary for even cooking. Transfer vegetables to baking sheet as they finish. Place bell peppers in bowl, cover with plastic wrap, and let steam to loosen skins, about 5 minutes.

6. When cool enough to handle, peel bell peppers and tomatoes. Using spoon, scoop eggplant flesh out of its skin; discard skin. Chop all vegetables into 1-inch pieces, transfer to bowl with vinaigrette, and toss to coat. Serve warm or at room temperature with lemon wedges.

> **TO MAKE AHEAD**
> - Grilled vegetable salad can be refrigerated for up to 2 days
> - To serve, bring salad to room temperature and season with salt and pepper to taste

Slow-Roasted Tomatoes

SERVES 4 **EASY**

ACTIVE TIME 15 MINUTES

TOTAL TIME 2 HOURS 15 MINUTES TO 2 HOURS 45 MINUTES

WHY THIS RECIPE WORKS Slow roasting is a great way to use up an abundance of garden tomatoes or to improve wan supermarket tomatoes, as it produces sweet, concentrated flavor with little effort. We started by cutting the tomatoes into thick slices and layering them into a baking dish. Drizzling them with plenty of extra-virgin olive oil infused them with bright, fruity flavor as they cooked. Thin slices of garlic mellowed and softened during the long cooking time, lending a rich, nutty flavor. A sprinkle of salt and pepper was all the seasoning these sweet tomatoes needed. The roasted tomatoes taste great as a side dish or as flavorful addition to salads, sandwiches, pizzas, and pastas. Leftover tomato oil can be used to make salad dressings or as a dipping oil for bread.

½ cup extra-virgin olive oil

4 garlic cloves, sliced thin

2 pounds ripe tomatoes, cored and cut crosswise into ½-inch-thick slices
   Salt and pepper

1. Adjust oven rack to middle position and heat oven to 325 degrees. Brush bottom of 13 by 9-inch baking dish with 2 tablespoons oil and sprinkle with half of garlic. Arrange tomato slices in pan, overlapping edges as needed to fit. Pour remaining 6 tablespoons oil over tomatoes, then sprinkle with salt and remaining garlic. Roast tomatoes until slightly shriveled and most of juices have been replaced with oil, 1½ to 2 hours.

2. Remove dish from oven and let tomatoes cool in oil for at least 15 minutes or up to 4 hours. To serve, remove tomatoes from oil with slotted spoon and season with salt and pepper to taste.

TO MAKE AHEAD

- Tomatoes in oil can be refrigerated for up to 4 days
- To serve, bring tomatoes to room temperature and season with salt and pepper to taste

Stuffed Plum Tomatoes

SERVES 8 **EASY**

ACTIVE TIME 30 MINUTES

TOTAL TIME 1 HOUR 30 MINUTES TO 2 HOURS

WHY THIS RECIPE WORKS We wanted stuffed tomatoes that tasted as good as they looked and could easily be made ahead of time. Plum tomatoes were a good starting point; their meaty, sweet flavor and small size were ideal for a side dish. Salting the tomatoes rid them of excess liquid and ensured that our stuffing wouldn't get soggy. Fresh, tangy goat cheese, lightly flavored with olive oil and basil, gave the tomatoes a creamy center and made a perfect base for our topping of fresh toasted bread crumbs. Do not overprocess the bread into fine, even crumbs; the rustic texture of coarse, slightly uneven bread crumbs is preferable here. To scoop out the seeds and ribs from the tomatoes, we found it easiest to use a sharp-edged spoon, such as a measuring spoon, grapefruit spoon, or melon baller. We prefer using kosher salt because residual grains can easily be wiped away from the tomatoes; if using table salt, be sure to reduce the amount of salt by half.

2 slices hearty white sandwich bread, torn into quarters
3 tablespoons extra-virgin olive oil
3 garlic cloves, minced
¼ cup grated Parmesan cheese
¼ cup chopped fresh basil
    Kosher salt and pepper
8 firm, ripe plum tomatoes (3 to 4 ounces each)
6 ounces goat cheese, softened

1. Adjust oven rack to middle position and heat oven to 325 degrees. Pulse bread in food processor to coarse crumbs, about 6 pulses. Toss crumbs, 2 tablespoons oil, and garlic together. Spread crumbs on rimmed baking sheet and bake, stirring occasionally, until lightly browned and dry, 15 to 20 minutes; set aside to cool. When cool, toss crumbs with Parmesan and 2 tablespoons basil and season with salt and pepper to taste.

2. Meanwhile, slice tomatoes in half lengthwise and scoop out inner ribs and seeds. Sprinkle insides of tomatoes with 1½ teaspoons salt, then lay cut sides down on several layers of paper towels. Let tomatoes sit at room temperature for 30 minutes to 1 hour to drain.

3. Mix goat cheese with remaining 1 tablespoon oil and remaining 2 tablespoons basil. Season with salt and pepper to taste, then transfer to small zipper-lock bag and cut off tip of bag.

4. Pat insides of tomatoes dry with paper towels. Pipe 1 teaspoon goat cheese mixture into bottom of each tomato, then spoon bread crumbs evenly into tomatoes, pressing gently to adhere. Arrange tomatoes in 13 by 9-inch baking dish.

5. Bake tomatoes until cheese is heated through and crumbs are crisp, 15 to 20 minutes. Serve.

TO MAKE AHEAD

Stuffed tomatoes, prepared through step 4, can be refrigerated for up to 2 days

SEEDING AND STUFFING PLUM TOMATOES

1. Slice tomatoes in half lengthwise and scoop out inner ribs and seeds. Salt and lay cut side down on paper towels to drain.

2. Pat drained tomatoes dry, then pipe 1 teaspoon goat cheese mixture into bottom of each tomato and top with bread crumbs.

Pureed Butternut Squash

SERVES 4 TO 6 `EASY`
ACTIVE TIME 15 MINUTES
TOTAL TIME 30 MINUTES

WHY THIS RECIPE WORKS With its silky-smooth texture and earthy, lightly sweet flavor, pureed butternut squash is a crowd-pleaser. But because of the simplicity of this dish, finding the right cooking method for the squash was key. We tested roasting, steaming, braising, and microwaving, and found that the microwave worked best. Not only was it one of the easiest methods, but tasters far preferred the clean, sweet squash flavor that the microwave produced. Plus, the microwave helped the squash release its liquid, which we drained away before pureeing so the finished dish didn't have a thin, watery texture. The squash puree needed only 2 tablespoons of half-and-half and 2 tablespoons of butter to help round out its flavor and add some richness.

> 2 pounds butternut squash, peeled, seeded, and cut into 1½-inch pieces (5 cups)
> 2 tablespoons half-and-half
> 2 tablespoons unsalted butter
> 1 tablespoon packed brown sugar
> Salt and pepper

1. Microwave squash in covered bowl until tender and easily pierced with fork, 15 to 20 minutes, stirring halfway through microwaving.

2. Drain squash in colander, then transfer to food processor. Add half-and-half, butter, sugar, and ½ teaspoon salt and process until squash is smooth, about 20 seconds, stopping to scrape down bowl as needed.

3. Transfer pureed squash to serving dish and season with salt and pepper to taste. Serve.

VARIATIONS

Pureed Butternut Squash with Sage and Toasted Almonds `EASY`

While squash microwaves, cook 1 tablespoon unsalted butter with ½ teaspoon minced fresh sage in 8-inch skillet over medium-low heat until fragrant, about 2 minutes. Substitute sage butter for butter added to food processor. Sprinkle with ¼ cup toasted sliced almonds before serving.

Pureed Butternut Squash with Orange `EASY`

Add 2 tablespoons orange marmalade to food processor with butter.

Pureed Butternut Squash with Honey and Chipotle Chiles `EASY`

Substitute honey for sugar. Add 1½ teaspoons minced canned chipotle chile in adobo sauce to food processor with butter.

> **TO MAKE AHEAD**
> • Pureed squash can be refrigerated for up to 2 days
> • To reheat, microwave squash in covered bowl, stirring often and adding additional half-and-half as needed, until hot throughout, 4 to 6 minutes

CUTTING UP BUTTERNUT SQUASH

1. After peeling squash, trim off top and bottom and cut squash in half where narrow neck and wide curved bottom meet.

2. Cut neck of squash into evenly sized planks. Cut planks into evenly sized pieces, according to recipe.

3. Cut squash base in half lengthwise, then scoop out and discard seeds and fibers.

4. Slice each base half into evenly sized lengths, then cut lengths into evenly sized pieces, according to recipe.

We give our classic Green Bean Casserole nuanced flavor by replacing canned soup with a creamy homemade sauce.

Green Bean Casserole

SERVES 10 TO 12   **FREEZE IT**

ACTIVE TIME 45 MINUTES

TOTAL TIME 3 HOURS 20 MINUTES

WHY THIS RECIPE WORKS Green bean casserole is a holiday staple, so we set out to develop a version that could be assembled in advance to make our holiday cooking easier. To ensure that the flavor of the casserole didn't become dull in the freezer, we boosted flavor by using plenty of garlic, white wine, and fragrant thyme. After testing a number of ways to parcook the beans, we discovered that the easiest solution was also the best: simply add them raw. Tossing the beans with a bit of cornstarch before putting them in the baking dish helped to thicken any liquid they exuded during cooking. We stuck with a classic crunchy topping of canned fried onions and bread crumbs.

TOPPING

- 2 slices hearty white sandwich bread, torn into pieces
- 2 tablespoons unsalted butter, melted
- ¼ teaspoon salt
- 2 cups canned fried onions

CASSEROLE

- 3 tablespoons unsalted butter
- 10 ounces white mushrooms, trimmed and sliced thin
- 1 teaspoon salt
- ½ teaspoon pepper
- 6 garlic cloves, minced
- ½ teaspoon dried thyme
- ¼ cup all-purpose flour
- 1½ cups chicken broth
- 1½ cups heavy cream
- ½ cup dry white wine
- 2 pounds green beans, trimmed and cut into 1-inch pieces
- ¼ cup cornstarch

1. FOR THE TOPPING Pulse bread, melted butter, and salt in food processor to coarse crumbs, about 6 pulses. Combine bread crumbs and fried onions in bowl. Set aside.

2. FOR THE CASSEROLE Adjust oven rack to middle position and heat oven to 400 degrees. Melt butter in 12-inch skillet over medium heat. Add mushrooms, salt, and pepper and cook until mushrooms release their liquid, about 5 minutes. Increase heat to medium-high and cook until liquid has evaporated, about 5 minutes. Add garlic and thyme and cook until fragrant, about 30 seconds. Stir in flour and cook until golden, about 1 minute. Slowly whisk in broth, cream, and wine and bring to boil. Reduce heat to medium and simmer, stirring occasionally, until sauce is thickened, about 10 minutes.

3. Toss green beans with cornstarch in large bowl and transfer to 13 by 9-inch baking dish. Pour warm mushroom mixture evenly over green beans. Let cool completely.

4. Cover with aluminum foil and bake until sauce is bubbling and green beans are tender, 40 to 50 minutes, stirring green beans halfway through baking. Remove foil and spread topping over green beans. Bake until golden brown, about 8 minutes. Serve.

TO MAKE AHEAD

- Casserole and topping, prepared through step 3, can be refrigerated separately for up to 24 hours
- Alternatively, casserole and topping, prepared through step 3, can be frozen separately for up to 1 month; to bake, continue with step 4, increasing baking time (before topping) to 1 hour 20 minutes

Summer Vegetable Gratin

SERVES 4 `EASY`

ACTIVE TIME 30 MINUTES
TOTAL TIME 2 HOURS

WHY THIS RECIPE WORKS We loved the idea of a rich bread crumb–topped gratin showcasing our favorite summer vegetables: zucchini, summer squash, and ripe tomatoes. But every version we tried ended up a watery, soggy mess thanks to the liquid the vegetables released. To fix this problem, we salted the vegetables and let them drain before assembling the casserole. We baked the dish uncovered so that the remaining excess moisture would evaporate in the oven. Layering the tomatoes on top exposed them to more heat so that they ended up roasted and caramelized. To flavor the vegetables, we tossed them with an aromatic garlic-thyme oil and added a layer of caramelized onions.Fresh bread crumbs tossed with Parmesan and shallots made an elegant topping. The success of this recipe depends on high-quality vegetables. Buy zucchini and summer squash of roughly the same diameter. We like the combination, but you can also use just zucchini or summer squash. We prefer using kosher salt because residual grains can easily be wiped away from the vegetables; if using table salt, be sure to reduce all of the salt amounts in the recipe by half.

Salting the vegetables and baking the gratin uncovered eliminates excess moisture in this summery casserole.

1 pound zucchini, sliced ¼ inch thick
1 pound yellow summer squash, sliced ¼ inch thick
    Kosher salt and pepper
1½ pounds ripe tomatoes, cored and sliced ¼ inch thick
6 tablespoons extra-virgin olive oil
2 onions, halved and sliced thin
2 garlic cloves, minced
1 tablespoon minced fresh thyme
1 slice hearty white sandwich bread, torn into quarters
2 ounces Parmesan cheese, grated (1 cup)
2 shallots, minced
¼ cup chopped fresh basil

1. Toss zucchini and summer squash with 2 teaspoons salt and let drain in colander until vegetables release at least 3 tablespoons liquid, about 45 minutes. Pat zucchini and summer squash dry firmly with paper towels, removing as much liquid as possible.

2. Meanwhile, spread tomatoes out over paper towel–lined baking sheet, sprinkle with 1 teaspoon salt, and let stand for 30 minutes. Thoroughly pat tomatoes dry with more paper towels.

3. Heat 1 tablespoon oil in 12-inch nonstick skillet over medium heat until shimmering. Add onions and 1 teaspoon salt and cook, stirring occasionally, until softened and dark golden brown, 20 to 25 minutes; set aside.

4. Combine 3 tablespoons oil, garlic, thyme, and ½ teaspoon pepper in bowl; set aside. Process bread in food processor until finely ground, about 10 seconds, then combine with 1 tablespoon oil, Parmesan, and shallots in separate bowl; set aside.

5. Adjust oven rack to upper-middle position and heat oven to 400 degrees. Grease 3-quart gratin dish (or 13 by 9-inch baking dish) with remaining 1 tablespoon oil. Toss zucchini and summer squash with half of garlic-oil mixture and arrange in greased baking dish. Sprinkle evenly with caramelized onions, then top with tomato slices, overlapping them slightly. Spoon remaining garlic-oil mixture evenly over tomatoes.

6. Bake until vegetables are tender and tomatoes are starting to brown on edges, 40 to 45 minutes. Remove gratin dish from oven and increase heat to 450 degrees. Sprinkle bread-crumb mixture evenly over top and continue to bake gratin until bubbling and cheese is lightly browned, 5 to 10 minutes. Let cool for 10 minutes, then sprinkle with basil and serve.

TO MAKE AHEAD

Gratin and bread-crumb mixture, prepared through step 5, can be refrigerated separately for up to 24 hours

To balance out the sweetness of the sweet potatoes in this gratin, we use earthy Swiss chard and savory Parmesan.

Sweet Potato and Swiss Chard Gratin

SERVES 4 TO 6
ACTIVE TIME 40 MINUTES
TOTAL TIME 1 HOUR 50 MINUTES

WHY THIS RECIPE WORKS For a new twist on a classic potato gratin, we created a decidedly savory and elegant sweet potato version. To mitigate some of the potatoes' sweetness we turned to earthy, bitter Swiss chard, which we sautéed with shallot, garlic, thyme, and butter. We shingled half the sliced potatoes along the bottom of the gratin dish, topped them with the chard, and then layered on the remaining potatoes. Pouring a combination of water, wine, and cream over the vegetables encouraged the potatoes to cook evenly and imparted a welcome richness. Covering the gratin dish for the first half of baking ensured the potatoes cooked through. We then uncovered the dish so that the excess liquid could evaporate and the cheesy topping could brown. We were happy to find that we could refrigerate the fully assembled gratin for up to a day, making it easy to bake and serve on a busy holiday. Slicing the potatoes ⅛ inch thick is crucial for the success of this dish; use a mandoline, a V-slicer, or a food processor fitted with a ⅛-inch-thick slicing blade.

2 tablespoons unsalted butter
2 shallots, minced
   Salt
2 pounds Swiss chard, stemmed and cut into
   ½-inch-wide strips
3 garlic cloves, minced
2 teaspoons minced fresh thyme
¾ teaspoon pepper
⅓ cup heavy cream
⅓ cup water
⅓ cup dry white wine
3 pounds sweet potatoes, peeled and sliced ⅛ inch thick
2 ounces Parmesan cheese, grated (1 cup)

1. Adjust oven rack to middle position and heat oven to 350 degrees. Melt butter in Dutch oven over medium-high heat. Add shallots and 1 teaspoon salt and cook until shallots are softened, about 2 minutes. Stir in chard and cook until wilted, about 2 minutes. Stir in garlic, thyme, and pepper and cook until fragrant, about 30 seconds; transfer to bowl.

2. Add cream, water, wine, and 1 teaspoon salt to now-empty pot and bring to simmer over medium-high heat. Remove pot from heat and cover to keep warm.

3. Shingle half of potatoes evenly into 3-quart gratin dish (or 13 by 9-inch baking dish). Spread wilted chard mixture evenly over potatoes, then shingle remaining potatoes over top. Pour cream mixture evenly over top and sprinkle with Parmesan.

4. Cover dish with aluminum foil and bake for 20 minutes. Uncover and continue to bake until gratin is golden and feels tender when poked with paring knife, 40 to 50 minutes. Let cool for 10 minutes before serving.

▶ TO MAKE AHEAD
Gratin, prepared through step 3, can be refrigerated for up to 24 hours

Modern Cauliflower Gratin

SERVES 8 TO 10
ACTIVE TIME 40 MINUTES
TOTAL TIME 1 HOUR 45 MINUTES

WHY THIS RECIPE WORKS To create a cauliflower gratin that was creamy and flavorful without being too rich, we relied on cauliflower's natural ability to become an ultracreamy puree, using it as a sauce to bind the florets together. To ensure that we had enough cauliflower to use in two ways, we used two heads. We removed the cores and stems and steamed these until soft; we then blended them to make the sauce. We cut the florets into slabs,

For a creamy yet light gratin with clean cauliflower flavor, we puree the stems and some florets into a silky sauce.

which made for a more compact casserole and helped them cook more evenly. For a streamlined, efficient cooking setup, we placed the cauliflower cores and stems in water in the bottom of a Dutch oven and set our steamer basket filled with florets right on top. Butter and Parmesan (plus a little cornstarch) gave the sauce a richer flavor and texture without making it too heavy, and a few pantry spices lent some complexity. Tossing the florets in the sauce before placing them in the dish ensured that they were completely coated. Topping the gratin with Parmesan and panko gave it savory crunch. When buying cauliflower, look for heads without many leaves. If your cauliflower does have a lot of leaves, buy slightly larger heads—about 2¼ pounds each. This recipe can be halved to serve 4 to 6; cook the cauliflower in a large saucepan and bake the gratin in an 8-inch square baking dish.

- 2 heads cauliflower (2 pounds each)
- 8 tablespoons unsalted butter
- ½ cup panko bread crumbs
- 2 ounces Parmesan cheese, grated (1 cup)
  Salt and pepper
- ½ teaspoon dry mustard
- ⅛ teaspoon ground nutmeg

Pinch cayenne pepper
1 teaspoon cornstarch dissolved in 1 teaspoon water
1 tablespoon minced fresh chives

1. Adjust oven rack to middle position and heat oven to 400 degrees.

2. Pull off outer leaves of 1 head of cauliflower and trim stem. Using paring knife, cut around core to remove; halve core lengthwise and slice thin crosswise. Slice head into ½-inch-thick slabs. Cut stems from slabs to create florets that are about 1½ inches tall; slice stems thin and reserve along with sliced core. Transfer florets to bowl, including any small pieces that may have been created during trimming, and set aside. Repeat with remaining head of cauliflower. (After trimming, you should have about 3 cups of sliced stems and cores and 12 cups of florets.)

3. Combine sliced stems and cores, 2 cups florets, 3 cups water, and 6 tablespoons butter in Dutch oven and bring to boil over high heat. Place remaining florets in steamer basket (do not rinse bowl). Once mixture is boiling, place steamer basket in pot, cover, and reduce heat to medium. Steam florets in basket until translucent and stem ends can be easily pierced with paring knife, 10 to 12 minutes. Remove steamer basket and drain florets. Re-cover pot, reduce heat to low, and continue to cook stem mixture until very soft, about 10 minutes longer. Transfer drained florets to now-empty bowl.

4. While cauliflower is cooking, melt remaining 2 tablespoons butter in 10-inch skillet over medium heat. Add panko and cook, stirring frequently, until golden brown, 3 to 5 minutes. Transfer to bowl and let cool. Once cool, add ½ cup Parmesan and toss to combine.

5. Transfer stem mixture and cooking liquid to blender and add 2 teaspoons salt, ½ teaspoon pepper, mustard, nutmeg, cayenne, and remaining ½ cup Parmesan. Process until smooth and velvety, about 1 minute (puree should be pourable; adjust consistency with additional water as needed). With blender running, add cornstarch slurry. Season with salt and pepper to taste. Pour puree over cauliflower florets and toss gently to evenly coat. Transfer mixture to 13 by 9-inch baking dish (it will be quite loose) and smooth top with spatula.

6. Scatter bread-crumb mixture evenly over top. Transfer dish to oven and bake until sauce bubbles around edges, 13 to 15 minutes. Let stand for 20 to 25 minutes. Sprinkle with chives and serve.

TO MAKE AHEAD

- Assembled gratin and bread-crumb mixture, prepared through step 5, can be refrigerated separately for up to 24 hours
- To bake, continue with step 6, increasing baking time to 25 to 30 minutes

Classic Mashed Potatoes

SERVES 4 EASY
ACTIVE TIME 15 MINUTES
TOTAL TIME 1 HOUR

WHY THIS RECIPE WORKS Many people would never consider consulting a recipe when making mashed potatoes; instead they just add chunks of butter and spurts of cream until their conscience tells them to stop. Little wonder, then, that mashed potatoes made this way are consistent only in their mediocrity. We wanted mashed potatoes that were perfectly smooth and creamy, with great potato flavor and plenty of buttery richness every time. We began by selecting russet potatoes for their high starch content. Boiling them whole and unpeeled yielded mashed potatoes that were rich, earthy, and sweet. We used a food mill or ricer for the smoothest texture (a potato masher can be used if you prefer your potatoes a little chunky). For smooth, velvety potatoes, we added melted butter first and then half-and-half. Melting, rather than merely softening, the butter enabled it to coat the starch molecules quickly and easily, so the potatoes turned out creamy and light. Russet potatoes make fluffier mashed potatoes, but Yukon Golds have an appealing buttery flavor and can be used instead.

    2 pounds russet potatoes, unpeeled
    8 tablespoons unsalted butter, melted
    1 cup half-and-half, warmed
       Salt and pepper

1. Place potatoes in large saucepan and add cold water to cover by 1 inch. Bring to boil over high heat, reduce heat to medium-low, and simmer until potatoes are just tender (paring knife can be slipped in and out of potatoes with little resistance), 30 to 45 minutes. Drain.

2. Using potholder or folded dish towel to hold potatoes, peel skins from potatoes with paring knife. For slightly chunky texture, return peeled potatoes to now-empty pot and mash smooth using potato masher. For creamy texture, set ricer or food mill over now-empty pot; cut peeled potatoes into large chunks and press or mill into saucepan in batches.

3. Stir in melted butter until incorporated. Gently whisk in warm half-and-half and season with salt and pepper to taste. Serve.

> ▸ TO MAKE AHEAD
> • Mashed potatoes can be refrigerated for up to 2 days
> • To reheat, microwave potatoes in covered bowl, stirring often and adding additional half-and-half as needed, until hot throughout, 6 to 9 minutes

We simmer russet potatoes with sautéed garlic, butter, and half-and-half to infuse them with flavor before mashing.

Garlic Mashed Potatoes

SERVES 8 TO 10 EASY
ACTIVE TIME 30 MINUTES
TOTAL TIME 1 HOUR

WHY THIS RECIPE WORKS Making mashed potatoes isn't typically a quick endeavor—add roasted garlic to the mix and you've really got a project on your hands. We wanted a streamlined recipe that could be made ahead of time. We started with the garlic. We found that sautéing minced garlic with a bit of sugar offered great roasted garlic flavor in a fraction of the time it would take to roast a whole head. We tested simply mixing the sautéed garlic with a batch of mashed potatoes, but tasters complained that the dish didn't seem cohesive. Instead, we decided to cook the potatoes with the garlic to infuse them with flavor from the start. Although our Classic Mashed Potatoes recipe calls for boiling the potatoes whole, that technique wouldn't work here. Instead, we peeled, cubed, and rinsed the potatoes to remove excess starch that could make the finished mash gluey. We then added the rinsed potatoes, half-and-half, butter, and a small amount of water to the pot with the sautéed garlic and let everything simmer together.

The small pieces of potato soaked up tons of garlic flavor, and since we were cooking them in a small amount of liquid, no flavor was lost in draining.

    4   pounds russet potatoes, peeled, quartered, and
        cut into ½-inch pieces
    12 tablespoons unsalted butter, cut into pieces
    12 garlic cloves, minced
    1   teaspoon sugar
    1½ cups half-and-half
    ½   cup water
        Salt and pepper

1. Place cut potatoes in colander. Rinse under cold running water until water runs clear. Drain thoroughly.

2. Melt 4 tablespoons butter in Dutch oven over medium heat. Add garlic and sugar and cook, stirring often, until sticky and straw colored, 3 to 4 minutes. Add rinsed potatoes, 1¼ cups half-and-half, water, and 1 teaspoon salt to pot and stir to combine. Bring to boil, then reduce heat to low and simmer, covered and stirring occasionally, until potatoes are tender and most of liquid is absorbed, 25 to 30 minutes.

3. Off heat, add remaining 8 tablespoons butter to pot and mash with potato masher until smooth. Using rubber spatula, fold in remaining ¼ cup half-and-half until liquid is absorbed and potatoes are creamy. Season with salt and pepper to taste. Serve.

TO MAKE AHEAD

- Garlic mashed potatoes can be refrigerated for up to 2 days
- To reheat, microwave potatoes in covered bowl, stirring often and adding additional half-and-half as needed, until hot throughout, 10 to 15 minutes

Creamy Mashed Sweet Potatoes

SERVES 4 TO 6   EASY
TOTAL TIME 15 MINUTES
ACTIVE TIME 50 MINUTES

WHY THIS RECIPE WORKS Deeply flavored, earthy, and subtly sweet, mashed sweet potatoes hardly need a layer of marshmallows to make them a tempting side. For a silky and full-flavored mash, we found the secret was to thinly slice the potatoes and cook them covered, on the stovetop, over low heat in a small amount of butter and cream. Once the sweet potatoes were fall-apart tender, they could be mashed right in the pot—no draining necessary. Adding another spoonful of cream when we mashed the potatoes enriched them even more. This recipe can be doubled and prepared in a Dutch oven, but the cooking time will need to be doubled as well.

    2   pounds sweet potatoes, peeled, quartered lengthwise,
        and cut into ¼-inch-thick slices
    4   tablespoons unsalted butter, cut into 4 pieces
    3   tablespoons heavy cream
    1   teaspoon sugar
        Salt and pepper

1. Combine sweet potatoes, butter, 2 tablespoons cream, sugar, ½ teaspoon salt, and ¼ teaspoon pepper in large saucepan. Cook, covered, over low heat until potatoes are fall-apart tender, 35 to 40 minutes. Off heat, mash sweet potatoes with potato masher.

2. Stir in remaining 1 tablespoon cream and continue to mash until smooth. Season with salt and pepper to taste, and serve.

VARIATIONS
Smokehouse Mashed Sweet Potatoes   EASY

Add ⅛ teaspoon cayenne pepper to saucepan in step 1. In step 2, mash ½ cup shredded smoked Gouda cheese with sweet potatoes and cover with lid until cheese melts, about 1 minute. Sprinkle with 6 slices chopped and cooked bacon and 1 thinly sliced scallion.

Herbed Mashed Sweet Potatoes with Caramelized Onions   EASY

If you prefer, substitute ¼ teaspoon dried thyme for the thyme sprig (but do not remove in step 2).

Add 1 sprig fresh thyme to saucepan in step 1. While sweet potatoes are cooking, melt 1 tablespoon butter in small nonstick skillet and add 1 chopped small onion, ¼ teaspoon sugar, and ¼ teaspoon salt. Cook over low heat until onion is caramelized, about 15 minutes. Discard thyme and mash potatoes as directed in step 1. Stir in onion and 1 tablespoon sour cream along with heavy cream in step 2.

Far East Mashed Sweet Potatoes   EASY

Substitute 2 teaspoons soy sauce for salt and add 1½ teaspoons minced fresh ginger and 1 minced garlic clove to saucepan in step 1. Sprinkle mashed sweet potatoes with 2 tablespoons chopped fresh cilantro before serving.

TO MAKE AHEAD

- Mashed sweet potatoes can be refrigerated for up to 2 days
- To reheat, microwave potatoes in covered bowl, stirring often and adding heavy cream as needed, until hot throughout, 6 to 9 minutes

Beating a few eggs into our mashed potatoes gives them a light and fluffy texture when baked.

Mashed Potato Casserole

SERVES 6 TO 8 **EASY**

ACTIVE TIME 30 MINUTES

TOTAL TIME 1 HOUR 50 MINUTES

WHY THIS RECIPE WORKS A great mashed potato casserole promises fluffy, buttery, creamy potatoes nestled under a savory golden crust. And with all the mashing and mixing done beforehand, it's the perfect convenience dish during the holiday season. Using half-and-half instead of heavy cream lightened the recipe, and cutting it with chicken broth kept the potatoes moist. Beating eggs into the potato mixture helped it achieve a fluffy, airy texture and allowed us to use a handheld mixer to mash the potatoes without them turning gluey. Garlic and Dijon mustard gave our casserole a flavorful bite. We like to use a shallow 2-quart gratin dish, which allows for the most surface area (and browned crust), but a 13 by 9-inch baking dish also works.

 4 pounds russet potatoes, peeled and cut into 1-inch chunks

 ½ cup half-and-half

 ½ cup chicken broth

 12 tablespoons unsalted butter, cut into pieces

 1 garlic clove, minced

 2 teaspoons Dijon mustard

 2 teaspoons salt

 4 large eggs

 ¼ cup minced fresh chives

1. Place potatoes in Dutch oven and add water to cover by 1 inch. Bring to boil over high heat. Reduce heat to medium and simmer until potatoes are just tender (paring knife can be slipped in and out of potatoes with little resistance), about 20 minutes.

2. Meanwhile, adjust oven rack to upper-middle position and heat oven to 375 degrees. Grease 2-quart gratin dish. Heat half-and-half, broth, butter, garlic, mustard, and salt in saucepan over medium-low heat until butter is melted, about 5 minutes; cover to keep warm.

3. Drain potatoes and transfer to large bowl. Using handheld mixer set at medium-low speed, beat potatoes while slowly adding half-and-half mixture until smooth and creamy, about 1 minute. Scrape down bowl, then beat in eggs, one at a time, until incorporated, about 1 minute. Using rubber spatula, gently fold in chives. Transfer potato mixture to prepared gratin dish and smooth top with rubber spatula.

4. Bake until potatoes rise and begin to brown, 35 to 45 minutes. Let casserole cool for 10 minutes. Serve.

TO MAKE AHEAD ▶

- Casserole, prepared through step 3, can be refrigerated for up to 24 hours
- To bake, let sit at room temperature for 1 hour and continue with step 4

Classic Scalloped Potatoes

SERVES 4 TO 6 **EASY**

ACTIVE TIME 30 MINUTES

TOTAL TIME 1 HOUR 15 MINUTES

WHY THIS RECIPE WORKS For our weeknight-friendly scalloped potato recipe, we used traditional russet potatoes to form cohesive layers, and mixed heavy cream with an equal amount of chicken broth to offset the typical heaviness of the dish. We parboiled the potatoes on the stove, then poured the mixture into a casserole dish and finished it in the oven. Prep and assemble all of the other ingredients before slicing the potatoes or they will begin to brown (do not store them in water; this will make the gratin bland and watery). If the potato slices do start to discolor, put them in a bowl and cover with the cream and chicken broth. Slicing the potatoes ⅛ inch thick is crucial for the success of this dish; use a mandoline, a V-slicer, or a food processor fitted with a ⅛-inch-thick slicing blade. You can substitute Parmesan for the cheddar if desired.

    2 tablespoons unsalted butter
    1 onion, chopped fine
    1 tablespoon minced fresh thyme or 1 teaspoon dried
    2 garlic cloves, minced
1¼ teaspoons salt
 ¼ teaspoon pepper
2½ pounds russet potatoes, peeled and sliced ⅛ inch thick
    1 cup chicken broth
    1 cup heavy cream
    2 bay leaves
    4 ounces cheddar cheese, shredded (1 cup)

1. Adjust oven rack to middle position and heat oven to 425 degrees. Melt butter in Dutch oven over medium-high heat. Add onion and cook until softened, 5 to 7 minutes. Stir in thyme, garlic, salt, and pepper and cook until fragrant, about 30 seconds. Add potatoes, broth, cream, and bay leaves and bring to simmer.

2. Cover, reduce heat to medium-low, and simmer until potatoes are almost tender (paring knife can be slipped in and out of potato slice with some resistance), about 10 minutes.

3. Discard bay leaves. Transfer mixture to 8-inch square baking dish and press into even layer.

4. Sprinkle evenly with cheddar. Bake until bubbling around edges and top is golden brown, about 15 minutes. Let casserole cool for 10 minutes before serving.

VARIATIONS

Scalloped Potatoes with Chipotle Chiles and Smoked Cheddar Cheese `EASY`
Add 2 teaspoons minced canned chipotle chile in adobo sauce to pot with potatoes. Substitute smoked cheddar for cheddar.

Scalloped Potatoes with Wild Mushrooms `EASY`
Add 8 ounces cremini mushrooms, trimmed and sliced ¼ inch thick, and 4 ounces shiitake mushrooms, stemmed and sliced ¼ inch thick, to pot with onion; cook as directed.

TO MAKE AHEAD
- Casserole, prepared through step 3, can be refrigerated for up to 24 hours
- To bake, cover dish tightly with greased aluminum foil and bake in 400-degree oven until hot throughout, about 45 minutes; uncover, top with cheddar, and continue to bake until cheddar is lightly browned, about 30 minutes; let casserole cool for 10 minutes before serving

A mix of cheddar, sour cream, and butter gives our twice-baked potato filling the right amount of richness and tang.

Twice-Baked Potatoes with Bacon, Cheddar, and Scallions
SERVES 8
ACTIVE TIME 45 MINUTES
TOTAL TIME 1 HOUR 45 MINUTES

WHY THIS RECIPE WORKS Twice-baked potatoes—essentially baked russet potatoes whose flesh has been removed from the shells, mashed with dairy products and seasonings, mounded back into the shells, and baked again—offer a variety of textures and flavors in a single bite. Done well, the skin is chewy and substantial without being tough, with just a hint of crispness to play off the smooth, creamy filling. Done poorly, the skin is flabby and the filling is dry and starchy or overloaded with bland cream. We wanted a perfect rendition that we could also prepare a day or two prior to serving. Tests revealed that tasters preferred a combination of sharp cheddar and sour cream enriched with 4 tablespoons of butter. To this, we added bacon, sautéed onion, and a final sprinkling of fresh scallions. We had initially feared that storing the stuffed potatoes in the refrigerator would result in their tasting dry or their skins being limp, but our fears turned out to be unfounded: The stored stuffed potatoes were identical to their freshly made counterparts. Buying evenly sized potatoes will help ensure that they cook at the same rate. Be sure to leave a layer of potato inside the potato skins; it helps them retain their shape when stuffed and baked.

4 russet potatoes (7 to 8 ounces each), unpeeled, rubbed lightly with vegetable oil, and poked several times with fork
4 slices bacon, chopped fine
1 onion, chopped fine
6 ounces sharp cheddar cheese, shredded (1½ cups)
1 cup sour cream
4 tablespoons unsalted butter, softened
Salt and pepper
2 scallions, sliced thin

1. Adjust oven rack to upper-middle position and heat oven to 400 degrees. Place potatoes directly on hot oven rack and bake until skins are crisp and deep brown and paring knife easily pierces flesh, about 1 hour, flipping potatoes halfway through baking. Transfer potatoes to wire rack and let cool slightly, about 10 minutes. Increase oven temperature to 500 degrees.

2. Meanwhile, cook bacon in 10-inch nonstick skillet over medium-high heat until crisp, about 8 minutes. Using slotted spoon, transfer bacon to paper towel–lined plate, leaving fat in skillet. Return skillet to medium heat, add onion, and cook, stirring occasionally, until softened and lightly browned, about 10 minutes; set aside. Line rimmed baking sheet with aluminum foil and set wire rack in sheet.

3. Using oven mitt to handle hot potato, cut each potato in half lengthwise. Using soupspoon, scoop flesh from each half into medium bowl, leaving ¼- to ½-inch thickness of flesh in each shell. Transfer potato shells to prepared wire rack.

4. Mash potato flesh with fork until smooth. Stir in 1 cup cheddar, sour cream, butter, and sautéed onion, and season with salt and pepper to taste. Spoon mixture into potato shells, mounding slightly at center. Sprinkle with remaining ½ cup cheddar and crisp bacon.

5. Bake until shells are crisp and filling is heated through, 10 to 15 minutes. Sprinkle with scallions and serve.

VARIATIONS

Twice-Baked Potatoes with Bacon, Blue Cheese, and Caramelized Onions

For more caramelized onion flavor, add an extra onion.

Substitute ½ cup crumbled blue cheese for cheddar. Add 1 tablespoon brown sugar to onion in step 2; cook until onion is very soft and deeply browned, about 20 minutes.

Southwestern Twice-Baked Potatoes

Substitute 1½ cups shredded pepper Jack cheese for cheddar. Add 3 minced garlic cloves to onion during final minute of cooking in step 2. Add 1 teaspoon minced chipotle chile in adobo sauce to mashed potato mixture in step 4.

TO MAKE AHEAD

- Baked stuffed potatoes, prepared through step 4, can be refrigerated for up to 2 days
- To bake, continue with step 5, increasing baking time to 15 to 25 minutes

Classic Bread Stuffing with Sage and Thyme

SERVES 8 TO 10   EASY
ACTIVE TIME 30 MINUTES
TOTAL TIME 2 HOURS 30 MINUTES

WHY THIS RECIPE WORKS Since a stuffed turkey takes longer to cook and often results in overcooked meat, we usually prefer to cook our stuffing outside the bird. For this recipe, we aimed to create a stuffing that would have a great balance of flavors and textures. The secret lay in the ratio of bread to liquid to aromatics and other flavorings. Half-inch cubes of bread made the stuffing pleasantly chunky and allowed the other ingredients to be distributed evenly throughout. Tasters preferred chicken broth to other liquid ingredients since it gave the stuffing clean, savory flavor, and a couple of eggs offered richness, moisture, and structure. Aromatics like celery, onion, and herbs gave the stuffing a classic flavor profile. Covering the stuffing for only part of the baking time ensured that it was moist throughout with a crispy, crunchy lid. Instead of oven drying in step 1, you can let bread stale overnight at room temperature. This recipe can be doubled and baked in a 15 by 10-inch baking dish for a larger crowd.

1½ pounds hearty white sandwich bread, cut into ½-inch cubes
6 tablespoons unsalted butter
2 celery ribs, minced
1 onion, chopped fine
¼ cup minced fresh parsley
1½ tablespoons minced fresh sage or 1 teaspoon dried
1½ tablespoons minced fresh thyme or ½ teaspoon dried
1½ teaspoons minced fresh marjoram or ½ teaspoon dried
2½ cups chicken broth
2 large eggs, lightly beaten
1 teaspoon salt
1 teaspoon pepper

Baking our stuffing covered for part of the cooking time ensures that it is moist throughout with a crunchy top.

1. Adjust oven rack to middle position and heat oven to 300 degrees. Grease 13 by 9-inch baking dish. Spread bread onto rimmed baking sheet and bake, stirring occasionally, until bread is dry, 45 minutes to 1 hour. Let bread cool completely on sheet, about 30 minutes.

2. Increase oven temperature to 400 degrees. Melt butter in 12-inch skillet over medium-high heat. Add celery and onion and cook until softened, about 10 minutes. Stir in parsley, sage, thyme, and marjoram and cook until fragrant, about 1 minute. Transfer to very large bowl.

3. Add dried, cooled bread, broth, eggs, salt, and pepper to vegetable mixture and toss to combine. Transfer mixture to prepared baking dish.

4. Cover with aluminum foil and bake for 25 minutes. Remove foil and continue to bake until golden, about 30 minutes longer. Let cool for 10 minutes and serve.

TO MAKE AHEAD

- Stuffing, prepared through step 3, can be refrigerated for up to 2 days
- To bake, continue with step 4, increasing covered baking time to 40 minutes

Homemade Cornbread Dressing

SERVES 10 TO 12

ACTIVE TIME 55 MINUTES

TOTAL TIME 3 HOURS (PLUS 2 HOURS TO COOL CORNBREAD)

WHY THIS RECIPE WORKS Cornbread and sausage stuffing is a compelling alternative to the usual bread-based dish. But the recipes we tried all called for store-bought cornbread, which had a fluffy texture that resulted in mushy stuffing. We'd have to make the cornbread from scratch. We began with our favorite cornbread recipe: Combine cornmeal with flour, leavener, salt, and sugar (which we omitted) before whisking in eggs, buttermilk, milk, and melted butter. Because our dressing would offer tons of flavor, we decided to eliminate the buttermilk and replace the butter with vegetable oil; tasters couldn't tell the difference. We cubed the cornbread and, while it worked fine to let it stale overnight, we found we could achieve the same results more quickly by drying it out in a low oven. We tried assembling the dressing and storing the whole casserole in the fridge overnight, but unfortunately the cornbread became too mushy. We opted instead to wait until just before baking to combine the cornbread with chicken broth, eggs, browned sausage, and aromatics. To increase richness, we added extra sausage, doubled the eggs to four, and replaced 1 cup of the chicken broth with half-and-half. We also drizzled melted butter over the dressing before baking it, which helped crisp the top. Instead of oven drying in step 3, you can let the cut cornbread stale overnight at room temperature.

CORNBREAD

2⅔ cups milk

½ cup vegetable oil

4 large eggs

2 cups (10 ounces) cornmeal

2 cups (10 ounces) all-purpose flour

4 teaspoons baking powder

1 teaspoon salt

DRESSING

1½ pounds bulk pork sausage

2 onions, chopped fine

3 celery ribs, chopped fine

6 tablespoons unsalted butter

4 garlic cloves, minced

1 teaspoon ground sage

1 teaspoon dried thyme

3½ cups chicken broth

1 cup half-and-half

4 large eggs

½ teaspoon salt

⅛ teaspoon cayenne pepper

1. FOR THE CORNBREAD Adjust oven racks to upper-middle and lower-middle positions and heat oven to 375 degrees. Grease and flour 13 by 9-inch baking pan. Whisk milk, oil, and eggs together in bowl.

2. In large bowl, combine cornmeal, flour, baking powder, and salt. Whisk in milk mixture until smooth. Pour batter into prepared pan and bake on lower rack until golden and toothpick inserted in center comes out clean, about 30 minutes. Let cool in pan on wire rack, about 2 hours.

3. Reduce oven to 250 degrees. Cut cornbread into 1-inch squares. Divide cornbread between 2 rimmed baking sheets and bake, stirring occasionally, until dry, 50 minutes to 1 hour. Let cornbread cool completely on sheets, about 30 minutes.

4. FOR THE DRESSING Cook sausage in 12-inch nonstick skillet over medium-high heat until no longer pink, about 5 minutes; transfer to paper towel–lined plate. Pour off all but 2 tablespoons fat left in pan. Add onions, celery, and 2 tablespoons butter to fat in pan and cook over medium-high heat until vegetables soften, about 5 minutes. Stir in garlic, sage, and thyme and cook until fragrant, about 30 seconds. Stir in broth, remove from heat, and let cool for 5 minutes.

5. In large bowl, whisk half-and-half, eggs, salt, and cayenne together. Slowly whisk in warm broth mixture until incorporated. Gently fold in dried cornbread and sausage. Let mixture sit, tossing occasionally, until cornbread is saturated, about 20 minutes.

6. Heat oven to 375 degrees. Grease 13 by 9-inch baking pan. Transfer cornbread mixture to prepared pan. Melt remaining 4 tablespoons butter and drizzle evenly over top. Bake on upper rack until top is golden brown and crisp, 30 to 40 minutes. Let cool for 15 minutes and serve.

TO MAKE AHEAD

Cornbread, prepared through step 2, can be stored at room temperature for up to 2 days

Wild Rice Dressing
SERVES 10 TO 12
ACTIVE TIME 40 MINUTES
TOTAL TIME 2 HOURS 40 MINUTES

WHY THIS RECIPE WORKS While developing our recipe for a dressing made with nutty wild rice, we discovered the amount of liquid that a given variety of wild rice absorbed varied drastically. To allow for this, we boiled the rice in extra liquid and then drained the excess, reserving the liquid. Cream and eggs bound the dressing but on their own were far too rich. Adding some of the rice cooking liquid lightened the dish and enhanced the nutty, earthy flavor of the rice. We found that toasted bread added color and crunch

Small pieces of toasted bread add color and crunch and don't overwhelm the nutty flavor of the wild rice in this dressing.

and eliminated the need for staling bread. Covering the casserole kept the surface from getting too crunchy.

     2 cups chicken broth
     2 cups water
     1 bay leaf
     2 cups wild rice
    10 slices hearty white sandwich bread, torn into pieces
     8 tablespoons unsalted butter
     2 onions, chopped fine
     3 celery ribs, chopped fine
     4 garlic cloves, minced
  1½ teaspoons dried sage
  1½ teaspoons dried thyme
  1½ cups heavy cream
     2 large eggs
   ¾ teaspoon salt
   ½ teaspoon pepper

1. Bring broth, water, and bay leaf to boil in medium saucepan over medium-high heat. Stir in rice. Reduce heat to low, cover, and simmer until rice is tender, 35 to 45 minutes. Strain rice through fine-mesh strainer, reserving 1½ cups cooking liquid. Discard bay leaf.

2. Adjust oven racks to upper-middle and lower-middle positions and heat oven to 325 degrees. Working in batches, pulse bread in food processor until coarsely ground, about 6 pulses. Spread crumbs onto 2 rimmed baking sheets and bake until golden, about 20 minutes, stirring occasionally. Let crumbs cool completely.

3. Melt 4 tablespoons butter in 12-inch skillet over medium heat. Add onions and celery and cook until golden, 8 to 10 minutes. Stir in garlic, sage, and thyme and cook until fragrant, about 30 seconds. Stir in reserved cooking liquid, remove from heat, and cool for 5 minutes.

4. In large bowl, whisk cream, eggs, salt, and pepper together. Slowly whisk in warm broth mixture. Stir in rice and bread crumbs. Transfer mixture to 13 by 9-inch baking dish.

5. Melt remaining 4 tablespoons butter in now-empty skillet and drizzle evenly over dressing. Cover dish with aluminum foil and bake on lower rack until set, 45 to 55 minutes. Remove foil and let cool for 15 minutes. Serve.

VARIATIONS
Wild Rice Dressing with Dried Fruit and Nuts
Add 1½ cups chopped dried apricots, cranberries, or cherries and 1½ cups chopped toasted pecans along with bread crumbs in step 4.

Wild Rice Dressing with Leeks and Mushrooms
Substitute 4 leeks (white and light green parts only), halved lengthwise and sliced thin, and 10 ounces cremini mushrooms, trimmed and sliced thin, for onions and celery.

> **TO MAKE AHEAD**
> - Dressing, prepared through step 4, can be refrigerated for up to 24 hours
> - To bake, continue with step 5, increasing baking time to 1 hour 5 minutes to 1¼ hours

Basmati Rice Pilaf
SERVES 4 TO 6   **EASY**
ACTIVE TIME 20 MINUTES
TOTAL TIME 55 MINUTES

WHY THIS RECIPE WORKS Although rice pilaf is simple to make, making it ahead can be a convenient time saver when company's coming, especially when making one of our dressed-up variations. In fact, we found that we didn't even need to turn on the stove on serving day, and instead could easily reheat the rice in the microwave. Rinsing the rice before cooking removed excess starch and

To ensure perfectly fluffy and flavorful rice pilaf, we rinse and then toast the grains before adding water to the pot.

ensured the fluffy, rather than clumpy, grains that we were after, and toasting it for a few minutes in the pan deepened its flavor. Instead of following the traditional ratio of 1 cup of rice to 2 cups of water, we found using a little less liquid delivered better results. Placing a dish towel under the lid while the rice finished steaming off the heat absorbed excess moisture and guaranteed perfectly fluffy rice. Long-grain white, jasmine, or Texmati rice can be substituted for the basmati. A nonstick saucepan works best here, although a traditional saucepan will also work. The recipe (and the variations) can be doubled and cooked in a Dutch oven—the cooking time will remain the same.

  2 tablespoons extra-virgin olive oil
  1 onion, chopped fine
    Salt and pepper
1½ cups basmati rice, rinsed
2¼ cups water

1. Heat oil in large saucepan over medium heat until shimmering. Add onion and ¼ teaspoon salt and cook until softened, about 5 minutes. Stir in rice and cook, stirring often, until grain edges begin to turn translucent, about 3 minutes.

2. Stir in water and bring to simmer. Reduce heat to low, cover, and continue to simmer until rice is tender and water is absorbed, 16 to 18 minutes.

3. Remove pot from heat and lay clean folded dish towel underneath lid. Let sit for 10 minutes. Fluff rice with fork, season with salt and pepper to taste, and serve.

VARIATIONS

Basmati Rice Pilaf with Currants and Cinnamon `EASY`

Add 1 minced garlic clove, ½ teaspoon ground turmeric, and ¼ teaspoon ground cinnamon to pot after cooking onion in step 1. Cook until fragrant, about 30 seconds. Sprinkle ¼ cup dried currants over cooked rice before letting rice sit in step 3.

Indian-Spiced Basmati Rice Pilaf with Dates and Parsley `EASY`

Add 1 minced garlic clove, 1½ teaspoons minced fresh ginger, ⅛ teaspoon ground cinnamon, and ⅛ teaspoon ground cardamom to pot after cooking onion in step 1. Cook until fragrant, about 30 seconds. Before serving, stir in ¼ cup chopped dried dates and 1½ tablespoons minced fresh parsley.

Saffron Basmati Rice Pilaf with Apricots and Almonds `EASY`

Add ¼ teaspoon saffron with onion in step 1. Sprinkle ¼ cup chopped dried apricots over cooked rice before letting rice sit in step 3. Before serving, stir in ¼ cup toasted slivered almonds.

TO MAKE AHEAD

- Pilaf can be refrigerated for up to 3 days
- To reheat, microwave pilaf in covered bowl until hot throughout, 3 to 5 minutes, fluffing with fork halfway through microwaving, then season with salt and pepper to taste

NOTES FROM THE TEST KITCHEN

Storing Rice, Grains, and Beans

To prevent open boxes and bags of rice, grains, and beans from spoiling in the pantry, store them in airtight containers, and, if you have space, keep rice and grains in the freezer. This is especially important for whole grains, which turn rancid with oxidation. Use rice and grains within six months. Though beans are less susceptible to pests and spoilage than rice and grains, and can be kept up to a year, you will get the best results if you use beans within the first month or two of purchase.

Baking brown rice in the oven is more foolproof and hands-off than cooking it on the stove thanks to the indirect heat.

Foolproof Baked Brown Rice

SERVES 4 TO 6 `EASY`
ACTIVE TIME 10 MINUTES
TOTAL TIME 1 HOUR 20 MINUTES

WHY THIS RECIPE WORKS Healthy, inexpensive, and conveniently shelf-stable, rice is a great pantry staple to keep on hand. There are as many different ways to cook rice as there are different types, and we were out to find a simple, foolproof method for cooking brown rice. We started by eliminating the stovetop method (and the risk of scorching) and instead cooked the rice in the oven to approximate the controlled, indirect heat of a rice cooker. In playing with proportions, we discovered why brown rice is typically sodden and overcooked: Most brown rice recipes call for a 2:1 water-to-rice ratio. For our brown rice recipe, we found that 2⅓ cups water to 1½ cups rice gave us perfectly cooked rice. Just a bit of extra-virgin olive oil, to help prevent the grains from sticking, and a bit of salt was all we needed to add to our simple rice. We covered the rice tightly with aluminum foil and popped it in the oven for about an hour. Happily, making the rice ahead worked well as reheating was as simple as microwaving for a few minutes. For an accurate measurement of boiling water, bring a full kettle of water to a boil and then measure out the desired amount. Medium or short-grain brown rice can be substituted for the long-grain rice.

2⅓ cups boiling water
1½ cups long-grain brown rice, rinsed
 2 teaspoons extra-virgin olive oil
    Salt and pepper

1. Adjust oven rack to middle position and heat oven to 375 degrees. Combine boiling water, rice, oil, and ½ teaspoon salt in 8-inch square baking dish. Cover dish tightly with double layer of aluminum foil. Bake until liquid is absorbed and rice is tender, about 1 hour.

2. Remove dish from oven, uncover, and fluff rice with fork, scraping up any rice that has stuck to bottom. Cover dish with clean dish towel and let rice sit for 5 minutes. Season with salt and pepper to taste, and serve.

TO MAKE AHEAD

- Rice can be refrigerated for up to 3 days
- To reheat, microwave pilaf in covered bowl until hot throughout, 3 to 5 minutes, fluffing with fork halfway through microwaving, then season with salt and pepper to taste

Cutting down on the amount of liquid called for in most recipes gives us tender quinoa with a satisfying bite.

Quinoa Pilaf with Herbs and Lemon

SERVES 4 TO 6 **EASY**
ACTIVE TIME 20 MINUTES
TOTAL TIME 50 MINUTES

WHY THIS RECIPE WORKS In theory, quinoa has an appealingly nutty flavor and a crunchy texture; in practice it often turns into a mushy mess with washed-out flavor and an underlying bitterness. We wanted a simple quinoa pilaf with light, distinct grains and great flavor. We found that most recipes for quinoa pilaf turned out woefully overcooked because they call for far too much liquid. We reduced the water to ensure tender grains with a satisfying bite. We also toasted the quinoa in a dry saucepan to develop its natural nutty flavor before simmering. We flavored our pilaf with some onion sautéed in butter and finished it with herbs and a squeeze of lemon juice. We like the convenience of prewashed quinoa; rinsing removes the quinoa's bitter protective coating (called saponin). If you buy unwashed quinoa (or if you are unsure whether it's washed), rinse it and then spread it out over a clean dish towel to dry for 15 minutes before cooking.

1½ cups prewashed white quinoa
 2 tablespoons unsalted butter or extra-virgin olive oil
 1 small onion, chopped fine
¾ teaspoon salt
1¾ cups water
 3 tablespoons chopped fresh cilantro, parsley, chives, mint, or tarragon
 1 tablespoon lemon juice

1. Toast quinoa in medium saucepan over medium-high heat, stirring frequently, until quinoa is very fragrant and makes continuous popping sound, 5 to 7 minutes; transfer to bowl.

2. Add butter to now-empty saucepan and melt over medium-low heat. Add onion and salt and cook, stirring frequently, until onion is softened and light golden, 5 to 7 minutes.

3. Stir in water and toasted quinoa, increase heat to medium-high, and bring to simmer. Cover, reduce heat to low, and simmer until grains are just tender and liquid is absorbed, 18 to 20 minutes, stirring once halfway through cooking. Remove pan from heat and let sit, covered, for 10 minutes.

4. Fluff quinoa with fork, stir in herbs and lemon juice, and serve.

Quinoa Pilaf with Olives, Raisins, and Cilantro `EASY`

Add ¼ teaspoon ground cumin, ¼ teaspoon dried oregano, and ⅛ teaspoon ground cinnamon to saucepan with onion and salt. Stir in ¼ cup golden raisins halfway through cooking quinoa. Substitute ⅓ cup coarsely chopped pimento-stuffed green olives and 3 tablespoons chopped fresh cilantro for chopped fresh herbs. Substitute 4 teaspoons red wine vinegar for lemon juice.

Quinoa Pilaf with Shiitakes, Edamame, and Ginger `EASY`

Substitute minced whites of 4 scallions for onion. Add 4 ounces thinly sliced shiitake mushrooms and 2 teaspoons grated fresh ginger to saucepan with scallion whites. Substitute thinly sliced greens of 4 scallions for fresh herbs and 4 teaspoons rice wine vinegar for lemon juice. Stir in ½ cup cooked, shelled edamame, and 1 tablespoon mirin in step 3.

> **TO MAKE AHEAD**
>
> - Quinoa, prepared through step 3, can be refrigerated for up to 3 days
> - To reheat, microwave quinoa in covered bowl until hot throughout, 3 to 5 minutes, fluffing with fork halfway through microwaving, and continue with step 4

Tart cranberries and toasted pecans put a festive spin on a simple side dish of warm farro.

Warm Farro with Orange and Herbs

SERVES 4 TO 6 `EASY`
ACTIVE TIME 25 MINUTES
TOTAL TIME 50 MINUTES

WHY THIS RECIPE WORKS Chewy, nutty farro is a great base for a unique and flavorful side dish. A few tests proved that the best way to achieve evenly cooked, tender farro was to cook it like pasta, in plenty of water. Garlic and onion together made an aromatic base for the simple side, bringing out some of the farro's natural sweetness. A splash of fresh orange juice provided a subtle acidity, which helped to bring out the nuttiness of the grains. A healthy sprinkle of fresh parsley and mint gave the dish a nice pop of color and brightness. We also created a simple variation using tart, sweet dried cranberries and toasted pecans. When we made this dish ahead, tasters preferred the texture of microwave-reheated farro to that of farro reheated on the stovetop. Do not substitute pearled farro for the whole farro in this recipe. If using quick-cooking or presteamed farro (read the ingredient list on the package to determine this), you will need to alter the farro cooking time in step 1.

1½ cups whole farro
    Salt and pepper
 3 tablespoons extra-virgin olive oil
 1 onion, chopped
 1 garlic clove, minced
 ¼ cup chopped fresh parsley
 ¼ cup chopped fresh mint
 1 tablespoon fresh orange juice

1. Bring 4 quarts water to boil in Dutch oven. Stir in farro and 1 tablespoon salt, return to boil, and cook until grains are tender with slight chew, 15 to 30 minutes. Drain farro, return to now-empty pot and cover to keep warm.

2. Heat 2 tablespoons oil 12-inch skillet over medium heat until shimmering. Add onion and ¼ teaspoon salt and cook until softened, about 5 minutes. Stir in garlic and cook until fragrant, about 30 seconds. Add remaining 1 tablespoon oil and farro and cook, stirring frequently, until heated through, about 2 minutes.

3. Off heat, stir in parsley, mint, and orange juice. Season with salt and pepper to taste. Serve.

Warm Farro with Cranberries and Pecans `EASY`

Omit fresh mint. Add ½ cup chopped dried cranberries to skillet with garlic in step 2. Stir in ½ cup toasted, chopped pecans with parsley in step 3.

`TO MAKE AHEAD` ▶

- Farro, prepared through step 2, can refrigerated for up to 3 days
- To reheat, microwave in covered bowl until hot throughout, 3 to 5 minutes, stirring halfway through microwaving, and continue with step 3

Barley Risotto with Mushrooms and Herbs

SERVES 4 TO 6

ACTIVE TIME 1 HOUR 15 MINUTES

TOTAL TIME 1 HOUR 15 MINUTES

WHY THIS RECIPE WORKS We found that preparing barley with a risotto cooking method was a wonderful way to bring out a new dimension of the grain. Because the hull and the bran are removed from pearl barley, the starchy interior is exposed, helping to create a supple, velvety sauce when simmered. We used the classic risotto cooking method, adding the liquid in batches and allowing it to be absorbed before adding more. Since barley takes longer to cook than Arborio rice, we found that we needed to use more liquid than we would in a regular risotto. Sautéed onion along with porcini and cremini mushrooms gave the risotto a savory, earthy backbone, and white wine added welcome acidity and brightness. Finally, we finished the dish with fresh parsley and Parmesan cheese for richness. Do not substitute hulled, hull-less, quick-cooking, or pre-steamed barley (read the ingredient list on the package to determine this) in this recipe. Serve with extra grated Parmesan cheese.

- 4 cups chicken broth
- 4 cups water
- 1 tablespoon extra-virgin olive oil
- 12 ounces cremini mushrooms, trimmed and sliced thin
- 1 onion, chopped fine
- ½ ounce dried porcini mushrooms, rinsed and minced
  Salt and pepper
- 1½ cups pearl barley, rinsed
- 1 cup white wine

Pearl barley works well in a risotto-style dish since its starchy interior is exposed, creating a velvety sauce when cooked.

- 1 teaspoon minced fresh thyme
- 2 ounces Parmesan cheese, grated (1 cup)
- 1 tablespoon unsalted butter
- 1 tablespoon minced fresh parsley

1. Bring broth and water to simmer in medium saucepan. Reduce heat to lowest setting and cover to keep warm.

2. Heat oil in large saucepan over medium heat until shimmering. Add cremini mushrooms, onion, porcini mushrooms, and ½ teaspoon salt and cook, stirring occasionally, until vegetables are just beginning to brown, about 4 minutes. Stir in barley and cook, stirring often, until lightly toasted and aromatic, about 4 minutes. Stir in wine and cook until fully absorbed, about 2 minutes.

3. Stir in thyme and 3 cups warm broth. Simmer, stirring occasionally, until liquid is absorbed and bottom of pan is dry, 22 to 25 minutes. Stir in 2 cups warm broth and simmer, stirring occasionally, until liquid is absorbed and bottom of pan is dry, 15 to 18 minutes.

4. Continue to cook risotto, stirring often and adding remaining broth as needed to prevent pan bottom from becoming dry, until barley is cooked through, but still somewhat firm in center, 15 to 20 minutes.

5. Off heat, stir in Parmesan, butter, and parsley. Season with salt and pepper to taste. Serve.

> **TO MAKE AHEAD** ▶
>
> • Barley risotto, prepared through step 4, can be refrigerated up to 3 days
> • To reheat, cook risotto in saucepan over medium heat, adding 1 to 2 cups additional broth or water as needed and stirring often, until hot throughout, about 10 minutes, and continue with step 5

French Lentils with Carrots and Parsley

SERVES 4 TO 6 `EASY`
ACTIVE TIME 25 MINUTES
TOTAL TIME 1 HOUR 20 MINUTES

WHY THIS RECIPE WORKS Smaller and firmer than the more common brown and green varieties, French lentils, or *lentilles du Puy*, are perfect for simple sides thanks to their rich, complex flavor and tender texture. To highlight the sweet, earthy flavor of the lentils, we took inspiration from their name and looked to France, slowly cooking the lentils with carrots, onion, and celery (a classic French combination called a *mirepoix*). Garlic and thyme added aromatic flavors that complemented the lentils. Lentilles du Puy, also called French green lentils, are our first choice for this recipe, but brown, black, or regular green lentils are fine, too (note that cooking times will vary depending on the type used).

 2 carrots, peeled and chopped fine
 1 onion, chopped fine
 1 celery rib, chopped fine
 2 tablespoons extra-virgin olive oil
   Salt and pepper
 2 garlic cloves, minced
 1 teaspoon minced fresh thyme or ¼ teaspoon dried
2½ cups water
 1 cup lentilles du Puy, picked over and rinsed
 2 tablespoons minced fresh parsley
 2 teaspoons lemon juice

1. Combine carrots, onion, celery, 1 tablespoon oil, and ½ teaspoon salt in large saucepan. Cover and cook over medium-low heat, stirring occasionally, until vegetables are softened, 8 to 10 minutes. Stir in garlic and thyme and cook until fragrant, about 30 seconds.

Small *lentilles du Puy* keep their shape and texture during cooking, making them a good base for this simple side dish.

2. Stir in water and lentils and bring to simmer. Reduce heat to low, cover, and simmer gently, stirring occasionally, until lentils are mostly tender, 40 to 50 minutes. Uncover and continue to cook, stirring occasionally, until lentils are completely tender, about 8 minutes.

3. Stir in parsley, lemon juice, and remaining 1 tablespoon oil. Season with salt and pepper to taste, and serve.

VARIATION

French Lentils with Swiss Chard `EASY`

Omit carrots, celery, and parsley. Separate stems and leaves from 12 ounces Swiss chard; finely chop stems and cut leaves into ½-inch pieces. Add chard stems to pot with onion and stir chard leaves into pot after uncovering in step 2.

> **TO MAKE AHEAD** ▶
>
> • Lentils, prepared through step 2, can be refrigerated for up to 3 days
> • To reheat, microwave in covered bowl until hot throughout, 3 to 5 minutes, stirring halfway through microwaving, and continue with step 3

Boston Baked Beans

SERVES 4 TO 6 · EASY
ACTIVE TIME 25 MINUTES
TOTAL TIME 5 HOURS 45 MINUTES TO 6 HOURS 15 MINUTES

WHY THIS RECIPE WORKS Heady with smoky pork and bittersweet molasses, authentic Boston baked beans are both savory and sweet, a combination of flavors brought together by a long simmer. We wanted to create a recipe for beans packed with multiple levels of intense flavor, yet traditional enough to make a New Englander proud. We started with a combination of salt pork and bacon and browned them in a Dutch oven before sautéing an onion in the rendered fat. After adding dried white beans and water, along with molasses and mustard, we finished the cooking in the oven, which ensured that the beans cooked through evenly and prevented scorching on the bottom of the pot. We removed the lid for the last hour of cooking to reduce the sauce to a syrupy, intensified state. A teaspoon of cider vinegar, stirred in at the end, gave our sauce tanginess, while another tablespoon of molasses boosted its flavor. Although the beans required a good amount of hands-off cooking time, we found they could easily be made a few days ahead. Be sure to use mild molasses; dark molasses will taste too strong. You will need a Dutch oven with a tight-fitting lid for this recipe.

    4 ounces salt pork, rind removed, cut into ½-inch pieces
    2 slices bacon, chopped fine
    1 onion, chopped fine
    9 cups water
    1 pound (2½ cups) dried small white beans, picked over and rinsed
    ½ cup plus 1 tablespoon molasses
    1½ tablespoons brown mustard
      Salt and pepper
    1 teaspoon cider vinegar

1. Adjust oven rack to lower-middle position and heat oven to 300 degrees. Cook salt pork and bacon in Dutch oven over medium heat until lightly browned and most fat has rendered, about 7 minutes. Stir in onion and cook until softened, 5 to 7 minutes. Stir in water, beans, ½ cup molasses, mustard, and 1¼ teaspoons salt. Increase heat to medium-high and bring to boil.

2. Cover pot and transfer to oven. Bake until beans are tender, about 4 hours, stirring every hour.

3. Remove lid and continue to bake until liquid has thickened to syrupy consistency, 1 to 1½ hours.

4. Remove pot from oven. Stir in vinegar and remaining 1 tablespoon molasses and season with salt and pepper to taste. Serve.

TO MAKE AHEAD

- Baked beans can be refrigerated for up to 3 days
- To reheat, bring beans, covered, to gentle simmer, stirring often and adjusting consistency with hot water, and season with salt and pepper to taste

Barbecue Baked Beans

SERVES 4 TO 6 · EASY
ACTIVE TIME 30 MINUTES
TOTAL TIME 6 HOURS TO 6 HOURS 30 MINUTES

WHY THIS RECIPE WORKS Most barbecue joints serve ladlefuls of smoky, deeply-flavored beans alongside the slabs of ribs and mounds of pulled pork. We wanted to make those creamy-textured, saucy beans at home to accompany our own barbecue, and we wanted to be able to make them in advance. To get there, we used dried pinto or navy beans. Bacon was a convenient substitute for smoky barbecued meat, and we blended barbecue sauce, brown sugar, and mustard for a sweet but spicy flavor—a fair amount of garlic and onion helped, too. The secret ingredient in our recipe was coffee. Its roasted, slightly bitter flavor tied all the elements together. We found that the oven provided steady, uniform heat, guaranteeing that the beans cooked through evenly and preventing the thick, sweet sauce from scorching on the bottom of the pot. To finish, we stirred in more barbecue sauce and then seasoned the beans with an extra splash of hot sauce to complement the sweet and tangy flavors. If you don't have time to make freshly brewed coffee, instant will do just fine. You will need a Dutch oven with a tight-fitting lid for this recipe.

    4 slices bacon, chopped fine
    1 onion, chopped fine
    4 garlic cloves, minced
    8 cups water
    1 pound (2½ cups) dried pinto or navy beans, picked over and rinsed
    1 cup brewed coffee
    ½ cup plus 2 tablespoons barbecue sauce
    ¼ cup packed dark brown sugar
    1½ tablespoons brown mustard
    1 tablespoon molasses
    ½ teaspoon hot sauce, plus extra to taste
      Salt and pepper

1. Adjust oven rack to lower-middle position and heat oven to 300 degrees. Cook bacon in Dutch oven over medium heat until beginning to crisp, about 5 minutes. Stir in onion and cook until softened, about 5 minutes. Stir in garlic and cook until fragrant, about 30 seconds. Stir in water, beans, coffee, ½ cup barbecue sauce, sugar, mustard, molasses, hot sauce, and 1¼ teaspoons salt. Increase heat to medium-high and bring to boil.

2. Cover pot and transfer to oven. Bake until beans are tender, about 4 hours, stirring every hour.

3. Remove lid and continue to bake until liquid has thickened to syrupy consistency, 1 to 1½ hours.

4. Remove pot from oven. Stir in remaining 2 tablespoons barbecue sauce and season with hot sauce, salt, and pepper to taste. Serve.

TO MAKE AHEAD

- Beans can be refrigerated for up to 3 days
- To reheat, bring beans, covered, to gentle simmer, stirring often and adjusting consistency with hot water, and season with salt and pepper to taste

NOTES FROM THE TEST KITCHEN

The Science of Salt-Soaking Beans

Most people think of brining as a way to keep lean meat juicy and tender, but brining isn't just for meat. When you soak dried beans in salted water, they cook up with softer skins and are less likely to blow out and disintegrate. Why? It has to do with how the sodium ions in salt interact with the cells of the bean skins. As the beans soak, the sodium ions replace some of the calcium and magnesium ions in the skins. Because sodium ions are more weakly charged than calcium and magnesium ions, they allow more water to penetrate into the skins, leading to a softer texture. During soaking, the sodium ions filter only partway into the beans, so their greatest effect is on the cells in the outermost part of the beans. Softening the skins also makes them less likely to split as the beans cook, keeping the beans intact. For 1 pound of dried beans, dissolve 3 tablespoons of table salt in 4 quarts of cold water. Soak the beans at room temperature for 8 to 24 hours. Drain and rinse them well before using.

FOR A QUICK SALT-SOAK If you are pressed for time, you can "quick-soak" your beans. Simply combine the salt, water, and beans in a large Dutch oven and bring to a boil over high heat. Remove the pot from the heat, cover, and let stand for 1 hour. Drain and rinse the beans well before using.

Cranberry Beans with Warm Spices
SERVES 4 TO 6 **EASY**
ACTIVE TIME 30 MINUTES
TOTAL TIME 2 HOURS TO 2 HOURS 30 MINUTES (PLUS 8 HOURS TO SOAK BEANS)

WHY THIS RECIPE WORKS Cranberry beans have a delicate flavor and a creamy texture similar to that of pinto or cannellini beans. We wanted to create a dish that would highlight these beans, and since they are common in Turkey, we took inspiration from there to create a gently spiced flavor profile. Since cranberry beans are rarely canned, we knew we'd have to start with dried beans. To help the beans cook up creamy and tender, we soaked them overnight in salt water. We sautéed aromatic vegetables along with tomato paste for depth of flavor; just a touch of cinnamon imparted a subtle yet distinctly Turkish flavor. White wine offered acidity. Letting the beans cook through in the gentle heat of the oven ensured that they were perfectly cooked without the need for constant monitoring. Lemon juice and fresh mint nicely balanced the warm, rich flavors of the beans. If cranberry beans are unavailable, you can substitute pinto beans. You can use vegetable broth in place of the chicken broth to make this recipe vegetarian. For more information on soaking beans, see "The Science of Salt-Soaking Beans." You will need a Dutch oven with a tight-fitting lid for this recipe.

Salt and pepper
1 pound (2½ cups) dried cranberry beans, picked over and rinsed
¼ cup extra-virgin olive oil
1 onion, chopped fine
2 carrots, peeled and chopped fine
4 garlic cloves, sliced thin
1 tablespoon tomato paste
½ teaspoon ground cinnamon
½ cup dry white wine
4 cups chicken broth
2 tablespoons lemon juice, plus extra for seasoning
2 tablespoons minced fresh mint

1. Dissolve 3 tablespoons salt in 4 quarts cold water in large container. Add beans and soak at room temperature for at least 8 hours or up to 24 hours. Drain and rinse well.

2. Adjust oven rack to lower-middle position and heat oven to 350 degrees. Heat oil in Dutch oven over medium heat until shimmering. Add onion and carrots and cook until softened, about 5 minutes. Stir in garlic, tomato paste, cinnamon, and ¼ teaspoon pepper and cook until fragrant, about 1 minute. Stir in wine, scraping up any browned bits. Stir in broth, ½ cup water, and beans and bring to boil. Cover, transfer pot to oven, and cook until beans are tender, 1 to 1½ hours, stirring every 30 minutes.

An overnight soak in salt water helps our cranberry beans cook up tender and creamy.

3. Stir in lemon juice and mint. Season with salt, pepper, and extra lemon juice to taste. Adjust consistency with extra hot water as needed. Serve.

TO MAKE AHEAD

- Beans, prepared through step 2, can be refrigerated for up to 2 days
- To reheat, bring beans, covered, to gentle simmer, stirring often, and continue with step 3

Spicy Chickpeas with Turnips

SERVES 4 TO 6 **EASY**

ACTIVE TIME 25 MINUTES

TOTAL TIME 1 HOUR

WHY THIS RECIPE WORKS Unlike most North African cooking, Tunisian food is known for being quite hot and spicy. We wanted to highlight the flavors of this cuisine with a chickpea dish that could be enjoyed as an accompaniment yet was hearty enough to be served all on its own as a vegetarian entrée. To start, we created a spicy and savory base of sautéed aromatics. In Tunisia, fresh Baklouti chiles are the main source of heat, but we opted for the more widely available jalapeño chile, which has a similar heat level. We also added extra punch with cayenne pepper. Once the aromatic foundation for this dish was in place, it was time to add the hearty vegetables. In an effort to keep our recipe streamlined, we opted for canned chickpeas; the chickpeas softened slightly with cooking, and the perfectly tender chickpeas were a hit with tasters. Including the starchy, seasoned liquid from the cans gave our sauce good flavor and body. To add bulk and earthy flavor to this dish, we tested a variety of root vegetables and landed on turnips, a common ingredient in Tunisian cuisine. We cut the turnips into bite-size pieces so they would cook quickly and evenly. A final touch of lemon juice was all this zesty bean dish needed before serving.

2 tablespoons extra-virgin olive oil
2 onions, chopped
2 red bell peppers, stemmed, seeded, and chopped
 Salt and pepper
¼ cup tomato paste
1 jalapeño chile, stemmed, seeded, and minced
5 garlic cloves, minced
¾ teaspoon ground cumin
¼ teaspoon cayenne pepper
2 (15-ounce) cans chickpeas
12 ounces turnips, peeled and cut into ½-inch pieces
¾ cup water, plus extra as needed
¼ cup chopped fresh parsley
2 tablespoons lemon juice, plus extra for seasoning

1. Heat oil in Dutch oven over medium heat until shimmering. Add onions, bell peppers, ½ teaspoon salt, and ¼ teaspoon pepper and cook until softened and lightly browned, 5 to 7 minutes. Stir in tomato paste, jalapeño, garlic, cumin, and cayenne and cook until fragrant, about 30 seconds.

2. Stir in chickpeas and their liquid, turnips, and water. Bring to simmer and cook until turnips are tender and sauce has thickened, 25 to 35 minutes.

3. Stir in parsley and lemon juice. Season with salt, pepper, and extra lemon juice to taste. Adjust consistency with extra hot water as needed. Serve.

TO MAKE AHEAD

- Beans, prepared through step 2, can be refrigerated for up to 2 days
- To reheat, bring beans, covered, to gentle simmer, stirring often, and continue with step 3

CHAPTER 10

Holiday and Brunch Classics

For more side dishes, see pages 288–315 in the Sides chapter

■ EASY (30 minutes or less active time)   ■ FREEZE IT
Photo: Roast Beef Tenderloin with Caramelized Onion and Mushroom Stuffing

Our foolproof way to prepare a moist, well-seasoned turkey is to brine it before roasting.

Classic Roast Turkey

SERVES 10 TO 22 **EASY**
ACTIVE TIME 25 MINUTES
TOTAL TIME 3 HOURS 15 MINUTES TO 4 HOURS 45 MINUTES
(PLUS 6 HOURS BRINING TIME)

WHY THIS RECIPE WORKS Roasting a turkey can be daunting for even the most experienced cook. The white meat can easily overcook since the dark meat needs to cook for longer. We overcame this challenge by brining our turkey. Brining adds moisture to the meat and helps it hold on to more of its natural juices. To ensure even cooking, we first roasted the bird breast side down, then flipped it breast side up to finish. Or you can skip this step and simply roast the turkey breast side up for the entire time and protect the breast with a piece of aluminum foil if it begins to overbrown. If using a disposable roasting pan, support it underneath with a rimmed baking sheet. Depending on the size of the turkey, total roasting time will vary from 2 to 3½ hours. If using a self-basting turkey (such as a frozen Butterball) or a kosher turkey, do not brine as it will be too salty. Serve with Turkey Gravy (page 324).

Salt and pepper
1 (12- to 22-pound) turkey, neck and giblets discarded
4 tablespoons unsalted butter, melted

1. For a 12- to 17-pound turkey, whisk 2 gallons cold water and 1 cup salt together in large container to dissolve salt. For an 18- to 22-pound turkey, whisk 3 gallons cold water and 1½ cups salt together in large container to dissolve salt. Add turkey and submerge completely, then cover and refrigerate or store in very cool spot (40 degrees or less) for at least 6 hours.

2. Adjust oven rack to lowest position and heat oven to 425 degrees. Line V-rack with aluminum foil and poke several holes in foil. Set rack inside large roasting pan and spray foil with vegetable oil spray. Remove turkey from brine, pat dry inside and out with paper towels, tie legs together with kitchen twine, and tuck wingtips behind back.

3. Brush breast side of turkey with half of butter and season with pepper. Lay turkey in rack breast side down. Brush back of turkey with remaining butter and season with pepper. Roast turkey for 1 hour.

4. Remove turkey from oven and lower oven temperature to 325 degrees. Tip juice from cavity of turkey into pan. Flip turkey breast side up using clean dish towels or wads of paper towels. Continue to roast turkey until breast registers 160 degrees and thighs register 175 degrees, about 1 to 2½ hours longer.

5. Tip turkey so that juice from cavity runs into roasting pan. Transfer turkey to carving board and let rest, uncovered, for 30 minutes. Carve and serve.

TO MAKE AHEAD ▶

Turkey, prepared through step 1, can be refrigerated in brine for up to 12 hours

NOTES FROM THE TEST KITCHEN ◀

Roasting Times for an Unstuffed Turkey

The times below are guidelines, but you should gauge whether your turkey is done by checking when the breast registers 160 degrees and the thighs reach 175 degrees. It's true—a 22-pound bird takes only 3½ hours at the most.

RAW TURKEY WEIGHT	NUMBER OF SERVINGS	APPROXIMATE ROASTING TIME
12 to 14 pounds	10 to 12	2 to 2½ hours
15 to 17 pounds	14 to 16	2½ to 3 hours
18 to 22 pounds	20 to 22	3 to 3½ hours

CARVING A TURKEY

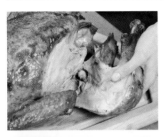

1. Remove leg quarters by pulling each one away from carcass. Gently press leg out to side and push up on joint. Carefully cut through joint.

2. Separate drumsticks from thighs by cutting through joint that connects them. Slice meat off drumsticks and thighs, leaving a bit of skin attached to each slice.

3. Pull wings away from carcass and cut carefully through joint between wing and breast. Cut wings in half for easier eating.

4. Remove breast meat by cutting down along each side of breastbone, pulling meat away from bone as you cut. Slice breast meat crosswise into thin slices for serving.

Roast Salted Turkey and Gravy

SERVES 10 TO 12

ACTIVE TIME 1 HOUR 15 MINUTES

TOTAL TIME 3 HOURS 10 MINUTES TO 3 HOURS 40 MINUTES (PLUS 24 HOURS SALTING TIME)

WHY THIS RECIPE WORKS Brining is the best way to guarantee a moist turkey, but it isn't always the most practical way, especially if you have limited refrigerator space. We wanted to develop an alternative method to brining that would both season the meat and keep it moist. Instead of brining, we turned to salting—it seasons the meat, but no bucket is required. An unconventional roasting method—preheating a baking stone under the empty roasting pan—ensured that the dark meat, which was in contact with the super-hot pan, cooked faster than the delicate breast meat. Covering the turkey breast with foil for part of the roasting time further shielded it from the heat and prevented overcooking. Rubbing the turkey with a small amount of baking powder just before it went into the oven encouraged deeply bronzed and crispy skin. Our ultraflavorful, concentrated drippings were the perfect base for a simple gravy. This recipe was developed and tested using Diamond Crystal Kosher Salt. If you have Morton Kosher Salt, which is denser than Diamond Crystal, reduce the salt in step 1 to 3 tablespoons and rub 1 tablespoon of the salt mixture into each breast, 1½ teaspoons into each leg, and the remainder into the cavity. If using a self-basting turkey (such as a frozen Butterball) or a kosher turkey, do not apply the salt mixture to the bird. The success of this recipe is dependent on saturating the baking stone and roasting pan with heat.

Kosher salt and pepper
4 teaspoons sugar
1 (12- to 14-pound) turkey, neck and giblets removed and reserved for gravy
2½ tablespoons vegetable oil
1 teaspoon baking powder
1 small onion, chopped fine
1 carrot, sliced thin
5 sprigs fresh parsley
2 bay leaves
5 tablespoons all-purpose flour
3¼ cups water
¼ cup dry white wine

1. Combine ¼ cup salt and sugar in bowl. Place turkey, breast side up, on counter. Using your fingers, carefully loosen skin covering breast and legs. Rub 4 teaspoons salt-sugar mixture under skin of each breast, 2 teaspoons under skin of each leg, and remaining salt-sugar mixture inside cavity. Tuck wingtips behind back and tie legs together with kitchen twine. Place turkey on wire rack set in rimmed baking sheet and refrigerate, uncovered, for 24 hours.

2. At least 30 minutes before roasting turkey, adjust oven rack to lowest position, set baking stone on rack, set roasting pan on baking stone, and heat oven to 500 degrees. Combine 1½ teaspoons oil and baking powder in small bowl. Pat turkey dry with paper towels. Rub oil mixture evenly over turkey. Cover turkey breast with double layer of aluminum foil.

3. Remove pan from oven and drizzle remaining 2 tablespoons oil into pan. Place turkey, breast side up, in pan and return pan to oven. Reduce oven temperature to 425 degrees and roast for 45 minutes.

4. Remove foil, reduce oven temperature to 325 degrees, and continue to roast until breast registers 160 degrees and thighs register 175 degrees, 1 to 1½ hours longer.

5. Using spatula, loosen turkey from pan; transfer to carving board and let rest, uncovered, for 45 minutes. While turkey rests, use wooden spoon to scrape up any browned bits from bottom of pan. Strain mixture through fine-mesh strainer set over bowl. Transfer drippings to fat separator and let rest for 10 minutes. Reserve 3 tablespoons fat and defatted liquid (you should have 1 cup; add water as needed to equal 1 cup). Discard remaining fat.

6. Heat reserved fat in large saucepan over medium-high heat until shimmering. Add reserved neck and giblets and cook until well browned, 10 to 12 minutes. Transfer neck and giblets to large plate. Reduce heat to medium; add onion, carrot, parsley sprigs, and bay leaves; and cook, stirring frequently, until vegetables are softened, 5 to 7 minutes. Add flour and cook, stirring constantly, until flour is well coated with fat, about 1 minute. Slowly whisk in reserved defatted liquid and cook until thickened, about 1 minute. Whisk in water and wine, return neck and giblets to saucepan, and bring to simmer. Simmer for 10 minutes, then season with salt and pepper to taste. Discard neck. Strain gravy through fine-mesh strainer, discarding solids, and transfer to serving bowl. Carve turkey and arrange on serving platter. Serve with gravy.

TO MAKE AHEAD

Salted turkey, prepared through step 1, can be refrigerated for up to 48 hours

NOTES FROM THE TEST KITCHEN

Thawing a Frozen Turkey

What's the best way to thaw a frozen turkey? Defrost the turkey in the refrigerator, calculating one day of defrosting for every 4 pounds of turkey. Say you're cooking a 12-pound turkey. The frozen bird should be placed in the refrigerator on Monday so that it's defrosted and ready to cook for Thanksgiving Day. If you plan on brining your bird the night before, start thawing that 12-pound bird on Sunday.

What if you forget to thaw your turkey ahead of time? Don't panic. You can still save the situation and quick-thaw the turkey in a large bucket with cold tap water. Place the turkey (still in its original wrapper) in the bucket and let it thaw for 30 minutes per pound; a 12-pound bird, for example, would take 6 to 8 hours. Change the cold water every half-hour to guard against bacteria growth.

For perfectly cooked beef tenderloin, we sear it last, not first, and then serve it with a flavored butter.

Roast Beef Tenderloin

SERVES 4 TO 6 **EASY**
ACTIVE TIME 30 MINUTES
TOTAL TIME 2 HOURS 30 MINUTES (PLUS 1 HOUR SALTING TIME)

WHY THIS RECIPE WORKS Many recipes sear, then roast, beef tenderloin. But it takes a long time to sear a tenderloin straight from the refrigerator because a lot of surface moisture has to evaporate before any browning can occur. During this time, too much heat is transferred to the roast and you end up with a band of overcooked gray meat below the surface. We wanted to remedy this problem and make sure the recipe was foolproof. Center-cut beef tenderloin roast is also known as Châteaubriand. Ask your butcher to prepare a trimmed center-cut Châteaubriand, as this cut is not usually available without special ordering. If you are cooking for a crowd, this recipe can be doubled to make two roasts. Sear the roasts one after the other, wiping out the pan and adding new oil after searing the first roast. Both pieces of meat can be roasted on the same rack. We prefer this roast cooked to medium-rare, but if you prefer it more or less done, see our guidelines on page 189. You can omit the Shallot and Parsley Butter and serve the tenderloin with one of the sauces on pages 324–325.

1 (2-pound) center-cut beef tenderloin roast, trimmed

2 teaspoons kosher salt

1 teaspoon coarsely ground pepper

2 tablespoons unsalted butter, softened

1 tablespoon vegetable oil

1 recipe Shallot and Parsley Butter (recipe follows)

1. Tie roast with kitchen twine at 1½-inch intervals, then sprinkle evenly with salt. Cover loosely with plastic wrap and let stand at room temperature for 1 hour. Meanwhile, adjust oven rack to middle position and heat oven to 300 degrees.

2. Pat roast dry with paper towels. Sprinkle roast evenly with pepper and spread unsalted butter evenly over surface. Transfer to wire rack set in rimmed baking sheet and roast until meat registers 120 to 125 degrees (for medium-rare), 40 to 55 minutes, flipping roast halfway through cooking.

3. Heat oil in 12-inch skillet over medium-high heat until just smoking. Place roast in skillet and sear until well browned on all sides, 4 to 8 minutes. Transfer roast to carving board and spread 2 tablespoons Shallot and Parsley Butter evenly over top; let rest for 15 minutes. Remove twine and slice ½ inch thick. Serve, passing remaining Shallot and Parsley Butter separately.

TO MAKE AHEAD

Cooked tenderloin can sit at room temperature for up to 2 hours

---

SHALLOT AND PARSLEY BUTTER

MAKES ABOUT ½ CUP **EASY** **FREEZE IT**

ACTIVE TIME 10 MINUTES

TOTAL TIME 10 MINUTES

4 tablespoons unsalted butter, softened

1 small shallot, minced

1 tablespoon minced fresh parsley

1 garlic clove, minced

¼ teaspoon salt

¼ teaspoon pepper

Whip butter in bowl with fork until light and fluffy. Mix in remaining ingredients and let rest to blend flavors, about 10 minutes.

TO MAKE AHEAD

Shallot and parsley butter can be wrapped tightly in plastic wrap and refrigerated for up to 4 days or frozen for up to 2 months

This flavorful tenderloin can be stuffed with the mushrooms, caramelized onion, and Madeira up to one day ahead.

Roast Beef Tenderloin with Caramelized Onion and Mushroom Stuffing

SERVES 4 TO 6

ACTIVE TIME 1 HOUR

TOTAL TIME 2 HOURS 30 MINUTES (INCLUDES SITTING TIME)

WHY THIS RECIPE WORKS Beef tenderloin is perfect holiday fare. Add a rich stuffing and you've got the ultimate main course. The tenderloin's thin, tapered shape, however, makes for uneven cooking; in the time it took us to develop a nice crust, the meat overcooked. Also, chunky fillings fell out of the meat when sliced. We wanted a stuffed beef tenderloin with a deeply charred crust, a tender, rosy-pink interior, and a flavorful stuffing that stayed neatly rolled in the meat. A center-cut tenderloin cooked more evenly than a whole one; plus, its cylindrical shape made the roast easier to stuff. Double-butterflying the meat gave us more space. Rubbing the stuffed, rolled, and tied roast with salt, pepper, and olive oil added flavor and helped develop a good crust when we seared the meat. We could fit just a cupful of stuffing, so we knew the flavors had to be intense. We decided on woodsy cremini mushrooms and caramelized onions, seasoned with Madeira and garlic; this luxurious combination made a savory-sweet jam-like filling that spread easily on the meat and held together well. Baby spinach added color and freshness. This recipe can be doubled to make two roasts. Sear the roasts one after the other, cleaning the pan and adding new oil after searing the first roast. Both pieces of meat can be roasted on the same rack. We prefer this roast cooked to medium-rare, but if you prefer it more or less done, see our guidelines on page 189.

STUFFING

- 8 ounces cremini mushrooms, trimmed and chopped
- ½ tablespoon unsalted butter
- 1½ teaspoons extra-virgin olive oil
- 1 onion, halved and sliced ¼ inch thick
- ¼ teaspoon salt
- ⅛ teaspoon pepper
- 1 garlic clove, minced
- ½ cup Madeira or sweet Marsala wine

BEEF ROAST

- 1 (2-pound) center-cut beef tenderloin roast, trimmed
  Kosher salt and pepper
- ½ cup baby spinach
- 3 tablespoons extra-virgin olive oil

HERB BUTTER

- 4 tablespoons unsalted butter, softened
- 1 tablespoon whole-grain mustard
- 1 tablespoon chopped fresh parsley
- 1 garlic clove, minced
- ¾ teaspoon chopped fresh thyme
- ⅛ teaspoon salt
- ⅛ teaspoon pepper

1. FOR THE STUFFING Pulse mushrooms in food processor until coarsely ground, about 6 pulses. Heat butter and oil in 12-inch nonstick skillet over medium-high heat. Add onion, salt, and pepper and cook, stirring occasionally, until onion begins to soften, about 5 minutes. Stir in mushrooms and cook until all the moisture has evaporated, 5 to 7 minutes. Reduce heat to medium and continue to cook, stirring frequently, until vegetables are deeply browned and sticky, about 10 minutes. Stir in garlic and cook until fragrant, about 30 seconds. Slowly stir in Madeira and cook, scraping up any browned bits, until liquid has evaporated, 2 to 3 minutes. Transfer to plate and let cool to room temperature, about 5 minutes.

2. FOR THE BEEF ROAST Insert knife one-third of way up from bottom of roast along 1 long side and cut horizontally, stopping ½ inch from edge. Open roast and press flat; 1 side will be twice as thick. Continue cutting thicker side of roast in half, stopping ½ inch from edge; open roast and press flat.

3. Pat roast dry with paper towels and season cut side with salt and pepper. Spread cooled mushroom mixture over cut side of

roast, leaving ½-inch border on all sides; spread spinach over top and press gently to compress. Roll roast into tight cylinder, then tie with kitchen twine at 1½-inch intervals.

4. Combine 1 tablespoon oil, 1½ teaspoons salt, and 1½ teaspoons pepper in small bowl, then rub roast with oil mixture; let sit at room temperature for 1 hour.

5. Adjust oven rack to middle position and heat oven to 450 degrees. Heat remaining 2 tablespoons oil in 12-inch skillet over medium-high heat until just smoking. Add roast to pan and cook until well browned on all sides, 8 to 10 minutes. Transfer roast to wire rack set in rimmed baking sheet and transfer to oven. Roast until meat registers 120 to 125 degrees (for medium-rare), 20 to 22 minutes.

6. FOR THE HERB BUTTER While meat roasts, combine all ingredients in small bowl. Transfer roast to carving board and spread half of herb butter evenly over top; let rest for 15 minutes. Remove twine and slice ½ inch thick. Serve, passing remaining herb butter separately.

TO MAKE AHEAD

Stuffed roast, prepared through step 3, can be refrigerated for up to 24 hours

BUTTERFLYING A BEEF TENDERLOIN

1. Insert knife one-third of way up from bottom of roast along 1 long side and cut horizontally, stopping ½ inch from edge.

2. Open roast and press flat; 1 side will be twice as thick.

3. Continue cutting thicker side of roast in half, stopping ½ inch from edge.

Best Prime Rib

SERVES 6 TO 8   **EASY**

ACTIVE TIME 30 MINUTES

TOTAL TIME 5 TO 6 HOURS (PLUS 24 HOURS SALTING TIME)

WHY THIS RECIPE WORKS The perfect prime rib should have a dark and substantial crisp crust encasing a juicy, rosy center. To achieve this perfect roast, we started by salting the roast and then refrigerating it uncovered for 24 hours. This not only seasoned the meat but also dried out the exterior; searing a superdry roast in a superhot skillet helped it develop a nice thick crust. Removing the bones from the roast made it easier to brown the meat. To further enhance tenderness, we cooked the roast at a very low temperature, which allowed the meat's enzymes to act as natural tenderizers. A quick trip under the broiler restored the crispness the crust had lost while the meat was resting. Look for a roast with an untrimmed fat cap (ideally ½ inch thick). We prefer the flavor and texture of prime-grade beef, but choice grade will work as well. Monitoring the roast with a meat-probe thermometer is best. If you use an instant-read thermometer, open the oven door as little as possible and remove the roast from the oven while taking its temperature. If the roast has not reached the correct temperature in the time range specified in step 3, heat the oven to 200 degrees, wait for 5 minutes, then shut it off, and continue to cook the roast until it reaches the desired temperature. Serve with Creamy Horseradish Sauce or Salsa Verde (page 325), if desired.

1 (7-pound) first-cut beef standing rib roast (3 bones), bones removed from roast and reserved
    Kosher salt and pepper
2 teaspoons vegetable oil
    Coarse salt

1. Using sharp knife, cut slits in surface layer of fat, spaced 1 inch apart, in crosshatch pattern, being careful to not cut into meat. Rub 2 tablespoons kosher salt over entire roast and into slits. Place meat back on bones (to save space in refrigerator), transfer to large plate, and refrigerate, uncovered, for at least 24 hours.

2. Adjust oven rack to middle position and heat oven to 200 degrees. Heat oil in 12-inch skillet over high heat until just smoking. Sear sides and top of roast (reserving bone) until browned, 6 to 8 minutes total (do not sear side where roast was cut from bone). Place meat back on ribs, so bones fit where they were cut, and let cool for 10 minutes; tie meat to bones with 2 lengths of kitchen twine between ribs. Transfer roast, fat side up, to wire rack set in rimmed baking sheet and season with pepper. Roast until meat registers 110 degrees, 3 to 4 hours.

3. Turn off oven; leave roast in oven, opening door as little as possible, until meat registers 115 to 120 degrees (for rare) or 120 to 125 degrees (for medium-rare), 30 minutes to 1¼ hours longer.

4. Remove roast from oven (leave roast on baking sheet), tent with aluminum foil, and let rest for at least 30 minutes or up to 1¼ hours.

5. Adjust oven rack 8 inches from broiler element and heat broiler. Remove foil from roast, form into 3-inch ball, and place under ribs to elevate fat cap. Broil until top of roast is well browned and crisp, 2 to 8 minutes.

6. Transfer roast to carving board. Slice meat into ¾-inch-thick slices. Season with coarse salt to taste, and serve.

> **TO MAKE AHEAD**
>
> Salted prime rib, prepared through step 1, can be refrigerated for up to 4 days

PREPARING BEST PRIME RIB

1. To remove bones from roast, use sharp knife and run it down length of bones, following contours as closely as possible. (Removing bones makes it easier to brown meat in skillet.)

2. After crosshatching fatcap, rub kosher salt thoroughly over roast and work it into slits. Place meat on bones and refrigerate for at least 1 day and up to 4 days.

3. Remove roast from bones and sear roast in hot skillet; do not brown side that was attached to bones. Fit browned roast back onto bones, let cool, then tie with twine between each rib.

4. Cook roast slowly in 200-degree oven until it reaches 110 degrees. Turn off oven until meat reaches desired internal temperature. After letting roast rest, broil roast until top is well browned and crisp.

CLASSIC HOLIDAY SAUCES

These flavorful sauces and condiments add a lot to the holiday table, and are perfect for topping roast turkey and mashed potatoes or dressing up a piece of meat.

TURKEY GRAVY

MAKES 2 QUARTS `EASY` `FREEZE IT`

ACTIVE TIME 30 MINUTES

TOTAL TIME 4 HOURS

The beauty of this recipe is that it can be made weeks in advance and frozen long before you've brought home your holiday bird. You can substitute nine turkey wings, separated at the joints, for the turkey thighs in this recipe.

- 6 turkey thighs, trimmed
- 2 carrots, chopped
- 2 celery ribs, chopped
- 2 onions, chopped
- 1 garlic head, outer papery skins removed and top third of head cut off and discarded
- 2 tablespoons vegetable oil
- 10 cups chicken broth, plus extra as needed
- 2 cups dry white wine
- 12 sprigs fresh thyme
  Unsalted butter, as needed
- 1 cup all-purpose flour
  Salt and pepper

1. Adjust oven rack to middle position and heat oven to 450 degrees. Toss turkey, carrots, celery, onions, garlic, and oil together in large roasting pan. Roast, stirring occasionally, until well browned, 1½ to 1¾ hours.

2. Transfer roasted turkey mixture to Dutch oven. Add broth, wine, and thyme sprigs and bring to boil over medium-high heat, skimming as needed. Reduce heat to medium-low and simmer gently until reduced to 8 cups, about 1½ hours. Strain broth through fine-mesh strainer into large container, pressing on solids to extract as much liquid as possible; discard solids.

3. Let strained broth settle for 5 minutes, then use large spoon to skim off fat (reserving ½ cup, and adding butter as needed to reach ½ cup). Heat fat in now-empty Dutch oven over medium-high heat until shimmering. Whisk in flour and cook, whisking constantly, until well browned, 3 to 7 minutes.

4. Slowly whisk in reserved broth and bring to boil. Reduce heat to medium-low and simmer until gravy is very thick, 10 to 15 minutes. Season with salt and pepper to taste.

TO MAKE AHEAD

- Broth, prepared through step 2, can be refrigerated for up to 2 days or frozen for up to 1 month; if frozen, thaw completely in refrigerator before continuing with step 3
- Alternatively, gravy can be refrigerated for up to 2 days; to reheat, bring to gentle simmer, adjusting consistency with hot water as needed

PORT WINE AND CHERRY SAUCE

MAKES 3 CUPS `EASY`

ACTIVE TIME 25 MINUTES

TOTAL TIME 1 HOUR 15 MINUTES

Use a good-quality medium-bodied wine, such as a Côtes du Rhône or Pinot Noir, for this sauce. This sauce goes well with roast beef or pork.

- 1 tablespoon vegetable oil
- 2 large shallots, minced
- 2 cups port
- 2 cups dry red wine
- 1½ cups chicken broth
- 1 cup dried tart cherries
- 4 sprigs fresh thyme
- 2 bay leaves
- 2 tablespoons water
- 4 teaspoons cornstarch
- 4 tablespoons unsalted butter, cut into 4 pieces
  Salt and pepper

1. Heat oil in medium saucepan over medium heat until shimmering. Add shallots and cook until softened, about 2 minutes. Stir in port, wine, broth, cherries, thyme sprigs, and bay leaves and bring to boil over medium-high heat. Reduce heat to medium-low and simmer until mixture measures about 3 cups, 50 minutes to 1 hour.

2. Whisk water and cornstarch together in small bowl to dissolve, then stir into simmering sauce. Cook until sauce has thickened slightly, about 2 minutes. Discard thyme sprigs and bay leaves.

3. Stir in butter, 1 piece at a time, and season with salt and pepper to taste.

TO MAKE AHEAD

- Sauce, prepared through step 2, can be refrigerated for up to 2 days
- To reheat, bring sauce to gentle simmer and continue with step 3

CREAMY HORSERADISH SAUCE

MAKES 1¼ CUPS **EASY**

ACTIVE TIME 10 MINUTES

TOTAL TIME 20 MINUTES

A classic with roasted beef, this sauce also tastes great with fresh salmon and a variety of smoked fish.

    1 cup sour cream
    3 tablespoons prepared horseradish
    1 tablespoon mayonnaise
    1 tablespoon lemon juice
    1 garlic clove, minced
    ¼ teaspoon sugar
      Salt and pepper

Combine all ingredients in bowl and season with salt and pepper to taste. Let sit at room temperature until flavors have blended, about 10 minutes.

TO MAKE AHEAD

- Sauce can be refrigerated for up to 3 days
- To serve, bring sauce to room temperature and stir to recombine

CRANBERRY SAUCE

MAKES 5 CUPS **EASY**

ACTIVE TIME 10 MINUTES

TOTAL TIME 20 MINUTES

You can use frozen cranberries in this recipe but do not thaw before using, and add about 2 minutes to the simmering time.

    2 cups sugar
    1½ cups water
    2 tablespoons grated orange zest
      (2 oranges)
    ½ teaspoon salt
    1½ pounds (6 cups) cranberries
    ¼ cup orange liqueur, such as
      triple sec or Grand Marnier

1. Bring sugar, water, orange zest, and salt to boil in medium saucepan over high heat, stirring occasionally to dissolve sugar. Stir in cranberries and return to boil. Reduce heat to medium and simmer until saucy and slightly thickened and about two-thirds of berries have popped open, about 6 minutes.

2. Transfer to bowl and stir in liqueur.

TO MAKE AHEAD

- Sauce, prepared through step 1, can be refrigerated for up to 3 days
- To serve, bring sauce to room temperature and continue with step 2

FRESH MINT RELISH

MAKES 2¼ CUPS **EASY**

ACTIVE TIME 15 MINUTES

TOTAL TIME 15 MINUTES

Consider using a food processor to mince the parsley and mint; it will be quicker. This relish is perfect with lamb.

    1 cup minced fresh parsley
    1 cup minced fresh mint
    1 cup extra-virgin olive oil
    ⅓ cup red wine vinegar
    ¼ cup water
    1 shallot, minced
    4 garlic cloves, minced
    1 tablespoon sugar
    1 teaspoon salt

Combine all ingredients in bowl.

TO MAKE AHEAD

- Relish can be refrigerated for up to 6 hours
- To serve, bring relish to room temperature and stir to recombine

SALSA VERDE

MAKES 1 CUP **EASY**

ACTIVE TIME 10 MINUTES

TOTAL TIME 10 MINUTES

Serve with roast beef, steak, or fish.

    3 cups fresh parsley leaves
    1 cup fresh mint leaves
    ½ cup extra-virgin olive oil
    3 tablespoons white wine vinegar
    2 tablespoons capers, rinsed
    3 anchovy fillets, rinsed
    1 garlic clove, minced
    ⅛ teaspoon salt

Pulse all ingredients in food processor until mixture is finely chopped (mixture should not be smooth), about 10 pulses, scraping down sides of bowl as needed. Transfer mixture to bowl.

TO MAKE AHEAD

- Sauce can be refrigerated for up to 2 days
- To serve, bring sauce to room temperature and stir to recombine

For a crisp crust and perfectly cooked interior we pan-sear the leg of lamb before putting it in the oven to finish.

Roast Boneless Leg of Lamb with Garlic-Herb Crust

SERVES 4 TO 6

ACTIVE TIME 50 MINUTES

TOTAL TIME 1 HOUR 50 MINUTES

WHY THIS RECIPE WORKS Boneless leg of lamb would seem to be an easy dinner; after all, it already comes boned, rolled, and tied. But it's not as simple as seasoning the lamb, throwing it in the oven, and then checking on it occasionally. We wanted a foolproof method for achieving a crisp crust and perfectly cooked interior every time. We first settled on a half leg as the right amount to serve four to six people. Searing the roast on the stovetop jump-started the cooking process and ensured a golden-brown crust, while finishing it in a 375-degree oven allowed the meat to cook through at an even rate, guaranteeing a juicy and tender interior. A savory crumb crust—flavored with fresh herbs, garlic, and some Parmesan—was a welcome addition to our roast. To prevent the crust

from falling apart once the twine was cut, we cut the twine halfway through cooking, after the lamb had roasted long enough to hold its shape and then applied the crust to the lamb. We prefer the sirloin end rather than the shank end for this recipe, though either will work well. We prefer this roast cooked to medium, but if you prefer it more or less done, see our guidelines on page 189. Serve with Fresh Mint Relish (page 325), if desired.

  1 slice hearty white sandwich bread
  ¼ cup extra-virgin olive oil
  ¼ cup minced fresh parsley
  3 tablespoons minced fresh rosemary
  2 tablespoons minced fresh thyme
  3 garlic cloves, peeled
  1 ounce Parmesan cheese, grated (½ cup)
  1 (3½- to 4-pound) boneless leg of lamb, trimmed
    Salt and pepper
  1 tablespoon Dijon mustard

1. Adjust oven rack to lower-middle position and heat oven to 375 degrees. Pulse bread in food processor until coarsely ground, about 10 pulses (you should have about 1 cup crumbs); transfer to bowl. In now-empty processor, process 1 teaspoon oil, parsley, rosemary, thyme, and garlic until minced, scraping down sides of bowl as needed, about 1 minute. Transfer 1½ tablespoons herb mixture to second bowl; set aside. Scrape remaining mixture into bowl with bread crumbs; stir in Parmesan and 1 tablespoon oil and set aside.

2. Lay lamb with rough interior side (which was against bone) facing up and pound to even ¾-inch thickness; rub with 2 teaspoons oil and season with salt and pepper. Spread reserved herb

PREPARING BONELESS LEG OF LAMB

1. Place rough side of meat (side that was closest to bone) facing up on counter or cutting board. Pound meat to ¾-inch thickness to ensure even cooking.

2. Rub meat with oil then season it with salt and pepper and spread with herb mixture. Roll meat into tight cylinder and tie it with twine at 1-inch intervals.

mixture evenly over meat, leaving 1-inch border around edge. Roll roast into tight cylinder, then tie with kitchen twine at 1-inch intervals. Season with salt and pepper, then rub with 1 tablespoon oil.

3. Set wire rack in rimmed baking sheet. Heat remaining 1 tablespoon oil in 12-inch skillet over medium-high heat until just smoking, about 3 minutes. Sear lamb until well browned on all sides, about 8 minutes. Using tongs, stand roast on each end to sear, about 30 seconds per end. Transfer to rack and roast until meat registers 120 degrees, 30 to 35 minutes.

4. Transfer roast to carving board and remove twine. Brush lamb exterior with mustard, then carefully press bread-crumb mixture onto top and sides of roast with your hands, pressing firmly to form solid, even coating that adheres to meat. Return coated roast to rack; roast until meat registers 130 to 135 degrees (for medium), 15 to 25 minutes longer.

5. Transfer roast to carving board, tent loosely with aluminum foil, and let rest for 15 minutes. Cut into ½-inch-thick slices and serve.

TO MAKE AHEAD

Stuffed lamb and bread-crumb mixture, prepared through step 2, can be refrigerated separately for up to 24 hours

Slow-Roasted Fresh Ham

SERVES 12 TO 14
ACTIVE TIME 40 MINUTES
TOTAL TIME 5 HOURS TO 6 HOURS 30 MINUTES (PLUS 12 HOURS SALTING TIME)

WHY THIS RECIPE WORKS Fresh ham is a meaty, uncured, unsmoked cut which turns tender and flavorful with slow-roasting. We wanted to figure out a foolproof way to cook the oddly shaped, thick-skinned shank-end ham. Removing the skin allowed the fat underneath to render, adding rich flavor to the meat. Rubbing the roast with a mixture of salt, brown sugar, and herbs seasoned it thoroughly and helped the meat retain moisture during cooking. To get the seasonings even deeper into the blocky ham, we cut a large pocket in the meaty end and rubbed the seasoning into it. Cooking the ham in an oven bag kept in moisture for the necessary long cooking time. A simple glaze broiled on before serving made for a flavorful, impressive finish. Use a turkey-size oven bag for this recipe.

A fresh ham is great for a large gathering because it can be prepared and refrigerated for up to 24 hours in advance.

1 (8- to 10-pound) bone-in, shank-end fresh ham
⅓ cup packed brown sugar
⅓ cup kosher salt
3 tablespoons minced fresh rosemary
1 tablespoon minced fresh thyme
1 large oven bag
2 tablespoons maple syrup
2 tablespoons molasses
1 tablespoon soy sauce
1 tablespoon Dijon mustard
1 teaspoon pepper

1. Place ham flat side down on cutting board. Using sharp knife, remove skin, leaving ½- to ¼-inch layer of fat intact. Cut 1-inch diagonal crosshatch pattern in fat, being careful not to cut into meat. Place ham on its side. Cut one 4-inch horizontal pocket about 2 inches deep in center of flat side of ham, being careful not to poke through opposite side.

2. Combine sugar, salt, rosemary, and thyme in bowl. Rub half of sugar mixture in ham pocket. Tie 1 piece of kitchen twine tightly around base of ham. Rub exterior of ham with remaining sugar mixture. Wrap ham tightly in plastic wrap and refrigerate for at least 12 hours.

3. Adjust oven rack to lowest position and heat oven to 325 degrees. Set V-rack in large roasting pan. Unwrap ham and place in oven bag flat side down. Tie top of oven bag closed with kitchen twine. Place ham, flat side down, on V-rack and cut ½-inch slit in top of oven bag. Roast until ham registers 160 degrees, 3½ to 5 hours. Remove ham from oven and let rest in oven bag on V-rack for 1 hour. Increase oven temperature to 450 degrees.

4. Whisk maple syrup, molasses, soy sauce, mustard, and pepper together in bowl. Cut off top of oven bag and push down with tongs, allowing accumulated juices to spill into roasting pan; discard oven bag. Leave ham sitting flat side down on V-rack.

5. Brush ham with half of glaze and roast for 10 minutes. Brush ham with remaining glaze, rotate pan, and roast until deep amber, about 10 minutes longer. Transfer ham to carving board, flat side down, and let rest for 20 minutes. Pour pan juices into fat separator. Carve ham into ¼-inch-thick slices, arrange on platter, and moisten lightly with defatted pan juices. Serve, passing remaining pan juices separately.

TO MAKE AHEAD

Ham, prepared through step 2, can be refrigerated for up to 24 hours

PREPARING A FRESH HAM

1. Cut 4-inch pocket in meaty flat end of ham and season inside pocket.

2. Tie twine around base to create more even shape, then season exterior.

Sheets of phyllo create a dough-like texture in this savory pumpkin and cheese vegetarian lasagna-like option.

Vegetarian Phyllo-Pumpkin Casserole

SERVES 10 TO 12
ACTIVE TIME 1 HOUR
TOTAL TIME 2 HOURS 30 MINUTES

WHY THIS RECIPE WORKS In Turkey, *borek* is a savory filled pastry that is traditionally made by layering sheets of thin dough with appealing fillings that can include a variety of vegetables and cheeses. We wanted to use this traditional dish as inspiration for a holiday-worthy vegetarian main. After testing several different recipes, we decided to make a casserole filled with winter squash and halloumi cheese, a fresh cheese found throughout the region. Boreks are traditionally made using *yufka* dough, which is thicker and doughier than phyllo but thinner than a flour tortilla. Because yufka dough is not widely available, we turned to phyllo to be our stand-in. Although we typically brush each layer of phyllo with oil to help crisp the sheets into individual flaky layers, we instead painted small stacks of phyllo with a mixture of egg and milk for this recipe. This saturated the thin layers and glued them together, forming a noodle-like dough that mimicked the chew and thickness of traditional yufka. Pumpkin is used frequently in Turkish cooking, and canned pumpkin puree made an ultrasimple and flavorful base for our filling. We seasoned the puree with white wine, garlic, and ginger and created a second filling layer with rich cottage cheese, salty halloumi, and fresh mint. Tasters couldn't get enough of the finished sweet, savory, chewy layers that came together into a presentation-worthy dish. Because this is a more involved project of a recipe, we were excited to find that the assembled casserole holds well in the refrigerator. Some tasters even preferred the made-ahead versions because the phyllo-stacks became fully saturated and even more tender and noodle-like. Phyllo dough is also available in larger 18 by 14-inch sheets; if using, cut them in half to make 14 by 9-inch sheets. Do not thaw the phyllo in the microwave; let it sit in the refrigerator overnight or on the counter for 4 to 5 hours. While working with the phyllo, cover the sheets with plastic wrap and place a damp dish towel on top to prevent drying.

FILLING

- 1 tablespoon extra-virgin olive oil
- 1 large onion, chopped
- 1½ teaspoons salt
- 3 garlic cloves, minced
- 1 teaspoon grated fresh ginger
- ½ teaspoon pepper
- 1½ cups dry white wine
- 3 (15-ounce) cans unsweetened pumpkin puree
- 5 large eggs
- 12 ounces halloumi cheese, shredded (3 cups)
- 8 ounces (1 cup) cottage cheese
- ½ cup heavy cream
- ½ cup chopped fresh mint

LAYERS

- ⅓ cup milk
- 1 large egg
- 2 pounds (14 by 9-inch) phyllo, thawed

1. FOR THE FILLING Heat oil in 10-inch skillet over medium-high heat until shimmering. Add onion and salt and cook until softened, about 5 minutes. Stir in garlic, ginger, and pepper and cook until fragrant, about 30 seconds. Stir in wine, bring to simmer, and cook, stirring occasionally, until onion is very tender and mixture has reduced slightly and measures 1¼ cups, 15 to 20 minutes.

2. Transfer onion mixture to food processor and let cool slightly, about 5 minutes. Add pumpkin and eggs and process until mixture is thoroughly combined and smooth, about 3 minutes, scraping down sides of bowl as needed. Combine halloumi, cottage cheese, cream, and mint in separate bowl.

3. FOR THE LAYERS Adjust oven rack to middle position and heat oven to 400 degrees. Whisk milk and egg together in bowl until combined. Trim 50 phyllo sheets to 12½ by 8½ inches.

4. Spread 1 cup pumpkin filling on bottom of greased 13 by 9-inch baking dish. Lay 5 phyllo sheets in dish, brush with egg mixture, then top with 5 more phyllo sheets.

5. Brush phyllo with egg mixture, then spread 2⅓ cups pumpkin filling evenly on top. Lay 5 more phyllo sheets in dish, brush with egg mixture, then top with 5 more phyllo sheets.

6. Brush phyllo with egg mixture, then spread half of cheese mixture evenly over top. Lay 5 more phyllo sheets in dish, brush with egg mixture, then top with 5 more phyllo sheets.

7. Working from center outward, use palms of your hands to gently compress layers and press out any air pockets. Repeat layering in steps 5 and 6, then brush top with egg mixture.

8. Trim 10 phyllo sheets to 13 by 9 inches. Spread remaining pumpkin filling evenly on phyllo layers. Lay 5 large phyllo sheets in dish, brush with egg mixture, then top with 5 more large phyllo sheets. Gently compress layers and wipe away excess filling that may have leaked out along sides of dish.

9. Brush top with remaining egg mixture and bake until casserole registers 165 degrees and top is puffed and golden brown, 40 to 45 minutes. Let cool for 30 minutes before serving.

> **TO MAKE AHEAD ▶**
> - Remaining egg mixture and casserole, prepared through step 8, can be refrigerated separately (casserole wrapped tightly with well-greased plastic wrap), for up to 24 hours
> - To bake, unwrap casserole and continue with step 9

LAYERING PHYLLO-PUMPKIN CASSEROLE

1. After making fillings, spread 1 cup pumpkin filling on bottom of greased baking dish. Then build layers of phyllo, egg mixture, pumpkin filling, and cheese filling.

2. Spread remaining pumpkin filling evenly on phyllo layers and top with remaining 10 phyllo sheets. Gently compress layers and wipe away any excess filling.

SPACE-SAVING SLOW-COOKER HOLIDAY SIDES

The holidays are a busy time for everyone, and it's easy to find yourself running out of space on your stovetop and in your oven. The slow cooker is a great way to lighten the load on your appliances, and can be used to prepare a range of classic holiday side dishes. Better yet, you can hold these dishes in the slow cooker on the warm setting, so they can truly conform to your schedule. You will need a 5- to 7-quart slow-cooker for these recipes.

▶ TO MAKE AHEAD

Sides can be held in slow cooker on warm or low setting for up to 2 hours

SLOW-COOKER CLASSIC MASHED POTATOES

SERVES 10 TO 12 **EASY**

COOKING TIME 5 TO 6 HOURS ON LOW OR 3 TO 4 HOURS ON HIGH

For an accurate measurement of boiling water, bring a full kettle of water to a boil and then measure out the desired amount.

- 5 pounds russet potatoes, peeled and sliced ¼ inch thick
- 2¾ cups boiling water
  Salt and pepper
- 3 tablespoons unsalted butter, melted, plus 9 tablespoons cut into 9 pieces
- ½ cup sour cream
- 3 tablespoons minced fresh chives

1. Combine potatoes, boiling water, and 2 teaspoons salt in slow cooker. Brush top layer of potatoes with melted butter. Press 16 by 12-inch sheet of parchment paper firmly onto potatoes, folding down edges as needed. Cover and cook until potatoes are completely tender, 5 to 6 hours on low or 3 to 4 hours on high.

2. Discard parchment. Mash potatoes with potato masher until smooth. Stir in sour cream, chives, and remaining 9 tablespoons butter until combined. Season with salt and pepper to taste. Serve.

SLOW-COOKER MASHED SWEET POTATOES

SERVES 10 TO 12 **EASY**

COOKING TIME 5 TO 6 HOURS ON LOW OR 3 TO 4 HOURS ON HIGH

For an accurate measurement of boiling water, bring a full kettle of water to a boil and then measure out the desired amount.

- 5 pounds sweet potatoes, peeled and sliced ¼ inch thick
- 2¼ cups boiling water, plus extra as needed
- 2½ teaspoons sugar
  Salt and pepper
- 3 tablespoons unsalted butter, melted, plus 9 tablespoons cut into 9 pieces
- ⅓ cup heavy cream

1. Combine potatoes, boiling water, sugar, and 1¼ teaspoons salt in slow cooker. Brush top layer of potatoes with melted butter. Press 16 by 12-inch sheet of parchment paper firmly onto potatoes, folding down edges as needed. Cover and cook until potatoes are tender, 5 to 6 hours on low or 3 to 4 hours on high.

2. Discard parchment. Mash potatoes with potato masher until smooth. Stir in cream and remaining 9 tablespoons butter until combined. Adjust consistency with extra boiling water as needed. Season with salt and pepper to taste. Serve.

SLOW-COOKER SCALLOPED POTATOES

SERVES 6 TO 8

COOKING TIME 4 TO 5 HOURS ON LOW OR 3 TO 4 HOURS ON HIGH

Do not soak the potatoes in water before using or the dish will be watery.

- 3 pound russet potatoes, peeled and sliced ¼ inch thick
- 1¼ cups heavy cream
- 1¼ cups chicken broth
- 4½ tablespoons cornstarch
- 4 garlic cloves, minced
- 2 teaspoons minced fresh thyme or ½ teaspoon dried
- ½ teaspoon salt
- ½ teaspoon pepper
- 3 ounces sharp cheddar cheese, shredded (¾ cup)
- 3 ounces Monterey Jack cheese, shredded (¾ cup)
- 2 tablespoons minced fresh chives

1. Line slow cooker with aluminum foil collar and lightly coat with vegetable oil spray. Microwave potatoes with 2 tablespoons cream in large covered bowl, stirring occasionally, until nearly tender, 8 to 10 minutes.

2. Whisk remaining cream, broth, cornstarch, garlic, thyme, salt, and pepper together in separate bowl. Microwave cream mixture, whisking occasionally, until thickened, about 5 minutes. Slowly whisk in ½ cup cheddar and ½ cup Monterey Jack until melted.

3. Add cream mixture to potatoes and gently toss to combine. Transfer potatoes to prepared slow cooker and press gently to compress into even layer. Cover and cook until potatoes are tender, 4 to 5 hours on low or 3 to 4 hours on high.

4. Remove foil collar. Sprinkle potatoes with remaining ¼ cup cheddar and ¼ cup Monterey Jack, cover, and let sit until melted, about 20 minutes. Sprinkle with chives before serving.

SLOW-COOKER CLASSIC THANKSGIVING STUFFING

SERVES 10 TO 12

COOKING TIME 3 TO 4 HOURS ON LOW

  2 pounds hearty white sandwich bread, cut into ½-inch pieces (16 cups)
 12 ounces Italian sausage, removed from its casing
  4 tablespoons unsalted butter
  2 onions, chopped fine
  3 celery ribs, minced
  2 tablespoons minced fresh thyme or 2 teaspoons dried
  2 tablespoons minced fresh sage or 2 teaspoons dried
2½ cups chicken broth
  2 large eggs
  1 teaspoon salt
  1 teaspoon pepper

1. Line slow cooker with aluminum foil collar and lightly coat with vegetable oil spray. Adjust oven racks to upper-middle and lower-middle positions and heat oven to 250 degrees. Spread bread over 2 rimmed baking sheets and bake, shaking sheets occasionally, until edges have dried but centers are slightly moist, about 45 minutes, switching sheets halfway through baking. Let bread cool for 10 minutes; transfer to very large bowl.

2. Brown sausage well in 12-inch skillet over medium-high heat, breaking up large pieces with wooden spoon, about 5 minutes; transfer to bowl with dried bread.

3. Add butter to sausage drippings left in skillet and melt over medium-high heat. Add onions, celery, thyme, and sage and cook until vegetables are softened and lightly browned, 8 to 10 minutes. Stir in ½ cup broth, scraping up any browned bits; transfer to bowl with bread.

4. Whisk remaining 2 cups broth, eggs, salt, and pepper together, then pour over bread mixture and toss gently to incorporate; transfer to prepared slow cooker. Cover and cook until stuffing is heated through, 3 to 4 hours on low.

5. Remove foil collar and let stuffing cool for 10 minutes before serving.

MAKING A FOIL COLLAR FOR A SLOW COOKER

Most slow cookers have a hotter side (typically the back side, opposite the side with the controls) that can cause stuffings and other dense dishes, such as casseroles, to burn. To solve this problem, we line the slow-cooker insert with an aluminum foil collar. Depending on the width of the foil, you will need either two or three sheets of foil. The food will help hold the collar in place during cooking, and the collar will prevent the food from cooking unevenly.

1. To make foil collar, fold sheets of heavy-duty aluminum foil into 6-layered rectangle roughly 16 by 4 inches. Press collar into back side of insert; food will help hold collar in place.

2. After potatoes or stuffing has cooked, remove foil collar and let food cool as directed in recipe before serving.

Our recipe produces perfect popovers whether you make and hold the batter or bake and then rewarm them.

Popovers

MAKES 6 POPOVERS **EASY**

ACTIVE TIME 20 MINUTES

TOTAL TIME 2 HOURS 30 MINUTES

WHY THIS RECIPE WORKS The perfect popover soars to towering heights without the addition of whipped egg whites or leavener for lift—but only if you get the baking magic just right. Skip a step or alter the timing slightly and you'll have squat, tough, or sunken popovers. Do they have to be this finicky? We aimed to develop a foolproof recipe that would produce tall popovers with a crisp exterior and an airy, custardy interior every time. Since many recipes turned out skimpy popovers, our first move was to double the ingredient amounts found in most recipes so we could fill the cups of the popover pan almost completely. We tested cake flour, all-purpose flour, and bread flour; because bread flour has the highest protein content of the three, it gave the popovers the strongest structure, and thus the highest rise and most crisp crust. The downside was that it sometimes caused the batter to set up too quickly, which impeded rise. Resting the batter for an hour before baking relaxed the proteins and prevented the popovers from setting up too quickly. Whole milk is traditional, but the fat weighed down our popovers; low-fat milk fixed the problem. Popovers can collapse as they cool, so we poked a hole in the top of each toward the end of baking and then again once they were out of the oven. The small holes enabled the popovers to release the steam slowly and maintain their crispness. Greasing the popover pan with shortening ensures the best release, but vegetable oil spray may be substituted; do not use butter. To monitor the popovers' progress without opening the oven door, use the oven light.

Shortening

2 cups (11 ounces) bread flour, plus extra for pan

3 large eggs, room temperature

2 cups warm 1 or 2 percent low-fat milk (110 degrees)

3 tablespoons unsalted butter, melted

1 teaspoon sugar

1 teaspoon salt

1. Grease 6-cup popover pan with shortening, then flour pan lightly. Whisk eggs in medium bowl until light and foamy. Slowly whisk in warm milk, melted butter, and sugar until incorporated.

2. Whisk flour and salt together in large bowl. Whisk three-quarters of milk mixture into flour mixture until no lumps remain, then whisk in remaining milk mixture.

3. Transfer batter to 4-cup liquid measuring cup, cover tightly with plastic wrap, and let rest for at least 1 hour.

4. Adjust oven rack to lower-middle position and heat oven to 450 degrees. Whisk batter to recombine, then pour into prepared pan (batter will not reach top of cups). Bake until just beginning to brown, about 20 minutes.

5. Without opening oven door, reduce oven temperature to 300 degrees and continue to bake until popovers are golden brown, 35 to 40 minutes.

6. Poke small hole in top of each popover with skewer and continue to bake until deep golden brown, about 10 minutes. Transfer pan to wire rack, poke popovers again with skewer, and let cool for 2 minutes. Remove popovers from pan and serve warm.

TO MAKE AHEAD

- Batter, prepared through step 3, can be refrigerated for up to 24 hours; to bake, let sit at room temperature for 1 hour and continue with step 4
- Baked popovers can be stored at room temperature for up to 2 days; to reheat, bake on rimmed baking sheet in 400-degree oven for 5 to 8 minutes until warmed through

Rustic Dinner Rolls

MAKES 16 ROLLS   EASY   FREEZE IT
ACTIVE TIME 30 MINUTES
TOTAL TIME 5 HOURS (INCLUDES RISING TIME)

WHY THIS RECIPE WORKS European-style dinner rolls are different from their rich, tender American cousins. The dough for these rustic rolls is lean and the crumb is open, with a yeasty, savory flavor. But the best part might be their crust—so crisp it practically shatters when you bite into it, yet chewy enough to offer satisfying resistance. It is this crust that keeps European-style dinner rolls in the domain of professionals, who use steam-injected ovens to expose the developing crust to moisture. We wanted a reliable recipe for rolls as good as any from a European bakery. Unfortunately, when we tasted our first batch, we found a dense, bland crumb beneath a leathery crust. The flavor was easy enough to improve: We added whole-wheat flour for earthiness (just 3 tablespoons did the trick) and honey for sweetness. Extra yeast opened the crumb slightly, but it wasn't enough. The crumb structure of artisan-style loaves is achieved with a wet dough, so we ultimately found success when we upped the hydration of our roll dough. The water created steam during baking, opening up the crumb and making it airier. For an ultracrisp crust, we came up with a two-step process that mimicked a steam-injected oven: First, we misted the rolls with water before starting them in a cake pan at a high temperature to help set their shape (since the dough was soft, individually baked rolls turned out squat). Next, we lowered the temperature, pulled the rolls apart, and returned them to the oven on a baking sheet until they were golden on all sides. We do not recommend mixing this dough by hand.

> 3 cups (16½ ounces) bread flour
> 3 tablespoons whole-wheat flour
> 1½ teaspoons instant or rapid-rise yeast
> 1½ cups plus 1 tablespoon water, room temperature
> 2 teaspoons honey
> 1½ teaspoons salt

1. Whisk bread flour, whole-wheat flour, and yeast together in bowl of stand mixer. Whisk water and honey together in 4-cup liquid measuring cup until honey has dissolved.

2. Using dough hook on low speed, slowly add water mixture to flour mixture and mix until cohesive dough starts to form and no dry flour remains, about 2 minutes, scraping down bowl and hook as needed. Cover bowl tightly with plastic wrap and let dough rest for 30 minutes.

3. Add salt to dough and mix on low speed for 5 minutes. Increase speed to medium and knead until dough is smooth and slightly sticky, about 1 minute. Transfer dough to lightly greased

These foolproof rustic rolls can be shaped and refrigerated overnight or baked and then frozen for up to a month.

large bowl or container, cover tightly with plastic, and let rise until doubled in size, 1 to 1½ hours.

4. Using greased bowl scraper (or your fingertips), fold dough over itself by gently lifting and folding edge of dough toward middle. Turn bowl 90 degrees and fold dough again; repeat turning bowl and folding dough 2 more times (total of 4 folds). Cover tightly with plastic and let rise for 30 minutes. Repeat folding, then cover bowl tightly with plastic and let dough rise until doubled in size, about 30 minutes.

5. Grease two 9-inch round cake pans. Press down on dough to deflate. Transfer dough to well-floured counter, sprinkle lightly with flour, and divide in half. Stretch each half into even 16-inch log and cut into 8 equal pieces (about 2 ounces each). Using your well-floured hands, gently pick up each piece and roll in your palms to coat with flour, shaking off excess. Arrange rolls in prepared pans, placing one in center and seven around edges, with cut side facing up and long side of each piece running from center to edge of pan. Cover loosely with greased plastic.

6. Let rolls rise until nearly doubled in size and dough springs back minimally when poked gently with your knuckle, about 30 minutes.

7. Adjust oven rack to middle position and heat oven to 500 degrees. Mist rolls with water and bake until tops are brown, about 10 minutes. Remove rolls from oven and reduce oven temperature to 400 degrees.

8. Carefully invert rolls out of pans onto baking sheet and let cool slightly. Turn rolls right side up, pull apart, and arrange evenly on sheet. Continue to bake until deep golden brown, 10 to 15 minutes, rotating sheet halfway through baking. Transfer rolls to wire rack and let cool completely, about 1 hour, before serving.

TO MAKE AHEAD ▶

- Shaped rolls, prepared through step 5, can be refrigerated for at least 8 hours or up to 16 hours; to bake, continue with step 6, increasing rising time to 1½ hours
- Baked and cooled rolls can be stored at room temperature for up to 2 days or frozen for up to 1 month; to reheat, thaw if frozen, wrap in aluminum foil and bake on rimmed baking sheet in 350-degree oven for 10 minutes until warmed through

PREPARING RUSTIC DINNER ROLLS

1. After cutting dough in half, stretch each half into 16-inch log, then cut each log into 8 equal pieces. Roll to coat with flour and arrange in pans.

2. To follow 2-step baking process, partially bake rolls in cake pan to help set their shape.

3. Separate rolls and return them to oven on baking sheet to ensure finished rolls are golden and crisp all around.

Honey-Wheat Dinner Rolls

MAKES 15 ROLLS   **FREEZE IT**
ACTIVE TIME 45 MINUTES
TOTAL TIME 4 HOURS (INCLUDES RISING TIME)

WHY THIS RECIPE WORKS Good honey-wheat dinner rolls have the softness of white rolls, with satisfying heft and a nutty whole-wheat flavor that's complemented by a touch of floral sweetness. That said, these appealing rolls rarely hit the mark: Commercial versions are soft but taste artificially sweet, while homemade rolls have good flavor but can be as dense as wet sand. What makes achieving great whole-wheat breads so difficult is the presence of the bran. This part of the grain, which is removed from white flour, gives whole-wheat flour its distinct hearty flavor. But the bran is sharp—so sharp that it cuts through the bread's gluten structure, leaving you with a dense product. To produce a light, fluffy whole-wheat roll, we'd have to incorporate some all-purpose flour—but not so much that we'd lose the roll's earthy, nutty whole-wheat flavor. We also had success when we made a very wet dough. The excess liquid softened the bran's edges, ensuring that it didn't wreak havoc on the dough's structure. To boost the honey flavor, we used 6 tablespoons instead of the 2 that many recipes call for. As a bonus, the liquid honey hydrated the dough further and contributed softness. And to make sure the flavor came through loud and clear, we brushed the warm baked rolls with honey butter. With this finishing touch, our fluffy, pleasantly sweet, nutty-tasting rolls really earned their honey-wheat title.

2½   cups (13¾ ounces) whole-wheat flour
1¾   cups (8¾ ounces) all-purpose flour
2¼   teaspoons instant or rapid-rise yeast
     Salt
1¾   cups whole milk, room temperature
 6   tablespoons plus 1 teaspoon honey
 5   tablespoons unsalted butter, melted
 2   large eggs, room temperature

1. Whisk whole-wheat flour, all-purpose flour, yeast, and 2¼ teaspoons salt together in bowl of stand mixer. Whisk milk, 6 tablespoons honey, 4 tablespoons melted butter, and 1 egg together in 4-cup liquid measuring cup until honey has dissolved.

2. Using dough hook on low speed, slowly add milk mixture to flour mixture and mix until cohesive dough starts to form and no dry flour remains, about 2 minutes, scraping down bowl as needed. Increase speed to medium-low and knead until dough is smooth and elastic and clears sides of bowl but sticks to bottom, about 8 minutes.

For tender, fluffy whole-wheat dinner rolls, we found we needed to include some all-purpose flour as well.

3. Transfer dough to lightly floured counter and knead by hand to form smooth, round ball, about 30 seconds. Place dough seam side down in lightly greased large bowl or container, cover tightly with plastic wrap, and let rise until doubled in size, 1½ to 2 hours.

4. Make foil sling for 13 by 9-inch baking dish by folding 2 long sheets of aluminum foil; first sheet should be 13 inches wide and second sheet should be 9 inches wide. Lay sheets of foil in dish perpendicular to each other, with extra foil hanging over edges of dish. Push foil into corners and up sides of dish, smoothing foil flush to dish, then spray foil with vegetable oil spray.

5. Press down on dough to deflate. Transfer dough to clean counter and stretch into even 15-inch log. Cut log into 15 equal pieces (about 2½ ounces each) and cover loosely with greased plastic. Working with 1 piece of dough at a time (keep remaining pieces covered), form into rough ball by stretching dough around your thumbs and pinching edges together so that top is smooth. Place ball seam side down on clean counter and, using your cupped hand, drag in small circles until dough feels taut and round. Arrange dough balls seam side down into 5 rows of 3 in prepared dish and cover loosely with greased plastic.

6. Let rolls rise until nearly doubled in size and dough springs back minimally when poked gently with your knuckle, 1 to 1½ hours.

7. Adjust oven rack to lower-middle position and heat oven to 350 degrees. Beat remaining 1 egg with 1 tablespoon water and pinch salt. Gently brush rolls with egg wash and bake until golden brown, 25 to 30 minutes, rotating dish halfway through baking.

8. Combine remaining 1 teaspoon honey and remaining 1 tablespoon melted butter in bowl. Let rolls cool in dish for 15 minutes. Using foil overhang, transfer rolls to wire rack and brush with honey mixture. Serve warm or at room temperature.

TO MAKE AHEAD

- Shaped rolls, prepared through step 5, can be refrigerated for at least 8 hours or up to 16 hours; to bake, continue with step 6
- Baked and cooled rolls can be stored at room temperature for up to 2 days or frozen for up to 1 month; to reheat, thaw if frozen, wrap in aluminum foil, and bake on rimmed baking sheet in 350-degree oven for 10 minutes until warmed through

Cream Biscuits

MAKES 8 BISCUITS **EASY** **FREEZE IT**
ACTIVE TIME 20 MINUTES
TOTAL TIME 45 MINUTES

WHY THIS RECIPE WORKS We were after a biscuit recipe that would be simpler than the traditional versions that require cutting butter or shortening into flour, rolling out dough, and stamping biscuits. Cream biscuits, which rely on plain heavy cream in lieu of butter or shortening, were our answer for easy-to-make light and tender biscuits. While most biscuit dough should be handled lightly, we found this dough benefited from 30 seconds of kneading. Although it was easy enough to quickly shape the dough with our hands and then stamp out rounds, alternatively we found we could shape the dough using an 8-inch cake pan, then turn the dough out onto the counter and cut it into wedges. Popping the shaped biscuits into the oven immediately kept them from spreading.

2 cups (10 ounces) all-purpose flour
2 teaspoons sugar
2 teaspoons baking powder
½ teaspoon salt
1½ cups heavy cream

1. Adjust oven rack to upper-middle position and heat oven to 450 degrees. Line rimmed baking sheet with parchment paper. Whisk flour, sugar, baking powder, and salt together in large bowl. Stir in cream with wooden spoon until dough forms, about 30 seconds.

2. Turn dough out onto lightly floured counter and gather into ball. Knead dough briefly until smooth, about 30 seconds. Pat dough into ¾-inch-thick circle.

3. Cut biscuits into rounds using 2½-inch biscuit cutter, dipping cutter in flour as needed. (Alternatively, press dough evenly into 8-inch round cake pan, unmold onto counter, and cut into 8 wedges with bench scraper.) Gather dough scraps together, pat gently into ¾-inch-thick circle, and cut out additional biscuits.

4. Place biscuits on prepared baking sheet. Bake until golden brown, about 15 minutes, rotating sheet halfway through baking. Transfer biscuits to wire rack, let cool for 5 minutes, and serve.

VARIATIONS

Cream Biscuits with Fresh Herbs `EASY` `FREEZE IT`

Stir 2 tablespoons minced fresh parsley, cilantro, chives, tarragon, dill, or basil into flour mixture before adding cream.

Cream Biscuits with Cheddar Cheese `EASY` `FREEZE IT`

Stir ½ cup cheddar cheese, cut into ¼-inch cubes, into flour mixture before adding cream.

TO MAKE AHEAD

- Shaped biscuits, prepared through step 3, can be refrigerated for up 2 hours or frozen for up to 1 month
- To bake, continue with step 4, increasing baking time to 20 to 25 minutes if frozen

24-Hour "Omelet"

SERVES 6 TO 8 `EASY`

ACTIVE TIME 25 MINUTES

TOTAL TIME 1 HOUR 25 MINUTES (PLUS 8 HOURS REFRIGERATING TIME)

WHY THIS RECIPE WORKS A 24-hour omelet is nothing like the omelet that you order at your favorite breakfast joint. Nor does it take a day to bake. It's meant to be assembled in the evening and then popped in the oven to bake while the coffee brews the next morning. Cheesy and golden, it puffs impressively above the rim of the baking dish. While similar to a breakfast strata, a 24-hour omelet is more about the eggs and less about the bread; it also usually forgoes the meats and vegetables that often star in a strata. Consisting of an eggy custard, bread, and cheese, the 24-hour

This eggy casserole gets it melt-in-the-mouth consistency from pieces of buttered bread and a rest in the refrigerator.

omelet is lighter than the fluffiest scrambled eggs and practically melts in your mouth. With the intent of keeping the ingredients and preparation simple, we set out to develop the tastiest 24-hour omelet possible. We started with the bread. Since we wanted the bread to "melt" into the custard, we went with a firm, dense white bread. Buttering the bread added good richness and flavor. As for the custard, we chose milk over cream and half-and-half, since it let the egg flavor shine. To flavor the casserole, we chose cheddar cheese because it melted well and had great flavor, a small amount of grated onion, and a bit of dry mustard and hot sauce for a hint of spiciness that nicely accentuated the creaminess of the eggs. Use the large holes of a box grater to grate the onion. The omelet needs to sit in the refrigerator, well covered, for at least 8 hours in order to achieve the desired consistency.

 3 tablespoons unsalted butter, softened
10 slices hearty white sandwich bread
12 ounces cheddar cheese, shredded (3 cups)
 8 large eggs
 3 cups whole milk
 1 small onion, grated
 1 teaspoon salt

½ teaspoon pepper
1 teaspoon dry mustard
½ teaspoon hot sauce

1. Grease 13 by 9-inch baking dish. Spread butter evenly over 1 side of bread slices, then cut into 1-inch pieces. Scatter half of bread evenly in prepared dish and sprinkle with half of cheddar. Repeat with remaining bread and cheese.

2. Whisk eggs, milk, onion, salt, pepper, mustard, and hot sauce together in bowl until well combined. Pour egg mixture evenly over bread and press lightly on bread to submerge. Wrap dish tightly with plastic wrap and refrigerate for at least 8 hours.

3. Adjust oven rack to middle position and heat oven to 350 degrees. Unwrap casserole and bake until puffed and golden, about 1 hour. Serve immediately.

VARIATIONS
24-Hour "Omelet" with Pepper Jack and Chipotle Chiles `EASY`
Substitute pepper Jack cheese for cheddar and 2 to 3 teaspoons minced canned chipotle chile in adobo sauce for dry mustard and hot sauce. Sprinkle 3 tablespoons minced fresh cilantro over top before serving.

24-Hour "Omelet" with Sun-Dried Tomatoes and Mozzarella `EASY`
Substitute mozzarella cheese for cheddar. Add ½ cup grated Parmesan cheese and ½ cup patted dry and chopped oil-packed sun-dried tomatoes between 2 layers of bread in step 1. Sprinkle 3 tablespoons minced fresh cilantro over top before serving.

> **TO MAKE AHEAD**
>
> Omelet, prepared through step 2, can be refrigerated for up to 24 hours

Breakfast Strata with Spinach and Gruyère
SERVES 4 TO 6 `EASY`
ACTIVE TIME 30 MINUTES
TOTAL TIME 2 HOURS 15 MINUTES (PLUS 1 HOUR REFRIGERATING TIME)

WHY THIS RECIPE WORKS Many recipes for this savory bread pudding are soggy and laden with excessive custard and ingredients, rendering this simple casserole an overindulgence. Looking for a breakfast or brunch casserole that was simple, with just enough richness to satisfy, we considered the bread. Whole dried bread slices had the best texture and appearance, and buttering

Strata is a perfect make-ahead holiday breakfast because it can be assembled and refrigerated for up to 24 hours.

them added richness. We carefully selected a few complementary ingredients for the filling, and we sautéed them to remove excess moisture and prevent the casserole from becoming waterlogged. Weighting down the assembled strata overnight improved its texture, and we could bake it the following morning for a perfect make-ahead breakfast. We found that two 1-pound boxes of brown or confectioners' sugar, laid side by side over the plastic wrap, make ideal weights. The recipe can be doubled and assembled in a greased 13 by 9-inch baking dish; increase the baking time to 1 hour and 20 minutes. Substitute any semisoft melting cheese, such as Havarti, sharp cheddar, or Colby, for the Gruyère.

8–10 (½-inch-thick) slices French or Italian bread
4 tablespoons unsalted butter, softened
4 shallots, minced
Salt and pepper
10 ounces frozen chopped spinach, thawed and squeezed dry
½ cup dry white wine
6 ounces Gruyère cheese, shredded (1½ cups)
6 large eggs
1¾ cups half-and-half

1. Adjust oven rack to middle position and heat oven to 225 degrees. Arrange bread in single layer on rimmed baking sheet and bake until dry and crisp, about 40 minutes, flipping slices halfway through baking. Let bread cool slightly, then spread 2 tablespoons butter evenly over 1 side of bread slices.

2. Meanwhile, melt remaining 2 tablespoons butter in 10-inch nonstick skillet over medium heat. Add shallots and pinch salt and cook until softened, about 3 minutes. Stir in spinach and cook until warmed through, about 2 minutes; transfer to bowl. Add wine to now-empty skillet and simmer over medium-high heat until reduced to ¼ cup, about 3 minutes; set aside to cool.

3. Grease 8-inch square baking dish. Arrange half of bread slices, buttered side up, in single layer in dish. Sprinkle half of spinach mixture and ½ cup Gruyère over top. Repeat with remaining bread, remaining spinach mixture, and ½ cup Gruyère to make second layer.

4. Whisk eggs, reduced wine, half-and-half, 1 teaspoon salt, and pinch pepper together in bowl, then pour evenly over top of bread and cheese in dish. Cover dish tightly with plastic wrap, pressing it flush to surface. Weight down strata and refrigerate for at least 1 hour.

5. Adjust oven rack to middle position and heat oven to 325 degrees. Meanwhile, let strata sit at room temperature for 20 minutes. Unwrap strata and top with remaining ½ cup Gruyère. Bake until edges and center are puffed and edges have pulled away slightly from sides of dish, 50 to 55 minutes. Let casserole cool for 5 minutes before serving.

VARIATION

Breakfast Strata with Sausage, Mushrooms, and Monterey Jack `EASY`

Chorizo, kielbasa, or hot or sweet Italian sausage can be substituted for the breakfast sausage.

Omit spinach, and substitute Monterey Jack cheese for Gruyère. Before cooking shallots, add 8 ounces crumbled bulk breakfast sausage to skillet and cook until no longer pink, about 2 minutes. Stir in 8 ounces trimmed and sliced white mushrooms and cook until lightly browned, 5 to 10 minutes. Stir in shallots and continue to cook as directed.

TO MAKE AHEAD

Strata, prepared through step 4, can be refrigerated for up to 24 hours

For superflavorful and easier huevos rancheros for a crowd, we poach eight eggs in the heated salsa in a casserole dish.

Huevos Rancheros

SERVES 4
ACTIVE TIME 40 MINUTES
TOTAL TIME 1 HOUR 35 MINUTES

WHY THIS RECIPE WORKS Huevos rancheros has made its way northward from Mexico, becoming common on breakfast menus around the United States. To make this crowd-pleasing but involved dish of fried eggs, cheese, and tomato-chile sauce manageable for a group, we roasted the sauce components to brown the vegetables and replicate the char from a cast-iron skillet. We then transferred everything to a casserole dish and nestled the eggs into the sauce so we could cook eight eggs at once. Moving this spicy dish of eggs and charred chiles to the oven gave us a perfectly timed meal that's not just for breakfast. Use a heavyweight rimmed baking sheet; flimsy sheets will warp. Our winning sheet pan is Nordic Ware Baker's Half Sheet. Serve with refried beans and hot sauce.

2 (28-ounce) cans diced tomatoes
1 tablespoon packed brown sugar
1 tablespoon lime juice
1 onion, chopped
½ cup chopped canned green chiles
¼ cup extra-virgin olive oil
3 tablespoons chili powder
4 garlic cloves, sliced thin
Salt and pepper
4 ounces pepper Jack cheese, shredded (1 cup)
8 large eggs
1 avocado, halved, pitted, and diced
3 scallions, sliced thin
⅓ cup minced fresh cilantro
8 (6-inch) corn tortillas, warmed

1. Adjust oven rack to middle position and heat oven to 500 degrees. Line rimmed baking sheet with parchment paper. Drain tomatoes in fine-mesh strainer set over bowl, pressing with rubber spatula to extract as much juice as possible. Reserve 1¾ cups tomato juice and discard remainder. Whisk sugar and lime juice into reserved tomato juice and set aside.

2. In separate bowl, combine onion, chiles, oil, chili powder, garlic, ½ teaspoon salt, and drained tomatoes. Transfer tomato mixture to prepared baking sheet and spread in even layer to edges of sheet. Roast until charred in spots, 35 to 40 minutes, stirring and redistributing into even layer halfway through baking. Reduce oven temperature to 400 degrees.

3. Transfer roasted tomato mixture to 13 by 9-inch baking dish and stir in tomato juice mixture. Season with salt and pepper to taste, then spread into even layer. Sprinkle pepper Jack over tomato mixture. Using spoon, hollow out 8 holes in tomato mixture in 2 rows. Crack 1 egg into each hole. Season eggs with salt and pepper.

4. Bake until whites are just beginning to set but still have some movement when dish is shaken, 13 to 16 minutes. Transfer dish to wire rack, tent with aluminum foil, and let sit for 5 minutes. Spoon avocado over top, then sprinkle with scallions and cilantro. Serve with warm tortillas.

TO MAKE AHEAD

- Roasted tomato mixture and tomato juice mixture, prepared through step 2, can be combined and refrigerated for up to 24 hours
- To bake, microwave sauce until hot, about 2 minutes (stirring halfway through), transfer to baking dish, and continue with step 3

NOTES FROM THE TEST KITCHEN

Buying Eggs

There are numerous—and often confusing—options when buying eggs at the supermarket. And when eggs are the focal point of a dish, the quality of the eggs makes a big difference. Here's what we've learned in the test kitchen about buying eggs.

CHOOSING EGGS According to the U.S. Department of Agriculture (USDA), the average American eats upward of 250 eggs every year. Theoretically, these eggs come in three grades (AA, A, and B), six sizes (from peewee to jumbo), and a rainbow of colors. But the only grade we could find in the market was grade A, the only colors were brown and white, and the only sizes were jumbo, extra-large, large, and medium. So how do we choose? After extensive tasting, we could not discern any consistent flavor differences. The size (and volume) of the egg, however, is important, particularly when baking. In all of our recipes, we use large eggs.

HOW OLD ARE MY EGGS? Egg cartons are marked with both a sell-by date and a pack date. The pack date is the day the eggs were graded and packed, which is generally within a week of when they were laid but may be as much as 30 days later. The sell-by date is within 30 days of the pack date, which is the legal limit set by the USDA. In short, a carton of eggs may be up to two months old by the end of the sell-by date. Even so, according to the USDA, eggs are still fit for consumption for an additional three to five weeks past the sell-by date.

EGG SIZES If you do not have large eggs on hand, substitutions are possible. See the chart below for help in making accurate calculations. For half of an egg, whisk the yolk and white together, measure, and then divide in half.

LARGE	JUMBO	EXTRA-LARGE	MEDIUM
1 =	1	1	1
2 =	1½	2	2
3 =	2½	2½	3½
4 =	3	3½	4½
5 =	4	4	6
6 =	5	5	7

Adding the filling to the quiche's pie shell while the crust is still warm ensures a velvety custard that bakes evenly.

Cheese Quiche

SERVES 6 TO 8
ACTIVE TIME 40 MINUTES
TOTAL TIME 3 HOURS 25 MINUTES (PLUS 1 HOUR COOLING TIME)

WHY THIS RECIPE WORKS Our ideal quiche has a tender, buttery pastry case embracing a smooth custard that is neither too rich nor too lean. We tested numerous combinations of dairy and eggs to find the perfect combination. The baking temperature was equally important; 350 degrees was low enough to set the custard gently, yet hot enough to brown the top before the filling dried out and became rubbery. To keep the crust from becoming soggy, we parbaked it before adding the filling. To avoid spilling the custard, we set the parbaked crust in the oven before pouring the custard into the pastry shell. For perfectly baked quiche every time, we pulled it out of the oven when it was still slightly soft and allowed it to set up as it cooled. Be sure to add the custard to the pie shell while the crust is still warm so that the quiche will bake evenly. You can substitute other fresh herbs for the chives, such as thyme, parsley, or marjoram. You can use store-bought pie dough in place of the homemade dough in this recipe.

    1 recipe Foolproof Single-Crust Pie Dough (page 370)
    5 large eggs
    2 cups half-and-half
    ¼ teaspoon salt
    ¼ teaspoon pepper
    4 ounces cheddar cheese, shredded (1 cup)
    1 tablespoon minced fresh chives

1. Roll dough into 12-inch circle on well floured counter. Loosely roll dough around rolling pin and gently unroll it onto 9-inch pie plate, letting excess dough hang over edge. Ease dough into plate by gently lifting edge of dough with your hand while pressing into plate bottom with your other hand. Trim overhang to ½ inch beyond lip of plate. Tuck overhang under itself; folded edge should be flush with edge of plate. Crimp dough evenly around edge of plate using your fingers. Wrap dough-lined plate loosely in plastic and refrigerate until dough is firm, about 30 minutes.

2. Adjust oven rack to middle position and heat oven to 400 degrees. Line chilled pie crust with double layer of aluminum foil, covering edges to prevent burning, and fill with pie weights. Bake until pie dough looks dry and is pale in color, 25 to 30 minutes.

3. Adjust oven rack to lower-middle position and reduce oven temperature to 350 degrees. Whisk eggs, half-and-half, salt, and pepper together in large bowl. Stir in cheddar.

4. Place warm pie shell on rimmed baking sheet and place in oven. Carefully pour egg mixture into warm shell until it reaches about ½ inch from top edge of crust (you may have extra egg mixture).

5. Bake quiche until top is lightly browned, center is set but soft, and knife inserted about 1 inch from edge comes out clean, 40 to 50 minutes. Let quiche cool for at least 1 hour, sprinkle with chives, and serve warm.

VARIATIONS
Quiche Lorraine
Substitute Gruyère for cheddar. Cook 4 slices finely chopped bacon in 10-inch skillet over medium heat until crisp, 5 to 7 minutes; transfer to paper towel–lined plate. Discard all but 2 teaspoons fat left in skillet, add 1 small finely chopped onion, and cook over medium heat until lightly browned, about 5 minutes; transfer to plate with bacon. Stir bacon mixture into egg mixture with cheese and chives.

Leek and Goat Cheese Quiche

Substitute 1 cup crumbled goat cheese for cheddar. Melt 2 table-spoons unsalted butter in 10-inch skillet over medium-high heat. Add 2 finely chopped leeks, white and light green parts only, and cook until softened, about 6 minutes; transfer to bowl. Stir leeks into egg mixture with cheese and chives.

TO MAKE AHEAD

- Baked quiche can be refrigerated for up to 2 days (crust will be less crisp)
- To reheat, bake in 400-degree oven for 10 to 15 minutes until hot throughout

NOTES FROM THE TEST KITCHEN

Storing Eggs

In the test kitchen, we've tasted two- and three-month-old eggs and found them perfectly palatable. However, at four months, the white was very loose and the yolk had off-flavors, though it was still edible. Our advice is to use your discretion; if eggs smell odd or are discolored, pitch them. Older eggs also lack the structure-lending properties of fresh eggs, so beware when baking.

IN THE REFRIGERATOR Eggs often suffer more from improper storage than from age. If your refrigerator has an egg tray in the door, don't use it—eggs should be stored on a shelf, where the temperature is below 40 degrees (the average refrigerator door temperature in our kitchen is closer to 45 degrees). Eggs are best stored in their cardboard or plastic carton, which protects them from absorbing flavors from other foods. The carton also helps maintain humidity, which slows down the evaporation of the eggs' moisture.

IN THE FREEZER Extra whites can be frozen for later use, but we have found their rising properties to be compromised. Frozen whites are best in recipes that call for small amounts (like an egg wash) or that don't depend on whipping (an omelet). Yolks can't be frozen as is, but adding sugar syrup (microwave 2 parts sugar to 1 part water, stirring occasionally, until sugar is dissolved) to the yolks allows them to be frozen. Stir a scant ¼ teaspoon sugar syrup per yolk into the yolks before freezing. Defrosted yolks treated this way will behave just like fresh yolks in custards and other recipes.

This elegant tart contains just enough custard to bind the ingredients together so the flavor of the salmon really shines.

Smoked Salmon and Leek Tart

SERVES 8 **EASY**

ACTIVE TIME 30 MINUTES

TOTAL TIME 1 HOUR (PLUS 2 HOURS COOLING TIME)

WHY THIS RECIPE WORKS Unexpected and elegant, each bite of this savory tart contains a trio of flavors and textures: flaky pastry, creamy custard, and briny, smoky salmon. Using half-and-half in the leek and custard filling added flavor and richness. Chopping up the salmon made the tart easier to both slice and eat. Once baked, this tart can sit out for up to 4 hours. You will need a 9-inch fluted tart pan with a removable bottom for this recipe. Buy smoked salmon that looks bright and glossy and avoid salmon that looks milky and dry. Serve chilled or at room temperature, with lemon wedges.

1 tablespoon unsalted butter

1 pound leeks, white and light green parts only, halved lengthwise, sliced thin, and washed thoroughly

Salt and pepper

2 large eggs

½ cup half-and-half

1 tablespoon minced fresh dill

1 recipe Press-In Tart Dough (page 282), baked and cooled

6 ounces thinly sliced smoked salmon, cut into ¼-inch pieces

1 tablespoon extra-virgin olive oil

1 tablespoon minced fresh chives

1. Adjust oven rack to middle position and heat oven to 375 degrees. Melt butter in 10-inch skillet over medium heat. Add leeks and ½ teaspoon salt and cook, covered, stirring occasionally, until leeks are softened, about 10 minutes. Remove pan from heat and let leeks cool uncovered for 5 minutes.

2. Whisk eggs, half-and-half, dill, and ¼ teaspoon pepper together in bowl. Stir in leeks until just incorporated. Place cooled tart shell on rimmed baking sheet and place in oven. Carefully pour egg mixture into cooled shell and bake until filling has set and center feels firm to touch, 20 to 25 minutes, Transfer sheet to wire rack and let tart cool completely, at least 2 hours.

3. Just before serving, toss salmon, oil, and chives together in bowl and season with salt and pepper to taste before sprinkling evenly over cooled tart. Slice and serve.

TO MAKE AHEAD ▶

- Baked tart, prepared through step 2, can sit at room temperature for up to 4 hours before continuing with step 3
- Baked tart, prepared through step 2, can be refrigerated for up to 24 hours; bring tart to room temperature before continuing with step 3

Gravlax

SERVES 8 TO 10   **EASY**

ACTIVE TIME 20 MINUTES

TOTAL TIME 25 MINUTES (PLUS 3 DAYS SALTING TIME)

WHY THIS RECIPE WORKS Homemade gravlax sounds like it would require an extravagant time commitment and specialty tools and ingredients, but in fact it's a supereasy and fun project that is a natural choice for making ahead. For gravlax that was evenly moist, tender, and consistently salted, we soaked the fish

Homemade gravlax makes a spectacular hors d'oeuvre when served on cocktail pumpernickel with crème fraîche.

in brandy, coated it in brown sugar, salt, and dill, and then pressed and refrigerated it. The salt drew liquid from the fish and cured it, while the brown sugar countered the harshness of the salt and added deep flavor. The brandy helped the rub adhere and added flavor. We basted the fish just once a day to keep it moist. Once it was finished, all we had to do was slice the salmon as thin as possible. This homemade gravlax has to cure for three days. It is ready when the fish is no longer translucent and its flesh is firm, with no give.

⅓ cup packed light brown sugar

¼ cup kosher salt

1 (1-pound) skin-on salmon fillet

3 tablespoons brandy

1 cup coarsely chopped fresh dill

1. Combine sugar and salt. Place salmon, skin side down, in 13 by 9-inch glass baking dish. Drizzle with brandy, making sure to cover entire surface. Rub salmon evenly with sugar mixture, pressing firmly on mixture to adhere. Cover with dill, pressing firmly to adhere.

2. Cover salmon loosely with plastic wrap, top with square baking dish, and weight down with several large, heavy cans. Refrigerate until salmon feels firm, about 3 days, basting salmon with liquid released into baking dish once a day.

3. Scrape dill off salmon. Remove fillet from dish and pat dry with paper towels. Slice salmon crosswise on bias into very thin pieces and serve.

TO MAKE AHEAD ▷

Gravlax, prepared through step 2, can be wrapped tightly in plastic wrap and refrigerated for up to 1 week

Yeasted Waffles

MAKES SIX 7-INCH WAFFLES   **EASY**
ACTIVE TIME 20 MINUTES
TOTAL TIME 55 MINUTES (PLUS 12 HOURS REFRIGERATING TIME)

WHY THIS RECIPE WORKS Raised waffles are barely on the current culinary radar, and that's a shame. They sound old-fashioned and require advance planning, but they are crisp, tasty, and easy to prepare. We wanted to revive this breakfast treat with yeasted waffles that were creamy and airy, tangy, and refined and complex. We settled on all-purpose flour, found the right amount of yeast to provide a pleasant tang, and added a full stick of melted butter for rich flavor. Refrigerating the batter overnight kept the growth of the yeast under control and produced waffles with superior flavor. Now all we had to do in the morning was heat up the waffle iron. While the waffles can be eaten as soon as they are removed from the iron, they will have a crispier exterior if rested in a warm oven for 10 minutes. (This method also makes it possible to serve everyone at the same time.) The batter must sit in the refrigerator for at least 12 hours.

1¾ cups milk
  8 tablespoons unsalted butter, cut into 8 pieces
  2 cups (10 ounces) all-purpose flour
  1 tablespoon sugar
1½ teaspoons instant or rapid-rise yeast
  1 teaspoon salt
  2 large eggs
  1 teaspoon vanilla extract

1. Heat milk and butter in small saucepan over medium-low heat until butter is melted, 3 to 5 minutes. Let mixture cool until warm to touch.

The batter for these crisp raised waffles can be made in advance and held in the refrigerator for up to 24 hours.

2. Whisk flour, sugar, yeast, and salt together in large bowl. In separate bowl, whisk eggs and vanilla together. Gradually whisk warm milk mixture into flour mixture until smooth, then whisk in egg mixture. Scrape down bowl with rubber spatula, cover tightly with plastic wrap, and refrigerate for at least 12 hours.

3. Adjust oven rack to middle position and heat oven to 200 degrees. Set wire rack in rimmed baking sheet and place in oven. Heat waffle iron according to manufacturer's instructions. Remove batter from refrigerator when waffle iron is hot (batter will be foamy and doubled in size). Whisk batter to recombine (batter will deflate).

4. Spray preheated waffle iron with vegetable oil spray. Add ⅔ cup batter to waffle iron and cook according to manufacturer's instructions until crisp, firm, and golden, 4 to 6 minutes. Serve immediately or transfer to wire rack in oven. Repeat with remaining batter.

TO MAKE AHEAD ▷

Waffle batter, prepared through step 2, can be refrigerated for up to 24 hours

For this rich and sweet breakfast casserole, we dry out the bread pieces in the oven before adding the custard.

French Toast Casserole

SERVES 6 TO 8 **EASY**

ACTIVE TIME 25 MINUTES

TOTAL TIME 2 HOURS 10 MINUTES (PLUS 8 HOURS REFRIGERATING TIME)

WHY THIS RECIPE WORKS When we're craving the flavors and richness of French toast without a fuss, we turn to French toast casserole, which can serve a crowd all at once, no batches necessary. Our French toast casserole has a built-in make-ahead element in that it has to be refrigerated for at least 8 hours to achieve the desired consistency. The ideal French toast casserole has layers of rich, creamy custard and soft but toothsome pieces of bread, all covered by a sweet topping of brown sugar, butter, and pecans. With this clear goal in mind, we set out to closely examine each component of the dish. We began our testing with the choice of bread. We found that supermarket French and Italian loaves, with their dense texture and thin, chewy crust, worked best. We also found that the recipe was best when we "staled" the bread in the oven, allowing it to dry and toast slightly before assembling

the dish. The casserole made with dry, toasted bread had a firmer texture and deeper flavor and was able to withstand a longer stay in the refrigerator before being baked. For the custard, we settled on eight whole eggs and a little less than twice as much whole milk as heavy cream, which gave us a rich and custardy but not cloying result. This was breakfast, after all, not dessert. Our tasters preferred a topping that called for combining brown sugar and butter with a dash of corn syrup, into which we folded pecans. The corn syrup kept the sugar and butter from separating during baking and turning greasy. Do not substitute low-fat or skim milk in this recipe. Be sure to use supermarket-style loaf bread with a thin crust and fluffy crumb; artisan loaves with a thick crust and a chewy crumb do not work well here.

1 pound French or Italian bread, torn into 1-inch pieces
8 large eggs
2½ cups whole milk
1½ cups heavy cream
1 tablespoon granulated sugar
2 teaspoons vanilla extract
½ teaspoon ground cinnamon
½ teaspoon ground nutmeg
8 tablespoons unsalted butter, softened
1⅓ cups packed (9⅓ ounces) light brown sugar
3 tablespoons light corn syrup
2 cups pecans, chopped coarse

1. Adjust oven racks to upper-middle and lower-middle positions and heat oven to 325 degrees. Spread bread out over 2 rimmed baking sheets and bake until dry and light golden, about 25 minutes, switching and rotating sheets halfway through baking. Let bread cool completely.

2. Grease 13 by 9-inch baking dish, then pack dried bread into dish. Whisk eggs, milk, cream, granulated sugar, vanilla, cinnamon, and nutmeg together in bowl. Pour egg mixture evenly over bread and press on bread lightly to submerge. Wrap dish tightly with plastic wrap and refrigerate for at least 8 hours.

3. Stir butter, brown sugar, and corn syrup together in bowl until smooth, then stir in pecans.

4. Adjust oven rack to middle position and heat oven to 350 degrees. Un wrap casserole and sprinkle evenly with topping, breaking apart any large clumps. Place casserole on rimmed baking sheet and bake until puffed and golden, about 1 hour. Let casserole cool for 10 minutes before serving.

TO MAKE AHEAD

Assembled casserole and topping, prepared through step 3, can be refrigerated separately for up to 24 hours

A lot of cake flour helps to make the ultimate crumb topping for this rich but tender cake.

New York–Style Crumb Cake

SERVES 8 TO 10 **EASY**

ACTIVE TIME 30 MINUTES

TOTAL TIME 1 HOUR 15 MINUTES

WHY THIS RECIPE WORKS The essence of crumb cake is the balance between the buttery cake and the thick, lightly spiced topping. Starting with our favorite yellow cake recipe, we realized we needed to reduce the amount of butter or the richness would be overwhelming. We also wanted our crumb topping to be soft and cookie-like, not a crunchy streusel. Don't be tempted to substitute all-purpose flour for the cake flour, as doing so will make a dry, tough cake. If you don't have buttermilk, you can substitute an equal amount of plain low-fat yogurt. Take care to not push the crumbs into the batter. This recipe can be doubled and baked in a 13 by 9-inch pan. If doubling, increase the baking time to about 45 minutes. We did not like the result when we froze this cake.

CRUMB TOPPING

8 tablespoons unsalted butter, melted
⅓ cup (2⅓ ounces) granulated sugar
⅓ cup packed (2⅓ ounces) dark brown sugar
¾ teaspoon ground cinnamon
⅛ teaspoon salt
1¾ cups (7 ounces) cake flour

CAKE

1¼ cups (5 ounces) cake flour
½ cup (3½ ounces) granulated sugar
¼ teaspoon baking soda
¼ teaspoon salt
6 tablespoons unsalted butter, cut into 6 pieces and softened
⅓ cup buttermilk
1 large egg plus 1 large yolk
1 teaspoon vanilla extract
Confectioners' sugar

1. Adjust oven rack to upper-middle position and heat oven to 325 degrees. Cut 16-inch length of parchment paper (or aluminum foil) and fold lengthwise to 7-inch width. Spray 8-inch square baking pan with vegetable oil spray and fit parchment into pan, pushing it up sides; allow excess to hang over edges of pan.

2. **FOR THE CRUMB TOPPING** Whisk melted butter, granulated sugar, brown sugar, cinnamon, and salt together in medium bowl to combine. Add flour and stir with rubber spatula or wooden spoon until mixture resembles thick, cohesive dough; set aside to cool to room temperature, 10 to 15 minutes.

3. **FOR THE CAKE** Using stand mixer fitted with paddle, mix flour, granulated sugar, baking soda, and salt on low speed to combine. With mixer running, add softened butter 1 piece at a time. Continue beating until mixture resembles moist crumbs, with no visible butter chunks remaining, 1 to 2 minutes. Add buttermilk, egg and yolk, and vanilla and beat on medium-high speed until light and fluffy, about 1 minute, scraping down bowl as needed.

MAKING NEW YORK–STYLE CRUMB CAKE

1. Make cake batter, scrape into prepared pan, and smooth top.

2. Break topping into large pea-size pieces and sprinkle evenly over batter.

4. Transfer batter to prepared pan. Using rubber spatula, spread batter into even layer. Break apart crumb topping into large pea-size pieces and spread in even layer over batter, beginning with edges and then working toward center.

5. Bake until crumbs are golden and toothpick inserted in center of cake comes out clean, 35 to 40 minutes, rotating pan halfway through baking. Let cool on wire rack for at least 30 minutes. Remove cake from pan by lifting parchment overhang. Dust with confectioners' sugar just before serving.

TO MAKE AHEAD

- Cake, prepared through step 4, can be wrapped tightly with plastic wrap and refrigerated for up to 24 hours
- To bake, continue with step 5, increasing baking time to 40 to 45 minutes

Sticky Buns

MAKES 12 BUNS

ACTIVE TIME 50 MINUTES

TOTAL TIME 3 HOURS 25 MINUTES (INCLUDES RISING TIME)

WHY THIS RECIPE WORKS Many recipes for sticky buns call for a firm, dry dough that's easy to manipulate into the required spiral, simple to slice, and sturdy enough to support a generous amount of topping. But firm, dry sticky buns aren't very appealing. To make a softer, more tender, and moist sticky bun, we added a cooked flour-and-water paste to the dough. The paste traps water, so the dough isn't sticky or difficult to work with, and the increased hydration converts to steam during baking, which makes the bread fluffy and light. The added water also keeps the crumb moist and tender. To ensure that the soft bread wouldn't collapse under the weight of the topping, we strengthened the crumb by adding a resting period and withholding the sugar and salt until the gluten was firmly established. Dark corn syrup plus water was the key to a topping that was substantial enough to sit atop the buns without sinking in but not so firm that it presented a danger to our teeth. For dough that is easy to work with and produces light, fluffy buns, we strongly recommend that you measure the flour for the dough by weight. The slight tackiness of the dough aids in flattening and stretching it in step 6, so resist the urge to use a lot of dusting flour. Rolling the dough cylinder tightly in step 7 will result in misshapen rolls; keep the cylinder a bit slack. Bake these buns in a metal, not glass or ceramic, baking pan. We like dark corn syrup and pecans here, but light corn syrup may be used, and the nuts may be omitted, if desired.

Using three sweeteners is the key to a topping for these moist buns that is perfectly sweet and just sticky enough.

FLOUR PASTE

⅔ cup water

¼ cup (1⅓ ounces) bread flour

DOUGH

⅔ cup milk

1 large egg plus 1 large yolk

2¾ cups (15⅛ ounces) bread flour

2 teaspoons instant or rapid-rise yeast

3 tablespoons granulated sugar

1½ teaspoons salt

6 tablespoons unsalted butter, softened

TOPPING

6 tablespoons unsalted butter, melted

½ cup packed (3½ ounces) dark brown sugar

¼ cup (1¾ ounces) granulated sugar

¼ cup dark corn syrup

¼ teaspoon salt

2 tablespoons water

1 cup pecans, toasted and chopped (optional)

FILLING

¾ cup packed (5¼ ounces) dark brown sugar

1 teaspoon ground cinnamon

1. FOR THE FLOUR PASTE Whisk water and flour together in small bowl until no lumps remain. Microwave, whisking every 25 seconds, until mixture thickens to stiff, smooth, pudding-like consistency that forms mound when dropped from end of whisk into bowl, 50 to 75 seconds.

2. FOR THE DOUGH In bowl of stand mixer, whisk flour paste and milk together until smooth. Add egg and yolk and whisk until incorporated. Add flour and yeast. Fit stand mixer with dough hook and mix on low speed until all flour is moistened, 1 to 2 minutes. Let stand for 15 minutes. Add sugar and salt and mix on medium-low speed for 5 minutes. Stop mixer and add butter. Continue to mix on medium-low speed for 5 minutes longer, scraping down dough hook and sides of bowl halfway through (dough will stick to bottom of bowl).

3. Transfer dough to lightly floured counter. Knead briefly to form ball and transfer seam side down to lightly greased bowl; lightly coat surface of dough with vegetable oil spray and cover bowl with plastic wrap. Let dough rise until just doubled in volume, 40 minutes to 1 hour.

4. FOR THE TOPPING While dough rises, grease 13 by 9-inch metal baking pan. Whisk melted butter, brown sugar, granulated sugar, corn syrup, and salt in medium bowl until smooth. Add water and whisk until incorporated. Pour mixture into prepared pan and tilt pan to cover bottom. Sprinkle evenly with pecans, if using.

5. FOR THE FILLING Combine sugar and cinnamon in small bowl and mix until thoroughly combined; set aside.

6. Turn out dough onto lightly floured counter. Press dough gently but firmly to expel air. Working from center toward edge, pat and stretch dough to form 18 by 15-inch rectangle with long edge nearest you. Sprinkle filling over dough, leaving 1-inch border along top edge; smooth filling into even layer with your hand, then gently press mixture into dough to adhere.

7. Beginning with long edge nearest you, roll dough into cylinder, taking care not to roll too tightly. Pinch seam to seal and roll cylinder seam side down. Mark gently with knife to create 12 equal portions. To slice, hold strand of dental floss taut and slide underneath cylinder, stopping at first mark. Cross ends of floss over each other and pull. Slice cylinder into 12 portions and transfer, cut sides down, to prepared baking pan.

8. Cover tightly with plastic wrap and let rise until buns are puffy and touching one another, 40 minutes to 1 hour. Meanwhile, adjust oven racks to lower-middle and lowest positions. Place rimmed baking sheet on lower rack to catch any drips and heat oven to 375 degrees.

9. Bake buns on upper rack until golden brown, about 20 minutes. Tent with aluminum foil and bake until center of dough registers at least 200 degrees, 10 to 15 minutes longer. Let buns cool in pan on wire rack for 5 minutes. Place rimmed baking sheet over buns and carefully invert. Remove pan and let buns cool for 5 minutes. Using spoon, scoop any glaze on baking sheet onto buns. Let cool for at least 10 minutes longer before serving.

TO MAKE AHEAD

- Buns, prepared through step 7, can be refrigerated for up to 14 hours
- To bake, remove buns from refrigerator and continue with step 8, increasing rising time to 1 to 1½ hours

MAKING STICKY BUNS

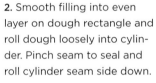

1. Pour topping mixture into prepared baking pan and tilt pan to cover bottom. Sprinkle evenly with pecans, if using.

2. Smooth filling into even layer on dough rectangle and roll dough loosely into cylinder. Pinch seam to seal and roll cylinder seam side down.

3. Slice cylinder into 12 equal portions. Transfer slices, cut sides down, to prepared baking pan. Let rise, then bake buns until golden brown and center of dough registers at least 200 degrees.

4. Let buns cool in pan on wire rack. Place rimmed baking sheet over buns and carefully invert. Remove pan and let buns cool. Using spoon, scoop any glaze on baking sheet onto buns.

Desserts

■ EASY (30 minutes or less active time)   ■ FREEZE IT
Photo: Rustic Walnut Tart

Hot melted butter and the food processor are keys to making our pound cake foolproof.

Easy Pound Cake

SERVES 8 **EASY** **FREEZE IT**

ACTIVE TIME 25 MINUTES

TOTAL TIME 1 HOUR 20 MINUTES (PLUS 2 HOURS COOLING TIME)

WHY THIS RECIPE WORKS Classic pound cake recipes tend to be very particular, requiring ingredients at certain temperatures and finicky mixing methods to ensure a proper emulsion of the eggs into the batter. For a simpler, foolproof pound cake, we discovered that hot melted butter (rather than softened) and the food processor were key. The fast-moving blade of the processor plus the hot melted butter emulsified the liquid ingredients quickly before they had a chance to curdle. Sifting the dry ingredients over our emulsified egg mixture in three additions, and whisking after each addition, allowed us to incorporate the dry ingredients easily and ensured no pockets of flour marred our final cake. The test kitchen's preferred loaf pan measures 8½ by 4½ inches; if you use a 9 by 5-inch loaf pan, start checking for doneness 5 minutes early.

1½ cups (6 ounces) cake flour
1 teaspoon baking powder
½ teaspoon salt

1¼ cups (8¾ ounces) sugar
4 large eggs, room temperature
1½ teaspoons vanilla extract
16 tablespoons unsalted butter, melted and hot

1. Adjust oven rack to middle position and heat oven to 350 degrees. Grease and flour 8½ by 4½-inch loaf pan. Whisk flour, baking powder, and salt together in bowl.

2. Process sugar, eggs, and vanilla together in food processor until combined, about 10 seconds. With processor running, add hot melted butter in steady stream until incorporated. Pour mixture into large bowl.

3. Sift flour mixture over egg mixture in 3 additions, whisking to combine after each addition until few streaks of flour remain. Continue to whisk batter gently until almost no lumps remain (do not overmix).

4. Scrape batter into prepared pan, smooth top, and gently tap pan on counter to settle batter. Bake cake until toothpick inserted in center comes out with few moist crumbs attached, 50 to 60 minutes, rotating pan halfway through baking.

5. Let cake cool in pan for 10 minutes. Run paring knife around edge of cake to loosen. Gently turn cake out onto wire rack and let cool completely, about 2 hours. Serve.

VARIATIONS
Easy Lemon Pound Cake EASY FREEZE IT
Add 2 tablespoons grated lemon zest (2 lemons) and 2 teaspoons lemon juice to food processor with sugar, eggs, and vanilla.

Easy Orange Pound Cake EASY FREEZE IT
Add 1 tablespoon grated orange zest and 1 tablespoon orange juice to food processor with sugar, eggs, and vanilla.

Easy Almond Pound Cake EASY FREEZE IT
Add 1 teaspoon almond extract and ¼ cup slivered almonds to food processor with sugar, eggs, and vanilla. Sprinkle 2 tablespoons slivered almonds over cake before baking.

Easy Ginger Pound Cake EASY FREEZE IT
Add 3 tablespoons minced crystallized ginger, 1½ teaspoons ground ginger, and ½ teaspoon ground mace to food processor with sugar, eggs, and vanilla.

TO MAKE AHEAD ▶

Pound cake can be stored at room temperature for up to 4 days or frozen for up to 1 month; if frozen, thaw completely at room temperature, 4 to 6 hours, before serving

Yellow Birthday Cake

SERVES 10 TO 12　**FREEZE IT**

ACTIVE TIME 1 HOUR

TOTAL TIME 2 HOURS 25 MINUTES

WHY THIS RECIPE WORKS Box mixes are famous for engineering cakes with ultralight texture. We set out to make an even fluffier cake without chemicals and additives. Chiffon cakes are especially weightless, springy, and moist, but unlike butter cakes, they are too light to stand up to a serious slathering of frosting. So we adapted a chiffon technique (using a large quantity of whipped egg whites to get a high volume and light texture) to combine the ingredients from our butter cake recipe. This gave us a light, porous cake that was sturdy enough to hold the frosting's weight. Using butter and a small amount of vegetable oil kept the butter flavor intact while improving the moistness of the cake. For extra tenderness, we increased the sugar and substituted buttermilk for milk. Be sure to use cake pans with at least 2-inch-tall sides.

2½　cups (10 ounces) cake flour
1¼　teaspoons baking powder
¼　teaspoon baking soda
¾　teaspoon salt
1¾　cups (12¼ ounces) sugar
10　tablespoons unsalted butter, melted and cooled
1　cup buttermilk, room temperature
3　tablespoons vegetable oil
2　teaspoons vanilla extract
3　large eggs, separated, plus large 3 yolks,
　　room temperature
　　Pinch cream of tartar
4　cups Quick and Rich Vanilla Frosting (page 353) or
　　Foolproof Chocolate Frosting (page 353)

1. Adjust oven rack to middle position and heat oven to 350 degrees. Grease two 9-inch round cake pans, line with parchment paper, grease parchment, and flour pans. Whisk flour, baking powder, baking soda, salt, and 1½ cups sugar together in bowl. In separate bowl, whisk melted butter, buttermilk, oil, vanilla, and egg yolks together.

2. Using stand mixer fitted with whisk attachment, whip egg whites and cream of tartar on medium-low speed until foamy, about 1 minute. Increase speed to medium-high and whip whites to soft billowy mounds, about 1 minute. Gradually add remaining ¼ cup sugar and whip until glossy, stiff peaks form, 2 to 3 minutes; transfer to bowl.

3. Add flour mixture to now-empty stand mixer bowl. With mixer on low speed, gradually add melted butter mixture and mix until almost incorporated (a few streaks of dry flour will remain), about 15 seconds. Scrape down bowl, then beat on medium-low speed until smooth and fully incorporated, 10 to 15 seconds.

4. Using rubber spatula, stir one-third of whites into batter. Gently fold remaining whites into batter until no white streaks remain. Divide batter evenly between prepared pans, smooth tops, and gently tap pans on counter to release air bubbles. Bake cakes until toothpick inserted in centers comes out clean, 20 to 22 minutes, switching and rotating pans halfway through baking.

5. Let cakes cool in pans for 10 minutes. Remove cakes from pans, discard parchment, and let cool completely on wire rack, about 2 hours.

6. Line edges of cake platter with 4 strips of parchment paper to keep platter clean, and place small dab frosting in center of platter to anchor cake. Place 1 cake layer on platter. Spread 1½ cups frosting evenly over top, right to edge of cake. Top with second cake layer, press lightly to adhere, then spread remaining frosting evenly over top and sides of cake. To smooth frosting, run edge of offset spatula around cake sides and over top. Carefully remove parchment strips before serving.

▶ TO MAKE AHEAD

- Unfrosted cake layers can be stored at room temperature for up to 24 hours or frozen for up to 1 month; if frozen, thaw completely at room temperature, 4 to 6 hours, before frosting (cake will be slightly tacky)
- Frosted cake can be refrigerated for up to 24 hours; bring to room temperature before serving

Devil's Food Layer Cake

SERVES 10 TO 12　**FREEZE IT**

ACTIVE TIME 1 HOUR

TOTAL TIME 2 HOURS 25 MINUTES

WHY THIS RECIPE WORKS Just what is devil's food cake? The name refers to the color of the cake, a very dark, almost black color, not the texture, taste, shape, or fancy decorations. Chocolaty and olate and Dutch-processed cocoa powder. Espresso also helped to intensify the chocolate, while brown sugar and sour cream deepened the flavor and helped keep the cake moist. Dissolving the cocoa in boiling water significantly enhanced the cocoa's flavor. Be sure to use cake pans with at least 2-inch-tall sides. For an accurate measurement of boiling water, bring a full kettle of water to a boil, then measure out the desired amount.

Blooming cocoa and espresso powder in boiling water gives our devil's food cake the deepest chocolate flavor.

½ cup (1½ ounces) Dutch-processed cocoa powder, plus extra for pan
1½ cups (7½ ounces) all-purpose flour
1 teaspoon baking soda
½ teaspoon baking powder
¼ teaspoon salt
1¼ cups boiling water
4 ounces unsweetened chocolate, chopped
1 teaspoon instant espresso powder or instant coffee powder
10 tablespoons unsalted butter, softened
1½ cups packed (10½ ounces) light brown sugar
3 large eggs, room temperature
½ cup sour cream, room temperature
1 teaspoon vanilla extract
4 cups Quick and Rich Vanilla Frosting (page 353) or Foolproof Chocolate Frosting (page 353)

1. Adjust oven rack to middle position and heat oven to 350 degrees. Grease two 9-inch round cake pans, then dust with cocoa powder and line bottoms with parchment paper.

2. Whisk flour, baking soda, baking powder, and salt together in bowl. In separate bowl, whisk boiling water, chocolate, cocoa, and espresso powder together until smooth.

3. Using stand mixer fitted with paddle, beat butter and sugar on medium-high speed until light and fluffy, about 3 minutes. Add eggs, 1 at a time, and beat until combined, about 30 seconds. Beat in sour cream and vanilla until incorporated.

4. Reduce speed to low and add flour mixture in 3 additions, alternating with chocolate mixture in two additions, scraping down bowl as needed. Give batter final stir by hand.

5. Scrape batter into prepared pans, smooth tops, and gently tap pans on counter to settle batter. Bake cakes until toothpick inserted in center comes out with few crumbs attached, 18 to 22 minutes, rotating pans halfway through baking.

6. Let cakes cool in pans for 10 minutes. Remove cakes from pans, discard parchment, and let cool completely on wire rack, about 2 hours.

7. Line edges of cake platter with 4 strips of parchment paper to keep platter clean, and place small dab frosting in center of platter to anchor cake. Place 1 cake layer on platter. Spread 1½ cups frosting evenly over top, right to edge of cake. Top with second cake layer, press lightly to adhere, then spread remaining frosting evenly over top and sides of cake. To smooth frosting, run edge of offset spatula around cake sides and over top. Carefully remove parchment strips before serving.

TO MAKE AHEAD

- Unfrosted cake layers can be stored at room temperature for up to 24 hours or frozen for up to 1 month; if frozen, thaw completely at room temperature, 4 to 6 hours, before frosting (cake will be slightly tacky)
- Frosted cake can be refrigerated for up to 24 hours; bring to room temperature before serving

NOTES FROM THE TEST KITCHEN

Freezing Layer Cakes

Freezing layer cakes is a great way to reduce the amount of work needed on serving day. To ensure that your cakes retain their quality, wrap the completely cooled, unfrosted cakes in double layer of plastic wrap, then aluminum foil, and freeze for up to one month. To defrost a frozen cake, thaw it completely at room temperature, 4 to 6 hours. Note that the surfaces of defrosted cakes will be a bit moist and tacky, so be sure apply the frosting gently to avoid tearing the crust.

FROSTINGS FOR LAYER CAKES

No layer cake is complete without a fluffy, decadent frosting to top it off. Both our vanilla and chocolate frostings go well with our Yellow Birthday Cake (page 351) or Devil's Food Layer Cake (page 351).

TO MAKE AHEAD

- Frosting can be held at room temperature for up to 3 hours
- Frosting can be refrigerated for up to 2 days; bring to room temperature and whisk briefly to re-fluff before using

QUICK AND RICH VANILLA FROSTING

MAKES 4 CUPS   EASY
ACTIVE TIME 15 MINUTES
TOTAL TIME 15 MINUTES

For a fun twist, consider adding some color to the vanilla frosting by stirring in a few drops of food coloring; be sure to add the food coloring sparingly because a little goes a long way.

 24 tablespoons (3 sticks) unsalted butter, cut into chunks and softened
  3 tablespoons heavy cream
 2½ teaspoons vanilla extract
  ¼ teaspoon salt
  3 cups (12 ounces) confectioners' sugar

1. Using stand mixer fitted with paddle, beat butter, cream, vanilla, and salt together on medium-high speed until smooth, about 1 minute. Reduce speed to medium-low, slowly add sugar, and beat until incorporated and smooth, about 4 minutes.

2. Increase mixer speed to medium-high and beat until frosting is light and fluffy, about 5 minutes.

VARIATIONS

COFFEE FROSTING   EASY
Add 2 tablespoons instant espresso or instant coffee to mixer with butter.

PEPPERMINT FROSTING   EASY
Add 2 teaspoons peppermint extract to mixer with butter.

ALMOND FROSTING   EASY
Add 2 teaspoons almond extract to mixer with butter.

COCONUT FROSTING   EASY
Add 1 tablespoon coconut extract to mixer with butter.

FOOLPROOF CHOCOLATE FROSTING

MAKES 4 CUPS   EASY
ACTIVE TIME 15 MINUTES
TOTAL TIME 15 MINUTES

Bittersweet, semisweet, or milk chocolate can be used in this recipe.

 26 tablespoons (3¼ sticks) unsalted butter, softened
 1⅓ cups (5⅓ ounces) confectioners' sugar
  1 cup (3 ounces) Dutch-processed cocoa powder
   Pinch salt
  1 cup light corn syrup
 1½ teaspoons vanilla extract
 10 ounces chocolate, melted and cooled

Process butter, sugar, cocoa, and salt in food processor until smooth, about 30 seconds, scraping down bowl as needed. Add corn syrup and vanilla and process until just combined, 5 to 10 seconds. Scrape down bowl, then add chocolate and process until smooth and creamy, 10 to 15 seconds.

FROSTING A LAYER CAKE

1. Place cake on platter and spread 1½ cups frosting evenly over top.

2. Place second cake layer on top and press lightly to adhere.

3. Spread more frosting over top layer, pushing it over edge of cake. Spread remaining frosting evenly over sides of cake.

4. To smooth frosting, run edge of offset spatula around cake sides and over top.

Individual Molten Chocolate Cakes

SERVES 8 **EASY** **FREEZE IT**

ACTIVE TIME 30 MINUTES
TOTAL TIME 40 MINUTES

WHY THIS RECIPE WORKS Molten chocolate cakes are a classic restaurant showstopper featuring an intense chocolate cake with a gooey, warm center. They also are an ideal make-ahead dessert, since the batter actually benefits from being frozen and baked later. For our recipe, we simplified the preparation by melting chocolate and butter together; whipping whole eggs and an extra yolk, sugar, and flavorings into a foam; then folding the two together. Serve with lightly sweetened whipped cream and fresh berries.

CAKE RELEASE

1 tablespoon unsalted butter, softened
1 tablespoon unsweetened cocoa powder

CAKES

8 ounces semisweet chocolate, coarsely chopped
8 tablespoons unsalted butter
4 large eggs plus 1 large yolk
1 teaspoon vanilla extract
¼ teaspoon salt
½ cup (3½ ounces) sugar
2 tablespoons all-purpose flour

1. FOR THE CAKE RELEASE Mix butter and cocoa together into paste, and brush it evenly inside eight 6-ounce ramekins.

2. FOR THE CAKES Adjust oven rack to middle position and heat oven to 400 degrees. Microwave chocolate and butter in bowl at 50 percent power, stirring occasionally, until melted, about 4 minutes. Let chocolate mixture cool slightly.

3. Using stand mixer fitted with whisk attachment, whip eggs, yolk, vanilla, salt, and sugar together on high speed until volume nearly triples, color is very light, and mixture drops from whisk in a smooth, thick stream, 5 to 7 minutes.

4. Scrape egg mixture over melted chocolate, then sprinkle flour over top. Gently fold batter together until it is uniformly colored. Pour batter into prepared ramekins and place on rimmed baking sheet.

5. Bake until cakes have puffed about ½-inch above rims of ramekins, have thin crust on top, and centers jiggle slightly when shaken gently, 10 to 15 minutes. Serve warm.

> **TO MAKE AHEAD** ▸
>
> Cakes, prepared through step 4, can be refrigerated for up to 8 hours or frozen for up to 1 month; if frozen, do not thaw before baking

Letting the batter rest allows us to pop air bubbles, ensuring a smooth top on our Flourless Chocolate Cake.

Flourless Chocolate Cake

SERVES 10 TO 12 **EASY**

ACTIVE TIME 25 MINUTES
TOTAL TIME 2 HOURS 25 MINUTES (PLUS 6 HOURS CHILLING TIME)

WHY THIS RECIPE WORKS To make a rich, fudgy flourless chocolate cake, we made a simple batter by microwaving the chocolate and butter and then incorporating the remaining ingredients. To ensure a smooth top, we strained and rested the batter and then popped any bubbles on the surface. We bypassed having to use a water bath by baking the cake in a low oven. Our favorite brand of bittersweet chocolate is Ghirardelli 60% Cacao Bittersweet Chocolate Premium Baking Bar. Top the cake with chocolate shavings, if desired. When cutting the cake, dip the blade of the knife into hot water and wipe it clean after each cut to help make neat slices.

12 ounces bittersweet chocolate, broken into 1-inch pieces
16 tablespoons unsalted butter
6 large eggs
1 cup (7 ounces) plus 2 teaspoons sugar
½ cup water
1 tablespoon cornstarch

1 tablespoon plus ½ teaspoon vanilla extract
1 teaspoon instant espresso powder
½ teaspoon salt
½ cup heavy cream, chilled

1. Adjust oven rack to middle position and heat oven to 275 degrees. Spray 9-inch springform pan with vegetable oil spray. Microwave chocolate and butter in bowl at 50 percent power, stirring occasionally, until melted, about 4 minutes. Let chocolate mixture cool for 5 minutes.

2. Whisk eggs, 1 cup sugar, water, cornstarch, 1 tablespoon vanilla, espresso powder, and salt together in large bowl until combined, about 30 seconds. Whisk in chocolate mixture until smooth and slightly thickened, about 45 seconds. Strain batter through fine-mesh strainer into prepared pan, pressing against strainer with rubber spatula to help batter pass through.

3. Gently tap pan on counter to release air bubbles, then let sit on counter for 10 minutes to allow air bubbles to rise before using tines of fork to pop bubbles. Bake cake until edges are set and center jiggles slightly when shaken gently, 45 to 50 minutes.

4. Let cake cool for 5 minutes, then run paring knife between cake and sides of pan. Let cake continue to cool in pan until barely warm, about 30 minutes. Cover cake tightly with plastic wrap, poke small hole in top, and refrigerate until cold and firmly set, at least 6 hours.

5. To unmold cake, remove sides of pan and slide thin metal spatula between cake bottom and pan bottom to loosen, then slide cake onto serving platter. Let cake stand at room temperature for 30 minutes.

6. Using stand mixer fitted with whisk attachment, whip cream, remaining 2 teaspoons sugar, and remaining ½ teaspoon vanilla on medium-low speed until foamy, about 1 minute. Increase speed to high and whip until stiff peaks form, 1 to 3 minutes. Serve with whipped cream.

TO MAKE AHEAD

Cake, prepared through step 4, can be refrigerated for up to 2 days

Triple-Chocolate Mousse Cake

SERVES 12 TO 16
ACTIVE TIME 1 HOUR 5 MINUTES
TOTAL TIME 6 HOURS 25 MINUTES (INCLUDES COOLING, CHILLING, AND SITTING TIME)

WHY THIS RECIPE WORKS Triple-chocolate mousse cake is a truly decadent dessert. Most times, though, the texture is exactly the same from one layer to the next and the flavor is so

For a light, creamy middle layer that wouldn't be overly rich, we take out the eggs and reduce the amount of chocolate.

overpoweringly rich it's hard to finish more than a few forkfuls. We aimed to create a triple-decker that was incrementally lighter in texture and richness. For simplicity's sake, we decided to build the whole dessert, layer by layer, in the same springform pan. For a base layer that had the heft to support the upper two tiers, we chose flourless chocolate cake instead of the typical mousse. Folding egg whites into the batter helped lighten the cake without affecting its structural integrity. For the middle layer, we started with a traditional chocolate mousse, but the texture seemed too heavy when combined with the cake, so we removed the eggs and cut back on the chocolate a bit—this resulted in a lighter, creamier layer. And for the crowning layer, we made an easy white chocolate mousse by folding whipped cream into melted white chocolate, and to prevent the soft mousse from oozing during slicing, we added a little gelatin to the mix. This recipe requires a springform pan with sides at least 3 inches tall. It's important to make each layer in sequential order. Be sure to let the bottom layer cool completely before adding the middle layer. Our favorite brand of bittersweet chocolate is Ghirardelli 60% Cacao Bittersweet Chocolate Premium Baking Bar, and our favorite brand of white chocolate chips is Guittard.

BOTTOM LAYER

6 tablespoons unsalted butter, cut into 6 pieces
7 ounces bittersweet chocolate, chopped fine
¾ teaspoon instant espresso powder
1½ teaspoons vanilla extract
4 large eggs, separated
Pinch cream of tartar
Pinch salt
⅓ cup packed (2⅓ ounces) light brown sugar

MIDDLE LAYER

7 ounces bittersweet chocolate, chopped fine
2 tablespoons Dutch-processed cocoa powder
5 tablespoons hot water
1½ cups heavy cream, chilled
1 tablespoon granulated sugar
⅛ teaspoon salt

TOP LAYER

¾ teaspoon unflavored gelatin
1 tablespoon water
6 ounces white chocolate chips
1½ cups heavy cream, chilled
Shaved chocolate or cocoa powder for serving (optional)

1. **FOR THE BOTTOM LAYER** Adjust oven rack to middle position and heat oven to 325 degrees. Spray 9½-inch springform pan with vegetable oil spray. Melt butter, chocolate, and espresso powder in large heatproof bowl set over saucepan filled with 1 inch of barely simmering water, stirring occasionally, until smooth. Remove from heat and let mixture cool slightly, about 5 minutes. Whisk in vanilla and egg yolks; set aside.

2. In stand mixer fitted with whisk attachment, whip egg whites, cream of tartar, and salt on medium-low speed until foamy, about 1 minute. Add half of sugar and whip until combined, about 15 seconds. Add remaining sugar, increase speed to high, and whip until soft peaks form, about 1 minute longer. Gently fold one-third of beaten egg whites into chocolate mixture to lighten. Fold in remaining egg whites until no white streaks remain. Carefully transfer batter to prepared springform pan and smooth top.

3. Bake until cake has risen, is firm around edges, and center has just set but is still soft (center will spring when gently pressed with finger), 13 to 18 minutes. Let cake cool completely in pan, about 1 hour. (Cake will collapse as it cools.)

4. **FOR THE MIDDLE LAYER** Melt chocolate in large heatproof bowl set over saucepan filled with 1 inch of barely simmering water, stirring occasionally until smooth; let cool slightly, 2 to 5 minutes. In small bowl, combine cocoa and hot water.

5. Using stand mixer fitted with whisk attachment, whip cream, sugar, and salt on medium-low speed until foamy, about 1 minute.

Increase speed to high and whip until soft peaks form, 1 to 3 minutes.

6. Whisk cocoa mixture into melted chocolate until smooth. Gently fold one-third of whipped cream into chocolate mixture to lighten. Fold in remaining whipped cream until no white streaks remain. Spoon mixture into cake pan on top of bottom layer, and smooth top. Wipe any drops of batter off sides of pan and gently tap pan on counter to release air bubbles. Refrigerate cake while preparing top layer.

7. **FOR THE TOP LAYER** In small bowl, sprinkle gelatin over water and let sit for at least 5 minutes. Place white chocolate in medium heatproof bowl. Bring ½ cup cream to simmer in small saucepan over medium-high heat. Off heat, add gelatin mixture and stir until fully dissolved. Pour cream mixture over white chocolate, cover, and let sit for 5 minutes. Whisk mixture smooth and let cool to room temperature, stirring occasionally.

8. Using stand mixer fitted with whisk attachment, whip remaining 1 cup cream on medium-low speed until foamy, about 1 minute. Increase speed to high and whip until soft peaks form, 1 to 3 minutes. Gently fold one-third of whipped cream into white chocolate mixture to lighten. Fold remaining whipped cream into white chocolate mixture until no streaks remain. Spoon mixture into cake pan on top of middle layer, and smooth top. Refrigerate cake until chilled and set, at least 2½ hours.

9. To serve, let cake soften at room temperature for 30 to 45 minutes. Run thin knife between cake and sides of pan; remove sides of pan. Run cleaned knife along outside of cake to smooth. If using, garnish top of cake with shaved chocolate and/or dust with cocoa. Using cheese wire (or dental floss), gently slice cake, wiping wire clean as needed between slices.

▶ TO MAKE AHEAD

Cake, prepared through step 8, can be refrigerated for up to 2 days

Icebox Cheesecake

SERVES 12 **EASY**
ACTIVE TIME 30 MINUTES
TOTAL TIME 1 HOUR 45 MINUTES (PLUS 6 HOURS CHILLING TIME)

WHY THIS RECIPE WORKS Icebox cheesecake is a great make-ahead dessert since it needs time to chill before serving. We wanted our icebox cheesecake to have a supple, creamy texture and great flavor. We tried all manner of recipes, and found it was best to stick to the tried-and-true combination of heavy cream and cream cheese thickened with gelatin. Allowing the gelatin to hydrate in a portion of the cream, then bringing it to a boil in the microwave fully activated its thickening power. We whipped the heavy cream

We soften gelatin in cream to give our no-bake cheesecake a supple, velvety texture.

and cream cheese before adding the cream and gelatin mixture to ensure even dispersal of the gelatin. Lemon juice, lemon zest, and vanilla added just enough spark to perk up the flavor of the tangy cream cheese, while a moderate amount of sugar kept the filling light. Do not substitute low-fat or nonfat cream cheese in this cake, or it will not set up properly. When cutting the cake, have a pitcher of hot tap water nearby; dipping the knife into the water and wiping it clean with a dish towel after each cut helps make neat slices. Serve with Strawberry Topping (page 359) if desired.

CRUST
- 8 whole graham crackers, broken into rough pieces
- 1 tablespoon sugar
- 5 tablespoons unsalted butter, melted

FILLING
- 1½ cups heavy cream
- 2½ teaspoons unflavored gelatin
- ⅔ cup (4⅔ cups) sugar
- 1 pound cream cheese, cut into 1-inch chunks and softened
- 1 teaspoon grated lemon zest plus 2 tablespoons juice

- 1 teaspoon vanilla extract
- Pinch salt

1. FOR THE CRUST Adjust oven rack to lower-middle position and heat oven to 325 degrees. Process graham cracker pieces in food processor to fine crumbs, about 30 seconds. Combine graham cracker crumbs and sugar in bowl, add melted butter, and toss with fork until evenly moistened. Pour crumbs into 9-inch springform pan and press into even layer with bottom of dry measuring cup. Bake crust until fragrant and beginning to brown around edges, about 13 minutes. Let crust cool, about 30 minutes.

2. FOR THE FILLING Pour ¼ cup heavy cream into liquid measuring cup. Whisk in gelatin and let stand until gelatin is softened, about 5 minutes. Microwave mixture until cream is bubbling and gelatin is completely dissolved, about 30 seconds.

3. Using stand mixer fitted with paddle, beat remaining 1¼ cups heavy cream and sugar at medium-high speed until soft peaks form, about 2 minutes. Reduce speed to medium-low, add softened cream cheese, and beat until combined, about 1 minute. Scrape bowl well. Add lemon juice, vanilla, and salt and beat on medium-low speed until combined, about 1 minute. Scrape bowl well. Increase speed to medium-high and beat until smooth, about 3 minutes. Add cream-gelatin mixture and lemon zest and beat until smooth and airy, about 2 minutes.

4. Pour filling into cooled crust and spread it out evenly using offset spatula. Refrigerate cake until firm, at least 6 hours.

5. To serve, wrap hot, damp kitchen towel around springform pan. Unlock pan and carefully lift off sides. Slip thin metal spatula under crust and carefully slide cheesecake onto serving platter.

VARIATIONS

Peppermint Chip Icebox Cheesecake EASY
For crust, substitute 16 Oreo Chocolate Mint Creme cookies for graham crackers, omit sugar, and reduce melted butter to 2 tablespoons. For cake, reduce sugar to ½ cup and omit lemon juice, lemon zest, and vanilla; add 2 tablespoons crème de menthe with salt, and stir 1 cup mini semisweet chocolate chips into filling before pouring into crust.

Peanut Butter Icebox Cheesecake EASY
For crust, substitute 16 Nutterbutter cookies for graham crackers, omit sugar, and reduce melted butter to 2 tablespoons. For cake, reduce sugar to ½ cup, omit lemon juice and zest, and stir ½ cup creamy peanut butter into finished filling. Before serving, press ½ cup chopped salted peanuts into sides of cheesecake.

TO MAKE AHEAD

Cheesecake, prepared through step 4, can be refrigerated for up to 2 days (crust will be less crisp)

DESSERT SAUCES AND TOPPINGS

An easy sauce or topping can make even the simplest dessert feel extra special. Try pairing these accompaniments with ice cream, pound cake, or cheesecake for a company-worthy after-dinner treat.

CHOCOLATE SAUCE

MAKES ABOUT 2 CUPS **EASY**
ACTIVE TIME 15 MINUTES
TOTAL TIME 20 MINUTES

For the best flavor, use good-quality chocolate here. Bittersweet or semi-sweet chips can be substituted.

- 1 cup heavy cream
- ¼ cup light corn syrup
- 4 tablespoons unsalted butter, cut into 4 pieces
  Pinch salt
- 8 ounces bittersweet or semisweet chocolate, chopped fine

Bring cream, corn syrup, butter, and salt to boil in small saucepan over medium-high heat. Off heat, stir in chocolate, cover, and let sit until chocolate is melted, about 5 minutes. Uncover and whisk gently until smooth, trying not to incorporate air bubbles. Serve warm or at room temperature.

> **TO MAKE AHEAD**
>
> Sauce can be refrigerated for up to 2 weeks; to reheat, microwave at 50 percent power, stirring often, until warm and smooth, 1 to 3 minutes

HOT FUDGE SAUCE

MAKES ABOUT 2 CUPS **EASY**
ACTIVE TIME 20 MINUTES
TOTAL TIME 20 MINUTES

Sifting the cocoa powder prevents lumps from forming in the sauce. For the best flavor, use good-quality chocolate here. Semisweet chips can be substituted.

- 10 ounces semisweet chocolate, chopped fine
- ⅓ cup (1 ounce) Dutch-processed cocoa powder, sifted
- ¾ cup light corn syrup
- ⅓ cup (2⅓ ounces) sugar
- ⅓ cup heavy cream
- ⅓ cup water
  Pinch salt
- 3 tablespoons unsalted butter, cut into 3 pieces
- 1 teaspoon vanilla extract

Microwave chocolate in bowl at 50 percent power, stirring occasionally, until melted, 1 to 3 minutes. Whisk in cocoa until dissolved. Meanwhile, simmer corn syrup, sugar, cream, water, and salt together in medium saucepan over medium heat, stirring often, until thickened, about 4 minutes. Off heat, whisk in butter and vanilla. Let mixture cool slightly, then stir in melted chocolate until smooth. Serve warm.

> **TO MAKE AHEAD**
>
> Sauce can be refrigerated for up to 2 weeks; to reheat, microwave at 50 percent power, stirring often, until warm and smooth, 1 to 3 minutes

CARAMEL SAUCE

MAKES ABOUT 1½ CUPS **EASY**
ACTIVE TIME 20 MINUTES
TOTAL TIME 20 MINUTES

Be careful when stirring in the cream, because the hot mixture may splatter.

- ½ cup water
- 1 cup (7 ounces) sugar
- 1 cup heavy cream
- ½ teaspoon vanilla extract
- ½ teaspoon lemon juice
- ⅛ teaspoon salt

1. Pour water into medium saucepan, then pour sugar into center of pan (don't let it hit sides of pan). Gently stir sugar with clean spatula to wet it thoroughly. Bring to boil over medium-high heat and cook, without stirring, until sugar has dissolved completely and liquid has faint golden color, 3 to 6 minutes.

2. Reduce heat to medium-low and continue to cook, stirring occasionally, until caramel has dark amber color, 1 to 3 minutes. Off heat, slowly whisk in cream until combined (mixture will bubble and steam vigorously). Stir in vanilla, lemon juice, and salt. Serve warm.

> **TO MAKE AHEAD**
>
> Sauce can be refrigerated for up to 2 weeks; to reheat, microwave at 50 percent power, stirring often, until warm and smooth, 1 to 3 minutes

BUTTERSCOTCH SAUCE

MAKES ABOUT 1½ CUPS **EASY**
ACTIVE TIME 10 MINUTES
TOTAL TIME 10 MINUTES

Be careful when stirring in the cream, because the hot mixture may splatter.

- 1 cup packed (7 ounces) light brown sugar
- 8 tablespoons unsalted butter, cut into 8 pieces
- ½ cup heavy cream
- 2 teaspoons light corn syrup
- 1 teaspoon vanilla extract

Cook sugar and butter together in medium saucepan over medium-high heat, stirring often, until mixture bubbles and becomes lighter in color, 3 to 5 minutes. Off heat, slowly whisk in cream until combined (mixture will bubble and steam vigorously). Stir in corn syrup and vanilla. Serve warm or at room temperature.

TO MAKE AHEAD ▶

Sauce can be refrigerated for up to 2 weeks; to reheat, microwave at 50 percent power, stirring often, until warm and smooth, 1 to 3 minutes

STRAWBERRY TOPPING

MAKES ABOUT 3 CUPS **EASY**
ACTIVE TIME 20 MINUTES
TOTAL TIME 1 HOUR 45 MINUTES
(INCLUDES COOLING TIME)

Do not substitute frozen strawberries in this recipe.

- 20 ounces (4 cups) fresh strawberries, hulled and sliced thin
- ¼ cup (1¾ ounces) sugar
   Pinch salt
- ½ cup strawberry jam
- 1 tablespoon lemon juice

1. Toss strawberries, sugar, and salt together in large bowl and let sit, stirring occasionally, until berries have released their juice and sugar has dissolved, about 30 minutes.

2. Process jam in food processor until smooth, about 8 seconds. Simmer jam in small saucepan over medium heat until no longer foamy, about 3 minutes. Stir warm jam and lemon juice into berries and let cool to room temperature, about 1 hour. Serve at room temperature or chilled.

VARIATION

BLUEBERRY TOPPING **EASY**

Substitute 3 cups fresh blueberries for strawberries, and blueberry jam for strawberry jam. Gently mash blueberries to help release their juices before letting them sit in step 1.

TO MAKE AHEAD ▶

Topping can be refrigerated for up to 24 hours; stir gently before serving

RASPBERRY SAUCE

MAKES ABOUT 1½ CUPS **EASY**
ACTIVE TIME 15 MINUTES
TOTAL TIME 1 HOUR 15 MINUTES
(INCLUDES COOLING TIME)

Blueberries, blackberries, or thinly sliced strawberries can be substituted for the raspberries.

- 15 ounces (3 cups) fresh or thawed frozen raspberries
- 5 tablespoons sugar, plus extra as needed
- ¼ cup water
- ⅛ teaspoon salt
- 2 teaspoons lemon juice

1. Bring raspberries, sugar, water, and salt to simmer, stirring occasionally, in large saucepan over medium heat. Simmer until sugar has dissolved and raspberries are heated through, about 1 minute.

2. Process warm mixture in food processor until smooth, about 20 seconds. Strain sauce through fine mesh strainer into bowl, pressing solids to extract as much puree as possible. Discard strained solids.

3. Stir in lemon juice, season with sugar to taste, and let cool to room temperature, about 1 hour. Serve at room temperature or chilled.

TO MAKE AHEAD ▶

Sauce can be refrigerated for up to 4 days; stir gently before serving

Baking our New York cheesecake in a dual-temperature oven without a water bath ensures that it doesn't crack.

New York–Style Cheesecake

SERVES 12 TO 16 **FREEZE IT**

ACTIVE TIME 35 MINUTES

TOTAL TIME 4 HOURS 30 MINUTES (PLUS 8 HOURS 30 MINUTES COOLING AND CHILLING TIME)

WHY THIS RECIPE WORKS We set out to find the secret to New York cheesecake with the plush, dense filling, impressive stature, and browned top that characterize this style. The secret turned out to be a long bake at a very low temperature to set the filling, then a final blast of heat at the end of baking to brown the top. This style of cheesecake is baked without a water bath, since that often causes it to crack across the top. Although this cheesecake took about 12 hours from to start to finish, much of that time is hands-off, making it an ideal make-ahead dessert. An accurate oven thermometer and instant-read thermometer are essential. To ensure proper baking, check that the oven thermometer is holding steady at 200 degrees and refrain from frequently taking the temperature of the cheesecake (unless it is within a few degrees of 165, allow 20 minutes between checking). Keep a close eye on the cheesecake in step 5 to prevent overbrowning. Serve with Strawberry Topping (page 359) if desired.

CRUST

6 whole graham crackers, broken into pieces
⅓ cup packed (2⅓ ounces) dark brown sugar
½ cup (2½ ounces) all-purpose flour
¼ teaspoon salt
7 tablespoons unsalted butter, melted

FILLING

2½ pounds cream cheese, softened
1½ cups (10½ ounces) granulated sugar
⅛ teaspoon salt
⅓ cup sour cream
2 teaspoons lemon juice
2 teaspoons vanilla extract
6 large eggs plus 2 large yolks

1. FOR THE CRUST Adjust oven racks to upper-middle and lower-middle positions and heat oven to 325 degrees. Process cracker pieces and sugar in food processor until finely ground, about 30 seconds. Add flour and salt and pulse to combine, 2 pulses. Add 6 tablespoons melted butter and pulse until crumbs are evenly moistened, about 10 pulses. Brush bottom of 9-inch springform pan with ½ tablespoon melted butter. Using your hands, press crumb mixture evenly into pan bottom. Using bottom of dry measuring cup or ramekin, firmly pack crust into pan. Bake on lower-middle rack until fragrant and beginning to brown around edges, about 13 minutes. Transfer to rimmed baking sheet and set aside to cool completely. Reduce oven temperature to 200 degrees.

2. FOR THE FILLING Using stand mixer fitted with paddle, beat cream cheese, ¾ cup sugar, and salt at medium-low speed until combined, about 1 minute. Beat in remaining ¾ cup sugar until combined, about 1 minute. Scrape beater and bowl well; add sour cream, lemon juice, and vanilla and beat at low speed until combined, about 1 minute. Add egg yolks and beat at medium-low speed until thoroughly combined, about 1 minute. Scrape bowl and beater. Add whole eggs two at a time, beating until thoroughly combined, about 30 seconds after each addition. Pour filling through fine-mesh strainer set in large bowl, pressing against strainer with rubber spatula or back of ladle to help filling pass through strainer.

3. Brush sides of springform pan with remaining ½ tablespoon melted butter. Pour filling into crust and set aside for 10 minutes to allow air bubbles to rise to top. Gently draw tines of fork across surface of cake to pop air bubbles that have risen to surface.

4. When oven thermometer reads 200 degrees, bake cheesecake on lower rack until center registers 165 degrees, 3 to 3½ hours. Remove cake from oven and increase oven temperature to 500 degrees.

5. When oven is at 500 degrees, bake cheesecake on upper rack until top is evenly browned, 4 to 12 minutes. Let cool for 5 minutes; run paring knife between cheesecake and side of springform pan. Let cheesecake cool until barely warm, 2½ to 3 hours. Wrap tightly in plastic wrap and refrigerate until cold and firmly set, at least 6 hours.

6. To unmold cheesecake, remove sides of pan. Slide thin metal spatula between crust and pan bottom to loosen, then slide cheesecake onto serving platter. Let cheesecake stand at room temperature for about 30 minutes. To slice, dip sharp knife in very hot water and wipe dry between cuts. Serve.

TO MAKE AHEAD

- Baked crust can be stored at room temperature for up to 24 hours before making cheesecake
- Baked cheesecake, prepared through step 5, can be refrigerated for up to 4 days or frozen for up to 1 month; if frozen, thaw completely in refrigerator, about 12 hours, before serving (crust will be less crisp)

Tiramisù

SERVES 10 TO 12   **FREEZE IT**

ACTIVE TIME 40 MINUTES

TOTAL TIME 40 MINUTES (PLUS 6 HOURS CHILLING TIME)

WHY THIS RECIPE WORKS Tiramisù is an Italian classic. We wanted to find a streamlined approach to tiramisù that high-lighted its luxurious combination of flavors and textures. Instead of making a fussy custard-based filling (called *zabaglione*), we instead simply whipped egg yolks, sugar, salt, rum, and mascarpone together. Whipped cream lightened the filling. We briefly moistened the ladyfingers in a mixture of coffee, espresso powder, and more rum. The test kitchen prefers a tiramisù with a pronounced rum flavor; for a less potent rum flavor, reduce the amount of rum in the coffee mixture. Brandy and even whiskey can be substituted for the dark rum. Do not let the mascarpone warm to room temperature before whipping, or else it might break. Dried ladyfingers are also called *savoiardi*; you will need between 42 and 60 savoiardi, depending on their size and brand.

2½ cups strong brewed coffee, room temperature

1½ tablespoons instant espresso powder

  9 tablespoons dark rum

  6 large egg yolks

⅔ cup (4⅔ ounces) sugar

¼ teaspoon salt

1½ pounds mascarpone, chilled

¾ cup heavy cream, chilled

14 ounces dried Italian ladyfingers

3½ tablespoons Dutch-processed cocoa powder

¼ cup grated semisweet or bittersweet chocolate (optional)

To streamline our tiramisù, we skip the fussy custard and use a simpler mix of egg yolks, mascarpone, and whipped cream.

1. Combine coffee, espresso powder, and 5 tablespoons rum in wide bowl or baking dish until espresso dissolves.

2. Using stand mixer fitted with whisk attachment, mix yolks at low speed until just combined. Add sugar and salt and mix at medium-high speed until pale yellow, 1½ to 2 minutes, scraping down bowl as needed. Reduce speed to medium, add remaining 4 tablespoons rum, and mix at medium speed until just combined, 20 to 30 seconds; scrape bowl. Add mascarpone and mix until no lumps remain, 30 to 45 seconds, scraping down bowl as needed. Transfer mixture to large bowl.

3. In now-empty mixer bowl (no need to clean mixer bowl), whip cream on medium-low speed until foamy, about 1 minute. Increase speed to high and whip until stiff peaks form, 1 to 3 minutes. Using rubber spatula, fold ⅓ whipped cream into mascarpone mixture to lighten, then gently fold in remaining whipped cream until no white streaks remain.

4. Working with 1 ladyfinger at a time, drop half of ladyfingers into coffee mixture, roll, remove, and transfer to 13 by 9-inch baking dish. (Do not submerge ladyfingers in coffee mixture; entire process should take no longer than 2 to 3 seconds for each cookie.) Arrange soaked cookies in single layer in baking dish, breaking or trimming ladyfingers as needed to fit neatly into dish.

5. Spread half of mascarpone mixture over ladyfingers, spreading it to sides and into corners of dish, and smooth top. Place 2 tablespoons cocoa in fine-mesh strainer and dust cocoa over mascarpone.

6. Repeat with remaining ladyfingers, mascarpone, and 1½ tablespoons cocoa to make second layer. Clean edges of dish, cover with plastic wrap, and refrigerate until set, at least 6 hours. Before serving, sprinkle with grated chocolate, if using.

TO MAKE AHEAD ▶

Tiramisù can be refrigerated for up to 24 hours or frozen for up to 1 month; if frozen, thaw completely in refrigerator before serving

Chocolate Pots de Crème

SERVES 8 **EASY**

ACTIVE TIME 30 MINUTES

TOTAL TIME 50 MINUTES (PLUS 4 HOURS CHILLING TIME)

WHY THIS RECIPE WORKS Classic *pots de crème* are truly decadent, with a satiny texture and intense chocolate flavor. We loved that we could make this impressive dessert up to 3 days ahead. A stovetop custard was easier to make than a baked one, and a combination of heavy cream, half-and-half, and egg yolks gave the right amount of richness and body. Bittersweet chocolate offered bold chocolate flavor. When developing this recipe, we used Ghirardelli Bittersweet Chocolate Baking Bar, which contains about 60 percent cacao. If you want to use a darker chocolate that contains about 70 percent bittersweet chocolate, see our variation, Premium Dark Chocolate Pots de Crème. Serve with Whipped Cream (page 365) and Chocolate Shavings (page 363) if desired.

```
10  ounces 60% cacao bittersweet chocolate, chopped fine
 1  tablespoon vanilla extract
 1  tablespoon water
 ½  teaspoon instant espresso powder
 5  large egg yolks
 5  tablespoons (2¼ ounces) sugar
 ¼  teaspoon salt
1½  cups heavy cream
 ¾  cup half-and-half
```

1. Place chocolate in medium bowl and set fine-mesh strainer over top. Combine vanilla, water, and espresso powder in small bowl.

2. Whisk egg yolks, sugar, and salt together in bowl until combined. Whisk in cream and half-and-half. Transfer mixture to medium saucepan and cook over medium-low heat, stirring

To achieve a decadent texture, we skip the oven and use a stovetop method to make a custard.

constantly and scraping bottom of pot with wooden spoon, until thickened and silky and registers 175 to 180 degrees, 8 to 12 minutes. (Do not let custard overcook or simmer.)

3. Immediately pour custard through fine-mesh strainer over chocolate. Let mixture stand to melt chocolate, about 5 minutes. Add espresso-vanilla mixture and whisk mixture until smooth. Divide mixture evenly among eight 5-ounce ramekins. Gently tap ramekins against counter to remove air bubbles.

4. Let pots de crème cool to room temperature, then cover with plastic wrap and refrigerate until chilled, about 4 hours.

5. Before serving, let pots de crème stand at room temperature for 20 to 30 minutes.

VARIATIONS

Milk Chocolate Pots de Crème **EASY**

Milk chocolate behaves differently in this recipe than bittersweet chocolate, and more of it must be used to ensure that the custard sets. And because of the increased amount of chocolate, it's necessary to cut back on the amount of sugar so that the custard is not overly sweet.

Substitute 12 ounces milk chocolate for bittersweet chocolate and reduce sugar to 2 tablespoons.

Premium Dark Chocolate Pots de Crème `EASY`

This recipe is designed to work with a boutique chocolate that contains a higher percentage of cacao than our master recipe.

Substitute 8 ounces 62% to 70% cacao bittersweet chocolate for 60% cacao bittersweet chocolate.

TO MAKE AHEAD

Pots de crèmes, prepared through step 4, can be refrigerated for up to 3 days

MAKING CHOCOLATE SHAVINGS

To make chocolate shavings, soften large block (not bar) of chocolate in microwave on lowest power setting for 1 minute (chocolate shouldn't melt). Run vegetable peeler over chocolate to create curls.

Crème Brûlée

SERVES 8
ACTIVE TIME 40 MINUTES
TOTAL TIME 1 HOUR 20 MINUTES (PLUS 6 HOURS COOLING AND CHILLING TIME)

WHY THIS RECIPE WORKS Crème brûlée is all about the contrast between the crisp sugar crust and the silky custard underneath. We found that the secret to a soft, supple custard was using egg yolks rather than whole eggs. Heavy cream gave the custard a luxurious richness. Sugar, a vanilla bean, and a pinch of salt were the only other additions. Many recipes use scalded cream, but we found that this resulted in overcooked custard, so we heated only half of the cream—enough to extract flavor from the vanilla bean and dissolve the sugar. For the crust, we used crunchy turbinado sugar. A torch worked better than the broiler for caramelizing the sugar. Separate the eggs and whisk the yolks after the cream has finished steeping; if left to sit, the surface of the yolks will dry and form a film. A vanilla bean gives the custard the deepest flavor, but 2 teaspoons of vanilla extract, whisked into the yolks in step 2, can be used instead. While we prefer turbinado or Demerara sugar for the caramelized sugar crust, regular granulated sugar will work, too, but use only 1 teaspoon for each ramekin. Once sugar on top is brûléed, serve within 30 minutes or the sugar crust will soften.

1 vanilla bean
4 cups heavy cream
⅔ cup (4⅔ ounces) granulated sugar
  Pinch salt
10 large egg yolks
8-12 teaspoons turbinado or Demerara sugar

1. Adjust oven rack to lower-middle position and heat oven to 300 degrees. Cut vanilla bean in half lengthwise. Using tip of paring knife, scrape out vanilla seeds. Combine vanilla bean and seeds, 2 cups cream, granulated sugar, and salt in medium saucepan. Bring mixture to boil over medium heat, stirring occasionally to dissolve sugar. Off heat, cover and let steep for 15 minutes, then stir in remaining 2 cups cream.

2. Whisk egg yolks in large bowl until uniform. Whisk about 1 cup cream mixture into yolks, then repeat with 1 cup more cream mixture. Whisk in remaining cream mixture until thoroughly combined. Strain mixture through fine-mesh strainer into large liquid measuring cup, discarding solids.

3. Meanwhile, place dish towel in bottom of large baking dish or roasting pan. Set eight 4- or 5-ounce ramekins (or shallow fluted dishes) on towel. Bring kettle of water to boil.

4. Divide cream mixture evenly among ramekins. Set baking dish on oven rack. Taking care not to splash water into ramekins, pour enough boiling water into dish to reach two-thirds up sides of ramekins. Bake until centers of custards are just barely set and register 170 to 175 degrees, 25 to 35 minutes depending on ramekin type, checking temperature 5 minutes early.

5. Transfer ramekins to wire rack and let cool to room temperature, about 2 hours. Set ramekins on baking sheet, cover tightly with plastic wrap, and refrigerate until cold, about 4 hours.

CARAMELIZING SUGAR ON A CRÈME BRÛLÉE

1. After sprinkling sugar over surface of custard, tilt and tap ramekin to distribute it evenly into thin layer. Pour out excess sugar and wipe inside rims clean.

2. To caramelize sugar, sweep flame from perimeter of custard toward middle, keeping flame about 2 inches above ramekin, until bubbling and deep golden brown.

6. Uncover ramekins and gently blot tops dry with paper towels. Sprinkle each with 1 to 1½ teaspoons turbinado sugar (depending on ramekin type). Tilt and tap each ramekin to distribute sugar evenly then dump out excess sugar and wipe rims of ramekins clean. Ignite torch and caramelize sugar. Serve.

VARIATIONS
Espresso Crème Brûlée
Crush the espresso beans lightly with the bottom of a skillet; don't use a coffee grinder or else the beans will be ground too fine.

Substitute ¼ cup lightly crushed espresso beans for vanilla bean. Whisk 1 teaspoon vanilla extract into yolks before adding cream.

Tea-Infused Crème Brûlée
Substitute 10 Irish Breakfast tea bags, tied together, for vanilla bean; after steeping tea in cream, squeeze bags with tongs or press into fine-mesh strainer to extract all liquid. Whisk 1 teaspoon vanilla extract into yolks before adding cream.

TO MAKE AHEAD
• Crème brûlée, prepared through step 5, can be refrigerated for up to 3 days

The right amount of gelatin is the secret to panna cotta that is set but not rubbery.

Panna Cotta
SERVES 8
ACTIVE TIME 35 MINUTES
TOTAL TIME 35 MINUTES (PLUS 4 HOURS CHILLING TIME)

WHY THIS RECIPE WORKS Panna cotta is a simple, refined dessert where sugar and gelatin are melted in cream and milk, and the mixture is chilled in individual ramekins. We set out to create a simple recipe that would guarantee a pudding with the rich flavor of cream and vanilla and a delicate texture. The amount of gelatin proved critical; we used a light hand, adding just enough to make the dessert firm enough to unmold. Because gelatin sets more quickly at cold temperatures, we minimized the amount of heat by softening the gelatin in cold milk, then heating it very briefly until it was melted. To avoid premature hardening, we gradually added cold vanilla-infused cream to the gelatin mixture and stirred everything over an ice bath to incorporate the gelatin. A vanilla bean gives the panna cotta the deepest flavor, but 2 teaspoons of vanilla extract can be used instead. Serve the panna cotta with lightly sweetened berries or Raspberry Sauce (page 359). Though traditionally unmolded, panna cotta may be chilled and served in wineglasses with the sauce on top.

  1 cup cold whole milk
2¾ teaspoons unflavored gelatin
  3 cups cold heavy cream
  1 vanilla bean
  6 tablespoons (2⅔ ounces) sugar
    Pinch salt

1. Pour milk into medium saucepan, sprinkle gelatin over top, and let sit until gelatin softens, about 10 minutes. Meanwhile, place cream in large measuring cup. Cut vanilla bean in half lengthwise. Using tip of paring knife, scrape out vanilla seeds. Add vanilla bean and seeds to cream. Set eight 4-ounce ramekins on rimmed baking sheet. Make large bowl of ice water.

2. Heat milk and gelatin mixture over high heat, stirring constantly, until gelatin is dissolved and mixture registers 135 degrees, about 1½ minutes. Off heat, stir in sugar and salt until dissolved, about 1 minute.

3. Stirring constantly, slowly pour cream into milk mixture. Transfer mixture to clean bowl and set over bowl of ice water. Stir mixture often until slightly thickened and mixture registers

WHIPPED CREAM

MAKES ABOUT 2 CUPS `EASY`
ACTIVE TIME 10 MINUTES
TOTAL TIME 10 MINUTES

Whipped cream is as much about texture as flavor. Be sure to use well-chilled cream and start whipping at medium-low speed. Once the cream is frothy, increase the speed to high and whip until the cream is thick and billowy. For lightly sweetened whipped cream, use less sugar. On very hot days, chill the bowl and beaters.

1 cup heavy cream, chilled
1 tablespoon sugar
1 teaspoon vanilla extract
Pinch salt

Using stand mixer fitted with whisk attachment, whip cream, sugar, vanilla, and salt on medium-low speed until foamy, about 1 minute. Increase speed to high and whip until soft peaks form, 1 to 3 minutes.

VARIATIONS
SMALL-BATCH WHIPPED CREAM

MAKES ABOUT 1 CUP `EASY`

This recipe yields just 1 cup of whipped cream, which is perfect for garnishing small desserts such as Chocolate Pots de Crème (page 362). This small batch will not work in large stand mixers; instead, use a hand mixer or whip the cream by hand.

Reduce cream to ½ cup, sugar to 2 teaspoons, and vanilla to ½ teaspoon.

TANGY WHIPPED CREAM

MAKES ABOUT 2½ CUPS `EASY`

Sour cream gives this whipped cream a slight tang that pairs well with many fruit desserts.

Add ½ cup sour cream to mixture before whipping.

BOURBON WHIPPED CREAM

MAKES ABOUT 2 CUPS `EASY`

Add 2 teaspoons bourbon to mixture before whipping.

BROWN SUGAR–BOURBON WHIPPED CREAM

MAKES ABOUT 3 CUPS `EASY`

Serve this sweet and tangy whipped cream with any dessert that has lots of nuts, warm spices, or molasses like gingerbread, pecan pie, or pumpkin pie.

Substitute ⅓ packed light brown sugar for sugar. Add ½ cup chilled sour cream and 2 teaspoons bourbon to mixture before whipping.

> **TO MAKE AHEAD**
> Whipped cream can be transferred to fine-mesh strainer set over small bowl, covered, and refrigerated for up to 8 hours

---

50 degrees, about 10 minutes. Strain mixture through fine-mesh strainer into large liquid measuring cup, then distribute evenly among ramekins.

4. Cover baking sheet with plastic wrap and refrigerate until custards are just set (mixture should wobble when shaken gently), about 4 hours.

5. To unmold, run paring knife around perimeter of each ramekin. Hold serving plate over top of each ramekin and invert; set plate on counter and gently shake ramekin to release custard. Serve.

VARIATION
Lemon Panna Cotta

Add four 2-inch strips lemon zest, cut into thin strips, to cream with vanilla bean. Add ¼ cup lemon juice (2 lemons) to strained cream mixture before dividing among ramekins.

> **TO MAKE AHEAD**
> Panna cotta, prepared through step 4, can be refrigerated for up to 24 hours

Cranberry-Apple Crisp

SERVES 8 `FREEZE IT`
ACTIVE TIME 50 MINUTES
TOTAL TIME 1 HOUR 30 MINUTES

WHY THIS RECIPE WORKS Although it's hard to imagine that apple crisp needs much improvement, we liked the tartness and texture that cranberries added to one of our favorite standard dessert recipes. The challenges were balancing the fruit flavors and making sure that the filling baked evenly while the topping stayed crisp. We achieved the perfect fruit mix by combining fresh and dried cranberries, and we precooked all the fruit and added tapioca to thicken the juices. This step shortened the oven time and ensured that the classic butter, flour, sugar, cinnamon, and oat topping lived up to the name "crisp." If you can't find Braeburn apples, Golden Delicious will work. While old-fashioned rolled oats are preferable in this recipe, quick oats can be substituted; do not use instant oats. Serve with vanilla ice cream or Whipped Cream.

Our stovetop-to-oven method concentrates the fruits' flavors and produces a topping that's truly crisp.

TOPPING

¾ cup (3¾ ounces) all-purpose flour

½ cup packed (3½ ounces) light brown sugar

½ cup (3½ ounces) granulated sugar

1 teaspoon ground cinnamon

12 tablespoons unsalted butter, cut into ½-inch pieces and chilled

¾ cup (2¼ ounces) old-fashioned rolled oats

FILLING

1 pound (4 cups) fresh or frozen cranberries

1¼ cups (8¾ ounces) granulated sugar

¼ cup water

2½ pounds Granny Smith apples, peeled, cored, and cut into ½-inch pieces

2½ pounds Braeburn apples, peeled, cored, and cut into ½-inch pieces

1 cup sweetened dried cranberries

3 tablespoons Minute Tapioca

1. FOR THE TOPPING Adjust oven rack to middle position and heat oven to 400 degrees. Pulse flour, sugars, cinnamon, and butter in food processor until mixture has texture of coarse crumbs (some pea-size pieces of butter will remain), about 12 pulses. Transfer to medium bowl, stir in oats, and use fingers to pinch topping into peanut-sized clumps. Refrigerate while preparing filling.

2. FOR THE FILLING Bring cranberries, ¾ cup sugar, and water to simmer in Dutch oven over medium-high heat and cook until cranberries are completely softened and mixture is jam-like, about 10 minutes; transfer to bowl. Cook apples, remaining ½ cup sugar, and dried cranberries in now-empty Dutch oven over medium-high heat until apples begin to release their juices, about 5 minutes. Off heat, stir in cranberry mixture and tapioca.

3. Transfer filling to 13 by 9-inch baking dish set on rimmed baking sheet. Smooth surface evenly with spatula and scatter topping evenly over filling. Bake until juices are bubbling and topping is deep golden brown, about 30 minutes. (If topping is browning too quickly, loosely cover with piece of aluminum foil.) Let cool slightly. Serve warm or at room temperature.

VARIATION

Cranberry-Pear Crisp `FREEZE IT`

We prefer to use Bartlett pears here, but Bosc pears can also be used.

Substitute 5 pounds Bartlett pears, peeled, cored, and cut into ½-inch pieces, for apples; cook as directed.

> **TO MAKE AHEAD** ▸
>
> • Raw topping and cooked filling, prepared through step 2, can be refrigerated separately for up to 2 days; to bake, continue with step 3, increasing baking time to 35 to 40 minutes and covering dish with aluminum foil for first 20 minutes
>
> • Alternatively, raw topping, prepared through step 1, can be frozen for up to 1 month; do not thaw before using
>
> • Fully baked crisp can be held at room temperature for up to 4 hours; serve at room temperature or reheat in 400-degree oven for 10 minutes

Blueberry Cobbler

SERVES 8 `EASY`

ACTIVE TIME 30 MINUTES

TOTAL TIME 1 HOUR 30 MINUTES

WHY THIS RECIPE WORKS We wanted a cobbler that put the blueberry flavor front and center, with a light, tender biscuit topping that could hold its own against the fruit filling. We started by preparing a filling using 6 cups of fresh berries and just enough sugar to sweeten them. Cornstarch worked well to thicken the fruit's juices.

Parbaking the biscuit topping ensured that the biscuits wouldn't become soggy once placed on top of the fruit, and precooking the fruit filling meant all we had to do was marry the parbaked biscuits and the precooked filling and heat them together for 15 minutes until bubbly. This recipe works best with very juicy fruit. Before preparing the filling, taste the fruit, adding a smaller amount of sugar if the fruit is on sweet side and more if the fruit is tart. Do not let the biscuit batter sit for longer than 5 minutes or so before baking. If you don't have a deep-dish glass pie plate, use a round baking dish of similar size; a round shape makes it easy to fit the biscuits on top.

BISCUIT TOPPING

- 1½ cups (7½ ounces) all-purpose flour
- ¼ cup (1¾ ounces) plus 2 teaspoons sugar
- 1½ teaspoons baking powder
- ¼ teaspoon baking soda
- ¼ teaspoon salt
- ¾ cup buttermilk, chilled
- 6 tablespoons unsalted butter, melted and hot
- ⅛ teaspoon ground cinnamon

FRUIT FILLING

- ⅓–⅔ cup (2⅓–4⅔ ounces) sugar
- 4 teaspoons cornstarch
- 30 ounces (6 cups) blueberries
- 1 tablespoon lemon juice
- ½ teaspoon ground cinnamon

1. FOR THE BISCUIT TOPPING Adjust oven rack to middle position and heat oven to 400 degrees. Line rimmed baking sheet with parchment paper. Whisk flour, ¼ cup sugar, baking powder, baking soda, and salt together in large bowl.

2. In medium bowl, stir buttermilk and melted butter together until butter forms small clumps. Using rubber spatula, stir buttermilk mixture into flour mixture until just incorporated and dough pulls away from sides of bowl.

3. Using greased ¼-cup measure, scoop out and drop 8 mounds of dough onto prepared baking sheet, spaced about 1½ inches apart. Combine remaining 2 teaspoons sugar with cinnamon, then sprinkle over biscuits. Bake biscuits until puffed and lightly browned on bottom, about 10 minutes, rotating sheet halfway through baking. Remove parbaked biscuits from oven; set aside.

4. FOR THE FRUIT FILLING Whisk sugar and cornstarch together in large bowl. Add blueberries, lemon juice, and cinnamon and toss gently to combine. Transfer fruit mixture to 9-inch deep-dish glass pie plate, cover with aluminum foil, and set on foil-lined rimmed baking sheet. Bake until filling is hot and berries have released their juice, 20 to 25 minutes.

Parbaking both the biscuits and the filling for our blueberry cobbler ensures that both elements are perfectly cooked.

5. Remove fruit from oven, uncover, and stir gently. Arrange parbaked biscuits over top, squeezing them slightly as needed to fit into dish. Bake cobbler until biscuits are golden brown and fruit is bubbling, about 15 minutes. Transfer to wire rack and let cool for 15 minutes before serving.

VARIATIONS

Peach or Nectarine Cobbler EASY

Substitute 3 pounds peaches or nectarines, peeled, halved, pitted, and cut into ½-inch-thick wedges, for blueberries, and 1 teaspoon vanilla extract for cinnamon. Reduce cornstarch to 1 tablespoon and lemon juice to 1 teaspoon.

Fresh Sour Cherry Cobbler EASY

Substitute 3 pounds pitted fresh sour cherries for blueberries. Omit lemon juice and cinnamon. Increase cornstarch to 4½ teaspoons and sugar to ¾ cup. Add 2 tablespoons red wine and ¼ teaspoon almond extract to bowl with cherries.

TO MAKE AHEAD

Biscuits and filling, prepared through step 4, can be held at room temperature separately for up to 4 hours

For the juiciest filling, we crush a portion of the berries before combining them with sugar.

Strawberry Shortcakes

SERVES 6 TO 8 **FREEZE IT**

ACTIVE TIME 50 MINUTES

TOTAL TIME 1 HOUR 20 MINUTES

WHY THIS RECIPE WORKS Strawberry shortcake is the perfect summer dessert, but too often it looks far better than it tastes. We wanted a juicy strawberry filling that would stay put in between our biscuits. The solution? We chose the ripest berries we could find (for the best flavor), then mashed some of them into a chunky sauce and sliced the rest. Left to sit for a bit with a little sugar, the berry mixture macerated, exuding even more flavorful juice, making for a thick, chunky filling that soaked into, and didn't slip off, our tender biscuits. Preparing the fruit first gave it a chance to become truly juicy—just what you want on the fresh-made biscuits. This recipe will yield six biscuits and scraps can be gathered and patted out to yield another biscuit or two; these, though, will not be as tender as the first.

2½ pounds (8 cups) strawberries, hulled

11 tablespoons sugar

2 cups (10 ounces) all-purpose flour

1 tablespoon baking powder

½ teaspoon salt

8 tablespoons unsalted butter, cut into ½-inch cubes and chilled

⅔ cup half-and-half

1 large egg plus 1 large egg white, lightly beaten

1 recipe Whipped Cream (page 365)

1. Crush 3 cups strawberries with potato masher. Slice remaining berries and stir into crushed berries with 6 tablespoons sugar. Let sit at room temperature until sugar has dissolved and berries are juicy, about 30 minutes.

2. Meanwhile, adjust oven rack to lower-middle position and heat oven to 425 degrees. Pulse flour, 3 tablespoons sugar, baking powder, and salt in food processor until combined. Scatter butter pieces over top and pulse until mixture resembles coarse cornmeal, about 15 pulses. Transfer to large bowl.

3. In separate bowl, whisk half-and-half and egg together. Add half-and-half mixture to flour mixture and stir with rubber spatula until large clumps form. Turn mixture onto lightly floured counter and knead lightly until dough comes together.

4. Using your fingertips, pat dough into 9 by 6-inch rectangle about 1 inch thick. Cut out 6 biscuits using floured 2¾-inch biscuit cutter. Pat remaining dough into 1-inch thick piece and cut out 2 more biscuits. Place biscuits on parchment-lined baking sheet, spaced 1 inch apart.

5. Brush top of biscuits with egg white and sprinkle with remaining 2 tablespoons sugar. Bake biscuits until golden brown, 12 to 14 minutes. Let biscuits cool on baking sheet for about 10 minutes.

6. Split each biscuit in half and place bottoms on individual serving plates. Spoon portion of fruit over each bottom, then top with dollop of whipped cream. Cap with biscuit tops and serve immediately.

TO MAKE AHEAD ▶

- Berries, prepared through step 1, can be held at room temperature for up to 2 hours
- Baked biscuits, prepared through step 5, can be stored at room temperature for up to 3 days or frozen for up to 1 month; to serve, refresh in 350 degree oven for 3 to 5 minutes (7 to 10 minutes for frozen biscuits) before continuing with step 6

Applesauce gives the filling for our turnovers the perfect consistency and boosts the apple flavor.

Apple Turnovers

MAKES 8 TURNOVERS   `FREEZE IT`
ACTIVE TIME 35 MINUTES
TOTAL TIME 1 HOUR 15 MINUTES

WHY THIS RECIPE WORKS We wanted to make the perfect apple turnover, with a flaky, crisp crust and firm, not mushy, apples. Granny Smith apples made the best filling, since they have great tart flavor and hold their shape well once baked. The food processor made quick work of chopping the apples; we also added sugar, cinnamon, and lemon juice for flavor, warmth, and brightness. To avoid soggy turnovers, we let the apple mixture drain before filling the pastry and then used the flavorful reserved juice to seal the turnovers. Applesauce gave the filling the right consistency and added another layer of apple flavor. Our unbaked turnovers held up beautifully in the freezer, making them a great option for preparing in advance. If you don't have a food processor, grate the peeled apples on the coarse side of a box grater before mixing them with the lemon juice, sugar, and salt. (Grating results in a less attractive appearance, but the texture will be fine.) To thaw frozen puff pastry, let it sit either in the refrigerator for 24 hours or on the counter for 30 minutes to 1 hour.

2 Granny Smith apples, peeled, cored, and chopped coarse
¾ cup (5¼ ounces) sugar
1 tablespoon lemon juice
⅛ teaspoon salt
½ cup applesauce
2 (9½ by 9-inch) sheets puff pastry, thawed
1 teaspoon ground cinnamon

1. Adjust oven racks to upper-middle and lower-middle positions and heat oven to 400 degrees. Line 2 rimmed baking sheets with parchment paper.

2. Pulse apples, ½ cup sugar, lemon juice, and salt in food processor until pieces measure no larger than ½ inch, 8 to 10 pulses. Transfer mixture to fine-mesh strainer set over bowl and let drain for 5 minutes, reserving drained juice. Transfer drained apples to bowl and stir in applesauce.

3. Working with one sheet of pastry at a time, roll into 10-inch square on lightly floured counter. Cut pastry into four 5-inch squares. Place 2 tablespoons apple mixture in center of each square and brush edges with reserved apple juice. Fold pastry over filling to form triangles. Press edges together and crimp with fork. Transfer to prepared baking sheet.

4. Combine remaining ¼ cup sugar and cinnamon in bowl. Brush top of turnovers with reserved juice and sprinkle with cinnamon sugar. Bake until well browned, 20 to 26 minutes, switching and rotating sheets halfway through baking. Transfer turnovers to wire rack and let cool slightly, about 15 minutes. Serve warm or at room temperature.

VARIATIONS
Caramel-Apple and Cream Cheese Turnovers   `FREEZE IT`
We like to use either Kraft Caramels or Brach's Milk Maid Caramels for this recipe, but any brand of soft caramels, not hard caramel candies, will do; you will need about 16 caramels.

MAKING TURNOVERS

1. Place 2 tablespoons apple mixture in center of each square and brush edges with reserved apple juice.

2. Fold pastry over filling to form triangle, press edges together, and crimp with fork.

Substitute ½ cup cream cheese for applesauce. Add two caramel candies, quartered, to each turnover before shaping.

Cranberry-Apple Turnovers FREEZE IT

Substitute ¼ cup thawed frozen orange juice concentrate for ¼ cup applesauce. Add ¾ cup dried cranberries to food processor with apples.

Cheddar-Apple Turnovers FREEZE IT

Substitute ½ cup shredded cheddar for applesauce. Omit cinnamon sugar and sprinkle ¼ cup shredded cheddar over juice-brushed turnovers before baking.

> ▶ **TO MAKE AHEAD**
>
> Unbaked turnovers, prepared through step 3, can be frozen for up to 1 month; before baking, let sit at room temperature for 20 minutes, recrimp edges with fork, and continue with step 4

Foolproof Single-Crust Pie Dough

MAKES ENOUGH FOR ONE 9-INCH PIE **EASY** **FREEZE IT**
ACTIVE TIME 20 MINUTES
TOTAL TIME 1 HOUR 30 MINUTES

WHY THIS RECIPE WORKS Since water bonds with flour to form gluten, too much water makes a crust tough. But rolling out dry dough is difficult. For a pie dough recipe that baked up tender and flaky and rolled out easily every time, we found a magic ingredient: vodka. Using vodka, which is just 60 percent water, gave us an easy-to-roll crust recipe with less gluten and no alcohol flavor, since the alcohol vaporizes in the oven. Vodka is essential to the tender texture of this crust and imparts no flavor—do not substitute water. This dough is moister than most standard pie doughs and will require lots of flour to roll out (up to ¼ cup). A food processor is essential to making this dough—we don't recommend making it by hand.

1¼ cups (6¼ ounces) all-purpose flour
1 tablespoon sugar
½ teaspoon salt
6 tablespoons unsalted butter, cut into ¼-inch pieces and chilled
4 tablespoons vegetable shortening, cut into 2 pieces and chilled
2 tablespoons vodka, chilled
2 tablespoons ice water

1. Process ¾ cup flour, sugar, and salt in food processor until combined, about 5 seconds. Scatter butter and shortening pieces over top and process until incorporated and mixture begins to form uneven clumps with no remaining floury bits, about 10 seconds.

2. Scrape down sides of bowl and redistribute dough evenly around processor blade. Sprinkle remaining ½ cup flour over dough and pulse until mixture has broken up into pieces and is evenly distributed around bowl, 4 to 6 pulses.

3. Transfer mixture to large bowl. Sprinkle vodka and ice water over mixture. Stir and press dough together, using stiff rubber spatula, until dough sticks together.

PREPARING A SINGLE-CRUST PIE SHELL

1. Trim all but ½ inch of dough overhanging edge of pie plate. Tuck dough underneath itself to form tidy, even edge that sits on lip of pie plate.

2. Use index finger of one hand and thumb and index finger of other hand to create fluted ridges perpendicular to edge of pie plate.

3. Wrap dough-lined pie plate loosely in plastic and refrigerate until firm.

4. Before baking crust, line chilled pie crust with double layer of aluminum foil, covering edges to prevent burning, and fill with pie weights or pennies.

4. Turn dough onto sheet of plastic wrap and flatten into 4-inch disk. Wrap tightly and refrigerate for 1 hour. Before rolling dough out, let it sit on counter to soften slightly, about 10 minutes.

VARIATION
Foolproof Double-Crust Pie Dough
MAKES ENOUGH FOR ONE 9-INCH PIE   **EASY**   **FREEZE IT**
Vodka is essential to the tender texture of this crust and imparts no flavor—do not substitute water. This dough is moister than most standard pie doughs and will require lots of flour to roll out (up to ¼ cup). A food processor is essential to making this dough—we don't recommend making it by hand.

2½ cups (12½ ounces) all-purpose flour
 2 tablespoons sugar
 1 teaspoon salt
12 tablespoons unsalted butter, cut into
    ¼-inch pieces and chilled
 8 tablespoons vegetable shortening, cut into
    4 pieces and chilled
 ¼ cup vodka, chilled
 ¼ cup ice water

1. Process 1½ cups flour, sugar, and salt in food processor until combined, about 5 seconds. Scatter butter and shortening pieces over top and process until incorporated and mixture begins to form uneven clumps with no remaining floury bits, about 15 seconds.

2. Scrape down sides of bowl and redistribute dough evenly around processor blade. Sprinkle remaining 1 cup flour over dough and pulse until mixture has broken up into pieces and is evenly distributed around bowl, 4 to 6 pulses.

3. Transfer mixture to large bowl. Sprinkle vodka and ice water over mixture. Stir and press dough together, using stiff rubber spatula, until dough sticks together.

4. Divide dough into 2 even pieces. Turn each piece of dough onto sheet of plastic wrap and flatten each into 4-inch disk. Wrap each piece tightly and refrigerate for 1 hour. Before rolling dough out, let it sit on counter to soften slightly, about 10 minutes.

> **TO MAKE AHEAD**
> Dough can be refrigerated for up to 2 days or frozen for up to 1 month; if frozen, thaw completely at room temperature before rolling

Pie Dough for Lattice-Top Pie
MAKES ENOUGH FOR ONE 9-INCH LATTICE-TOP PIE
EASY   **FREEZE IT**
ACTIVE TIME 20 MINUTES
TOTAL TIME 1 HOUR 30 MINUTES

WHY THIS RECIPE WORKS When making a lattice, it's actually helpful to have a dough with a little more structure than the usual flaky pastry. To achieve this, our recipe calls for a few more tablespoons of water and a little less fat than usual, both of which help create a sturdy dough that can withstand the extra handling involved in making a lattice. Just as important, this dough still manages to bake up tender and taste rich and buttery.

 3 cups (15 ounces) all-purpose flour
 2 tablespoons sugar
 1 teaspoon salt
 7 tablespoons vegetable shortening, cut into ½-inch
    pieces and chilled
10 tablespoons unsalted butter, cut into ¼-inch pieces
    and chilled
10-12 tablespoons ice water

MAKING A DOUBLE CRUST PIE

1. Loosely roll second piece of dough round around rolling pin and gently unroll it onto filling.

2. Trim overhang to ½ inch beyond lip of plate, then pinch edges of top and bottom crusts firmly together.

3. Tuck overhang under itself; folded edge should be flush with edge of plate.

4. Crimp dough evenly around edge of plate using your fingers.

1. Process flour, sugar, and salt in food processor until combined, about 5 seconds. Scatter shortening over top and process until mixture resembles coarse cornmeal, about 10 seconds. Scatter butter over top and pulse until mixture resembles coarse crumbs, about 10 pulses. Transfer to bowl.

2. Sprinkle 5 tablespoons ice water over flour mixture. With rubber spatula, use folding motion to evenly combine water and flour mixture. Sprinkle 5 tablespoons ice water over mixture and continue using folding motion to combine until small portion of dough holds together when squeezed in palm of your hand, adding up to 2 tablespoons remaining ice water if necessary. (Dough should feel quite moist.)

3. Divide dough in half and form each half into 4-inch disk. Wrap disks tightly in plastic wrap and refrigerate for 1 hour. Let chilled dough sit on counter to soften slightly, about 10 minutes, before rolling.

TO MAKE AHEAD

Dough can be refrigerated for up to 2 days or frozen for up to 1 month; if frozen, thaw completely at room temperature before rolling

Graham Cracker Pie Crust

MAKES ENOUGH FOR ONE 9-INCH PIE   **EASY**
ACTIVE TIME 15 MINUTES
TOTAL TIME 30 MINUTES

WHY THIS RECIPE WORKS While store-bought graham cracker pie crusts are tempting (all you have to do is fill, chill, then serve), they often taste stale and bland. We wanted a fresh-tasting homemade crust that wasn't too sweet, with a crisp texture. Turns out, a classic graham cracker crust couldn't be easier to make: combine crushed crumbs with a little melted butter and sugar to bind them, then use a measuring cup to pack the crumbs into the pie plate. And producing a perfect graham cracker crust has a lot to do with the type of graham crackers used. After experimenting with the three leading brands, we discovered subtle but distinct differences among them and found that these differences carried over into crumb crusts made with each kind of cracker. In the end, we preferred Keebler Grahams Crackers Original in our crust. We don't recommend using store-bought graham cracker crumbs here as they can often be stale.

8 whole graham crackers, broken into 1-inch pieces
3 tablespoons sugar
5 tablespoons unsalted butter, melted and cooled

1. Adjust oven rack to middle position and heat oven to 325 degrees. Process graham cracker pieces and sugar in food processor to fine, even crumbs, about 30 seconds. Sprinkle melted butter over crumbs and pulse to incorporate, about 5 pulses.

2. Sprinkle mixture into 9-inch pie plate. Using bottom of dry measuring cup, press crumbs into even layer on bottom and sides of pie plate. Bake until crust is fragrant and beginning to brown, 12 to 18 minutes; transfer to wire rack. Following particular pie recipe, use crust while it is still warm or let it cool completely.

TO MAKE AHEAD

Baked crust can be stored at room temperature for up to 24 hours

PRESSING CRUMBS INTO A PIE SHELL

Sprinkle crumb mixture into 9-inch pie plate. Using bottom of dry measuring cup, press crumbs into even layer on bottom and sides of pie plate.

Classic Tart Dough

MAKES ENOUGH FOR ONE 9-INCH TART   **EASY**   **FREEZE IT**
ACTIVE TIME 15 MINUTES
TOTAL TIME 1 HOUR 25 MINUTES

WHY THIS RECIPE WORKS While regular pie crust is tender and flaky, classic tart crust should be fine textured, buttery rich, crisp, and crumbly—it is often described as being shortbreadlike. We set out to achieve the perfect tart dough, one that we could use in a number of tart recipes. We found that using a stick of butter made tart dough that tasted great and was easy to handle, yet still had a delicate crumb. Instead of using the hard-to-find superfine sugar and pastry flour that many other recipes call for, we used confectioners' sugar and all-purpose flour to achieve a crisp texture. Rolling the dough and fitting it into the tart pan was easy, and we had ample dough to patch any holes.

1 large egg yolk
1 tablespoon heavy cream
½ teaspoon vanilla extract
1¼ cups (6¼ ounces) all-purpose flour

⅔ cup (2⅔ ounces) confectioners' sugar

¼ teaspoon salt

8 tablespoons unsalted butter, cut into ¼-inch pieces and chilled

1. Whisk egg yolk, cream, and vanilla together in bowl. Process flour, sugar, and salt together in food processor until combined, about 5 seconds. Scatter butter over top and pulse until mixture resembles coarse cornmeal, about 15 pulses. With machine running, add egg mixture and continue to process until dough just comes together around processor blade, about 12 seconds.

2. Turn dough onto sheet of plastic wrap and flatten into 6-inch disk. Wrap tightly and refrigerate for 1 hour. Before rolling dough out, let it sit on counter to soften slightly, about 10 minutes.

TO MAKE AHEAD ▶

Dough can be refrigerated for up to 2 days or frozen for up to 1 month; if frozen, thaw completely at room temperature before rolling

MAKING A TART SHELL

1. Loosely roll dough around rolling pin and gently unroll it onto 9-inch tart pan with removable bottom, letting excess dough hang over edge.

2. Lift dough and gently press it into corners and fluted sides of pan.

3. Run rolling pin over top of pan to remove any excess dough.

Free-Form Tart Dough

MAKES ENOUGH FOR ONE 9-INCH TART **EASY** **FREEZE IT**
ACTIVE TIME 25 MINUTES
TOTAL TIME 1 HOUR 35 MINUTES

WHY THIS RECIPE WORKS A free-form tart—a single layer of buttery pie dough folded up around fresh fruit—is a simpler take on pie. But without the support of a pie plate, tender crusts are prone to leaking juice, and this can result in a soggy bottom. For our crust, we used a high proportion of butter to flour, which provided the most buttery flavor and tender texture without compromising the structure. We then turned to the French *fraisage* method to make the pastry: Chunks of butter are pressed into long, thin sheets that create lots of flaky layers when the dough is baked.

1½ cups (7½ ounces) all-purpose flour

½ teaspoon salt

10 tablespoons unsalted butter, cut into ½-inch pieces and chilled

4–6 tablespoons ice water

1. Process flour and salt in food processor until combined, about 5 seconds. Scatter butter pieces over top and pulse until mixture resembles coarse sand and butter pieces are about size of small peas, about 10 pulses. Continue to pulse, adding water 1 tablespoon at a time, until dough begins to form small curds that hold together when pinched with fingers, about 10 pulses.

2. Turn mixture onto lightly floured counter and gather into rectangular-shaped pile. Starting at farthest end, use heel of hand to smear small amount of dough against counter, pushing it away from you. Continue to smear dough until all crumbs have been worked. Gather smeared pieces of dough together into another rectangular-shaped pile and repeat process.

MAKING FREE-FORM TART DOUGH

1. Turn mixture onto lightly floured counter and gather into rectangular-shaped pile.

2. Starting at farthest end, use heel of your hand to smear small amount of dough against counter. Continue to smear dough until all crumbs have been worked.

3. Press dough into 6-inch disk, wrap tightly in plastic wrap, and refrigerate for 1 hour. Before rolling dough out, let it sit on counter to soften slightly, about 10 minutes.

TO MAKE AHEAD ▶

Dough can be refrigerated for up to 2 days or frozen for up to 1 month; if frozen, thaw completely at room temperature before rolling

Deep-Dish Apple Pie
SERVES 8 **FREEZE IT**

ACTIVE TIME 1 HOUR

TOTAL TIME 2 HOURS 45 MINUTES (PLUS 2 HOURS COOLING TIME)

WHY THIS RECIPE WORKS We wanted our deep-dish apple pie to be packed with tender, juicy apples fully framed by a buttery, flaky crust. But recipes for deep-dish pies are riddled with issues: The apples are often unevenly cooked and the fruit's exuded juice produces a bottom crust that is pale and soggy. Then there is the gaping hole left between the shrunken apples and the top crust. Precooking the apples solved the shrinking problem, helped the apples hold their shape, and prevented a flood of juices from collecting in the bottom of the pie plate, thereby producing a nicely browned bottom crust. We were surprised that cooking the apples twice didn't cause them to turn to mush; we learned that when apples are gently heated, their pectin is converted to a heat-stable form that helps them keep their shape. This allowed us to boost the quantity of apples to 5 pounds. You can substitute Empire or Cortland apples for the Granny Smith apples and Jonagold, Fuji, or Braeburn for the Golden Delicious apples.

    1 recipe Foolproof Double-Crust Pie Dough (page 371)
 2½ pounds Granny Smith apples, peeled, cored, and sliced
       ¼ inch thick
 2½ pounds Golden Delicious apples, peeled, cored, and
       sliced ¼ inch thick
   ½ cup (3½ ounces) plus 1 tablespoon granulated sugar
   ¼ cup packed (1¾ ounces) light brown sugar
   ½ teaspoon grated lemon zest plus 1 tablespoon juice
   ¼ teaspoon salt
   ⅛ teaspoon ground cinnamon
    1 large egg white, lightly beaten

1. Roll 1 disk of dough into 12-inch circle on well floured counter. Loosely roll dough around rolling pin and gently unroll it onto 9-inch pie plate, letting excess dough hang over edge. Ease dough into plate by gently lifting edge of dough with your hand while pressing into plate bottom with your other hand. Wrap dough-lined

Precooking the apples for our deep-dish pie eliminates excess liquid and allows the bottom crust to brown nicely.

plate loosely in plastic and refrigerate until dough is firm, about 30 minutes. Roll other disk of dough into 12-inch circle on lightly floured counter, then transfer to parchment paper–lined baking sheet; cover with plastic and refrigerate for 30 minutes.

2. Meanwhile, toss apples, ½ cup granulated sugar, brown sugar, lemon zest, salt, and cinnamon together in Dutch oven. Cover and cook over medium heat, stirring often, until apples are tender when poked with fork but still hold their shape, 15 to 20 minutes. Transfer apples and their juices to rimmed baking sheet and let cool completely, about 1 hour.

3. Adjust oven rack to lowest position and heat oven to 425 degrees. Line rimmed baking sheet with aluminum foil. Drain cooled apples in colander, reserving ¼ cup drained juice. Stir lemon juice into reserved apple juice.

4. Spread apples into dough-lined pie plate, mounding them slightly in middle, and drizzle with juice mixture. Loosely roll remaining dough round around rolling pin and gently unroll it onto filling. Trim overhang to ½ inch beyond lip of plate. Pinch edges of top and bottom crusts firmly together. Tuck overhang under itself; folded edge should be flush with edge of plate. Crimp dough evenly around edge of plate using your fingers. Cut four 2-inch vents in top of dough.

5. Brush surface with beaten egg white and sprinkle with remaining 1 tablespoon granulated sugar. Place pie on prepared sheet and bake until crust is light golden brown, about 25 minutes. Reduce oven temperature to 375 degrees, rotate baking sheet, and continue to bake until juices are bubbling and crust is deep golden brown, 30 to 40 minutes. Let pie cool on wire rack for 2 hours before serving.

TO MAKE AHEAD ▶

- Unbaked pie, prepared through step 4, can be frozen until firm, then wrapped in double layer of plastic wrap followed by aluminum foil and frozen for up to 2 weeks; to bake, continue with step 5, increasing baking time at 375 degrees to 40 to 50 minutes
- Baked pie can be held at room temperature for up to 8 hours or refrigerated for up to 24 hours; to serve, refresh in 350 degree oven for 10 to 15 minutes (crust will be less crisp)

Ultimate Blueberry Pie

SERVES 8 **FREEZE IT**

ACTIVE TIME 50 MINUTES

TOTAL TIME 2 HOURS 50 MINUTES (PLUS 4 HOURS COOLING TIME)

WHY THIS RECIPE WORKS We wanted a blueberry pie that had a firm filling full of fresh, bright flavor and still-plump berries. To thicken the pie, we favored tapioca, which allowed the blueberry flavor to shine through. Too much of it, though, and we had a congealed mess. Cooking and reducing half of the berries helped us cut down on the tapioca required, but not enough. A second inspiration came from a peeled and shredded Granny Smith apple. Apples are high in pectin, which acts as a thickener when cooked. Combined with a modest 2 tablespoons of tapioca, the apple thickened the filling to a soft, even consistency. Baking the pie on the bottom oven rack produced a crisp, golden bottom crust. To vent the steam from the berries, we cut circles in the top crust with a biscuit cutter. We were happy to find that the pie held beautifully for up to 24 hours as long as we refreshed it in the oven before serving. Use a coarse grater to shred the apple. Grind the tapioca to a powder in a spice grinder or mini food processor.

1 recipe Foolproof Double-Crust Pie Dough (page 371)
30 ounces (6 cups) blueberries
1 Granny Smith apple, peeled, cored, and shredded
¾ cup (5¼ ounces) sugar
2 tablespoons Minute Tapioca, ground
2 teaspoons grated lemon zest plus 2 teaspoons juice

We found that a peeled and grated apple, rich in pectin, helps to thicken and flavor the blueberries in our pie.

Pinch salt
2 tablespoons unsalted butter, cut into ¼-inch pieces
1 large egg white, lightly beaten

1. Roll 1 disk of dough into 12-inch circle on well floured counter. Loosely roll dough around rolling pin and gently unroll it onto 9-inch pie plate, letting excess dough hang over edge. Ease dough into plate by gently lifting edge of dough with your hand while pressing into plate bottom with your other hand. Wrap dough-lined plate loosely in plastic and refrigerate until dough is firm, about 30 minutes. Roll other disk of dough into 12-inch circle on lightly floured counter, then transfer to parchment paper–lined baking sheet; cover with plastic and refrigerate for 30 minutes.

2. Meanwhile, place 3 cups berries in medium saucepan and set over medium heat. Using potato masher, mash berries several times to release juices. Continue to cook, stirring often and mashing occasionally, until about half of berries have broken down and mixture is thickened and reduced to 1½ cups, about 8 minutes. Transfer berries to large bowl and let cool completely, about 1 hour.

3. Adjust oven rack to lowest position and heat oven to 400 degrees. Line rimmed baking sheet with aluminum foil. Place shredded apple in dish towel and wring dry. Stir apple, remaining

3 cups berries, sugar, tapioca, lemon zest and juice, and salt into cooked berries. Spread mixture into dough-lined pie plate and scatter butter over top.

4. Using 1¼-inch round cookie cutter, cut hole in center of top crust. Cut 6 more holes evenly around edge of crust, about 1½ inches from edge of center hole. Loosely roll top crust round around rolling pin then gently unroll it over filling. Trim overhang to ½ inch beyond lip of plate. Pinch edges of top and bottom crusts firmly together. Tuck overhang under itself; folded edge should be flush with edge of plate. Crimp dough evenly around edge of plate using your fingers.

5. Brush surface with beaten egg white. Place pie on prepared sheet and bake until crust is light golden brown, about 25 minutes. Reduce oven temperature to 350 degrees, rotate baking sheet, and continue to bake until juices are bubbling and crust is deep golden brown, 35 to 50 minutes. Let pie cool on wire rack for 4 hours before serving.

VARIATION

Ultimate Blueberry Pie using Frozen Berries FREEZE IT

Substitute 30 ounces frozen blueberries for fresh blueberries. In step 1, cook half of frozen berries over medium-high heat, without mashing, until reduced to 1¼ cups, 12 to 15 minutes.

> **TO MAKE AHEAD**
>
> - Unbaked pie, prepared through step 4, can be frozen until firm, then wrapped in double layer of plastic wrap followed by aluminum foil and frozen for up to 2 weeks; to bake, continue with step 5, increasing baking time at 350 degrees to 45 to 55 minutes
> - Baked pie can be held at room temperature for up to 8 hours or refrigerated for up to 24 hours; to serve, refresh in 350 degree oven for 10 to 15 minutes (crust will be less crisp)

Fresh Peach Pie

SERVES 8 FREEZE IT

ACTIVE TIME 45 MINUTES

TOTAL TIME 2 HOURS 40 MINUTES (PLUS 3 HOURS COOLING TIME)

WHY THIS RECIPE WORKS In our opinion, a perfect slice of peach pie is a clean slice of pie, with fruit that's tender yet intact. But juicy summer peaches usually produce soupy pies. We corralled the moisture that peaches give off during cooking by first macerating the peaches to draw out some of their juices and then adding a measured portion back to the filling. Using a combination of

A lattice crust is not just decorative; it allows moisture to evaporate, keeping our peach pie from becoming soggy.

cornstarch and pectin to thicken the filling gave it a clear, silky texture without any of the gumminess or gelatinous texture that larger amounts of either one alone produced. Finally, we used a reliable, delicious lattice crust, the open nature of which let moisture cook off as the pie baked. If your peaches are too soft to withstand the pressure of a peeler, cut a shallow X in the bottom of the fruit, blanch them in a pot of simmering water for 15 seconds, and then shock them in a bowl of ice water before peeling. For fruit pectin we recommend either Sure-Jell for Less or No Sugar Needed Recipes or Ball RealFruit Low or No-Sugar Needed Pectin.

3 pounds peaches, peeled, quartered, and pitted, each quarter cut into thirds
½ cup (3½ ounces) plus 3 tablespoons sugar
1 teaspoon grated lemon zest plus 1 tablespoon juice
⅛ teaspoon salt
2 tablespoons low- or no-sugar-needed fruit pectin
¼ teaspoon ground cinnamon
  Pinch ground nutmeg
1 tablespoon cornstarch
1 recipe Pie Dough for Lattice-Top Pie (page 371)

1. Toss peaches, ½ cup sugar, lemon zest and juice, and salt in bowl and let stand at room temperature for at least 30 minutes or up to 1 hour. In small bowl, combine pectin, cinnamon, nutmeg, and 2 tablespoons sugar.

2. Meanwhile, roll 1 disk of dough into 12-inch circle on lightly floured counter. Loosely roll dough around rolling pin and gently unroll it onto 9-inch pie plate, letting excess dough hang over edge. Ease dough into plate by gently lifting edge of dough with your hand while pressing into plate bottom with your other hand. Wrap dough-lined plate loosely in plastic and refrigerate until dough is firm, about 30 minutes.

3. Roll other disk of dough into 12-inch circle on lightly floured counter and transfer to parchment paper–lined baking sheet. With pizza wheel, fluted pastry wheel, or paring knife, cut dough into ten 1¼-inch-wide strips. Freeze strips on sheet until firm, about 30 minutes.

4. Adjust oven rack to lowest position and heat oven to 425 degrees. Transfer 1 cup peach mixture to bowl and mash into coarse paste with fork. Drain remaining peaches in colander, reserving ½ cup drained juice. Return peach pieces to bowl and toss with cornstarch. Whisk reserved juice and pectin mixture together in 12-inch skillet. Cook over medium heat until slightly thickened and pectin is dissolved, 3 to 5 minutes. Off heat, stir in drained peaches and mashed peaches.

5. Transfer peach mixture to dough-lined pie plate. Remove dough strips from freezer; if too stiff, let stand at room temperature until malleable but still very cold. Lay 2 longest strips across center of pie, perpendicular to each other. Arrange 4 shortest strips around edge of pie in shape of square. Lay remaining 4 strips between strips in center and around edge to make lattice design. Trim overhang to ½ inch beyond lip of plate. Pinch edges of top crust and lattice strips together firmly together and fold under. Folded edge should be flush with edge of pie plate. Crimp dough evenly around edge of pie using your fingers.

6. Using spray bottle, mist lattice with water and sprinkle with remaining 1 tablespoon sugar. Place pie on foil-lined rimmed baking sheet and bake until crust is set and begins to brown, about 25 minutes. Reduce oven temperature to 375 degrees, rotate baking sheet, and continue to bake until juices are bubbling and crust is deep golden brown, 30 to 40 minutes. Let pie cool on wire rack for 3 hours before serving.

TO MAKE AHEAD

- Unbaked pie, prepared through step 5, can be frozen until firm, then wrapped in double layer of plastic wrap followed by aluminum foil and frozen for up to 2 weeks; to bake, continue with step 6, increasing baking time at 375 degrees to 40 to 50 minutes
- Baked pie can be held at room temperature for up to 8 hours or refrigerated for up to 24 hours; to serve, refresh in 350 degree oven for 10 to 15 minutes (crust will be less crisp)

Pecan Pie

SERVES 8 **EASY** **FREEZE IT**
ACTIVE TIME 30 MINUTES
TOTAL TIME 2 HOURS (PLUS 2 HOURS COOLING TIME)

WHY THIS RECIPE WORKS Our ideal pecan pie has a smooth-textured, not-too-sweet filling and a crisp bottom crust. Using brown sugar gave the pie deep flavor, and reducing the amount allowed the pecans to take center stage. It was important to add the hot filling to a warm pie crust; this helped keep the crust from getting soggy. We discovered that simulating a double boiler when melting the butter and making the filling was an easy way to maintain gentle heat, which helped ensure that the filling didn't curdle.

MAKING A LATTICE-TOP PIE

1. Lay 2 longest strips across center of pie, perpendicular to each other.

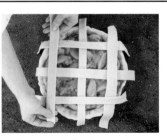

2. Arrange 4 shortest strips around edge of pie in shape of square.

3. Lay remaining 4 strips between strips in center and around edge to make lattice design.

4. Trim dough to ½ inch beyond edge of plate and press edges together to seal. Fold seam under and crimp edge using your fingers.

1 recipe Foolproof Single-Crust Pie Dough (page 370)

6 tablespoons unsalted butter, cut into 6 pieces

1 cup packed (7 ounces) dark brown sugar

½ teaspoon salt

3 large eggs

¾ cup light corn syrup

1 tablespoon vanilla extract

2 cups pecans, toasted and chopped fine

1. Roll dough into 12-inch circle on well floured counter. Loosely roll dough around rolling pin and gently unroll it onto 9-inch pie plate, letting excess dough hang over edge. Ease dough into plate by gently lifting edge of dough with your hand while pressing into plate bottom with your other hand. Trim overhang to ½ inch beyond lip of plate. Tuck overhang under itself; folded edge should be flush with edge of plate. Crimp dough evenly around edge of plate using your fingers. Wrap dough-lined plate loosely in plastic and refrigerate until dough is firm, about 30 minutes.

2. Adjust oven rack to middle position and heat oven to 400 degrees. Line chilled pie crust with double layer of aluminum foil, covering edges to prevent burning, and fill with pie weights. Bake until pie dough looks dry and is pale in color, 25 to 30 minutes.

3. Meanwhile, melt butter in heatproof bowl set in skillet of water maintained at just below simmer. Remove bowl from skillet and stir in sugar and salt until butter is absorbed. Whisk in eggs until smooth, then whisk in corn syrup and vanilla. Return bowl to hot water and stir until mixture is shiny, hot to touch, and registers 130 degrees. Off heat, stir in pecans.

4. Transfer pie crust to wire rack and remove weights and foil. Reduce oven temperature to 275 degrees. Pour warm pecan mixture into warm pie crust.

5. Place pie on rimmed baking sheet lined with aluminum foil. Bake until filling looks set but yields like Jell-O when gently pressed with back of spoon, 50 minutes to 1 hour, rotating sheet halfway through baking. Let pie cool on wire rack until filling has set, about 2 hours, before serving.

MAKING PECAN PIE FILLING

Cook filling in heatproof bowl set in skillet of water maintained at just below simmer until mixture is shiny, hot to touch, and registers 130 degrees.

VARIATION

Maple Pecan Pie EASY   FREEZE IT

The maple syrup in this pie yields a softer, more custardlike texture. Toasted walnuts can be substituted for pecans.

Omit vanilla. Reduce butter to 4 tablespoons and pecans to 1½ cups. Substitute ½ cup granulated sugar for brown sugar and 1 cup maple syrup for corn syrup.

▶ TO MAKE AHEAD

- Cooled unbaked pie, prepared through step 4, can be frozen until firm, then wrapped in double layer of plastic wrap followed by aluminum foil and frozen for up to 1 month; to bake, continue with step 5, increasing baking time at 275 degrees to 1½ hours
- Baked pie can be held at room temperature for up to 8 hours or refrigerated for up to 2 days; if refrigerated, bring to room temperature before serving (crust will be less crisp)

Pumpkin Pie

SERVES 8

ACTIVE TIME 45 MINUTES

TOTAL TIME 1 HOUR 45 MINUTES (PLUS 2 HOURS COOLING TIME)

WHY THIS RECIPE WORKS We wanted to create a pumpkin pie with a velvety smooth texture and great pumpkin flavor. To concentrate its flavor, we cooked canned pumpkin with sugar and spices, then whisked in heavy cream, milk, and eggs. For more complex flavor, we also added canned candied yams to the filling. To make sure our custard was evenly baked from edge to center, we started the pie at a high temperature for 10 minutes, then reduced the temperature for the remainder of the baking time. We found that it's important to add the hot filling to a warm pie crust as this helps keep the crust from getting soggy. Make sure to buy unsweetened canned pumpkin; avoid pumpkin pie mix. If candied yams are unavailable, regular canned yams can be substituted.

1 recipe Foolproof Single-Crust Pie Dough (page 370)

1 cup heavy cream

1 cup whole milk

3 large eggs plus 2 large yolks

1 teaspoon vanilla extract

1 (15-ounce) can unsweetened pumpkin puree

1 cup canned candied yams, drained

¾ cup (5¼ ounces) sugar

¼ cup maple syrup

2 teaspoons grated fresh ginger

1 teaspoon salt

½ teaspoon ground cinnamon
¼ teaspoon ground nutmeg

1. Roll dough into 12-inch circle on well floured counter. Loosely roll dough around rolling pin and gently unroll it onto 9-inch pie plate, letting excess dough hang over edge. Ease dough into plate by gently lifting edge of dough with your hand while pressing into plate bottom with your other hand. Trim overhang to ½ inch beyond lip of plate. Tuck overhang under itself; folded edge should be flush with edge of plate. Crimp dough evenly around edge of plate using your fingers. Wrap dough-lined plate loosely in plastic and refrigerate until dough is firm, about 30 minutes.

2. Adjust oven rack to middle position and heat oven to 400 degrees. Line chilled pie crust with double layer of aluminum foil, covering edges to prevent burning, and fill with pie weights. Bake until pie dough looks dry and is pale in color, 25 to 30 minutes.

3. Meanwhile, whisk cream, milk, eggs and yolks, and vanilla together in bowl. Bring pumpkin, yams, sugar, maple syrup, ginger, salt, cinnamon, and nutmeg to simmer in large saucepan over medium heat and cook, stirring constantly and mashing yams against sides of pot, until thick and shiny, 15 to 20 minutes. Off heat, whisk in cream mixture. Strain mixture through fine-mesh strainer, using rubber spatula to help work puree through strainer.

4. Transfer pie crust to wire rack and remove weights and foil. Pour warm pumpkin mixture into warm pie crust. Place pie on rimmed baking sheet lined with aluminum foil. Bake for 10 minutes. Reduce oven temperature to 300 degrees, rotate baking sheet, and continue to bake until edges of pie are set and center registers 175 degrees, 20 to 35 minutes. Let pie cool on wire rack until filling has set, about 2 hours, before serving.

TO MAKE AHEAD

Baked pie can be held at room temperature for up to 8 hours or refrigerated for up to 2 days; if refrigerated, bring to room temperature before serving (crust will be less crisp)

Summer Berry Pie

SERVES 8

ACTIVE TIME 45 MINUTES

TOTAL TIME 45 MINUTES (PLUS 3 HOURS CHILLING TIME)

WHY THIS RECIPE WORKS A fresh berry pie might seem like an easy-to-pull-off summer dessert, but most of the recipes we tried buried the berries in gluey thickeners or bouncy gelatin. Our goal was to make a pie with great texture and flavor—and still keep it simple. We started with our easy homemade graham cracker crust, which relies on crushed graham crackers. For the filling,

Processing some of the berries and thickening the puree with cornstarch gives this pie great texture and flavor.

we used a combination of raspberries, blackberries, and blueberries. After trying a few different methods, we found a solution that both bound the berries in the graham cracker crust and intensified their bright flavor. We processed a portion of berries in a food processor until they made a smooth puree, then thickened the puree with cornstarch. Next, we tossed the remaining berries with warm jelly for a glossy coat and a bit of sweetness. Pressed gently into the puree, the berries stayed put and tasted great. Feel free to vary the amount of each berry as desired as long as you have 6 cups of berries total; do not substitute frozen berries here. Serve with Whipped Cream (page 365).

10 ounces (2 cups) raspberries
10 ounces (2 cups) blackberries
10 ounces (2 cups) blueberries
½ cup (3½ ounces) sugar
3 tablespoons cornstarch
⅛ teaspoon salt
1 tablespoon lemon juice
1 recipe Graham Cracker Pie Crust (page 372), baked and cooled
2 tablespoons red currant or apple jelly

1. Gently toss berries together in large bowl. Process 2½ cups of berries in food processor until very smooth, about 1 minute (do not underprocess). Strain puree through fine-mesh strainer into small saucepan, pressing on solids to extract as much puree as possible (you should have about 1½ cups); discard solids.

2. Whisk sugar, cornstarch, and salt together in bowl, then whisk into strained puree. Bring puree mixture to boil, stirring constantly, and cook until it is as thick as pudding, about 7 minutes. Off heat, stir in lemon juice and let cool slightly.

3. Pour warm berry puree into cooled pie crust. Melt jelly in clean small saucepan over low heat, then pour over remaining 3½ cups berries and toss to coat. Spread berries over puree and lightly press them into puree. Cover pie loosely with plastic wrap and refrigerate until filling is chilled, about 3 hours, before serving.

TO MAKE AHEAD

Pie can be refrigerated for up to 24 hours (crust will be less crisp)

Key Lime Pie

SERVES 8   **EASY**

ACTIVE TIME 20 MINUTES

TOTAL TIME 50 MINUTES (PLUS 4 HOURS COOLING AND CHILLING TIME)

WHY THIS RECIPE WORKS We set out to create a recipe for classic Key lime pie with a fresh flavor and silky filling. Using juice and zest from fresh limes rather than bottled, reconstituted lime juice gave us a pie that was refreshing, cool yet creamy, and very satisfying. Traditional Key lime pie is usually not baked; instead, the combination of egg yolks, lime juice, and sweetened condensed milk firms up when chilled. However, we discovered that it set much more nicely after being baked for only 15 minutes. We found that it's important to add the hot filling to a warm pie crust as this helps keep the crust from getting soggy. Despite this pie's name, we found that most tasters could not tell the difference between pies made with regular supermarket limes (called Persian limes) and true Key limes. Since Persian limes are easier to find and juice, we recommend using them.

4 large egg yolks

4 teaspoons grated lime zest plus ½ cup juice (5 limes)

1 (14-ounce) can sweetened condensed milk

1 recipe Graham Cracker Pie Crust (page 372), baked and still warm

1 cup heavy cream, chilled

¼ cup (1 ounce) confectioners' sugar

A short stint in the oven helps to set the filling for our creamy and flavorful Key lime pie.

1. Adjust oven rack to middle position and heat oven to 325 degrees. Whisk egg yolks and lime zest together in medium bowl until mixture has light green tint, about 2 minutes. Whisk in condensed milk until smooth, then whisk in lime juice. Cover mixture and let sit at room temperature until thickened, about 30 minutes.

2. Pour thickened filling into warm crust. Bake until center is firm but jiggles slightly when shaken, 15 to 20 minutes. Let pie cool on wire rack for 1 hour. Cover pie loosely with plastic wrap and refrigerate until filling is chilled, about 3 hours.

3. Before serving, use stand mixer fitted with whisk attachment to whip cream and sugar on medium-low speed until foamy, about 1 minute. Increase speed to high and whip until soft peaks form, 1 to 3 minutes. Spread whipped cream attractively over top of pie.

TO MAKE AHEAD

Pie, prepared through step 2, can be refrigerated for up to 24 hours (crust will be less crisp)

Lemon Meringue Pie

SERVES 8

ACTIVE TIME 1 HOUR 15 MINUTES

TOTAL TIME 2 HOURS 40 MINUTES (PLUS 2 HOURS COOLING TIME)

WHY THIS RECIPE WORKS We wanted a pie with a flaky crust and a rich filling that was soft but not runny, firm but not gelatinous, and that balanced the airy meringue. Most important, we wanted a meringue that didn't break down and puddle on the bottom or "tear" on top. We learned that the puddling underneath the meringue is from undercooking, the beading on top from overcooking. We discovered that if the filling is piping hot when the meringue is applied, the underside of the meringue will not undercook; if the oven temperature is relatively low, the top of the meringue won't overcook. Baking the pie in a relatively cool oven also produces the best-looking, most evenly baked meringue. To further stabilize the meringue and keep it from weeping, we beat in a small amount of cornstarch. In terms of timing, you want to assemble the pie and get it into the oven as quickly as possible; the filling must be warm when added to the pie crust.

CRUST AND FILLING

- 1 recipe Foolproof Single-Crust Pie Dough (page 370)
- 1½ cups water
- 1 cup (7 ounces) sugar
- ¼ cup cornstarch
- ⅛ teaspoon salt
- 6 large egg yolks
- 1 tablespoon grated lemon zest plus ½ cup juice (3 lemons)
- 2 tablespoons unsalted butter, cut into 2 pieces

MERINGUE

- ⅓ cup water
- 1 tablespoon cornstarch
- 4 large egg whites
- ½ teaspoon vanilla extract
- ¼ teaspoon cream of tartar
- ½ cup (3½ ounces) sugar

1. FOR THE CRUST AND FILLING Roll dough into 12-inch circle on well floured counter. Loosely roll dough around rolling pin and gently unroll it onto 9-inch pie plate, letting excess dough hang over edge. Ease dough into plate by gently lifting edge of dough with your hand while pressing into plate bottom with your other hand. Trim overhang to ½ inch beyond lip of plate. Tuck overhang under itself; folded edge should be flush with edge of plate. Crimp dough evenly around edge of plate using your fingers. Wrap dough-lined plate loosely in plastic and refrigerate until dough is firm, about 30 minutes.

2. Adjust oven rack to middle position and heat oven to 400 degrees. Line chilled pie crust with double layer of aluminum foil, covering edges to prevent burning, and fill with pie weights. Bake until pie dough looks dry and is pale in color, 25 to 30 minutes. Remove weights and foil and continue to bake until crust is deep golden brown, 7 to 12 minutes. Transfer pie plate to wire rack, remove weights and foil, and let cool completely; place on rimmed baking sheet lined with aluminum foil.

3. Decrease oven temperature to 325 degrees. Bring water, sugar, cornstarch, and salt to simmer in large saucepan over medium heat, whisking constantly. When mixture starts to turn translucent, whisk in egg yolks, two at a time. Whisk in lemon zest and juice and butter. Return mixture to brief simmer, then remove from heat. Press plastic wrap flush to surface to prevent skin from forming.

4. FOR THE MERINGUE Bring water and cornstarch to simmer in small saucepan over medium-high heat and cook, whisking occasionally, until thickened and translucent, 1 to 2 minutes. Remove from heat and let cool slightly.

5. Using stand mixer fitted with whisk, whip egg whites, vanilla, and cream of tartar on medium-low speed until foamy, about 1 minute. Increase speed to medium-high and beat in sugar, 1 tablespoon at a time, until incorporated and mixture forms soft, billowy mounds. Add cornstarch mixture, 1 tablespoon at a time, and continue to beat to glossy, stiff peaks, 2 to 3 minutes.

6. Meanwhile, remove plastic from filling and return to very low heat during last minute or so of beating meringue (to ensure filling is hot).

7. Pour warm filling into cooled crust. Using rubber spatula, immediately distribute meringue evenly around edge and then center of pie, attaching meringue to pie crust to prevent shrinking. Using back of spoon, create attractive swirls and peaks in meringue. Bake until meringue is light golden brown, about 20 minutes, rotating sheet halfway through baking. Let pie cool on wire rack until filling has set, about 2 hours, before serving.

TO MAKE AHEAD

Baked pie can be held at room temperature for up to 6 hours before serving

Fresh Fruit Tart

SERVES 8 **FREEZE IT**

ACTIVE TIME 1 HOUR

TOTAL TIME 6 HOURS (INCLUDES COOLING AND CHILLING TIME)

WHY THIS RECIPE WORKS We set out to create a buttery, crisp crust filled with rich, lightly sweetened pastry cream and topped with fresh fruit. We started with our Classic Tart Dough and baked it until it was golden brown. We then filled the tart with pastry cream made with half-and-half that was enriched with butter and thickened with just enough cornstarch to keep its shape without becoming gummy. For the fruit, we chose a combination of sliced kiwis, raspberries, and blueberries. The finishing touch: a drizzle of jelly glaze for a glistening presentation.

 1 recipe Classic Tart Dough (page 372)
 2 cups half-and-half
½ cup (3½ ounces) sugar
   Pinch salt
 5 large egg yolks
 3 tablespoons cornstarch
 4 tablespoons unsalted butter, cut into 4 pieces
1½ teaspoons vanilla extract
 2 large kiwis, peeled, halved lengthwise, and sliced ⅜ inch thick
10 ounces (2 cups) raspberries
 5 ounces (1 cup) blueberries
½ cup red currant or apple jelly, melted and warm

1. Roll dough into 11-inch circle on lightly floured counter. Loosely roll dough around rolling pin and gently unroll it onto 9-inch tart pan with removable bottom, letting excess dough hang over edge. Lift dough and gently press it into corners and fluted sides of pan. Run rolling pin over top of pan to remove any excess dough. Wrap loosely in plastic, place on large plate, and freeze until dough is fully chilled and firm, about 30 minutes.

2. Adjust oven rack to middle position and heat oven to 375 degrees. Line chilled crust with double layer of aluminum foil, covering edges to prevent burning, and fill with pie weights. Bake until tart shell is golden and set, about 30 minutes. Carefully remove weights and foil and continue to bake until tart shell is fully baked and golden brown, 5 to 10 minutes. Transfer tart shell to wire rack and let cool completely.

3. Bring half-and-half, 6 tablespoons sugar, and salt to simmer in medium saucepan over medium heat, stirring occasionally. In medium bowl, whisk egg yolks, cornstarch, and remaining 2 tablespoons sugar until smooth.

4. Slowly whisk 1 cup simmering half-and-half mixture into yolk mixture to temper, then slowly whisk tempered yolk mixture back into remaining half-and-half mixture. Cook, whisking vigorously, until mixture is thickened and few bubbles burst on surface, about 30 seconds. Off heat, whisk in butter and vanilla. Transfer pastry cream to clean bowl, lay sheet of plastic wrap directly on surface, and refrigerate until chilled and firm, about 3 hours.

5. Whisk chilled pastry cream briefly, then spread over bottom of cooled tart shell. Shingle kiwi slices around edge of tart, then arrange 3 rows of raspberries inside kiwi. Finally, arrange mound of blueberries in center. Using pastry brush, dab melted jelly over fruit. To serve, remove outer metal ring of tart pan, slide thin metal spatula between tart and tart pan bottom, and carefully slide tart onto serving platter or cutting board.

TO MAKE AHEAD

- Dough-lined tart pan can be frozen for up to 1 month; thaw completely at room temperature before baking
- Baked, unfilled tart shell can be held at room temperature for up to 24 hours
- Pastry cream can be refrigerated for up to 2 days
- Assembled tart can be refrigerated for up to 6 hours

ASSEMBLING A FRESH FRUIT TART

1. Whisk chilled pastry cream briefly, then spread evenly over bottom of cooled tart shell.

2. Shingle kiwi around edge of tart, arrange 3 rows of raspberries inside kiwi, and mound blueberries in center.

Lemon Tart

SERVES 8 `EASY` `FREEZE IT`

ACTIVE TIME 30 MINUTES

TOTAL TIME 1 HOUR 30 MINUTES (PLUS 2 HOURS COOLING TIME)

WHY THIS RECIPE WORKS Despite its apparent simplicity, there is much that can go wrong with a lemon tart. It can slip over the edge of sweet into cloying; its tartness can grab at your throat; it can be gluey or eggy or, even worse, metallic tasting. Its crust can be too hard, too soft, too thick, or too sweet. We wanted a proper tart, one in which the filling is baked with the shell. For us, that meant only one thing: lemon curd. For just enough sugar to off-set the acid in the lemons, we used 3 parts sugar to 2 parts lemon juice, plus a whopping ¼ cup of lemon zest. To achieve a curd that was creamy and dense with a vibrant lemony yellow color, we used a combination of whole eggs and egg yolks. And for a smooth, light texture, we strained the curd and then stirred in heavy cream just before baking. Once the lemon curd ingredients have been combined, cook the curd immediately; otherwise it will have a grainy finished texture. We found that it's important to add the hot filling to a warm crust as this helps keep the crust from getting soggy. Serve with Whipped Cream (page 365).

    1 recipe Classic Tart Dough (page 372)
    2 large eggs plus 7 large yolks
    1 cup (7 ounces) granulated sugar
    ¼ cup grated lemon zest plus ⅔ cup juice (4 lemons)
      Pinch salt
    4 tablespoons unsalted butter, cut into 4 pieces
    3 tablespoons heavy cream
      Confectioners' sugar

1. Roll dough into 11-inch circle on lightly floured counter. Loosely roll dough around rolling pin and gently unroll it onto 9-inch tart pan with removable bottom, letting excess dough hang over edge. Lift dough and gently press it into corners and fluted sides of pan. Run rolling pin over top of pan to remove any excess dough. Wrap loosely in plastic, place on large plate, and freeze until dough is fully chilled and firm, about 30 minutes.

2. Adjust oven rack to middle position and heat oven to 375 degrees. Line chilled crust with double layer of aluminum foil, covering edges to prevent burning, and fill with pie weights. Bake until tart shell is golden and set, about 30 minutes.

3. Meanwhile, whisk eggs and yolks together in medium sauce-pan. Whisk in sugar until combined, then whisk in lemon zest and juice and salt. Add butter and cook over medium-low heat, stir-ring constantly, until mixture thickens slightly and registers

A simple lemon curd enriched with cream is easy to make on the stovetop and is the filling for this bracing lemon tart.

170 degrees, about 5 minutes. Immediately pour mixture through fine-mesh strainer into bowl. Stir in cream.

4. Remove baking sheet from oven and remove weights and foil from tart shell. Pour warm lemon filling into warm tart shell. Bake until filling is shiny and opaque and center jiggles slightly when shaken, 10 to 15 minutes.

5. Let tart cool on sheet to room temperature, about 2 hours. To serve, remove outer metal ring of tart pan, slide thin metal spatula between tart and tart pan bottom, and carefully slide tart onto serv-ing platter or cutting board. Dust with confectioners' sugar.

`TO MAKE AHEAD`

- Dough-lined tart pan can be frozen for up to 1 month; thaw completely at room temperature before baking
- Baked tart can be held at room temperature for up to 6 hours; dust with confectioners' sugar just before serving

A little bourbon cuts the sweetness of this elegant nut tart, and a hefty amount of vanilla gives it rounded flavor.

Rustic Walnut Tart

SERVES 8 **EASY** **FREEZE IT**

ACTIVE TIME 25 MINUTES
TOTAL TIME 2 HOURS (PLUS 2 HOURS COOLING TIME)

WHY THIS RECIPE WORKS This elegant nut tart is surprisingly easy to prepare, thanks to the very simple filling. For the filling, we used a pecan pie base but swapped in walnuts, reduced the amount of sugar, and added a hefty amount of vanilla as well as a hit of bourbon (or rum). The liquor cuts through the sweetness and intensifies the flavor of the nuts. We found that it's important to add the filling to a warm pie crust as this helps keep the crust from getting soggy. Pecans can be substituted for the walnuts if desired.

1 recipe Classic Tart Dough (page 372)
½ cup packed (3½ ounces) light brown sugar
⅓ cup light corn syrup
4 tablespoons unsalted butter, melted and cooled
1 tablespoon bourbon or dark rum
2 teaspoons vanilla extract
½ teaspoon salt
1 large egg
1¾ cups walnuts, chopped coarse
1 recipe Bourbon Whipped Cream (page 365), optional

1. Roll dough into 11-inch circle on lightly floured counter. Loosely roll dough around rolling pin and gently unroll it onto 9-inch tart pan with removable bottom, letting excess dough hang over edge. Lift dough and gently press it into corners and fluted sides of pan. Run rolling pin over top of pan to remove any excess dough. Wrap loosely in plastic, place on large plate, and freeze until dough is fully chilled and firm, about 30 minutes.

2. Adjust oven rack to middle position and heat oven to 375 degrees. Line chilled crust with double layer of aluminum foil, covering edges to prevent burning, and fill with pie weights. Bake until tart shell is golden and set, about 30 minutes. Carefully remove weights and foil and continue to bake until tart shell is fully baked and golden brown, 5 to 10 minutes.

3. Meanwhile, whisk sugar, corn syrup, butter, bourbon, vanilla, and salt together in large bowl until sugar dissolves. Whisk in egg until combined. Pour filling into warm tart shell and sprinkle with walnuts, pressing them into the filling. Bake until filling is set and walnuts begin to brown, 30 to 40 minutes, rotating sheet halfway through baking.

4. Let tart cool on sheet to room temperature, about 2 hours. To serve, remove outer metal ring of tart pan, slide thin metal spatula between tart and tart pan bottom, and carefully slide tart onto serving platter or cutting board. Serve with whipped cream, if using.

TO MAKE AHEAD

- Dough-lined tart pan can be frozen for up to 1 month; thaw completely at room temperature before baking
- Baked, unfilled tart shell can be held at room temperature for up to 24 hours
- Baked tart can be refrigerated for up 2 days; to serve, bring to room temperature before serving (crust will be less crisp)

Our rustic fruit tart combines stone fruits and berries for appealing flavors and textures.

Free-Form Summer Fruit Tart

SERVES 6 **EASY**

ACTIVE TIME 25 MINUTES
TOTAL TIME 1 HOUR 15 MINUTES

WHY THIS RECIPE WORKS For a simple summer fruit tart that's every bit as good as harder-to-prepare pie, we started with our foolproof recipe for free-form tart dough. To make sure our dough was easy to work with, we rolled it out into a circle, transferred it to a baking sheet, and chilled it until firm. A mix of stone fruits and berries produced an especially nice contrast in flavors and textures. We rolled the dough into a 12-inch circle, which produced a crust that was thick enough to contain a lot of fruit but thin enough to bake evenly. We placed the fruit in the middle, then lifted the dough over the fruit (leaving the center exposed) and pleated it loosely. To help prevent the tart from leaking, we found it crucial to leave a small swath of dough (about ½-inch wide) between the fruit and the edge of the tart to act as a barrier. The bright summer fruit needed only a bit of sugar for enhancement. Do not toss the fruit with the sugar until you are ready to assemble the tart. Feel free to alter the amount of sugar in step 2 to compensate for fruit that is either very sweet or very tart. Serve with vanilla ice cream or Whipped Cream (page 365).

1 recipe Free-Form Tart Dough (page 373)
1 pound peaches, nectarines, apricots, or plums, halved, pitted, and sliced thin
5 ounces (1 cup) blackberries, blueberries, or raspberries
¼ cup (1¾ ounces) plus 1 tablespoon sugar
Water, as needed

1. Adjust oven rack to middle position and heat oven to 375 degrees. Line rimmed baking sheet with parchment paper. Roll dough into 12-inch circle on lightly floured counter. Loosely roll dough around rolling pin and gently unroll it on prepared sheet. Cover loosely with plastic wrap and refrigerate until firm, 15 to 30 minutes.

2. Gently toss fruit and ¼ cup sugar together in bowl. Mound fruit in center of dough, leaving 2½-inch border around edge of fruit. Fold outermost 2 inches of dough over fruit, pleating it every 2 to 3 inches as needed; be sure to leave ½-inch border of dough between fruit and edge of tart. Gently pinch pleated dough to secure, but do not press dough into fruit.

3. Brush top and sides of dough lightly with water and sprinkle with remaining 1 tablespoon sugar. Bake until crust is golden brown and fruit is bubbling, about 1 hour, rotating sheet halfway through baking.

4. Let tart cool on sheet for 10 minutes. Use parchment to transfer tart to wire rack, then discard parchment. Let tart cool until filling thickens, about 25 minutes, before serving.

TO MAKE AHEAD ▶

Baked tart can be held at room temperature for up to 8 hours or refrigerated for up to 24 hours; to serve, refresh in 350 degree oven for 10 to 15 minutes before serving (crust will be less crisp)

MAKING A FREE-FORM FRUIT TART

Mound fruit in center of dough, leaving 2½-inch border around edge of fruit. Fold outermost 2 inches of dough over fruit, pleating every 2 to 3 inches; leave ½-inch border between fruit and edge of tart.

Browning some of the butter gives our chocolate chip cookies nutty, toffeelike flavor.

Chocolate Chip Cookies

MAKES 16 COOKIES **FREEZE IT**
ACTIVE TIME 35 MINUTES
TOTAL TIME 1 HOUR (PLUS COOLING TIME)

WHY THIS RECIPE WORKS Cookies are an ideal make-ahead treat, so we set out to refine the classic Toll House recipe to create a moist and chewy chocolate chip cookie with crisp edges and deep notes of toffee and butterscotch. The foundation for building both the right texture and flavor turned out to be melted butter. After browning a portion of the butter for nutty flavor, we stirred in the remaining butter until it was melted and then added both brown and white sugar. The sugar dissolved in the liquid butter, which enhanced its caramelization as the cookies baked. The freed-up liquid in the fat also encouraged a bit of gluten development, making our cookies chewier. Using two egg yolks, but only one white, added richness without a cakey texture. Knowing they would continue to firm up as they cooled, we made sure to bake the cookies just until they were golden brown and set, but still soft in the center. Light brown sugar can be used in place of the dark, but the cookies will be less full-flavored; make sure the brown sugar is fresh and moist.

1¾ cups (8¾ ounces) all-purpose flour
½ teaspoon baking soda
14 tablespoons unsalted butter
¾ cup packed (5¼ ounces) dark brown sugar
½ cup (3½ ounces) granulated sugar
2 teaspoons vanilla extract
1 teaspoon salt
1 large egg plus 1 large yolk
1¼ cups (7½ ounces) semisweet or bittersweet chocolate chips
¾ cup pecans or walnuts, toasted and chopped (optional)

1. Adjust oven rack to middle position and heat oven to 375 degrees. Line 2 baking sheets with parchment paper. Whisk flour and baking soda together in bowl.

2. Melt 10 tablespoons butter in 10-inch skillet over medium-high heat. Continue to cook, swirling constantly, until butter is dark golden brown and has nutty aroma, 1 to 3 minutes.

3. Transfer browned butter to large bowl and stir in remaining 4 tablespoons butter until melted. Whisk in brown sugar, granulated sugar, vanilla, and salt until incorporated. Whisk in egg and yolk until smooth with no lumps, about 30 seconds.

4. Let mixture stand for 3 minutes, then whisk for 30 seconds. Repeat process of resting and whisking 2 more times until mixture is thick, smooth, and shiny. Using rubber spatula, stir in flour mixture until just combined, about 1 minute. Stir in chocolate chips and pecans, if using.

5. Working with 3 tablespoons dough at a time, roll into balls and space 2 inches apart on prepared sheets.

6. Bake cookies, 1 sheet at a time, until golden brown and edges have begun to set but centers are still soft and puffy, 10 to 14 minutes, rotating sheet halfway through baking. Let cookies cool completely on sheet and serve.

TO MAKE AHEAD ▶

- Cookie dough, prepared through step 4, can be refrigerated for up to 3 days; to bake, bring to room temperature and continue with step 5
- Shaped dough balls, prepared through step 5, can be frozen for up to 1 month; to bake, arrange frozen cookies on parchment-lined baking sheet, place on top of second baking sheet (to prevent bottoms from burning), and increase baking time to 15 to 20 minutes
- Baked cookies can be stored at room temperature for up to 3 days; to refresh, place in 425-degree oven for 4 to 5 minutes

Melting the butter and mixing the dough by hand develops more pronounced chew.

Chewy Oatmeal Cookies

MAKES 20 COOKIES ▮**FREEZE IT**
ACTIVE TIME 35 MINUTES
TOTAL TIME 50 MINUTES (PLUS COOLING TIME)

WHY THIS RECIPE WORKS To make oatmeal cookies that were dense and chewy instead of dry and cakey, we used a combination of unsaturated fat (vegetable oil) and saturated fat (butter), and we reduced the proportion of flour. Adding an extra egg yolk boosted moistness and richness, while a touch more salt than most recipes call for tempered the sweetness and complemented the oaty flavor. Most recipes call for using a stand mixer, but we found this counterproductive to our goal of chewy, dense cookies because the mixer beats air into the dough. Instead we made our dough by hand, melting the butter for easier mixing. Browning the butter delivered more complexity, and blooming a small amount of cinnamon in the butter rounded out its flavor. Raisins added pops of brightness and reinforced the chewy texture. Regular old-fashioned rolled oats work best in this recipe. Do not use extra-thick rolled oats, as they will bake up tough in the cookie. For cookies with just the right amount of spread and chew, we strongly recommend that you weigh your ingredients. If you omit the optional raisins, the recipe will yield 18 cookies.

1 cup (5 ounces) all-purpose flour
¾ teaspoon salt
½ teaspoon baking soda
4 tablespoons unsalted butter
¼ teaspoon ground cinnamon
¾ cup packed (5¼ ounces) dark brown sugar
½ cup (3½ ounces) granulated sugar
½ cup vegetable oil
1 large egg plus 1 large yolk
1 teaspoon vanilla extract
3 cups (9 ounces) old-fashioned rolled oats
½ cup raisins (optional)

1. Adjust oven rack to middle position and heat oven to 375 degrees. Line 2 rimmed baking sheets with parchment paper. Whisk flour, salt, and baking soda together in medium bowl.

2. Melt butter in 8-inch skillet over medium-high heat. Continue to cook, swirling constantly, until butter is dark golden brown and has nutty aroma, 1 to 2 minutes. Transfer browned butter to large bowl and stir in cinnamon.

3. Whisk brown sugar, granulated sugar, and oil into browned butter until combined. Whisk in egg and yolk and vanilla until mixture is smooth. Using rubber spatula, stir in flour mixture until fully combined, about 1 minute. Stir in oats and raisins, if using (mixture will be stiff).

4. Working with 3 tablespoons dough at a time, roll into balls and space 2 inches apart on prepared sheets. Using your damp hand, press each ball into 2½-inch cookie.

5. Bake cookies, 1 sheet at a time, until edges are set and lightly browned and centers are still soft but not wet, 8 to 10 minutes, rotating sheet halfway through baking. Let cookies cool for 5 minutes on sheet, then transfer to wire rack and let cool completely. Serve.

▸ **TO MAKE AHEAD**

- Cookie dough, prepared through step 3, can be refrigerated for up to 3 days; to bake, bring to room temperature and continue with step 4
- Shaped dough balls, prepared through step 4, can be frozen for up to 1 month; to bake, arrange frozen cookies on parchment-lined baking sheet, place on top of second baking sheet (to prevent bottoms from burning), and increase baking time to 13 to 15 minutes
- Baked cookies can be stored at room temperature for up to 3 days; to refresh, place in 425-degree oven for 4 to 5 minutes

Storing Cookies

We rarely go through an entire batch of cookies the day they're made, so to maximize their freshness for several days, we store them in an airtight container at room temperature. You can restore that just-baked freshness to cookies (with the exception of cookies that have been glazed or dusted with confectioners' sugar) by recrisping them in a 425-degree oven for 4 to 5 minutes. Let the cookies cool on the baking sheet for a couple of minutes before removing them and serving them warm.

Peanut Butter Cookies

MAKES 24 COOKIES   **FREEZE IT**
ACTIVE TIME 35 MINUTES
TOTAL TIME 45 MINUTES (PLUS COOLING TIME)

WHY THIS RECIPE WORKS Our ideal peanut butter cookie is soft and chewy, with a strong peanut flavor. The problem is, the more peanut butter added to the dough, the sandier and crumblier the cookies become. After hitting the limit with 1 cup of extra-crunchy, we packed extra peanut flavor into our dough by adding a cup of salted, dry-roasted peanuts, which we processed to fine crumbs. To sweeten the cookies, we included both granulated and brown sugars, which yielded crisp-edged cookies with great flavor. We prefer extra-crunchy peanut butter for these cookies, but crunchy peanut butter or creamy peanut butter also works.

2½ cups (12½ ounces) all-purpose flour
 1 teaspoon salt
 ½ teaspoon baking powder
 ½ teaspoon baking soda
 1 cup dry-roasted salted peanuts
16 tablespoons unsalted butter, softened
 1 cup packed (7 ounces) light brown sugar
 1 cup (7 ounces) granulated sugar
 1 cup extra-crunchy peanut butter
 2 teaspoons vanilla extract
 2 large eggs

1. Adjust oven racks to the upper-middle and lower-middle positions and heat oven to 350 degrees. Line 2 baking sheets with parchment paper. Whisk flour, salt, baking powder, and baking soda together in bowl. Pulse peanuts in food processor to fine crumbs, about 14 pulses.

2. Using stand mixer fitted with paddle, beat butter, brown sugar, and granulated sugar on medium speed until light and fluffy, about 3 minutes. Beat in peanut butter until fully incorporated, about 30 seconds. Beat in vanilla, followed by eggs, one at a time, until combined, about 30 seconds, scraping down bowl as needed.

3. Reduce mixer speed to low and slowly add flour mixture until combined, about 30 seconds. Mix in peanuts until incorporated. Give dough final stir by hand to ensure that no flour pockets remain.

4. Working with 3 tablespoons dough at a time, roll into balls and space 2 inches apart on prepared sheets. Using fork, make cross-hatch design on cookies.

5. Bake cookies until edges are golden and centers have puffed but beginning to deflate, 10 to 12 minutes, switching and rotating sheets halfway through baking. Let cookies cool on sheets for 10 minutes. Serve warm or transfer to wire rack and let cool completely.

TO MAKE AHEAD

- Cookie dough, prepared through step 3, can be refrigerated for up to 3 days; to bake, bring to room temperature and continue with step 4
- Shaped dough balls, prepared through step 4, can be frozen for up to 1 month; to bake, arrange frozen cookies on parchment-lined baking sheet, place on top of second baking sheet (to prevent bottoms from burning), and increase baking time to 15 to 17 minutes
- Baked cookies can be stored at room temperature for up to 3 days; to refresh, place in 425-degree oven for 4 to 5 minutes

Brown Sugar Cookies

MAKES 24 COOKIES   **EASY**   **FREEZE IT**
ACTIVE TIME 30 MINUTES
TOTAL TIME 1 HOUR 5 MINUTES (PLUS COOLING TIME)

WHY THIS RECIPE WORKS To turn up the volume on a standard sugar cookie we switched out the granulated sugar in favor of dark brown sugar. Browning the butter produced a range of butterscotch and toffee flavors in our dough. A full tablespoon of vanilla offered sweet caramel notes. For the signature crystalline coating, we stuck with brown sugar but added a little white sugar to the rolling mix to prevent clumping. The right baking technique proved essential to the success of this recipe; we baked the cookies one sheet at a time, and pulled them from the oven when they were still soft. Avoid using a nonstick skillet to brown the butter; the dark color of the nonstick coating makes it difficult to gauge when the butter is sufficiently browned. Using fresh, moist brown sugar is crucial to the texture of these cookies.

14 tablespoons unsalted butter
 2 cups plus 2 tablespoons (10⅔ ounces) all-purpose flour
 ½ teaspoon baking soda

This cookie's rich flavor comes from a combination of browned butter, dark brown sugar, vanilla, and salt.

¼ teaspoon baking powder
1¾ cups packed (12¼ ounces) dark brown sugar, plus
    ¼ cup for rolling
½ teaspoon salt
1 large egg plus 1 large yolk
1 tablespoon vanilla extract
¼ cup granulated sugar

1. Melt 10 tablespoons butter in 10-inch skillet over medium-high heat. Continue to cook, swirling pan constantly, until butter is dark golden brown and has nutty aroma, 1 to 3 minutes. Transfer browned butter to large bowl and stir in remaining 4 tablespoons butter until melted; let cool for 15 minutes.

2. Meanwhile, adjust oven rack to middle position and heat oven to 350 degrees. Line 2 baking sheets with parchment paper. Whisk flour, baking soda, and baking powder together in bowl.

3. Whisk 1¾ cups brown sugar and salt into cooled butter until smooth with no lumps, about 30 seconds. Whisk in egg, yolk, and vanilla until incorporated, about 30 seconds. Using rubber spatula, stir in flour mixture until just combined, about 1 minute.

4. Combine remaining ¼ cup brown sugar and granulated sugar in shallow dish. Working with 2 tablespoons dough at a time, roll into balls then roll in sugar to coat; space 2 inches apart on prepared sheets.

5. Bake cookies, 1 sheet at a time, until edges have begun to set but centers are still soft, puffy, and cracked (cookies will look raw between cracks and seem underdone), 12 to 14 minutes, rotating sheet halfway through baking. Let cookies cool on baking sheet for 5 minutes, then transfer to wire rack and let cool completely before serving.

TO MAKE AHEAD

- Cookie dough, prepared through step 3, can be refrigerated for up to 3 days; to bake, bring to room temperature and continue with step 4
- Uncoated dough balls, prepared through step 4, can be frozen for up to 1 month; to bake, roll frozen dough balls in sugar and arrange on parchment-lined baking sheet, place on top of second baking sheet (to prevent bottoms from burning), and increase baking time to 17 to 20 minutes
- Baked cookies can be stored at room temperature for up to 3 days; to refresh, place in 425-degree oven for 4 to 5 minutes

MAKING BROWNED BUTTER

1. Place butter in skillet or saucepan with light-colored interior. Turn heat to medium-high and cook, swirling pan occasionally, until butter melts and begins to foam.

2. Continue to cook, swirling pan constantly, until butter is dark golden brown and has nutty aroma, 1 to 3 minutes.

3. Immediately transfer browned butter to heat-proof bowl.

Holiday Cookies

MAKES ABOUT 36 COOKIES   **FREEZE IT**
ACTIVE TIME 35 MINUTES
TOTAL TIME 1 HOUR 40 MINUTES (PLUS COOLING TIME)

WHY THIS RECIPE WORKS We wanted a simple recipe that would produce cookies sturdy enough to decorate yet tender enough to be worth eating. Superfine sugar helped to achieve a fine, delicate texture, while a little cream cheese assisted in making the dough workable without turning the cookies tough. Finally, using the reverse-creaming method of beating the butter into the flour-sugar mixture made for flat cookies, without any air pockets, that were easy to decorate. Baking them one sheet at a time ensured that they all baked evenly. If you can't find superfine sugar in the supermarket, simply process 1 cup granulated sugar in a food processor for about 30 seconds and then measure out ¾ cup. The dough scraps can be patted together, chilled, and rerolled one time only.

2½ cups (12½ ounces) all-purpose flour
¾ cup (5¼ ounces) superfine sugar
¼ teaspoon salt
16 tablespoons unsalted butter, cut into ½-inch pieces and softened
2 tablespoons cream cheese, softened
2 teaspoons vanilla extract

1. Whisk flour, sugar, and salt together in bowl of stand mixer. Fit mixer with paddle and beat in butter, 1 piece at a time, on medium-low speed until dough looks crumbly and slightly wet, 1 to 2 minutes.

2. Beat in cream cheese and vanilla until dough just begins to form large clumps, about 30 seconds. Knead dough in bowl by hand few times until it forms large cohesive mass.

3. Transfer dough to clean counter and divide into 2 equal pieces. Press each piece into 4-inch disk, wrap tightly in plastic wrap, and refrigerate until dough is firm yet malleable, about 30 minutes.

4. Working with 1 piece of dough at a time, roll dough out between 2 large sheets of parchment paper to even ⅛-inch thickness. Slide dough, still between the parchment, onto baking sheet and refrigerate until firm, about 10 minutes.

5. Adjust oven rack to middle position and heat oven to 375 degrees. Line 2 baking sheets with parchment paper. Working with 1 sheet of dough at a time, remove top piece of parchment and stamp out cookies using cookie cutters. Using thin offset spatula, transfer cookies to prepared baking sheet, spaced about 1 inch apart.

6. Bake cookies, 1 sheet at a time, until light golden brown, about 10 minutes, rotating sheet halfway through baking. Let cookies cool on sheet for 3 minutes, then transfer to wire rack and let cool completely. Repeat with remaining dough using freshly lined baking sheets.

TO MAKE AHEAD

- Dough, prepared through step 3, can be refrigerated for up to 2 days or frozen for up to 2 weeks; if frozen, thaw completely in refrigerator and continue with step 4
- Baked cookies can be stored at room temperature for up to 5 days

---

COOKIE GLAZES   **EASY**

Glazes are an easy way to decorate Holiday Cookies. To make the glaze, just whisk all the ingredients together until smooth; all glazes will make about 1 cup and need to be used immediately. Spread the glaze onto completely cooled cookies using the back of a spoon or pipe the glaze onto cookies to form a pattern or design. Let the glaze dry completely, about 30 minutes, before serving.

EASY ALL-PURPOSE GLAZE
2 cups (8 ounces) confectioners' sugar
3 tablespoons milk
2 tablespoons cream cheese, softened
Food coloring, as needed (optional)

CITRUS GLAZE
2 cups (8 ounces) confectioners' sugar
3 tablespoons fresh lemon, lime, or orange juice
2 tablespoons cream cheese, softened

NUTTY GLAZE
2 cups (8 ounces) confectioners' sugar
3 tablespoons milk
2 tablespoons cream cheese, softened
½ teaspoon almond or coconut extract

COFFEE GLAZE
2 cups (8 ounces) confectioners' sugar
3 tablespoons milk
2 tablespoons cream cheese, softened
1¼ teaspoons instant espresso powder or instant coffee

BITTERSWEET CHOCOLATE GLAZE
5 ounces bittersweet chocolate, melted
4 tablespoons (½ stick) unsalted butter, melted
2 tablespoons corn syrup
1 tablespoon vanilla extract

Almond Biscotti

MAKES 30 COOKIES
ACTIVE TIME 35 MINUTES
TOTAL TIME 1 HOUR 45 MINUTES (PLUS COOLING TIME)

WHY THIS RECIPE WORKS Since they keep for about a month, biscotti can be made far in advance. Our ideal biscotti is somewhere in between the dry, hard Italian original and the buttery, tender American version. Knowing that the crunch level depended, in part, on the amount of butter, we settled on just enough to give us a dough that was neither too hard nor too lean. Without enough butter to effectively cream with the sugar, we needed to find another way to aerate the dough. Whipping the eggs until they were light in color and then adding the sugar did the trick. To moderate the biscotti's crunchiness we ground part of the nuts (lightly toasted) in a food processor and substituted them for a portion of the flour. We baked the dough in two neat rectangles, then sliced them and baked the slices on a wire rack set in a baking sheet. The rack allowed air circulation around the cookies, making them evenly crisp. Be sure to toast the almonds just until fragrant; they will continue to toast while the biscotti bake.

1¼ cups whole almonds, lightly toasted
1¾ cups (8¾ ounces) all-purpose flour
2 teaspoons baking powder
¼ teaspoon salt
2 large eggs, plus 1 large white beaten with pinch salt
1 cup (7 ounces) sugar
4 tablespoons unsalted butter, melted and cooled
1½ teaspoons almond extract
½ teaspoon vanilla extract
Vegetable oil spray

1. Adjust oven rack to middle position and heat oven to 325 degrees. Using ruler and pencil, draw two 8 by 3-inch rectangles, spaced 4 inches apart, on piece of parchment paper. Grease baking sheet and place parchment on it, pencil side down.

2. Pulse 1 cup almonds in food processor until coarsely chopped, 8 to 10 pulses; transfer to bowl. Process remaining ¼ cup almonds in food processor until finely ground, about 45 seconds. Add flour, baking powder, and salt and process to combine, about 15 seconds; transfer to separate bowl.

3. Process 2 eggs in now-empty food processor until lightened in color and almost doubled in volume, about 3 minutes. With processor running, slowly add sugar until thoroughly combined, about 15 seconds. Add melted butter, almond extract, and vanilla and process until combined, about 10 seconds. Transfer egg mixture to medium bowl. Sprinkle half of flour mixture over top and fold gently with rubber spatula until just combined. Add remaining flour mixture and chopped almonds and gently fold until just combined.

Ground nuts in place of some flour moderate the biscotti's crunchiness so that they are crisp but not hard.

4. Divide dough in half. Using your floured hands, form each half into 8 by 3-inch rectangle, using lines on parchment as guide. Spray each loaf lightly with oil spray. Using rubber spatula lightly coated with oil spray, smooth tops and sides of rectangles. Gently brush tops of loaves with egg white wash. Bake loaves until golden and just beginning to crack on top, 25 to 30 minutes, rotating sheet halfway through baking.

5. Let loaves cool on sheet for 30 minutes. Transfer loaves to cutting board. Using serrated knife, slice each loaf on slight bias into ½-inch-thick slices. Space slices, cut side down, about ¼ inch apart on wire rack set in rimmed baking sheet. Bake until crisp and golden brown on both sides, about 35 minutes, flipping slices halfway through baking. Let cool completely before serving.

VARIATIONS
Anise Biscotti

Add 1½ teaspoons anise seeds to food processor with flour. Substitute anise-flavored liqueur for almond extract.

Pistachio-Spice Biscotti

Substitute shelled pistachios for almonds. Add 1 teaspoon ground cardamom, ½ teaspoon ground cloves, ½ teaspoon pepper,

¼ teaspoon ground cinnamon, and ¼ teaspoon ground ginger to food processor with flour. Substitute 1 teaspoon water for almond extract and increase vanilla extract to 1 teaspoon.

Hazelnut-Orange Biscotti

Substitute lightly toasted and skinned hazelnuts for almonds. Add 2 tablespoons minced fresh rosemary to food processor with flour. Substitute orange-flavored liqueur for almond extract and add 1 tablespoon grated orange zest to food processor with butter.

> **TO MAKE AHEAD**
>
> Biscotti can be stored at room temperature for up to 1 month

MAKING BISCOTTI

1. Using ruler and pencil, draw two 8 by 3-inch rectangles, spaced 4 inches apart, on piece of parchment paper. Grease baking sheet and place parchment on it, pencil side down.

2. After preparing dough, divide in half and with floured hands form each half into 8 by 3-inch loaf on parchment-lined sheet using lines as guide. Bake until golden.

3. Transfer partially baked loaves to cutting board. Using serrated knife, slice each loaf on slight bias into ½-inch-thick slices.

4. Space slices, with 1 cut side down, about ¼ inch apart on wire rack set in rimmed baking sheet. Bake until crisp and golden brown on both sides, about 35 minutes, flipping slices halfway through baking.

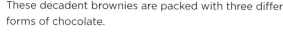

These decadent brownies are packed with three different forms of chocolate.

Chewy Brownies

MAKES 24 BROWNIES **EASY** **FREEZE IT**
ACTIVE TIME 30 MINUTES
TOTAL TIME 1 HOUR (PLUS 1 HOUR COOLING TIME)

WHY THIS RECIPE WORKS We cracked the code for perfectly chewy brownies and the key was fat—specifically, the right amounts of saturated and unsaturated fats. Once we figured out that a 1:3 ratio of saturated fat (butter) to unsaturated fat (vegetable oil) produced the chewiest brownies, we fine-tuned the other sources of fat (eggs and chocolate) to preserve the balance. Two extra egg yolks, along with two whole eggs, provided emulsification that prevented the brownies from turning greasy. We whisked unsweetened cocoa, along with some espresso powder, into boiling water, and then stirred in unsweetened chocolate. The heat unlocked the chocolate's flavor compounds, increasing its impact. Looking for even more chocolate punch, we realized that we could stir chunks of chocolate into the batter without affecting the balance of fats we'd worked hard to achieve. Our brownies now had pockets of gooey chocolate. For the chewiest texture, it is important to let the brownies cool thoroughly before cutting. If your baking dish is glass, cool the brownies 10 minutes, then remove them promptly from the pan (otherwise, the superior heat retention of glass can lead to overbaking). For an accurate measurement of boiling water, bring a full kettle of water to a boil and then measure out the desired amount.

½ cup plus 2 tablespoons boiling water
⅓ cup (1 ounce) Dutch-processed cocoa powder
1½ teaspoons instant espresso powder (optional)
2 ounces unsweetened chocolate, chopped fine
½ cup plus 2 tablespoons vegetable oil
4 tablespoons unsalted butter, melted
2 large eggs plus 2 large yolks
2 teaspoons vanilla extract
2½ cups (17½ ounces) sugar
1¾ cups (8¾ ounces) all-purpose flour
¾ teaspoon salt
6 ounces bittersweet chocolate, cut into ½-inch pieces

1. Adjust oven rack to lowest position and heat oven to 350 degrees. Make foil sling for 13 by 9-inch baking pan by folding 2 long sheets of aluminum foil; first sheet should be 13 inches wide, and second sheet should be 9 inches wide. Lay sheets of foil in pan perpendicular to each other, with extra foil hanging over edges of pan. Push foil into corners and up sides of pan, smoothing foil flush to pan, and grease foil.

2. Whisk water, cocoa, and espresso powder, if using, together in large bowl until smooth. Add unsweetened chocolate and whisk until chocolate is melted. Whisk in oil and melted butter. (Mixture may look curdled.) Whisk in eggs, yolks, and vanilla until smooth and homogeneous. Whisk in sugar until fully incorporated. Add flour and salt and mix with rubber spatula until combined. Fold in chocolate pieces.

3. Scrape batter into prepared pan and smooth top. Bake brownies until toothpick inserted halfway between edge and center comes out with few moist crumbs attached, 30 to 35 minutes, rotating pan halfway through baking. Let brownies cool in pan for 1½ hours.

4. Using foil overhang, lift brownies from pan. Transfer to wire rack and let cool completely, about 1 hour. Cut into squares and serve.

TO MAKE AHEAD
Brownies can be stored at room temperature for up to 4 days or frozen for up to 1 month; if frozen, thaw completely at room temperature before serving

The shortbread crust on our raspberry bars does double duty as part of the buttery streusel topping.

Raspberry Streusel Bars
MAKES 24 BARS   `EASY`   `FREEZE IT`
ACTIVE TIME 25 MINUTES
TOTAL TIME 55 MINUTES (PLUS 2 HOURS COOLING TIME)

WHY THIS RECIPE WORKS We wanted the right balance of bright, tangy fruit filling and rich, buttery shortbread crust for these bars—and we wanted an easy topping. For a fresh-tasting fruity filling, we combined fresh raspberries with raspberry jam. Adding a dash of lemon juice to the jam brightened the filling further. We made a butter-rich shortbread dough that did double duty as the bottom crust and as a base for our streusel topping. After pressing part of the mixture into the pan, we added oats, brown sugar, nuts, and a little extra butter to the rest, and pinched it into clumps. To prevent soggy-bottomed bars, we baked the bottom crust on its own before adding the raspberries and streusel and baking it all together. Frozen raspberries can be substituted for fresh, but be sure to defrost them before using. Quick oats will work in this recipe, but the bars will be less chewy and flavorful. Do not use instant oats.

2½ cups (12½ ounces) all-purpose flour
⅔ cup (4⅔ ounces) granulated sugar
½ teaspoon salt
18 tablespoons (2¼ sticks) unsalted butter, cut into 18 pieces and softened
½ cup (1½ ounces) old-fashioned rolled oats
½ cup pecans, toasted and chopped fine
¼ cup packed (1¾ ounces) light brown sugar
¾ cup raspberry jam
3¾ ounces (¾ cup) fresh raspberries
1 tablespoon lemon juice

1. Adjust oven rack to middle position and heat oven to 375 degrees. Make foil sling for 13 by 9-inch baking pan by folding 2 long sheets of aluminum foil; first sheet should be 13 inches wide and second sheet should be 9 inches wide. Lay sheets of foil in pan perpendicular to each other, with extra foil hanging over edges of pan. Push foil into corners and up sides of pan, smoothing foil flush to pan, and grease foil.

2. Whisk flour, granulated sugar, and salt together in bowl of stand mixer. Fit mixer with paddle and beat in 16 tablespoons butter, 1 piece at a time, on medium-low speed until mixture resembles damp sand, 1 to 1½ minutes. Reserve 1¼ cups mixture separately in medium bowl for topping.

3. Sprinkle remaining mixture into prepared pan and press into even layer with bottom of dry measuring cup. Bake until edges of crust begin to brown, 14 to 18 minutes, rotating pan halfway through baking.

4. Meanwhile, stir oats, pecans, and brown sugar into reserved topping mixture. Add remaining 2 tablespoons butter and pinch mixture with your fingers into clumps of streusel. In small bowl, mash jam, raspberries, and lemon juice together with fork until few berry pieces remain.

5. Spread berry mixture evenly over hot crust, then sprinkle with streusel. Bake bars until filling is bubbling and topping is deep golden brown, 22 to 25 minutes, rotating pan halfway through baking.

6. Let bars cool completely in pan, about 2 hours. Using foil overhang, lift bars from pan. Cut into squares and serve.

VARIATIONS
Strawberry Streusel Bars EASY FREEZE IT
Thawed frozen strawberries will also work here.

Substitute strawberry jam for raspberry jam and ¾ cup chopped fresh strawberries for raspberries.

Blueberry Streusel Bars EASY FREEZE IT
Thawed frozen blueberries will also work here.

Substitute blueberry jam for raspberry jam and ¾ cup fresh blueberries for raspberries.

TO MAKE AHEAD

Streusel bars can be stored at room temperature for up to 3 days or frozen for up to 1 month; if frozen, thaw completely at room temperature before serving (crust and streusel will be less crisp)

NOTES FROM THE TEST KITCHEN

Washing and Storing Berries
Washing berries before you use them is always a safe practice, and we think that the best way to wash them is to place the berries in a colander and rinse them gently under running water for at least 30 seconds. As for drying berries, we've tested a variety of methods and have found that a salad spinner lined with a buffering layer of paper towels is the best approach.

It's particularly important to store berries carefully, because they are prone to growing mold and rotting quickly. If the berries aren't to be used immediately, we recommend cleaning them with a mild vinegar solution (3 cups water mixed with 1 cup distilled white vinegar), which will destroy the bacteria, then drying them and storing them in a paper towel–lined airtight container.

Lemon Bars
MAKES 16 BARS FREEZE IT
ACTIVE TIME 35 MINUTES
TOTAL TIME 1 HOUR (PLUS 2 HOURS COOLING TIME)

WHY THIS RECIPE WORKS Successful lemon bars, with bright lemon flavor, depend on ample amounts of lemon juice and lemon zest. We used four lemons in our filling, along with two whole eggs and seven yolks for thickening. To tame the curd's pucker power and make it creamy, we added a small dose of heavy cream and some butter. Confectioners' sugar contributed a tender texture to the crust. We found that it was important to pour the warm filling over a warm crust to ensure that the filling cooked through evenly. If you live in a humid climate, dust the lemon bars with the confectioners' sugar right before serving. Humidity tends to make the sugar melt and turn splotchy.

Two whole eggs and seven egg yolks give the lemon curd a richness that balances the tangy lemon flavor.

CRUST

- 1¼ cups (6¼ ounces) all-purpose flour
- ½ cup (2 ounces) confectioners' sugar
- ½ teaspoon salt
- 8 tablespoons unsalted butter, cut into 8 pieces and softened

FILLING

- 2 large eggs plus 7 large yolks
- 1 cup (7 ounces) plus 2 tablespoons granulated sugar
- ¼ cup grated zest plus ⅔ cup lemon juice (4 lemons)
  Pinch salt
- 4 tablespoons unsalted butter, cut into 4 pieces
- 3 tablespoons heavy cream
  Confectioners' sugar

1. Adjust oven rack to middle position and heat oven to 350 degrees. Make foil sling for 8-inch square baking pan by folding 2 long sheets of aluminum foil so each is 8 inches wide. Lay sheets of foil in pan perpendicular to each other, with extra foil hanging over edges of pan. Push foil into corners and up sides of pan, smoothing foil flush to pan, and grease foil.

2. FOR THE CRUST Process flour, sugar, and salt in food processor until combined, about 3 seconds. Sprinkle butter over top and pulse until mixture is pale yellow and resembles coarse cornmeal, about 8 pulses. Sprinkle mixture into prepared pan and press firmly into even layer using your fingers. Bake until crust starts to brown, about 20 minutes, rotating pan halfway through baking.

3. FOR THE FILLING Meanwhile, whisk egg and yolks together in medium saucepan. Whisk in granulated sugar until combined, then whisk in lemon zest and juice and salt. Add butter and cook over medium-low heat, stirring constantly, until mixture thickens slightly and registers 170 degrees, about 5 minutes.

4. Strain mixture immediately through fine-mesh strainer into bowl and stir in cream. Pour warm lemon curd over hot crust. Bake until filling is shiny and opaque and center jiggles slightly when shaken, 10 to 15 minutes, rotating pan halfway through baking.

5. Let bars cool completely in pan, about 2 hours. Using foil overhang, lift bars from pan. Cut into squares, dust with confectioners' sugar, and serve.

TO MAKE AHEAD

Lemon bars can be refrigerated for up to 2 days or frozen for up to 1 month; if frozen, thaw completely at room temperature before serving (crust will be less crisp)

MAKING A FOIL SLING

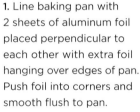

1. Line baking pan with 2 sheets of aluminum foil placed perpendicular to each other with extra foil hanging over edges of pan. Push foil into corners and smooth flush to pan.

2. Use foil handles to lift baked bar cookies from pan.

CONVERSIONS AND EQUIVALENTS

Some say cooking is a science and an art. We would say that geography has a hand in it, too. Flours and sugars manufactured in the United Kingdom and elsewhere will feel and taste different from those manufactured in the United States. So we cannot promise that the loaf of bread you bake in Canada or England will taste the same as a loaf baked in the States, but we can offer guidelines for converting weights and measures. We also recommend that you rely on your instincts when making our recipes. Refer to the visual cues provided. If the dough hasn't "come together, in a ball" as described, you may need to add more flour—even if the recipe doesn't tell you to. You be the judge.

The recipes in this book were developed using standard U.S. measures following U.S. government guidelines. The charts below offer equivalents for U.S. and metric measures. All conversions are approximate and have been rounded up or down to the nearest whole number.

EXAMPLE

1 teaspoon = 4.9292 milliliters, rounded up to 5 milliliters
1 ounce = 28.3495 grams, rounded down to 28 grams

VOLUME CONVERSIONS	
U.S.	METRIC
1 teaspoon	5 milliliters
2 teaspoons	10 milliliters
1 tablespoon	15 milliliters
2 tablespoons	30 milliliters
¼ cup	59 milliliters
⅓ cup	79 milliliters
½ cup	118 milliliters
¾ cup	177 milliliters
1 cup	237 milliliters
1¼ cups	296 milliliters
1½ cups	355 milliliters
2 cups (1 pint)	473 milliliters
2½ cups	591 milliliters
3 cups	710 milliliters
4 cups (1 quart)	0.946 liter
1.06 quarts	1 liter
4 quarts (1 gallon)	3.8 liters

WEIGHT CONVERSIONS	
OUNCES	GRAMS
½	14
¾	21
1	28
1½	43
2	57
2½	71
3	85
3½	99
4	113
4½	128
5	142
6	170
7	198
8	227
9	255
10	283
12	340
16 (1 pound)	454

CONVERSION FOR COMMON BAKING INGREDIENTS

Baking is an exacting science. Because measuring by weight is far more accurate than measuring by volume, and thus more likely to produce reliable results, in our recipes we provide ounce measures in addition to cup measures for many ingredients. Refer to the chart below to convert these measures into grams.

INGREDIENT	OUNCES	GRAMS
Flour		
1 cup all-purpose flour*	5	142
1 cup cake flour	4	113
1 cup whole-wheat flour	5½	156
Sugar		
1 cup granulated (white) sugar	7	198
1 cup packed brown sugar (light or dark)	7	198
1 cup confectioners' sugar	4	113
Cocoa Powder		
1 cup cocoa powder	3	85
Butter†		
4 tablespoons (½ stick, or ¼ cup)	2	57
8 tablespoons (1 stick, or ½ cup)	4	113
16 tablespoons (2 sticks, or 1 cup)	8	227

*U.S. all-purpose flour, the most frequently used flour in this book, does not contain leaveners, as some European flours do. These leavened flours are called self-rising or self-raising. If you are using self-rising flour, take this into consideration before adding leavening to a recipe.

†In the United States, butter is sold both salted and unsalted. We generally recommend unsalted butter. If you are using salted butter, take this into consideration before adding salt to a recipe.

OVEN TEMPERATURES

FAHRENHEIT	CELSIUS	GAS MARK
225	105	¼
250	120	½
275	135	1
300	150	2
325	165	3
350	180	4
375	190	5
400	200	6
425	220	7
450	230	8
475	245	9

CONVERTING TEMPERATURES FROM AN INSTANT-READ THERMOMETER

We include doneness temperatures in many of the recipes in this book. We recommend an instant-read thermometer for the job. Refer to the above table to convert Fahrenheit degrees to Celsius. Or, for temperatures not represented in the chart, use this simple formula:

Subtract 32 degrees from the Fahrenheit reading, then divide the result by 1.8 to find the Celsius reading.

EXAMPLE

"Roast chicken until thighs register 175 degrees."
To convert:
$175°F - 32 = 143°$
$143° ÷ 1.8 = 79.44°C$, rounded down to 79°C

Index

Note: Page references in *italics* indicate photographs.

■ indicates 30 minutes or less active time   ■ indicates recipe can be frozen